The Piano Improvisation Handbook

A practical guide to musical invention

CARL HUMPHRIES

A BACKBEAT BOOK
First edition 2009
Published by Backbeat Books
An Imprint of Hal Leonard Corporation
7777 West Bluemound Road,
Milwaukee, WI 53213
www.backbeatbooks.com

Devised and produced for Backbeat Books by
Outline Press Ltd
2A Union Court, 20-22 Union Road,
London SW4 6JP, England
www.jawbonepress.com

ISBN: 978-0-87930-977-0

Text copyright © 2009 by Carl Humphries. Volume copyright © 2009 by Outline Press Ltd.
All rights reserved. No part of this book may be reproduced in any form without written permission, except by a reviewer quoting brief passages in a review. For more information you must contact the publisher.

A discography, bibliography, glossary, and other supporting material for this book are available at www.pianoimprovisationhandbook.com. Updated information about the author, including tuition, workshops and other events, online exercises, and related publications, is available at www.carlhumphries.com.

DESIGN: Paul Cooper Design
EDITOR: John Morrish

Origination and print by Everbest Printing Co Ltd, China

09 10 11 12 13 5 4 3 2 1

CONTENTS

■ **PREFACE** 4

■ **INTRODUCTION** The history and practice of piano improvisation 7

■ SECTION ONE

UNIT ONE
22 BASIC THEORY
  22 The keyboard
  23 Notation
  26 Timing
  30 Scales
  37 Chords
  40 Keys

UNIT TWO
43 BASIC TECHNIQUE
  44 Posture and hand shape
  46 Finger independence
  47 Fingering
  48 Controlling sound
  52 Legato & staccato
  58 Practising scales
  66 Practising chords
  78 Pedal

■ SECTION TWO

UNIT THREE
81 EXPLORING MELODY
  82 Melody and improvisation
  83 Scale theory
  90 Simple melodic movement
  99 Simple melodic continuation

UNIT FOUR
104 EXPLORING CHORDS
  105 Chord layout
  108 Connecting chords
  122 Progressions

UNIT FIVE
139 EXPLORING KEYS
  140 Key relations
  141 Major and minor
  147 Transposition
  151 Modulation

UNIT SIX
159 EXPLORING RHYTHM
  160 Counting
  167 Syncopation and swing
  172 Coordinating the hands
  179 Rhythm and melody
  185 Rhythm and harmony

■ SECTION THREE

UNIT SEVEN
188 THE CLASSICAL APPROACH
  189 Solo melody
  205 Countermelody
  224 Melody and bass
  236 Chords and bass
  244 Extended harmony
  251 Melody and chords (I)
  260 Melodic variation
  264 Melody and chords (II)

UNIT EIGHT
268 THE JAZZ APPROACH
  269 Jazz harmony and scale theory
  281 The II-V-I progression
  292 Embellishing the II-V-I
  299 Left-hand voicings
  310 Licks and improvised melody
  331 Standards and lead sheets
  337 Reharmonisation
  356 Alternative structures
  361 Alternative voicings

■ SECTION FOUR

UNIT NINE
366 DEVELOPING MATERIAL
  367 The goal-note approach
  373 Phrase structure
  381 Improvising from scratch
  391 Melodic and harmonic reduction
  416 Working with ideas
  430 Colour and texture
  447 Arranging and improvising

UNIT TEN
455 FORM & STYLE IN IMPROVISATION
  456 Form in classical music
  464 Style in classical music
  470 Form in jazz and rock
  473 Style in rock, jazz, and blues

488 ON THE CD

Preface

The driving idea behind this book is that learning to improvise will greatly enhance your experience of learning to play the piano. It can be a fruitful alternative to the traditional approach, which focuses almost exclusively on learning to play written music. This doesn't mean there's anything wrong with that approach; it's just a recognition that in our times people often come to the piano with different priorities and passions already in place. And you don't have to choose between the two approaches. You can learn in the traditional way and study improvisation at the same time – for example, by using this book alongside lessons with a qualified teacher.

Apart from the fact that a lot of people specifically want to learn to improvise at the piano, there are other reasons for a book like this. Firstly, the art of improvisation is being rediscovered by musicians who are learning in the traditional way. The widespread influence of popular culture makes it natural for younger students to want the option of studying part-improvised styles like jazz and rock alongside the great classical works of the past. Piano teachers typically respond to this demand by going to their local music store and buying some easy written pieces that imitate the more obviously recognisable features of those styles, such as rock harmonies or jazz rhythms. But you can't really get to grips with these styles without confronting an awkward fact: performers play the lead role in making this music, not composers.

Recognising that fact can be an important step towards becoming interested in musical improvising. But that's not the only reason classical musicians are turning to it. Many are starting to recognise that there's something wrong with teaching a classical approach that apparently doesn't allow even highly skilled performers to explore their own musical inventiveness on their instruments.

Furthermore, teachers are now aware that being able to improvise in classical styles makes for a more natural, imaginative, and emotional relationship between the performer and the stylistic elements in classical compositions, and promotes a deeper understanding of form and structure. (They've also been influenced by the

PREFACE

rapid rise of music therapy as a way of promoting social interaction and self-expression – chiefly through group improvisation.)

Moreover, musicologists in recent years have shown that improvisation always played an important role in the classical tradition itself. Bach, Handel, Mozart, and Beethoven were as famous in their time as improvisers as they were as composers. In earlier styles of classical music the assumption was that the performer would embellish the written music he or she received from the composer. A piece of music was often judged on how well it prepared the ground for this, rather than as a self-contained work of art. In medieval music, even essential aspects of composition were studied through vocal improvisation under the guidance of a teacher. The idea that making and listening to music centres around a written musical work being realised on different occasions, rather than around the event of the musical performance itself, is now thought to be relatively modern. This conception has pushed improvisation to the margins of classical musical culture in the last couple of centuries. (The only areas of classical music where it survives are church organ playing and accompaniments for social dancing and ballet.)

Unfortunately the effect of this has been to push classical music away from being a living culture, in which possibilities for musical invention are thrown up by the day-to-day practice of music making, towards something more like a museum culture, dedicated to recreating the past in ways that appear academic and artificial.

This brings us to another set of reasons for a book like this. We can learn to improvise in the styles of classical music of the past, but if the point of going back to improvisation is that we want to rediscover our musical inventiveness and breathe new life into our musical traditions, that seems the wrong way to go about it. A similar problem shows up when learning to improvise jazz or rock. These can really only work as improvised styles when players are immersed in a common musical culture – interacting with one another in rehearsals and concerts, trading musical ideas, recordings, and so on. Even if you've got access to that sort of live musical scene, you probably won't feel confident enough to get involved from the early stages of your career as a pianist. So unless you opt to focus first on learning classical works and then switch to improvised styles later – which is pretty illogical – you will be dependent on recordings, text books, and tutors for guidance and inspiration. (If you're really lucky, you may find a teacher familiar with one or more of those styles; that's not easy, though, as most musicians who are serious about improvising prefer to be giving concerts than tutoring others.)

Unfortunately, without involvement in a living musical scene it's hard to get much practical use out of recordings, while textbooks give little more than raw materials (scales, riffs, licks, exercises, and harmonic tips), leaving it to you to figure

PREFACE

out how to apply these to create a performance. It is ironic, then, that as with the attempt to improvise in classical styles, what emerges tends to be academic and artificial – not at all the revitalising artistic experience that improvisation can and should be. That's why this book takes a new approach: it teaches improvisation as way of making music at the piano that is, to some extent, independent of any one style, whether this be classical, jazz, or rock. This means looking below the surface of individual musical styles to their organising principles and what they have in common at a conceptual, artistic, or purely technical level. The book presents nearly all those familiar styles as resources that you, the student, can use in the way that works best for you. Unfortunately, it is a fact of nature that there are a few styles, such as boogie-woogie and hard rock, that are so physically demanding that you can't learn them without compromising the muscular flexibility needed for other kinds of playing; for this reason they are not included.

Before starting this book you should be aware that there are two basic ways of learning to improvise, each with its own pros and cons. The first, which you'll find in many books on how to learn jazz and rock, focuses on scales and their relationship to established chord structures. It leads quickly to a certain kind of improvisational freedom, but only within a limited range of harmonic structures and stylistic contexts. It says little about the hardest problem in musical improvisation – achieving structural continuity and coherence while maintaining musical interest. Students who adopt this method usually hit a 'ceiling' that they can't get beyond; that is because their ability to improvise relies on reusing the same limited set of melodic and harmonic materials. This limits their inventiveness.

The second approach, which focuses on exploring the evolution of melodic phrases, harmonic progressions, rhythmic development, and textural contrast in an improvised context, takes us more gradually towards an improvised way of playing. It does so by creating a continuity between improvisation and composition. This leads to more creative possibilities in the long term, because the student is less reliant on a given set of structures and stylistic formulas.

This book aims to combine these two approaches. On the one hand it tries to fulfil students' need to achieve self-confidence early on in the learning process, which is essential for motivation. On the other, it aims to nurture their longer-term potential; that is, their potential to explore and enjoy improvising at the piano in ways that will have artistic merit. That means taking piano improvisation seriously, rather than seeing it as a sideline to learning the classics; but as you'll find out as you work through this book, it can be a lot of fun too.

Carl Humphries – 2009

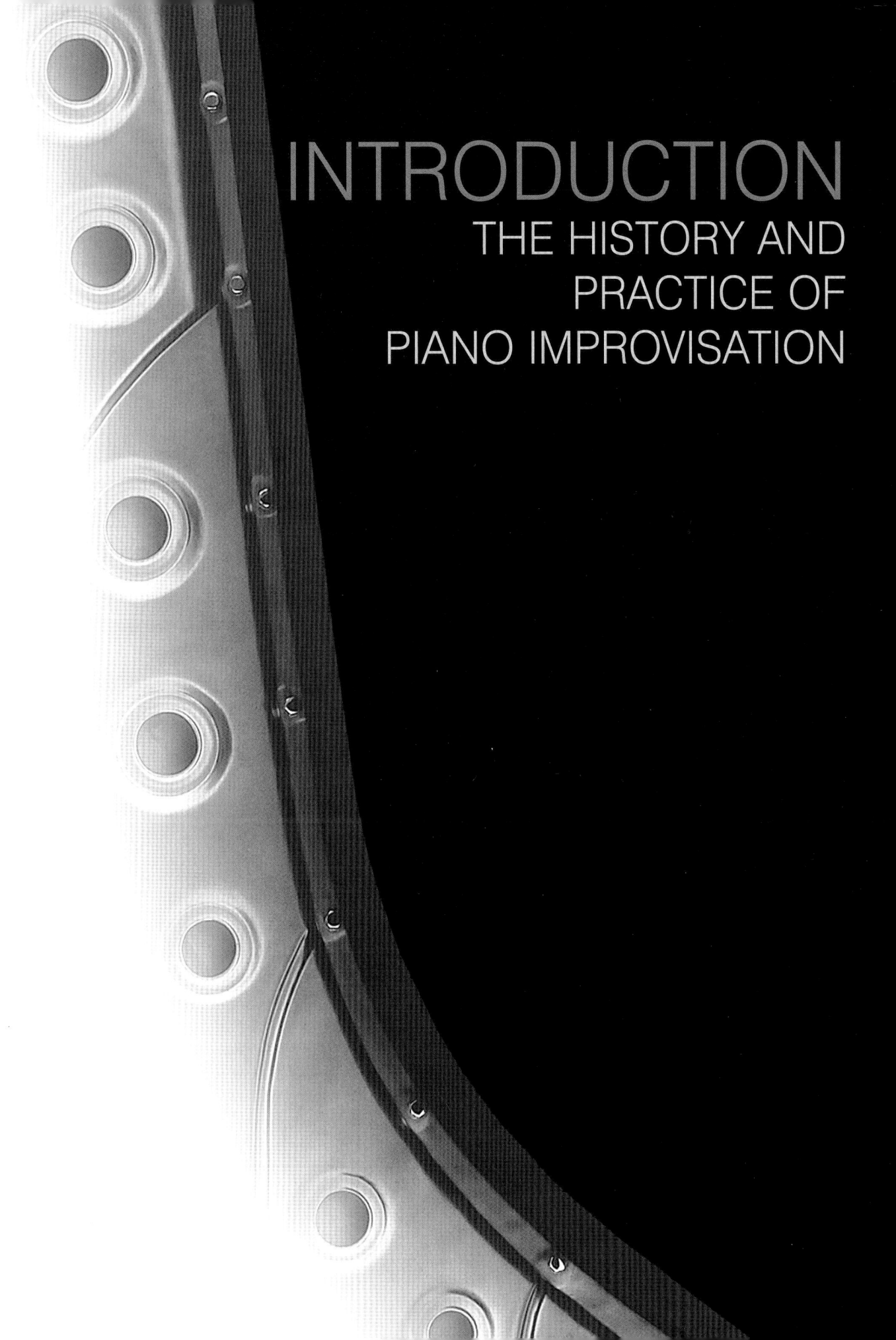

INTRODUCTION
THE HISTORY AND PRACTICE OF PIANO IMPROVISATION

INTRODUCTION

This introductory section is intended to help you understand what we mean when we talk about improvisation in music, and to provide an overview of the important role that improvisation has played in shaping musical cultures and traditions – especially in the Western world. If you like, you can jump over this and proceed with the rest of the book. However, it's designed to help you put the task of learning piano improvisation in a wider context and relate it more effectively to your experiences as a listener.

The concept of musical improvisation

When we talk about improvisation in music we generally mean a way of creating music in which at least some of the important aspects of the resulting music are determined as it is being played – 'on the fly', so to speak. But this doesn't say anything about which aspects of music are fixed in advance, or how they might be determined, or how they relate to those aspects that only take shape in performance. These things can all be quite different, depending on the kind of music being improvised. And what about the term 'performance'? This is ambiguous. It can refer to any event of making music through actual playing (as opposed to, say, configuring pre-recorded or synthetic sounds on a tape or computer), or to something more specific, like a one-off concert or recording session, in which a particular performance is given that may be unique and unrepeatable.

Some great jazz musicians – Louis Armstrong, for instance – created their solos through improvisation in rehearsal, but then changed hardly anything from one performance to the next. Others – Charlie Parker, for example – produced new improvisations on the same material with each and every concert.

In the Western classical tradition improvisation is also hard to pin down. To begin with, improvisation and composition were indistinguishable. This changed with time, especially as a result of the development of musical notation in the 15th century, which led to the idea of a 'musical work' defined by what the composer wrote down. Improvisation was then redefined specifically as a contrast to this, as whatever was thought to be unique and spontaneous in a particular performance. In the first half of the 19th century this emphasis reached an extreme, with players having to prove they were 'really improvising' by making use of musical ideas given to them there and then by audience members.

In another great tradition of musical improvising, Indian classical music, improvisation has always been defined as what is unique to the individual performance. In this case, though, the contrast is not with a written score, but between the loose rules governing the unfolding of improvised music and the much stricter rules involved in non-improvised music – rules which in both cases have been committed to memory by musicians, thanks to years of practice.

INTRODUCTION

These days many people tend to think of certain styles of music – particularly jazz – as essentially improvised, so that even when they rely heavily on elements worked out in advance of performance (through composition or other means) they're still heard as improvisations. And most people tend to think of Western classical music as essentially not improvised: if something is improvised in a classical concert, we tend to think that it is part of the performer's interpretation rather than part of the musical work itself, and therefore only of secondary importance. Yet the reality in both cases is more complex, for two reasons.

Firstly, as we'll see in a moment when we consider its history, the role of improvisation in any one kind of music making can evolve over time. That's because it is linked to other developments, such as changes in the musical language or in the role that such music plays in the wider culture for which it is created.

Secondly, while some musical traditions identify improvised music with an entirely distinctive style or kind of music, others treat it as an alternative method for arriving at broadly similar forms of musical structure and expression. Even within the same culture, some improvising musicians want their musical creations to sound as close as possible to their favourite non-improvised music, while others don't. Instead, the latter believe that how one makes music affects what one creates, so improvising is important as a way to produce music that sounds significantly different in some way, or at least sounds improvised.

All of this makes the essence of musical improvisation rather elusive, but there's a positive side to this: it forces us to focus on some of the more fundamental features of music making that come to the fore in improvised music, even if they're not strictly unique to it. For example, one thing improvising ought to have is an element of risk. There's something exciting and involving about playing or listening to music when one knows it reflects decisions being made as the music unfolds. Because such decisions have immediate consequences for where the music goes next, this creates an ever-present possibility of encountering something new and unexpected around the next corner. But the unfamiliar and the unexpected must still eventually be reconciled with the underlying structure of the music, which means that it poses a challenge. So then we have the thrill of hearing how that challenge is met by the players (who may also be ourselves).

That brings to light another essential feature of improvised music. A great improviser makes the music take a turn in an unexpected direction before bringing it back to something more familiar and resolved. We can only appreciate that if we are in a position to distinguish between those aspects of the music that provide a fixed framework – a basis for stability, coherence, and predictability in the musical style – and those that can be varied freely. In other words, we need to know in advance – based on previous musical experience – that certain features are obligatory for the player, just as others are not. This is possible because players and listeners belong to a shared musical culture that provides received models, each associated with a set of

INTRODUCTION

unchanging features and implicit rules with which we are intuitively familiar. What differentiates the various traditions of musical improvisation around the world and across the ages is, above all, the nature of these models and the kinds of musical invention during performance they make available.

Comparing different musical traditions in terms of how they use models as points of departure for improvising can give us a good sense of the different approaches to improvisation that have existed so far. It can also help us to realise that some of the practices we associate with relatively contemporary styles such as jazz have existed since ancient times, while others that we think of as distinctively Western are also found in cultures that may seem remote from ours.

Probably the two oldest kinds of model are those that involve melody types, and those that involve repetitive variation of a single phrase. In the first case, the improviser begins from a scale that's already linked to a standard set of melodic ideas – ideas that can then be more or less freely combined to make a continuous melody line. You can hear a lot of this sort of thing in classical Indian music (based on the raga) and music of the Middle East (Turkey, Iran, and the Arabic countries – based on the maqaam), but it's also likely that the religious chanting that is the earliest beginnings of European classical music reflected a similar practice. As we'll see, this use of melodic formulas that can be combined and recombined in many different ways is also one of main methods used in jazz. In the second case a single melodic phrase is varied each time it is repeated. This is possible either because it is performed without accompaniment or because it corresponds to a unit whose length is fixed relative to an underlying rhythmic framework that organises the overall texture. You'll hear lots of examples of this in the traditional musics of sub-Saharan Africa, from which the technique was transmitted into Afro-American styles such as blues and jazz, as well as into Latin-American music.

Then there are a large number of orally transmitted forms of traditional folk music (including most of those found in Europe) that may well have involved both types of model, but to an extent that's hard to determine. That's because in these cases it's not clear how far variations occurred in individual performances, as improvisation, or as a result of adaptations made during the process of oral transmission between performers. The result was a large body of melodies, each with a rather fluid identity but nevertheless clearly showing various degrees of similarity to one another; they are sometimes known as tune families. Such melodies naturally lend themselves to loose and creative forms of rendition that border on improvisation, as you'll hear for yourself if you make your way to one of those places in Europe where Celtic, Slavic, or Nordic folk music is still performed in an authentic way.

To understand how such fixed points of departure for improvisation have featured in Western classical music and jazz, however, we must look beyond these basic differences. It's necessary to consider how these models, and other aspects of the practice of improvisation, have evolved as a consequence of other developments in the musical language. This can help us to understand, and be critical of, fashionable assumptions about how improvisation relates to the different styles of music practised today, such as classical and jazz, not to mention the other styles covered in this book.

Improvisation in Western classical music

For Western classical musicians, the meaning of 'improvisation' has changed a lot over the centuries. It generally refers to those elements that change from one performance to another, as opposed to those that stay the same; in Western classical music the latter have come to be more and more identified with the concept of a music 'work'. The strict concept of a musical work only appeared in the late middle ages (at the end of the 15th century, to be precise). Since then its significance has evolved to reflect other developments, including the evolution of musical notation, new ideas about how music should be performed, and changes in the musical language that influence which aspects can be decided by performers without radically altering the music's underlying form.

Because our conception of a musical work has changed, our understanding of improvisation as a way of varying aspects of a work in performance has also changed. In the period of Western music before the appearance of this concept of a musical work, we can't identify improvisation as a distinct form of music making, even though what we now call improvising played an important role in almost all forms of music making. Equally, once the idea of a musical work became firmly established, it complicated the role of improvising. That's because it soon led to the composing of written works meant to sound like improvisations, and also to improvisations aimed at reproducing the distinctive features of composed music.

Throughout most of the Middle Ages it was common to learn the art of combining melodies through vocal 'discanting', which meant improvising a new melodic line (known as a 'countermelody') over a given series of held notes (called a 'cantus'). Moreover, when we study written musical manuscripts from the 12th and 13th centuries, they sometimes look just like written-out improvisations. (We can tell this because where several melody lines sound together they are worked out to sound good against the basic line (cantus), but not to sound equally good against one another.) By the 14th century, keyboard virtuosi were engaged in a similar practice, improvising new melodies over both religious chants and secular songs.

Apart from this kind of improvising, early Western music also suggests the use of melodic formulas linked to a given scale – the basic model for improvising that we referred to earlier as melody type. We can see this from the fact that music based on each of the scales used in early church music (known as the 'church modes') tends to be associated with a particular set of recurring melodic shapes, just as with the Indian ragas. Furthermore, descriptions from as far back as the 4th century talk about early forms of Christian chanting ending with a spontaneous expression of religious ecstasy through melodic decoration (called the 'Jubilus'). This connection between melodic vocal improvisation and the spontaneous expression of religious feeling is still around

INTRODUCTION

today in some forms of Christian worship. You can hear it, for example, in the spontaneous decoration by individual members of the congregation in choral singing on some of the more remote Scottish islands. Something related to this, which you're probably more familiar with, is the practice at Pentecostal church services of breaking suddenly and unexpectedly into ecstatic individual or group vocalising.

By the 16th century, when Renaissance music was at its height in Europe (and especially in Italy), improvised combinations of melodic lines were a regular feature of choral singing in Italian church services. But as stricter demands came to be made on how these lines should be related, a shift began towards purely composed textures. Even so, these techniques also influenced instrumental musicians, who used similar techniques to improvise music for traditional Italian dances (such as the 'saltarello') over a series of lower-sounding held notes (called a 'tenor').

Textbooks from this time also show examples in which a series of given notes form the basis for chords that then provide a melodic outline for the improvising musician. This reflects changes to the musical language occurring at the start of the 17th century, when Western music started to move towards a more chord-based approach centred around the harmonic implications of bass lines. Patterns consisting just of a sequence of bass notes, and sometimes chords as well, could be continually repeated while musicians improvised over them – a technique that was developed to extremes of virtuosity by English keyboard players, who called it 'making divisions on a ground'. The resulting method of variation over a repeated structure quickly came to be applied to the chords and/or melodies of well-known songs as well, using either or both as a 'theme' – a basis for ongoing variation. The technique has remained as a basic model for improvisation in classical music ever since: in the 20th century it was taken over and applied in jazz, as well as by other non-classical musicians.

Another important development, at the peak of the Renaissance, was the increasing use of ornamentation by performers to make an existing melody line more decorative. This technique was a form of improvised embellishment, and consisted of substituting faster runs of notes (known as diminutions) for the longer notes in the original melody. The musicians would take turns to be the one whose part could be varied in this way – rather as jazz musicians do when taking turns to 'solo'.

This way of embellishing a given melody gained a special significance with the emergence of a new musical culture and style in 17th century Europe. Baroque music stressed the expressive character of solo melodies as a vehicle for setting words, especially in the dramatic context provided by opera, which also became important around this time. The musical emphasis therefore shifted away from textures of simultaneously unfolding melodic lines ('polyphony'), and towards a single line heard over a background texture of supporting chords with an underlying bass line ('homophony'). This gave soloists more freedom to embellish a melody in performance, allowing them to show off their skills in extravagant ways that made them hugely popular with audiences (and very rich). Although some later Baroque composers, such as J.S.

Bach, attempted to contain this new element of freedom in how music was performed (by writing out the embellishments they wanted in their scores), most music at this time was composed on the assumption that it was open to the performer to add whatever they needed to impress listeners.

The result was a new and exciting culture of musical performance in which improvisation played an important role; it's not surprising that most of the great composers of this era were highly celebrated as improvisers. It was the ability to improvise that distinguished professional solo musicians from amateurs; while the former often reassembled their musical ideas into new pieces for each performance, the latter relied on printed versions of the works produced by composers, whose written music often reflected their own practice as professional improvising musicians. It's a huge contrast to the situation today. Nowadays the classical music world tends to treat improvisation is something amateurish that is only good for those who can't make the grade as composers or as performers of other people's music, and who are assumed to have no serious artistic aspirations.

Baroque music also brought in a new system for organising the relationship of different parts in a musical texture to a common bass line: 'basso continuo'. Its main point was to specify the harmonic implications of a bass line using a numerical shorthand (known as 'figured bass'), leaving it open to performers to decide exactly how melodic and chordal aspects of the texture should be realised. Freely improvising a melody line over a continuo bass was common in instrumental music of this time, especially in 17th-century Italy. What's more, it gave a lot of scope for melodies to be freely embellished on the spot by performers. That was standard practice in slow movements, where expressive flourishes known as 'graces' were extravagantly applied, especially by singers and violinists. In faster music a tradition evolved known as the 'varied reprise', in which a soloist would vary the melody line on its repeat. In both cases musicians made use of an extensive repertoire of standard melodic formulas, which could be used to ornament or otherwise vary an existing line, but also to generate new material to be played over the same bass line. One consequence was that short movements could easily be lifted out of longer works and used as basis for freely improvising new sets of 'variations'. This was the forerunner of the 'Theme and Variations', an important form in the later 18th century, when Western art music entered its so-called Classical period. Indeed, all of these practices lasted well into the 18th century, when the tradition of improvised embellishment fell into decline as composers increasingly tended to write out the exact ornamentation they wanted.

Of course, the element in Western classical music that's most famous for being improvised is the 'cadenza'. This is also something that evolved in the context of Baroque music, thanks to the popularity of instrumental concertos – works for a solo instrumentalist accompanied by an orchestra – as well as vocal arias. In both cases it was customary to pause on the chord just before the final harmonic resolution of a movement, while the soloist improvised freely, playing around with ideas from the

INTRODUCTION

preceding music in order to show off his virtuosity. Such cadenzas were also sometimes used to link movements in larger works. The tradition of the improvised concerto cadenza was maintained by the great composer-musicians of the Classical period, Mozart and Beethoven, and only fell into neglect in the mid 19th century, when it became normal for composers to write out cadenzas, and for the cadenzas in earlier music to be provided by historical specialists.

Like the cadenza, the tradition of keyboard improvisation associated with the 'free fantasia' first appeared in the 17th century, but lasted right through the Baroque and Classical periods and well into the 19th century. The idea of such a fantasia – essentially an entire piece improvised from start to finish – probably emerged from the Italian Baroque form known as the 'partimento'. This was a type of piece in which only the figured bass was given, with the performer expected to improvise a melody line over it. By the middle of the 18th century, when C.P.E. Bach wrote his famous *Essay On The True Art Of Playing Keyboard Instruments*, the keyboard fantasia had evolved into an important genre, with lots of possibilities for both technical virtuosity and expressive drama. This had important implications, since keyboard instruments, and the piano in particular, came to be regarded as the ideal medium for musical improvisation.

Pianist-composers such as Mozart, Clementi, and Beethoven were admired in their own day as much for their adventurous styles of solo piano improvisation as for their compositions, and were widely imitated. Apart from the fantasia, it was common to improvise variations on a theme or introductory preludes. The latter, 'preluding', was practised well into the second half of the 19th century by great names such as Clara Schumann, often being used to link consecutive works in a programme in different keys.

In the early 19th century, improvisation became hugely popular. This was partly because it appealed to the imagination of middle-class audiences, who were influenced by the cultural movement known as Romanticism. It was also due to the emergence of the piano as the most important instrument for concert soloists, made possible by technical advances in construction.

We know from piano improvisation textbooks published around this time that performers had a range of harmonic and textural formulas that they could call upon. (We'll explore some of these later in this book.) Often they involved loosely filling in a sequence of chord changes with scale-based or chord-based patterns that were so familiar to the pianist that they could be used and reused without requiring any thought at all. This allowed Romantic improvisers to 'surrender to the moment' with an almost dreamlike intensity, but did not stop them from following an overall plan that was usually worked out in advance. Such structures usually centred on contrasts between thematic ideas, and tended to alternate lyrical and virtuosic passages, using connections at the level of smaller melodic ideas ('motives') to establish continuity and coherence.

The great piano compositions of Romantic-era giants like Chopin and Liszt often display approaches to form and pianistic texture that are clearly derived from their improvised performances. This was sometimes reflected in their titles: for example

INTRODUCTION

Chopin's *Fantasie* and *Polonaise-Fantasie*, or Liszt's *Sonata (Quasi una Fantasia)*.

At the same time, the fact that the distinctive features of Romantic piano improvisation were gradually absorbed into written compositions undoubtedly contributed to the decline of improvisation in the mid 19th century. That also reflected the evolution of Romantic music towards a looser style: the special qualities of spontaneity and freedom previously associated with improvisation simply became the norm for all music of that time.

It's often claimed that since the mid 19th century classical music has been marked by an absence of improvisation. That's not quite true. In the late 19th century improvisation did drop out of the spotlight as far as classical music is concerned; it ceased to be a feature of celebrity performances in concert halls, at a time when public concerts were becoming the focus of classical musical life. In fact classical improvisation continued to be practised, chiefly by amateurs, but also by those whose professional responsibilities involved improvising music for specific circumstances, as with piano music for social dances and organ music for church ceremonies.

Both of these practices continue to the present day. A school of organ improvisation flourished among church organists in the late 19th and early 20th centuries, especially in France, providing the musical background for one of the most important and influential classical composers of the 20th century, Olivier Messiaen. (His organ improvisations were a feature of the musical and religious life of Paris for several decades in the 20th century.) In European countries like Britain and France you can still hear church organists improvise in ways that show they've been trained in that tradition. In many countries around the world a pianist who can improvise classically is certain to be in demand as an accompanist for dancers – especially wherever ballet is taught. Classical improvisation also enjoyed a brief renaissance in the first part of the 20th century in another area – that of live piano accompaniments to silent films.

But there was another development in the 20th century that was destined to have dramatic implications for the relationship of classical music to improvisation. This was the emergence of jazz, a new kind of music, often very obviously improvised. Jazz influenced the harmonic and rhythmic styles of many classical composers (including Debussy and Stravinsky), but its overall effect was to distance classical music from improvisation even more. It suggested a strong contrast between the faithful and precise interpretation of written scores by classical performers and the fluid and flexible approach adopted by jazz musicians towards their source materials.

This contrast has certainly encouraged the widespread perception that music that 'sounds classical' must be composed while music that 'sounds like jazz' must be improvised. That's plainly untrue, though it's become almost a self-fulfilling prophecy thanks to the reluctance of 20th-century classical musicians to acquire the skills needed to improvise. What is true is that improvisation has ceased to be the important element within classical musical life that it once was, especially at the level of public concert performances.

INTRODUCTION

The 1960s saw a brief return to improvisation at the experimental end of classical music, thanks to avant-garde modernist composers such as Karlheinz Stockhausen and Cornelius Cardew, as well as the interest in creating 'open-form' works displayed by composers such as Pierre Boulez and Witold Lutoslawski. For a short while these developments promised to give a certain kind of independence back to the performer, but they expected classically trained players with little or no experience of improvising to produce musically interesting results that made no references to conventional models. It's perhaps not surprising that this rarely, if ever, happened.

Groups of performers certainly exist today, and have existed in recent times, who specialise in the kinds of improvisation associated with the experimental wing of contemporary 'serious' music. These often now centre on using electronic sound-generating equipment and computers in live concert settings. However, they've yet to gain the attention of a wider public, and it's significant that their approach to improvisation is based on rejecting the kind of traditional harmonic and/or melodic materials that are associated with longstanding traditions of improvised music-making throughout the world. They have not arrived at anything that audiences are willing to recognise as a musical language that would also lend itself to being explored through improvisation.

In spite of the fact that classical music has drifted away from improvisation in the course of the last 150 years or so, there's been a striking revival of interest in recent years. Why? One factor has been the growing realisation – partly in response to the desire to reproduce earlier classical styles of performance as accurately as possible – that European art music of previous centuries relied much more heavily on the creativity of performers than was previously thought. Another reason, perhaps, has been growing concern for the future of classical music in times when the appeal of other styles of music – especially to young people – seems to have eclipsed much of the importance that Western art music once had for society.

Classical music survives as a composed art among those who are prepared to write music for an extremely small and specialised audience, mainly consisting of professional critics and other composers. And it can still be pursued as a publicly performed art amongst those who make it on to the international circuit of celebrity performers responsible for delivering authoritative interpretations of the classics. But something essential to any living musical culture seems to be missing from both of these spheres where classical music is concerned, or, at least, has come to be increasingly neglected. It's the sense of participation in a shared musical culture whose roots lie not in the past or in a specialised training, but in the everyday experiences, tastes, and music-making activities of ordinary people.

Looking back over the history of classical music, it's easy to see that these roots existed while the tradition acknowledged improvisation as something central – something that we need if we are to stay fully attuned to our creative instincts and passions. And it's clear that these same roots began to fade at around the time improvisation disappeared from the heart of classical music. This has led more thoughtful classical musicians to try to put improvisation back at the centre of music making, as a potentially revitalising source not just for performing practices but also for the musical language itself. Most notably, for the last two decades the pianist Robert Levin has sought to bring improvisation back into the performance of classical compositions, improvising cadenzas, preludes and fantasias in historical styles that match the works performed alongside them. More generally, improvisation is now back as part of the teaching programmes at many of the more forward-thinking music conservatoires around the world.

Improvisation in jazz and non-classical Western music
In modern times, jazz, more than any other musical style, has come to be closely identified in people's minds with improvisation. In fact not all jazz is improvised, and improvisation in jazz, just as in other styles, involves a balance between elements that are fixed in advance of a performance and others that are not. However, the style and forms of jazz have, right from the beginning, been mainly orientated towards improvisation. Even jazz styles that are not improvised tend to use a musical language that reflects the priorities of improvisation, focusing on simple chord progressions and loosely defined melodic formulas that can be endlessly varied and easily embellished without destroying the underlying coherence of the music.

Improvisation in jazz traditionally centres around a practice known as soloing, in which individual players in an ensemble take turns to improvise solo melodic lines while the remainder of the group provides an accompaniment. A solo normally runs across one or more sections known as choruses, and each chorus corresponds to one statement of the basic structure of the music. This structure, which is repeated over and over again, is most often taken from a popular song (typically from a Broadway musical), known as a standard, but it may be based on a version of the chords associated with the blues, or be composed by jazz musicians themselves. Where it includes an existing melody, the original form of this is known as the 'head', while jazz musicians like to refer to the structure of chord progressions as the 'changes'. This provides the immediate source material for a jazz performance, but not the only form of model used. Whatever their models, jazz players use a variety of techniques in order to produce interesting improvisations. One important resource they have is their knowledge of previous improvisations on the same source material by other musicians, which they get to know through repeated listening to recordings, often committing what they hear to memory or transcribing it into written notation so that it can function as a model.

The most important technique used by jazz musicians is the varying of a given melody line. This means that the latter plays a role roughly similar to that of the theme in a classical Theme and Variations. An inventive jazz musician will rework this line on every occasion, frequently varying its melodic shapes and rhythmic qualities to the point where they are no longer recognisable, though normally retaining just enough of its distinctive features to make us hear it with reference to the original melody. Sometimes it's only thanks to the supporting chord structure that we can identify it as related to the original version. Yet these chords can also be varied, using a set of techniques known as 'reharmonisation'.

The other main technique used is the stringing together of small melodic fragments, known as 'licks', to make extended musical phrases, whose connection to the overall structure is principally governed by an understanding of what scales can be used for improvising over particular chords. This means that the improvised material need not be constrained by the need to be heard as related to an original melody line, and can be explored more freely. However, the performer must continually recombine his or her musical ideas in fresh and unfamiliar ways. This is the only way to avoid the sense of cliché that rapidly emerges if listeners realise they are hearing the same underlying ideas being used and reused.

A contrasting approach to this is also used by some improvisers, especially in less traditional styles of jazz. This occurs when the player seeks to draw the attention of listeners to an underlying motif that recurs, with or without variation, and which is used to give a sense of unity to an improvisation that in other respects may be quite free or highly complex.

In fact, and especially in jazz as practised today (which is often a fusion of elements taken from diverse earlier styles), most improvising combines aspects of all of these techniques, often employing several simultaneously. It may also be defined by its use of more specific techniques. In 'modal improvisation', for example, the improviser plays over a series of chords derived from one of the scales used in early European church music (first used by the ancient Greeks, and known as modes), and keeps closely to the implications of these. In 'modal jazz', on the other hand, these and other artificially constructed scales are used as raw material for melodic improvising that may depart quite radically from the traditional implications of the accompanying chords, or which may involve substituting more complex chord structures derived from these same scales, whose implications may be ambiguous.

The improvisation techniques used in jazz have naturally been carried over into fusions between jazz and other non-classical styles, such as jazz-rock and Latin-jazz. Nevertheless, where these other styles originate from traditions in which improvisation plays a smaller a role (or none at all), it's not surprising to find that there's less scope for the techniques found in jazz itself.

Outside of jazz, the most important non-classical style for improvisation is blues (or 'the blues'), although elements of improvisation also appear in country and gospel, as well as in pop and rock music more generally. Blues improvisation, however, can mean two different things: blues-style improvisation, and improvisation based on the blues chord-progression. The latter can take the form of almost any style, though this is most commonly jazz or rock (or something derived from these), sometimes mixed with elements of the blues style itself. On the other hand, blues-style improvisation, like blues music generally, is a distinct style from jazz, and it's partly thanks to its influence that jazz reflects Afro-American musical influences in the striking way that it does.

You can hear the transition from blues to early jazz in piano idioms like boogie-woogie, where the right-hand improvises freely and loosely over driving left-hand rhythms and/or repeated bass-line patterns, which partly resemble the accompanying textures in traditional jazz. Although blues-style playing is an important style of improvised music making in its own right, especially on piano, styles like boogie-woogie require a fairly extreme level of physical exertion, partly to achieve the necessary rhythmic independence of the hands. That makes it impossible for most people to also cultivate the finger dexterity needed for successful jazz and classical playing. Because the latter represent the mainstream of improvised music, blues-style improvising will only be explored in this book in forms that avoid making these potentially damaging physical demands.

Improvisation and the piano
Ever since its invention by Bartolomeo Cristofori in the early 18th century, the piano has been at the centre of developments in Western music that have been important for improvising musicians. To see why, it is necessary to know something about its origins.

The piano emerged as a successor to a variety of other keyboard instruments, including the clavichord and the harpsichord. Like the piano, the clavichord produced musical tones by using hammers to strike strings, but the resulting sounds were too weak for any sort of public performance. By contrast, the harpsichord was the largest of a family of keyboard instruments that used a mechanism that plucked strings but also 'damped' them to stop the sound when keys were released. The harpsichord was powerful enough to be used in public solo recitals, but lacked the singing tone of the clavichord. Also, as with all keyboard instruments before the piano itself, there was no way for the player to vary the volume of individual notes. (Musicians nowadays would say that it wasn't 'touch sensitive'.)

Cristofori's achievement, which represented a breakthrough in instrument design, was to find a way to join the advantages of the clavichord with those of the harpsichord, so that an expressive singing tone could be combined with the volume needed for public concerts, while at the same time introducing a mechanism that would allow hammers to hit the strings at a speed controlled by the player. This meant that volume could be varied, but it also required him to develop a completely new mechanism for damping notes. The end result was that the keyboard player found himself (or herself) in almost total control of the character of the resulting notes, which could now be shaped expressively, just like with other less mechanical instruments (for example wind and stringed instruments), or the singing voice. At the same time, though, the piano preserved the enormous advantage of keyboard instruments generally: it allowed a single player to produce harmony and melody, sounding several notes or melody lines

INTRODUCTION

at the same time. In this way the piano put control of the entire texture of music into the hands of a single individual for the first time in the history of Western music.

It's no coincidence that the piano soon emerged as the instrument of choice for improvising musicians. This occurred in the 18th century, when a new conception of music (and art in general) was just emerging, focused on the arousal of strong feelings in audiences and on personal expression. That naturally favoured an individualistic approach on the part of performing artists: soloists were encouraged to present themselves as gripped by a spontaneous outpouring of emotion, with inspiration striking during the performance itself. New technical advances at the end of the century enabled larger, more powerful instruments to be built. Together with the invention of a sustaining pedal that could produce more resonant textures, these meant that the piano was even more suited to the style of musical Romanticism that developed in the 19th century.

Romantic performers such as Liszt and Chopin were then able to use the piano to open up the language of Western music to a much wider palette of colouristic possibilities, involving new harmonies, richer textures, and a wider range of registers. This made for a looser, more flexible approach to combining melody and harmony – one that left more scope for improvisation than earlier styles. The Romantic craze for improvisation was so intense that it had burned itself out by the mid 19th century. Nevertheless, this looser approach to relating harmony and melody, which was taken further by early 20th-century composers such as Ravel and Debussy, provided the essential basis for the improvised approach typical of jazz.

By now you should have realized that improvisation, and especially piano improvisation, has its own rich and exciting history. It is a history that has been hidden from view, partly by contemporary prejudices about the differences between classical and non-classical music in the West, and partly by the fact that until the invention of recording, which coincided with the birth of jazz, improvised music could not be preserved in any lasting form. So if you're serious about learning to improvise on the piano, you may well find that this history can provide a stimulating background against which to appreciate and evaluate your own achievements. But that will only happen if you are willing to bring that history back to life, and the best way to do this is to search out and listen to the recordings that can give you a glimpse of what improvised music actually sounded like in the past. That way you can start to piece together in your own mind the true nature of the tradition of piano improvisation, which includes not just the achievements of jazz 'greats' but also the classical approaches that existed before this, and which achieved equally interesting results as well as making the latter possible.

Why not start by hunting down some recordings of the old piano rolls made by pupils of Franz Liszt – who himself was surely the greatest keyboard improviser of the Romantic era? Hear how pianists like Alfred Reisenauer and Bernhard Stavenhagen adapt Liszt's own compositions freely to suit the inspiration of the moment, just as Liszt himself is said to have done. Notice also how their approach to timing and expressive

INTRODUCTION

interpretation is far looser and more natural sounding – and far riskier – than anything you're likely to hear from a classical pianist today. These contrasts can open up your mind to the spirit of Romantic piano improvisation.

After this, you might try listening to some of the classic recordings of Mozart piano concertos made by the American pianist Robert Levin (with The Academy of Ancient Music, directed by Christopher Hogwood). Unlike the vast majority of modern classical pianists, Levin takes seriously the element of improvisation implied in Mozart's scores, where the piano part is often left incomplete, to be filled out by the soloist on the spur of the moment. During cadenzas you can hear him executing genuine improvisations, which reflect painstaking historical research into the improvised style of the time, recreating the spirit and technique of classical improvisation.

Stepping even further back in time brings us to the tradition of improvised decorative embellishment of melody that was a central feature of Baroque operatic arias, and which was copied by instrumental soloists in Baroque concertos. Although little of this has survived into modern performance practice, we can gain a glimpse of what it might have sounded like from some of the earliest recordings of Italian opera. In some cases these include performances by singers at the end of their careers, who would have received their training as far back as the first half of the 19th century, when ornamentation was still regarded as an improvised art. (In Italy itself some of these musicians continued to perform like this right to the end of their lives, long after the tradition of operatic performance had evolved in a different direction.)

Of course the one area where improvisation (including piano improvisation) has been extensively recorded is jazz. As you work through this book, you'll certainly want to supplement your study of piano improvisation by listening to the great jazz pianists of the last 100 years or so. But where to start? A good place might be with Bill Evans, whose lyrical, introverted, and minimalist style of jazz, dating from the 1950s and 1960s, reflects classical influences alongside a nicely balanced mix of traditional and modern jazz approaches. On the other hand, if you want to hear improvising in the non-classical tradition extended to more ambitious proportions, try to get hold of the live recording of Keith Jarrett's 1975 Köln [Cologne] Concert. Jarrett, whose style also reflects more than just traditional jazz influences, is one of the few performers able to perform improvisations from scratch that extend to symphonic proportions. Whether you happen to enjoy his style or not, you should find it interesting and instructive to hear how he addresses the psychological and dramatic challenges involved in producing large-scale improvisations.

A discography is available at www.pianoimprovisationhandbook.com.

UNIT 1
BASIC THEORY

The keyboard

Notation

Timing

Scales

Chords

Keys

SECTION 1

SECTION 1 | UNIT 1

The keyboard

This unit provides the basic musical knowledge needed if you want to progress through the rest of the book. Glance through the topics: if you're confident that you already know about these things then you can skip ahead to Unit Two.

Let's start by getting familiar with the piano keyboard.

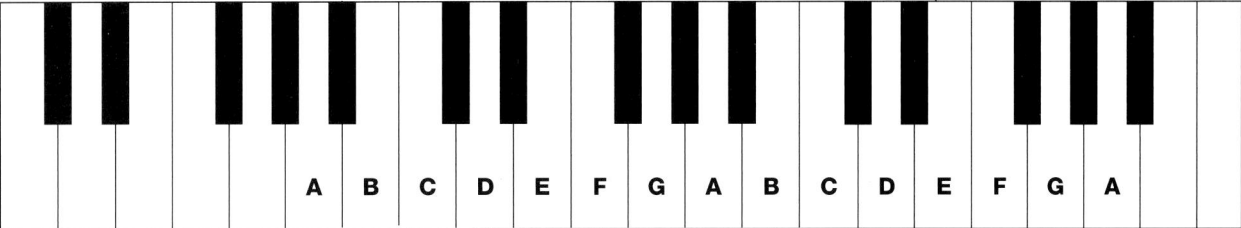

You can see from the illustration how black keys mostly alternate with white keys, except for where two white keys lie next to each other without a black key between them. This results in larger gaps between some of the black keys than others, so they fall into a clear alternating pattern of groups of two and three. It's this pattern we use to locate the different notes or pitches.

When it comes to naming the notes or pitches, we use the first seven letters of the alphabet to refer just to the white notes. (Black notes are more complicated, so we'll learn about them a little later in this unit.) What's important is that when we come back to the same place in the pattern of groups of two and three black notes, we reach the same letter-name again. This distance between two notes that have the same place in the pattern and the same letter-name is known as an **octave**.

So the first thing you need to do is to learn to recognise these different notes immediately from their place in the pattern. Try finding every A on the piano, then every B, then every C, and so on. Because the C right in the middle of the piano keyboard serves as an important reference point, it's known as **Middle C**. (It's usually parallel with the keyhole for locking the lid on a piano keyboard.)

Notation

Although this is a book about how to use the piano to improvise, and we don't normally think of improvising as playing from written music, you do need to read music to learn from this book. We're going to be using written musical examples to learn about the theory of music, to show examples of how different improvising techniques work, and to provide musical materials. You'll need to play through these examples as well as understanding them by looking at them. Sometimes they'll also take the form of exercises that require practice or provide starting points for your own creative explorations. So before we can really get started on learning to improvise, let's spend a bit of time learning about how music is written down.

If you've tried playing your instrument, you probably already know that as we move

UNIT 1 | SECTION 1

to the right side the keyboard notes sound progressively higher, and as we move to the left they sound progressively lower. This sense of higher and lower, which we call **pitch**, is reflected in how they are written. We indicate particular notes through how they are placed vertically in relation to a set of five horizontal lines known as the **stave** or **staff** (always pronounced 'stave'). A note can appear on a line, so that a line runs right through the middle of the sign for the note, or in a space between the lines, so that the lines run above and below the note.

In piano music there are normally two staves running across the page in parallel to one another – the upper one for notes that the right hand will play, the lower one for left-hand notes. Each has its own sign, which comes at the start of every line of music and is known as a **clef**. The letter-names come in different places on the staff depending on whether they are written in treble clef or bass clef. Also, whereas notes in treble clef refer to notes above (ie, to the right of) Middle C on the piano, notes in bass clef refer to notes below (ie, to the left of) Middle C. That's why treble clef is mostly used for right-hand notes (on the upper stave) and bass clef for left-hand notes (on the lower stave).

Taking just the notes on spaces or on lines in ascending order gives a pattern of letter names we can memorize: either the pattern makes a word, or each letter corresponds to the first letter of a word in a phrase. Here they are, for treble and bass clefs:

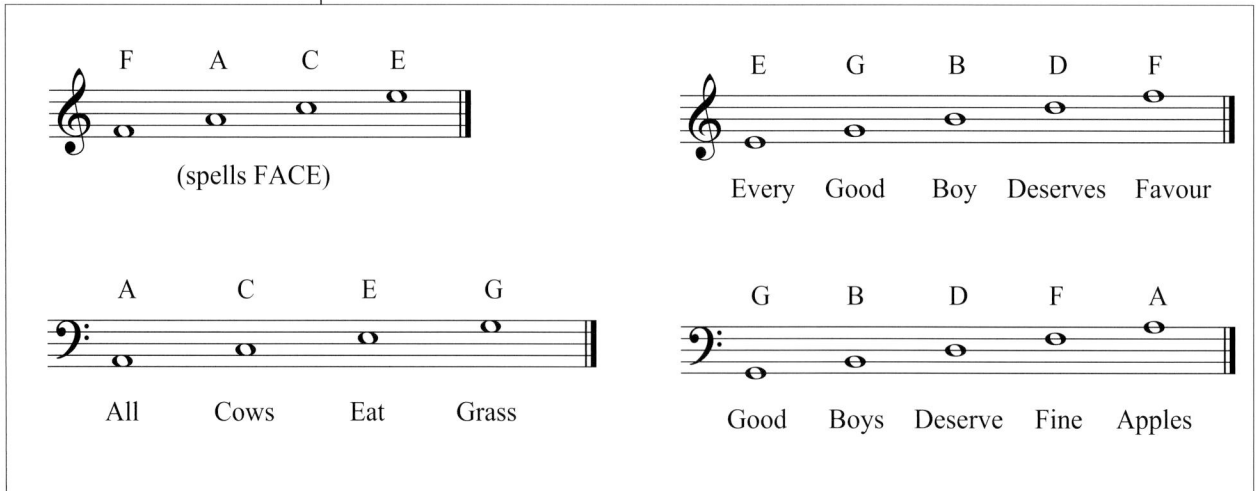

Now we need to understand how the two clefs fit together. Middle C comes above the bass clef and below the treble clef, with a small line through it. It's called a **leger line**, and represents an extra horizontal line which is only shown when needed for particular notes. Normally the gap between the staves is quite large, so it's not clear that this leger line is actually part of the same line when it's below the treble clef as when it's above the bass clef. The diagram (top right) makes this easier to see.

SECTION 1 | UNIT 1

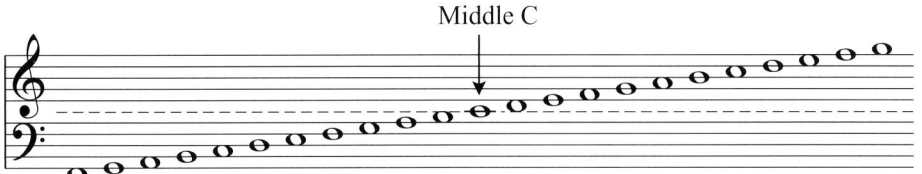

Sometimes the notes go beyond the staves, so extra leger lines are added to accommodate them. This happens when the notes are too high or low to be shown on the staves.

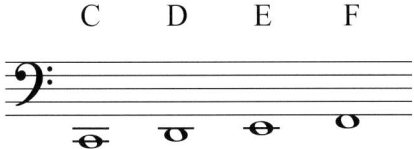 

We also have to use leger lines for notes above Middle C in the bass clef, and notes below Middle C in the treble clef.

 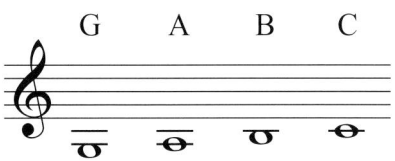

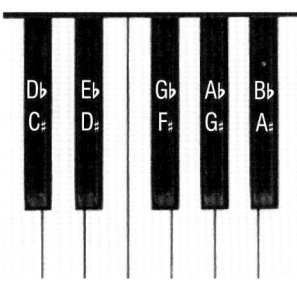

Names of the black notes

Now it's time to learn how to read and find the black notes. The key point to remember is that we basically think of black notes as **alterations** of neighbouring white notes. This means we can treat the same black note on the piano as an alteration of the white note either to the left (ie, just below) or to the right (ie, just above). In the former case it's as if we were slightly raising the pitch of the white note, so we call it a **sharp**. In the latter case it's as if we were slightly lowering it, so we call it a **flat**. The result is that each of the five different black notes that appear in the space of one octave can have two possible names, as shown in the diagram.

There are special signs to indicate sharps and flats. Sometimes we also use a **natural** sign, which cancels a sharp or flat and tells you to play the normal white note. We put these signs just in front of the notehead, on the same line or space.

the piano improvisation handbook | 25

UNIT 1 | SECTION 1

Timing

Now let's look at how **rhythm** in music can be written down. In order to know when to play a note and how long it should last for, we relate it to a regular underlying **pulse**, which we feel or just count silently to ourselves. This pulse falls into regular cycles of beats, corresponding to the **metre** of the music.

The way the music is written reflects this: it uses regular divisions, called **bars** or **measures,** which are separated by vertical lines called **barlines**. Each bar corresponds to a metrical cycle. A **double barline** shows the end of a piece. (Look ahead to the exercises in subsequent units of this book to see examples of how the music is divided up in this way.)

Rhythms are expressed as different time-values. These correspond to successive divisions into half of the longest time-value that's in common use. In northern Europe and America the names for time-values simply reflect these divisions, but in Britain and some other countries different names are used, derived from French and Latin.

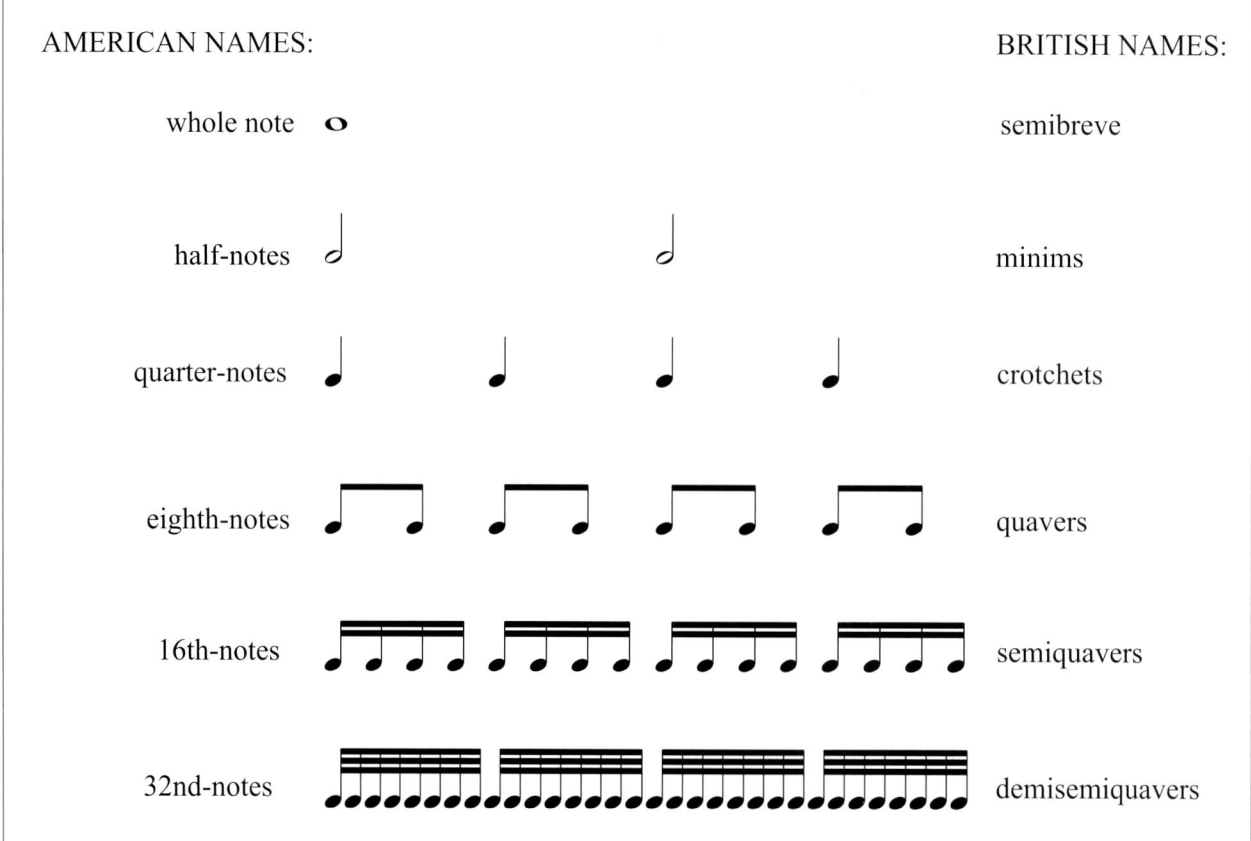

When actually reading and playing music, however, we think of time-values as divisions or multiples of the time-value that represents the actual pulse of the music. This time-value, along with the metre (the number of beats per bar), is always shown at the start of a piece of music, as a **time signature** – two numbers which look and work rather like a fraction. The lower number states which time-value counts as one unit of the pulse, treating it as a division of the longest time-value just like in the diagram above. The upper number shows how many of these fit into a single bar or measure.

Here are the most common time signatures. (Note that there are alternative signs for some of them.)

Also, each time-value has an equivalent sign for a gap in playing (in one hand or the other) of the same length. These gaps or silences are called rests. (A rest lasting for a whole bar is always shown with the sign for a whole-note rest, even when the bar itself is longer or shorter.)

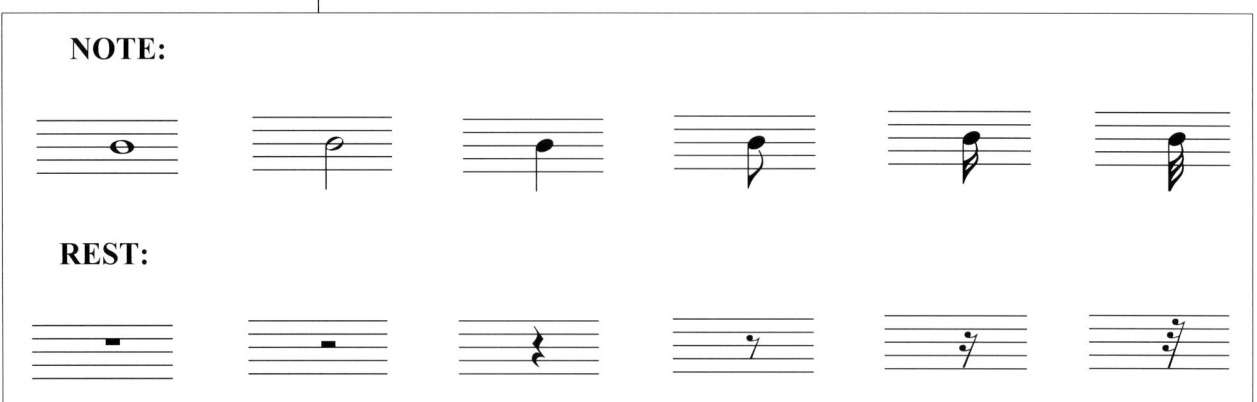

Notes and their equivalent rests

Sometimes we place a dot after a time-value: this adds half as much again to the value of the note. Likewise, placing a dot after a rest also adds half as much again to its length.

Some durations can't be expressed using the basic time-values with or without dots, so we have to join notes together, using a curved line called a **tie**. This is also necessary whenever a note gets held on through into the next measure.

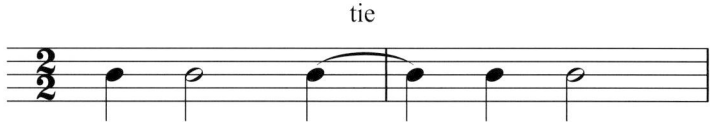

Another way of producing more time values is by altering the division of the beat. The most common way to do this is to divide it into three equal parts instead of into two. We show this by placing a numeral '3' above or below the notes: then it's called a **triplet**. Remember that each of the notes will be slightly faster than a division into half, because we're playing three notes in the time of two.

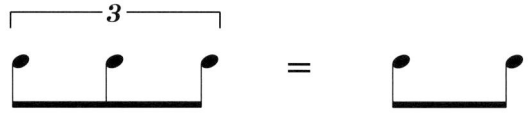

If we want this effect throughout a whole piece, as the standard division of the beat, then it's easier to use a special time signature that gives the beat itself the value of a dotted note, so that it already has three subdivisions rather than two. We express this using the lower number in the time signature by showing the value of the subdivisions rather than the value of the beat (though still as a fraction of a whole note). Then we put the total number of subdivisions per bar above it. (This equals the number of beats in a bar multiplied by three.) This is called **compound time**, while the more normal time signatures that naturally divide beats into halves rather than thirds are known as **simple time**. There are three basic possibilities with compound time:

Compound duple: 6/8 = six eighth-notes = 3 + 3 = two dotted quarter-note beats per bar

Compound triple: 9/8 = nine eighth-notes = 3 + 3 +3 = three dotted quarter-note beats per bar

Compound quadruple: 12/8 = twelve eighth-notes = 3 + 3 + 3 + 3 = four dotted quarter-note beats per bar

It's also worth noting that just as with simple time we can vary the time value that counts as one beat. In the case of compound time we do this by varying the time value that represents one subdivision of the beat, and which appears as the lower number in the time signature. So just as we can have 3/2 or 3/8 instead of 3/4 in simple triple time, we could have 6/4 or 6/16 instead of 6/8 in compound duple time, and so on.

These are the general principles for notating musical rhythm. In Unit Three we'll look at what's involved in learning to read rhythm fluently and play music in time.

Apart from metre and rhythm, the other important aspect to musical timing is the overall speed of the pulse – what musicians like to call **tempo**. That's an Italian term, roughly meaning 'time', but understood here as referring to the overall pace of the music. Classical musicians in particular like to use Italian terms to describe aspects of how music is played, and in some cases these have become the standard terms for players in any style. For example, Italian expressions are often used to indicate not just the music's speed, but its character as well.

Italian:	Explanation:
Prestissimo	very fast
Presto	quick
Vivace	lively
Allegro	fast
Allegretto	quite fast
Moderato	moderate
Andantino	slightly faster (or slower) than *Andante*
Andante	leisurely, at a walking pace
Largo	fairly slow
Adagio	slow
Lento	very slow
accelerando (accel.)	gradually getting faster
ritardando (ritard.)	gradually getting slower
rallentando (rall.)	gradually getting slower
ritenuto (rit.)	hold back
a tempo	return to the original speed

UNIT 1 SECTION 1

Whether we use Italian or English terms for tempo and expression depends on the style – we generally use Italian more for classical and English for non-classical styles. However, some Italian terms are universal and are used in all Western music.

Scales

Now let's turn to the most important resource for piano improvising: scales. These are the particular selections of notes we use as raw material for creating melodies and harmonies. There are two important aspects that define any particular scale: the note it starts (and finishes) on, and the sequence of larger or smaller steps that take us from this note to the note with the same name one octave higher and back again.

The simplest scale begins on C. It consists of just the white notes and is known as **C major**. Try playing through the notes slowly one at a time – maybe using just your right-hand index finger, starting on Middle C. (When you reach the top you can turn round and play the notes in descending order as well, until you arrive back where you started.)

Scale of C major

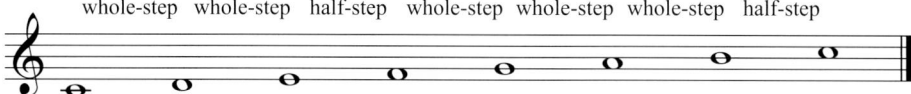

Note how it passes through each of the letter names – all seven – before reaching the octave. This means that it's what we call a **diatonic scale**. It's named C major because major scales all have the same pattern of larger and smaller steps. But wait a minute, you're probably thinking that in this case all the steps are the same, as it only consists of white notes. That's not true. In fact on the piano any two notes directly next to one another are the same distance apart, whether black or white. This means that two white notes separated by a black note, or two black notes separated by a white note, are actually twice as far apart as a white and a black note that sit right next to each other, or two white notes with no black note between them. In the first two cases we say that the two notes are a **whole-step** apart, in the second two cases a **half-step** apart.

You can see that in the scale of C major the white notes that come next to each other sometimes have a black note between them and sometimes not. When we start the scale on C, playing just white notes produces the particular pattern of whole and half-steps shown in the example above, which is the pattern for a **major scale**. (Ascending, it consists of two whole-steps followed by a half-step, then three whole-steps followed by a half-step.)

Note that if we start the scale on any note other than C and play just white notes, the pattern changes. Either we get a different scale or, if we change one of the notes to a black note, we can get the same pattern but starting on a different note.

For example here's another major scale, starting on G. Note how F has been raised to F-sharp so that the second half-step comes just before we reach the octave, as in C major. Play through the notes of the scale slowly, first with F-sharp and then with F-natural. Can you hear how adding the F-sharp is necessary to produce a scale with the same feel as C major?

Scale of G major

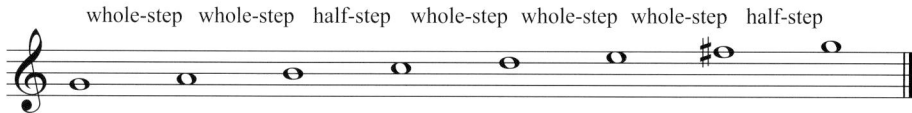

Note how the scale of G major starts four scale degrees higher than where C major started, and requires us to add one black note (a sharp). Another four steps up from G takes us to D. To get a major scale on this note we add one more sharp, also on the note just before the octave. That means we raise C to C-sharp. Note how we retain the F-sharp from G major.

Scale of D major

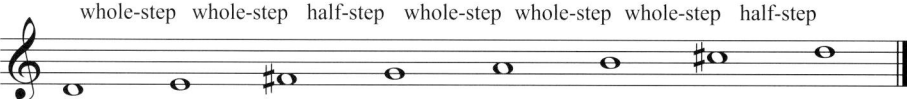

You can use this method to arrive at a few other major scales yourself – for example scales starting on A, E, and B. However, we can also begin a scale four steps lower. For example if go down four steps from C we arrive at F. The next example shows the scale of F major, but you can see that this time something different has happened: the fourth step has been lowered to B-flat, in order that the first half-step comes where it should. Once again, try comparing how it sounds, first with B-flat and then with B-natural. Which sounds better?

Scale of F major

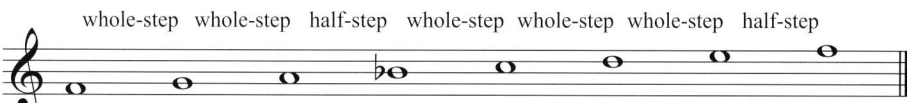

Although it may not be immediately obvious, this is just the same operation in reverse. You can see this if you ask what change must be made to the notes of F major to get back to the notes of C major. The answer is that the scale of C major will change the B-flat back to B-natural – in other words it raises the note before the octave in the new scale by a half-step from what it was in the old scale, just as when moving from C to G major, or G to D major.

It's worth going through this a few times, until you're clear in your own mind about how it works. This is your first taste of 'scale theory'.

> **Scale theory** is important for all kinds of music making, but it's especially important for improvising. Whereas musicians who just want to play composed music mostly treat scales as exercises for improving playing technique, in improvisation scales are the raw materials from which melodies and harmonies are created, so it's essential to understand how they work.

Changing the pattern of larger and smaller steps, keeping one note for each letter name, gives us another kind of diatonic scale: the **minor scale**. A good way to understand how minor scales work is to think of them as major scales with some notes (or **degrees** of the scale) lowered by a half-step. The third note of the scale is always lowered, and the sixth and/or seventh may also be lowered, but there are several different versions. Which one we use depends on several factors, including the style we are improvising in and what sort of expressive feel we're looking for. Generally minor key music sounds sadder, major key music happier.

> Lowering or raising a note by a half-step in a scale or chord produces what is known as an alteration. Alterations change the expressive character of the music, and often correspond to the most strikingly expressive notes in a melody or chord.

In classical music the minor scale appears in two forms, **harmonic minor** and **melodic minor**. As the names suggest, the first is used more for harmony (ie, chord structures), the latter for melody lines. In both cases the third is lowered, but because the harmonic minor scale lowers the sixth and not the seventh it creates an extra-large gap (of one-and-a-half steps) between these.

C harmonic minor

This can be a problem in melodies, but the melodic minor version avoids this, by not lowering the sixth on the way up and lowering both the sixth and seventh on the way down.

C melodic minor

In jazz and rock, however, other versions of the minor scale are more common. The **jazz minor** scale has the same notes as the ascending form of the melodic minor scale, but uses these in both directions.

C jazz minor

Similarly, the **rock minor** scale has the same alterations as the descending form of the classical melodic minor scale, again in both directions. Used in this way, this scale is also sometimes known by its old name, the **Aeolian mode**. (The term 'mode' refers to the old names for scales used in ancient church music, such as plainchant. However, this term is also used in jazz scale theory, so we'll return to it later in this book – see Unit Five.)

C rock minor

Jazz and rock also sometimes use another scale with a lowered third step that gives it a minor feel, known as the **Dorian mode**. (It's common in jazz-rock fusion styles, but also appears in earlier classical music.) Notice how this scale lowers the seventh from the major scale rather than the sixth.

C Dorian

Another type of scale that plays an important role in almost all kinds of music, and especially in folk and popular styles, is the **pentatonic scale**. This scale passes through only five different notes before reaching the octave, so two of the letter-names are omitted. Note how it contains a mix of whole-steps and one-and-a-half steps. It exists in two basic forms, major and minor:

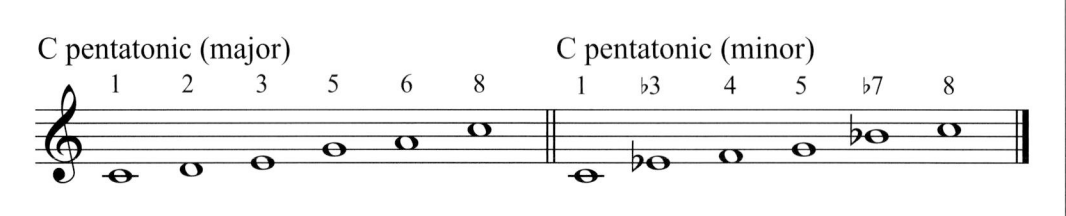

The above example shows both major and minor pentatonic scales on C, so you can see how the two scales compare when they start on the same note. Can you see that it's not just a question of lowering some notes by a half-step? The major and minor pentatonic scales each omit different notes from the normal seven-note major and minor scales. The major pentatonic leaves out the fourth and seventh notes, whereas the minor pentatonic leaves out the second and sixth. The numbers in these examples show which notes in the original seven-note scales they correspond to. However, it is a convention of the type of modern scale theory used in jazz and popular music that by themselves these numbers always refer to the notes of the original major scale. That's why some of the numbers above the minor pentatonic scale in the above example are preceded by flat signs. These signs tell us that while these notes correspond to the third and seventh notes of one of the versions of the C minor scale, they have also been lowered by a half-step (semitone) from what they are in the scale of C major. We write this because in scale theory for jazz and popular music all scales are treated as alterations from the major scale. (The same is true to a lesser extent in classical music as well.)

Now look at the next example. This shows another minor pentatonic scale, this time starting on A. Can you see how it contains exactly the same notes on the piano as the major pentatonic on C? This shows how closely related the two forms of the scale are. By the way, you can also find pentatonic scales if you play up and down just the black notes on the piano, starting on F sharp (for major pentatonic) or D sharp (for minor pentatonic).

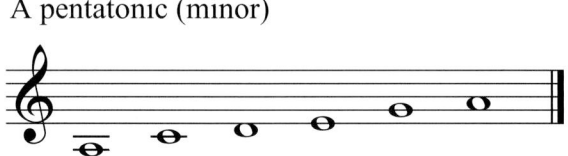

A scale which contrasts with all of the diatonic scales (whether major and minor) is the **chromatic scale**. This contains all the black and white notes, so it proceeds entirely in half-steps. Here it is, first in ascending form, then in descending form. (Notice how we tend to use sharps for the black notes on the way up, flats on the way down.)

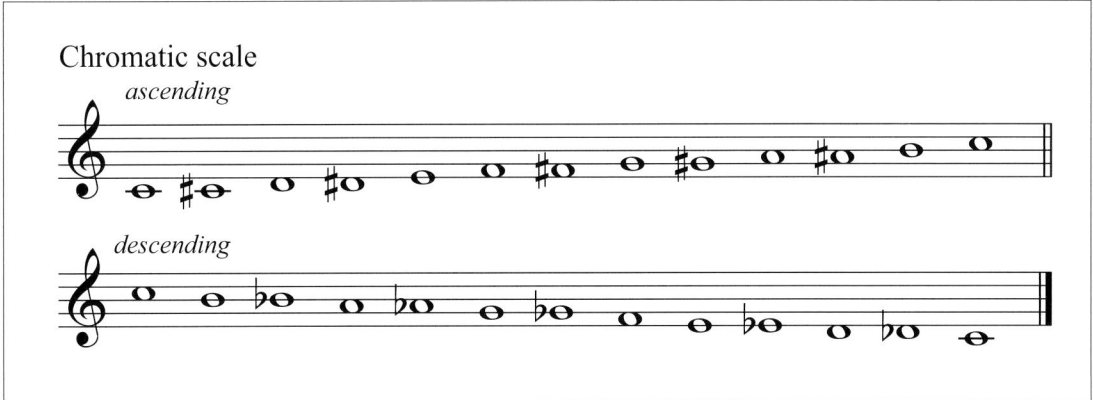

Now that we've had a taste of the variety of different scales available, it's time to learn about **intervals**. These are the distances between different notes in a scale. We normally name an interval by referring to the number of scale-steps in the major or minor scale needed to pass from the lower note, taken as the first note of the scale, to the higher note. Intervals in major and minor scales are called **diatonic intervals**. They are shown here for both the major scale and the descending melodic minor scale. (Remember: the harmonic minor scale has a raised seventh, forming an interval of a major seventh like that in the major scale, while the ascending form of the melodic minor scale has both the sixth and seventh degrees raised, so it has intervals of a major sixth and major seventh.)

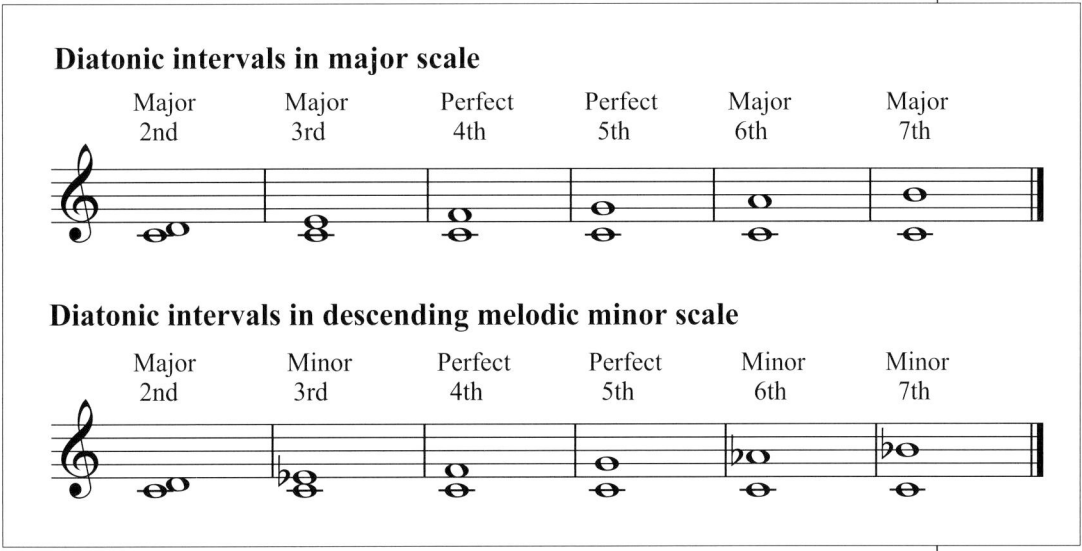

There are a few other intervals that do not appear in either the major or minor scales as intervals from the first note to other notes in the scale. We think of them as derived either from the chromatic scale or by **chromatic alteration** from diatonic intervals (ie, by lowering or raising the upper note by a half-step). These are **chromatic intervals**. In a few cases two chromatic intervals that look different on paper may correspond to the same two keys on the piano. We call these **enharmonic equivalents**. (They sound the same in isolation, but the way they are written reflects how they function in context, which in turn affects how we hear them.)

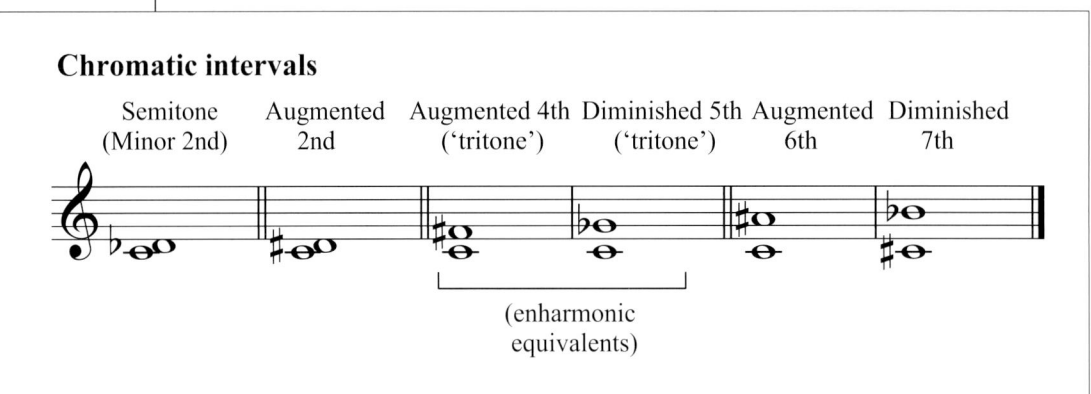

You should be able to see that the notes forming the interval of the minor second are right next to each other on the piano, so it's the same as what we've been calling a half-step until now. Another name for this – the smallest possible interval on the piano – is **semitone**. Similarly, the major second is the same as what we've been calling a whole-step, and is often referred to as a **whole tone** (or just **tone** for short).

Just as there are special names for different intervals in music, there's a technical name for each note in a diatonic (ie, seven-note) scale that reflects its position in the scale. This means we can talk about how notes relate to a certain type of scale without having to refer to particular notes, and then apply this knowledge to any scale we choose. Being able to do this is a crucial skill when learning how to improvise. The different positions that a note can have in a scale are known as **scale degrees**. Counting upwards from the first note, there are just seven names for these, the same for major and minor scales:

1 = tonic
2 = supertonic
3 = mediant
4 = subdominant
5 = dominant
6 = submediant
7 = leading tone

You should learn these names; as we'll see below, they're important for understanding how scales can be used to create harmony.

Chords

Western music has harmony as well as melody. Harmony is made up of chords – particular groups of notes played together that the ear learns to recognise as a single unit thanks to their distinctive sound. The most basic types of chord consist of three notes, each spaced two steps apart – that's an interval of a third. We call them **triads**. However, we can also change the sound of a triad by varying which of the three notes is placed at the bottom. This creates **inversions**.

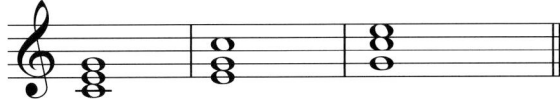

The lowest note of the original position of the chord, on which the triad is built, is called the **root**. (Hence the term **root position** when this note remains at the bottom.)

The three notes of a **triad**, then, are separated by intervals of a third, but as we've just seen, there are major and minor thirds. This actually gives four possible combinations of interval in a triad, which means four **chord types**:

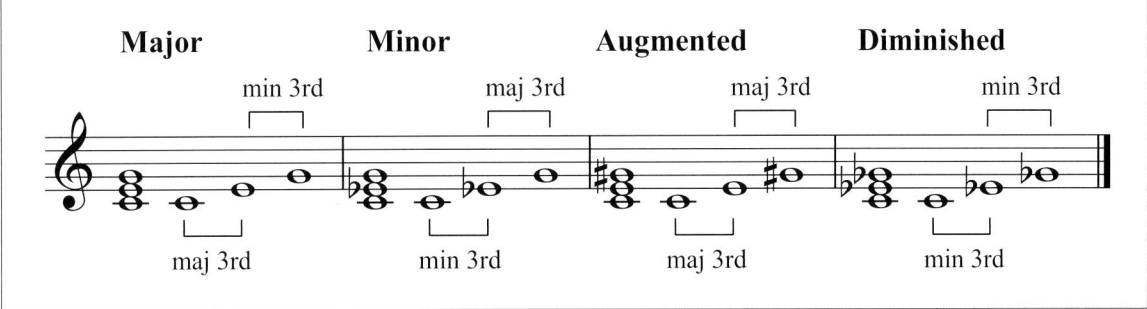

If we build a triad on each step of the major or minor scale, just using notes from that scale, we get different chord types for triads on different scale degrees. Often the chord type on a particular scale degree will differ, depending on whether the scale itself is major or minor and which version of the minor scale is used (see over.)

> Note how the degrees of the scale are shown below each staff as Roman numerals. We use this way of referring to scale degrees, especially in classical scale theory, whenever we want to think of scale degrees as the roots of chords rather than just as notes in the scale. That way we can use the scale degree to identify the chord built on it. When Roman numerals are used like this they don't automatically refer to the major scale; instead they refer to the scale actually in use in the music. So we don't need to indicate which scale degrees have been altered from the major scale.

UNIT 1 | SECTION 1

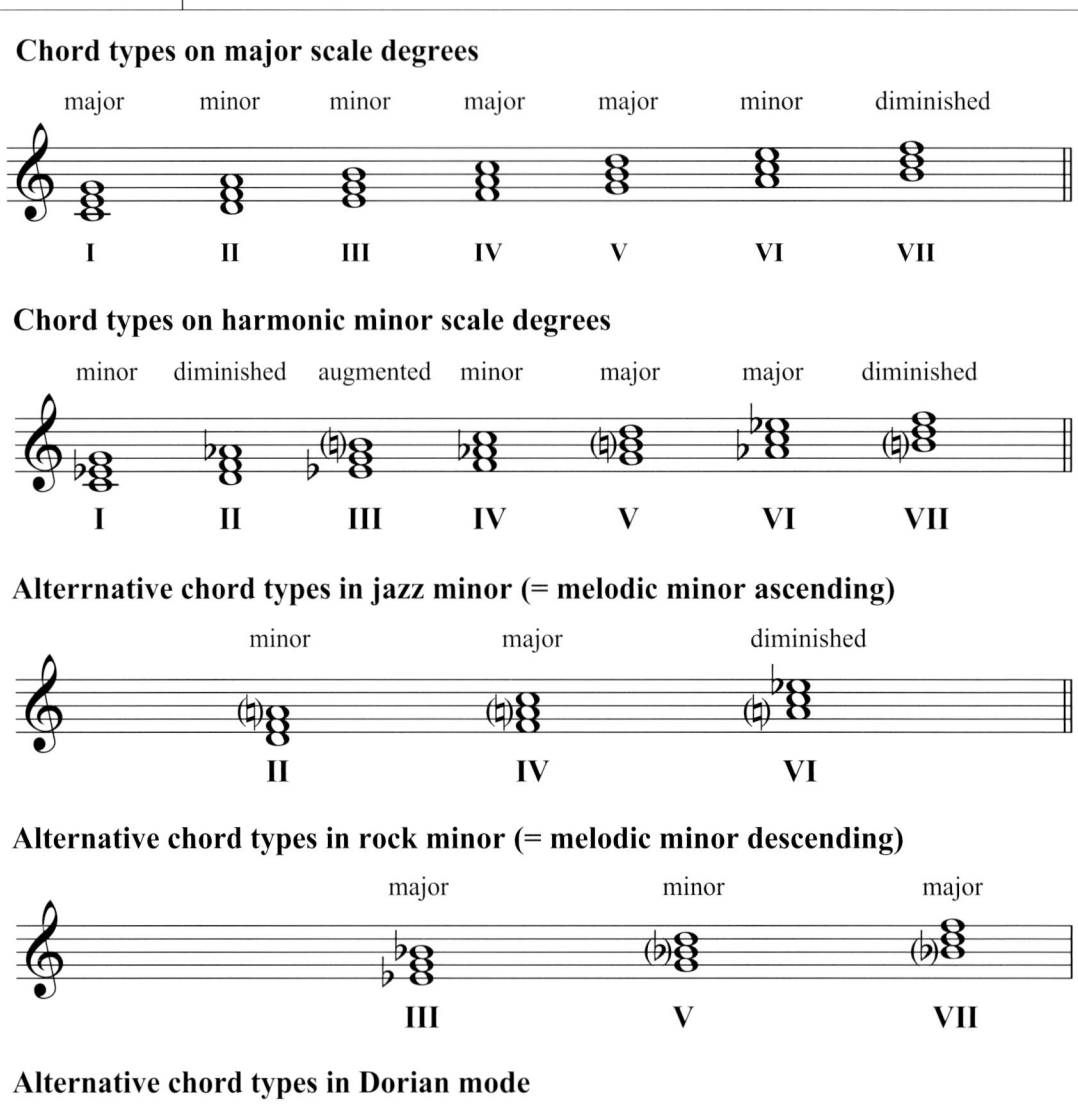

Don't be intimidated by the number of different possibilities for the minor scale here. Which version of the minor scale we use as the source of our chord types depends on which style of music we are improvising in, as you can see from the table on the opposite page.

Most of the time it's very simple: we use the harmonic minor for minor-scale chords in classical music, and the rock minor for minor-scale chords in rock and pop music. (Of

	Classical music	Jazz	Rock (& pop) styles
Harmonic minor scale	MAIN source of minor-scale chords	OCCASIONAL source of minor-scale chords	OCCASIONAL source of minor-scale chords
Jazz minor scale	OCCASIONAL source of chords, when individual parts use *ascending* melodic minor scale	Source of alternatives to major-scale chord-types (in advanced jazz only)	*Hardly used*
Rock minor scale	OCCASIONAL source of chords, when individual parts use *descending* melodic minor scale	*Hardly used*	MAIN source of minor-scale chords
Dorian mode	OCCASIONAL source of chords in *early* classical music	Used occasionally in jazz, more often in rock, and especially in jazz-rock fusion	

Scales used as sources of minor-scale chord-types in different styles.

course, we also have major-scale chords in both types of music.) Jazz mostly uses just major-scale chords: minor-scale chords only get used in advanced jazz, as a source of more complex alternative harmonisations. (We'll look at how that works, but much later in the book.)

To really grasp how chords work in music you need to understand how chords built on different scale degrees are related to one another. At any one time the music you play will mainly involve chords taken from a single (diatonic) scale: we then say that the music is in the **key** corresponding to that scale. (For example, if the chords are taken from the scale of C major, we say that the music is in the key of C major, with C as the **keynote**, and so on.) Each of these chords will have a particular function relative to the others, reflecting which scale-degree it's built on and what sort of chord-type it is. The table over the page uses the technical names for scale-degrees mentioned earlier to identify the different chords and specify their functions, which are independent of which type of scale the chords are derived from. Note that we treat chords separated by an interval of a fifth as closely related to one another.

Regardless of whether the music uses a major or a minor scale, the most important chords are always the **primary triads**, I, IV, and V. The tonic chord (I) is the most important chord of all, as it provides a sense of resolution and closure relative to the others. The principal source of tension and contrast with the tonic is the dominant chord (V), whose root is a fifth higher, but the subdominant chord (IV) also acts as a source of tension with both of these, with its root lying a fifth below the tonic (I).

If we think of how these chords are related from the point of view of the intervals of a fifth separating their roots, then dominant and subdominant lie on opposite sides of the tonic. They therefore function like opposed magnetic poles, each pulling the harmonic centre of gravity away from the tonic, but in opposite directions. In this way they also counterbalance each other.

The **secondary triads** II, III, and VI are also used, but a little less often. In a major

Chord functions

Degree	Technical Term	Function
I	TONIC	**Tonal centre;** (most important chord)
		Point of maximum harmonic resolution
II	SUPERTONIC	Fifth above dominant
		Substitutes for subdominant chord
III	MEDIANT	Fifth above submediant
		Substitutes for dominant chord
IV	SUBDOMINANT	**Fifth below tonic;**
		Main source of harmonic tension with dominant
V	DOMINANT	**Fifth above tonic;** (second most important chord)
		Main source of harmonic tension with tonic
VI	SUBMEDIANT	Fifth above supertonic
		Substitutes for tonic chord
VII	LEADING TONE	Fifth above mediant
		Rarely used chord

key these are all minor triads, so they introduce a contrast of harmonic colour to the primary triads, which are all major. It can also be helpful to think of them as substituting for the major triads whose roots are two scale-steps higher, which means the primary triads, IV, V or I. How they stand in relation to the tension between tonic, dominant, and subdominant is dependent on which of these primary triads they substitute for.

We haven't mentioned chord VII yet. That's because it's a more problematic chord that's only used in rather special circumstances. However, you need to understand the functions of these chords to know which **chord progressions** will sound good and which won't.

Keys

As we've just seen, most music uses a set of chords taken from a single major or minor scale, which defines the key of the music. However, music may change to another key, which occurs when the centre of gravity created by the chords shifts away from chord I. Hence we can talk about **key relationships** (that hold between different keys) as well as **chord relationships** (within a key). Although we sometimes use similar terms (such as tonic, dominant, etc.) in both cases, they are not referring to the same thing.

We've already seen how the same scale has a different mix of white and black notes depending on where it starts (ie, depending on what key it's in). Well, the more notes two keys have in common when using the same type of scale, the more closely related they are.

We've also learned how to recognise the signs for sharps, flats, and naturals in front of individual notes. These are known as **accidentals**, and affect just the particular note in front of which they are placed, for the remainder of the bar, unless cancelled by another sign. (So if the same note comes later in the bar, we don't need to repeat the accidental.) However because most music stays in the same key for significant periods of the time this can be inefficient. It's simpler to show the sharps or flats for that key at the beginning of each line of music, as what we call a **key signature**.

Here are the key signatures for the most common major keys. Note how sharps or flats accumulate in one given sequence for all the keys with sharps, and in another for all those with flats. As the example shows, minor scales also use these key signatures, but with some additional accidentals that vary depending on which version of the minor scale is involved. We'll learn more about these later. (C major and A minor are not shown as they have no sharps or flats at all in their key signatures.)

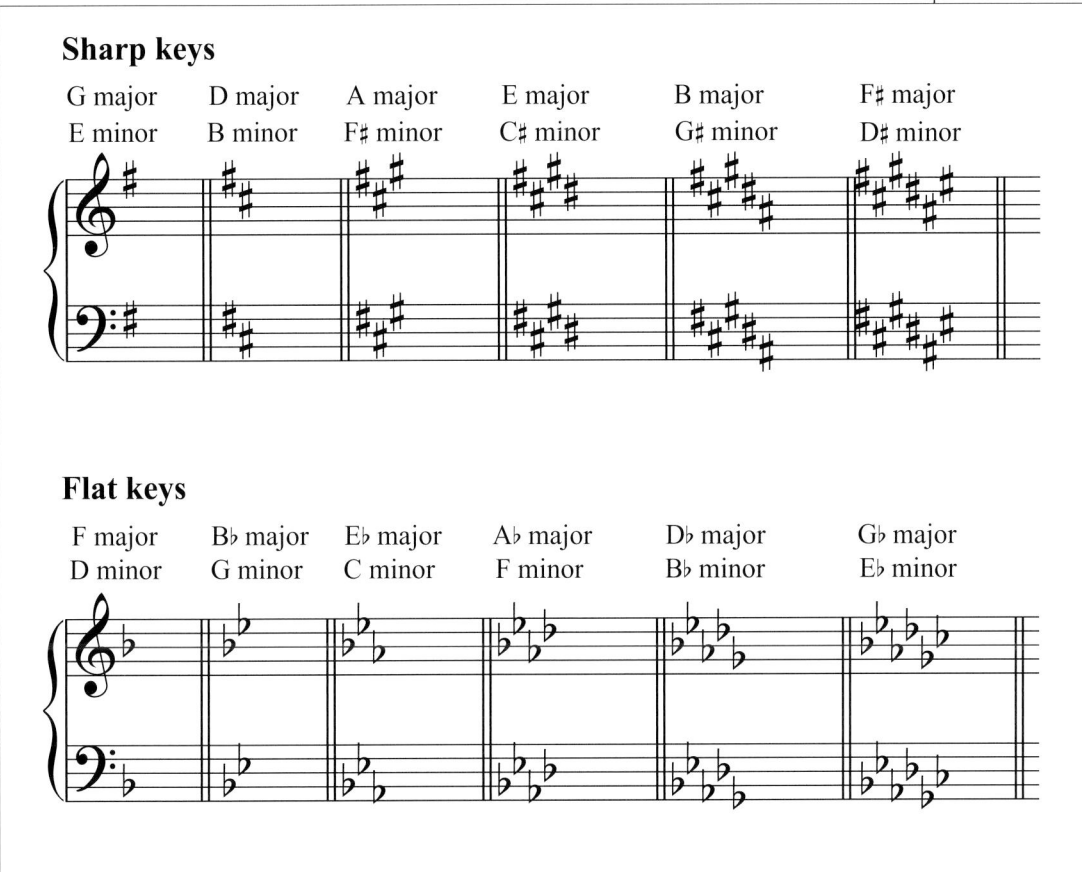

A key signature tells you to apply the necessary alterations automatically to any note in the music with the corresponding letter-name (in any octave). However, these signs can still be overridden by accidentals in the music, which will affect a particular note right up to the end of the bar in which the accidental appears.

Key relationships in music based on major and minor scales fall into a neat order, reflected in the key signatures. We show this by laying out the keys in a circle, in order of increasing numbers of sharps in one direction, and flats in the other. For every major key there's a minor key with the same key signature, a minor third down. (We call this the **relative minor**. The major key is then known as the **relative major** of that minor key.) These minor keys can be arranged around the inside of the circle. For both major and minor this gives a series of keys, each a perfect fifth away from the next. The whole sequence is known as the **Circle of Fifths**, and is incredibly important for anyone who wants to understand how music that uses the major-minor system works – especially improvisers.

The Circle of Fifths

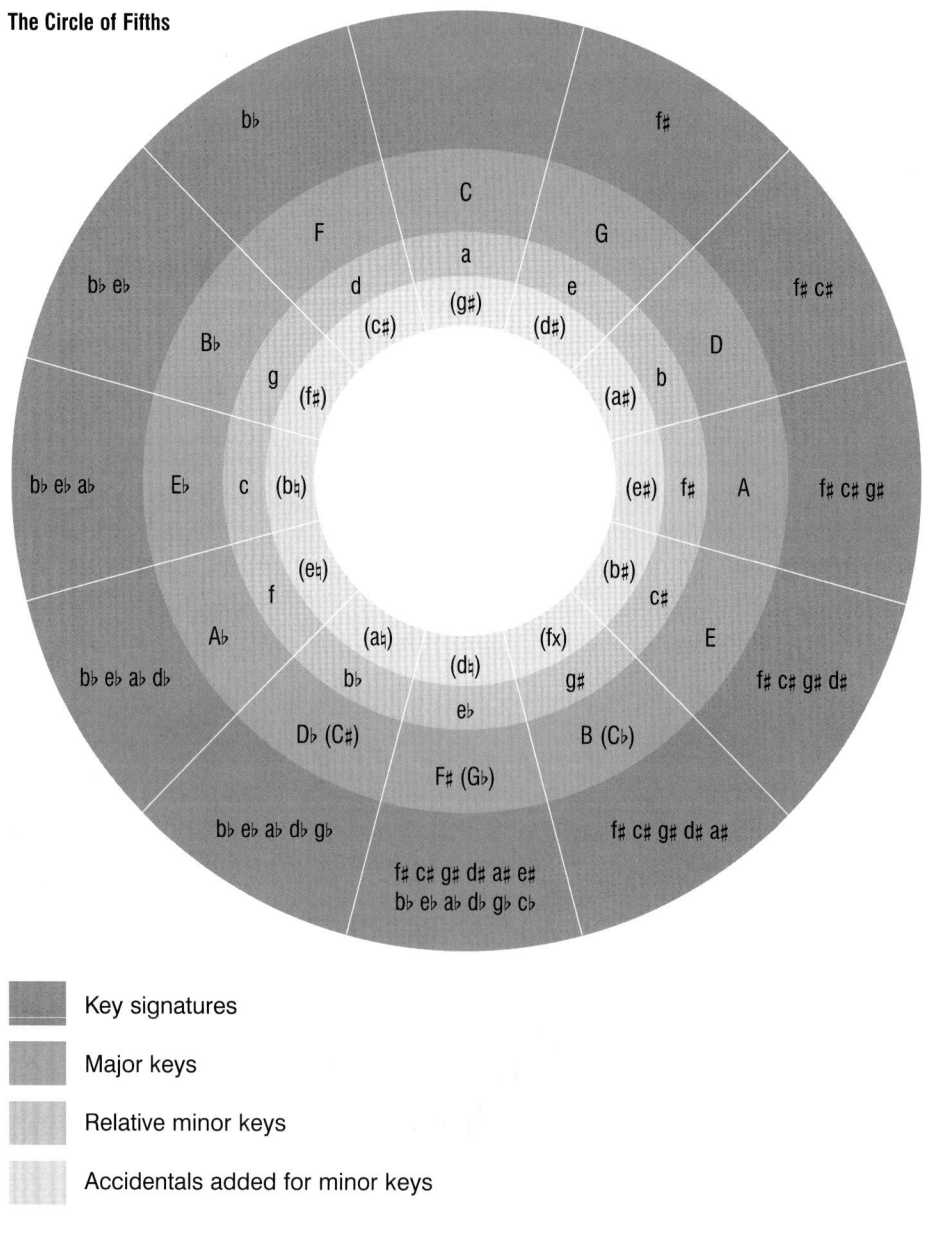

- Key signatures
- Major keys
- Relative minor keys
- Accidentals added for minor keys

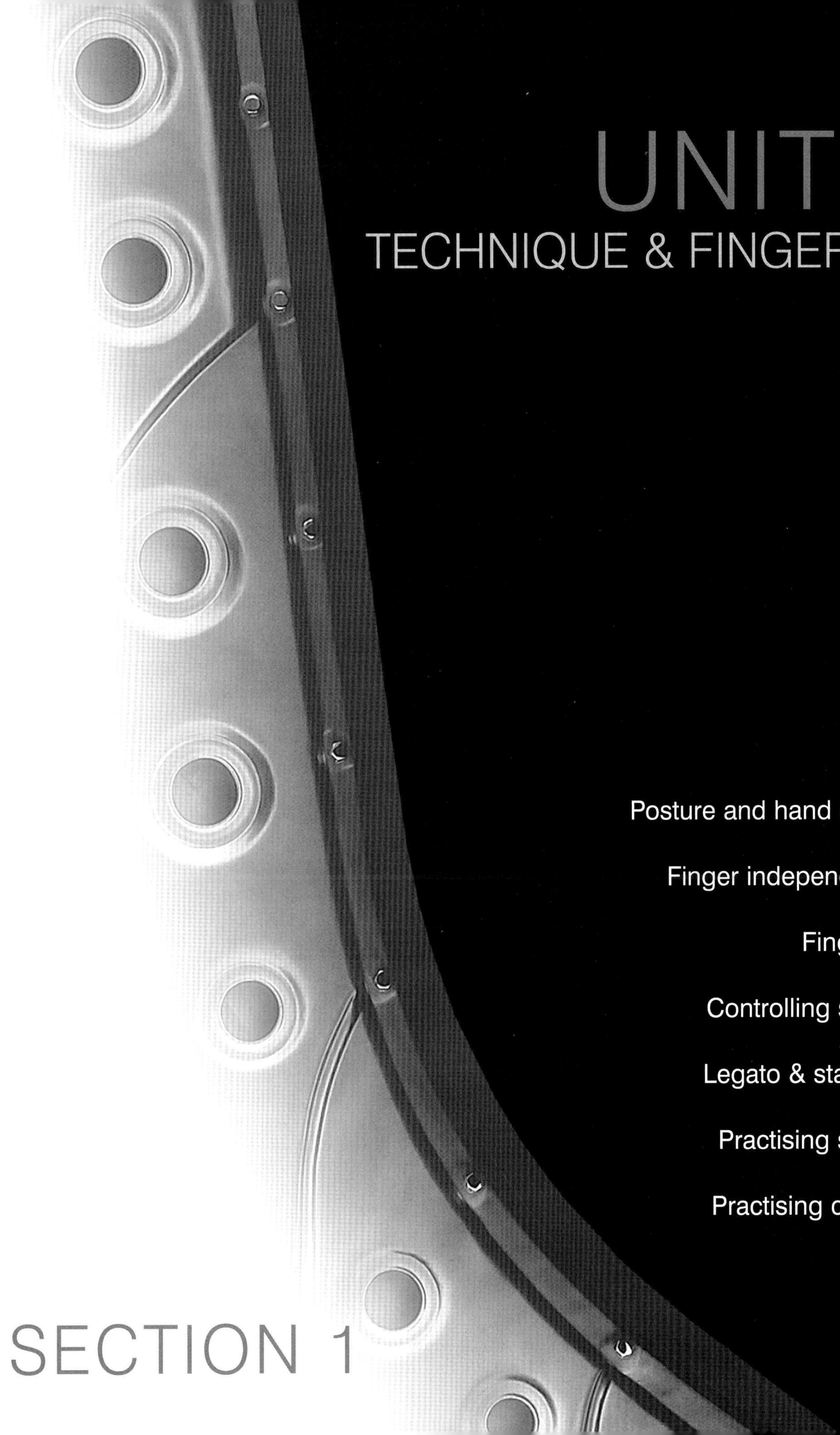

UNIT 2
TECHNIQUE & FINGERING

Posture and hand shape

Finger independence

Fingering

Controlling sound

Legato & staccato

Practising scales

Practising chords

Pedal

SECTION 1

UNIT 2 SECTION 1

Posture and hand shape

This unit outlines the basic issues connected with physical aspects of piano playing, which we call **technique**. It also deals with related aspects of musical notation, such as the symbols used in written music to indicate that a particular level of volume or method of playing is called for, or that particular fingers should be used. Finally it introduces the basic principles for which fingers to use when playing common patterns such as scales and chords. As with the previous unit, if you've already had experience of learning the piano in the recent past, and feel confident that you're already familiar with these things, then skip ahead to Unit Three. If not, you'll need to work through this material carefully: it's just as important for improvising as for any other kind of piano playing.

> **Good technique.** Some people think this is really only a must for classical pianists who want to perform the works of composers from the past in a stylistically refined way. Wrong! Technique has very little to do with style: it's there to help you achieve maximum physical control, along with ease and flexibility, playing in any style. How far you succeed is clearly audible in the sound of the resulting music, which is partly the sound of your playing. That's the same whether you're playing a written composition or improvising.

To get the most from your instrument when improvising at the piano it's best to get into the habit of sitting in the correct way as soon as possible. Ideally, you should have an adjustable piano stool, but if you have to make do with an ordinary chair, use newspapers to bring it up to exactly the right height rather than cushions – the latter are too soft and will upset your balance. If the chair's too high, find a different one!

How you sit when playing is known as your **posture**. Ideally, you should check it every time you sit at the piano before improvising. It's important to get your **height**, **distance**, and **angle** just right. First of all make sure your back is straight (but not stiff). Then put your hands on the keyboard (somewhere near the middle), adjusting the height of your stool (or chair) until there's only a very slight downward slope from the elbow to the wrists. At the same time be prepared to adjust the distance of the stool (or chair) from the keyboard, checking whether you can play comfortably across the whole keyboard without having to lean backwards, and that you don't have to lean forwards just to play at all. When you think you've got it right try to memorise how the arrangement looks and feels, so you can reproduce it easily the next time you sit at the piano. After you've been playing for a while your body may tell you things are not yet quite right, in which case some further adjustments will be necessary.

Another really important issue is hand shape. Take a look at the fingers on one of your hands: each one's a different size and shape, but somehow they've all got to work equally well when playing. We have to get used to holding each hand on the keyboard in such a way that the differences between fingers are reduced to a minimum.

To achieve this you need to apply the two golden rules of hand shape for pianists: level knuckles and rounded fingers. Let's see how these work.

If you position either hand on the white keys somewhere near the middle you'll see how the knuckles slope down away from the index and middle fingers in the direction of the smaller fingers. This means that the smaller, weaker fingers have no room to play. So you need to twist the hand round slightly from the wrist (towards the thumb) until you have level knuckles. When you do this you should find that the fingers themselves have to be less flat to continue resting on the keys – as if the hand were being cupped slightly to hold an object such as a tennis ball in the palm. Now try the same with the other hand.

Keeping both hands on the keyboard, try positioning each finger over an adjacent white key. Then take a look at your thumbs. You'll probably find they curve out a bit away from the rest of the hand, which means they aren't sitting squarely on the key they should be covering. If it's to align precisely with a key, the thumb therefore needs to be trained to curve in slightly towards the hand. Try as well to resist the temptation to let it rest on the wood in front of the keys.

 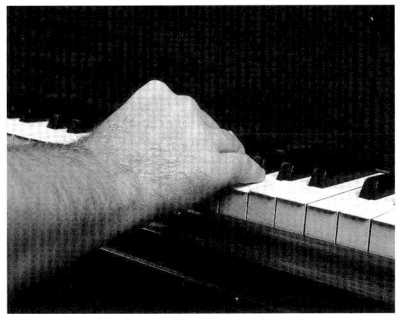 

HAND SHAPES
LEFT: a good hand position means level knuckles and rounded fingers. CENTRE: letting your knuckles slope to the right leaves no room for your shorter fingers to play. RIGHT: the high wrist is a sign of a tense hand. Time to take a break.

The next really important issue is **relaxation**. Let's start with your wrists. Each one should be slightly lower than the rest of the hand – so that there's a gentle slope upwards towards the knuckles. Try to keep it as relaxed as possible, but not so much that it causes the hand to collapse onto the keys. It still needs to support the hand. When the hand tenses up the knuckles tend to get pushed downwards, which makes the wrist rise and tense up as well.

Adult learners especially tend to have this problem when playing. It's made worse if you're in a hurry and try to play music that's too hard or too fast, as this usually means forcing your fingers to do things they are not yet ready to cope with. When it happens, stop playing and give your hand a good shake so the wrist goes floppy. If you try playing the same music again, do it more slowly. It may also be time to take a break.

The other main area where tension shows up is in the shoulders. If they're relaxed, then you should be able to feel your arms hanging quite loosely down from them, and the shoulders themselves should be quite low relative to your neck. (Check your elbows too: don't let them stick out sideways when the hands are on the keyboard – instead they should find their natural place fairly close in to the sides of your body.) As you play you'll sometimes find your shoulders have tensed up very gradually and risen without your being aware of it. In that case you need to consciously release the tension by 'letting them go', feeling them fall back down and become looser again.

Keep checking for signs of tension in your wrist and shoulders while improvising. Especially when playing a lot, take regular breaks, and give your wrists a shake to make sure they're loose. If you feel pain or tension in your arms, wrist, or hand, don't force yourself to carry on – you might injure yourself and your playing certainly won't benefit.

Of course, some tension is required for your body to operate at all, and for you to control it.

There are also some tension-related issues specifically relevant to improvisers. These involve the tendency to tense up when thinking about what to play next. This is a general problem that you'll need to be aware of throughout the process of learning to improvise, but it's usually more connected with the psychology of improvisation than pure physical technique. The way to avoid or minimise it is to familiarise yourself properly and thoroughly with all the techniques that piano improvisers use before putting yourself on the spot and expecting perfectly fluent and musically interesting improvisations to emerge.

Finger independence

The principal source of tension is the habit that most beginners have of forcing the fingers to play in ways for which they are not yet properly prepared. This is largely (though not exclusively) a matter of how two quite separate factors come together: the speed of the music and the degree of finger independence possessed by the player. (Finger independence means the ability to move any one finger without it being constrained by others.) The more muscular independence your fingers have from one another, the easier it is to play fast or difficult passages in a unforced way, without generating the sort of tension that gets passed along from the hand to the wrist, forearm, and shoulders.

Moving a finger shouldn't produce a reaction in the other fingers, but neither should it produce one in the hand as a whole. The problem is that students often think it's enough to suppress the reactions of other fingers by force – by tensing up the hand – and this tensing up is itself an uncontrolled reaction of the hand to the movement of the finger. Although it looks as though your fingers are perfectly under your control, a sensitive listener will hear the resulting tension manifested in the resulting music, which will sound awkward or aggressive.

In this book we'll develop finger independence above all through systematically exploring the melodic materials and other techniques involved in improvising. However, it's best to start with a really simple exercise designed to make you aware of what's really going on even when you play even the simplest things, namely individual notes.

Exercise 2.1

The idea here is to use extremely slow practice to make you aware that each stage of playing a note needs to be executed in an entirely natural and relaxed way.

Let's break the exercise down into stages to make it as clear as possible.
1. First just position one hand on the keys so that each finger (including the thumb) sits on an adjacent white note. Check that hand, wrist, arm and shoulders are all relaxed (with fingers rounded, knuckles level, etc.).
2. Now lift one finger, holding it raised well above the key for a few seconds, keeping all others resting on the keys, and the hand, wrist, and forearm relaxed.
3. Then let go of the finger so it falls onto the key, relaxing your hand sufficiently to release enough of the weight of the finger to depress the key.
4. Now hold the note for several seconds, feeling the hand weight pressing down through the finger into the resistance of the fully depressed key, with the hand relaxed and supported from the wrist, and other fingers just sitting on the keys, knuckles level.
5. Then release the key by taking the weight of the finger back into the hand, so that the hand itself is now once again entirely supported from the wrist.
6. Concentrate on relaxing for a few more seconds (in the playing position).
7. Begin again with the next finger.

Try to make a mental note of how all this feels as you're doing it. When you feel that you need to rest your hand, switch over to the other one. As you play each note, passing through stages 2-4, think "lift – play – relax!" It's easiest the very first time round if you start with your index and middle fingers, as these possess the greatest natural independence already. Note how the ring finger (next to the little finger) and the thumb are especially problematic. Don't force the former to play any more than it wants to – the muscles that control it are especially sensitive and can easily be injured. On the other hand it's worth spending some extra time working on the thumbs to make sure they lift for themselves and are not raised from the key by simply skewing the whole hand over in the direction of the little finger. At the same time, though, you'll need to be especially alert here to problems of tension in the hand, wrist, and forearm, so give the thumbs regular rests.

Fingering

If you take a look at written-out pieces of piano music you'll often see small numbers placed directly above or below the notes on the staff. These indicate which fingers you should use to play those notes.

Whether you're reading music or just improvising it, you need to know the numbering system that we use to refer to the different fingers. You will also need to learn some basic rules about which fingers we use when performing commonly recurring musical patterns. (We'll learn those in stages as we go along.)

Standard finger numbering works like this. Each hand is numbered outwards from the thumb (=1), through the index (=2) and middle (=3) fingers to the ring finger (=4) and then little finger (=5). This means that fingering is symmetrical between the hands.

UNIT 2 | SECTION 1

Controlling sound

An important aspect of piano technique relates to the way we control the amount of sound we produce when playing – the degree of loudness. A pianist playing classical compositions will typically follow both written instructions in the score and unwritten conventions for how loud or soft to play in certain situations. Obviously matters are different when improvising, as you are creating the music as you go along. This means developing a feel for what's appropriate and how to achieve it in the right way. In this book, wherever possible, suggestions will be given for this, and for other aspects of how material should be played and developed that fall under the general category of what musicians call expression (ie, all aspects of how you play a given series of notes or chords in order to enhance its expressive character). The idea is to prevent you from forgetting that these aspects of music continue to be essential even when your focus happens to be on what chord to reach for next, or what direction to take a melody in right now.

As far as loudness is concerned, it's not enough to know what level you want – you need to know how to produce it without jeopardising other aspects of playing. A common tendency is to want to strike the keys harder each time you want more sound. Seems logical, doesn't it? But this will make your arms and wrists tense up: then they'll get stiff and lose the freedom of movement they have when relaxed. Also your muscles may tire more quickly and get strained, leading to injuries. Soon you'll find you can't stop yourself playing everything too loudly in an awkward and tense way. (You may even feel you have to make a special physical effort just to play quietly, which adds even more to your state of physical tension.) So from the very start you need to get used to the idea that we can produce different levels of volume in a relaxed way. We do this by controlling how much of the dead weight of our body is released into the keys as we are playing them. Let's explore some simple exercises to help you with this.

Exercise 2.2

Check that you're sitting up straight, with relaxed, loose shoulders. Shut the piano lid and hold up your arms – so your hands are shoulder-high above the lid and ready to fall and land where the keys would be. Let go completely so they just drop down, noticing how hard the impact feels when they hit the lid. Then try the same thing, but when your hands reach the lid, keep them resting there for a bit, with the weight still pressing down so you can feel the lid actually taking your weight and supporting you, like when you lean against something. Sense the weight of the upper part of your body and arms pressing down on the lid through your hands! Remember how that feels!

Now open the lid and try the same thing with each hand in turn, but so that you end up holding down a simple triad with your thumb, middle finger and fifth finger. Can you feel the weight pressing through your hands and fingers and into the keys?

The next thing is to learn to control how much of your own weight you release – and thus how loud your playing will be. Think of different parts of the body as having their own weight. Then it's quite simple: letting go of more of the body releases more weight, starting from the hands, then working upwards to include the forearms, whole arms and even the shoulders. For maximum loudness, we tilt forwards (keeping a straight back), throwing the entire weight of the upper part of the body into the keys. Try adjusting the amount of weight as you play the chords in the next exercise.

Exercise 2.3
Try playing and holding the chords in each hand, adding more weight with each one, then gradually taking the weight back up into your body until you are left with just the gentle pressure of the hands and fingers. Notice how the wrist plays the role of a support throughout, keeping the hand from collapsing under the weight of the arms.

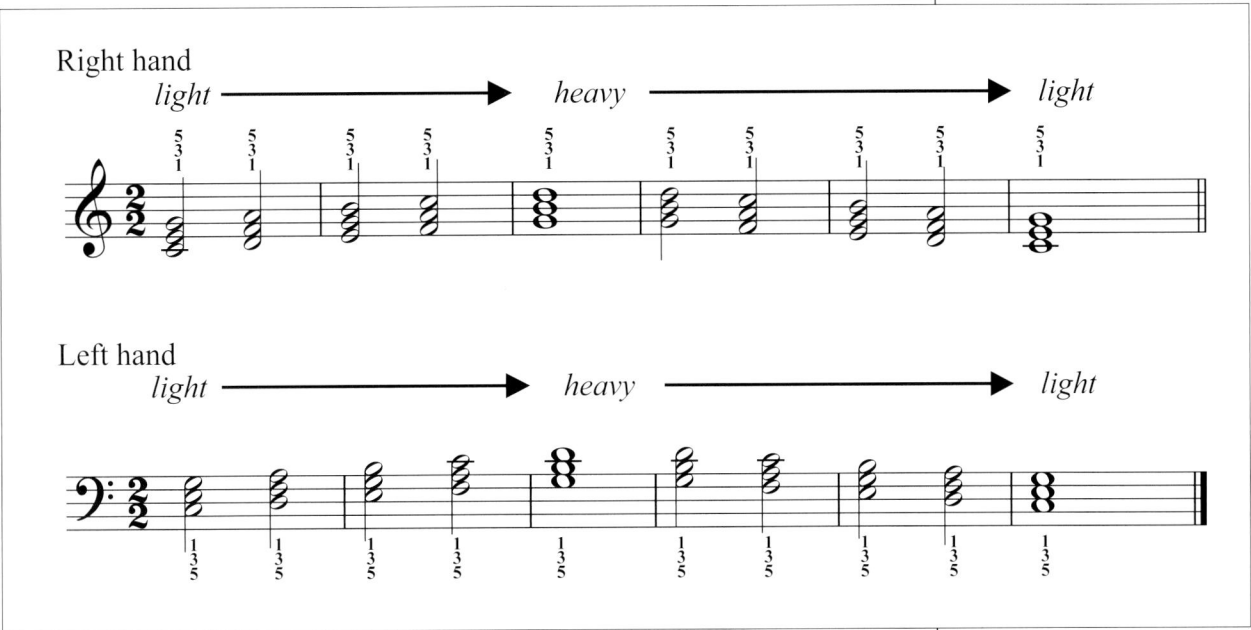

The technical name for the whole process of controlling how much sound one produces is **gradation of tone**. The resulting changes in the loudness of the music are known as **dynamics**, and these are sometimes indicated in written music using **dynamic markings**. These normally take the form of Italian terms, or abbreviations for these, as well as certain other symbols.

UNIT 2 | SECTION 1

Here are the main dynamic levels:

Italian	Abbreviation	Explanation
pianissimo	*pp*	very soft
piano	*p*	soft
mezzo piano	*mp*	fairly soft
mezzo forte	*mf*	fairly loud
forte	*f*	loud
fortissimo	*ff*	very loud

For gradual changes of volume the following hairpin signs are often used:

Italian	Sign	Explanation
crescendo	&lt;	getting gradually louder
diminuendo	&gt;	getting gradually softer

The terms below can be used to modify any of those mentioned above:

Italian	Explanation
molto	very, much
poco	slightly, a little
poco a poco	gradually
subito	suddenly
sempre	always
piu	more
meno	less

> **Dynamics, dynamics, dynamics!** A pianist who performs from written music normally follows the dynamic markings in a score, but when you're improvising there is no score. Instead you're thrown back on your own sense of what does or doesn't work musically. To some degree this is just a matter of becoming familiar with the standard ways in which dynamics are used in particular styles of piano playing: so listen to how lots of other musicians use dynamics and note what works and what doesn't. However, you also need to develop your own awareness of what sounds effective, which means listening carefully to your own playing. (Recording and listening to yourself can be really helpful here.) Many improvisers master difficult things like harmony but end up sounding poor because they've fallen into bad habits like playing everything at one dynamic level or too loudly.

the piano improvisation handbook

SECTION 1 | UNIT 2

The first step in developing your awareness of dynamics is to acquire a sense of what counts as an appropriate level for each of the basic dynamic markings (*pp, p, mp, mf, f, ff*). This should give a sort of scale of evenly spaced degrees of loudness.

Exercise 2.4
Now let's see if we can take the previous exercise further and establish a sense of level for each of the basic dynamic markings. In this case, play through each set of chords three times, following the different dynamic markings, and try to remember how much weight you released for each dynamic level, so that when you return to it you know in advance how much to use. Now play the same chords one or two octaves higher or lower, and you'll notice that different registers of the instrument have different volume characteristics: the lower and middle registers require more care in producing softer levels, the upper register (one to two octaves above middle C) is bit softer, and the topmost register is bright but with limited dynamic range. The double bar preceded by two dots at the end of each exercise is a 'repeat sign' that tells you to return to the beginning and start again.

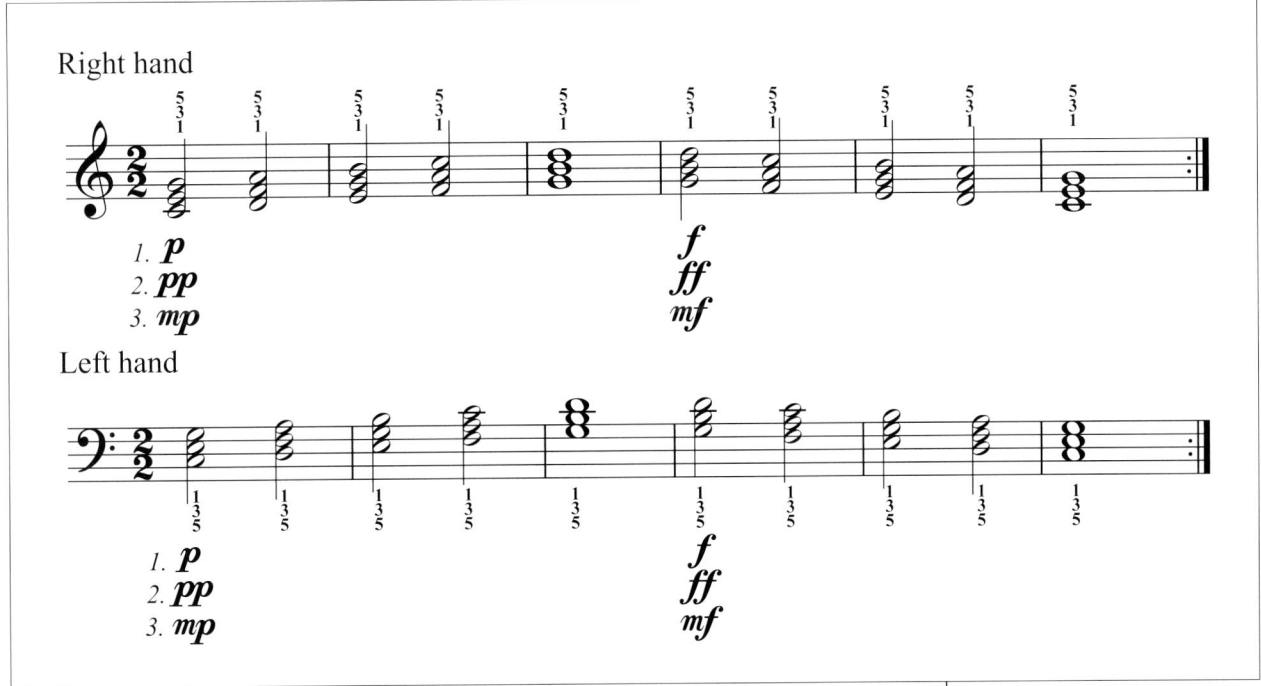

You should now have a sense of the different levels – of what it feels like to produce them as well as what they sound like – so it's time to see if you can make smooth transitions between them. The golden rule is not to change too suddenly. Crescendo and diminuendo are always gradual processes of getting louder or softer.

the piano improvisation handbook

Exercise 2.5

Here we take the same material as in the last exercise and introduce gradual changes of level between the different dynamic markings. Remember that this means a gradual change in the amount of weight as you pass through the sequence of chords.

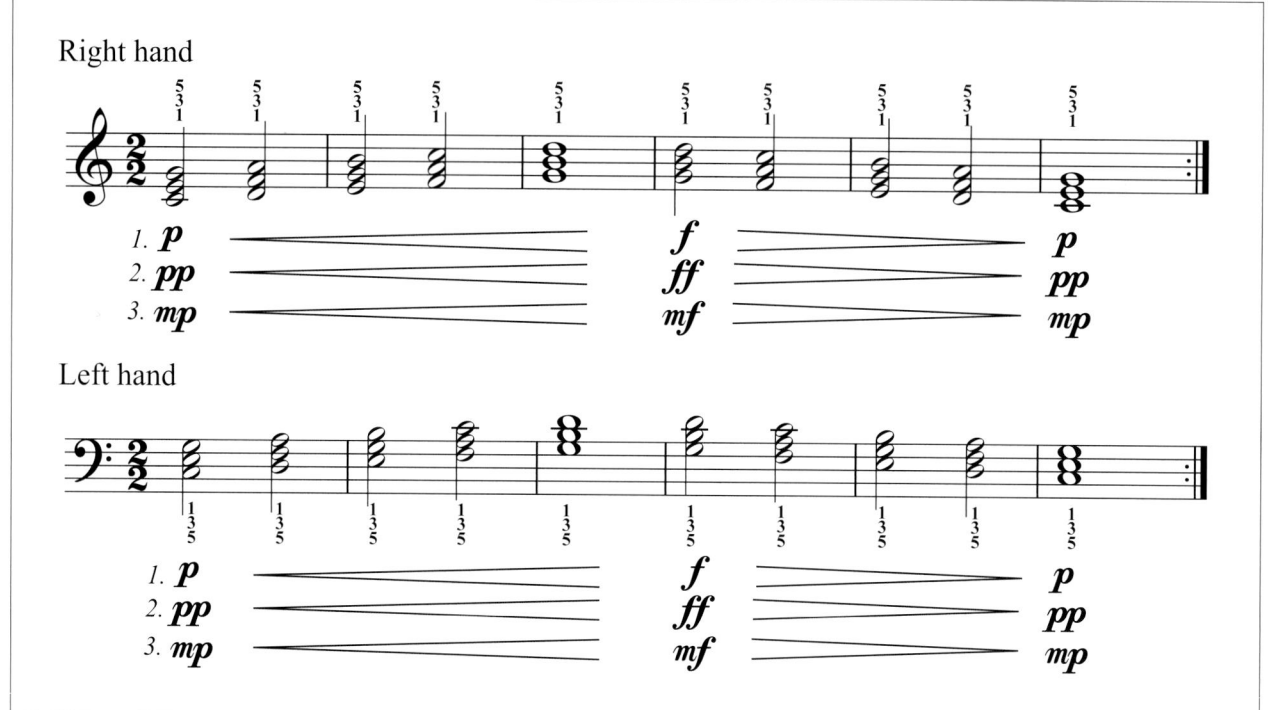

Legato & staccato

When we play music from a score there are also signs to tell us about other aspects of how the composer wanted particular notes or groups of notes to be played. These are mainly concerned with whether the notes should be joined smoothly, or played and released quickly, leaving a gap before the next note, and with whether they should be accented (ie, stressed) or not. We call this aspect of playing **articulation**, and it's just as important when we improvise on the piano. We use it to create contrasts of texture, but also to convey structural divisions within a musical passage. The two basic forms of articulation in piano playing both have Italian names.

Legato playing involves connecting or joining notes smoothly, so there's no audible gap between the end of one note and the start of the next. The idea is to create an effect similar to that of a singer executing two or more notes in a single uninterrupted breath. We do this by releasing each note just fractionally after we play the next one, creating a momentary overlap of the two sounds. (However, this isn't possible when a note gets immediately repeated. In such cases we actually have to shorten the first note slightly to allow extra time for the finger and key to return to their original position, so they are ready in time for the second note to be played.) Releasing a bit of the dead weight of the hand (or forearm) into the keys as you play will make for a stronger legato join, as it makes the fingers release the keys more slowly, which in turn slightly lengthens the overlap between notes.

Staccato playing, on the other hand, involves the deliberate releasing of a note immediately (or almost immediately) after we've struck it with a finger. This means there's usually a gap before the next note sounds. However, it's important to know that there are various kinds of staccato effect, which are distinguished by the way in which this sudden release of a note is brought about. With **finger staccato** we just release the finger itself, keeping the hand and wrist in a fixed position (but not stiff). With **hand staccato** the whole hand flicks first upwards and then downwards to create an attack that is immediately released as the hand rebounds back up again. When repeated over and over again at sufficient speed this amounts to a flapping movement which is useful for achieving staccato in faster melodic passages or with repeated notes. **Wrist staccato** is reserved for a more relaxed staccato effect, suited to more leisurely passages: a gentle lifting of the wrist as the note is played results in a 'follow-through' of the playing action, with the finger being drawn slightly upwards and inwards towards the hand itself, leading to the release of the key. Hand staccato and wrist staccato in particular are only possible with an extremely loose wrist.

Legato playing is often indicated in music with a curved line running between either two notes or between the first and last notes of a group that are to be joined together to make a single continuous **phrase**. This line is called a **slur**, and looks similar to a tie. (It's important to be able to distinguish a slur from a tie: if it only connects two consecutive notes on the same line or space, then it's a tie; otherwise it's a slur.) Staccato playing is indicated by dots placed above or below the individual notes, as in the following example:

The accent signs placed above notes in the next example indicate that the notes in question should be individually stressed for special emphasis.

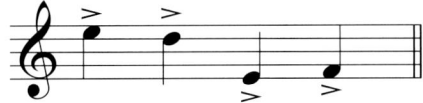

Occasionally we want to specify that a note should be held for its full length, even though it's not joined to another one. This is indicated with dashes as follows:

Finally, at the end of a piece of written music you will sometimes see the following sign, which requires you to pause on the note in question, holding it beyond its written value.

When the same articulation is required throughout a long passage of music, we give the articulation markings for the first few notes, followed by the marking 'simile' (Italian for 'in the same manner').

> **Don't forget articulation!** Yes, it's the same problem as with dynamics. When you improvise you need to decide about articulation for yourself, and the danger is that you simply fall into a habit of articulating everything in the way that involves least effort, so you can focus on other things that seem more important, like harmony and melody. You may feel this is OK, but for other listeners your playing will start to sound one-dimensional, and no amount of inspired harmonic or melodic improvisation will compensate for that. So learn about the different possibilities for articulation and stay on the lookout for new ways of articulating musical ideas and textures as they happen.

Now here's a simple five-finger running exercise that you can use to practise legato. It's also good for developing finger independence, so you can use it as a warm-up exercise each time you sit down to practise.

Exercise 2.6
Position one hand on the piano at a time, so that the thumb is placed over the first note of the exercise and the other fingers sit on adjacent white notes. Check that your knuckles are level and that your fingers are well-rounded. Feel your finger-tips touching the keys, waiting to play. As you play try to make sure that you only release each note fractionally after playing the next one, and keep your wrist and shoulders loose and relaxed throughout. Allow a little bit of the weight of your hand and forearm to be released into the keys through your fingers as

you play, and try to feel this weight being transferred from one finger to the next as you play them. Start the exercise extremely slowly and gradually speed up. Note how the right-hand part begins with the thumb on Middle C, while the left-hand thumb starts on the G below middle C but covers exactly the same five notes as the right hand, one octave lower.

Now let's see if you can do this with both hands playing together at the same time.

Exercise 2.7

Here's the same five-finger exercise, with the hands playing together, first in opposite directions, then in the same direction. Keep relaxed throughout and don't rush. Remember, when you play hands together you have twice as much to think about, so you need to take things much more slowly to begin with. Only then can you gradually bring it up to the same speed as when playing hands separately.

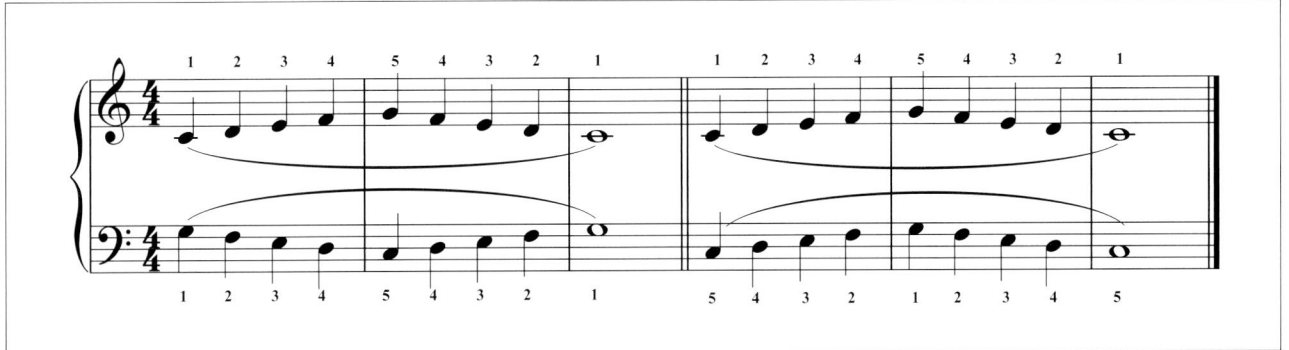

UNIT 2 | SECTION 1

Use the next exercise to practise the different kinds of finger and hand staccato.

Exercise 2.8
Start by playing individual notes with a crisp finger staccato (a). (It can help to imagine yourself touching a red-hot object and drawing your finger away as quickly as possible. However, you must also make sure to bring your hand immediately back into position over the keys, so that it's ready to play the next note.) Then switch to hand staccato for repeated notes (b). Then try to use the same technique, with the wrist just as loose, for faster runs (c). When using hand staccato, it can help if you have the wrists slightly raised above the level of the rest of the hands. Aim to keep the wrists as relaxed and loose as possible throughout.

Finally let's try wrist staccato. Because this is more difficult, it's best to approach it indirectly by first practising another form of articulation that's also important: the **couplet**. Couplets are pairs of notes in which the first is joined smoothly to the second while the second is released staccato. What's important is that we don't treat this as two separate actions but perform the whole thing as a single gesture. The result is that the first note is slightly stressed, while the second is both lightened and shortened. Pianists like to refer to this as 'tailing off'.

SECTION 1 | UNIT 2

Exercise 2.9

As we play the first note we let the wrist relax downwards as far as possible (but without causing the hand to collapse onto the keys). This releases some weight into the key through the finger. Then as we play the second note we draw the wrist back up, withdrawing the weight as we do so. At this point the hand is only loosely supported by the wrist and flops down a little. The result is that the finger gets drawn upwards and inwards slightly towards the hand, which naturally causes the note to be released, just as in wrist staccato. It's easier to learn this releasing movement in the context of the overall gesture involved in playing couplets than when performing staccato notes in isolation. Once you're confident about it, try playing section (a) of the previous exercise again, but this time with wrist staccato instead of finger staccato.

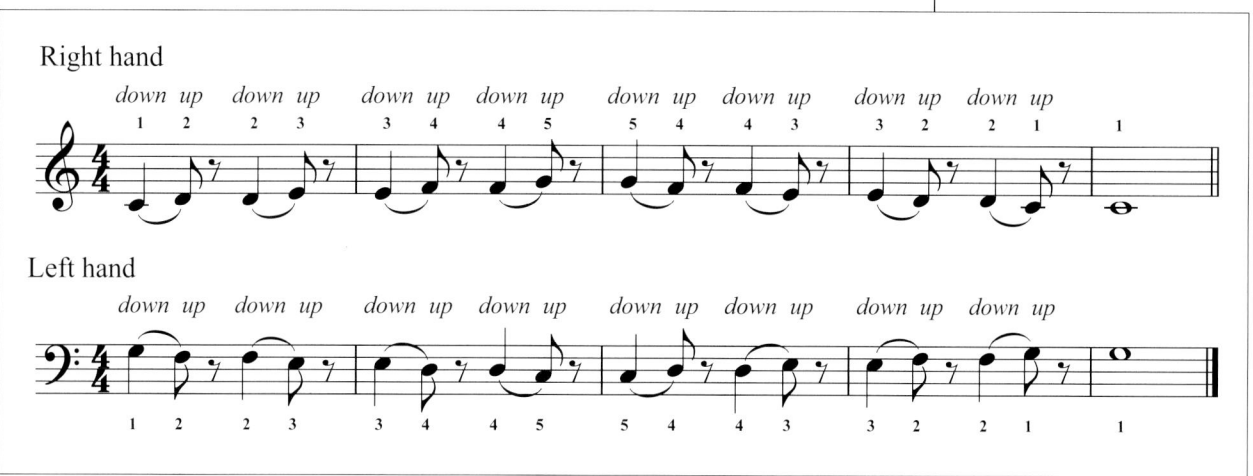

Saving the daylight. Most mainstream styles of piano improvisation focus on unfolding a melody over a sustained harmonic texture. This makes it natural to think of legato as the normal or 'default' way of playing everything, with staccato just used for contrast or to punctuate the texture. The big trap here – which even quite skilled improvisers sometimes fall into – is that everything ends up automatically being played legato: you simply forget about the need for gaps in the melody line or harmonic texture to mark phrase divisions or punctuate the texture. Although these gaps may seem unimportant, they are actually of immense psychological importance for listeners, as they provide moments of 'daylight' within the unfolding musical texture: these make it possible for us to keep our attention focused on what we are hearing.

It's worth remembering that we don't just use articulation to create contrasts of texture. Joining groups of notes into phrases separated by short breaks is useful for making audible the structural divisions of the music. We call this **phrasing**. Articulating musical phrases in a sensitive way adds to the expressive interest of the music by suggesting some of the characteristics of heightened speech, just like singing.

Phrasing also requires a sensitivity to subtle changes of dynamics and accentuation: for example we tend to get slightly louder as a melody ascends or approaches a highpoint, and slightly quieter as it falls back down. Accentuation tends to reflect metre – we normally stress the note or notes that fall on the first beat or 'strong' beats of a measure – but we sometimes also stress a note because we want to make sure that it will go on sounding clearly for longer. This is sometimes necessary on the piano – especially in the higher registers – as notes die away naturally once they've been played. (We'll explore how accent relates to rhythm and metre in the next unit.)

Practising scales

In the previous unit we've seen how scales are created, but how do we play them? We've only got five fingers, but we know that scales normally have more than five notes and continue for at least an octave. There's a special fingering pattern we use, so we can continue playing the scale smoothly and evenly, without a break in the rhythm or legato, over one or more octaves. We also use this pattern when playing scales staccato.

The example below shows a scale of C major over one octave in each hand. Note how as we ascend in the right hand we follow the normal sequence of fingers until we reach the third finger, and then begin again with the thumb. How do we do this? Well, what we do is pass the thumb under the second and third fingers as they are playing, so we can play it once again on the next note just before releasing the third finger. This creates a nice smooth join, and is called the **passing thumb**: remember, it's important to move the thumb into position over the new note before it's actually required to play to avoid a sudden jerking of the hand that will disrupt the rhythm. (You will find that your wrist naturally adjusts its angle in order to help the thumb pass through – that's okay, but try to avoid moving the elbow as well.) Once we've used the thumb on the new note the other fingers can easily move back into their natural position adjacent to the thumb to give us the additional fingers needed to play right up to the octave. As the right hand descends it goes through exactly the same pattern in reverse, but this means that when we arrive on the thumb we need to bring the third finger over onto the next note before releasing the thumb itself. It can help to think of the fingers as describing an arc as they are brought over the thumb, and once again it's important to accomplish this stretch with the help of the wrist rather than through moving the elbow. You can see how the left hand follows exactly the same pattern too, but in a reverse direction: thumb passes under as we descend the scale, and the third finger is brought back over as we ascend back up.

C major

When you've tried each hand separately a few times you can combine the hands. There are two ways you can do this. The hands can move in opposite directions at the same time, starting together on Middle C, or in the same direction with each hand starting on C, separated by an octave. We call the former **contrary motion** and the latter **similar motion**. The example below shows both options. When both hands start on the same note, as in contrary motion, you need only play the first note with your thumb in one hand. Before trying the scale hands together in similar motion, try playing through just the left hand a few times to get used to how it feels starting at the bottom.

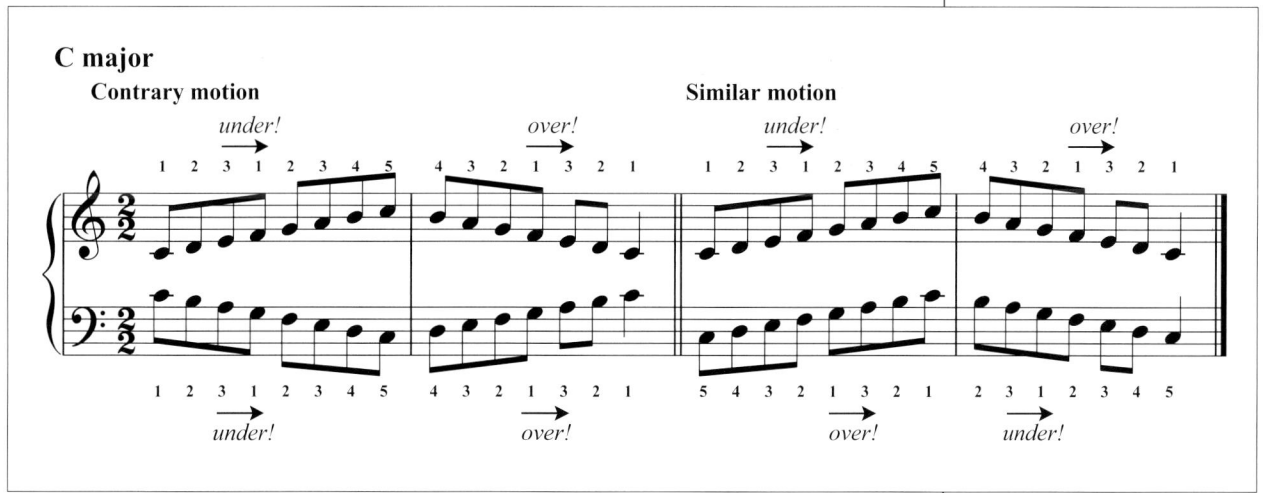

UNIT 2 | SECTION 1

We often want to play a scale over more than one octave. To do this we make a similar move with the passing thumb, this time just before reaching the end of the first octave. Instead of using the fifth finger to play the note an octave above where we started we pass the thumb under the preceding fourth finger and use it instead. Once the other fingers are brought back into their natural position next to the thumb we can then begin the whole pattern once more in the new octave, only using fifth when we have gone up as far as we want to go. As with a one-octave scale the pattern is simply reversed to come back down. Here it is for C major to two octaves, for each hand separately. Note how the left hand is given starting from the bottom – this is the usual way in which it is practised by itself. You can also try combining the two hands in contrary and similar motion.

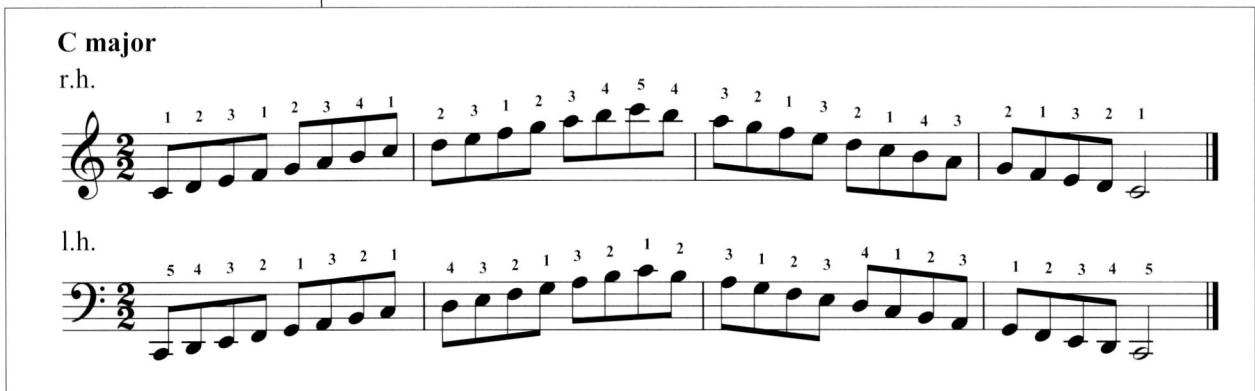

Passing the thumb under the third or fourth fingers is awkward and can easily disrupt the flow of a scale, producing unwanted hesitations, accents or breaks in the smooth joining of notes that are supposed to be played legato. Here are some exercises for developing mobility of the thumb and flexibility of the wrist in order to help with this.

Exercise 2.10

In (a) we pass the thumb to and fro under second and third fingers, while in (b) we pass it under second, third, and fourth fingers. Focus on keeping the elbows close to the sides of the body: your wrist should be flexible enough to assist the thumb in moving under, and should remain low and relaxed.

If we return once more to the scale of C major, you should be able to see that the fingering of the scale over two octaves has a pattern: first we pass the third finger under, then the fourth, then the third again, or, in the opposite direction, first we bring third finger over the thumb, then fourth, and then third again. We can reduce this fingering pattern to the simple formula 3-4-3. This is the standard fingering in either hand for most major and minor scales starting on white notes.

However, there are two exceptions to this, which are scales on F and B. In each of these scales one hand reverses the fingering pattern, which becomes 4-3-4, while the other hand sticks to the standard 3-4-3 formula.

Here's F major. In this case the right hand uses the alternative pattern to having to pass the thumb under onto a black note, which would be very awkward. Note how this means that the right hand reaches the highest note of the scale on fourth finger, and turns round without having used fifth finger at all. The left hand follows the normal fingering. (F minor is also like this.)

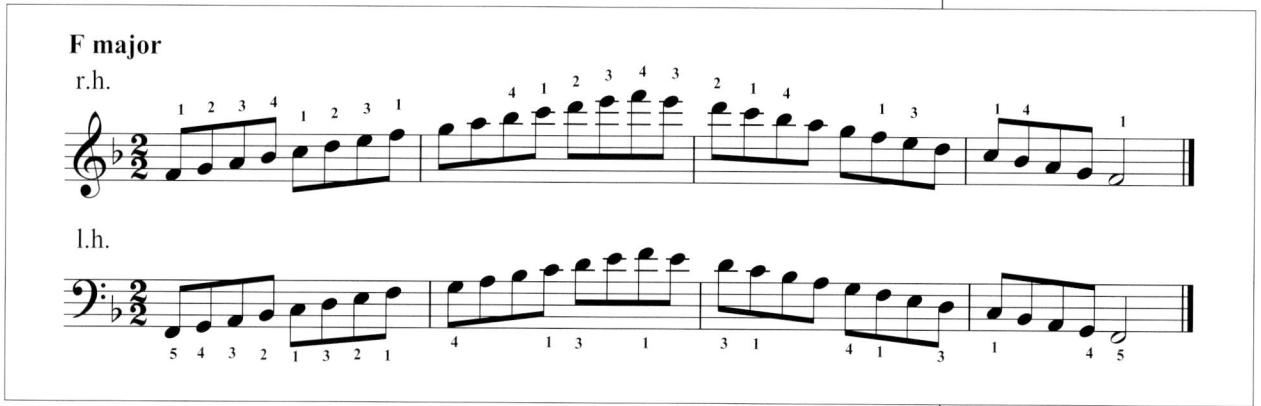

UNIT 2 | SECTION 1

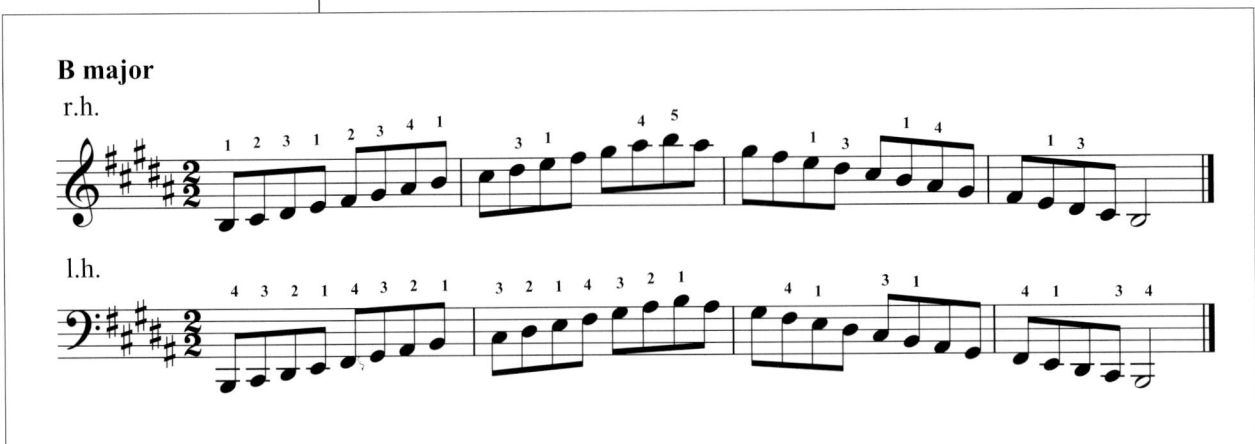

Now here's B major. This time it's the left hand that uses 4-3-4. Because it starts at the bottom of the scale, which in terms of fingering is equivalent to the right hand starting at the top, it begins with fourth finger, and fifth finger is once again omitted. The right hand follows the normal fingering. (B minor is also like this.)

B major uses this alternative fingering pattern in the left hand because it's the only way to make sure the thumb consistently plays on white notes. This is also an important principle for fingering scales starting on black notes. Basically, passing the thumb under after the third finger means we've covered three notes in a single hand position, while passing it under after the fourth means we've covered four notes. Because diatonic (ie, major and minor) scales have seven notes per octave, alternating between these two possibilities will mean we get to cover all the notes in the scale while repeating the same fingering pattern from one octave to the next, which is exactly what we want. This leaves one problem, which is where to start in the pattern: it depends on where the black notes come, as we must avoid putting the thumb on a black note wherever possible. The fingering is normally arranged so we pass the thumb under to a white note coming immediately after a black note, as this is when the passing thumb movement is at its easiest.

You can see these principles in the next scale, E-flat major: the thumb always begins a new hand position on a white note just after one or more black notes. (Note that when the right hand starts with a single black note at the bottom, or the left hand arrives on a single black note at the very top of the scale, we use second finger instead of the normal finger demanded by the pattern – it's easier on the thumb and there are no additional notes to play beyond the black note.)

This sometimes gives rise to right-hand and left-hand fingerings that are related in a fairly straightforward way, as the hands share a common principle. (The best way to see this is to compare the right hand ascending with the left hand descending.) For example in E-flat major, which has three black notes per octave, each hand passes the thumb under the third after a single black note and under the fourth after two consecutive black notes. In A-flat major, with four black notes per octave, the common

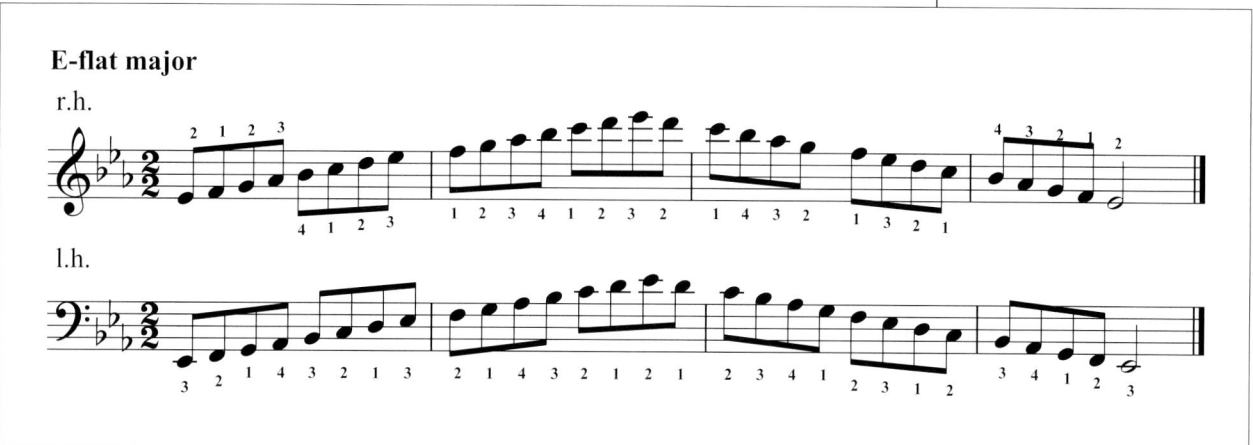

principle is that we pass the thumb under the third after a sequence consisting of one white and two black notes, but under the fourth after two white and two black notes. In B-flat major, with just two black notes per octave, the principle is that we pass the thumb under the third after a sequence of two white notes and one black note, but under the fourth after three white notes and one black note. Apart from E-flat major, though, the patterns are not that easy to combine into hands-together playing in similar motion, as each hand uses different fingers to play the same black notes, so you'll need to practise a great deal hands separately before attempting to combine the hands.

There's another grouping of scales that cuts across the distinction between scales starting on white notes and those starting on black notes. These are the scales that have all five black notes, and just two white notes, per octave. B major is an example, as are D-flat and G-flat majors. In these scales the need to ensure that the thumbs always play on the white notes (except for the first note of B major in the left hand, where the thumb is replaced by fourth as there are no notes to play beyond it), produces a new rule of fingering, which reflects the fact that the black notes on the keyboard fall into alternating groups of two and three.

The group of two black notes is fingered in such a way that we then pass the thumb under after the third finger, while the group of three black notes is fingered so that we then pass the thumb under after the fourth finger. This is more easily grasped when we look at how the fingering works in the opposite direction, with the right hand descending with the left hand ascending: we bring third finger over the thumb to begin the group of two black notes, but fourth finger over to start the group of three black notes. Don't be frightened by the number of black notes in these scales – while it makes them look difficult on paper they're actually among the easiest to play.

When you come to learn minor scales starting on black notes you'll find they sometimes also use fingerings derived from this pattern, even when they don't use all five of the black keys. In the case of these scales you will occasionally find that there are one or two small differences in the fingering depending on whether the harmonic or melodic form of the minor scale is used.

UNIT 2 SECTION 1

> **Scales for improvisers.** It's important to become familiar with the fingerings and notes for all of the major and minor scales through regular practising: this has long been recognised as one of the essential foundations of a sound technique, whether you want to play written compositions or improvise. With improvising, though, it's also important as the starting point for exploring and getting to know the particular combinations of white and black notes and related fingerings that we encounter in each key. Because these are different depending on the key we are playing in, you're going to have to familiarise yourself with the most common melodic and harmonic sequences (and their fingerings) as these appear in each and every key. Scale practice will play an important role in preparing you for this.

To be a successful improviser you'll ultimately need to be equally confident about playing in any key. That means being familiar with the major and minor scales for all twelve possible key centres. However, some keys are used less frequently than others, and some scales are technically more difficult to master than others, so it doesn't make sense to try to learn all of them right away. Use the diagram below as a guide to which scales to begin practising now and which ones to leave till later. Note how major scales such as B-flat, E-flat, and A-flat appear earlier in the list than D-flat and G-flat, even though the latter are technically easier to play. This is because the latter correspond to less frequently used keys.

Level	Group	Scales
1	Major scales on white notes with 3-4-3 fingering in both hands	C, G, D, A, E majors
2	Major scales on white notes where 3-4-3 is combined with 4-3-4	F and B majors
3	Minor scales on white notes with 3-4-3 fingering in both hands	C, G, D, A, E minors
4	Minor scales on white notes where 3-4-3 is combined with 4-3-4	F and B minors
5	Major scales on black notes not containing all five black keys	B-flat, E-flat, A-flat majors
6	Major scales on black notes containing all five black keys	D-flat, G-flat/F-sharp majors
7	Minor scales on black notes	B-flat, E-flat, G-sharp, C-sharp, F-sharp minors

Which keys occur most often can depend on what style of music you're working in and, especially, what other instruments (if any) you're most likely to play alongside. Classical music uses the entire range of keys, with a slight preference for those with less sharps or flats. On the other hand, guitar-dominated styles such as rock and pop tend to keep mainly to the keys that are easiest for guitarists, such as D, A, and E majors. Jazz can also cover the full range of keys, but the prominence of instruments such as the clarinet and saxophone in that kind of music makes keys such as F, B-flat, and E-flat more attractive, as these are the easiest keys for those instruments to play in.

Apart from the diatonic major and minor scales, you should also practise the fingering for a chromatic scale. Note how we use the third finger on all of the black

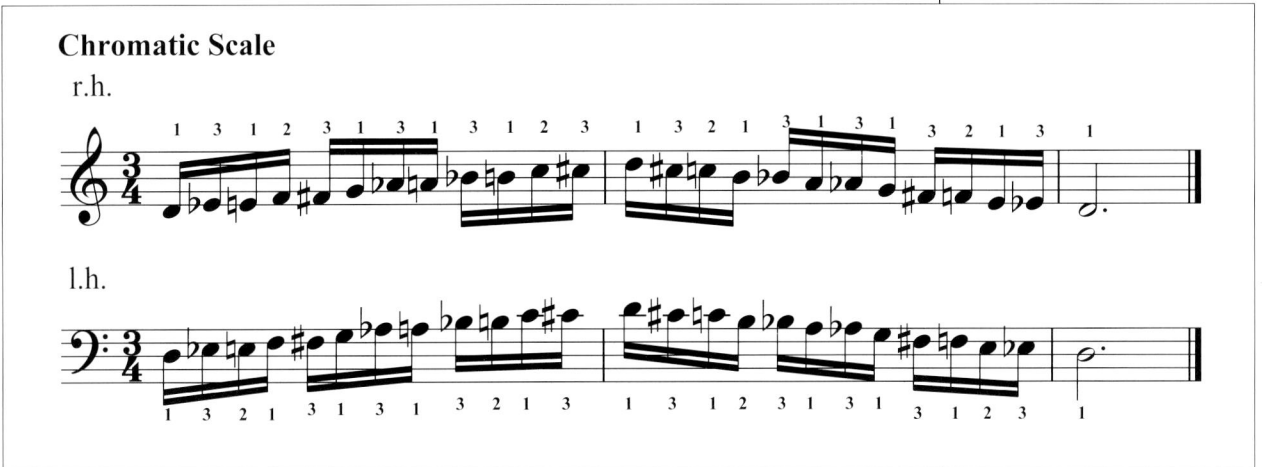

notes, alternating with the thumb on white notes, and introduce the second finger between these whenever we come to two directly adjacent white keys on the piano.
Some pianists like to make use of pentatonic scales in the right hand when improvising. This is particularly common in rock-based and folk-related piano styles, and also occurs in jazz. If you are keen to improvise in those styles, it might be worth learning the fingerings for these too, so you can practise them along with other scales. The downside of this is that these scales involve consecutive notes that are irregularly spaced, so practising them extensively can interfere with the learning of the major and minor scales, which for most styles of music are more fundamental. That's why classical players in particular prefer not to practise them as separate scales in their own right. Also, there's no universal fingering for these scales. Even so, here's a typical pattern for C major pentatonic:

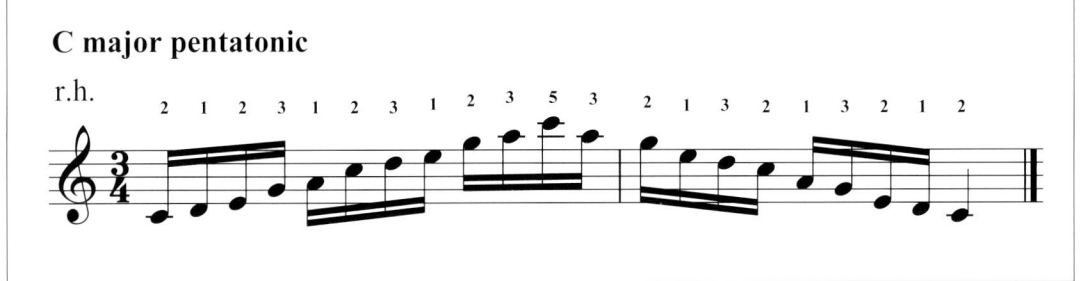

UNIT 2 | SECTION 1

The same goes for other scales that have been specially created or adapted to suit particular styles of music. The most important example is the **blues scale**: this is based on the minor pentatonic scale, with one extra note added – the flattened fifth of the scale. Here it is in the right hand for C major:

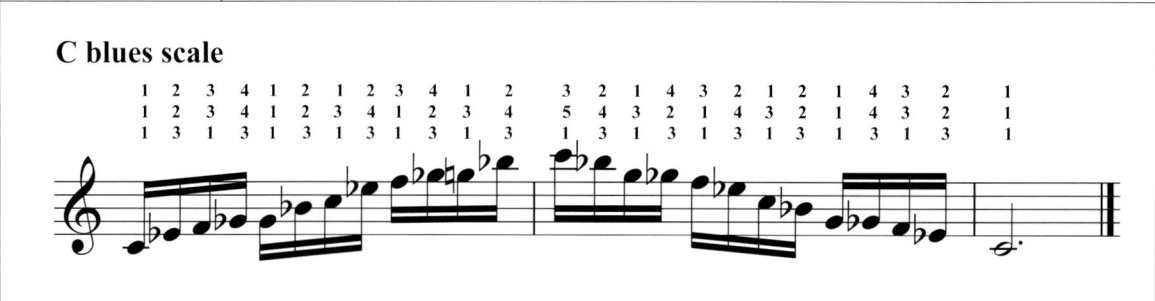

Once again, there's no standard fingering, and many blues players will have their own individual way of doing this, which may also be different for each key. The example above shows three different fingerings: the first imitates a diatonic scale fingering by reproducing the same pattern in each octave, the second minimizes the number of times that the thumb is passed under, and the third imitates a chromatic scale fingering with its alternation of thumb and middle finger. All of these might be useful, depending on the context. (We'll be looking at blues-style improvising in Unit Ten.)

Jazz also introduces a variety of additional scales through altering or adding notes to existing scales. The most important examples are **bebop scales**. (We'll also have a look at these in Unit Ten.) Once again, whether or not you practise these systematically for their own sake is up to you. If you intend to make a great deal of use of them it makes sense, but otherwise not, as it does complicate the process of getting to know the more common and basic scales.

Practising chords
1) Triads and three-note broken chords

Chords don't just appear in music as 'blocks' of notes played together, though that's probably their most common form. Often the notes of a chord are played one after another in immediate succession, forming a melodic pattern. The rules for fingering chords are determined by the need to be able to play all the notes of the chord at the same time, should we want to, but in practice these rules get applied differently, depending on whether we're dealing with successions of block chords or chord-based melodic patterns.

We've already learned (in Unit One) that a simple three-note chord, a **triad**, can appear in three different positions or inversions – root position, first inversion, and second inversion – depending on which note is at the bottom. Each position is associated with a basic three-note fingering pattern. The example below shows the three major triads and three minor triads on the piano that have just white notes, all fingered this way. Notice how in each case the fingering for first and second inversions is different depending on which hand is playing. (Note that these chords can also be played in other octaves apart from those given here.)

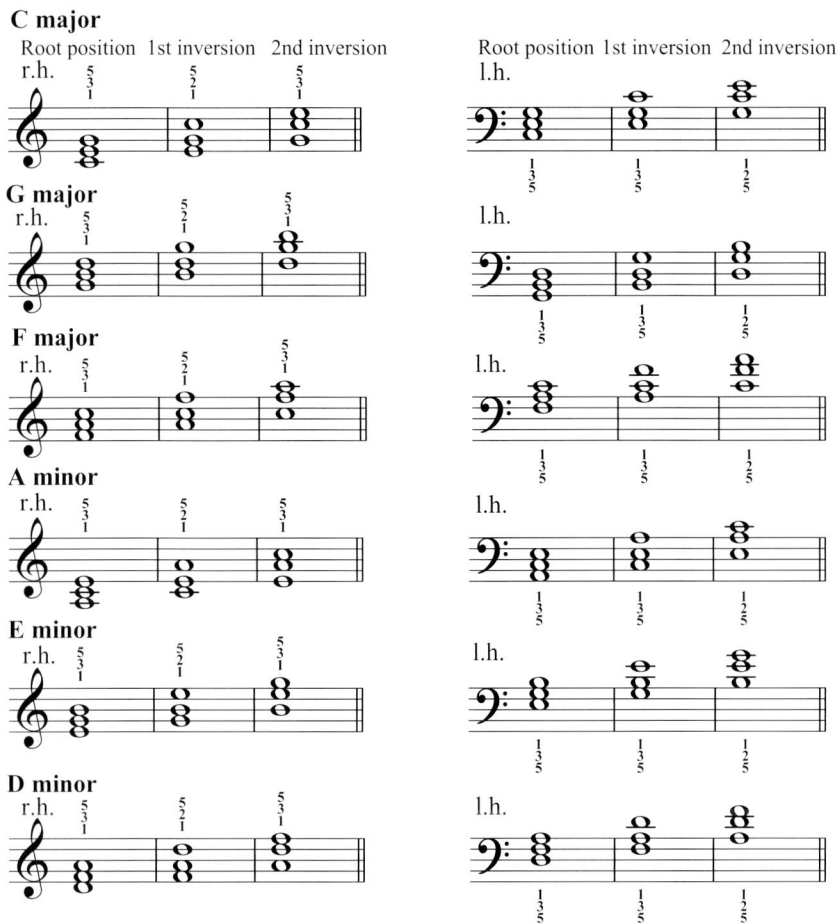

Now let's take a look at a simple chord-based melodic pattern based on this. It involves playing through the notes of each position of the chord before shifting the hand up to the next position. At the top we come to rest on the octave, before reversing the pattern and finally ending up on the fifth of the scale. This sort of sequence, where we pass melodically through each of the inversions in turn, is known as a **broken chord**. In this case it's a three-note broken-chord pattern. Over the page is the sequence for each of the major and minor triads shown in the previous example.

UNIT 2 | SECTION 1

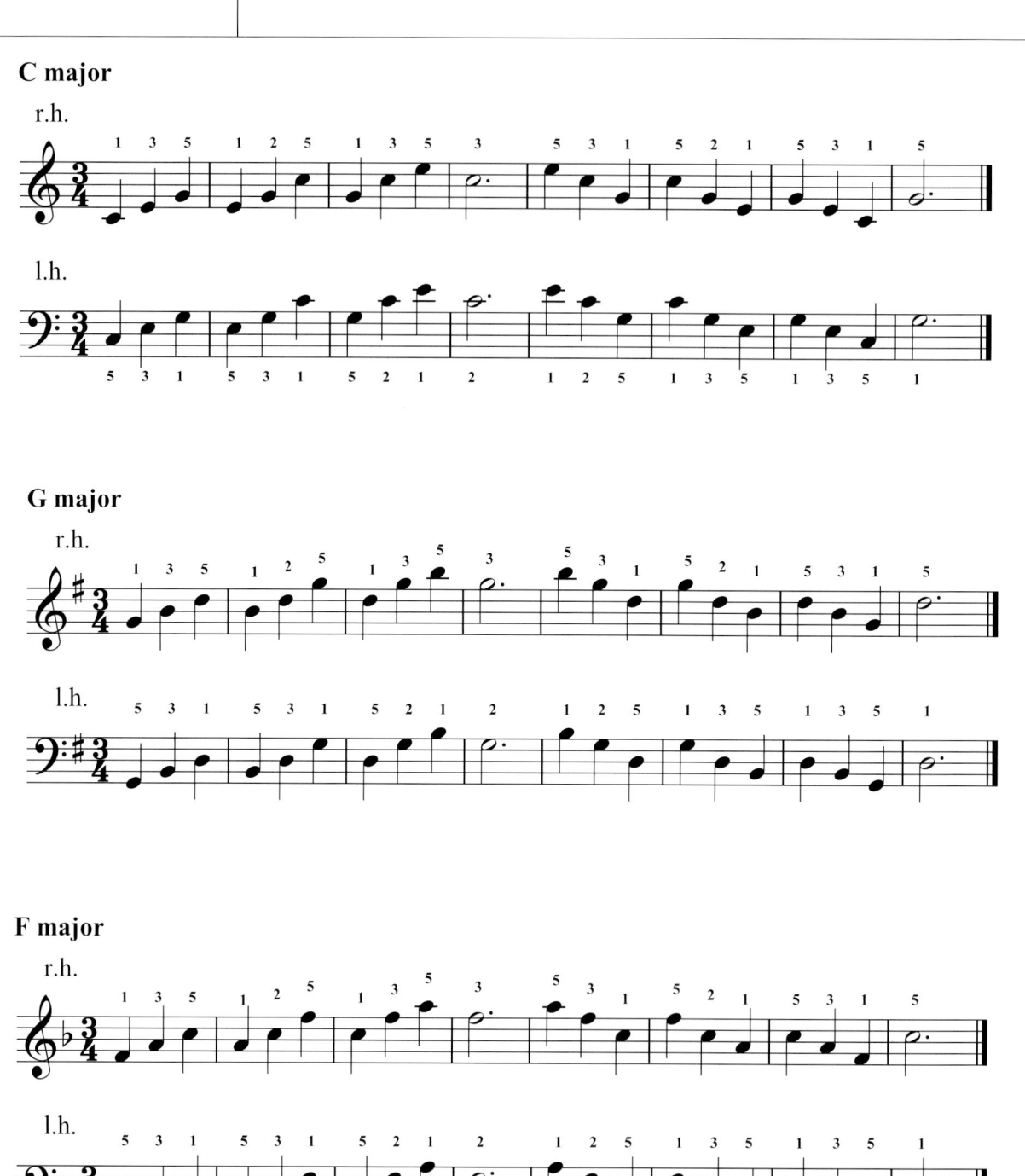

A minor

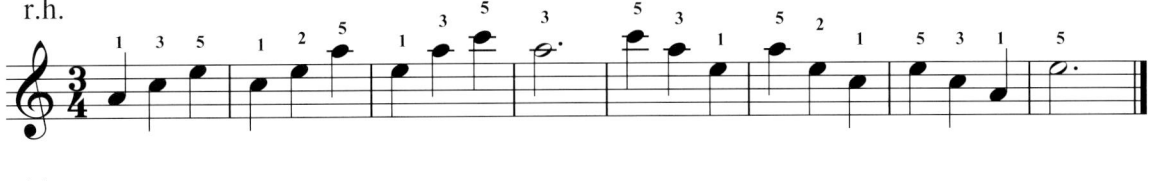

E minor

D minor

> **Chord-based patterns** often show up in melodic improvising, where they tend to be interwoven with stepwise movement. (They also appear as a feature of accompanying textures in some kinds of piano music – especially 19th-century classical and 20th-century rock styles.) Learning these patterns will give you the most effective preparation for dealing with the challenges involved in fingering block chords. That's important because the latter often prove to be the first major barrier to success for aspiring piano improvisers.

It's really worth practising these broken-chord patterns. Note that the same fingerings are also often used for three-note chords involving one or more black notes, but the corresponding chord-based melodic patterns are awkward to play, as they involve moving the thumb in and out of the black notes a great deal. So it's really only worth practising these patterns on chords that don't contain any black notes.

2) Connecting up the triads

Let's look now at how simple triads can be connected to each other as blocks. At this stage all we're interested in is mastering the basic fingerings and shifts of position that this involves. (We'll explore chord progressions themselves in Unit Three.) There are two simple rules we apply wherever possible. The first concerns the choice of position for the chords, while the second concerns fingering.

RULE 1: for a smooth-sounding transition between chords, always move to an inversion of the new chord as close as possible to where the preceding chord was located.

RULE 2: when moving between chords, always use fingerings that result in a minimum of adjustment to the hand position.

Once again, let's stick to chords with just white notes. As there are no sharps or flats in the key of C major, we'll focus on linking together triads in that key. The most common chord juxtapositions in a major key involve the primary triads, I, IV, and V. Starting from I in each of its three positions, we can see how it links up with either V or IV. Note how we don't necessarily use the same fingerings as when playing these triads in isolation or in the chord-based melodic patterns shown above. That's because we finger the connection, not the chord.

Of course you'll notice straight away that it's impossible to join all the notes in one chord smoothly to all of those in the next – mainly because the thumb has to release the first note it plays before sliding into position over a new one, making an overlap impossible. Normally one, if not two, of the other notes can be joined smoothly with an overlap in the fingers. (You can usually spot the possible joins by looking out for where

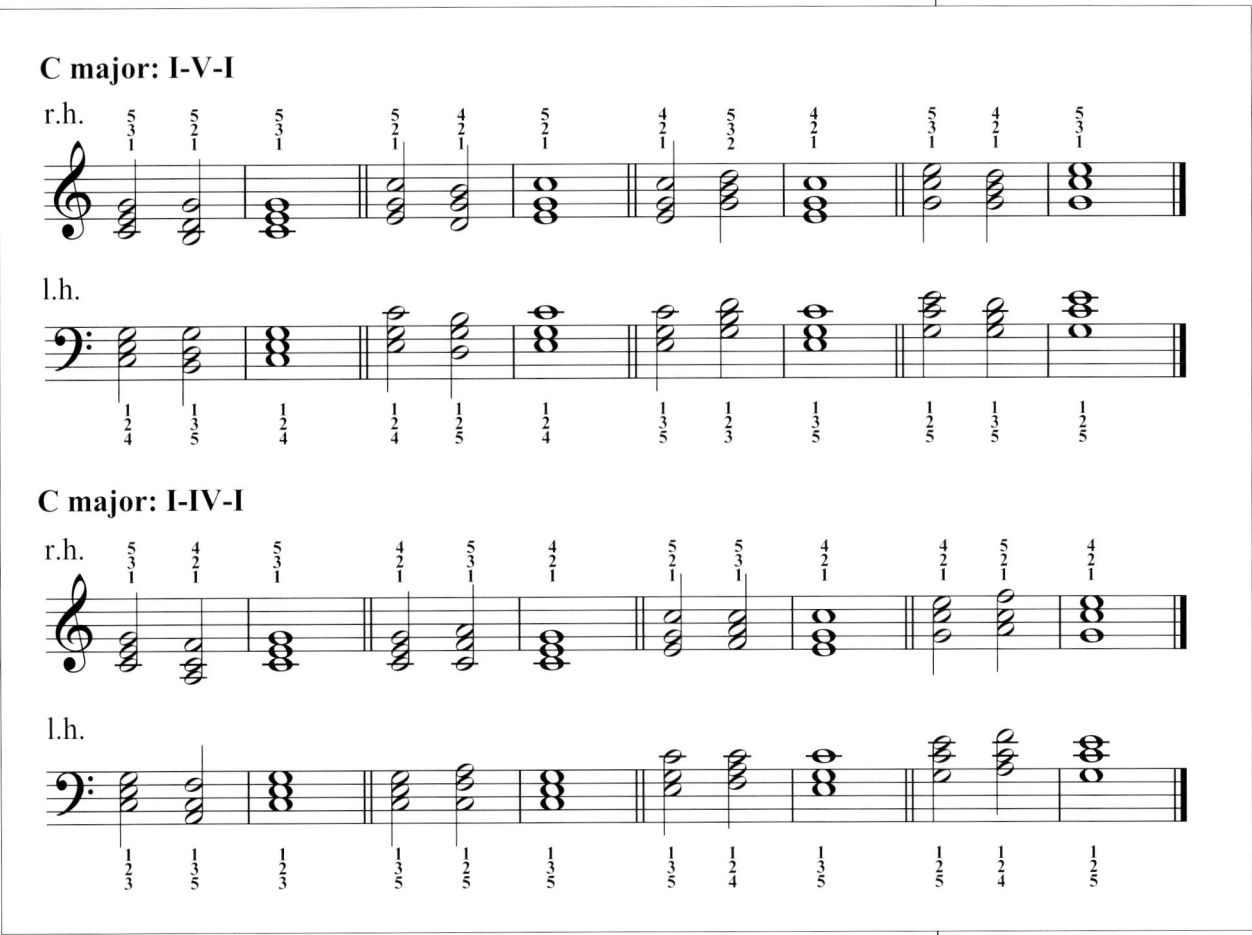

one chord uses fourth and the other fifth, or one uses second and the other third.) Play the chords slowly, but try to execute the actual shift from one chord to another as quickly as possible – yet without tensing up the hand. Make sure you play all three notes exactly together. (It can help to feel all three fingers in contact with the keys for a fraction of a second before you play them. Once they have played the notes and are holding them, feel the wrist relax so that some of the dead weight of the hand is released into the keys.)

At this stage you may feel tempted to try playing these chords using the right-hand pedal (also known as the sustaining pedal) at the same time. Resist the urge to do so. Regardless of whether you eventually end up playing chord sequences with pedal or not, the only way to learn these connections properly and make them sound good is to practise them without pedal. (We'll discuss the role that the pedal can play in the final section of this unit.)

The next example shows how exactly the same set of shifts between chords, made two scale-steps lower on the keyboard, produces a parallel set of connections, this time between secondary triads. (Remember, in a major key these are minor triads.) This time the connections are from VI to III and from VI to II.

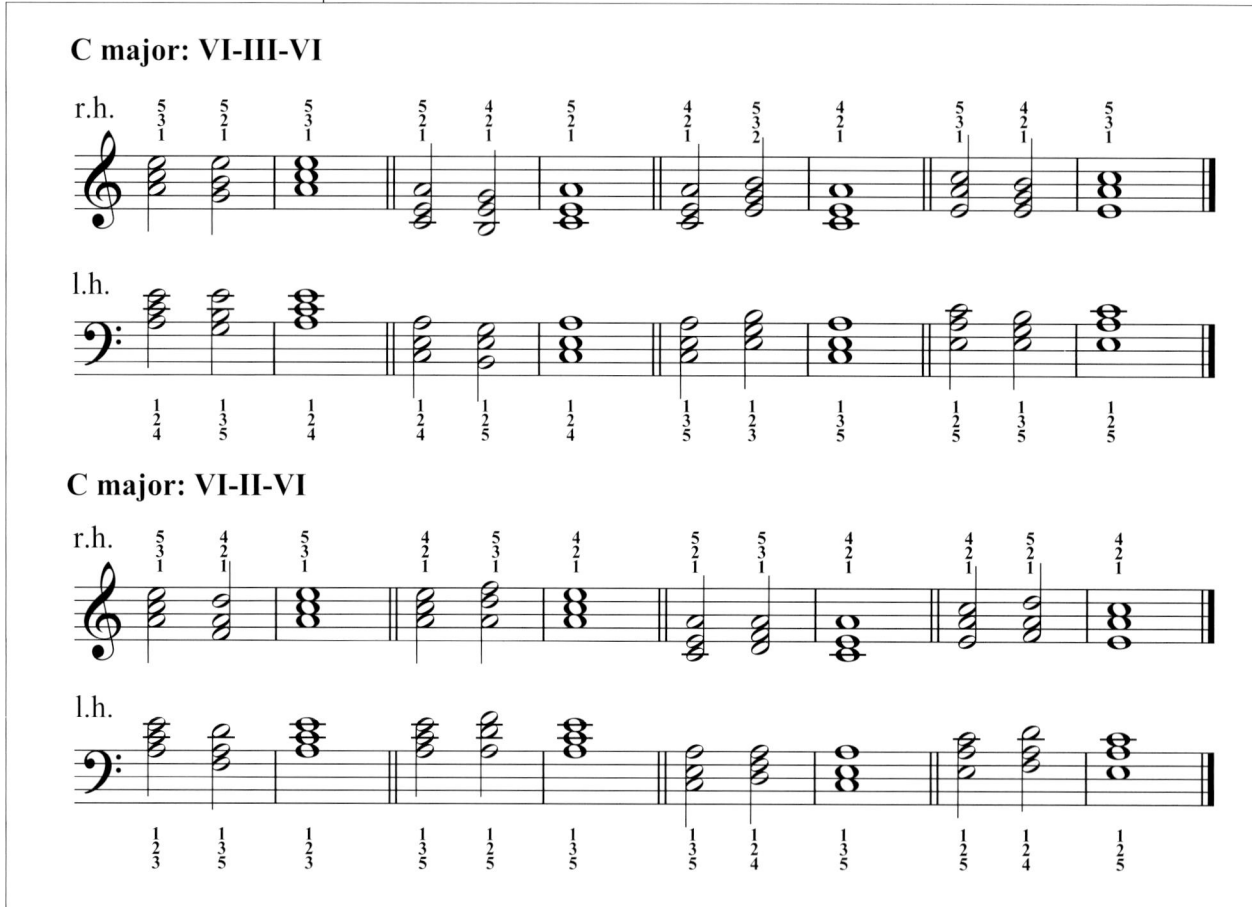

In the above examples we are always moving to and fro between triads with roots a fifth apart. As we'll see in due course, these are the strongest and commonest kinds of chord progression in music. However, another important connection is from a given chord to the chord with a root two scale-steps lower (opposite page, top). This enables us to connect up primary and secondary triads together. (Note that this kind of shift only proceeds in one direction. The reverse movement is also possible, but corresponds to a less commonly used kind of progression.)

Another kind of connection involves chords built on adjacent scale steps (opposite page, bottom). Moving to the chord with a root one step higher is an important and common progression in all styles of mainstream music, especially when this takes us from IV to V or from V to VI. However, in the former case the reverse movement is

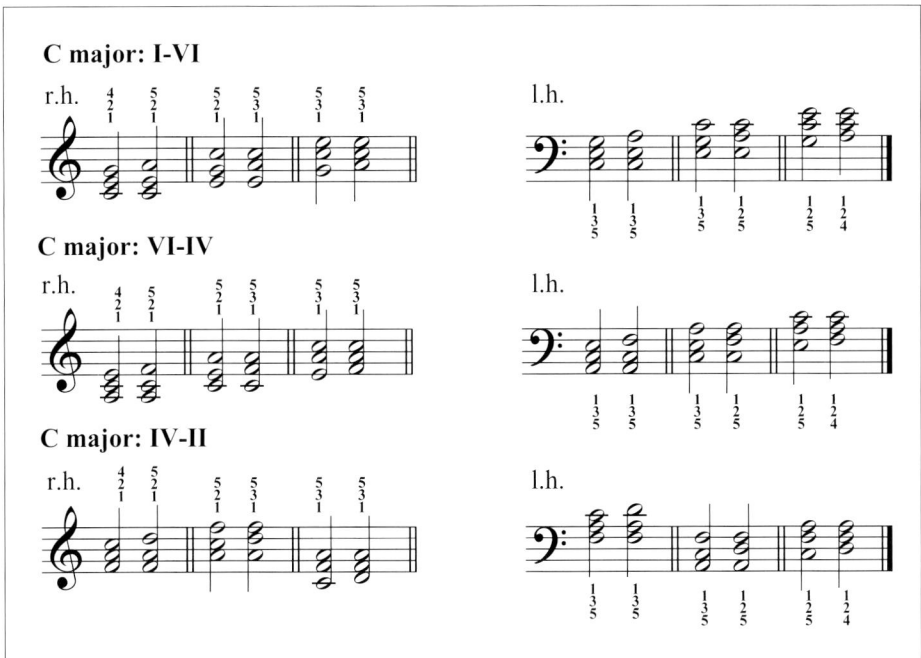

generally avoided, as it normally results in an ineffective progression. The exceptions are blues and blues-influenced rock or jazz styles, in which the progression from V to IV has a special role. Using the same kind of connection to link the secondary triads II and III gives an archaic-sounding 'churchy' effect that is also used occasionally.

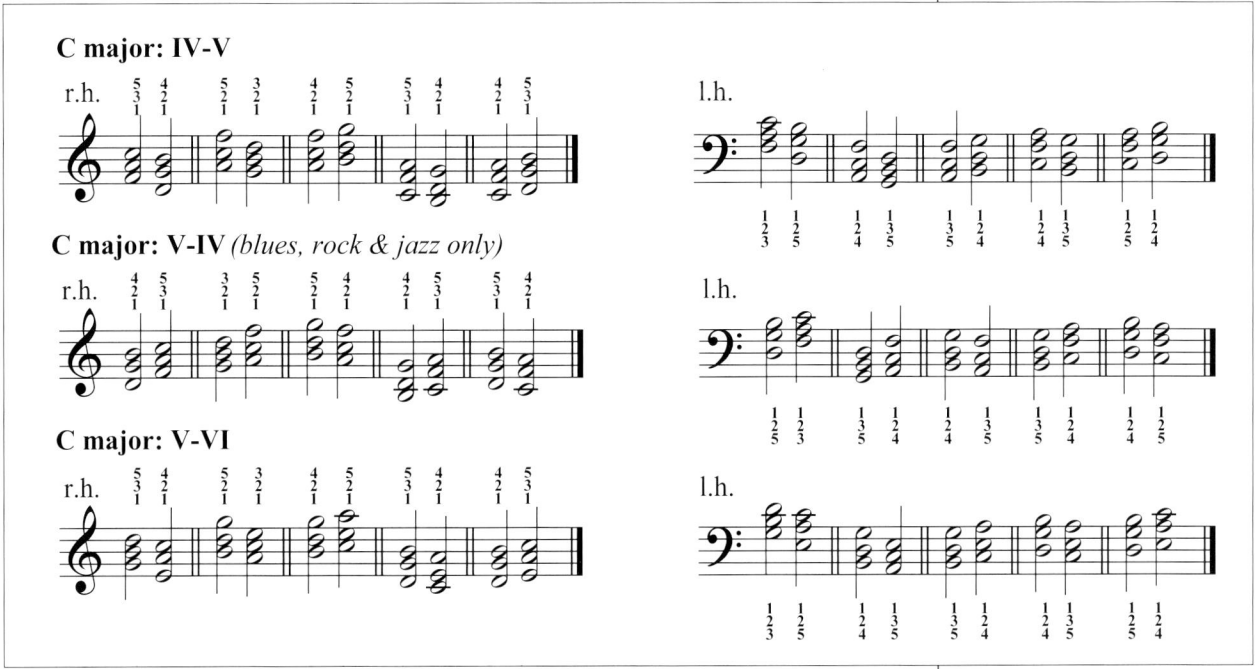

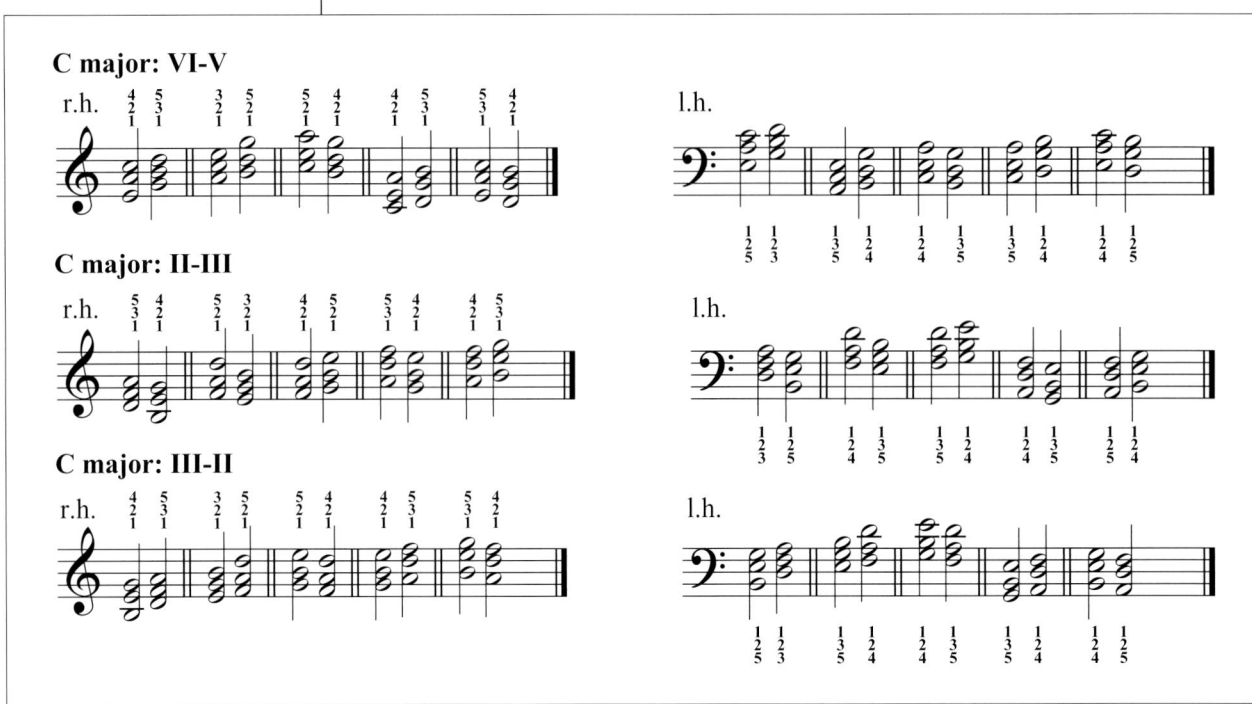

With the connections in the above example there's a temptation to just move the whole triad up or down a step. That's okay if it's in first or second inversion, but not if it's in root position, as a root position triad always contains two notes a perfect fifth apart. Moving from one chord containing this interval of a fifth straight to another with the same interval (between corresponding notes) generates an effect which in most contexts sounds unpleasant. It's called **parallel fifths**.

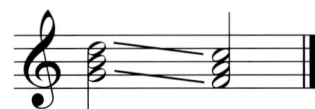

Parallel fifths

Of course these examples only show the most common connections between triads in a major key, and in C major, which has no sharps or flats. However, most of the time you'll find the fingerings for connecting triads together as blocks remain the same, regardless of whether they involve black notes or not. That's why it's important to first learn to relate the fingerings just to the kinds of connection between the chords. Practise all of the above examples (hands separately) until you can really play them easily, without having to think about the fingerings at all but keeping relaxed. You'll have a chance to practise these connections in other keys in due course.

SECTION 1 | UNIT 2

3) Four-note chord patterns and broken chords

Many of the three-note chord fingerings used to join triads together in the preceding examples are actually derived from four-note chord patterns in which the hand plays the chord with one of the notes **doubled** at the octave. Here are the three positions of a C major chord as four-note block chords. Note the fingering for each position, which once again is different depending on the hand.

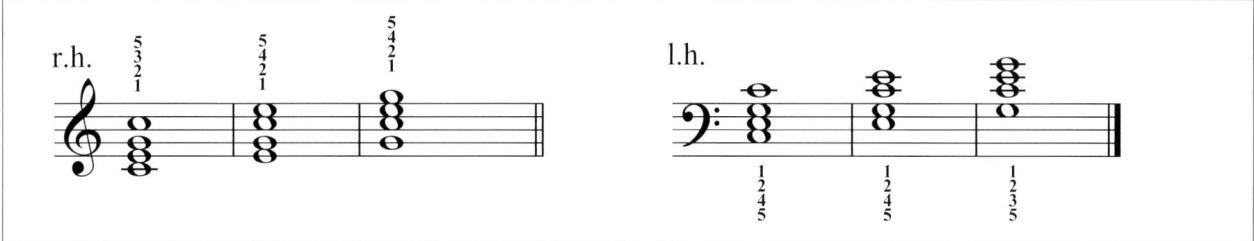

Although we won't be making use of four-note block chords in actual improvising until much later, they are an important source of fingering patterns, so it's worth practising them as broken-chord patterns as soon as you feel ready to do so (over the page, top). Nevertheless, the patterns are quite hard to play, so start by playing up and down each position by itself. In fact there's no need to cover all the notes at once. Instead, as you move through the chord (and back again), let the wrist swing round sideways to help the hand cover the notes it needs to play. We call this a **lateral movement**. Try keeping the elbows fairly close in to the body as you do it.

The pictures show the lateral, left-to-right movement of the wrist in playing a right-hand arpeggio. Once the thumb has played (left), the wrist swings right to support the central fingers (centre) and then the little finger (right).

the piano improvisation handbook

UNIT 2 | SECTION 1

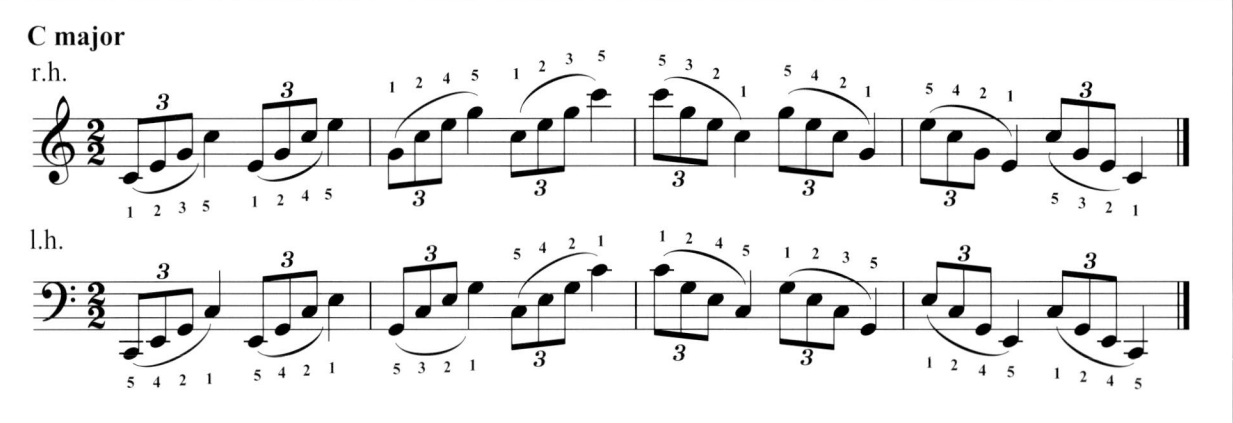

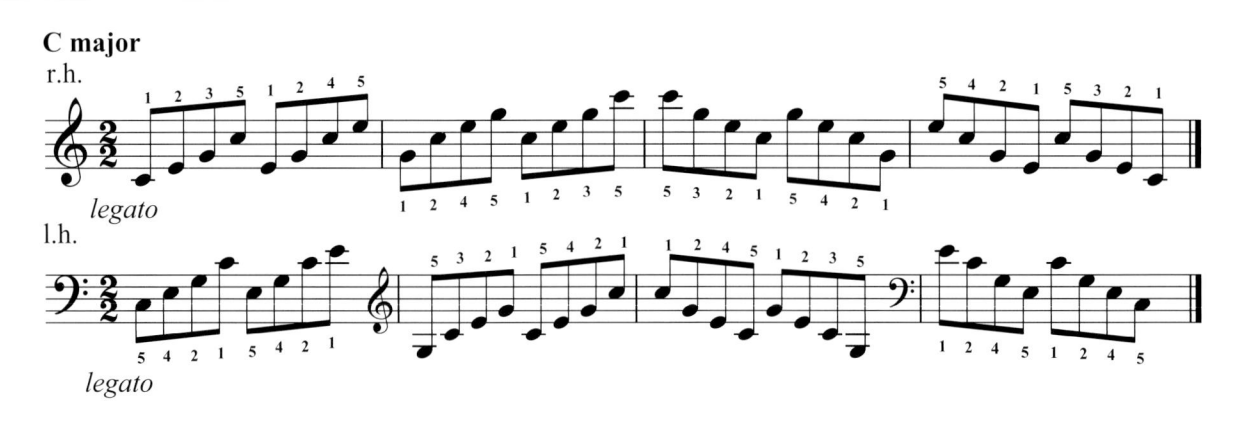

Now here's the four-note broken chord exercise itself (opposite page, middle). First let's make it slightly easier for ourselves: we'll pause for a moment on the last note in each position. This gives us a little bit more time for making the shift.

Let's see if we can do it without pausing. This means going fluently from one position into the next, assisted by swifter lateral movements of the wrist (opposite page, bottom).

4) Two-octave arpeggios
There's another kind of chord-based melodic pattern based on fingerings for four-note chords. This time it involves crossing directly from one octave to the next. It's known as an **arpeggio**. Because arpeggios can be played in all keys, they're useful for familiarising yourself further with four-note chord fingerings, and for seeing how these are affected by playing in the different keys. As with scales, we avoid using the thumb on black notes wherever possible. Here's an arpeggio of C major. First practise it hands separately for a while, and then try hands together. It's important to maintain a smooth join as you stretch the thumb under into the next octave, so don't rush, and keep the elbows close to the sides of your body. Notice how we stress the first of every four notes, rather than the first of every three, so the accent falls on a different note and different fingers in each octave.

Other arpeggios containing just white notes (ie, G and F majors, A, E, and D minors) follow the same fingering pattern in each hand, so try these right away too.

However, the fingering gets complicated once we introduce black notes. Chords starting on a white note but with a black note as the third of the chord will use third instead of fourth finger in the left hand if the black note is a sharp (as in D, A, and E majors), but not if it's a flat (as in G, C, or F minors). Arpeggios starting on black notes require different fingerings again. (You'll find these in any standard classical guide to playing scales and arpeggios.)

Arpeggios are important if you want to develop your technique to an advanced level – especially in the area of classical playing. They help with developing increased wrist suppleness and hand-eye coordination, and encourage you to become familiar with moving up and down the keyboard at speed.

Note that arpeggios involving one or two black notes per octave will require you to position the hands further into the black keys: rather than moving in and out of the keyboard, depending on whether you are playing white or black notes, we simply play the white keys further in (ie, between the black keys). That way the hands and fingers retain a consistent position and shape throughout. This is taken further in those arpeggios consisting of just black notes, ie, G-flat (or F-sharp) major and E-flat minor. Those are played on just the black notes, but using fingerings derived from arpeggios with white notes. So we finger the black notes as if they were white notes. These are the hardest arpeggios of all and you should leave them to last before attempting them.

Pedal

A standard modern piano has two pedals: the left-hand **soft pedal**, and the right-hand **sustaining pedal**. The soft pedal makes the sound softer and duller, and is used only for special effects where a muted quality of sound is required. (Resist the temptation to use it as a substitute for genuine soft playing, which you ought to be able to achieve just through the hands and fingers.)

The **sustaining pedal** is much more important, so when pianists just talk about "pedalling" without further qualification it's this one they're talking about. Pressing it down with your right foot de-activates the dampers for the whole keyboard in one go. Normally these would automatically cut off a note, as soon as the key is released by your finger. With the pedal down, notes will instead carry on sounding until you let go of the pedal, even after the keys have been released. Among other things this frees up your fingers to play other notes while the previous ones are still sounding. It also creates an echoing ambience within the instrument – the result of the sympathetic resonance of other strings, which are also no longer damped. So using the right pedal also changes the quality of sound. Unless it's released or 'cleared' regularly, notes and harmonies and textures simply accumulate.

There are two principal ways of using the pedal. The simpler one is **direct pedalling**. Here the pedal is pressed down at the same time as a note or chord is sounded. Then we either release it at the same time as the key(s), or continue holding it down while other notes are sounded as well, only releasing it later. The immediate effect is to make the note(s) more sonorous, but it also causes a sequence of notes to overlap with one another, producing a smoother and richer texture. This can sound good, but the danger is it can undermine the harmonic structure of the music by allowing notes from successive chords to overlap, producing a muddy effect that's best avoided.

This is one of the reasons why we also need the other technique – **legato pedalling**. Here we use pedal to create a legato join that would be impossible using fingers alone. We do it by 'catching' the first note or chord in the pedal, keeping the latter held down so that the sound(s) carry on, even when we've let go of the key(s) so as to get ready to play the next one(s). Then, just after sounding the new note or chord, we release the pedal. The important thing is to make sure the pedal goes down some time before you release the fingers from playing the first note or chord, but up just after actually playing the next one. Once we've sounded the new note or chord with our fingers, releasing the pedal just after doing so, we can then put the pedal straight back down again, preparing us for a similar move to the next note or chord. The effect of doing this for each note or chord in a sequence is that we end up keeping the pedal down most of the time, but 'clearing' it with a momentary 'up-down' movement (of the right foot) every time we begin a new note or chord.

> **Pedalling technique.** Yes, you guessed it: we use the right foot for the right pedal, the left foot for the left one. The pedal should be covered by the front part of the foot, including a little more than just the toes, but with the heel resting on the ground as a support. This way depressing the pedal with the foot should not affect the rest of your body. If the pedal isn't in use for a significant period of time the right foot can go back to the normal position of resting entirely on the ground. The left foot remains firmly on the ground throughout, except when the left pedal is in use.

The main challenge is to make sure that when you depress the pedal it doesn't affect the volume of your playing. In particular, you should try to avoid producing an unintended accent every time you put the pedal down. What kind of pedalling, if any, we use, is partly a matter of style, but is often dictated by the structure of the music as well:

- Piano textures that involve clearly defined changes from one harmony to the next, but which require the use of the pedal to assist with maintaining a legato texture, generally call for legato pedalling.
- Direct pedalling is often reserved for altering the sonority of individual chords, but is also used when an accumulation of sound or texture is called for.

A major issue with both kinds of pedalling concerns how they affect the way melodies sound. You should always keep in mind that the basic way of presenting a melody line on the piano is as a sequence of notes joined smoothly in the fingers, not as a sequence of notes that overlap because they are accumulating thanks to pedal. Often, though, a melody unfolds over a single harmony, and if the harmonic texture has to be sustained with the help of pedal this will mean that the notes of the melody are also affected. They will no longer each be released just as the next one sounds, as in normal legato playing. In such circumstances we often have no choice but to try to find a compromise between melodic clarity and harmonic continuity. It helps to bear in mind the following:

When successive melody notes belong to the same harmony the effect of them overlapping is usually OK, as they sound good together anyway. (Technically, we say they form a **consonance**. Intervals of major or minor third or sixth, and of a perfect fourth or fifth, are consonant.)

Stepwise melodic movement is usually problematic, as the overlapping of notes one step apart produces a clashing affect. (Technically, a **dissonance** – as with major and minor seconds and sevenths, as well as augmented and diminished intervals.)

In almost all piano playing there's a strong temptation to use pedal to compensate for technical insecurities. However, the simple truth is that listeners 'hear through' the effect of the pedal to the quality of the playing itself. This means that if the music has not been mastered properly independently of the pedal, a listener will be aware of this even when pedal is used.

When you're learning to play written compositions, mastering the music means learning to play what's written with the correct fingering, etc, through repeated practice. With improvising, however, things are different, as you're often making up the music on the spot. Above all it means being familiar in advance with the fingering patterns and notes for all of the basic harmonic and melodic sequences likely to be used in the style of music you're exploring, in any of the keys you could find yourself playing in. If you don't do this, you'll find yourself using pedal to cover up the gaps that result when you hesitate about where to go next or what fingering to use, and this will make your playing sound slushy and amateurish. That's why it's important to really get to know the raw materials of music before you try to make your own music with them – exactly what we'll be doing in Section Two of this book.

UNIT 3
EXPLORING MELODY

- Exploring melody
- Melody and improvisation
- Scale theory
- Simple melodic movement
- Simple melodic continuation

SECTION 2

UNIT 3 SECTION 2

Melody and improvisation

In this unit we'll look at the basis for melody: how simple, short melodic sequences or shapes can be created out of scales, without any chord structures or rhythm being involved. Only after having done this will we be in a position to appreciate how chord structures, keys, rhythm, and metre can further enrich melodic improvising.

Improvising generally centres around an unfolding melody line – a succession of notes or tones. The relationship between these notes depends on the intervals between them, which in turn depends on the scale they come from. So the raw materials of melodic improvising are basically notes arranged into scales. That's true, but only up to a point, as it ignores a couple of important things:

Intervals more than notes create the musical interest and expressive character of a line. Individual notes do have an expressive character or colour, but as far as melody is concerned this is less important than that of intervals. (Intervals are more than just distances between pitches: each has a particular sounding quality as a result of how it relates to the scale.)

Intervals occur in a melody as melodic movements – going from one note to another. It's the movements involving these intervals that create the recognisable shape (or contour) of a melody line, not just the intervals themselves.

How this melodic shape is organised is our chief concern when learning to improvise melody. It can be more fluid and open-ended, or more sharply defined. In the second case it gives rise to melody lines that feel relatively complete and self-contained – the sort associated more with composed than improvised music.

Most melody lines in Western classical and non-classical music have a clear beginning, middle, and end. In many cases they're also built up from smaller motifs or phrases. That's true whether the music is improvised or composed. Even jazz, which may sound like a continuous stream of notes, is usually based on an underlying melody with these features. Yet musical styles in which improvising plays an important role tend to treat melody more fluidly: they focus on how shapes unfold as stages or moments in a single continuous line. For example, Indian classical music, in which improvisation

> **Raw ingredients.** Although improvising is often made to seem harder than it really is, the fact remains, it's not always easy. So it's better to take the elements one by one and explore how each works before putting them together. Creating not just a good melody, but also original chords, key structures, and rhythmic textures all at once is a lot less difficult if you've first explored each aspect by itself. Musicians who don't do so usually end up with a one-sided style: maybe their melodies are great, but their chord arrangements are sadly predictable, or maybe they've got some original harmonic twists but use rhythm in a way that's stiff and mechanical. That's why each of the next four units focuses on just one of the elements of music.

> **Playing around.** Wherever you want to take your improvising, you'll need to first spend time playing around with scales to discover their potential yourself. Only then is it worth trying to create 'completed' melodies. It's at this level of free play that an improvising musician develops his or her own relationship to the melodic possibilities of scales – the basis for a truly personal style and sound. The best way to guarantee your playing lacks individuality is to ignore this and jump straight into improvising melodies that sound 'finished'.

plays a central role, works more like this than Western music – especially Western classical music from the 18th century onwards, when the idea of a composed musical work became prevalent. Actually earlier Western classical music is also a bit more fluid in its approach, as are modern rock and jazz soloing, which are mainly improvised. These differences don't depend so much on whether the music is actually improvised or composed, as on the status of improvisation and composition in the musical culture at a particular time.

Most improvising falls between the two extremes of creating neatly structured melodies, which often sound 'composed', and just playing around freely with shapes as they unfold from one moment to the next. When you're learning, though, it's best to start with a more fluid style, as this encourages a more relaxed and playful mindset that makes it easier to be creative in the early stages. We'll be focusing here on what is involved when melodies unfold in a fairly loose and free way.

Scale theory
1. The major scale
Let's start with the most widely used scale in Western music: the major scale. There are some things we need to know before we can use it properly. First let's recall the sequence of whole-steps and half-steps (tones and semitones) that define it as major. This shows that it consists of two matching segments, or **tetrachords**.

Scale of C major

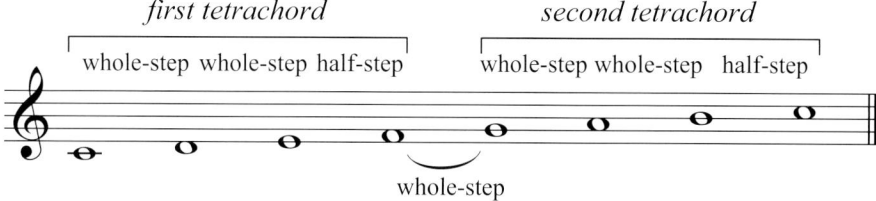

UNIT 3 SECTION 2

Within any diatonic scale, whether major or minor, the different scale degrees stand in a hierarchy of importance. This is because the scale itself creates a context (by establishing a particular key or **tonality**) in which we hear certain degrees as more or less 'resolved'. (In practice the more resolved a note is, the less need we feel for it to be followed straight away by another note with less harmonic tension - what we call a 'resolution'.) At the top of the hierarchy comes the most resolved degree, its first note – the tonic or keynote. Then come the remaining notes of the tonic triad: the third and fifth. Then come those notes of the pentatonic (major) scale starting on the keynote not already given as part of the tonic triad: the second and sixth. Then we're left with those notes of the major scale not already given as part of the pentatonic scale: the fourth and seventh. (This gives us the whole hierarchy within the major scale, but it can also sometimes be helpful to think of this process of elaboration as being taken one step further, with the addition of the five remaining notes of the chromatic scale – those not already present within the major scale.)

It's much easier to grasp this from the table below, which makes use of the standard system for naming scale degrees in modern jazz scale theory. In this system the major scale functions as a yardstick for all other scales. The seven degrees of the major scale – any major scale – are simply assigned the Arabic numerals 1 to 7. We then indicate how other scales differ from this by treating the differences as chromatic alterations – ie, raised or flattened by a semitone – from what the corresponding scale degrees would be in the major scale itself.

Hierarchy of scale degrees in a major scale.

Tonic (keynote)	1										
Tonic triad (major)	1				3		5				
Major pentatonic scale	1		2		3		5		6		
Diatonic (major) scale	1		2		3	4	5		6		7
Chromatic scale	1	♯1/♭2	2	♯2/♭3	3	4	♯4/♭5	5	♯5/♭6	6	♯6/♭7	7

Certain scale degrees are important for another reason: they correspond to the keynotes of closely related alternative keys. In Unit Two we saw how the strongest relations exist between keys separated by a fifth. (The relations were represented using the Circle of Fifths diagram, in which more closely related keys appear as closer or adjacent.) Because these relations make themselves felt within a key too, the corresponding scale degrees are themselves experienced as potential alternative 'centres of gravity', competing with the actual key centre and thus with the tonic. This mainly affects the fifth and fourth of the scale, which correspond to key centres one step removed on the Circle of Fifths from the actual key centre. (However, it can also affect any scale degrees corresponding to key centres two steps removed on the Circle of Fifths – eg, the second of the major scale.) This mainly affects the chords built on these scale degrees, but can also affect how the scale degrees themselves figure in pure melody. The diagram (opposite page) helps to visualize this. It uses Roman numerals to show how keys nearby on the Circle of Fifths are related, but Arabic numerals for corresponding scale degrees within a key. (Note how each key is pictured as having its own parallel hierarchy.)

Finally, this hierarchy of scale degrees within a key is affected by any harmony sounding as notes succeed one another melodically. A note that's less resolved relative to the hierarchy may nevertheless be more resolved relative to the chord sounding at that moment (or even relative to the particular inversion of that chord) or vice versa. But we'll worry about this in the next section, as it concerns harmony too.

The implications of these factors for how melodic movement works in a major key

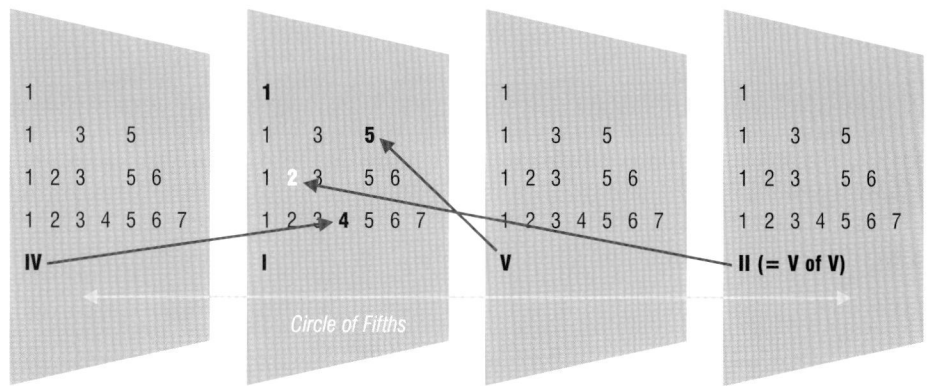

Major scale degrees corresponding to key centres close by on the Circle of Fifths. NOTE: additional text & arrows superimposed on a preformatted diagram here!]

are not that simple, so let's take them one step at a time, starting with the tetrachords.

Each tetrachord is a sequence of larger and smaller steps. Ascending stepwise through the first takes us to the fourth of the scale (F in C major), a relatively unresolved note but nevertheless important as it corresponds to the subdominant pole, and thus to one of the nearest alternative key centres on the Circle of Fifths (see the above diagram). The sense of arrival we have as we reach it is heightened by the tetrachord, because the ascending sequence of steps that the latter gives us means we reach this scale degree via a half-step preceded by two whole-steps. So the final step is smaller, but takes just as long as the others – as if the last note were somehow delayed or harder to get to. In the case of the second tetrachord there's an even stronger version of the same, as the sense of delayed arrival created by the tetrachord involves reaching the keynote itself (an octave above the starting note). Just play through the ascending form of the tetrachords slowly and you should be able to hear this for yourself:

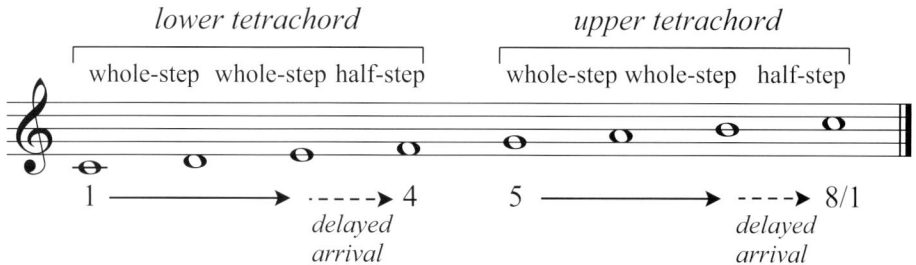

Descending stepwise through the upper tetrachord takes us first through the half-step and then the two whole-steps: in this case the effect is of a more gradual descent followed by a more rapid one. This creates a downwards momentum that comes to rest on the bottom note of the tetrachord, the structurally important fifth of the scale (G in C major). This is a note that's relatively resolved in terms of the internal hierarchy of the scale, and is also an important counter-pole to the keynote as it, too, corresponds to one of the nearest alternative key centres. Then, as we pass through the lower tetrachord, we experience a stronger version of the same, as the descending movement comes to rest on the keynote itself. Once again, play slowly through the tetrachords – this time descending – and try to experience this for yourself:

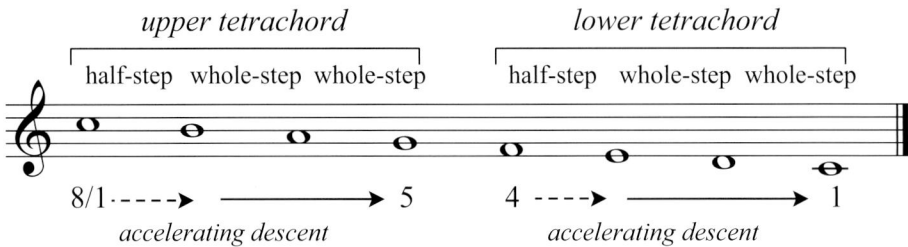

Now let's look at the implications of the hierarchy itself. Remember, it reflects how resolved different notes are, given their particular function in the scale. At any one point, a melody can move either to a note that's functionally more resolved than the preceding one, or to a note that's functionally less resolved. In the former case there's a convenient name for this: it's a melodic **resolution**. But there's no opposite term in our language for the latter case, so in the discussion which follows we'll just have to talk about resolving and non-resolving movements. (Think of 'non-resolving' here as meaning what 'un-resolving' would mean, if such a term existed.)

The other point to bear in mind is that whether the overall effect of a melodic movement is a sense of resolution or a sense of increased tension is not just a matter of its functional character. It's also affected by the melodic **direction** of the movement: the sense that upwards or ascending movements tend to feel more like non-resolving ones, while downwards or descending movements tend to feel more like resolving ones. This means that the character of a particular melodic movement also depends on how it relates to the overall shape of the melody line in which it occurs, which will also be affected by things such as rhythm and metre.

We'll explore the role of shape more fully in subsequent units, when we look at how melodies are created that also have a definite rhythm and metre, as well as chord structure. It's important to realise, though, that the functional character of melodic movements is not altered by this, as it is something more basic. This can be illustrated by considering what happens when we take individual movements and move one of the notes up or down an octave, something which both reverses the direction of melodic movement and changes the size of interval between the notes. (The technical name for this is **interval inversion**.) The example below shows each interval in the major scale involving the tonic as a melodic movement, followed by its inversion. You should be able to hear that the sense of functional resolution or non-resolution remains unchanged in each case. (The same goes for intervals not involving the tonic, and for intervals in minor scales.)

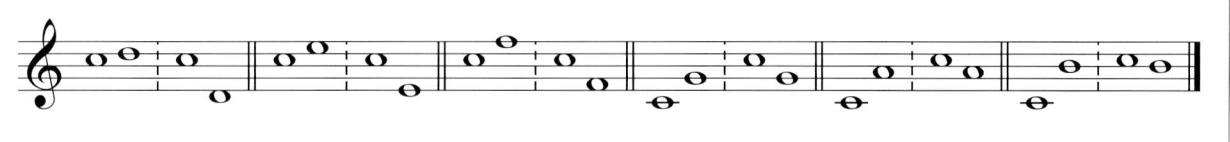

So as far as understanding the raw materials of melody are concerned – ie, scales, notes, intervals, and the kinds of melodic movement they produce – it's just the functional aspect that we're concerned with right now. The basic principle of functional resolution in melodies is that a melodic movement to a more basic note in the functional hierarchy of the scale will be heard as resolving, and a melodic movement to a less basic note will be heard as the opposite. This aspect will be complicated as soon as we add chords.

As far as the melodic implications of the hierarchy are concerned, the simplest case is where one of the two notes involved is the keynote. In functional terms, any movement away from the keynote is experienced as the opposite of a resolution, and any movement to the keynote as a resolution. In the case of movements to and from the fourth and fifth degrees, however, things are complicated by the importance that these scale degrees possess as counter-poles to the tonic, and by the tetrachords. The latter reinforce the sense that the fourth and fifth degrees represent alternative points of resolution to the keynote. This is a result of the presence of audible parallels between

Parallel resolving movements

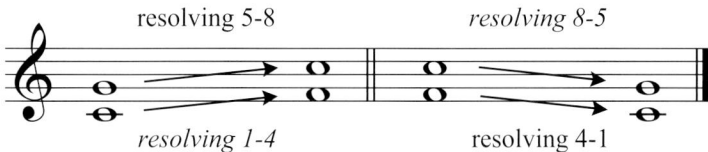

> **Proto-scales.** The parallels between the tetrachords show us something important, which is that the tetrachords actually represent a more basic level of scale-structure than the diatonic scale itself – one from which the latter is thought to have evolved (in ancient history). Indeed, one of the best ways to fine-tune your awareness of the potential of pure melody is to deliberately ignore the overall structure of the scale for a while and focus on how melodic movements relate just to the tetrachords themselves.

the upper and lower tetrachords. For example, the fact that the fourth occupies an equivalent place within the lower tetrachord to the keynote at the octave in the upper tetrachord enables us to sometimes feel that moving up to the fourth from the keynote is like moving up to the keynote (at the octave) from the fifth, and is therefore actually a kind of resolution. Equally, the fact that the keynote at the octave has an equivalent position in the upper tetrachord to the fourth in the lower one means that we can sometimes feel that moving down to the fifth from the keynote (at the octave) is like moving down to the keynote from the fourth, ie, a resolution.

This introduces some ambiguity into our sense of whether certain melodic movements amount functionally to resolutions or not. In such cases it's the wider harmonic, rhythmic, and melodic context that tends to determine this. Even so, in most cases it is clear, and anyway it's only by exploring this aspect that we can hope to grasp why some sequences of movements have a better sense of underlying direction than others, regardless of their shape. First, though, we must consider how the minor scale differs from the major scale with regard to the features we've just been looking at.

2. Minor scales

In Unit One we saw that different versions of the minor scale may be used, depending on style and context. Here we're only concerned with the purely melodic potential of scales, so we can ignore those versions mainly used for creating chords or for coordinating melody with harmony. For example, although the classical harmonic minor scale is used especially for chords, and the classical melodic minor scale for certain kinds of melodic movement, both primarily reflect the kind of chords classical music uses, so it's not so interesting to explore pure melodic improvising with them. The jazz minor scale is different again: rather than serving as a basis for the overall unfolding of melody and chords in a minor key, it's used for producing alternative, less familiar-sounding harmonisations in major-key music, or as scale material for improvising over individual minor chords. (We'll explore these much later.) Of the versions of the minor scale covered in Unit One, this leaves us with just two: the rock minor and Dorian minor. It's no coincidence that both of these correspond to **modes** – the kind of scales used before chords and harmony were discovered, in early Western music from the Middle Ages, as well as in Ancient Greek, Roman, and Byzantine music.

These two minor scales display similar characteristics to the major scale, but there are some differences too. The first concerns the tetrachords. On the opposite page are the two minor scales, with the tetrachords shown. Notice how the rock minor (or Aeolian mode) has two identical tetrachords, just like the major scale, but the sequence of larger and smaller steps they share is now different. Meanwhile the Dorian minor (or Dorian mode) has a quite different upper tetrachord from its lower one.

With the rock minor, the fact that the semitone now occurs in the middle of the tetrachord means that we no longer feel such a strong sense of arrival as we ascend towards the top of each tetrachord, or descend towards the bottom. With the Dorian minor the fact that the upper and lower tetrachords are different makes it harder to

Scale of C rock minor (Aeolian mode)

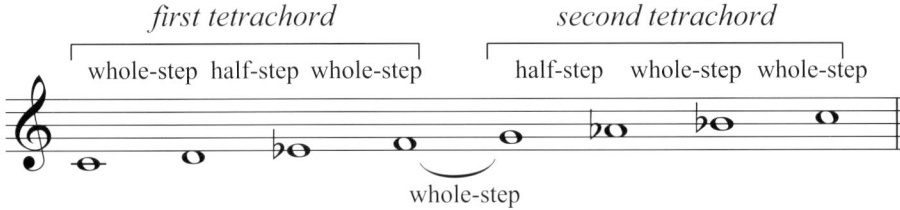

Scale of C Dorian minor (Dorian mode)

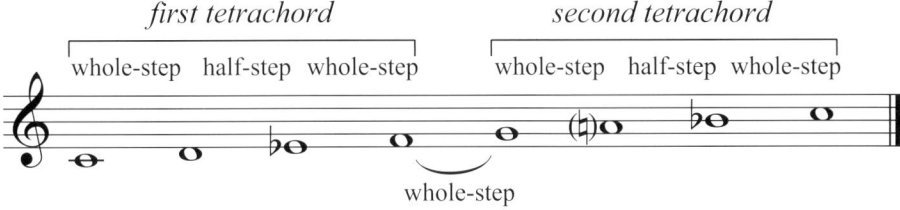

experience the kind of parallels between them audible in the major scale. Apart from the overall feeling of sadness associated with minor scales generally (which is mainly a result of the flattened third), this gives them a rather static and timeless quality.

At the same time, the internal hierarchy of these scales looks different, though it follows the same logic. First comes the keynote, then the tonic triad, but then after this comes the minor pentatonic scale, which is followed by the remaining notes of the diatonic scale itself. (We could then have included the remaining notes of the chromatic scale as a further level, as before, but for the sake of simplicity we've chosen not do that this time.) Because the minor pentatonic is different from the major pentatonic, the fourth and seventh degrees are now more important than the second and sixth. However, this hierarchy counts for less with minor scales than with the major scale, as it no longer simply reflects the natural order of harmonic relations between scale degrees and the keynote. Instead it's an attempt to create a parallel structure to that

Tonic (keynote)	1							
Tonic triad (major)	1		♭3		5			
Major pentatonic scale	1		♭3	4	5			♭7
Rock minor scale	1	2	♭3	4	5	♭6		♭7
Dorian minor scale	*1*	*2*	*♭3*	*4*	*5*		*6*	*♭7*

Hierarchy of scale degrees in rock minor and Dorian minor scales.

within the major scale. In particular, the relative importance given to the notes of the minor pentatonic scale here is mainly a feature of modern styles such as jazz and rock.

It's worth noting that the only note that's actually different between the two versions of the minor scales here is the sixth, which is flattened (from the major) in the rock minor, but not in the Dorian minor. The diagram shows both scales, using Arabic numerals and alterations to show where they differ from the major scale.

UNIT 3 | SECTION 2

There's also a slight difference in how key relations affect our awareness of how certain scale degrees function as counter-poles to the tonic. The fourth and fifth keep the same significance as in a major key, but another scale step acquires some added significance as a result of its being only two steps removed from the keynote on the Circle of Fifths: the flattened seventh. Here's a diagram similar to that given above for major scales, to help you visualize how key relations get projected into the hierarchy of the minor scales themselves.

Minor scale degrees corresponding to key centres close by on the Circle of Fifths – use relative minor descending

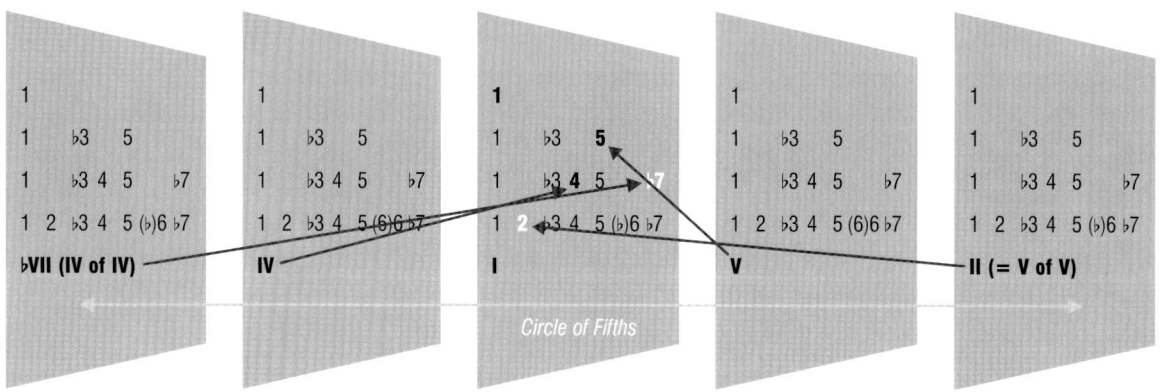

Simple melodic movement

Now we're ready to explore how melodic movement works – what happens when we combine individual melodic movements into simple sequences. (The term 'sequence' just refers here to any succession of melodic movements. It's also used to refer to the practice of immediately restating a melodic shape, starting on a higher or lower scale degree.)

> **The failed genius problem.** A common mistake is to think that if you just play around with the notes of the scale for long enough, you'll come up with wonderfully inspired new melody lines that everyone thinks are amazingly brilliant and cool. But it just doesn't happen like that, so it's only a matter of time before you get disillusioned, decide you're not quite the genius you thought, and give up piano improvisation. What a waste! You never gave yourself a proper chance, because you never found out how melody lines work. Understanding how melodic movements fit together to make shapes with definite structure and direction can help you avoid this.

In this section, try to play slowly through all of the examples here, joining the notes smoothly and listening carefully to how they sound. It's also worth singing along as you play, as this gives a stronger feel for the effect. (The examples all use a special type of note-symbol that implies no specific time-value. For the time being we'll keep things simple: all examples will be in the key of C, beginning first with the major scale.)

Let's start by joining melodic movements in pairs. This involves three notes, of which at least two must be different. The number of possible three-note combinations using just the seven notes of a diatonic scale is quite large, but in practice only some of these are suited to the loose, purely melodic improvising we want to explore right now. A sensible strategy, then, is to try first to sort out which are suitable and which are not.

It can help just to let the tonic triad sound on the piano for a few moments before you play each set of examples. This helps to establish the context implied by the scale itself. In examples based on the major scale this will be a chord of C major (CEG). In subsequent examples based on the minor scale it will be A minor (ACE).

Here are some examples of the simplest kind of three-note sequence. In these cases the second movement simply reverses the first:

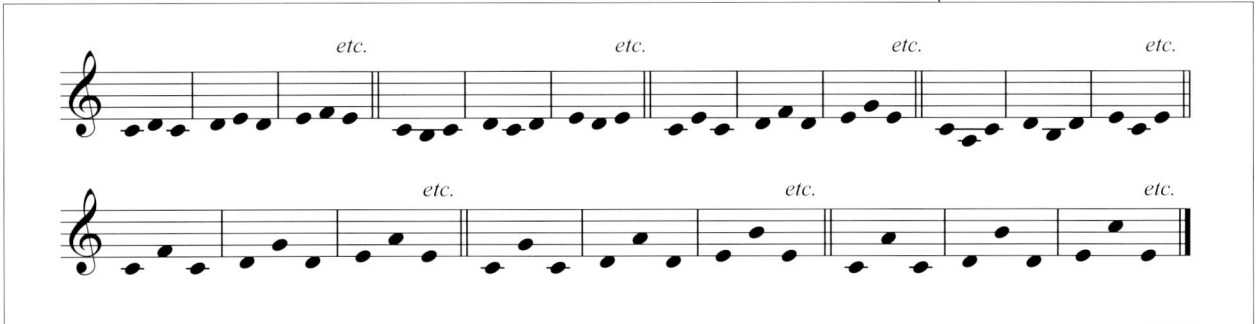

If the movement is stepwise, as in the first set of examples, we just hear a melodic decoration of the first note. That's fine, but it doesn't take the melody anywhere new. On the other hand, if it's a larger interval that's reversed, as in the other examples, we get a sequence that's so self-contained it doesn't really call for any continuation. Such sequences can be useful when building neatly structured melodies (or patterns that repeat themselves) from short motives or phrases – something we'll explore later – but they're not so good for exploring how melodic movements link together at a more basic level (or as part of a more fluid melody line), as once again they don't really go anywhere.

The next set of examples (over the page) show shapes that begin and end with notes from the tonic triad. Consequently they sound very resolved.

Unlike the previous sequences, these do go somewhere, but to a place so closely related to where they started that the resulting sense of movement is weak. In the first set this is because the sequence simply passes through the notes of a triad, so it's hard to hear the individual notes of a melody as really displacing one another: instead we tend to hear them as outlining a chord in which all of them are implied together. From the point of view of melodic movement the effect is static. Sometimes we might want that, but it's better to focus initially on sequences with a strong sense of directedness and movement, as it's easier to feel how these could be continued.

In the second set of examples above, the sequence takes us from one note of the tonic triad to another, via a note that isn't part of the triad, so there's a stronger sense of displacement as we pass from one note to the next, but the fact that the underlying movement from the first to the third note is between two notes belonging to the same triad still means that the overall quality of movement is quite static. The exception is when we move between the first and fifth degrees of the scale, as in the third set. These two scale degrees displace each other quite powerfully because they're counter-poles on the Circle of Fifths.

At the other extreme are sequences involving those scale degrees that, in terms of the internal hierarchy of the scale, are the least resolved. The clearest examples are those that make use of the seventh step – the **leading tone** or **leading note**. This scale degree stands out not only because it's so unresolved, but also because it comes right next to the most resolved scale degree, the tonic, and is only separated from the latter by a half-step. The result is that we mainly use it to approach or depart from the tonic in a stepwise fashion:

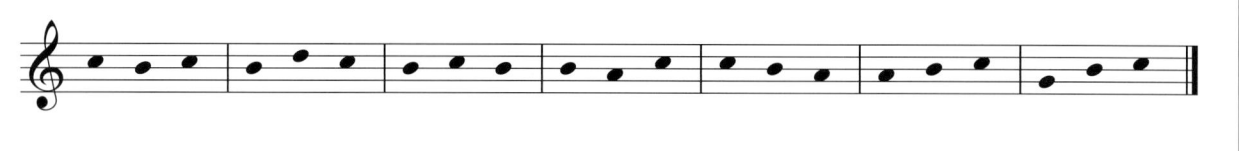

Notice how the stepwise movement here can amount to just a decorated restatement of the first note, or can occur between the first and third notes with the note between heard as a decorative diversion. (The last of the above examples is an exception, as it doesn't approach the seventh by step: this is acceptable here because of the especially close harmonic relationship between the seventh and the fifth, the former being the third of the triad built on the latter. However, it still has to resolve by step to the tonic.)

In the case of sequences using the fourth of the scale, matters are slightly more complicated; while this degree is located on the least resolved level of the internal hierarchy it can nevertheless take on importance as a counter-pole to the keynote, and as the top note of the lower tetrachord. (As we've already seen, the latter encourages us to hear it as an important point of melodic arrival when approached from below.)

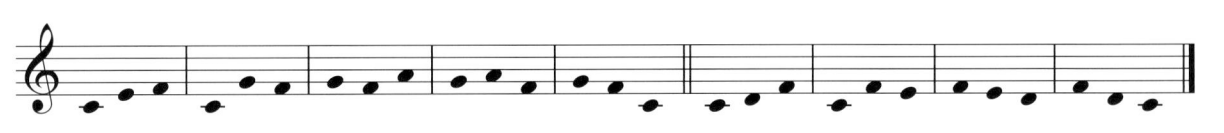

In the first set of examples above the melodic context encourages us to hear the fourth as relatively resolved, while in the second it's heard as more of an unresolved note that, like the seventh, must therefore move to a more resolved note close by. (This ambiguity means it is more affected by the wider melodic, harmonic, and rhythmic context than other scale degrees.)

The Devil's interval. Note that none of the sequences here move between the fourth and the seventh, either directly or indirectly. That's because the interval formed between these two degrees of the scale is particularly uncomfortable on the ear. It's an augmented fourth (or diminished fifth, or just 'tritone' for short), and we try to avoid it in most melodic contexts. Medieval musicians called this 'diabolus in musica' – 'the devil in music'.

Things are pretty similar with the rock and Dorian minor scales. For example, sequences that involve simply reversing the first melodic movement with the second don't lead anywhere, and when the movement is stepwise we just hear them as decorations of the starting note. (In the next few examples a sharp sign above a note indicates the option of playing the sequence either with the sixth as a natural, as in the rock minor, or as a sharp, as in the Dorian. A sharp or natural sign before the note indicates that it is only acceptable when played as shown.)

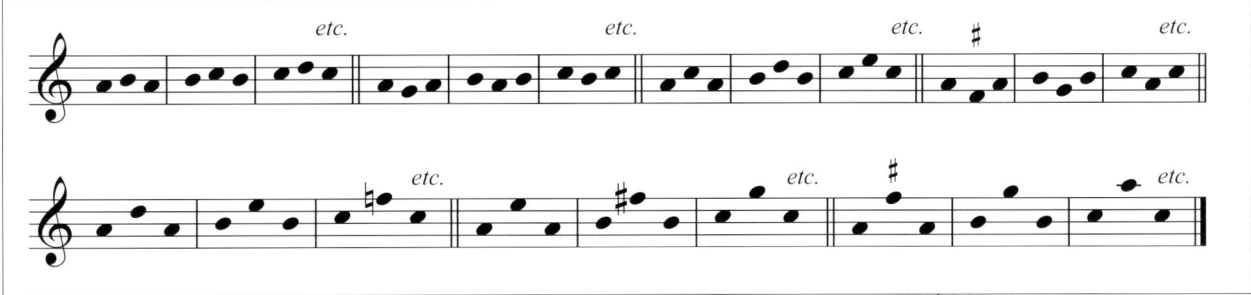

Sequences that pass through the notes of a triad again generate a weak sense of movement and so sound static, as do sequences that start and finish on notes that both belong to the tonic triad, unless these are just the tonic and fifth:

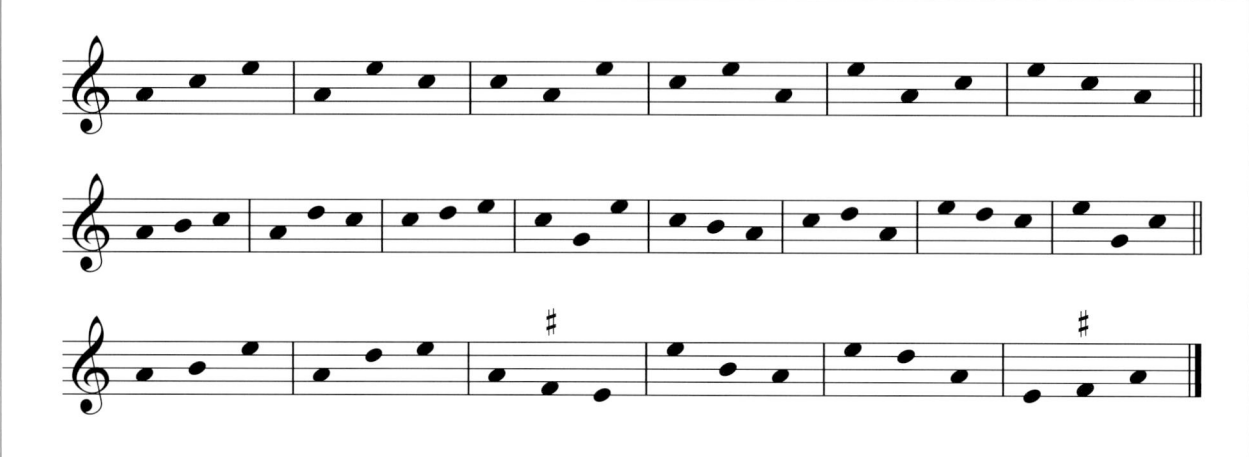

On the other hand, movements involving the seventh step are now much less of a problem. In some of the examples below we are even aware of this scale degree as a potential counter-pole to the tonic, two steps away on the Circle of Fifths:

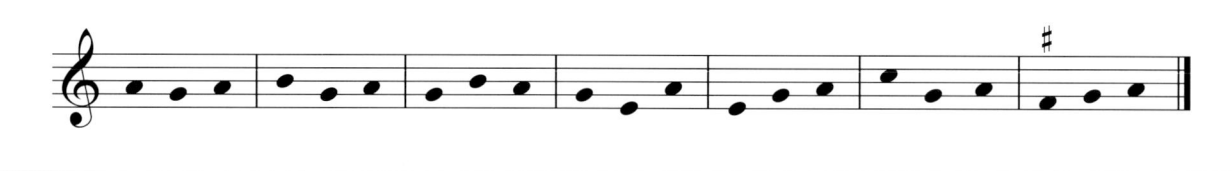

The fourth is less ambiguous than in a major key, owing to the altered structure of the tetrachords: there's less feeling that it has to resolve downwards to the third, but still a sense that it's a counter-pole to the tonic, so its function within the scale is more stable. Movement between the fourth and seventh no longer involves the problematic interval of the tritone and so is fine as well:

Nevertheless, the tritone is still present in these minor scales: in the rock minor it occurs between the second and sixth degrees, in the Dorian minor between the third and sixth, so we must avoid moving directly or indirectly between these notes.

Now let's consider another aspect of how melodic movements can fit together to produce longer sequences. We've already seen that there are two sorts of movement: resolving and non-resolving. If you find yourself unsure which movements are resolving and which not, remember this is simply a question of which of the two notes forming the movement is more basic in the hierarchy of the scale used: consult the tables at the start of the unit, showing the hierarchies for major and minor scales. When we join two movements together in a three-note sequence there are four possibilities:

- a resolving movement followed by another resolving movement
- a non-resolving movement followed by another non-resolving movement
- a non-resolving movement followed by a resolving movement
- a resolving movement followed by a non-resolving movement

What sort of melodic effects can these combinations give rise to? Well, let's return to the major scale once again and see how each combination can work using the various acceptable movements that we still have available to us. Here, first, are sequences that consist of a resolving movement followed by another resolving movement:

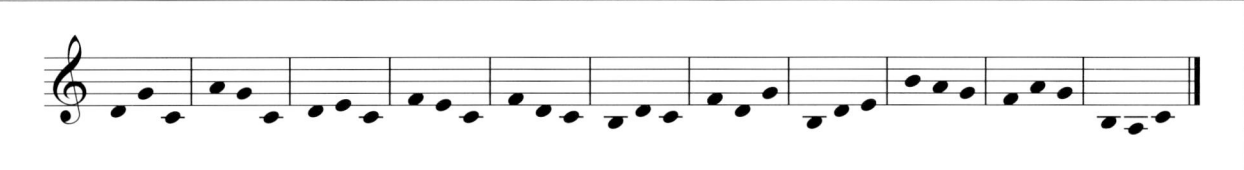

Such sequences generate a strong sense of movement towards and arrival at their final note, but don't seem to have come from anywhere of matching significance. This makes them feel rather one-sided and incomplete – like fragments that belong at the end of longer phrases. Hence they're not really suited to being used as a starting point for melodic improvising, though as we'll see they're certainly useful for other things.

Now here are the sequences in which a non-resolving movement is followed by another non-resolving movement:

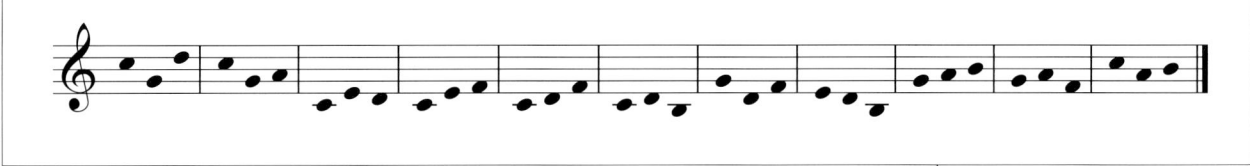

These ones display the opposite characteristic: they produce a strong sense of departure from and movement away from their initial note, but don't seem to take us to anywhere of equivalent significance. They also feel one-sided and incomplete – this time in a way that reminds us of fragments belonging at the start of longer phrases. We could certainly use them as part of more extended melodic lines that subsequently arrive at some sort of resolution. However, this would mean working with melody on a larger, more ambitious scale, whereas right now we just want melodic movements that can be combined into the simplest possible sequences. So once again these are best left for later.

The next set of examples illustrate what happens when a non-resolving movement is followed by a resolving movement:

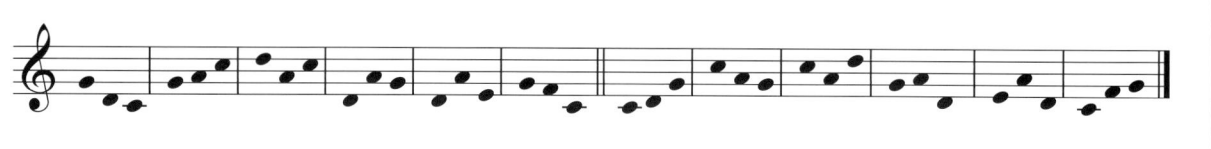

Each sequence here possesses its own feeling of completeness. This is because the resolving and non-resolving movements seem to balance one another. So these sequences are really worth exploring at this stage: they can serve as building blocks for creating a line. As you play through each of these sequences you should also find that you hear the two melodic movements as being 'framed' by the relationship between the first and third notes: we also hear this as a kind of indirect melodic movement, that can either be resolving or not. This helps to give each sequence an overall sense of direction. In the above examples the first group are framed by a resolving movement, the second by a non-resolving one.

Let's compare this to what happens when a resolving movement is followed by a non-resolving movement:

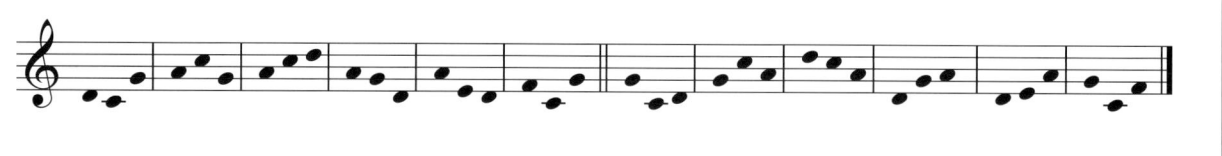

Although these sequences lack the sense of closure that comes from ending with a resolution, they do display some feeling of completeness, as the resolving and non-resolving movements still counterbalance one another. Here too, then, we have simple sequences that are definitely worth exploring at this stage. Once again the individual movements are framed by an indirect movement between first and third notes that gives an overall directional character to each sequence. (Again, the first group shows sequences framed by a resolving movement, the second sequences framed by a non-resolving movement.)

What about in minor scales? Here the possible combinations are similar, though the scale degrees involved in each will sometimes differ to reflect differences between the scales hierarchies. Here, first, are sequences that involve a resolving movement followed by another resolving movement:

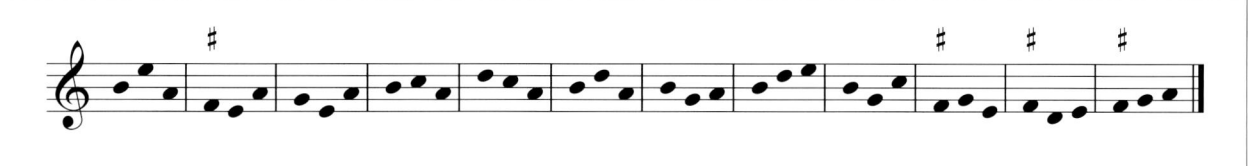

Once again we have a feeling that these lack a clearly defined point of departure, even though they create a strong sense of arrival.

Here now are sequences in which a non-resolving movement is followed by another non-resolving movement:

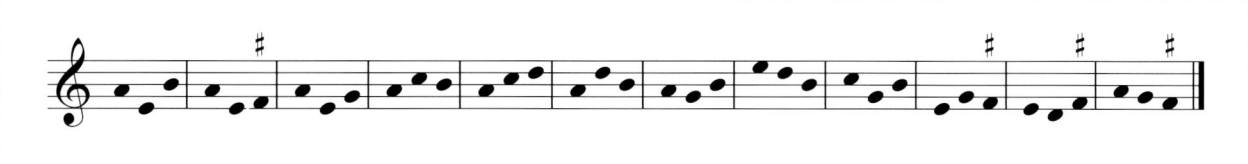

Conversely, as with the major scale, these have a powerful sense of departure but no sense of arrival.

Now here we have non-resolving movements that in each case are followed by a resolving movement:

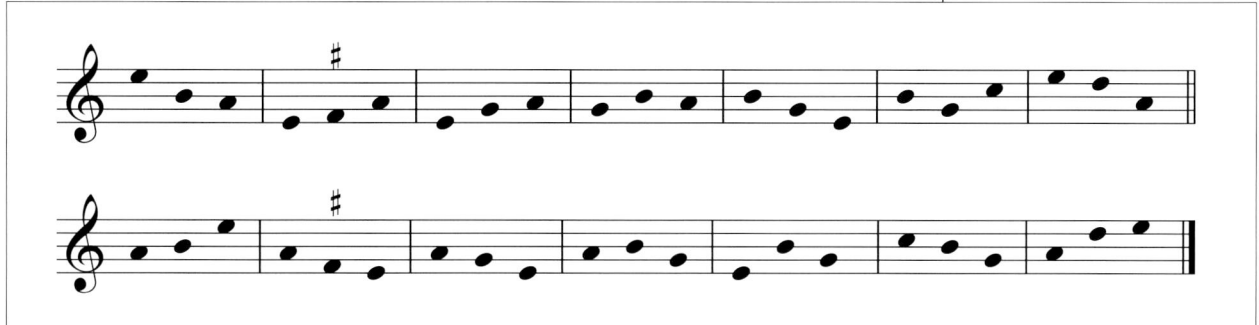

As in the major scale, this combination creates a sense of internally balanced departure and arrival. (Once again, the first group are framed by a resolving movement between the first and third notes, the second group by a non-resolving movement.)

Finally, here are resolving movements being followed by non-resolving movements:

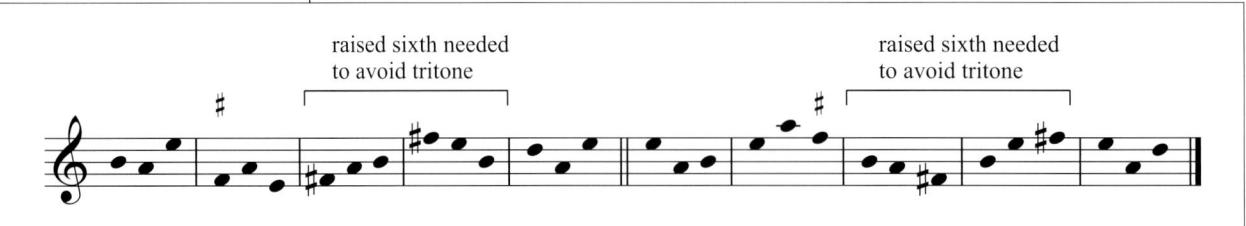

Again, there's a sense here that the arriving or resolving movement is counterbalanced by the subsequent departing or non-resolving movement, even though the sequences don't end with a resolution. (Here, too, the first group are framed by a resolving movement, the second by a non-resolving movement.)

Exercise 3.1
Explore each of the following sets of three notes in turn, trying out all the possible sequences of movements it can be used to create. Which of them do you think sound good in themselves, and which sound incomplete? Which lack a clear sense of direction and which have it?

As soon as we combine movements together into sequences we encounter another basic feature of music: **melodic shape**. Although many aspects of how this works will only become clear later, when we're dealing with sequences of more than three notes and with ones that have a definite metre and rhythm, we can already grasp the two most basic rules of thumb for good melodic shapes:

- Balance steps with leaps (and vice versa).
- Balance upward with downward movement (and vice versa).

In certain situations these two rules of thumb combine to produce fairly precise implications for what works and what doesn't: for example a large ascending leap – say, a sixth or bigger – should almost always be followed by one or more descending steps, a large descending leap by one or more ascending steps. This means that in practice we try to avoid a succession of melodic leaps in the same direction. We also try to avoid long, unbroken successions of stepwise movements (except where these have a purely decorative or textural function).

We'll talk about various other aspects of melodic shape in due course. First, however, we need to look at how longer sequences of melodic movements can be created that make musical sense.

Simple melodic continuation

Now we've familiarized ourselves with the basic options for combining melodic movements into short sequences it's time to start learning how to continue these, so as to make a slightly more extended line. Basically, we treat sequences as building blocks that can be combined into larger phrases, and the simplest way to do this, of course, is just to play them one after another.

Once again, we'll focus at this stage on how this can be explored without any specific harmony, metre, or rhythm. That's the best way to make sure it feeds straight into your exploration of melody at the most basic level – at the level of the sort of free and fluid playing around with melodic lines that provides the best starting point when learning to improvise.

It's at this point that the overall resolving or non-resolving character of individual sequences becomes significant. A three-note sequence 'framed' by a resolving movement between its first and last notes will generally sound better when followed by one 'framed' by a non-resolving movement, and vice versa. In other words, the logic that governed which combinations of individual melodic movements work best repeats itself here at the level of how two sequences fit together. On the other hand, once two such sequences are combined together a third level of melodic movement appears, in the form of the overall movement from the first to the last note of the newly created longer sequence. Let's take one example (over the page) and look at how this works. The notes forming the framing movements within each shorter sequence are highlighted using unfilled note-heads:

UNIT 3 | SECTION 2

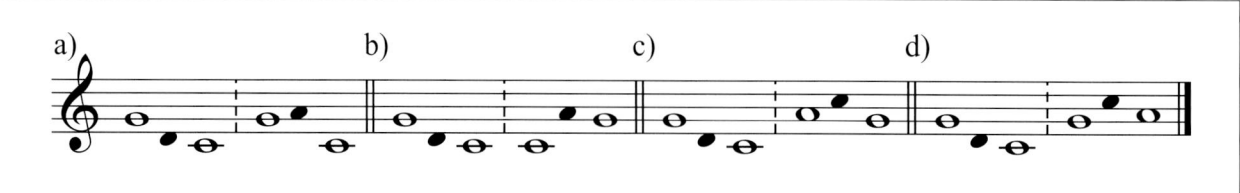

In each case we get a different overall effect:

- In (a), in spite of the difference between the two sequences, the framing movements are both resolving in character, so there's no sense that the second counterbalances the first. Moreover, in fact they're identical, so there's no sense of underlying melodic development at all, and the overall movement from the first to last note of the six-note sequence simply repeats the first framing movement at a higher level.

- In (b), the situation is a bit better: the resolving character of the first framing movement is answered by the non-resolving character of the second. Yet the latter simply reverses the former – like a person taking one step forward, then one step backwards, so there's no sense that the melody takes us anywhere new.

- In (c), as in (a), both framing movements are resolving, but the second is different from the first. Although the second doesn't counterbalance the first in terms of resolution, there is some sense of melodic development even if it still only leads us back to the note we started on, so it's as if we had moved in a circle.

- In (d), as in (b), the initial framing movement, which is resolving, is answered by a second one that's non-resolving. The overall movement from the first to the last note of the entire six-note sequence is now a non-resolving movement too – one that takes us somewhere new, so the whole sequence now calls out to be answered by whatever comes next.

All in all, then, (a) and (b) are relatively uninteresting, (c) has some interest, but only (d) achieves a really interesting sense of melodic development, with clear implications for what could follow.

There are two variations on this method of extending a sequence that deserve brief consideration: **dovetailing** and **embedding.**

Instead of simply following one short sequence with another, we can dovetail two such sequences together by making the last note (or two notes) of the first sequence count as the first note (or two notes) of the second, resulting in five-note or four-note sequences. Play through the following examples:

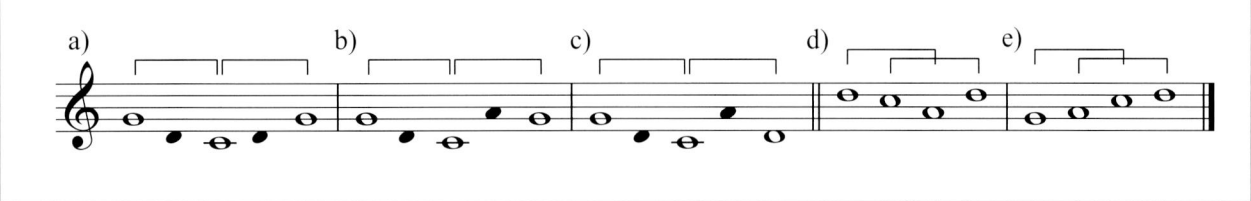

Once again, it's clear that some of these produce better results than others:

- In (a) the second sequence simply reverses the first.

- In (b) the same is true at the level of the framing movements, even if there's some variation, so neither of these represents an interesting melodic development.

- In (c) we also have a resolving framing movement followed by a non-resolving one, but this time the latter takes us somewhere new, while the overall movement from the first to the fifth note is also a non-resolving movement to a new place. This means that on both levels the melody has really gone somewhere, thus creating expectations for what is likely to follow.

With examples (d) and (e) the dovetailing involves two notes rather than just one, and in each case produces quite the opposite melodic effect:

- In (d) the result is a four-note sequence that moves in circular fashion back to where it started: there's no overall framing movement, so even though each of the component sequences is framed by a non-resolving movement the effect is static, if unresolved.

- In (e) a resolving framing movement dovetails with another resolving one, but the overall framing movement is a non-resolving one, taking us to somewhere new, so the effect is of something internally quite resolved that nevertheless moves forward.

Alternatively, we can embed one sequence within another, providing that the first and last notes of one of the two sequences correspond to the first and second, or second and third notes of the other. In the examples below the filled note-head is the one that belongs to just the embedded sequence, while the three unfilled note-heads taken together correspond to the embedding sequence:

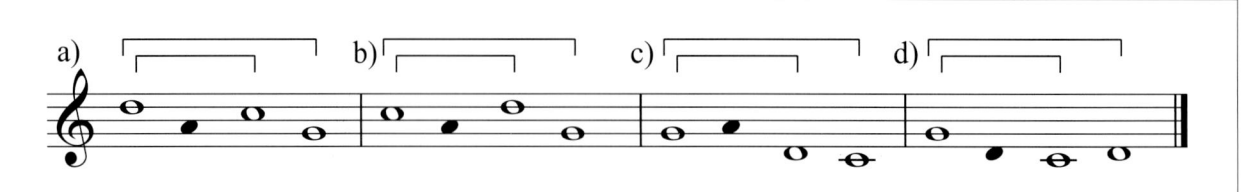

Once again, the overall melodic effect will reflect the relationship between the framing movements of the two component sequences, keeping in mind that the framing movement of the embedding sequence is also that of the new longer sequence:

- In (a) both framing movements are resolved. At the same time the overall framing movement resolves onto the fifth of the scale – the principal counter-pole to the tonic. The combined effect of these features is to give the phrase a strong sense of internal resolution that makes the final note sound oddly resolved, given its powerful unresolved relationship to the tonic itself.

- In (b) both framing movements are unresolved, intensifying our sense that the phrase as a whole requires a resolution of the final fifth back to the tonic.

- In (c) the framing movement of the embedded sequence is non-resolving, while that of the embedding sequence is resolving. The result is a sense of overall resolution that's heightened by the contrast with the movement of the embedded phrase.

- In (d) the framing movement of the embedded sequence is resolving, while that of the embedding sequence is non-resolving. This throws the unresolved character of the phrase as a whole into relief.

Note how in the last of the above examples we hear the note belonging to just the embedded sequence as a decoration of the embedding sequence. This is because it proceeds stepwise to a note that belongs to the latter. This brings us to another aspect of how melodic sequences can be elaborated into more complex and extended lines, which is through **embellishment**. However, we won't be in a position to explore that topic until we've first got to know how the other raw materials of musical improvising work.

Exercise 3.2

The chart below shows the most common (and unproblematic) three-note sequences based on the major scale that are internally balanced (from a functional point of view), in that they contain both a resolving and a non-resolving movement. Reading across each row gives the four possible combinations of resolving and non-resolving movements for the same set of three notes, while looking down each column gives the different possible forms each combinations can have in the scale (of C major). Use this as a reference point as you play around and explore the sequences to see how they can be combined. Listen carefully as you play, and try to determine for yourself what the resulting musical effects are, along the lines just discussed. Make a note of any sequences you find especially pleasing. Doing that will be your first and most important step towards developing a personal vocabulary of musical ideas, and with it your own individual voice as a creative musician. Don't worry about rhythm, or about creating melodies that sound 'complete', for now.

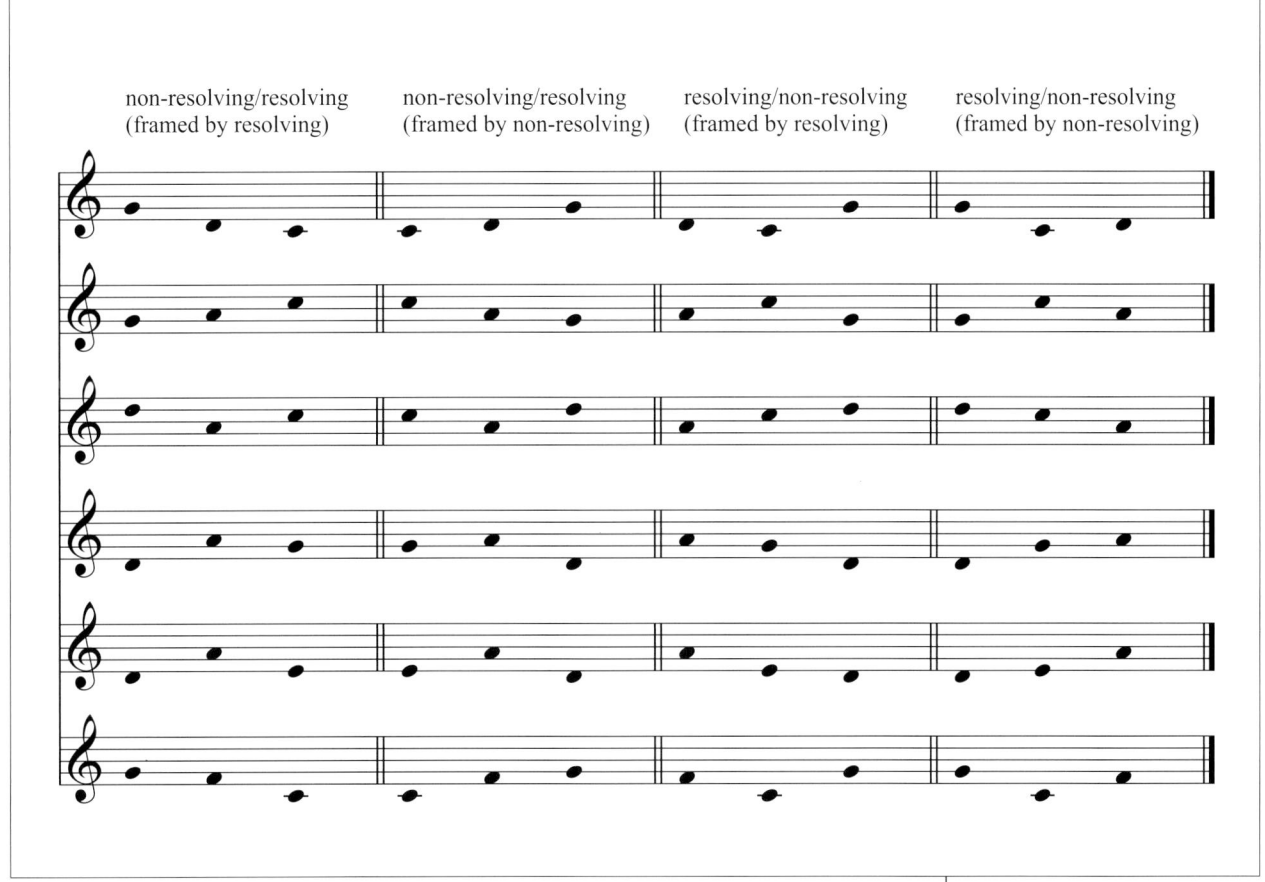

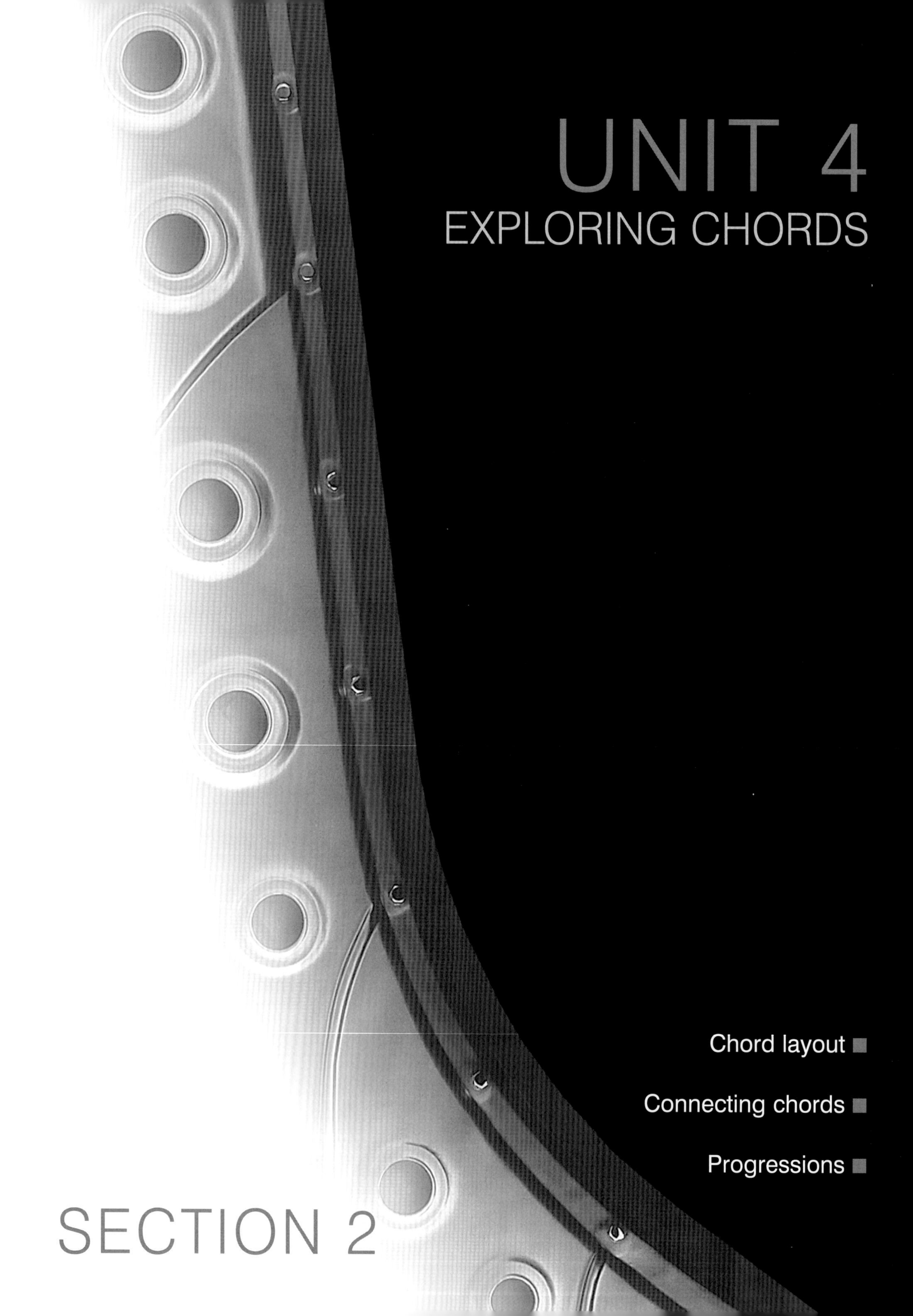

UNIT 4
EXPLORING CHORDS

Chord layout ■

Connecting chords ■

Progressions ■

SECTION 2

SECTION 2 | UNIT 4

Chord layout

It's tempting to think that the easiest way to play chords on the piano is to play them in your left hand, as this leaves your right hand free to focus on playing the melody. That's especially so when you want to improvise: putting all the harmony in the left hand creates a neat divide and lets you focus on the right hand, which tends to do most of the melodic playing as it is in a higher register than the left hand. Unfortunately it doesn't work in practice.

Harmony didn't originally develop around the possibilities of the keyboard: instead it first evolved out of the choral textures of early Western classical music, which involved four different kinds of voice – soprano, alto, tenor, and bass (or SATB for short) – singing together. Because of this, the most basic way to lay out chords between the hands on the piano still uses a four-part texture. So for each chord we actually need to play four notes, not just the three that a triad provides. Hence one note normally gets to be used in two different octaves at the same time. We say it's **doubled**.

At the same time, four-part harmony on the piano sounds best with the three upper voices located close together in the octave above or the area just below Middle C, and with the lowest voice, the **bassline**, located somewhere in the octave-and-a-half below this. (Allowing the upper parts to move down too close to the bassline produces a muddy texture that spoils the harmony and drowns out the melody.)

All of this means the best way to lay out chords is with one note in the left hand and three in the right. But if your right hand has to play three notes of each chord, how will it also have room to explore melody? That's a big issue, especially when improvising. The solution is to first learn the basic method of laying out chords in four parts, and then see how these can be adapted where necessary, either by reducing the number of parts or by moving more notes into the left hand to take the pressure off the right.

Take a look at the example below. It shows a chord of C major. In every case the chord is in root position, so the root must be in the bass, ie, the left hand. In the first five examples, just playing a right-hand triad in any inversion over this means the root is automatically doubled, which is fine. (In these cases the notes of the right hand triad are as close together as possible – we call this **close position**). That's the simplest route to a good four-part layout, but sometimes we want to double a different note, either because it alters the feel of the chord itself in a way that we like, or because it's needed for a smooth connection with the preceding or succeeding chord. In that case the right hand must open out and play either the third or the fifth in two octaves at once, rather than the triad.

Root position

UNIT 4 | SECTION 2

The choice of right hand position often depends on which note you want on top, as this is the one most likely to be part of the melody. With root position chords, we normally double the root or fifth, but may occasionally double the third instead. (We may also omit the fifth, but not the third.)

Sometimes, though, we also want to use chords in first or second inversion. These sound less resolved, and the rules are different for which notes you can or should double. For first inversion chords, double the root or fifth, but never the third (ie, don't double the bass). For second inversion chords, double the bass (ie, the fifth). (In these cases it's not advisable to omit any notes of the triad.) In practice this means we can't use close position triads over first inversion chords, but must use them over second inversion chords:

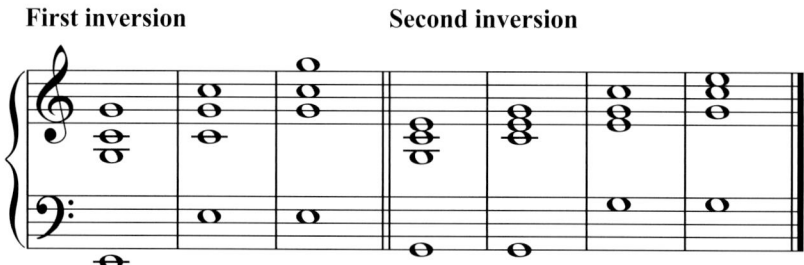

Now let's see how the layout of these chords can be adapted so that we have just two notes in the left hand and two in the right.

We can further reduce the number of notes in the right hand by reducing the overall number of parts in the texture from four to three, but there's a tricky trade-off between opening up the right hand for freer melodic improvising and limiting the options for connecting chords together smoothly (something we'll consider in the next part of this unit).

As far as individual chords are concerned, two notes in the left and one in the right works, so long as the left hand can provide the required notes of the chord without forcing the middle part down too low. (Whether it's OK to have the third directly above the root, as in the first case here, depends on how high or low the root is. Any lower than is shown here is to be avoided.) On the other hand, moving the third up an octave, which is also shown, creates a large stretch (known as a tenth). Left-hand tenths used to be very popular amongst those jazz pianists with large hands, but most players find them a strain and end up taking the middle note back into the right hand.

Root position   **First inversion**   **Second inversion**

You should now be able to see that having all three notes of the chord in the left hand is actually the most radical departure of all from the standard four-part layout. This opens up the right hand even more for playing around with melody, but leaves very limited possibilities for chord connection. It plays an important role in jazz (see the section on left-hand voicings in Unit Eight), thanks to the particular kind of chord structures used there, which are different from those used in other kinds of non-classical music or in mainstream classical music. However, outside of jazz it has limited usefulness.

In classical music, chords can also be played by just the left hand, but this is because the notes of the chord are played as a sequential pattern instead of simultaneously as a block chord. The result is a rhythmic-harmonic texture that may provide a pleasing background for a melody, but the scope of the right hand for melodic improvising remains fairly limited, as the melody must be kept relatively simple in order to be coordinated with the left hand pattern. In spite of this, 19th-century piano improvisers such as Chopin and Liszt were able to produce virtuosic improvisations over such patterns, partly through a deliberate loosening of the rhythmic relationship between the hands. (We'll consider the role these kinds of texture can play in improvisation in Unit 12.)

All of the examples shown so far feature a chord of C major. As far as chord layout is concerned, the same rules will apply equally to major and minor chords, and do so regardless of their function within a key. Different rules apply, though, to chords based on diminished or augmented triads.

Diminished chords are normally laid out in first inversion, and in contrast to other first inversion chords if a note is doubled it should be the bass note (the third). This is especially relevant to chord VII in a major key, and to chord II in a minor key when this uses either the harmonic minor or rock minor scale, as these chords are diminished.

Augmented chords sound the same in any inversion, and it makes no difference which note is doubled. This is relevant to chord III in a minor key, when this uses either the harmonic minor or jazz minor scale. However, don't worry about these cases too much right now: you won't be making much use of these chords for the time being.

UNIT 4 SECTION 2

Connecting chords

Because the effect of a chord is different depending on how it's approached, how we connect up one chord to the next is important. In classical music this is called **voice-leading**, a term which refers to the way each note in one chord can be heard as moving melodically to a corresponding note in the next. The idea is that even when all of the notes are just played on the piano we still hear them as we do when each singer (or group of singers) in a vocal ensemble (or choir) takes responsibility for sounding one particular note in the chord, and then the equivalent note in the next chord, and so on: ie, we hear a texture of separately moving melodic parts.

No matter what style of music you want to improvise in, you'll need to take some account of voice-leading, though how far you go with this depends on the style and the wider musical context. For example:

- Solo piano improvising generally requires fairly precise treatment of voice-leading if the harmony is to avoid sounding crude and amateurish – especially in classical.
- Improvising piano alongside amplified and percussive instruments (eg, electric guitar, synthesizers, drum kit) will mean your harmony is much less exposed, and you may be playing with other chord-producing instruments for which voice-leading simply isn't an option – so here it makes sense to adopt a looser, freer approach.
- Jazz has a special system of standardised voicings for the most common progressions, so you don't have to worry about voice-leading very much here.

> **Classical connoisseur or hard-core rebel?** It's all in the voice-leading. Voice-leading allows us to hear chord progressions as combinations of unfolding lines or 'parts'. This way of hearing harmony reflects the history of Western classical music, so it's strongly associated with the latter. How you approach voice-leading tells listeners a huge amount about where you're positioning yourself stylistically and culturally. Careful, smooth voice-leading evokes a sense of musical tradition, emotional sophistication, and classical refinement, while musicians who don't bother about voice-leading are likely to be seen as rejecting tradition in favour of something more coarse and direct, as in blues, reggae, punk, and hard rock.

The rules for voice-leading can be complex, but whatever your musical preferences it's worth getting to know at least the core principles. The golden rule is that wherever possible, each part moves from a note in one chord to the nearest note in the next.

There are three different ways in which the movement in one part may relate to that in the others occurring at the same time: **parallel motion**, **oblique motion**, and **contrary motion**. In parallel motion two parts move together in the same direction, while in oblique motion one part moves while the other stays fixed, and in contrary motion the two parts move in opposite directions:

The main challenge when aiming for good voice-leading is to avoid an effect which results when two melodic parts or 'voices' move in parallel and are separated by an interval of a perfect fifth or octave. Because these intervals are so resolved, the two parts merge to form an independent texture within the overall movement of voices. This disrupts the sense of balance between the parts, and we lose the feeling of a smooth progression. These undesirable effects are called **parallel** (or **consecutive**) **fifths** and **octaves**. Composers have time to look through their harmony and remove these, but when you're improvising chords as well as melody that's not an option. The best way to minimise the risk of these is to follow these two principles:

- Learn standard voice-leading arrangements for the most common progressions.
- Aim where possible for contrary or oblique motion between upper voices and bass.

If you want your harmony to have a more nuanced classical feel, bear in mind that we tend to treat the inner parts slightly differently from the top part and the bass. Since the top line mostly carries the melody, its voice-leading will often be a function of the latter. (You can also think of a melody as just an embellishment of the voice-leading in whichever part carries it – ie, usually the top part.)

The **bassline** also plays a special role, as it must provide the right note for the chord to count as the particular position or inversion that it's supposed to be. This means it must also have a certain degree of melodic freedom. This is often taken further – especially in classical music – by treating it as a kind of **countermelody** to the principal line: ie, an independent and contrasting melody unfolding at the same time. (We'll examine this more in Unit Seven.) Hence the bassline may contain melodic leaps from one chord to the next, and these in turn are often decorated with stepwise melodic movement.

Now it's time to take a look at how these connections work in practice. We'll stick to the key of C major for the time being.

In the following examples the chord functions are indicated using the classical system of Roman numerals (which identify the scale-degree corresponding to the root of the chord within a given key – here C major). Note that in the modern version of this system, used here, inversions are indicated as follows:

Root position:	I	II	III	IV	etc.
First inversion:	I^b	II^b	III^b	IV^b	etc.
Second inversion:	I^c	II^c	III^c	IV^c	etc.

(The symbols for root positions chords are thus really short for I^a, II^a, III^a, IV^a, etc.)

It's worth knowing that the more traditional version of this classical system used numbers placed after the numerals to indicate chord inversions. These showed the intervals formed between the upper notes of the chord and the bass, just like in the old figured-bass system that was the basis for keyboard harmony in the Baroque period. (You can learn about how this relates to the history of keyboard improvisation in the Introduction.) However, in practice only those numbers that differed from the root position form appeared in the music, and these in turn gave rise to names for the chord inversions that are still sometimes used (eg, in older harmony textbooks). The table below shows how the different names and notations are related:

	Root position:	First inversion:	Second inversion:
Modern notation:		a	b
Intervals from bass:	5 3	6 3	6 4
Old notation:		6	6 4
Old name:		'sixth chord'	'six-four chord'

As we'll see shortly, these older names are also reflected in the names given to harmonic formulas.

> **Pedalling chords.** In practice you'll find most chord progressions involving four-part harmony end up being legato pedalled throughout, for the sake of achieving a smooth and even texture. Although some of the chord connections can usually be joined quite smoothly using fingers alone, the need for a consistent sound means that if just one of them needs legato pedalling, then the whole sequence will have to pedalled for a consistent quality of sound. Even so, practising (and memorising) chord connections first without pedal is essential: it forces you to apply fingering patterns consistently in order to achieve those smooth connections that are possible without pedal, and this heightens awareness of the audible effects of what your fingers are doing. Moreover, a smooth join achieved in the fingers always sounds better, even when accompanied by pedalling, as it allows for more precise control over dynamics, which play an important role in making audible the melodic connection between notes in successive chords.

SECTION 2 | UNIT 4

a) Connecting root position chords

When connecting chords in root position, the options depend on the interval between the roots. So even when the chords themselves are different, if the interval between the roots is the same, you use the same kind of connection. This is essential when improvising, as you won't have time to think through the voice-leading afresh for each and every progression. You need to be able to look at the interval from the root of the chord you're playing now to that of the chord you're about to play, and tell straight away what connections you can use. With practice your hands and fingers will learn this too, and they'll do most of the work – you won't have to think about it.

Let's start with connections between chords laid out with one note in the left hand and three in the right. Take a look at the first set of examples (p112). These show how to connect a chord to another with a root a perfect fourth lower (or fifth higher), followed by the reverse movement.

On p113 there is another set of examples, this time showing how to connect a chord to another with a root a perfect fourth higher (or fifth lower), followed by the reverse movement. In fact these are the same connections as in the first example, but this time presented with the second chord as the starting and finishing chord. Movements between chords with roots a fourth or fifth apart are the most basic connections of all, so it's worth practising the connections both ways round, so you get really familiar with how they work.

The examples on p114 (top) show connections leading from one chord to another with a root a third lower (or sixth higher). This kind of progression is also very effective, so you should become familiar with it. The reverse movement to a chord with the root a third higher is less common and its effectiveness depends on the particular chords. However, practising the reverse shift here will also help to consolidate your knowledge of the connection.

Connections leading between chords with roots a second apart are only sometimes effective – once again it depends on which particular chords are involved. As we'll see in the next section, IV-V and V-VI are important progressions, while V-IV can be very important in blues-based styles. Nevertheless, practising these connections moving to and fro between a variety of different chords is the best way to entrench the movement in your muscular memory (p114, bottom). Note how the right-hand fingerings for chord connections here are basically the same as in Unit Two. Try practising them first without pedal, and then with legato pedal (changing or clearing the pedal with each new chord).

For connections between chords laid out with two notes in each hand we also have a set of standard possibilities for each kind of root-movement. The fingerings will be more complex, since we can no longer simply apply the right-hand fingerings for connecting triads learned earlier. (Bear in mind that fingerings will often need to be adjusted to reflect the need to connect with chords coming before and after those shown in the examples. Hence those shown here are for guidance only.)

The examples on p115 show how to move to a chord with a root a perfect fourth lower (or fifth higher) and back again.

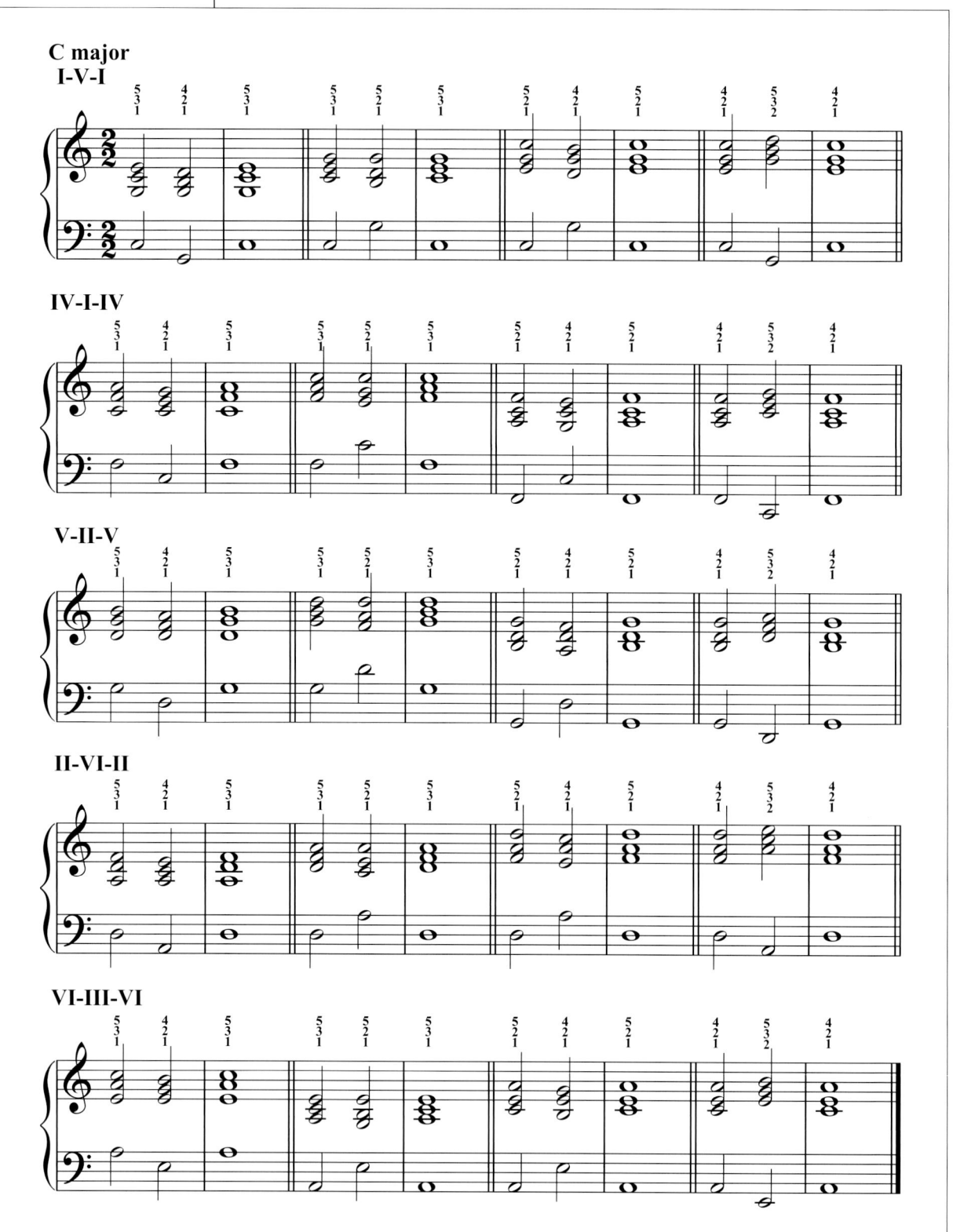

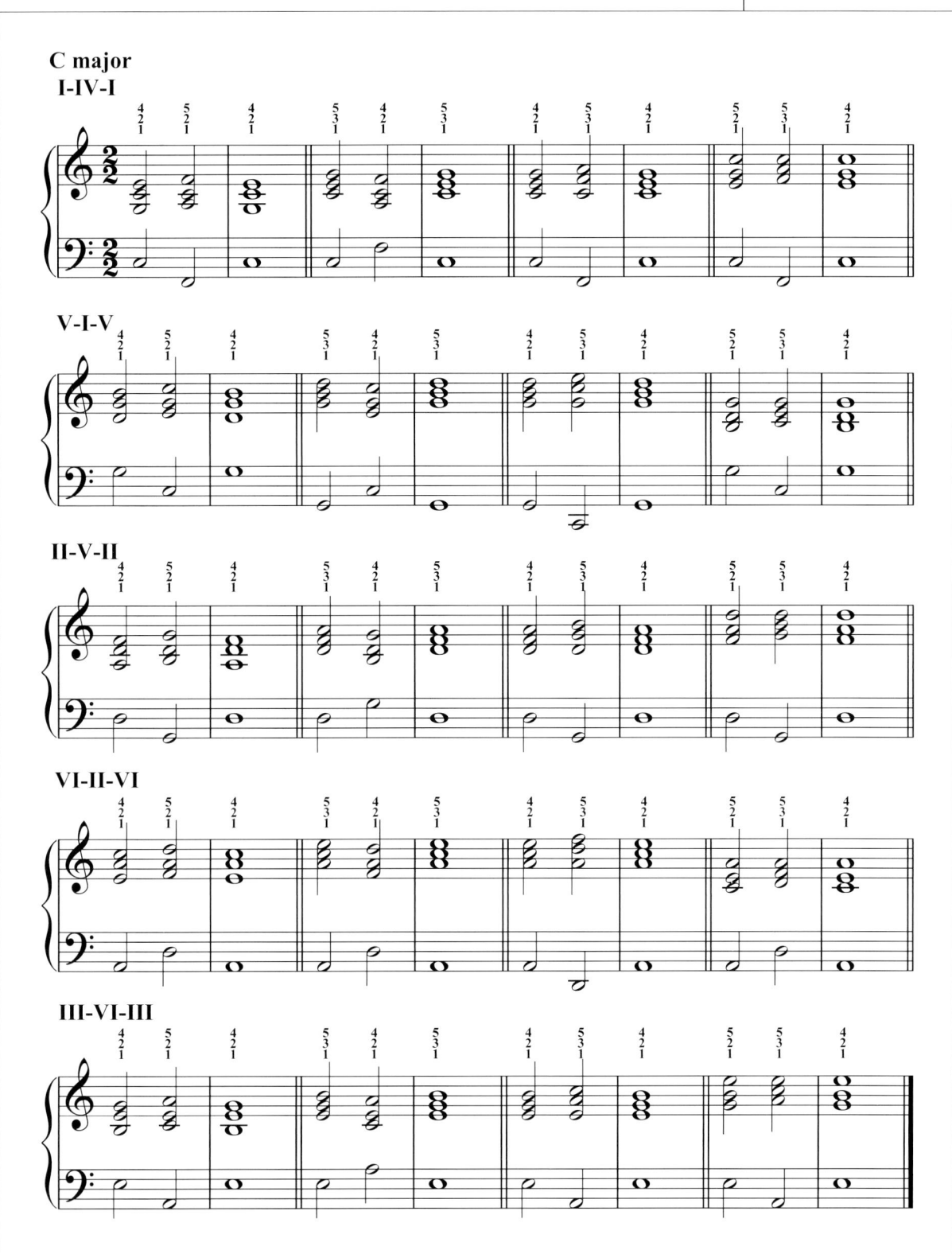

C major
I-VI-I
IV-II-IV
V-III-V

C major
V-VI-V
I-II-I
IV-V-IV
III-IV-III

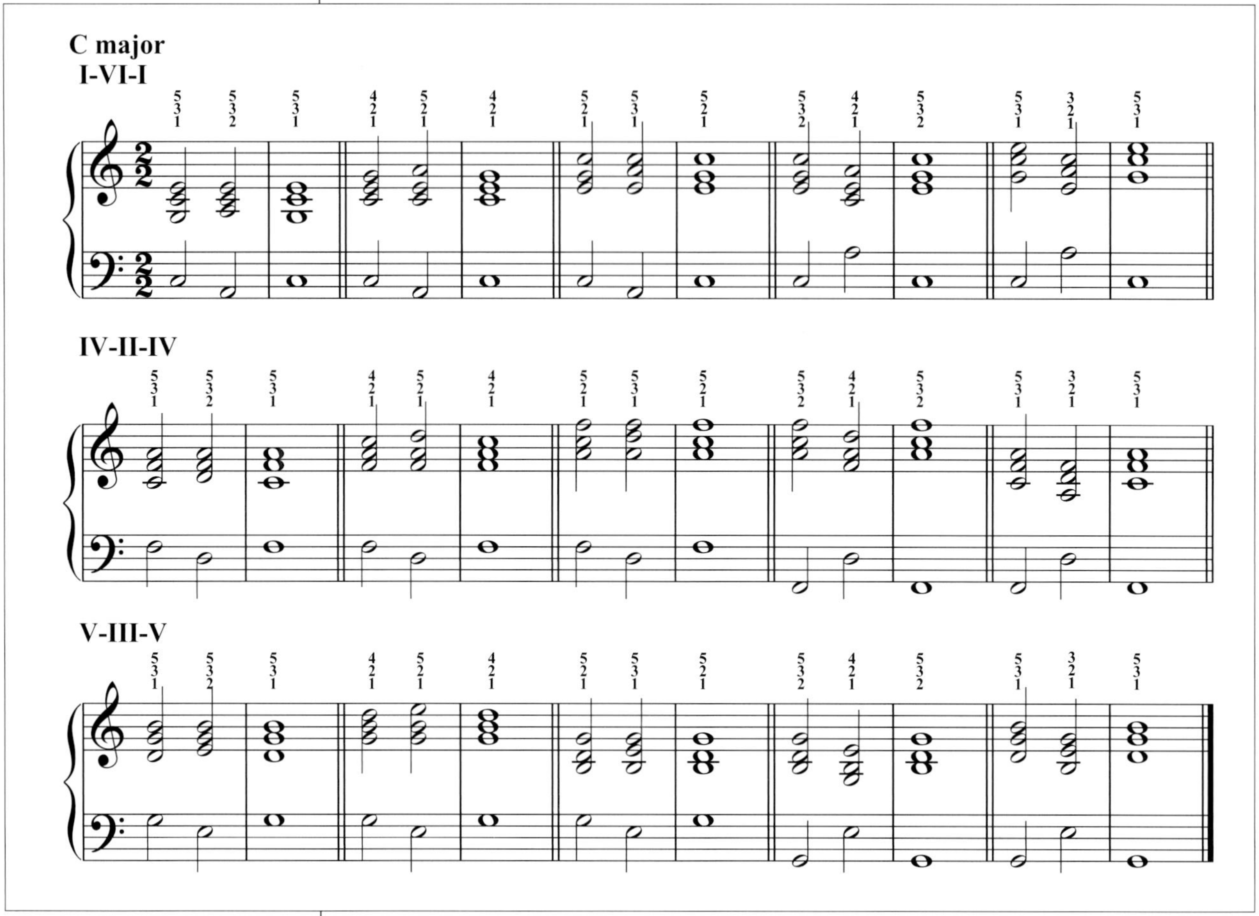

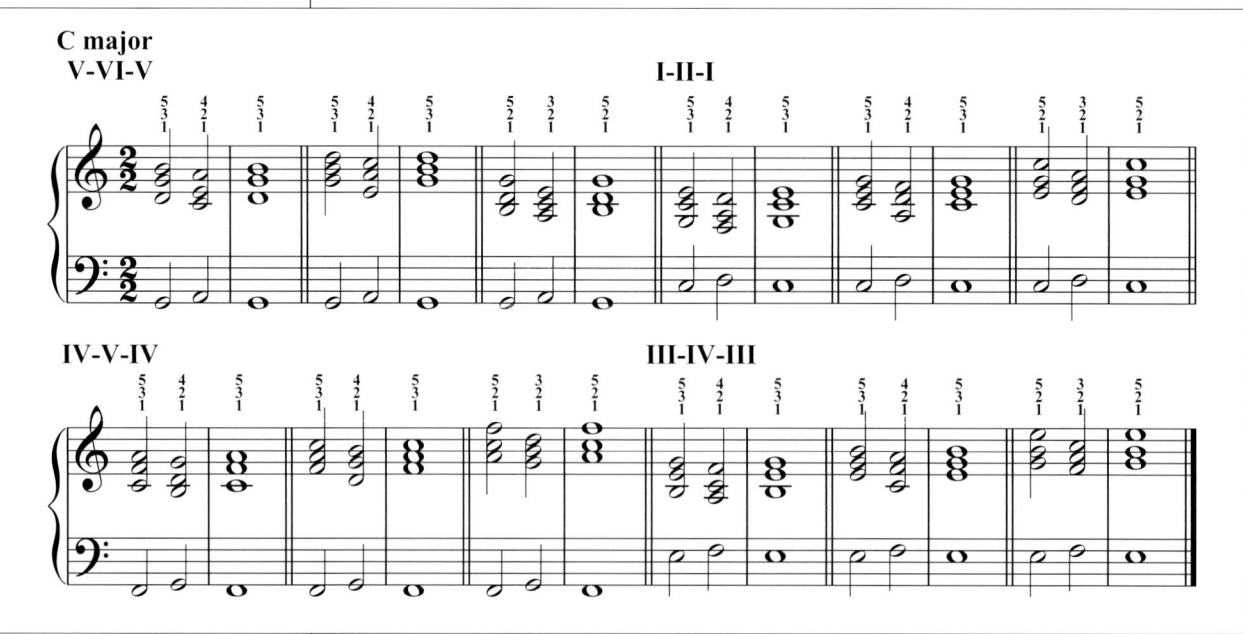

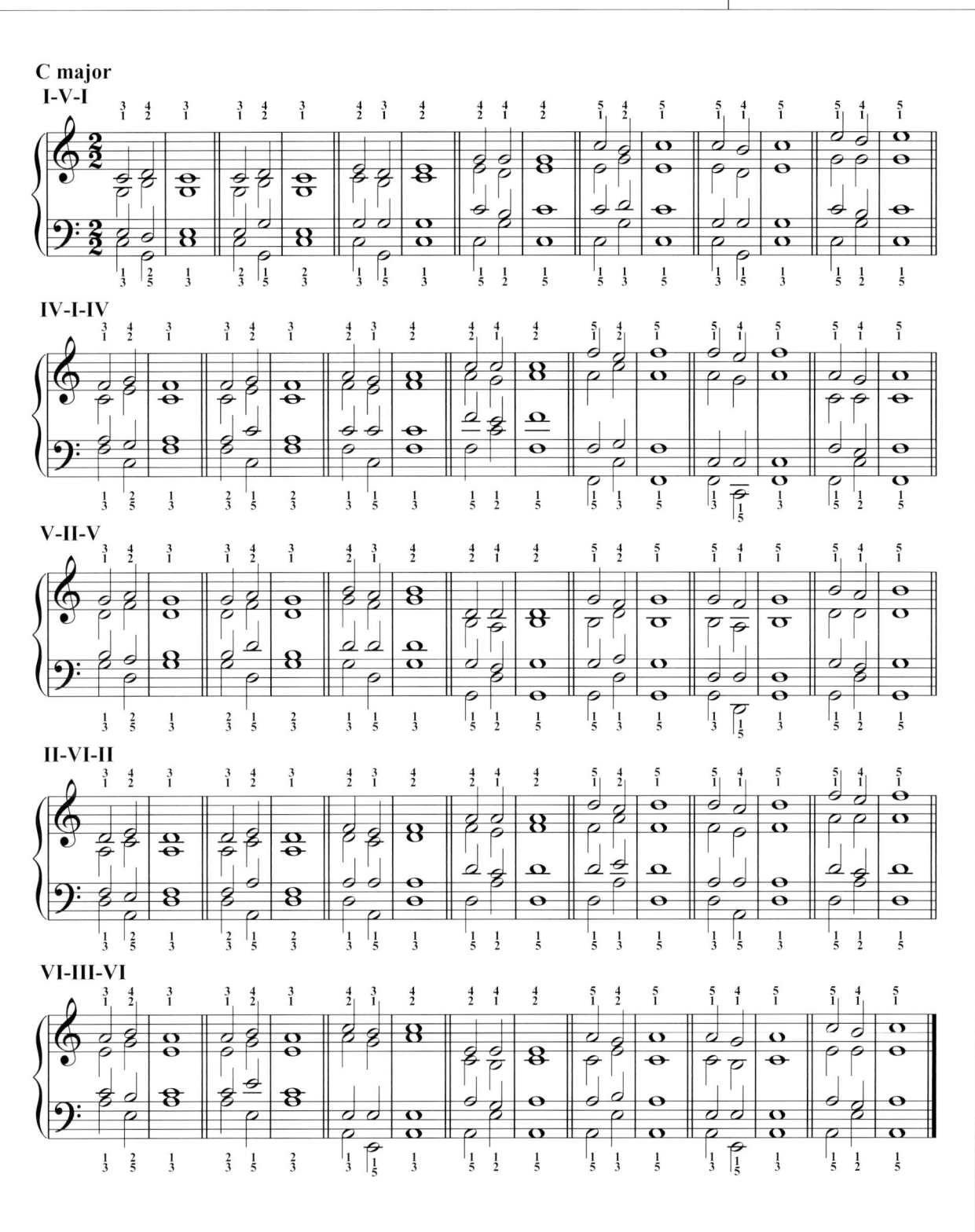

UNIT 4 SECTION 2

SECTION 2 | UNIT 4

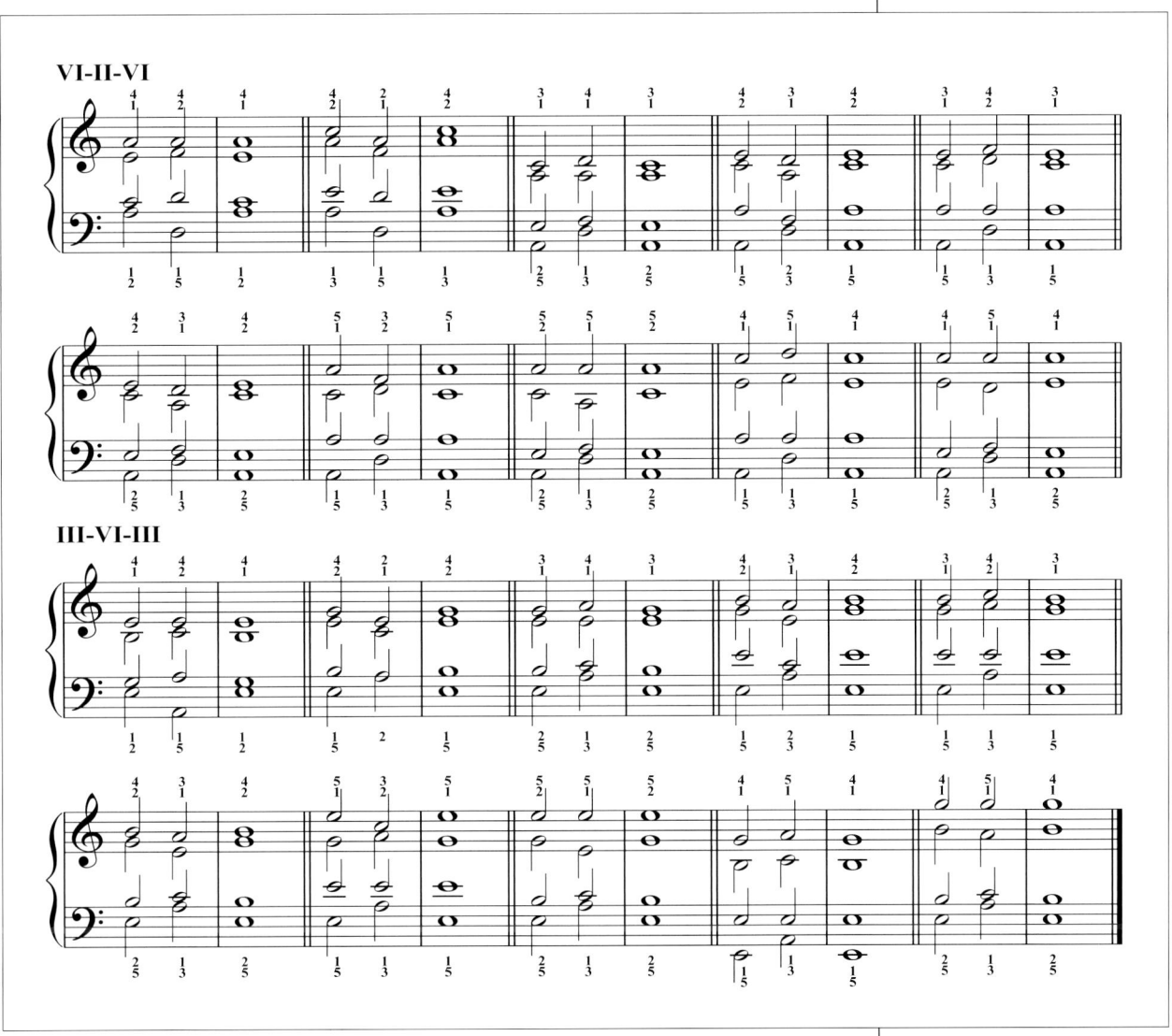

The examples on these two pages show how to move to a chord with a root a perfect fourth higher (or fifth lower), and back again.

UNIT 4 SECTION 2

Here are examples of connections to a chord with a root a third lower (or sixth higher) and back again:

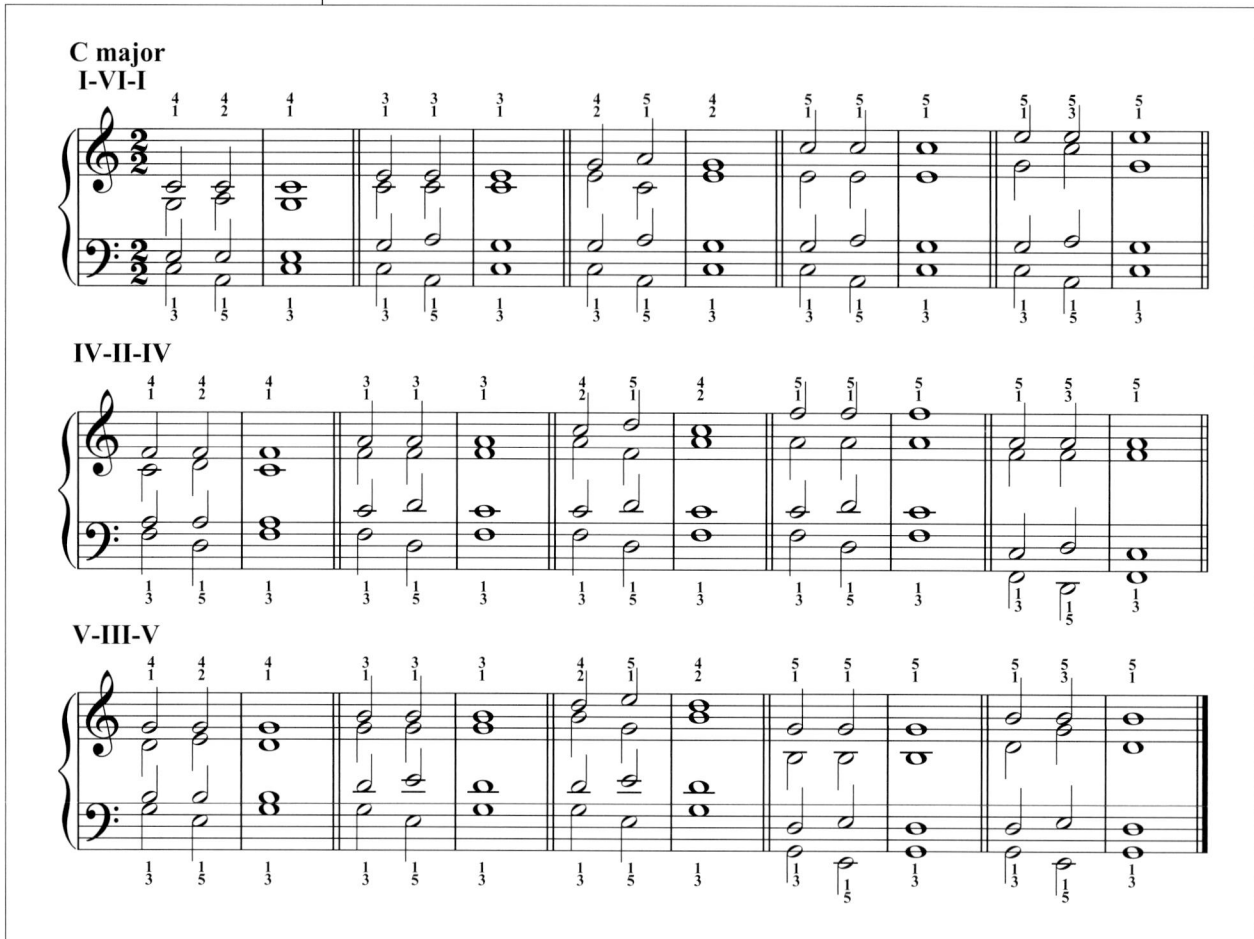

Finally, the examples opposite show connections from a chord to another chord whose root is a second higher, and back again.

You'll find that playing connections this way makes you more aware of the inner parts. That's especially good if you want a more classical and refined feel. In that case it's worth knowing about a voice-leading rule for moving from V to I, which is one of the most important chord progressions of all: the seventh of the scale should resolve up by step to the keynote. (However, there are also quite a few cases where that doesn't happen: instead, it moves back down to the fifth of the scale. This is because there's another rule that says that we can make an exception to this if the top part is moving down by step to the keynote. In the next section we'll see that this is an important feature of certain progressions.)

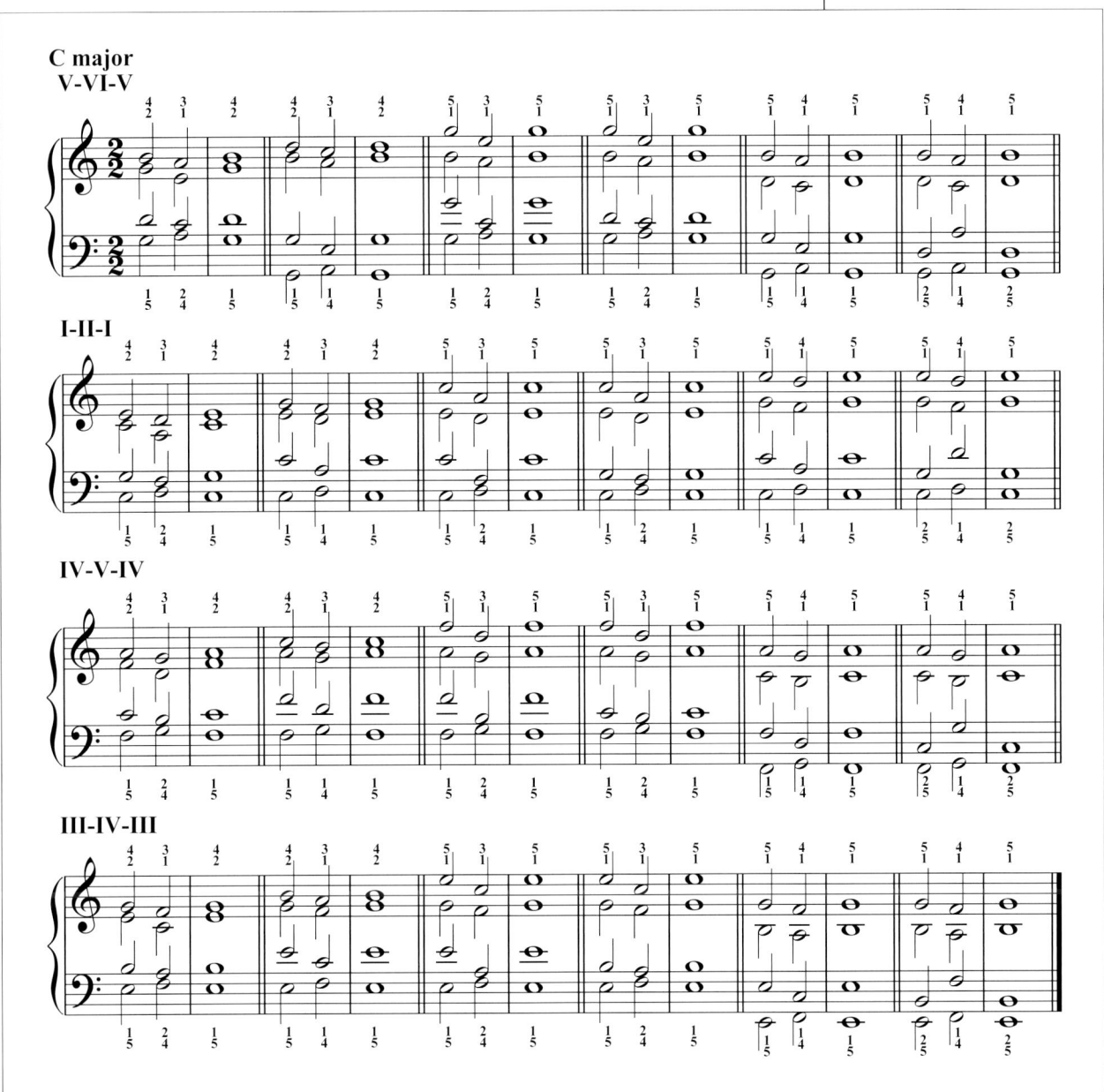

UNIT 4 | SECTION 2

b) Connections with first-inversion chords

Connections involving first-inversion chords tend to be easier to manage from the point of view of voice-leading. The simplest move is to go from root position to first inversion of the same chord, or the reverse of this. You can do this with any chord, but the example here just shows the different ways of doing this for a chord of C major (which is also chord I in the key of C major.) First it shows examples with one note in the left and three in the right, and then examples with two notes in the left and two in the right.

Another common move involving root-position and first-inversion chords involves connecting a root-position chord to the first-inversion chord whose root is a fourth lower. This means that the bassline actually only moves one scale-step. If this is just a semitone it's especially effective: we hear the third of the first-inversion in the bassline as a kind of leading-note relative to the root of the other chord (opposite page).

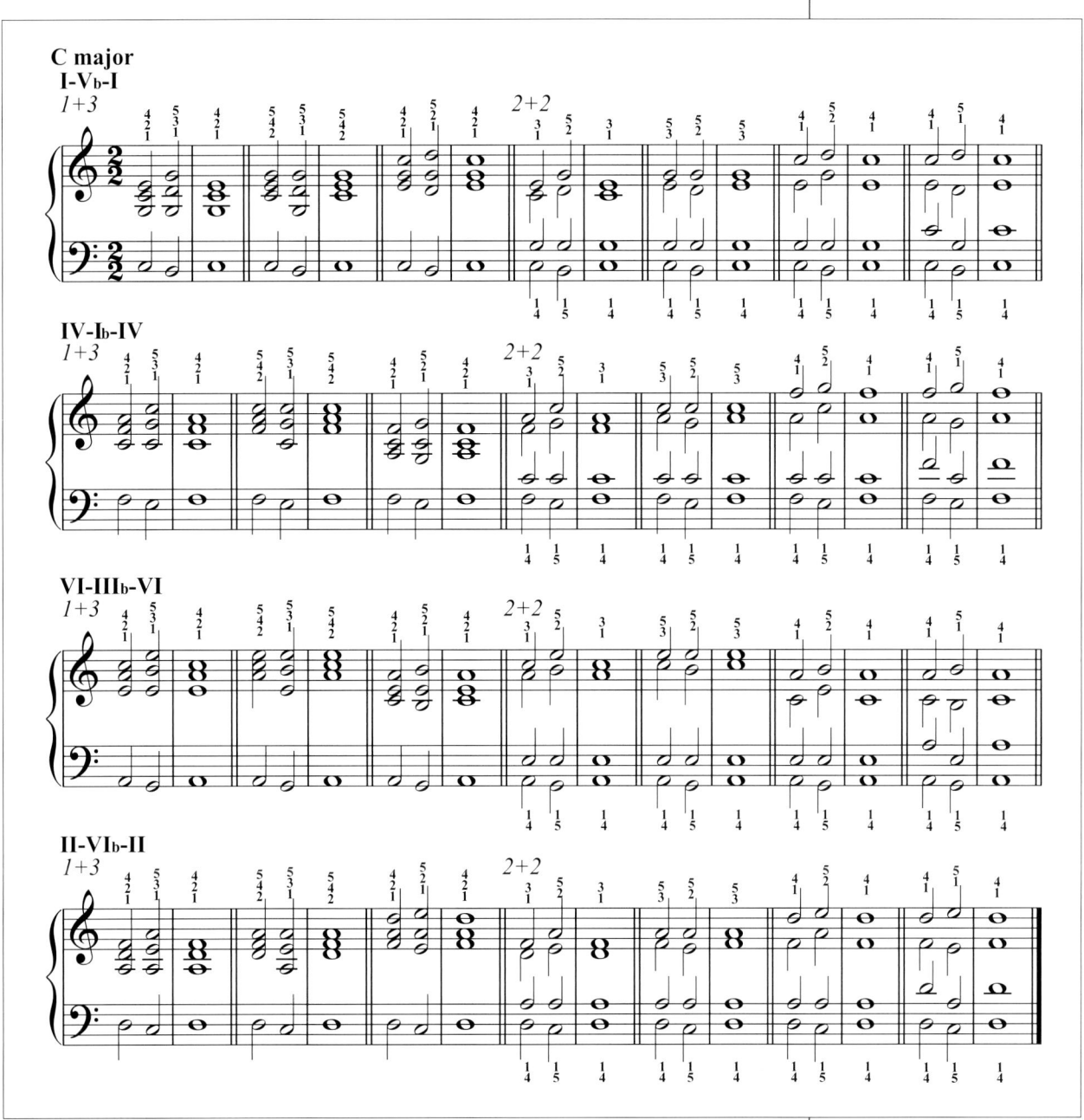

We can also join first-inversion chords to one another. In strict classical voice-leading you must then focus on the upper parts themselves, to make sure parallel fifths and octaves are avoided, rather than on the relationship between these parts and the bass. However, in more relaxed approaches (eg, later classical music and non-classical music) these tend to be tolerated, as the prominence of the third in the bass in first-inversion chords helps to counterbalance this effect.

Here are just some of the possibilities, with one note in the left and three in the right, then the same with two in the left and two in the right (opposite page). The brackets show which notes should be omitted for stricter classical voice-leading. In contrast to chords in first inversion, second-inversion chords are only used in certain special kinds of harmonic progression, which function as standard formulas that every improviser must learn, so it's best to just learn the voice-leading patterns and fingering for these as they relate to those formulas. We'll do that in the next section.

Progressions

Any series or sequence of chords played one after another forms a harmonic progression, but of course not all progressions sound equally good. In fact, aside from very simple ones that involve just a couple of chords, it's quite hard to create progressions that work. That's why this is an area where formulas play an essential role – at least for most improvisers. Even those who do create new progressions from scratch tend to do so in advance of an actual improvised performance, so they can explore alternative possibilities and see what works and what doesn't in a way that just isn't possible 'on the fly'.

In this section we'll start with some general advice about different kinds of progression at the simplest level – two-chord progressions. Then we'll look at formulas. Finally we'll consider some of the factors involved when creating new progressions from scratch.

a) Two-chord progressions

Just like voice-leading and fingering patterns for connections between chords, the progressions themselves are best understood in terms of the relationship between the roots of the chords involved. In other words, for most purposes we think of them as different sorts of **root progression**. For a particular two-chord root progression to work in itself, it must be strong enough to displace the first chord with the second, but not so strong as to also destroy any underlying sense of harmonic continuity between the two chords. Let's summarise the key points that you need to remember about these:

■ The best root-progressions are between chords with roots a perfect fifth or fourth apart.

■ Root-progressions to chords with the root two scale-steps (ie, a third) lower are good.

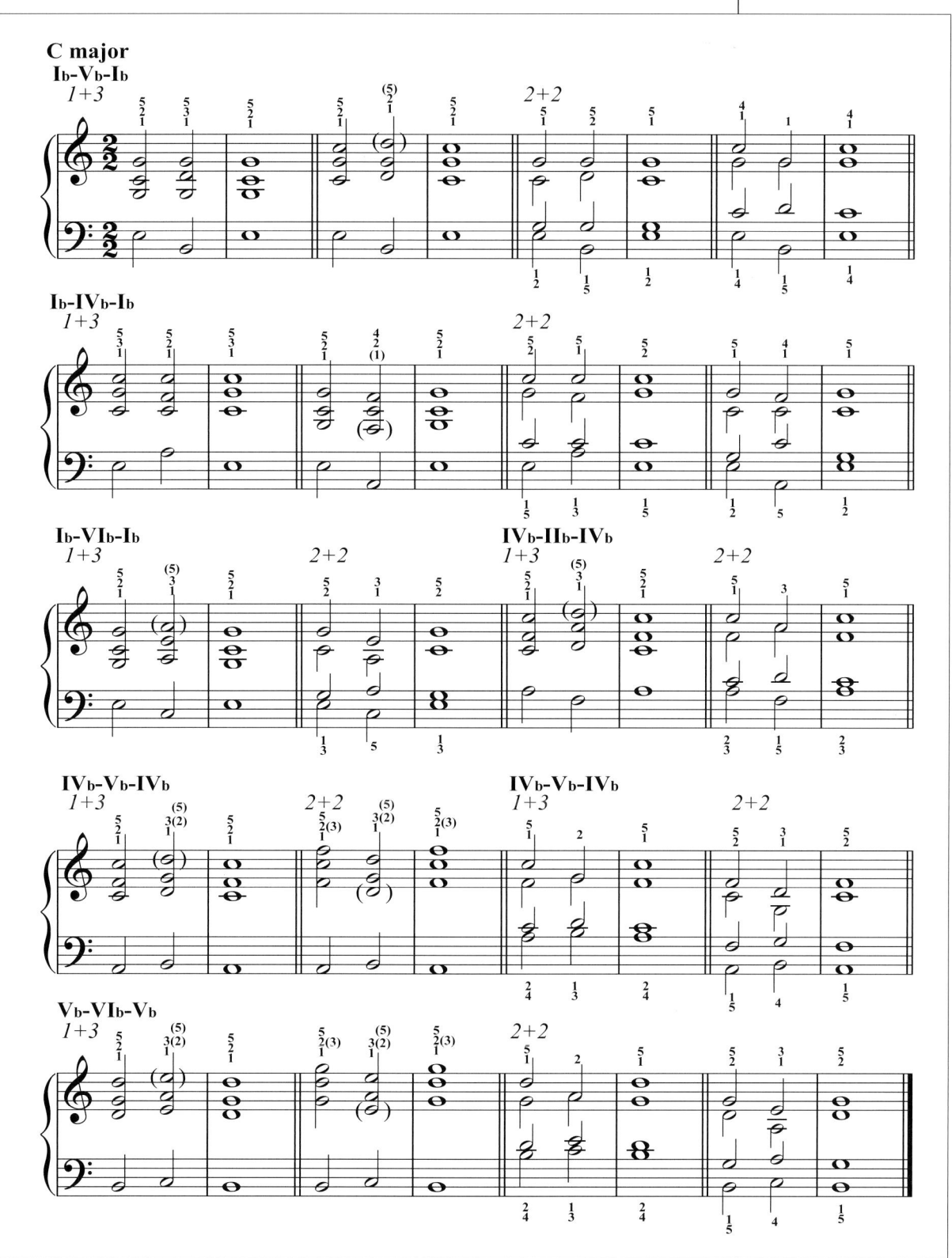

- Root-progressions to chords one scale-step (ie, a second) higher or lower can sound nice, but the displacement of the first chord by the second in such cases is more powerful, so this will depend on the context and the particular chords used:

- In classical music IV-V works well, but V-IV is usually avoided;

- V-IV is used a lot in blues-based music, including jazz and rock; that's because blues emphasises the subdominant region of tonal harmony, whereas classical music typically emphasises the dominant.

- V-VI corresponds to a certain formula, but it's one whose normal function is as a surprise resolution (see the next section).

- Moving between secondary triads (like II and III in a major key) can also work, but needs to be handled with care: the displacement is so strong that the connection to the underling structure of the major scale is weakened and a rather static effect results – but this can be useful for creating **modal harmony**.

b) Cadences & formulas

When it comes to chord progressions the most important formulas are definitely **cadences** (or 'cadential progressions'). These generally mark the end of a phrase or section, and create varying degrees of harmonic closure – rather like punctuation marks (ie, commas, semicolons, and full stops) in written texts. They offer an improviser useful landmarks to aim for, as they and the chords that immediately precede them tend to follow familiar patterns, even when these are varied. Because of this, they also offer the best starting point for learning to improvise extended chord sequences at the keyboard.

There are four basic kinds of cadence, with varying degrees of finality:

- PERFECT: this is the most common cadence, and generates a strong sense of finality in both a major or minor key. It always consists of a V-I progression.

- IMPERFECT: this is also a commonly used cadence, but the sense of closure incomplete. It always ends on V, which is usually preceded by I.

- PLAGAL: this is a slightly less common cadence, which nevertheless generates a strong sense of finality. This is especially effective in a major key, where it has the familiar 'Amen' flavour encountered in many hymns. It always consists of a IV-I progression.

- INTERRUPTED: this is slightly less common, and the expected sense of closure is replaced by a surprise resolution whose purpose is to withhold any sense of finality. This is achieved through substituting chord VI for chord I, in what would otherwise be a perfect cadence. In a major key this means arriving unexpectedly on a minor chord, while in the minor it means arriving unexpectedly on a major chord. This is also an example of **chord substitution** – a more general phenomenon that is especially important in jazz (see Unit Eight).

Let's take each of these in turn and explore the most typical examples of how they work. It's important to realise from the start that while the chords involved in the cadence itself tend to be mostly fixed, the voice-leading can still be varied. On the other hand, the chords just before the cadence, known as the 'preparation', are more open-ended, and can themselves be varied too, even though they tend to follow certain standard sequences. This means that when improvising it's generally best to operate according to the following sequence:

1 First decide what cadence you are aiming for.
2 Then decide what voice-leading you want for that cadence.
3 Then decide what preparatory sequence you want.
4 Then decide the voice-leading for the preparatory sequence.

In other words, in aiming to arrive at a cadence we start with the cadence and think backwards to the preparation – the reverse of the order in which we play the resulting material. This is an essential skill, one that every improviser must master, so it's best to tackle it right at the beginning, when you first try putting chords together to make progressions or longer sequences.

The following examples are all given with suggested fingerings as an aid to practice. For the purposes of improvisation one of the major tasks at this stage is to get so familiar with these formulaic progressions that your hands simply find the right notes automatically (ie, without strain or hesitation). The best way of doing this is to memorise a fixed fingering for each sequence. The resulting associations between fingering patterns and chord structures will be the foundation for many of the subsequent skills you'll want to work on – in particular the ability to move across different keys or between major and minor keys (see the next unit). Hence you should aim to practise all the examples here systematically – until you can execute them fluently from memory.

A perfect cadence involves V-I, so it can use any of the connections for root progressions to a chord with a root a perfect fifth lower (or perfect fourth higher) given earlier in this unit. The standard preparation for this is to precede it with IV, or with similar progressions involving roots descending in fifths. Adding one such progression gives us the sequence II-V-I, which is also used widely in jazz, and takes on a special function there (see Unit Eight). Adding one more gives us the commonly occurring sequence VI-II-V-I. Because II is actually just a substitution for IV here, we can also use the progression VI-IV-V-I. Using IV creates a very emphatic cadence, as it acts as a foil for V. (That's because these two chords correspond to competing counter-poles within the

UNIT 4 | SECTION 2

key.) Using II brings in a secondary triad that makes for a less emphatic effect. (NB: for reasons of space all subsequent examples in this unit feature just the most straightforward and commonly used division between the hands: ie, one note in the left and three in the right.)

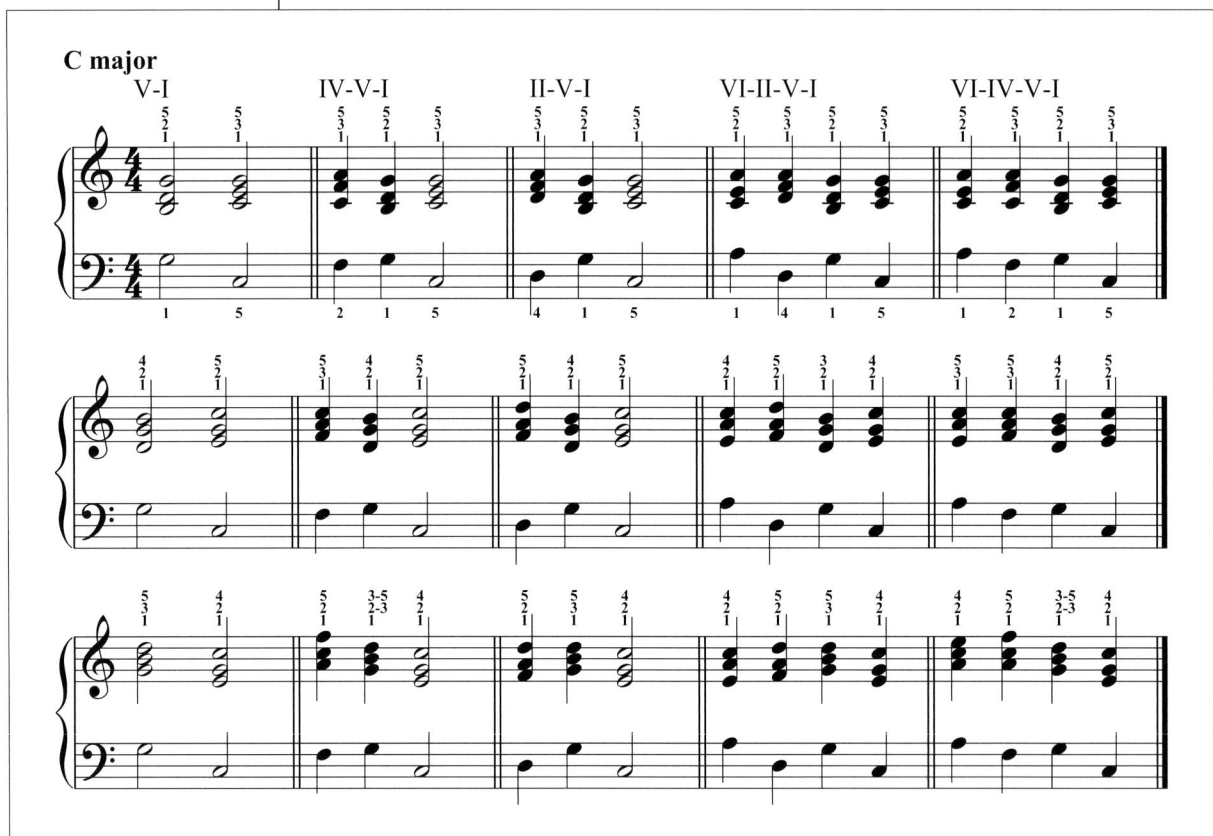

There are two additional variations here – both of them standard in classical music but not in jazz. This difference reflects a basic contrast we'll be exploring later (see Unit Seven and Unit Eight), but which you should start to be aware of now:

- Classical music tends to use chords that are simpler in themselves, but makes more use of first (and second) inversions, both to vary the level of tension in the harmonic texture and to achieve melodic continuity in the bassline.

- Jazz tends to use chords that are internally more complex, but mainly thinks of these just as root position chords (regardless of the actual melodic movement occurring in the bass).

The first variation is to precede V with I in second inversion (I^c). This creates a kind of harmonic decoration, in which upper voices descend by step over the bass note, which is the same for both I^c and V. This effect is the first of the two standard formulas in which second inversion chords can be used, and is know as a **cadential six-four**. (Note that the cadential six-four requires I^c to come on a stronger beat and V on a weaker beat.)

The second variation is to use II in first inversion (II^b), creating a stepwise movement in the bass as it moves from the third of this chord to the root of V.

As the examples below show, these two options can be used separately or together:

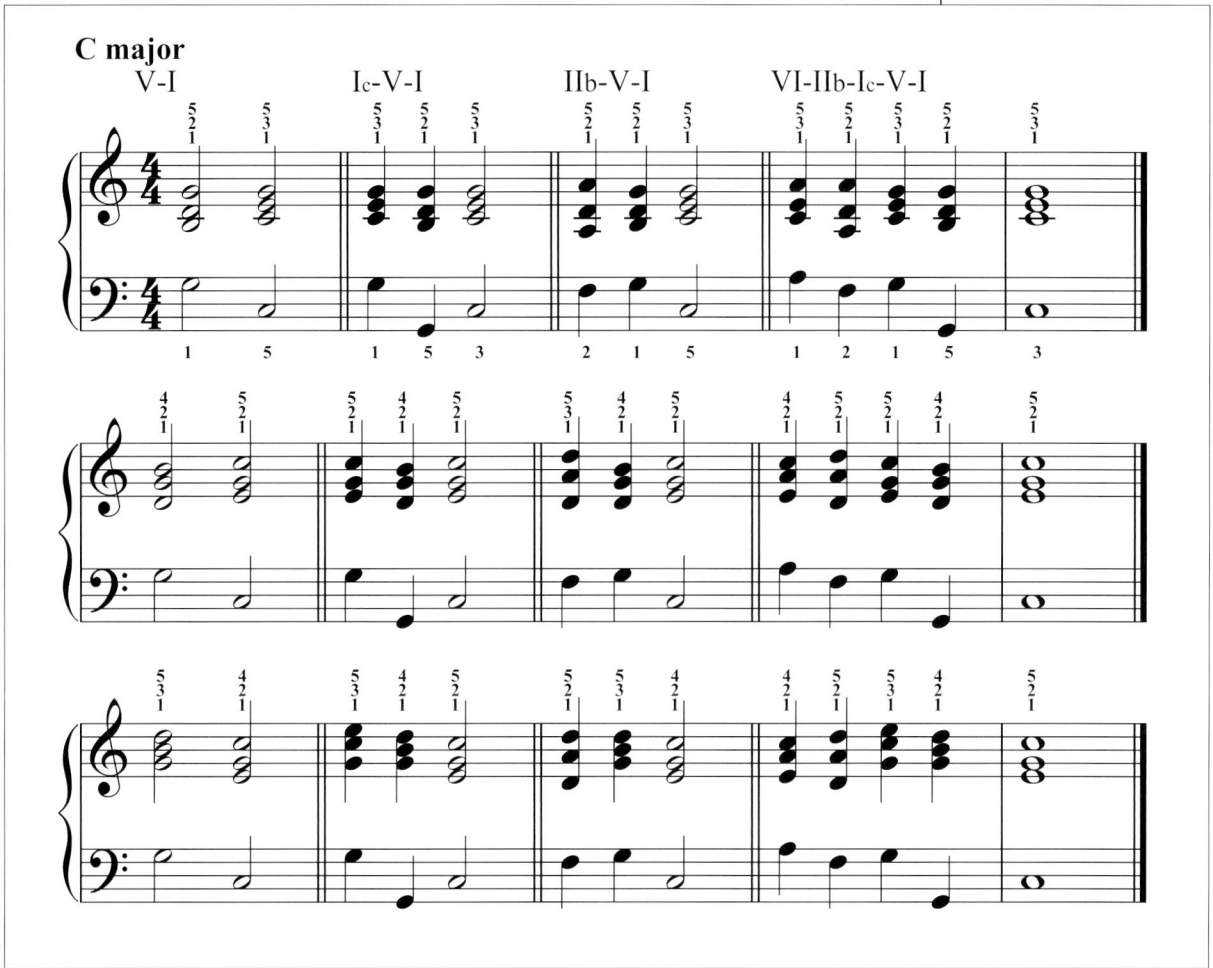

With the exception of the cadential six-four, it's best to steer clear of chord I in the preparatory sequence leading up to a perfect cadence, as otherwise the effect of the resolution onto I in the cadence itself is weakened.

An imperfect cadence must end on V. In principle any progression ending this way that delivers an inconclusive resolution is okay. In practice, the most common chord to precede V is I. However, II or II^b are also possible, and arriving from IV or VI can also be effective.

These in turn are best preceded by progressions whose roots move by intervals of a fifth or a third (or their inversions). I-V is best preceded by IV, as this throws the presence of V in the perfect cadence into relief, due to the fact that, as we've already noted, V and IV compete as counter-poles within the key. Then IV can in turn be followed

by II, the secondary triad that is its standard substitute:

Meanwhile II-V or II^b-V can be preceded by VI, as when preparing a perfect cadence, and either IV-V or VI-V can be preceded by I. These can in turn be preceded by chords with roots a fifth or a third higher (opposite page).

SECTION 2 UNIT 4

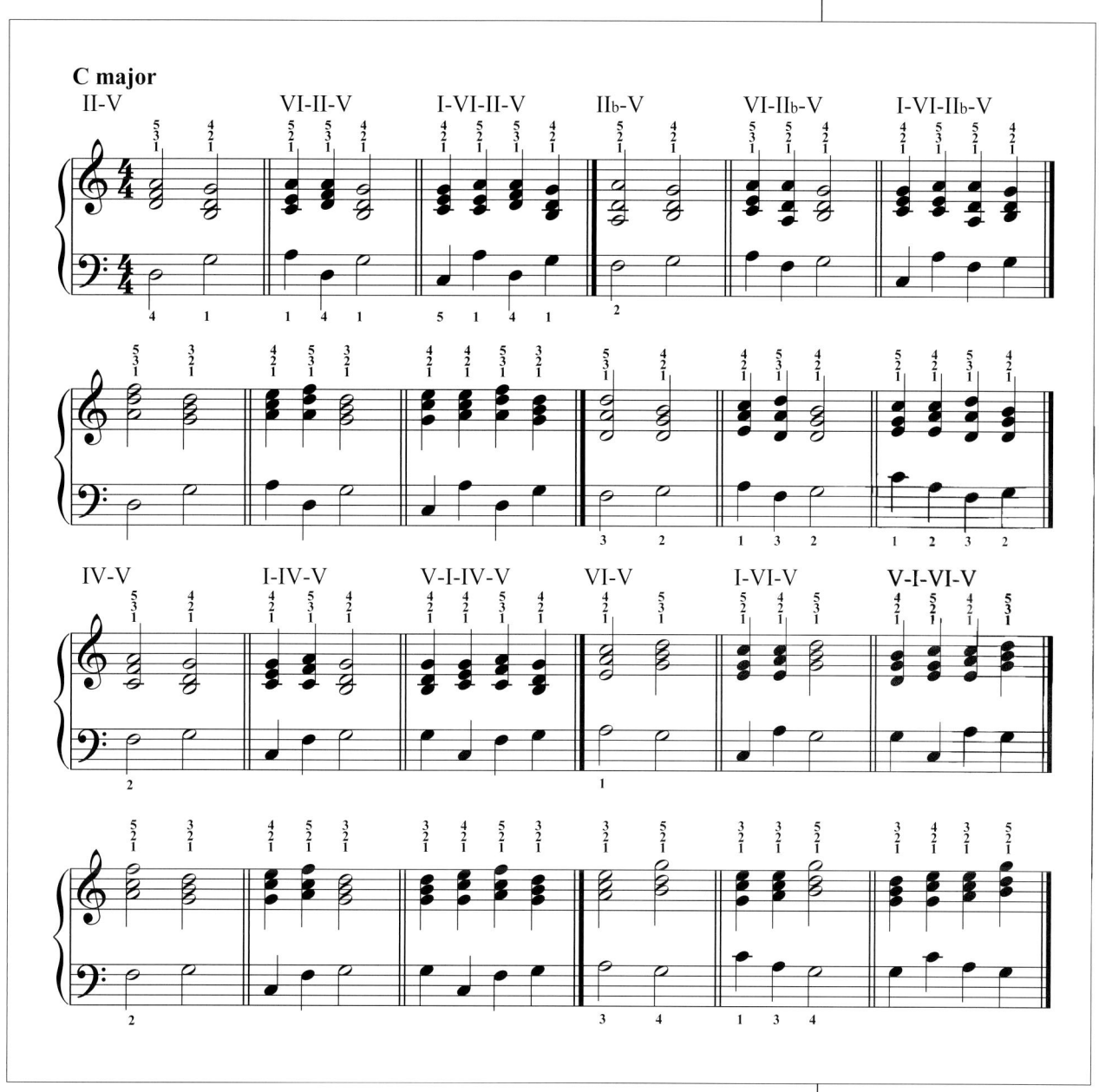

Again the cadence can be decorated by introducing I^c in place of V (on the strong beat where the latter was expected), and only then moving to V (on a weaker beat). (However, this is less effective when preceded by I, as we lose the change of root as the progression moves into the cadence.)

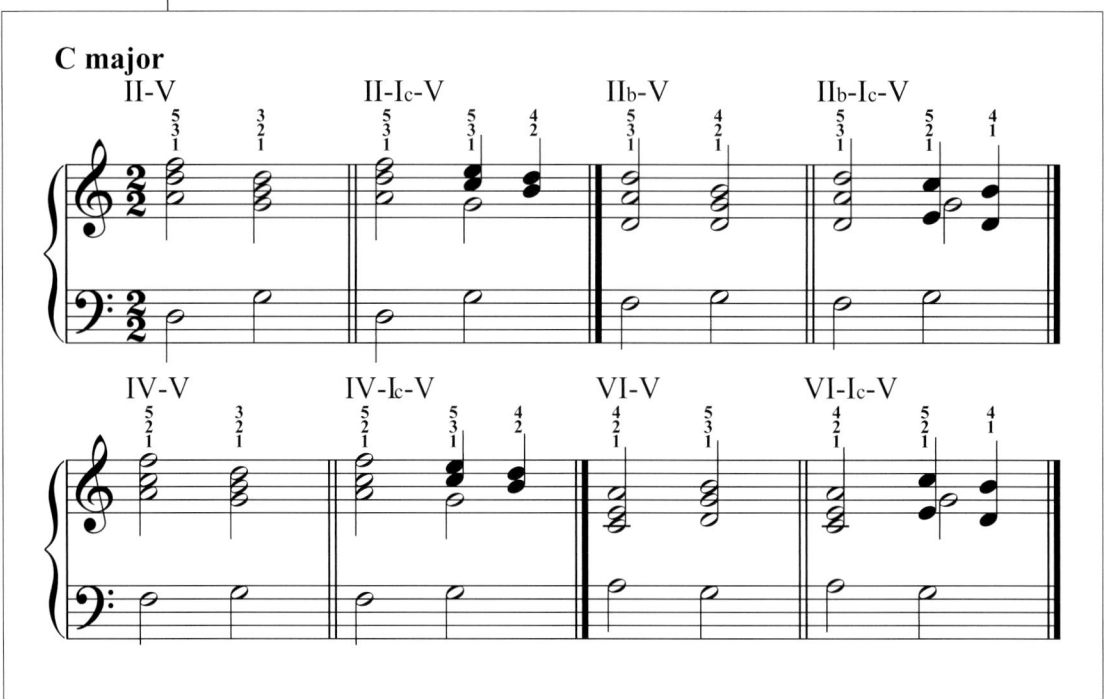

A plagal cadence involves IV-I, so it can use any of the connections to a chord with a root a perfect fourth lower (or perfect fifth higher) given earlier in this unit. The strongest progressions for approaching the cadence will once again be those that involve a movement to a chord whose root is a fifth or a third lower, which means approaching IV from I or VI.

However, as with the perfect cadence, using I in the preparatory phase weakens the effect of the ensuing resolution onto I in the cadence itself, so the way to avoid this is to use I^c. Here we must use the other standard formulas in which second inversion chords can be used, known as the **passing six-four**. This formula requires the bass note of the second inversion chord to be approached and left by step, which usually means placing the root position and first inversion of a chord whose root is a fifth lower on either side of this. Here are some typical examples. Note that we can move the formula around to produce a variety of progressions while retaining the same underlying connections and fingering (opposite page).

In the case of the plagal cadence, the passing six-four will be IV^b-I^c-IV, with the final IV also counting as the first chord of the cadence. On the other hand, if IV is preceded by VI, then the most effective preparation is for this in turn to be preceded by V. (Having V in the preparation throws IV into relief in the plagal cadence itself, as these represent competing counter-poles within the key.) A more direct movement from V to IV is also possible, but as we've already seen this is more likely to be encountered in blues-influenced styles such as jazz and rock than in classical harmony. When moving directly

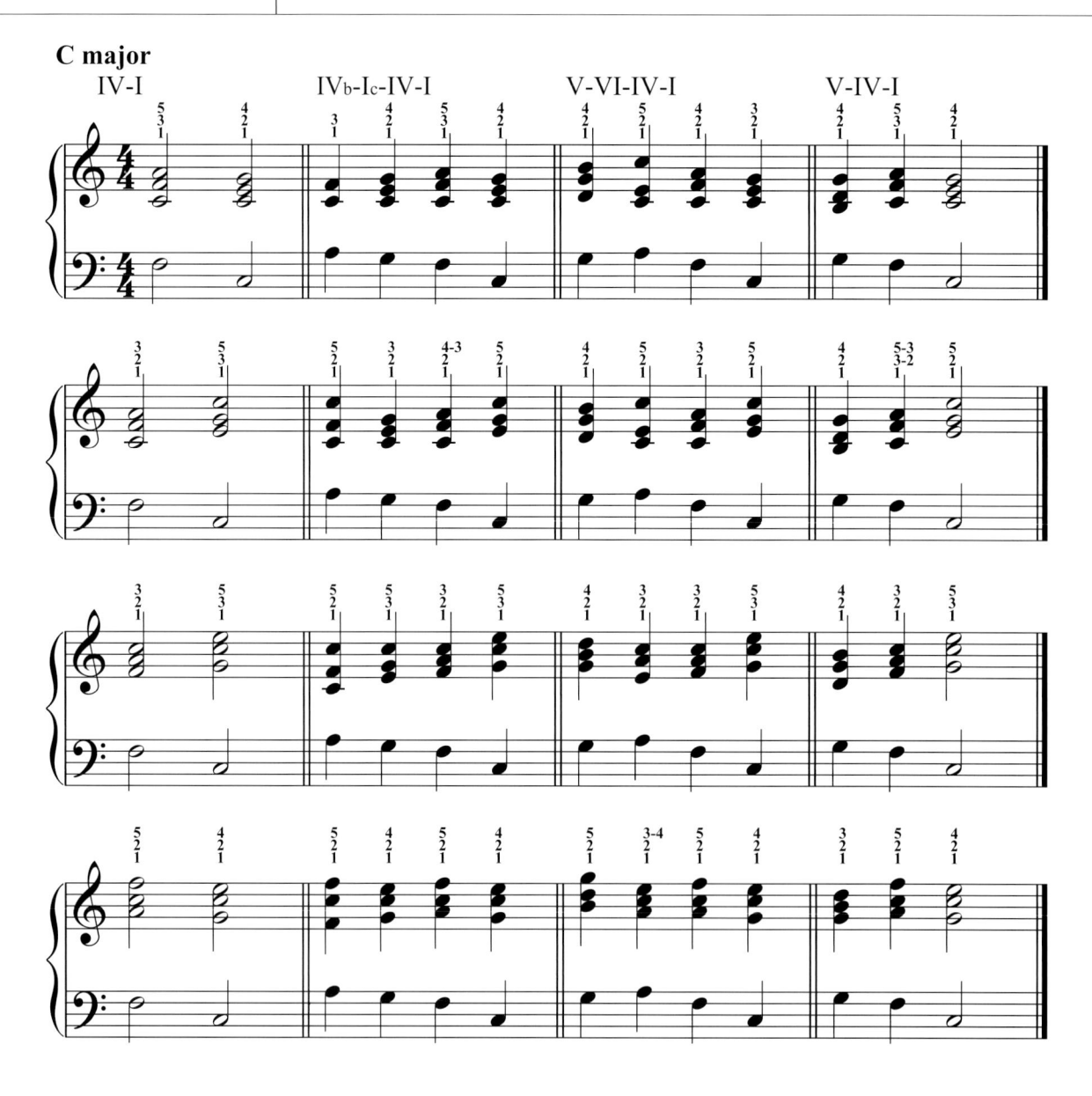

between chords with roots one step apart, as with V-IV or V-IV, take particular care to ensure the hands move in contrary motion: that way you can be sure none of the upper parts will form parallel fifths or octaves with the bass (opposite page).

An interrupted cadence involves V-VI. Normally this might be considered a rather weak progression, but it's effective here because VI functions as a surprise substitute for I, in what would otherwise be a powerful V-I perfect cadence. The possible preparations will be the same as for the latter, except that it is now VI that we seek to avoid in the preparation, in order not to anticipate and weaken the surprise effect of the cadence itself (above).

Once again we can vary these by decorating the dominant chord with a cadential six-four formula or by replacing IV or II with II♭ (which in both cases is better preceded by I than IV or VI). We can also use both of these techniques at once:

c) Opening chord sequences

Now we're ready to look at the aspect of improvising chord sequences that is complementary to that involved in cadences. Whereas cadences call for us to plan backwards from a point of arrival to the chords that precede them, the progressions that we use to open a phrase or section require us to plan forwards from a point of departure to whatever comes next. Organising chords into longer sequences requires us to think about the relationship between harmony on the one hand, and metre and rhythm on the other – something we'll only be ready to explore properly in Unit Six. However, there are some basic points relating to how such progressions unfold that we can consider right away.

> You might think it's weird that we looked first at how to use chord progressions to end phrases or sections, and only afterwards considered how they can be used to start them. Actually there's a good reason for that. It's because the greatest challenges for improvising always come after you've started a new passage – what's difficult is almost always continuing or completing what you've started. So the progressions that can take you through to the end of a phrase or section are the real lifesavers – the ones you need to know best.

Any good chord sequence has to generate a sense of forward unfolding (hence the term 'pro-gression'). The standard way is to follow a harmonic trajectory that takes us from I to one or other of the two remaining primary triads, V or IV. Conversely, if it happens to begin with one of the latter, it normally traces a route back to I. This gives four options in all:

1 From I to V
2 From I to IV
3 From V to I
4 From IV to I

In the majority of cases your opening chord progression will start with I, so the forward unfolding will consist of a movement that ends with V or IV. This allows us to focus on the first two options – at least for the present. As far as these are concerned, it's best to begin by focusing on what's possible using just primary triads (I, IV, and V), as these offer the clearest guide to harmonic structure in simple progressions. Secondary triads (II, III, and VI) should then be introduced just as alternatives for these, through what we've already learned to refer to as chord substitution. (Remember, each primary triad can be substituted for by the secondary triad whose root is a third lower.)

As with cadences, we tend to avoid anticipating the chord that's the ultimate goal of the progression. At the same time, because IV and V correspond to competing counter-

UNIT 4 | SECTION 2

poles to the tonic within the key, passing through one of these to the other (ie, I-IV-V or I-V-IV V) creates a stronger sense of progression, while passing directly from I (or its substitute) to IV or V gives a milder effect.

If the goal is V, progressions such as those below, which can also be thought of as involving imperfect cadences, will make musical sense. (Don't pay too much attention to rhythm here. We'll be exploring the rhythmic aspect of chord sequences separately in Unit Six.)

A similar logic means that if the goal is IV, passing through V (or its substitute, III) will also make for strong progressions (opposite, top).

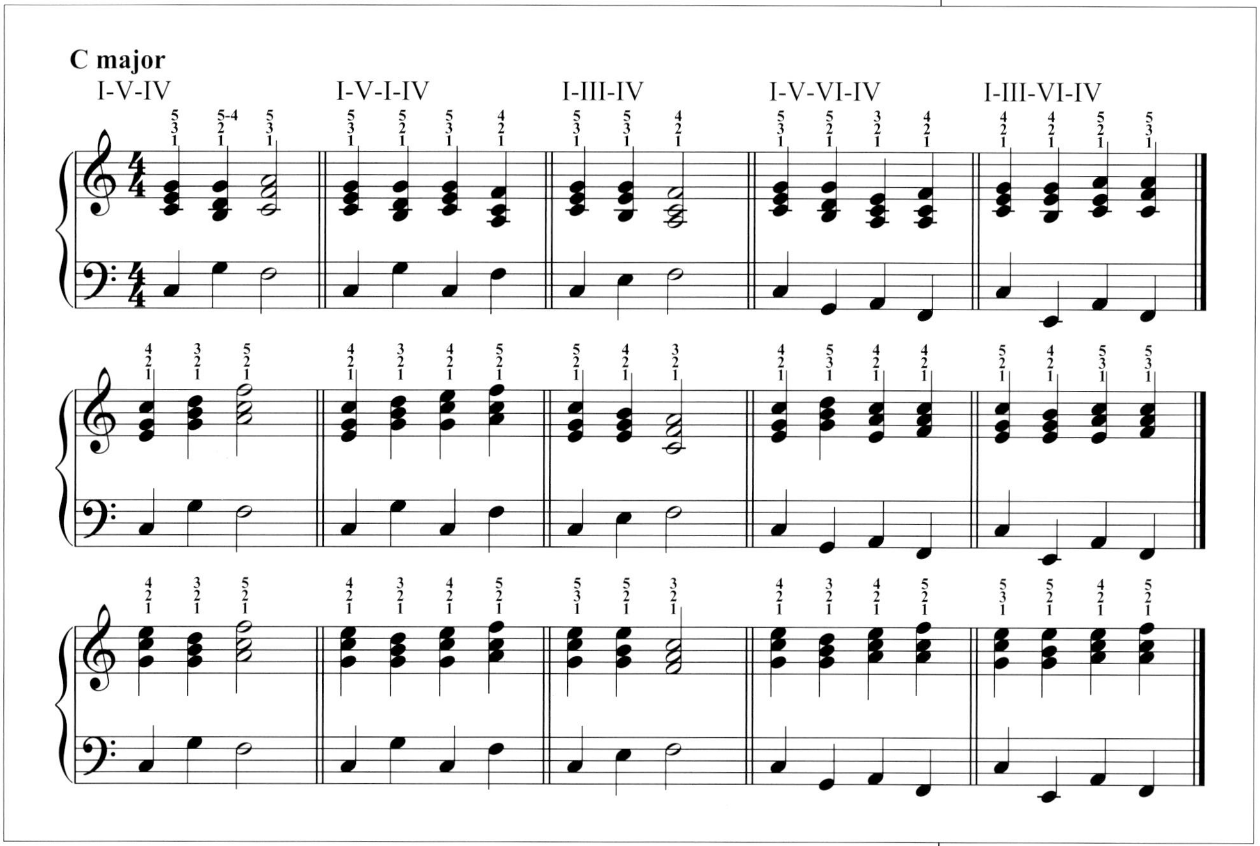

However, while this second group are fine for blues-influenced styles like rock and jazz, they're problematic for classical harmony. Whereas blues treats the subdominant as the chief counter-pole to the tonic, classical harmony treats it as less important than the dominant – something which conflicts with the idea that V could function as just a transition stage on the way to IV. Because of this, classical progressions tend to stick to the milder kinds of progression that go from I to IV without passing through V. In that case any chords between I and IV are most likely to be either an inversion of or substitute for I itself:

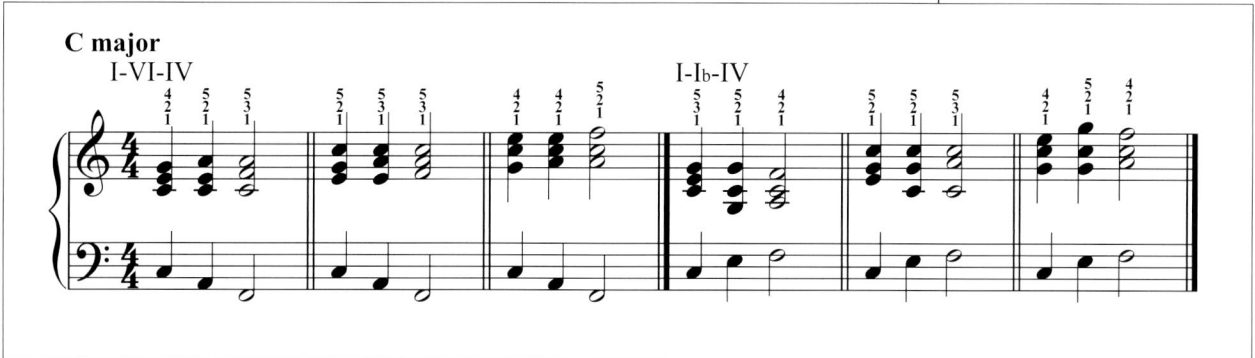

UNIT 4 | SECTION 2

Now for the remaining two possibilities. When we find ourselves moving from IV or V to I the options are fairly straightforward. Since the arrival at I will most probably involve either a perfect or plagal cadence, we can see straight away that the strongest effects will be achieved when the cadence does not repeat the chord which is the point of departure for the sequence. Hence a move from V to I is strongest when it passes through IV by closing with a plagal cadence, while a move from IV to I can effectively pass through V by closing with a perfect cadence. In each case chord substitutes can also be used:

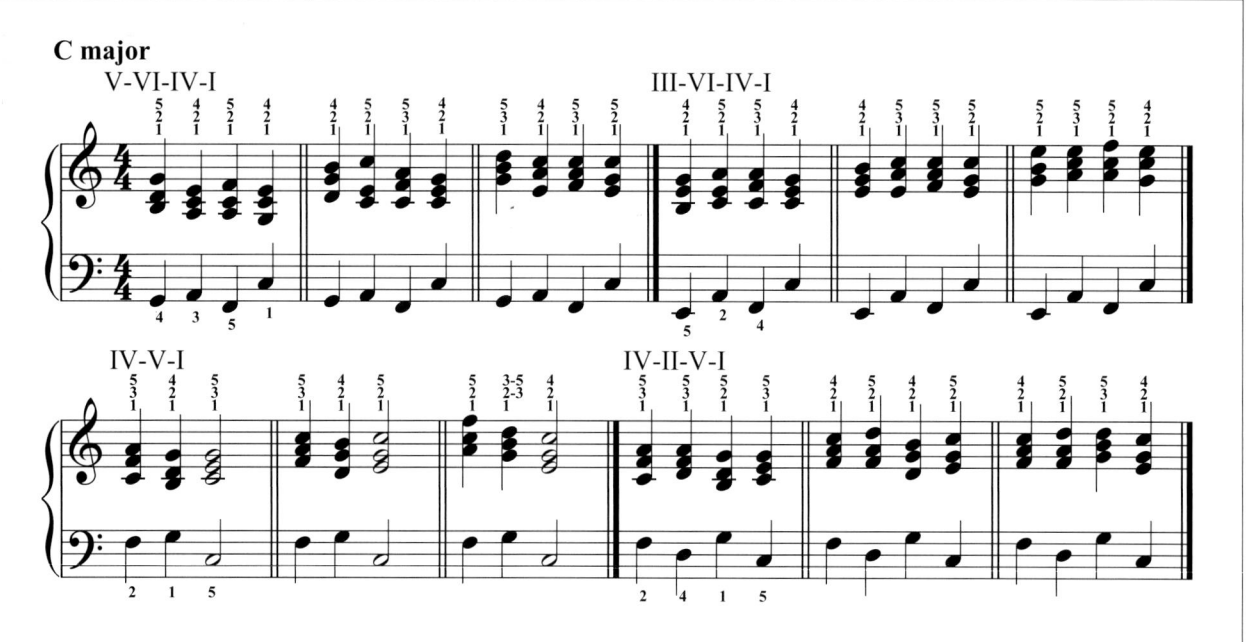

What follows after any of these progressions is another matter, as it will depend on the larger structure you're aiming to create as you improvise.

> **From major to minor.** All of the examples in this unit use harmony in a major key. But what about minor-key harmony? We could just present all of the structures and connections shown in this chapter once again, this time in a minor key. However, experience shows this isn't the best way to approach minor-key harmony when learning improvisation. It's more useful to understand how each particular structure can be realised in a major or a minor key, and the best way to do this is for you to learn for yourself how to transfer each structure from a major-key into the equivalent minor key. Since this is closely related to what you do when transferring a structure from one key to a different key, we'll explore these two important issues together (in the next unit).

UNIT 5
EXPLORING KEYS

Key relations

Major and minor

Transposition

Modulation

SECTION 2

UNIT 5 SECTION 2

Key relations

So far all the melodic movements and chord progressions we've explored have been in C major. But there are twelve different major keys and twelve different minor keys – one of each for every note of the chromatic scale. So we've still got some work to do to get familiar with how melody and harmony work in some or all of these other keys.

The logical way to approach this is to practise reproducing the harmonic structures we've looked at in the previous unit in as many of these other keys as possible. However, from the point of view of the particular skills an improviser needs, taking one key after another and trying to recreate what we've learned in C major isn't so fruitful.

It's better to concentrate on what happens when we move material from a given key to another one that's in a particularly close relation to the first key. If we follow this approach systematically, we can still eventually explore all the keys. At the same time, though, we'll be learning something else that's also crucial for improvising, which is how a particular relationship between keys determines what changes we have to make when we switch material between them.

In Unit One we learned about how keys are related in terms of the Circle of Fifths, and how each major key is also closely related to a minor key with which it shares most of its notes and, importantly, the same key signature. These, you'll remember, are known as each other's relative major and minor, and the latter always corresponds to a keynote two scale-steps (ie, three half-steps/semitones or a minor third) below that of the former. However, a major key is also related to the minor key on the same keynote, even though this has a different key signature. So C major, for example, can be understood as directly related to two different minor keys at the same time: A minor (the relative minor), and C minor (the minor key on the same keynote, known as the **tonic minor**).

In effect, then, a major key stands in an immediate relationship to two minor keys and two major keys – the latter being the two major keys adjacent to it on the Circle of Fifths. A good way to visualise this is to think of the keys as located in a kind of two-dimensional 'tonal space', with major-minor relations laid out along the horizontal axis, and relations corresponding to the Circle of Fifths positioned on the vertical axis.

Diagram 5.1 shows how this works for just the keys most immediately related to C major. (In key-diagrams such as this we'll follow a standard convention, indicating major keys with capital letters, minor keys with small letters.)

For the sake of comparison, Diagram 5.2 shows how a similar set of relationships looks when another key is chosen as the starting point – in this case the key one step higher on the Circle of Fifths, G major:

And Diagram 5.3 shows the relationships for the key a step lower on the Circle of Fifths – F major.

Now let's come back to C major again, and look at how other keys relate to it. The next diagram, Diagram 5.4, shows what happens if we extend our initial network of relations to include keys two steps removed from C major, both on the Circle of Fifths and on the major-minor axis. In the former case this introduces the keys of B-flat and D major, whose keynotes are just one scale-step higher or lower than that of C major itself.

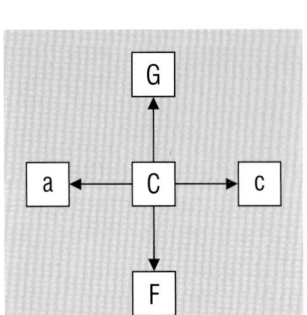

Diagram 5.1

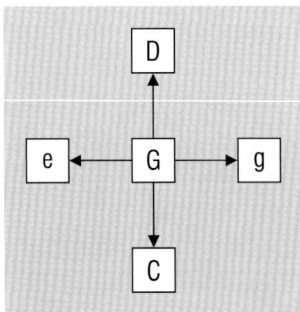

Diagram 5.2

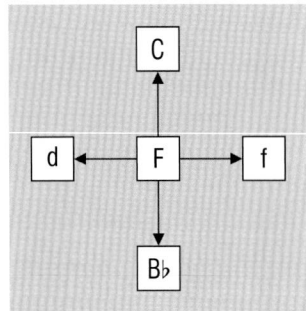

Diagram 5.3

In the latter case we can extend the axis of major-minor relations by realising that A minor, as well as being the relative minor of C major, is the tonic minor of A major, while C minor, in addition to being the tonic minor of C major, is the relative minor of E flat major. This brings in another couple of new major keys, whose keynotes are, respectively, a minor third lower and higher than that of C major.

In addition to these relations, there are two other sets that are important. The first involves keys whose keynotes are a major third lower or higher than C: these are E major and A flat major. (In each case one of the keys in the relation will have a keynote corresponding to the third of the major triad built on the keynote of the other, and this represents another way in which keys can be directly related. Notice, though, that these keys can also be linked to C major via a combination of moves along the axis of major-minor relations and Circle-of-Fifths relations, or simply through a larger series of moves along the Circle of Fifths itself.)

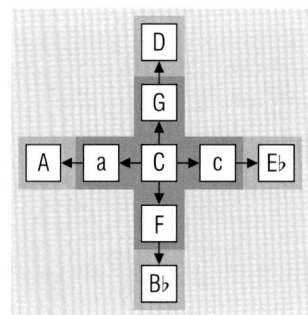

Diagram 5.4

The second involves pairs of keys whose keynotes are adjacent to one another in the chromatic scale. One of the distinctive features of jazz harmony is that it regards this as enough to mean they are immediately related. Classical music, by contrast, does not, so the relation is then seen as a more indirect one, corresponding to a series of moves involving both the major-minor axis and the Circle of Fifths (as shown in the diagram below) or a larger series of moves along just the Circle of Fifths. As Diagram 5.5 indicates, by this stage the whole procedure has given us a total of ten different major keys and two minor keys related to C major.

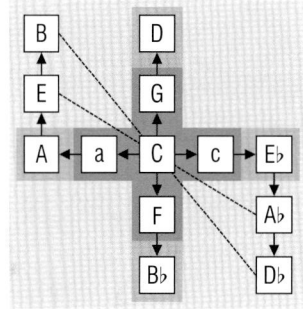

Diagram 5.5

In fact the only remaining major keys are those whose keynotes are a tritone (ie, an augmented fourth or diminished fifth) away from C: these are F-sharp major and its enharmonic equivalent, G-flat major. (Remember, enharmonic equivalence means these are just two different ways of referring to the same set of notes on the keyboard.) Although not shown in the above diagram, this relation is also worth exploring, due to its special role in jazz, so it will be the final relation in the sequence we've unfolded.

It's this sequence of key relations that will serve as our guide in the rest of this unit as we explore what's involved in playing the same harmonic material in a variety of keys.

First we'll focus on what happens when we transfer material from a major key into one or other of the closely related minor keys mentioned above. After this we'll explore what happens when we try to reproduce material in all the remaining major keys. Finally, we'll consider how to include other minor keys as well.

Major and minor

As we've just discovered, when taking material to and fro between major and minor keys there are two important relationships: between a major key and its relative minor, and between a major key and its tonic minor. At the same time, when dealing with minor keys there's an additional factor to consider, which is the different versions of the minor scale available, each one more or less associated with certain styles of music. However, for most purposes it's sufficient to keep in mind that while Classical music mainly uses the harmonic minor, rock and pop styles are more likely to use the rock minor (Aeolian). As

UNIT 5 | SECTION 2

we noted in Unit One, the minor scale plays a different role in jazz, whose harmonic structures are usually based on a major key, even when minor scales are used as a source for certain kinds of chord, or for improvising over these.

Let's take one of the most widely used progressions – a perfect cadence with a standard preparation – and see how it transfers into the minor from C major. First here it is in C major, followed by an equivalent series of chords in the relative minor (A minor), using the classical harmonic minor, then the rock minor:

Now here's the same progression in C major, this time followed by an equivalent series of chords in the tonic minor (C minor), also using both versions of the scale. Note how in this and other subsequent examples key signatures have been replaced by accidentals in order to show more clearly exactly which notes change between major and minor. (Remember: an accidental affects all subsequent instances of the note in front of which it is placed, up to the end of the measure in which it appears.)

Now let's analyse exactly what happens when we move material over to major or minor in the way demonstrated by these examples:

1 In all cases the fingering sequence remains unchanged.

2 Moving to the relative minor involves:
   - a shift of hand position (down two scale-steps)
   - introducing no new sharps, flats or naturals, except for the seventh of the new minor scale, which is raised by a semitone in the harmonic minor but not in the rock minor.

3 Moving to the tonic minor involves:
   - no shift of hand position
   - flattening of the third and sixth of the major scale in the harmonic minor, plus also the seventh in the rock major.

Just occasionally things aren't quite so simple. Most of the time we don't need to adapt the layout of chords as we shift from a major key to a minor key, even though this results in some minor chords becoming major, and some major chords becoming minor. But if a minor chord changes into a diminished chord, adjustments do have to be made, owing to the fact that the rules for chord layout are different for diminished triads. This mainly affects II, which is a minor triad in a major key but a diminished triad in a minor key (regardless of whether we use the classical harmonic minor or rock minor scale).

Let's see how this works in practice. In the following examples chord II must be changed to II^b to reflect the fact that a diminished triad is usually placed in first inversion:

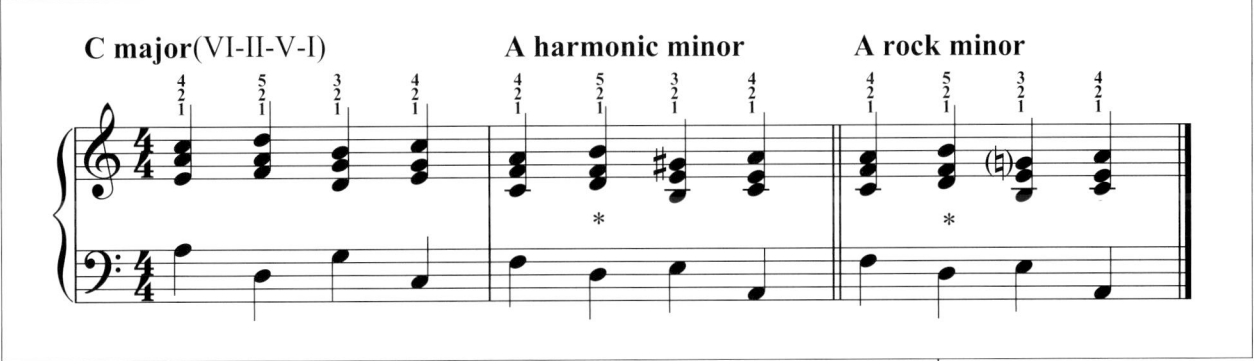

[Example 5.0.5]

[Example 5.0.6]

In the next couple of examples chord II^b is already present in the original major key progression. Nevertheless, a change to the chord layout is still required: the fact that it's now a diminished triad means the third should be doubled rather than the root or fifth.

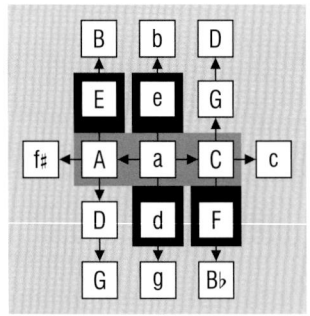

Diagram 5.6: network of key relations for A classical harmonic minor.

You should note how in the preceding examples the use of the right-hand thumb on a black note (E-flat) in C minor requires the hand to move further into the black keys than when making the equivalent move in C major or A minor. Whether the thumb plays on a black or a white note is a significant feature that may change even when the fingering itself stays the same, so that identical fingering of identical chords in different keys can still sometimes call for adjustments to be made to the positioning of the hand.

So far we've discussed how major keys can lie at the centre of networks of key relations, but not how minor keys might do so. There are two reasons for that. The first is practical: we normally first learn how harmony works in a major key, and only afterwards how it works in a minor key, so the most common direction of transfer is major-to-minor, not the other way round. The second is that with minor keys things are slightly more complicated, as within the network of keys immediately related to a particular minor key their importance is a little different, depending on which version of the minor scale is in use. Even so, once you're familiar with all the keys and key-relations you'll find that sometimes you do want to move material from a minor key to a major one. Diagrams 5.6 and 5.7 show how the most important relations differ for the two commonly used forms of the minor scale.

SECTION 2 | UNIT 5

Of course you can practise moving back and forth between the major and minor key versions of the progressions already given above, as well as trying similar moves with the other progressions outlined in the previous unit. However, simply making the same moves in reverse to get back to the original C major version won't teach you much about what's involved when we change a minor-key progression into a major-key one. That's because you'll already be familiar with the latter and so won't be forced to go through the steps involved in getting there. It's better, then, to take the minor-key versions you already have and try moving them to the other major keys to which they're immediately related. A minor is the relative minor of C major, but it's also the tonic minor of A major. C minor is the tonic minor of C major, but it's also the relative minor of E flat major, so we can also try moving material over from A minor to these major keys. Let's do that now with the progressions we've just been looking at.

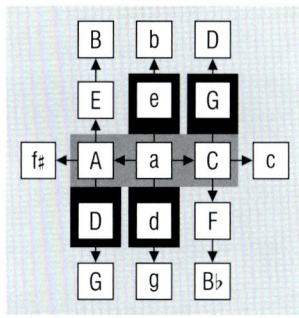

Diagram 5.7: network of key relations for A rock/Aeolian minor

Here's the first of those – the one whose chord layout was completely unaffected when moved from major to minor. Now it's being changed from A minor (given here in both versions) to A major (the tonic major):

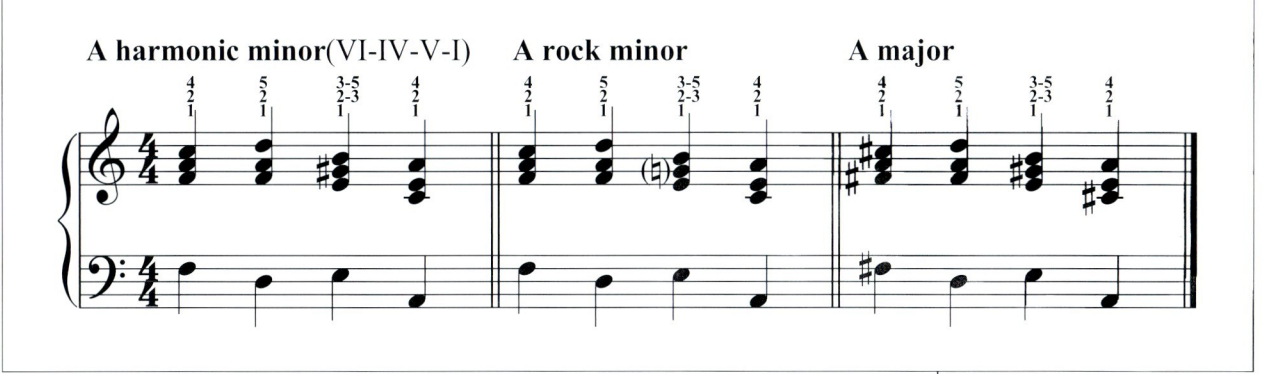

Here it is again, this time being changed from C minor (given here in both versions) to E-flat major (the relative major):

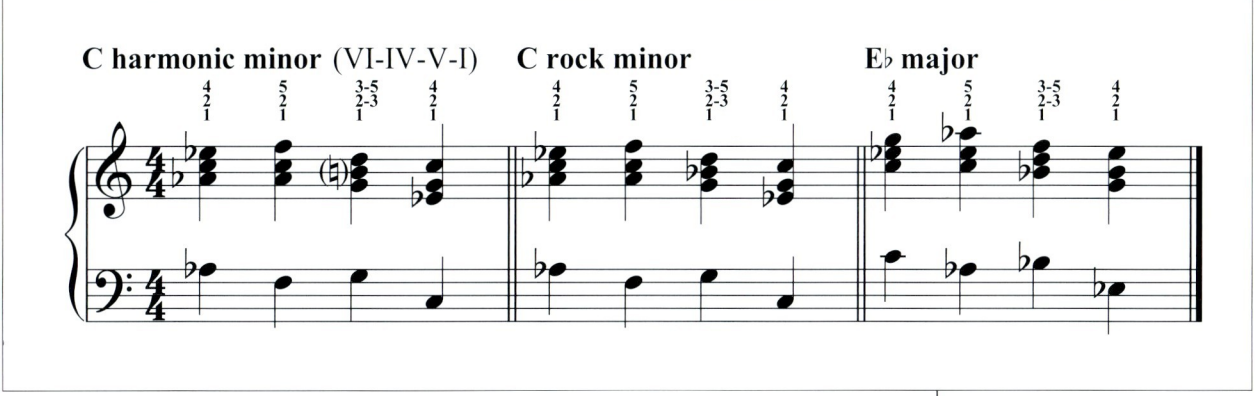

the piano improvisation handbook | 145

Now here's a similar procedure for the second progression, which originally started out with II in the major-key version, but replaced this with II^b in the minor-key versions above. Note that we don't have to make the same change in reverse. Although II^b will now change from a diminished triad back to a minor one as we take the progression back into a major key again, it works perfectly well in first inversion there as well, so we keep this change. However, we're still affected by the different rules for doubling for minor and diminished chords, so we must replace a layout in which the third is doubled with one in which the root or fifth are. First let's see how that works, changing from A minor to A major:

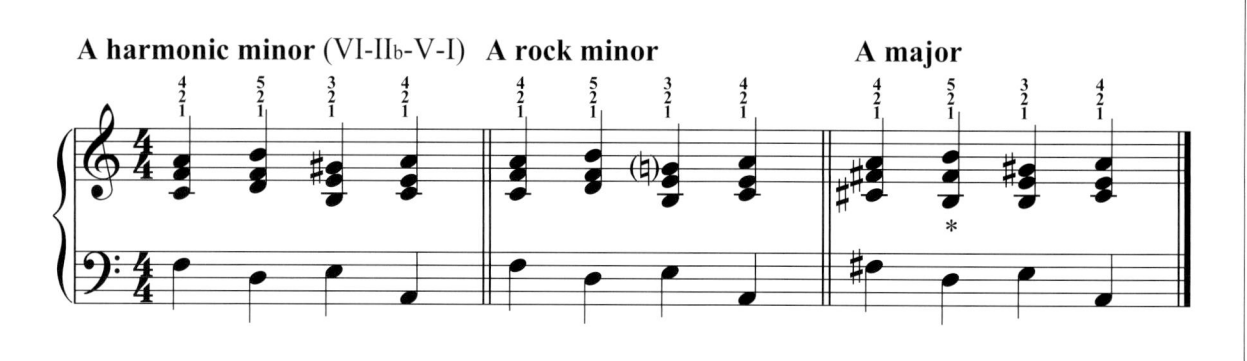

And now the same thing, changing from C minor to E-flat major:

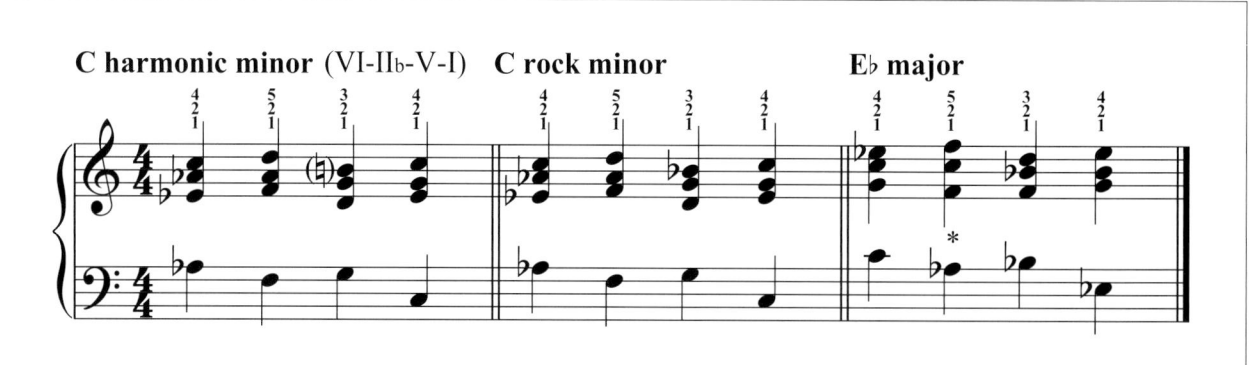

Exercise 5.1
Now take as many as possible of the major-key progressions in the previous unit and see if you can recreate them as minor-key progressions, following the above models. When you've reproduced a progression in the relative minor, try moving it back to the major, but to the tonic major rather than the relative major. When you've reproduced a progression in the tonic minor, try moving it back to the major, but to the relative major rather than the tonic major.

SECTION 2 | UNIT 5

Transposition

So far we've looked at what's involved when we move a progression from a major key to a related minor key, and then from that minor key to another related major key. However, when we perform both of these moves in sequence (eg, C major to A minor to A major, or C major to C minor to E-flat major), we are in effect moving material from one major key to another major key. This means that the material is internally unchanged: all that's happened is that we've reproduced it (in another key) one or more scale-steps higher or lower on the piano. The same is true when we move material from one minor key to another minor key. In both cases we're dealing with **transposition**.

Being able to transpose material freely between different keys is one of the most essential skills you'll need if you're going to be a competent improviser. In fact, if we had to choose just one specific skill whose possession differentiates improvising musicians from others, it would probably have to be this one. Why? Because it's through transposing ideas and material between keys that one becomes familiar with it in the kind of way that's necessary when improvising: so familiar that you can make use of it whenever you want, no matter what key you happen to find yourself in.

Using the key-relation diagrams shown earlier in this unit as a guide, it's easy to see which are the most important intervals for transposing. Here they are, listed in order of importance:

- Transposition to keys one step removed on the Circle of Fifths – ie, up or down a perfect fifth.
- Transposition to keys two steps removed on the Circle of Fifths – ie, up or down a major second.
- Transposition to keys a major third higher or lower.
- Transposition to keys two steps removed on major-minor axis – ie, a minor third higher or lower.
- Transposition to keys a semitone higher or lower – ie, to keys whose keynotes are adjacent to one another in the chromatic scale (mainly useful in jazz).
- Transposition to the two enharmonically equivalent keys a tritone away from the starting key (also mainly useful in jazz).

The next example (p148) shows the VI-IV-V-I progression transposed through all of the intervals, following this same sequence. (Normally each shift of key would be expressed in the form of a key signature. However, in the examples here, as in the previous section, the sharps and flats are all shown as accidentals, without a key signature, in order to highlight more clearly the changes that occur as we shift from one key to another. Remember, this is not how such progressions would normally be written out. The original version of the progression is repeated before each transposition here to make clear that in each case the transposition is from C major to another key.)

The example on p149 shows the slightly more complex VI-II^b-I^c-V-I cadential progression from the last section, transposed in the same way.

UNIT 5 | SECTION 2

[Example 5.0.11]

[Example 5.0.12]

You can practice each transposition more effectively by repeating the same procedure more than once in succession. Indeed, some useful correspondences show up when you try to repeat each transposition more than once:

- Transposing twice by a perfect fifth = transposing once by a major second.
- Transposing twice by a major second = transposing once by a major third.
- Transposing twice by a major third = transposing once by a major third in the opposite direction.
- Transposing twice by a minor third = transposing once by a tritone.
- Transposing twice by a minor second = transposing once by a major second.
- Transposing twice by a tritone brings you back to where you started.

Exercise 5.2
Now try out a similar series of transpositions for as many of the progressions given in the previous unit as possible.

Exercise 5.3
Once you've tried out these progressions in each of the major keys, it's time to see how they look in the remaining minor keys. Take each progression from the previous exercise, this time starting with the version in the major key into which you transposed it there. Then change it again, first into its relative minor, then into its tonic minor (as described and practised in the previous section).

So far we've only practised transposing chord progressions. We've seen that even when the notes change, the fingering generally doesn't. But what about melodic material? This is more complex, because although sometimes melodic shapes are fingered in ways that remain unaffected by changes to the particular notes involved, in other cases they use fingering derived from that of the particular scale (or broken chord or arpeggio) that the melody is based on. As we know, different scales, broken chords

> **Trapped in C major.** The saddest thing that can happen to an improvising pianist is to get trapped in one key, so all their ideas and chords have to be played there. One reason transposition is crucial for improvisers is that it enables you to get fluent in all the keys, so you avoid this fate. Otherwise it's not just that your ideas will be limited to the keys you know: their quality and variety will suffer. That's because it's the subtle variations across keys in terms of how fingering, notes, and harmonic or melodic functions correlate with one another that are the real source of variety and inspiration for improvising musicians – and especially for pianists. Each key opens up a new perspective on the harmonic and melodic possibilities of the style you're involved with.

and arpeggios often involve different fingering patterns. (There's no fixed or general rule about this, but it helps to think of the scales for the two keys involved and try to memorise how each note of the first scale maps onto an equivalent note in the second – ie, one that represents the corresponding scale-degree.) In practice the best way to master melodic transposition is to first master the transposition of chord progressions. Why? Because this is the best way to acquire a good grasp of the function of the different notes in each key, which is ultimately also what you must rely on when transposing melodies.

Modulation

So far we've learned how to switch between major and minor keys and transpose material to other keys without changing its structure. Now it's time to learn how to bring about a change from one key to another that forms part of the continuous unfolding of the music itself. Changing key in this way is known as **modulation**.

Once again, the best way to approach this is to begin by just working with simple chord progressions, as these provide the clearest view of what's involved. (When we come to look at the ways melody and harmony can fit together in classical and jazz, as we'll do in Unit Seven and Unit Eight, we'll see that the same basic principles apply no matter how richly developed the melodic aspect is.)

It's important to realise from the outset that modulations are defined in terms of the functional relationship between the new key and the old key. This relationship is identified by thinking of the tonic chord of the new key as if it were a chord appearing within the old key and then asking what function it would have there. Hence we employ the same terms used for describing the functions of different chords within a key (dominant, subdominant, mediant, etc.) to describe the functional relationship of a new key to the initial key.

Depending on whether we start out from a major or a minor key, different modulations appear as the most straightforward options:

- Modulations from a major key to another major key most often go to the dominant or subdominant.

- Modulations from a major key to a minor key most often go to the relative minor (= the submediant minor), but may also go to the supertonic or mediant.

- Modulations from a minor key to another minor key most often go to the subdominant, but may also go to the dominant (minor).

- Modulations from a minor key to a major key most often go to the relative major (= the mediant), but may also go to the submediant or dominant (major).

These are the ones we'll be focusing on here. In the longer run, though, it's worth also knowing about some other possibilities associated more closely with specific styles:

- In classical music (especially of the late Romantic period and after) more exotic modulations are often created by moving to one of the above keys but substituting the corresponding minor key for the expected major one on the new keynote, or vice versa – as when passing from a major key to the submediant or mediant majors, or from a minor key to the mediant or submediant minors.

- In jazz, as we've already noted, keys a semitone apart are seen as directly related, so switching to another major or minor key a semitone higher or lower is common.

- Rock and pop often favour a sudden change to a key a whole tone higher or lower, used to dramatically notch up the tension as a verse in a song is repeated for the final time; however, this is typically accomplished without any transition.

In the last two instances the key changes tend to occur without any structured preparation, reflecting the looser approach to harmonic continuity that is a feature of these non-classical styles. Hence one should not think of these as modulations in the strict sense of the word. Even so, it's worth keeping in mind that conventional modulations play an important role in these styles too.

To understand what's involved in executing the different modulations you'll need to know about a few techniques additional to those covered so far. These are:

- pivot chords
- functional displacement
- dominant seventh chords
- interchangeability of major and minor

To carry out a modulation from one key to another we first need to find at least one chord common to both starting and finishing keys: a chord all of whose notes appear in the scales for both keys. This provides the point of harmonic transition between the two keys, and is what we call a **pivot chord**. For example, when modulating from C major to G major, we can use any chord in C major that doesn't include an F, as this is the one note that differs between the scales of C and G majors. (Chords with an F in C major will have an F sharp in G major.) As the most common modulations are to keys closely related, the keys normally do have most of their notes in common. (In cases where only one note is different between the two scales, this leaves four possible pivot chords, but where two or more notes are different the number of possible pivot chords will be reduced.)

The next technique we need to make use of is **functional displacement**. Here we deliberately introduce (at least) one note that belongs to the scale of the new key but not to that of the old key. Where possible we make this happen in a melodic voice in which the note in the old key with the same letter-name appeared not long before. (For example, when modulating from C major to G major we'll need to introduce an F sharp in a melodic part that, prior to the appearance of the pivot chord, contained an F natural.) This has the effect of cancelling out the latter, which we hear as displaced by the new version of this note. This signals to the listener that the old key-centre has ceased to operate and a new one has come into force.

The next resource you need to know about is the **dominant seventh chord**. In addition to being useful for modulations, this represents the first and most important of a series of additions to the repertoire of chords we've already learned to use – the series of three-note triads built on different degrees of the scale. Unlike these, the dominant seventh chord consists of four notes. It's created by adding an extra note to a major triad whose root is the dominant of a major or minor scale, a seventh above the root. Because triads are themselves created by superimposing notes a third apart, adding this new note can be considered an extension of this process. For this reason it's known as a **chord extension**.

What's striking about this new chord is that the seventh is a harmonically dissonant interval, so the result is a chord containing a dissonance as part of the chord. (It's worth bearing in mind that this idea of a chord including a dissonance that need not be resolved while that same chord continues to sound, so that it only resolves with the resolution of the chord itself, was considered controversial and shocking when it first appeared in classical music during the Renaissance.) The point of it is that it allows composers and improvisers to achieve more heightened levels of harmonic tension, leading in turn to more striking resolutions.

The example below shows some possible layouts and voice-leading for a dominant seventh resolving to a tonic chord in C major.

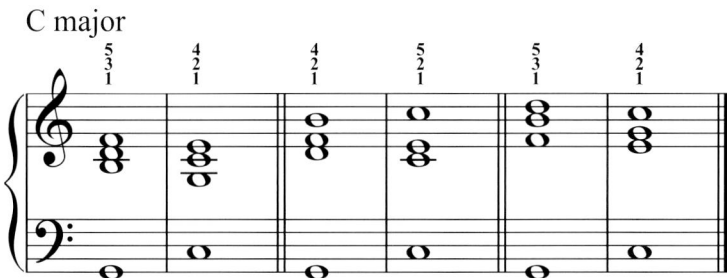

Note how the seventh (here, the F) of chord V invariably resolves downwards by a semitone to the third of chord I (the E), while the third (the B) of the dominant chord can be heard as rising by a semitone to arrive at the root of the tonic chord, which is also the tonic itself (C). (The latter is known as a 'leading tone effect'. Note that we can hear it this way even if the actual voice-leading requires the leading tone to move down to the fifth of the next chord.)

UNIT 5 SECTION 2

These movements of just a semitone give rise to unusually powerful voice-leading effects. In the 19th century, composers such as Wagner used them to introduce more and more chromatic notes into the harmony and, as we'll see later, similar effects play a big role in jazz. Indeed, this ultimately led to the dissolution of tonality in modern classical music, as well as paving the way for the looser relationship between melody and harmony that makes jazz improvisation possible.

The dominant seventh chord is especially useful when modulating into major keys, as in one stroke it unambiguously establishes a new major key with reference to its place on the Circle of Fifths. (That's because it contains both the fourth and seventh degrees of the new scale – the two scale degrees whose combination is unique to that major key. As we move 'down' the Circle in the direction of keys with less sharps or more flats it's the seventh that gets lowered by a semitone to become the seventh of the new scale, while moving up the Circle in the direction of keys with more sharps or less flats leads to the fourth being raised by a semitone to become the seventh of the new scale.) Sometimes it can perform a similar function when modulating to minor keys as well.

Finally, you should know about a trick that, from the early 19th century onwards, has been increasingly used by composers and improvisers in order to enlarge the range of possible modulations. This is the idea of **major-minor interchangeability**. The idea here is that a major key can 'borrow' chords from the minor scale based on the same keynote, and vice versa. These **borrowed chords** (see Unit Seven for more on these) greatly enlarge the number of possible pivot chords available to link keys together, as well as allowing us to use diminished chords more freely to modulate to major as well as minor keys.

Now it's time to see how this works in practice. Bear in mind that the examples below show just a few of the many different possible ways of handling standard modulations. They are also somewhat artificial as, for reasons of space, in each case the modulation occurs almost immediately within a very short stretch of music. It's normal for a piece of music to spend more time establishing the initial key, and this would also provide the context within which a particular modulation is then heard as making musical sense.

We'll begin with modulations from major to major. The first example shows a couple of standard opening progressions that modulate to the dominant and end with perfect

> In this and subsequent examples you'll see the chord functions marked beneath the lower staff with **Roman numerals**. This is the method used in traditional harmonic analysis: it has the advantage of showing you the chord structure independently of the particular key the music happens to be in. Large Roman numerals indicate major and augmented triads, small numerals minor or diminished ones. Pivot chords are shown as having a function in both the starting and ending keys (separated by a horizontal line).

cadences involving dominant seventh chords. Note how in both cases here the F-sharp is heard as displacing an F-natural that appeared earlier in the same melodic part.

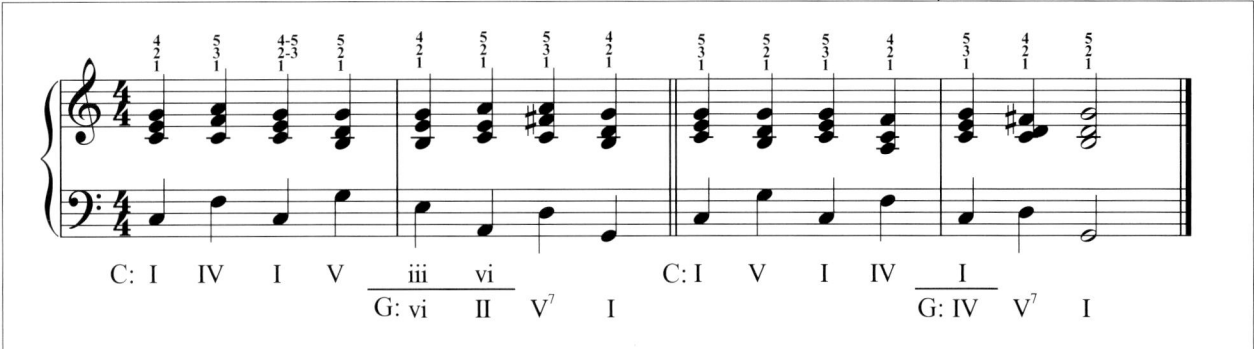

The next example shows two standard progressions that modulate to the subdominant, also ending with perfect cadences involving dominant seventh chords. Note how the first sequence introduces chord VI in the starting key to create a strong root progression to chord II, which in turn functions as the first chord of the VI-II-V^7-I cadential progression in the new key.

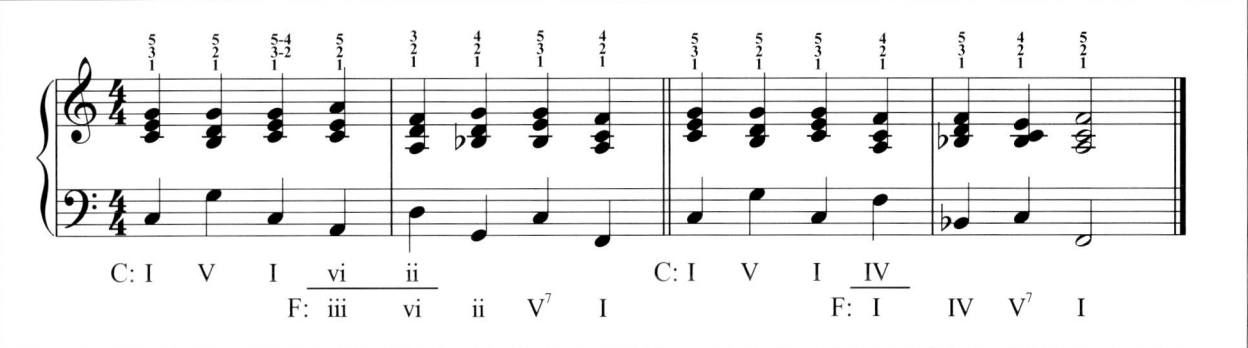

Now we'll consider modulations from major to minor. Here are examples of a progression modulating to the relative (ie, submediant) minor and supertonic minor:

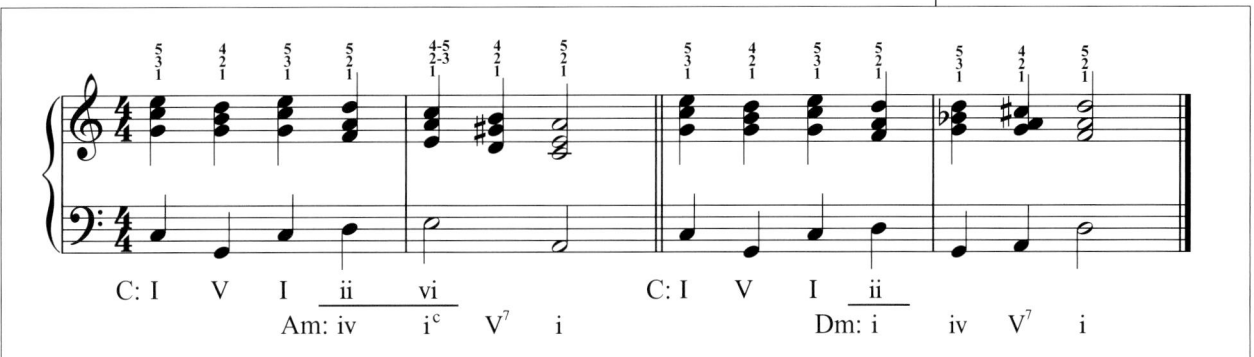

UNIT 5 | SECTION 2

Let's take modulations that start out from a minor key next. In traditional harmony the most common modulations of this sort are from minor to major, so we'll begin with these. The next example shows modulations to the relative (ie, mediant) major and submediant major. (Note how the second modulation uses chord II^b in the new key to displace both the G-sharp and B-natural of A harmonic minor with the G-natural and B-flat of F major.)

Finally we'll look at modulations from minor to minor. Here the examples show typical modulations to the subdominant and dominant minors:

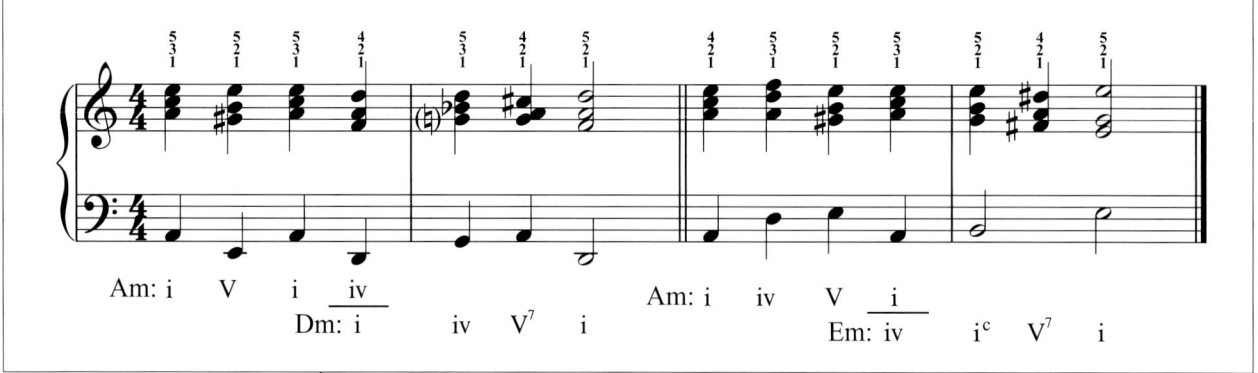

Now let's take a brief look at how major-minor interchangeability can help us achieve some more tricky modulations. The example at the top of the opposite page shows how modulations from a major key to the submediant and mediant majors can be accomplished, even though these keys are quite distant from the starting key, borrowing pivot chords from more closely related minor keys with the same keynotes.

Another resource that can sometimes be useful for modulations is the **diminished seventh chord**. Like the dominant seventh chord, this is created through chord extension. We just take a diminished triad (such as appears on the seventh step of both the major and harmonic minor scales) and add an extra note a minor third above the already flattened fifth of the chord. (The resulting interval between the new note and the

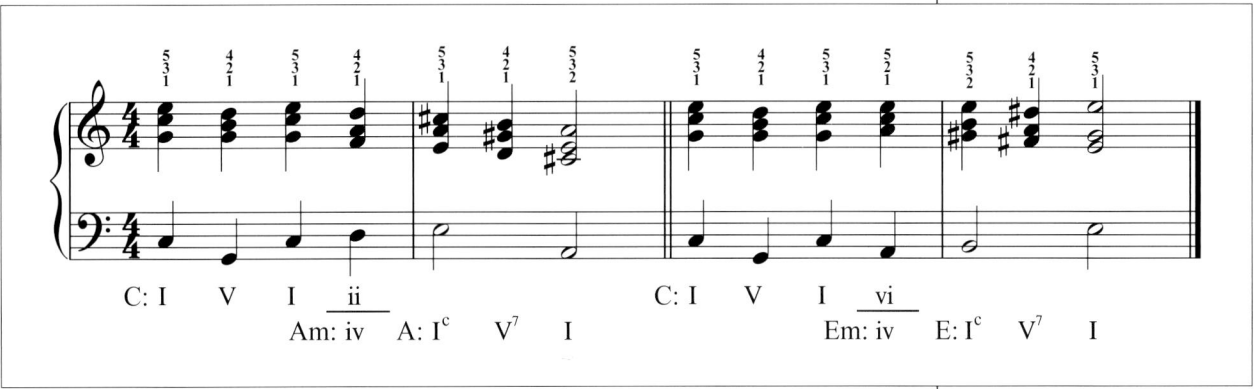

root is two semitones smaller than a major seventh, and one semitone smaller than a minor seventh, but still counts as a seventh because of the number of scale steps it corresponds to – hence the name 'diminished seventh'.) This chord is especially useful for modulating to minor keys as it contains both the flattened sixth and raised seventh of the harmonic minor scale – a combination unique to the minor key in question. The example below shows some possible layouts and voice-leading for a diminished seventh chord resolving to a tonic chord in C minor:

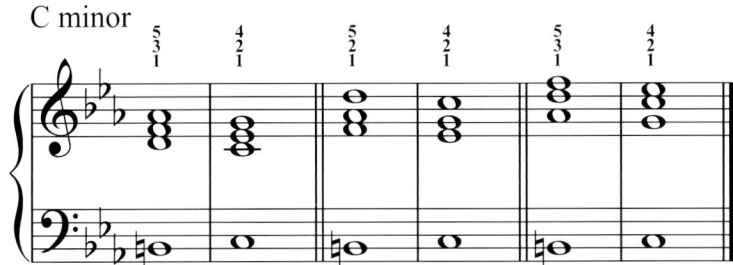

We can also understand this chord as a further extension of the dominant seventh, if we think of it as adding a further note a third above the seventh of the latter while omitting the root of the dominant chord itself. This allows us to think of it as an incomplete dominant seventh with flattened ninth. Hence the resolution to the tonic can be heard as a perfect cadence.

The diminished seventh chord possesses a feature which makes it extremely useful for certain kinds of modulation: because it consists entirely of superimposed minor thirds, the same chord can be understood as belonging to any one of four different keys with keynotes likewise separated by one or more minor thirds. The next example shows how the same diminished seventh chord can thus be made to resolve to four different tonic chords, allowing it to function ambiguously as a pivot chord between any of these keys. (To grasp this, keep in mind the idea of enharmonic equivalence: the same pitch can be written differently in different keys, so G-sharp = A-flat, E sharp = F, C-flat = B. The example is given without key signatures to make it easier to see the notes in common.)

UNIT 5 SECTION 2

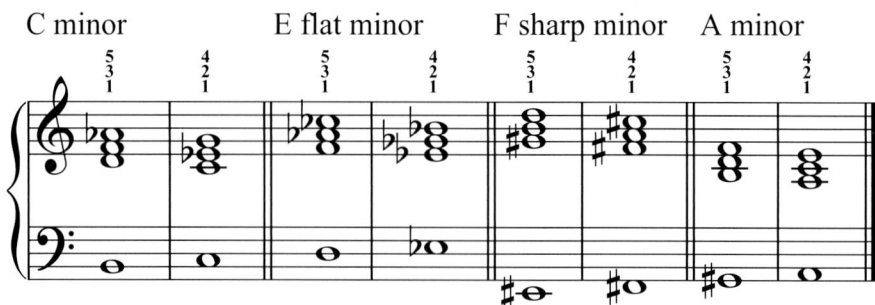

You can see how useful this is from the next example, which shows a modulation from a minor key to the mediant minor. What would otherwise be difficult is made simple by the fact that both keys share the same diminished seventh chord. Note also how the voice-leading is arranged so that the outer voices both move stepwise by semitones to the next chord.

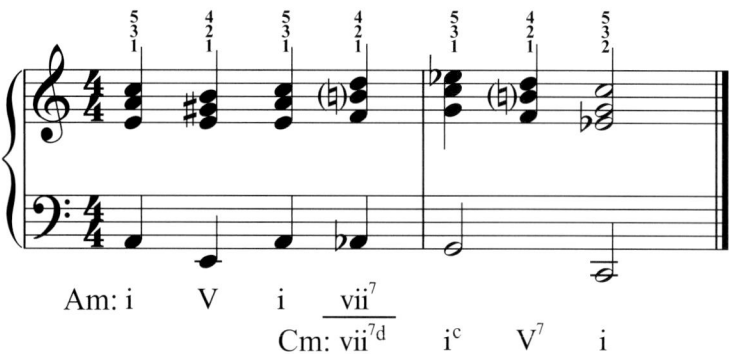

Not all modulations should be thought of as displacing the initial key irreversibly with a new one. Some kinds of music (especially 19th-century classical music) make use of what are known as **passing modulations**. These are temporary changes of key that don't last long enough to really displace the original key centre, and which are normally immediately followed by a return to the latter. Such modulations create heightened contrast within an overall key centre, often by highlighting a minor chord as a temporary key centre against the background of an overarching major key, or vice versa.

Exercise 5.4
Try executing your own modulations following the models given above, but using other opening and cadential progressions taken from the previous unit. In each case play the progression VERY slowly: allow as much time as you need to work out the next chord. Then try transposing the examples given here, and any others you've created, into as many other keys as possible.

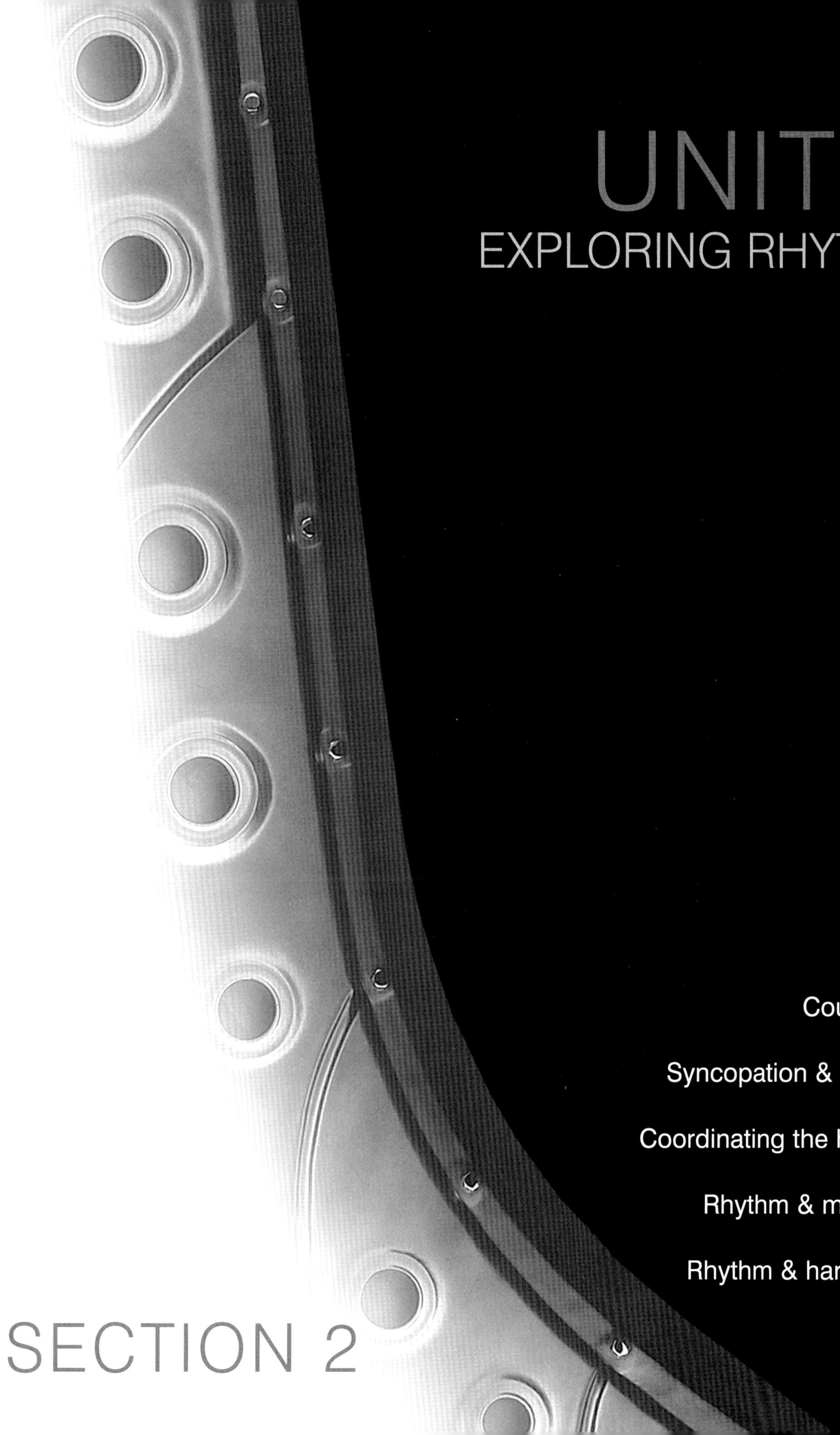

UNIT 6
EXPLORING RHYTHM

- Counting
- Syncopation & swing
- Coordinating the hands
- Rhythm & melody
- Rhythm & harmony

SECTION 2

UNIT 6 | SECTION 2

Counting

So far we've explored the basics of melodic unfolding and harmonic structure, but probably the most basic aspect in all music is yet to come: rhythm. Only when you've grasped how each of these other elements fits into the rhythmic organisation of music can you understand how they also fit with one another to create a larger unity – something we're likely to recognise as 'music'.

In order to make sense of how melody and harmony relate to rhythm, though, we must first get a feel for rhythm itself. This means learning how to control the speed of the notes you play by relating them to a stable pulse, and understanding exactly how different rhythms relate to the underlying metre of the music.

In the first section we'll work through some of the most commonly used rhythmic possibilities available in Western music. We'll practise clapping different rhythms while counting the beats of the bar aloud at the same time. That way we can hear and understand how the rhythms relate to the metre. This should give you a basic 'rhythmic vocabulary'. Afterwards we'll explore some more specific aspects of how rhythm works, including its role in melody and harmony.

There's a standard way of counting rhythm in music: with each new bar we start over again, counting from 'one'. We can also count divisions within a beat if necessary: the halfway point is counted by saying 'and', a quarter of the way through the beat is counted by saying 'er', and three-quarters of the way through is counted by saying 'a'. So if we wanted to count aloud the division of the first beat of a bar into four equal subdivisions we would say 'one-er-and-a'. Mostly, however, we just count the beats themselves and try to feel how the subdivisions relate to them.

It's important to know that when a note is held for more than a beat (or is followed by a rest) we continue to count the beats of the bar while holding it (or waiting to play the next note). Also, the metrical organisation of music means the first beat of each bar is always the strongest, and with four beats per bar the third beat is also slightly emphasised.

Work through the exercises below, repeating each pattern over and over again until you feel confident about how it relates to your counting and to the underlying pulse. Each one-bar pattern can be repeated as many times as you wish, but of course any of these can also be combined with others to produce larger patterns. (As a final test, you can even try clapping sequentially through the whole sequence of rhythms for each exercise!) Then try working out some rhythms of your own. (In order to understand rhythms you've made up yourself it helps to try and write them down. This forces you to think about exactly how they relate to the musical metre.)

SECTION 2 | UNIT 6

Exercise 6.1
Here are typical rhythms in the simplest metre of all: simple duple time. The simplest rhythm of all is a straightforward stating of the pulse itself. Others are then derived from this by either subdivision of one or more beats in the bar, holding on individual notes for more than one beat, or both of these.

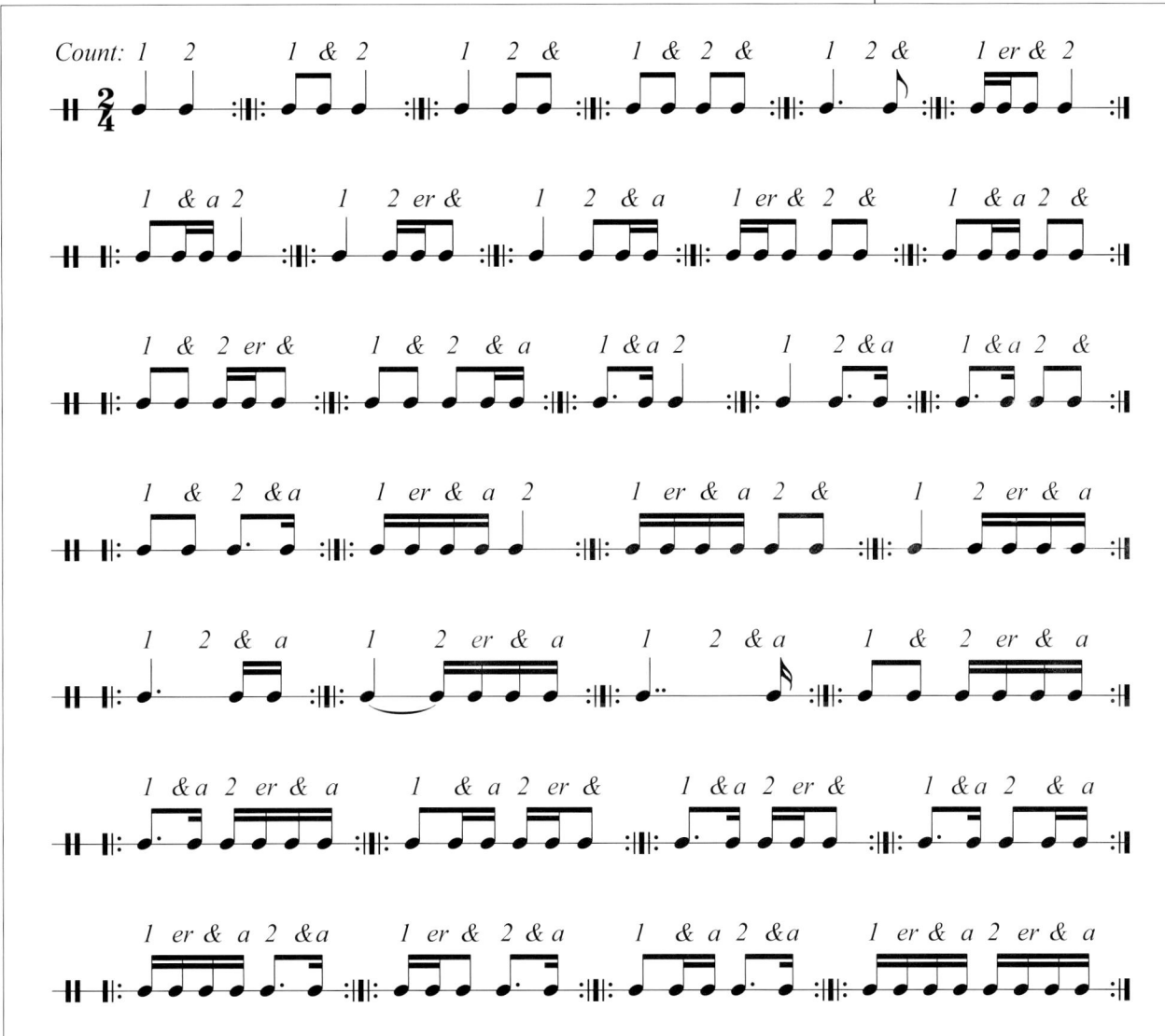

UNIT 6 | SECTION 2

Exercise 6.2
Now here are rhythms in simple triple time. Note especially the lilting effect of rhythms that contain a dotted rhythm spread over two of the three beats of a bar.

Exercise 6.3

Next come rhythms in simple quadruple time. Many of these will be the same as two-bar rhythms in simple duple time, except that here we are aware of a difference of stress between the first and third beats of the bar, which then defines the four-beat character of the rhythm itself.

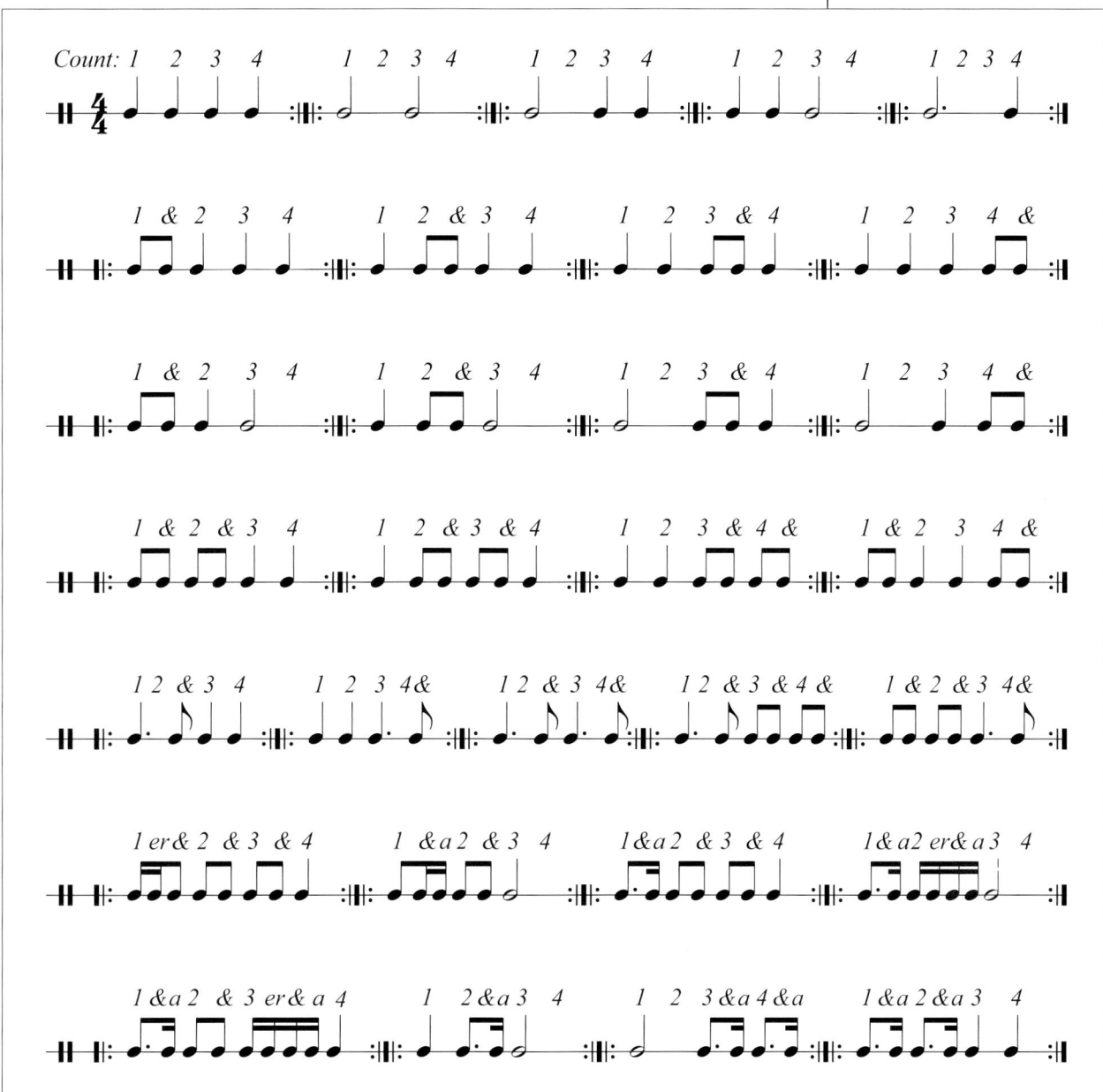

UNIT 6 | SECTION 2

Exercise 6.4
Now let's take a look at the simplest form of compound time, which is compound duple time. Here it's important to remember that a single beat or count is represented by a dotted note (in this case a dotted crotchet), which naturally then divides into three equal subdivisions rather than two. Note especially the use of dotted rhythms within individual beats, starting on either the first or second subdivision of the beat itself. Divisions into thirds are counted as 'one-and-a-two-and-a'.

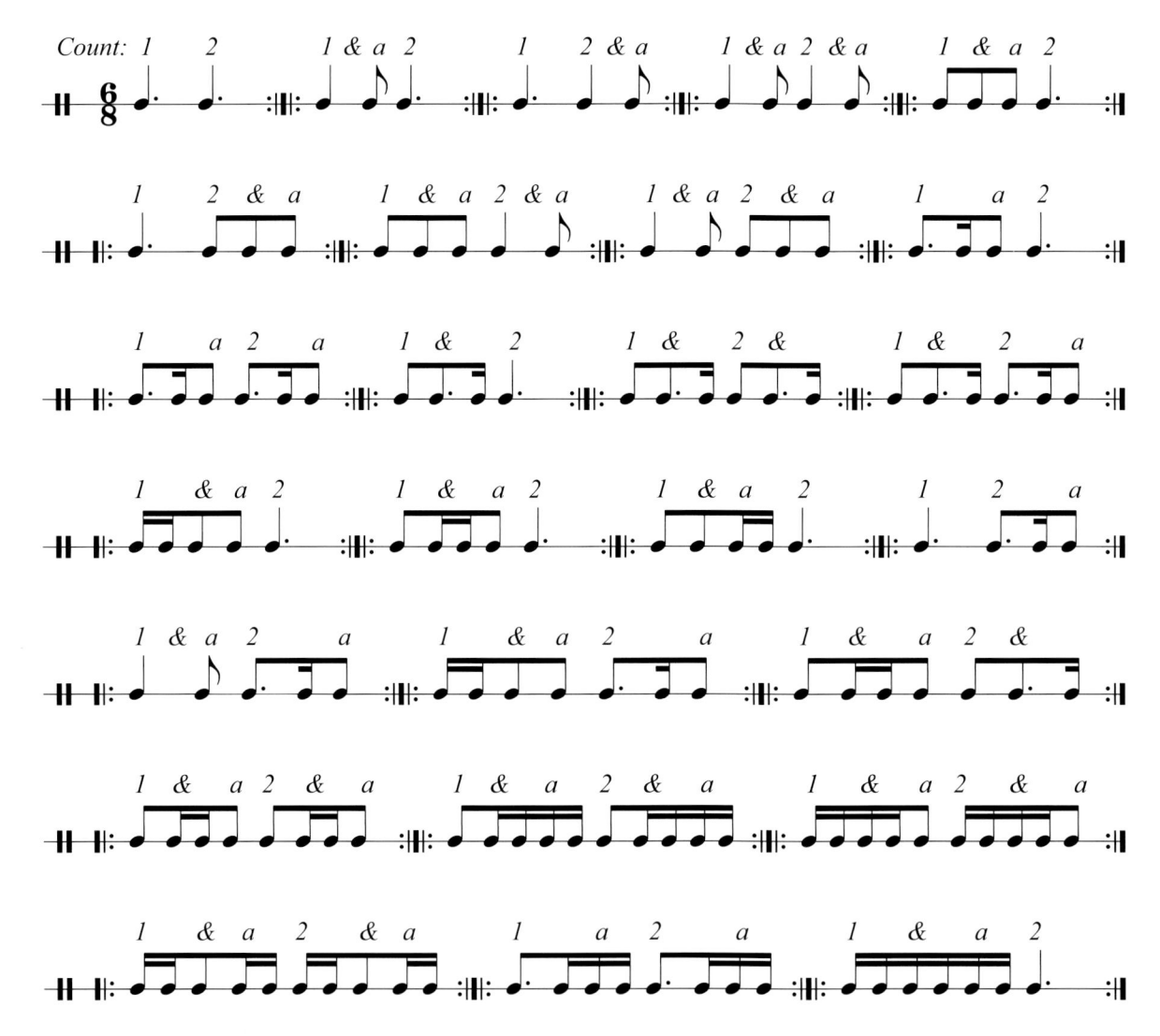

Exercise 6.5
Now here are rhythms in compound triple time. Many of the rhythmic possibilities here will be related to those in compound duple time, as the possibilities for subdividing individual beats will be the same.

Exercise 6.6
Finally here come rhythms in compound quadruple time. Many of these will be the same as two-bar rhythms in compound duple time, except that once again we feel here a difference of stress between the first and third beats of the bar. Here, too, you'll find that many of the rhythmic possibilities are related to those in compound duple or triple time, as the possibilities for subdividing individual beats are essentially the same.

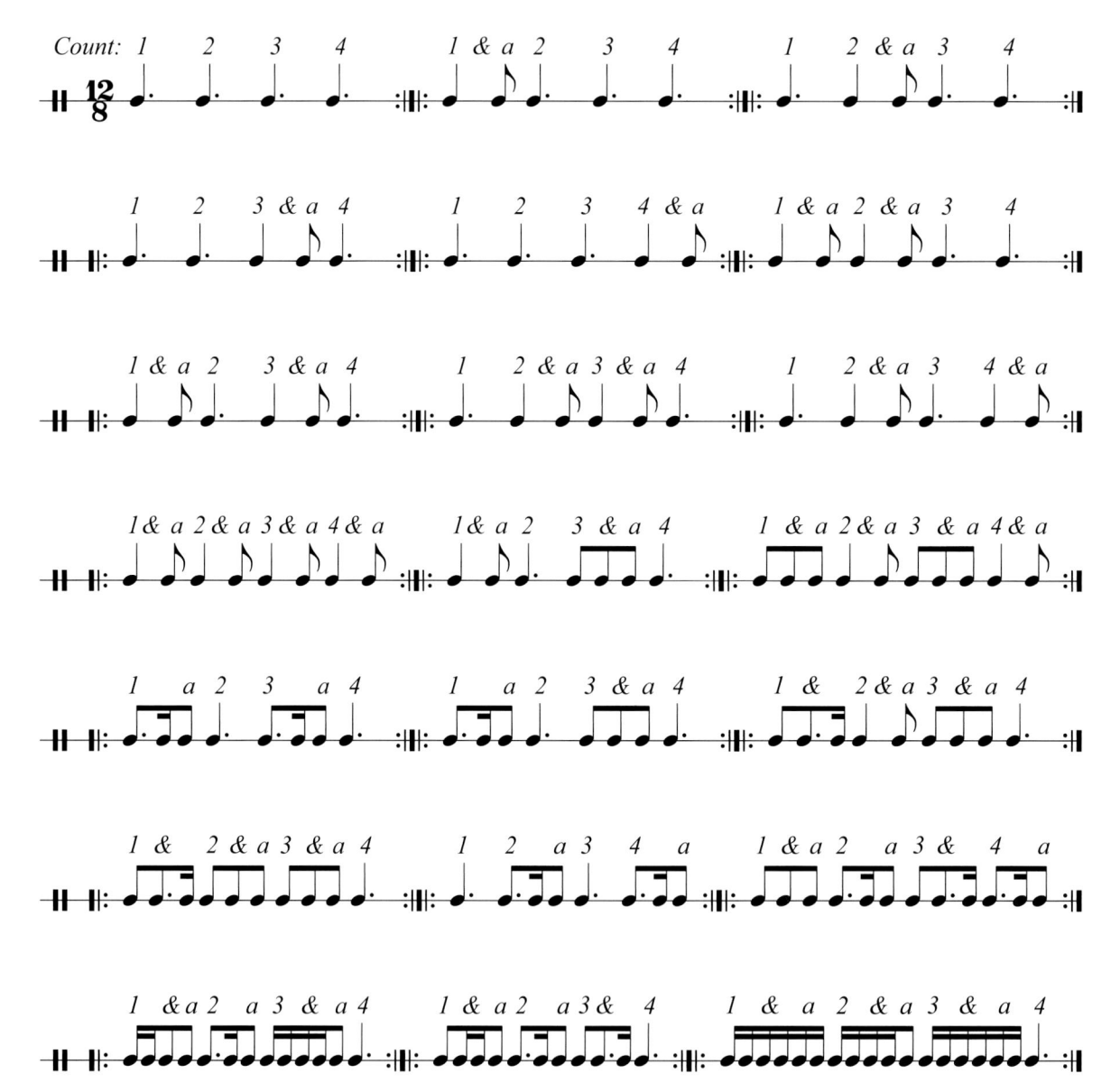

Syncopation & swing

1. Syncopation

You should have realised by now that rhythms in music derive their character from how they relate to an underlying metre, which itself is a repeating pattern of stronger and weaker beats. These beats form a hierarchy, with stronger and weaker beats and subdivisions corresponding to greater and lesser degrees of stress. (The first beat is the strongest point in the metrical hierarchy, and those subdivisions that fall between beats are the weakest.) However, the relationship of rhythm to the metrical hierarchy isn't simply one of subordination. Sometimes rhythm follows the underlying metrical hierarchy, but it can also work against it as a way of generating rhythmic tension. (If it fails to do so the music may lack rhythmic interest.)

The most straightforward way in which rhythm can depart from the metrical hierarchy is through **weak-beat** or **offbeat accents**: stresses placed on weak beats or subdivisions that would not normally be stressed. This takes the form of accents that are marked in written music. A similar effect is often created in another way, by employing rhythms that themselves deliberately work against the normal stress pattern of the metre. We can create such rhythms by placing melodically and/or harmonically important notes on the subdivisions before or after a beat rather than on the beat itself – or by placing them on a weak beat just before or after a strong beat, rather than on the strong beat itself). The effect is often reinforced by holding such notes over to the next beat, so that no new note sounds on the latter at all. Taken as a whole this technique is known as **syncopation**.

It's a popular misconception that the presence of syncopation is the essential thing that distinguishes modern non-classical styles (such as jazz, rock, pop, blues, etc) from classical music. That's not true: classical music also makes a lot of use of syncopation. Even so, there is a grain of truth in it: the contrast between the way syncopation works in Western classical music on the one hand and in modern non-classical styles on the other is one of the most basic features that differentiates these two kinds of music from one another.

Basically, classical music treats syncopation as a feature that arises out of the rhythmic unfolding and development of particular melodic lines. By contrast, non-classical styles treat syncopation as a more or less fixed and constant feature of the rhythmic texture of the music, just like the metrical hierarchy itself.

This difference reflects the contrasting historical origins of classical music and modern non-classical styles:

- Classical music evolved gradually over centuries in a culture whose musical language was shaped by the need to set words to music in ways that would preserve their metre and thus their comprehensibility – mainly for religious purposes.

- Styles like jazz, rock, pop, and blues originated from a fusion of elements of that same European tradition with African musical influences that arrived in America as a result of the slave trade. (The use of syncopation as a permanent feature of rhythmic textures is one of the hallmarks of traditional African music.)

At the same time it's worth keeping in mind that this difference of approach is not absolute. A continuum exists between these two ways of treating the relationship between rhythm and metre, and as an improviser you're free to situate yourself wherever you like along it, so long as you keep in mind that how you handle syncopation will have strong implications for the cultural and stylistic associations your music has for listeners.

Let's have a look at some typical examples of how syncopation works, starting with the kind we are more likely to encounter in classical music. Note how classical syncopations tend to occur only after the metre has first been clearly established, and are immediately followed by a return to unsyncopated rhythm. The first example shows a standard syncopation effect in simple duple time.

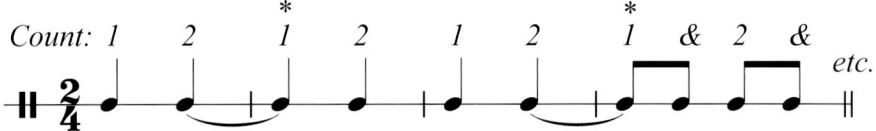

Now a couple of examples in simple triple time:

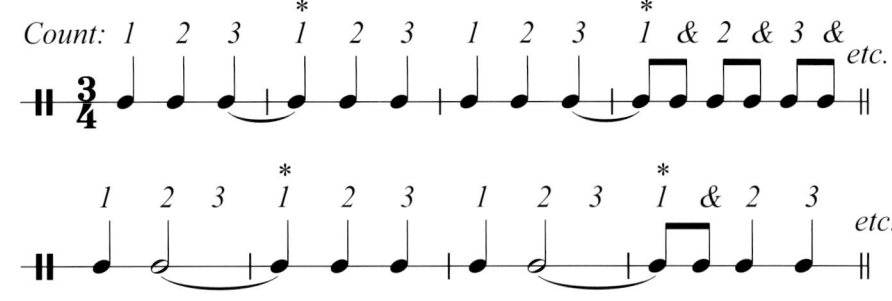

And in simple quadruple time:

Syncopation is also possible in compound time. Here's are examples in compound duple time:

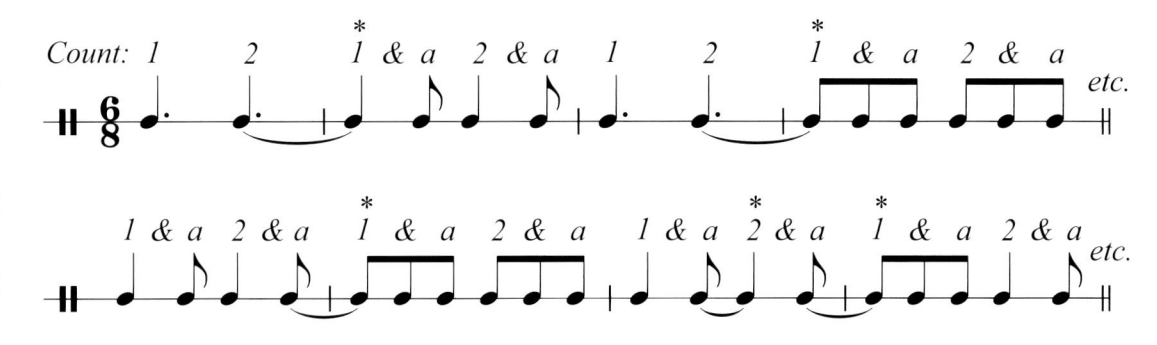

And now compound triple time:

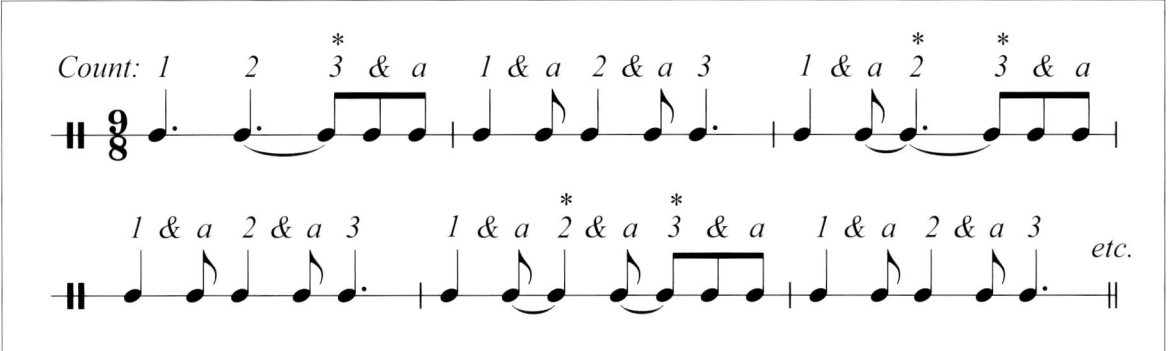

Finally, here's syncopation in compound quadruple time:

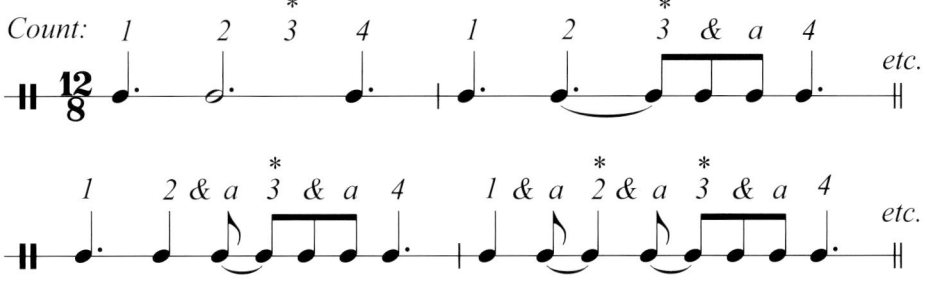

Now let's turn to the kind of syncopated rhythm effects you're more likely to come across in non-classical styles with Afro-American influences. This kind of syncopation usually takes one or other of two forms: notes are consistently placed either just before certain beats in each bar or just after them. The former is known as **pushing the beat**

and is associated with an 'upbeat' feel of the sort found in ragtime and American country music. The latter is known as **leaning on the beat** and is associated more with the 'downbeat' feel of the blues and blues-related styles. Modern rock and pop styles make use of both kinds of syncopation, as well as a number of standardised forms of syncopation associated with particular dance genres or dance grooves. One of the richest sources of syncopated rhythmic patterns for non-classical music is Latin-American music, thanks to musical styles such as salsa and popular dance-based styles like samba.

Pushing and leaning on the beat often take the form of subtle shifts in timing that mean that notes fall just before or after the beat. (In non-classical styles the beat is often independently maintained by a rhythmic section, but in solo piano styles it's implied or maintained by the left hand, while the right hand works more freely around the pulse with a degree of rhythmic independence.)

These kinds of timing shifts can't be accurately shown in musical notation, which must therefore either show unsyncopated rhythms or a simplified version of the syncopation – one in which these notes are presented as if they were falling on the nearest regular subdivision of the beat. The latter method is more useful here as it allows us to make use of some written examples to gain an approximate sense of where the syncopations come in different rhythmic patterns. However, you should keep in mind that this needs to be supplemented by listening to the different styles of music in which it appears.

The most common metre for modern rock and pop styles is simple quadruple time, which is also the easiest metre for practising syncopations. Here are some syncopated patterns in simple quadruple time typical of modern rock and pop styles.

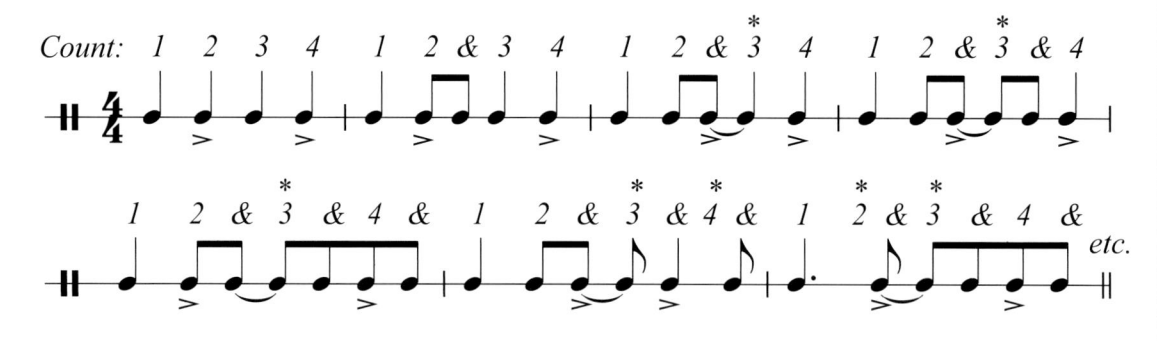

As the above example illustrates, rock and pop styles often also make use of regular accents on the second and fourth beats of the bar – the weak beats of the metrical pattern. Like syncopations, these weak-beat accents are maintained as a fixed feature of the rhythmic texture, and are known as **backbeats**. The stronger the backbeat, the greater the 'heavy rock' feel.

Jazz makes extensive use of syncopated rhythmic patterns, but these have to be understood in the context of a more general concept of rhythm in jazz that centres around the notion of **swing**. This needs to be considered separately, so we'll look at it next.

2. Swing

As we've just mentioned, jazz uses a special kind of rhythm known as 'swing'. The basic idea is that rhythms get a more swinging feel if we consistently delay the second subdivision of each beat. However, in jazz these rhythms are still written out in musical notation as equal divisions of the beat. What we see written thus doesn't correspond to what we play or hear.

Below are some typical examples of 'swung' rhythms, including syncopations. In order to help understand these rhythms they are shown first in jazz notation (which shows how they are normally written) and then in classical notation (which gives a more accurate approximation of how they sound.) Note how a division of the beat in which all three subdivisions are played still gets written as triplet quavers, even in jazz.

It's important to keep in mind that the exact rhythmic character of swung rhythms can vary quite considerably, depending on the mood and tempo of the music. Faster, more upbeat music tends to flatten out the rhythms, bringing them closer to equal subdivisions. On the other hand slower, more downbeat music tends to exaggerate the contrast between longer and shorter notes, bringing the rhythms closer to classical-style dotted rhythms. In jazz terminology the opposite of playing music with 'swing' is to play it 'straight' (ie, strictly as written).

Coordinating the hands

One of the biggest challenges for anybody learning the piano is playing 'hands together', especially when each hand has to play in a way that is rhythmically independent from what the other is doing. When learning to play written compositions there's a well-known method for dealing with this: first we practise each hand separately, then we combine the hands at a greatly reduced speed, and finally we practise gradually bringing the music up to the speed called for by the composer. This makes sense, but only because you're playing off written music – exactly what you're not doing when you improvise. So as improvisers we have to find other ways of developing rhythmic independence between the hands. The best way is to get really familiar with the most common formulas for combining the hands, but in ways open-ended enough to leave room for lots of free variation when actually improvising.

The most basic kind of coordination between rhythmically independent parts is where each hand plays material based on a different recurring time-value. What matters here is the relationship between the time values: how many notes in one part fit against a single note in the other. The simplest is one-against-two, but we may also have one-against-three, one-against-four, etc.

Exercise 6.7
Try playing the following patterns slowly, focusing on maintaining rhythmic evenness. Keep the hands relaxed and avoiding hesitating at points where the two hands play together. Putting a slight stress on the first beat of each bar will help you to maintain a sense of metrical regularity. When you feel confident about the timing, gradually increase the speed.

SECTION 2 | UNIT 6

The next exercise presents a similar relationship between the hands, but with unequal time-values in one of the parts.

Exercise 6.8
Once again, start by playing the patterns slowly. Take care that you don't flatten out the dotted rhythms by hesitating just before points where the hands coincide. Keep the fingers rounded and firm. Aim for a crisp and precise rhythmic feel.

SECTION 2 | UNIT 6

UNIT 6 | SECTION 2

Now here's a version of the same thing in which the held notes are replaced with chords sounding on the beats left empty by the melody. This establishes a relationship of **rhythmic complementation** between the two hands – a commonly used technique that allows them to fit together neatly and form a single continuous rhythmic texture.

Exercise 6.9 (opposite page)
In this exercise stress the first beat of the bar clearly throughout, while making sure that the chords on the weak beats don't sound too heavily. Watch the shape of the hand when the weaker fingers are playing faster notes, making sure the fingers stay rounded and the knuckles level. Keep the shoulders, wrists, and hands relaxed throughout.

Dotted rhythms often occur against a regular on-the-beat accompaniment, producing a tricky combination of time-values that needs to be handled with care. The next exercise practises this.

Exercise 6.10
Feel a clear accent as the hands play together on the strong beat. Then hold the dotted note on while the other hand plays on the weak beat, fitting the quaver in afterwards to arrive hands together on the next strong beat. Judge the timing carefully so the quaver comes exactly halfway between the weak beat and the next strong beat.

UNIT 6 | SECTION 2

Now let's take a look at what's involved in coordinating the hands when one of them is playing syncopated rhythms. The best way to master this is to first practise the rhythms away from the keyboard, either by slapping each hand on the corresponding leg or drumming out the rhythms on a flat surface (like the lid of the piano keyboard itself). This exaggerates the physical movements involved, which in turn makes it easier for your body to develop a feel for how the rhythms fit together. The next exercise features some of the most common syncopated rhythms, first in one hand, then in the other.

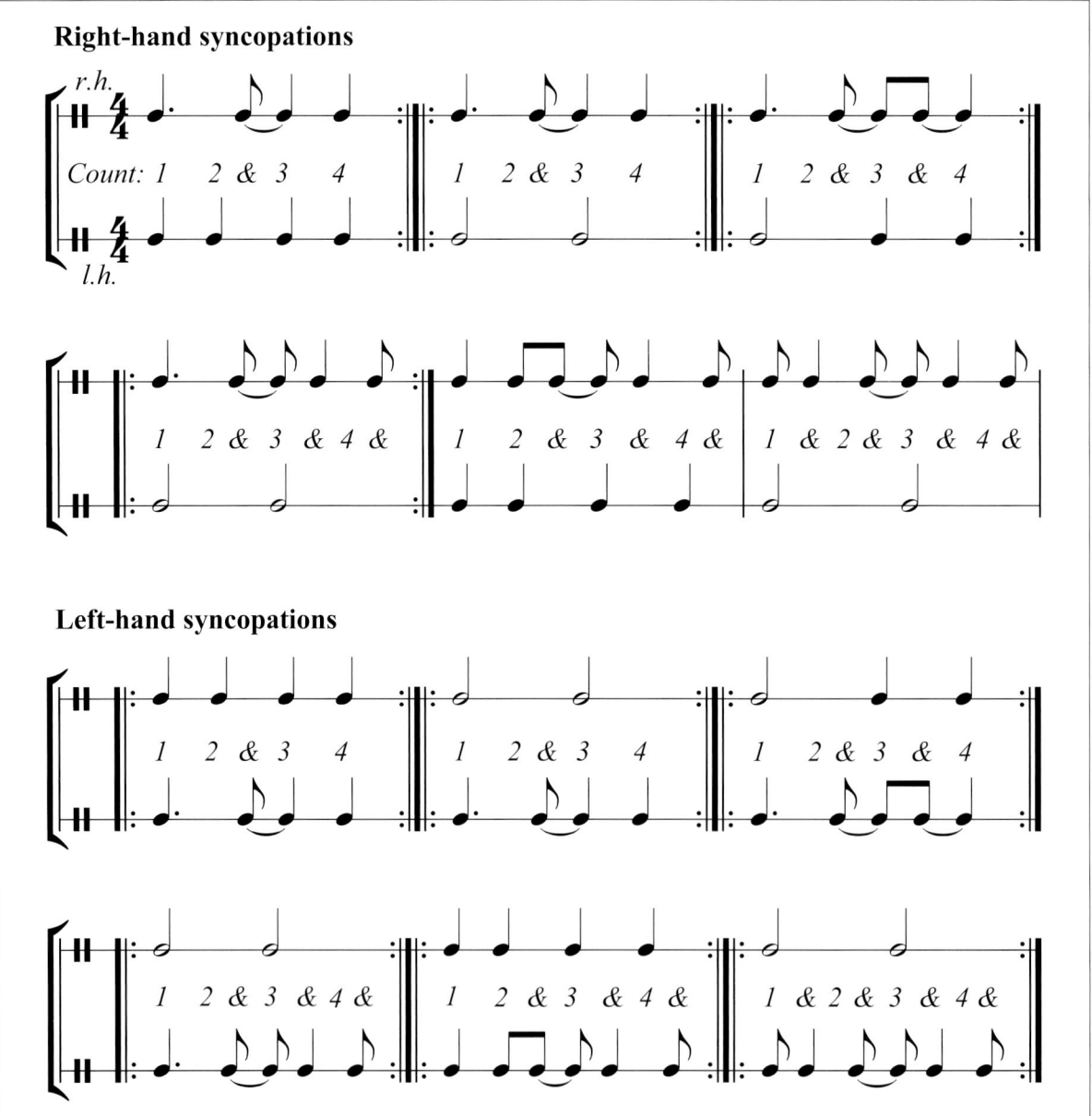

SECTION 2 | UNIT 6

Exercise 6.11 (opposite page)
Practise tapping out these syncopations, first straight and then with swing.

Rhythm & melody

Now we're ready to begin looking at how rhythm works in relation to melody. The relationship between these can be quite hard to pin down as it's rather complex and can vary depending on the style of the music. However, there are basically two possibilities, which we can loosely call rhythm-as-melody and melody-as-rhythm:

- Rhythm-as-melody is what we find in music where the main source of rhythm or rhythmic texture in the music is not the melody itself, so the rhythmic unfolding of the melody need only work as an aspect of the melody itself.
- Melody-as-rhythm is what we find especially in dance music – the melody itself is the main source of rhythm or rhythmic texture, and this requires its melodic unfolding to fit with its rhythmic character rather than the other way round.

Let's look at some examples to get a feel for how this works in practice and what possibilities it offers for improvising. We'll start with an example of rhythm-as-melody. In this case the rhythm only sounds interesting when heard as part of the melody itself – not when heard on its own as a purely rhythmic texture. That leaves us free to experiment with varying the rhythm in pretty much any way we want, just as long as the resulting melody still works. As an illustration, the exercise below shows how syncopation can be used in different ways to vary the overall effect of a melody of this sort. Note how the melody remains recognisable in spite of the changes introduced.

Exercise 6.12 CD Tracks 1–4
Here are several versions of an English folksong classic, 'What Shall We Do With The Drunken Sailor?' The first (a) keeps to the traditional rhythm, with no syncopations. Note how the melody essentially consists of two contrasting elements: on the one hand there are the more insistently rhythmic repetitions of a single pitch, on the other the smoother shapes outlining chords. The second (b) applies syncopations to repeated notes only, whereas the third (c) applies it to just the chordal shapes. In the fourth version (d) both aspects of the melody are syncopated. Play through all of the versions. Then experiment, adding syncopations of your own to the original and seeing how they sound. (Look out for the small eighth-note/quaver E-sharp in bar 30: its what's called a 'grace note'. Such notes are decorative additions, and in this case the diagonal slash through the stem means it should be played as fast as possible. The technical name for this is an acciaccatura – an Italian term meaning 'crushed note'. Remember also that enharmonic equivalence means that E-sharp is the same as F-natural on the keyboard.) Finally, take some other well-known tunes and explore different ways of adding syncopations to see what happens.

UNIT 6 SECTION 2

THE DRUNKEN SAILOR
Traditional

SECTION 2 | UNIT 6

Now let's turn to a contrasting example. The next exercise shows a perfect instance of melody-as-rhythm – it's a traditional Irish folk tune. In cases like this we can experiment creatively by varying the purely melodic aspect of the line (the pitches and intervals), but not by varying the rhythm.

Exercise 6.13 CD Tracks 5

First learn to play the tune ('The Irish Washerwoman') as written. Note how the melody in the second section is different, but the underlying rhythm (consisting of continuous quavers) remains the same. Can you now make up a tune yourself for the right hand, using the same rhythm and in the same key?

UNIT 6 | SECTION 2

The next exercise shows a tune in which the melody is one of the main sources of the rhythmic texture of the music as a whole. However, in this case it's not the only one, as there's also a rhythmic left-hand accompaniment. This makes it possible to be a little more flexible in how the rhythm of the melody is treated, as you can see from the repeated notes introduced into the repetitions of the opening four-bar phrase. Note how the accompaniment is also varied the second time round, with left-hand notes on the first beat of the bars omitted to produce a syncopated 'backbeat' effect.

Exercise 6.14 CD Tracks 6 (opposite page)
'Kalinka' is a well-known Russian folk-dance melody. First run through the first part a few times so that you're confident with the notes. Notice that the rhythmic variations introduced in the repetitions of the original four-bar phrase are just repetitions of existing notes, and introduce no new time-values. Put a strong accent on the first beat of the bar throughout, but especially in the second part.

Now let's look at how syncopation can work as an essential element within a melody, rather than as just a means for varying it. A good starting point is to take a tune that everyone knows, with lots of syncopation, but begin from a version that has the syncopations removed. Then we can reintroduce them to see what difference they make.

Exercise 6.15 CD Tracks 7–8 (p184)
Here we have two versions of the classic Mexican folk tune 'La Cucaracha'. The first (a) has had the syncopations removed from both the melody and the accompaniment. The second (b) has them in, just like in the original version of the tune. Try playing both versions yourself. Which of them do you think sounds best? Now try adding some more syncopations of your own. What effect do they have on the character of the melody?

Notice that the melody in the last of the above exercises always starts in the middle of the bar (on an 'upbeat'). This is a common effect, known as **anacrusis**, and usually means that each phrase or section likewise ends in the middle of a bar. (In written music with this feature there's a rule that says that the first and last bars should add together to make a single whole bar in the given metre, as in the above examples.)

Working through the above exercises should give you a good initial feel for some of the different ways in which rhythm and melody can be related. Ultimately, though, you'll need to break free from models like these and begin to explore this relationship for yourself. You can do this by taking the many short melodic phrases shown in the examples in Unit Three and combining them in any way you want with the rhythms shown in the examples at the beginning of this unit.

Exercise 6.16
Using the melodic shapes given in Unit Three and the rhythms given in this unit as your source material, try applying a range of different rhythmic forms to individual melodic figures, loosely at first. Each time play around freely at first, using any rhythm you want. Afterwards try to work out exactly what the rhythms are, so you can play them more precisely. Writing down rhythms is especially useful for understanding the exact nature of what you are playing.

UNIT 6 | SECTION 2

LA CUCARACHA

Traditional

Rhythm and harmony

We mostly think of rhythm as affecting how melodies and textures unfold over time. But it also affects harmony, in ways that are independent of melody and other aspects of musical texture. This is because a chord sequence can't be truly effective unless it makes good use of what we call **harmonic rhythm**. Harmonic rhythm is the effect created when the timing of chord changes in the music takes on its own musically significant rhythmic pattern.

In the simplest cases such a pattern just corresponds to the harmony changing at regular intervals of time. The following example consists of a fairly typical chord sequence moving with an underlying harmonic rhythm of one chord per bar, but presented in three different time signatures. Play through the different versions and you'll surely hear for yourself that the underlying effect – the rhythm of the chord changes themselves – stays the same, regardless of the number of beats per bar or any

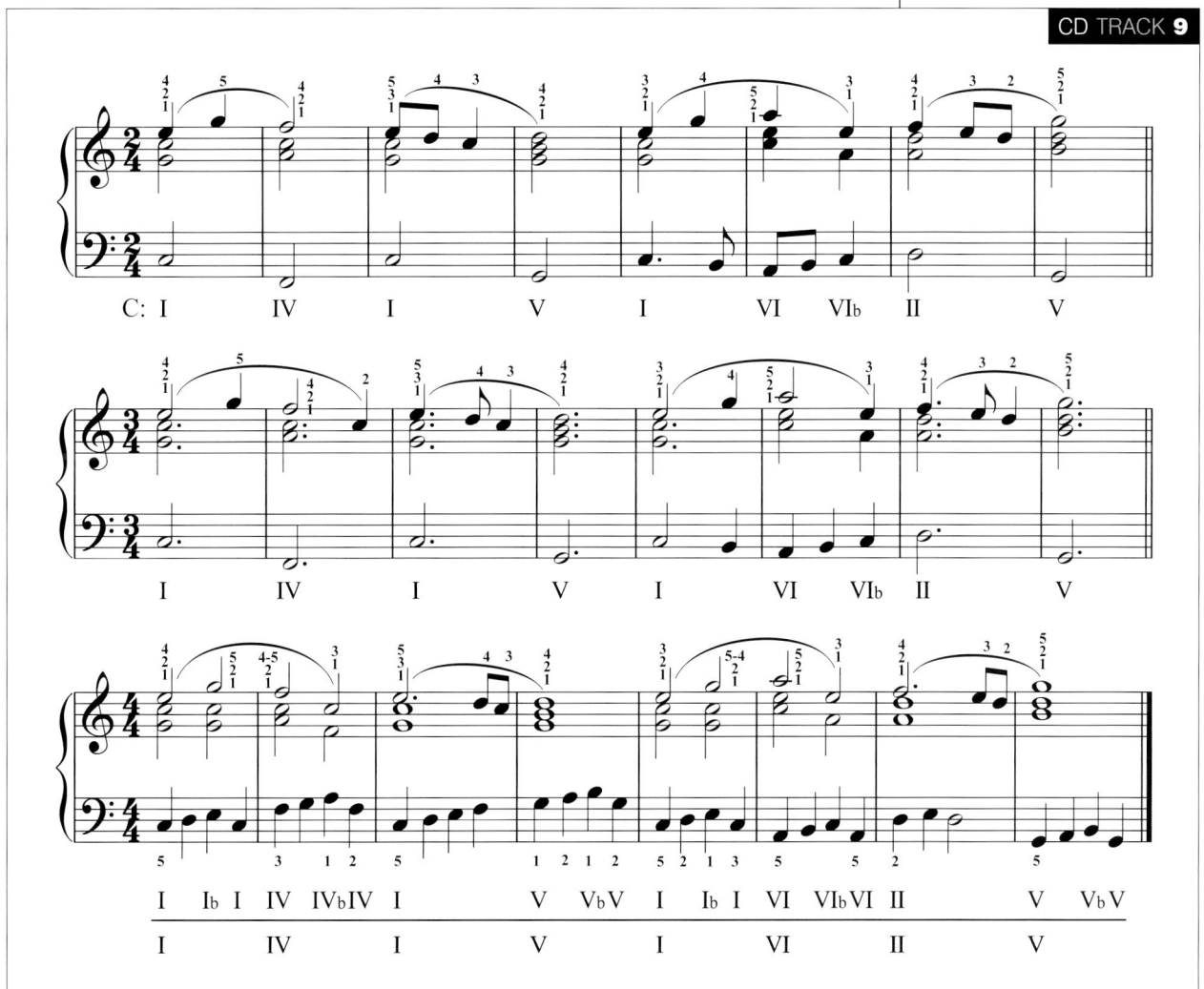

CD TRACK 9

other differences. Note that the additional chord change in bar six doesn't affect the underlying harmonic rhythm. That's because it's only a change of inversion. The same goes for the changes on the third and fourth beats in the bar in the third version. (In the latter case a simplified chord structure is shown beneath the actual chord structure to make clear how the harmonic rhythm is preserved.)

What this shows is that harmonic rhythm is more basic than other aspects of the music's rhythmic structure, since the latter may vary without really affecting it.

Another important consideration is that harmonic rhythm, like almost everything else, develops as the music unfolds. The most common way for this to occur is that the music begins with a regular but fairly relaxed harmonic rhythm. Then, as soon as the pattern starts to sound predictable or an increase in tension is called for, we can increase the pace of harmonic change. Starting off with chord changes spaced fairly widely apart in time leaves lots of room for this, and knowing when to do this is also an important skill – a bit like an actor's sense of timing. Conversely, slowing the harmonic rhythm down can be an effective way of diffusing tension after a climax. In practice most good players quickly come to realise that proper development of the harmonic rhythm is an indispensable tool for maintaining musical interest over the course of their improvisations.

The next example (opposite page, CD track 10) uses the chord structure of a well-known American tune to illustrate how this works even within a relatively short stretch of music. It's worth getting familiar with the chords and melody here: they provide a neat starting point for jazz improvising, similar to those explored later in this book.

In order to get a clearer picture of how the harmonic rhythm develops in the example, let us lay out the chord changes in a diagram:

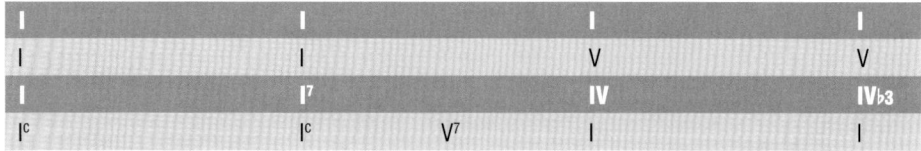

I		I		I		I
I		I		V		V
I		I⁷		IV		IV♭3
Iᶜ		Iᶜ	V⁷	I		I

What this shows is that the rate of harmonic change gradually increases, even while keeping the original pattern as a reference point. The tune as a whole corresponds to 16 bars of music, and naturally divides up into four phrases, each four bars in length. The first of these stays on the tonic (chord I) throughout. The second establishes a rhythm of one change for every two bars, which is maintained by the return to chord I two bars later at the start of the third phrase. The third phrase itself introduces a faster rate of harmonic change, with a new chord in every single bar, but note that the chords in the second and fourth bars of this phrase are no more than variations of the chords on the preceding bars. This means that the underlying harmonic rhythm here is still one change for every two bars. The fourth phrase introduces a further level of development: first it reverts to holding the initial chord for more than a bar, then it introduces a change halfway through the bar, before closing with a return to the more basic rhythm of one

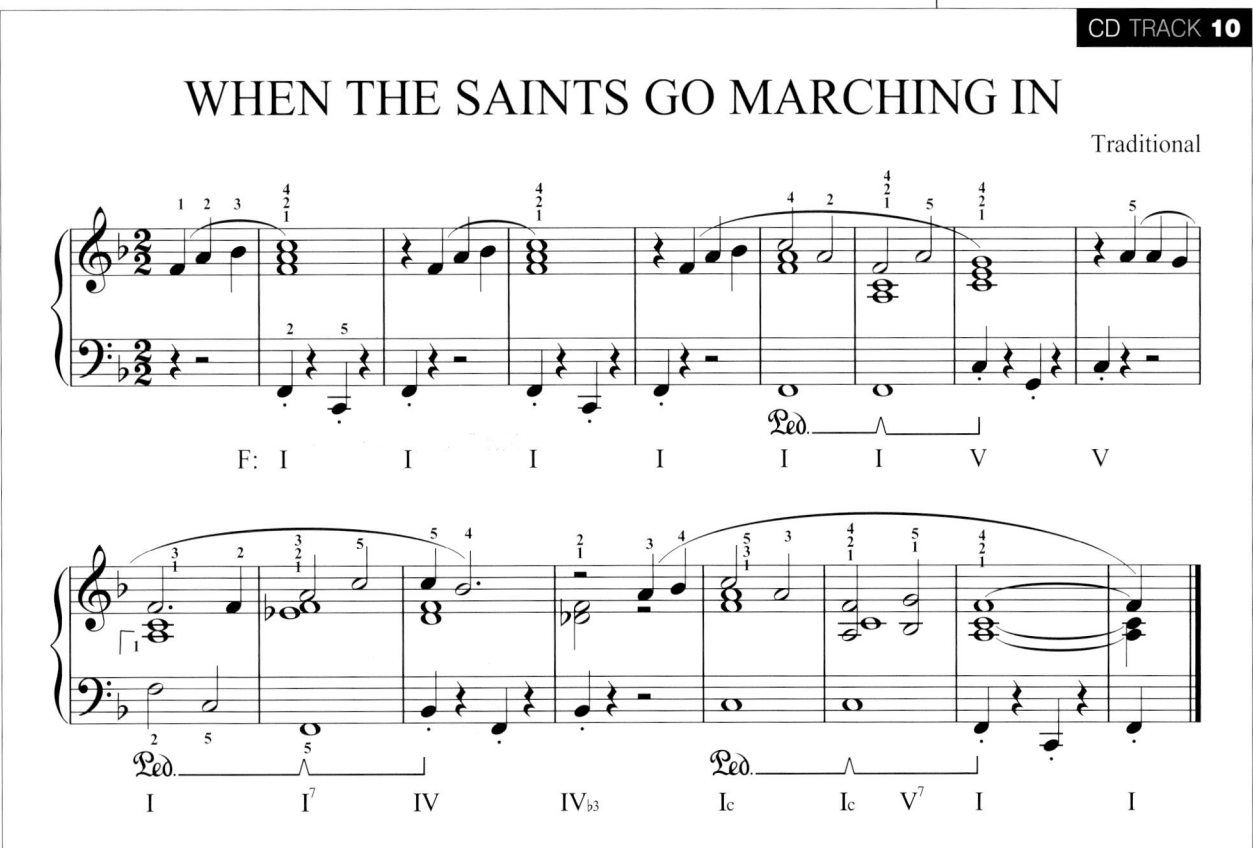

chord for two bars. However, even here there's a sense in which the underlying rhythm is maintained. That's because the I^c and V^7 chords together make up a cadential six-four progression. We know from Unit Four that this is heard less as a chord progression and more as a kind of resolution of dissonant upper parts over a stable dominant in the bass. Hence there's a sense in which these two bars are also heard as a single underlying harmony.

Exercise 6.17.
Now try creating some chord sequences of your own in which the harmonic rhythm is first clearly established and then developed through introducing variations in how rapidly the chord changes occur. You can also try borrowing the opening chord patterns from some well-known tunes, and seeing how those patterns can be developed in terms of their harmonic rhythm – independently of the tunes they were originally created for.

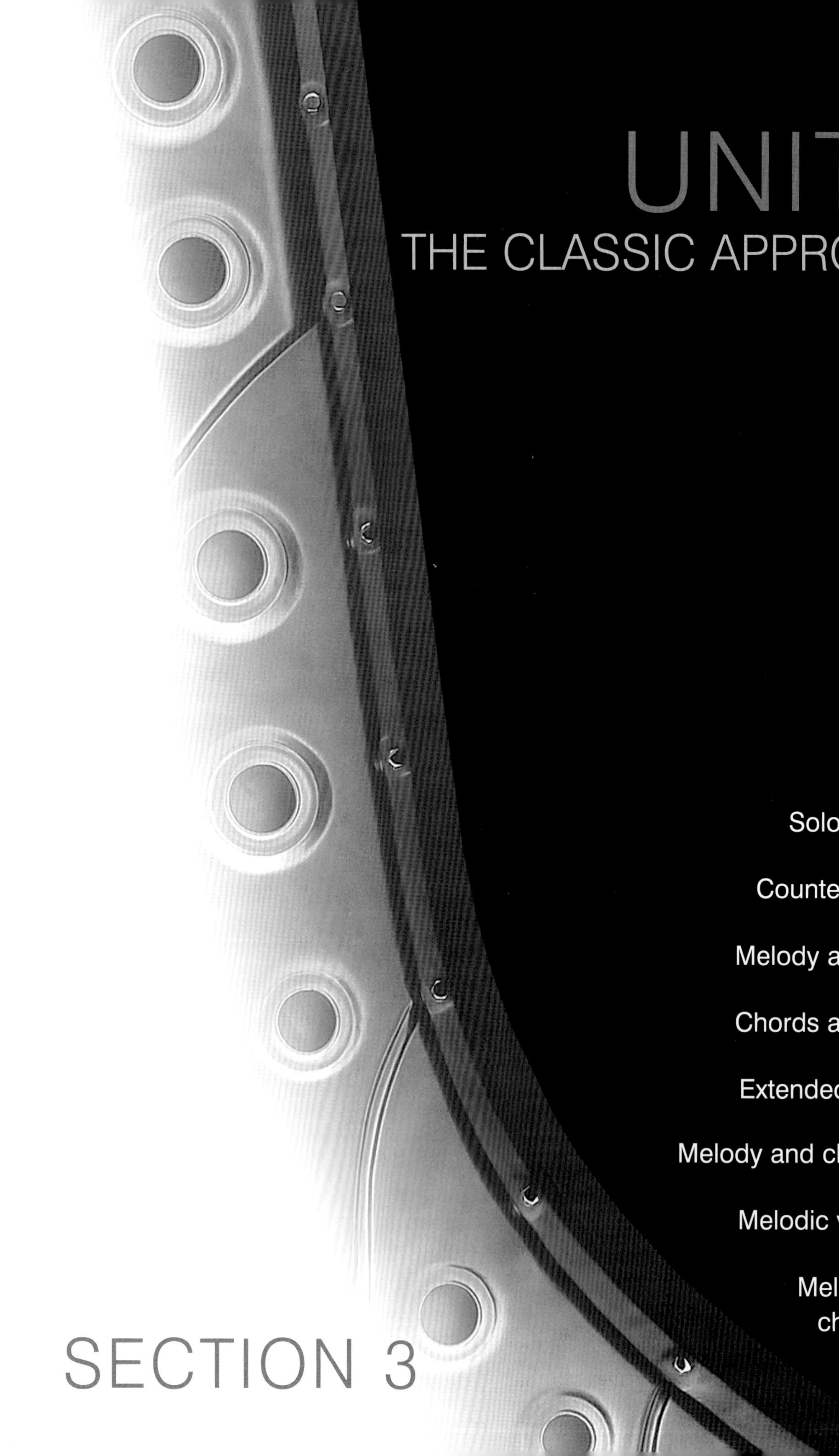

UNIT 7
THE CLASSIC APPROACH

- Solo melody
- Countermelody
- Melody and bass
- Chords and bass
- Extended harmony
- Melody and chords (I)
- Melodic variation
- Melody and chords (II)

SECTION 3

SECTION 3 | UNIT 7

Adopting and exploring the classical approach to improvising needn't involve copying specific musical styles from the past, though it can also serve as a basis for that. There's a set of more basic features of the classical approach that you can learn independently of these styles, and this then leaves you free to apply them to whatever style – classical or contemporary – you wish. The same goes for the jazz approach, and in both cases, the key idea is that mastering the basics independently of this or that style gives you the freedom to make creative use of them as you evolve your own style. (Understanding the classical approach at this level will also better equip you to handle the rock and pop styles explored in the last unit of the book, as these mix elements of both approaches. As we'll see over the course of this unit and the next, what essentially differentiates the classical approach from that of jazz is a different way of thinking about the relation between melody and harmony – especially as regards the role of counterpoint and the treatment of dissonance.)

Solo melody

> **Which first, classical or jazz?** This unit aims to cover the basics of improvisation in mainstream classical music. The next explores the fundamentals of jazz improvisation. In a sense they run parallel to each other. If you're mainly interested in just one of the two styles you can, in principle, skip the other. Alternatively you can choose for yourself which style to explore first, or which to explore in more depth. Bear in mind that the two approaches are complementary – each enriches the other. It's also worth knowing that historically jazz evolved out of a combination of classical music and other influences – not the other way around. So learning about classical improvisation first may give you a better understanding of the origins of jazz. Either way, the remaining units of this book will be a lot more meaningful if you're familiar with the essentials of both approaches.

1) Basic principles of melodic shape

The place to start when learning about the classical approach to improvisation is solo (ie, unaccompanied) melody, for which the technical term is **monody**.

In Unit Three we looked at different kinds of melodic movement, but an actual melody involves far more than just a series of these. Apart from the fact that such movements need to form a satisfying and coherent **shape** or **contour**, there's also the rhythmic and metrical aspect, and harmonic implications to think about too. Although these are all present together in a melody, it's easier to learn about them one by one. We'll start by considering how simple melodic shapes work.

As we've already said, a good melodic shape balances **ascending** with **descending** movements, smaller **steps** with larger **leaps**. It usually has a clearly defined overall shape that involves a **high-point** (ie, a melodic 'climax'), though this may sometimes be withheld to increase the sense of expectation.

When learning to improvise melodies it is important to develop a feel for how these principles of good shape work independently of the scale or harmony used. So it is best to try applying them over a variety of different scales straight away. At the same time, this gives us a chance to start exploring the different possible scales from the very outset.

It is also a good idea to begin by using just fragments of scales – the sort that correspond to standard hand-positions (and their extensions) on the piano. We can do this by initially limiting the melodic **range** or **compass** of the melody. Then we can gradually expand this until we reach the interval of an octave, at which point a complete scale becomes available. Here are some other useful rules of thumb you should know about for good melodic shape:

- Always follow a large leap (eg, a sixth or greater) in one direction with stepwise movement in the opposite direction.
- Always follow a sequence of two successive leaps in the same direction with stepwise movement in the opposite direction.
- Avoid leaps of a tritone (= augmented fourth or diminished fifth), a major seventh, or any interval greater than an octave.
- Avoid two or more movements in the same direction that together form a tritone, a major seventh, or any interval greater than an octave.

> **Strict or free?** It's important to realise that just as there are a variety of styles within classical music, there are a variety of versions of the rules governing things like melody and harmony – some stricter, some freer. Generally, the older the style the stricter the rules. The principles given here are meant to serve as a sensible compromise between the extremes of early classical music on the one hand and modern approaches on the other. We'll discuss differences of style within classical music in more depth in Unit Ten. At that point you'll be in a position to decide whether you want to take your approach further in the direction of earlier or later styles of classical improvising.

2) Getting started

Okay, so you've decided to try improvising a solo melody, and you've read through the rules in the section above. You're sitting at the keyboard, and you're looking at all those black and white piano keys. At this point you're bound to have the same thought as every student of improvisation who comes up against a similar situation: "Where on earth do I start?"

It seems like the six million dolllar question, but actually there's a simple and obvious answer. The secret is to begin by thinking of each and every melodic shape as unfolding with reference to a single dominant melodic movement. Let's call this the **guiding movement**.

For the sake of musical interest this guiding movement normally tends to be a leap rather than a step. What this means in practice is that for each melodic shape we first take one particular leap as a point of departure; then we explore the different ways in which the melody can unfold, after we have committed ourselves to allowing this particular movement to play a guiding role.

The simplest thing is to just begin with the guiding movement itself: just play it! Then follow it straight away with stepwise movement, keeping in mind the rules for melodic shape mentioned above.

> The **guiding movement technique** is widely used in Indian classical improvisation – probably the most sophisticated tradition of improvisation there is; yet actually it works in any style when the focus is on monody (ie, solo melody). The basic idea is that we treat each melodic phrase as a melodic embellishment or decoration of a single interval.

There's another important aspect to consider. The guiding movement you use and how you go about unfolding a shape around it will be determined in part by what notes you can easily get to, given the particular hand position from which you start. (We're assuming here that you want to play legato, so issues of fingering connected with joining notes smoothly to one another definitely apply.) For this reason it's best to start by focusing on shapes that can be developed using a given set of notes corresponding to either a single standard hand-position, one of its extensions, or a combination of positions that we can move between easily.

This is the focus of the exercises below. In each case the same positions and guiding movements are reproduced over several scale-fragments to illustrate how basic features of melodic contour remain unaffected by differences in the scale material used. Some sample shapes are given, just as a guide to get you started with your own explorations. These are rhythmically free, but you can vary timing as well. Also, why not try transposing your own melodic shapes to other keys?

(You'll probably want to focus mainly on playing melodies with your right hand, so the examples are given in treble clef with right-hand fingering above the stave. But there's nothing to stop you using these exercises as a starting point for left-hand melodic improvising too: just follow the fingering below the stave, playing the notes an octave lower than written.)

Exercise 7.1
We'll begin with a standard five-finger hand position covering a range of a fifth. First play through the examples, listening for how the different kinds of movement used fit together to make a musically satisfying shape. Then improvise your own shapes using the same hand positions. Be sure to try out each shape over all of the scale-fragments given in the model examples.

Exercise 7.2

Now here's something similar, but this time extending the five-finger hand position so that it covers a range of a sixth. Once again first try the examples given, then improvise your own.

UNIT 7 | SECTION 3

Exercise 7.3
Now one more set, this time extending the hand position to cover a seventh.

Expanding the melodic range to an octave or more when improvising brings with it the need to be aware of fingering issues. It's usually at this stage that you need to start to think of the melodic compass as breaking down into two or more of the sort of hand positions you've just been exploring. These can then be linked by the same sort of techniques used when fingering scales: ie, the passing of the thumb under the third or fourth finger, and the reverse movement, where we bring the third or fourth finger over the thumb. Alternatively, we can shift hand position more gradually by bringing the thumb up next to the third or fourth finger (or to the second finger in cases where this has already moved away from the thumb).

Once the compass of the melody extends to an octave we find we're looking at a complete scale, which means we can now vary the source material in another way – through the choice of which type of scale we're going to use. The simplest way is to take the major scale, but start on notes other than the tonic. The resulting scales are similar to those used in early classical music – known as the **church modes**. (These also show up in jazz, as we'll see in the next unit. From now on we'll refer to them just as **modes**.) Here are the basic seven modes of the major scale, the first of which corresponds to the major scale itself:

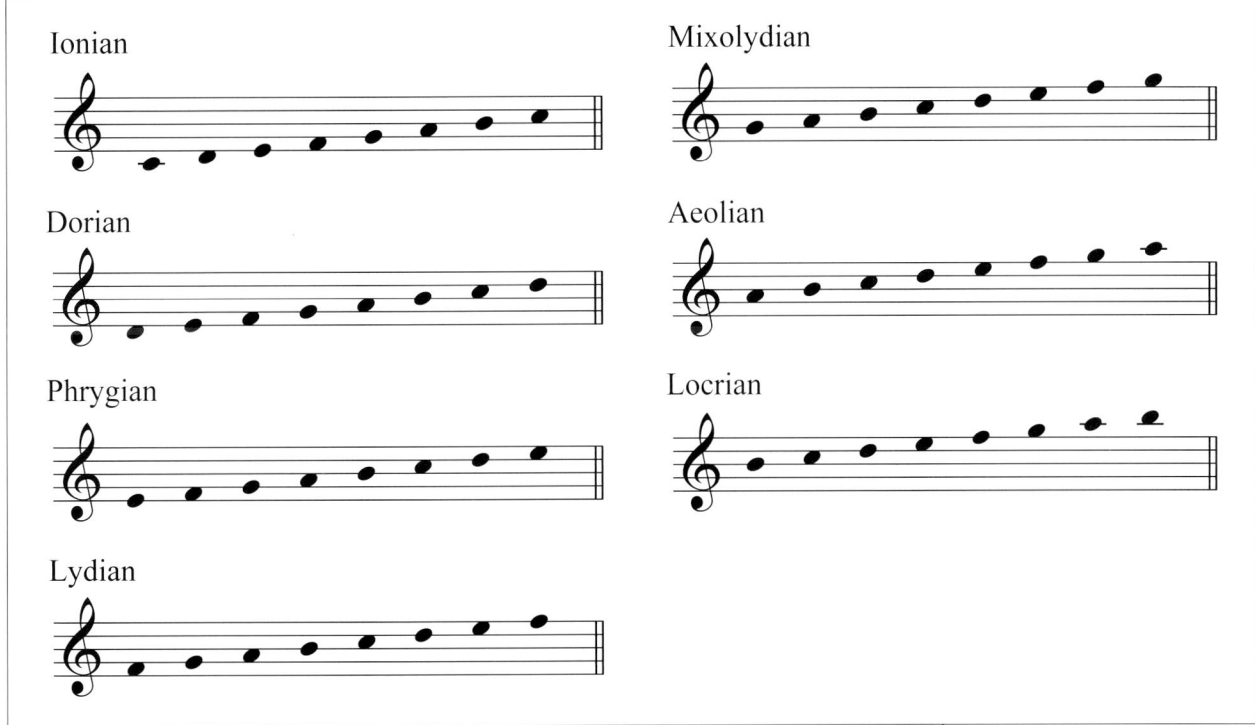

Of these the ones you're most likely to use (apart from the Ionian, which is just the same as C major) are the Dorian and Aeolian, which we now mostly hear as variants of the minor scale. (You should remember from Unit One that the Aeolian mode corresponds to the form of the minor scale used in a lot of rock music – the 'rock minor'

– as well as to the descending form of the classical melodic minor scale.) Hence it makes sense to think of these as forming an expanded set of options, together with classical minor scales, for minor-key improvisation. This is how these look, based on a common starting note of A:

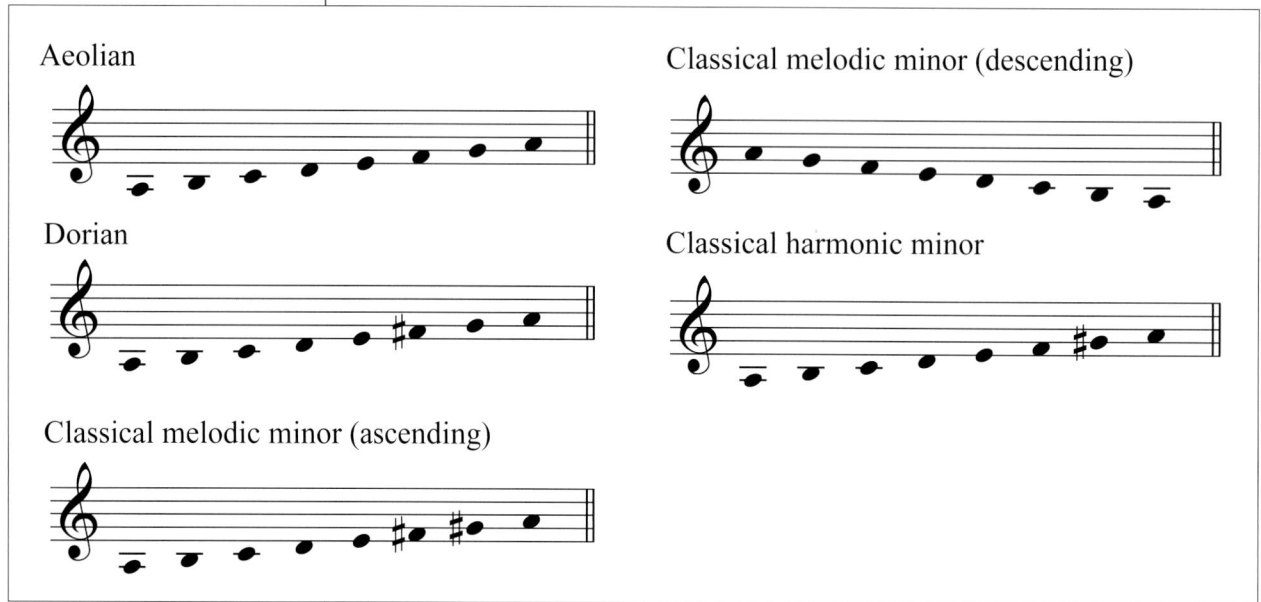

Taking these together with the major scale itself gives us a good range of scale-types as source material. At this stage it can be instructive to explore putting individual melodic shapes through a variety of different modes and scales based on the same starting note. This will give you a heightened awareness of how the choice of scale material affects the expressive character of particular shapes. (Note that some intervals have to be changed to accommodate the fact that tritones occur in different places depending on the scale used.)

3) Adding rhythm, metre, and phrase structure
When improvising solo melodies there are two approaches you can take:

- Melodic shape comes first, rhythm after.
- Melodic shape and rhythm come together from the start.

In the first case, we initially focus just on finding good melodic shapes, without worrying about rhythm. This is a lot easier in the earlier stages of learning to improvise, and it also allows you to play around afterwards with different rhythmic possibilities for the same melodic shape. (Keeping the rhythm loose and vague in the early stages is also good if you're the sort of person who could benefit from a more relaxed approach to improvising – this can help classical musicians especially.) However, you'll pretty quickly find that many of your melodic ideas come with their rhythmic character clearly defined right from the outset: in these cases it makes sense to treat rhythm and melodic shape as equally basic. Either way, as soon as you introduce rhythm you'll need to think about metre and phrase structure too.

A melody with a definite rhythm will always imply a definite metre (corresponding to one of the time signatures when written out), and you'll need to know what this is in order to continue the melody in a rhythmically consistent and satisfying way. Unless you plan to note down your ideas, though, you won't need to determine the exact time values. What you must decide right away is just whether the music you're creating has two, three, or four beats to a bar, and whether the typical subdivision of these beats is into halves (simple time) or thirds (compound time).

You must also be aware of where each melodic phrase starts and finishes in relation to the metrical cycle. As soon as you've got a melodic idea you want to take further, ask yourself whereabouts in it the first beat of the bar (the strong beat) comes. Although most phrases start and finish at the same point in the cycle, this need not correspond to the first beat of the bar.

Melodies frequently start on an upbeat, just before the downbeat at the beginning of the bar (and the metrical cycle). In such cases you'll normally find each successive phrase starts at a similar point (at least within one section or stretch of music), and the last phrase ends just before such a point is reached. This is **anacrusis**. (In written music it corresponds to the practice of writing an incomplete bar at the start and end of a piece that together add up to one complete bar of music.)

You also need to consider **phrase structure**. Most melodies consist of short phrases that link together to make a longer line. Successive phrases are heard as complementing and balancing one another, usually in pairs: these in turn tend to be heard as forming larger phrases which likewise complement and balance one another, and so on. Within each pair the most common relationship between phrases is one which resembles a **question and answer** in spoken discourse: the first phrase opens out or ascends in a way that raises expectations, and these are then fulfilled or answered by the second phrase, which returns back roughly to where the first phrase began, often with a descending movement.

4) Harmonic implications

More often than not the particular scale that serves as source material for a melody will result in it having certain harmonic implications: that is, at certain points we can't help feeling the implied presence of a particular chord derived from the scale. We tend to be aware of these implications even if the melody is played without any actual accompanying texture. This means that in order to make a solo melody sound good we must take account of these implications while improvising. So improvising a solo melody usually means creating not just a logical series of melodic movements, a satisfying melodic shape, and a coherent rhythmic and metrical structure, but also an implied chord structure that would make sense when realised as sounding chords.

> **Remember:** a melody is always more than the sum of its parts. It's really something unique that emerges from the interaction of melodic movement and shape, timing, rhythm, and metre, and harmonic implications – not to mention the expressive nuances of volume, texture, colour, articulation, and timing resulting from the way it is played.

This connection between melody and implied harmony is actually a two-way relationship. While the melody itself implies a harmonic structure, it's also the case that we hear the structure of the melody in terms of how it relates to the harmony. This is especially important in classical music, which makes an important distinction between those notes in a melody which belong to the harmony and those that don't. The former are called **harmony notes**, the latter **non-harmony notes**. To explore what this means in practice let's take a few well known melodies and see how they work.

> One of the main differences between classical music and other styles is the fact that in the former there are precise rules for how non-harmony notes should occur in a melody. Even so, just how strictly these rules are applied can vary, depending on the nature of the melody and the particular style involved. This is especially the case when the melody has originated as a folk tune: folk melodies and styles have often evolved with only limited reference to the harmonic system of Western classical music.

The first example is a major-key tune: 'Camptown Races'. (This is a popular choice amongst beginners as a jumping-off point for improvising because of its very straightforward implied chord structure.) The upper staff shows the melody. The lower staff shows the implied harmony, written out just as simple root position chords without any attempt at voice-leading. (The implied chords are also indicated using Roman numerals, but showing the actual notes of each implied chord allows us to see more easily which notes in the melody are harmony notes and which not. This is something you should be able to do in your own mind before too long, based on just the chord symbols or your own reading of the harmonic implications of the melody itself. You'll get a chance to practise that later in the book.)

The chords follow a simple but effective pattern, which nevertheless maintains variety and interest with a change in the harmonic rhythm in bars 7, 11, and 15 (from one chord change for every two bars to one per bar) and by using chord IV as a further contrast to I in the second half, above and beyond chord V as in the first half. Only primary triads are used. Non-harmony notes are marked with an asterisk. (Note how few there are.) In classical music non-harmony notes are almost always followed

SECTION 3 UNIT 7

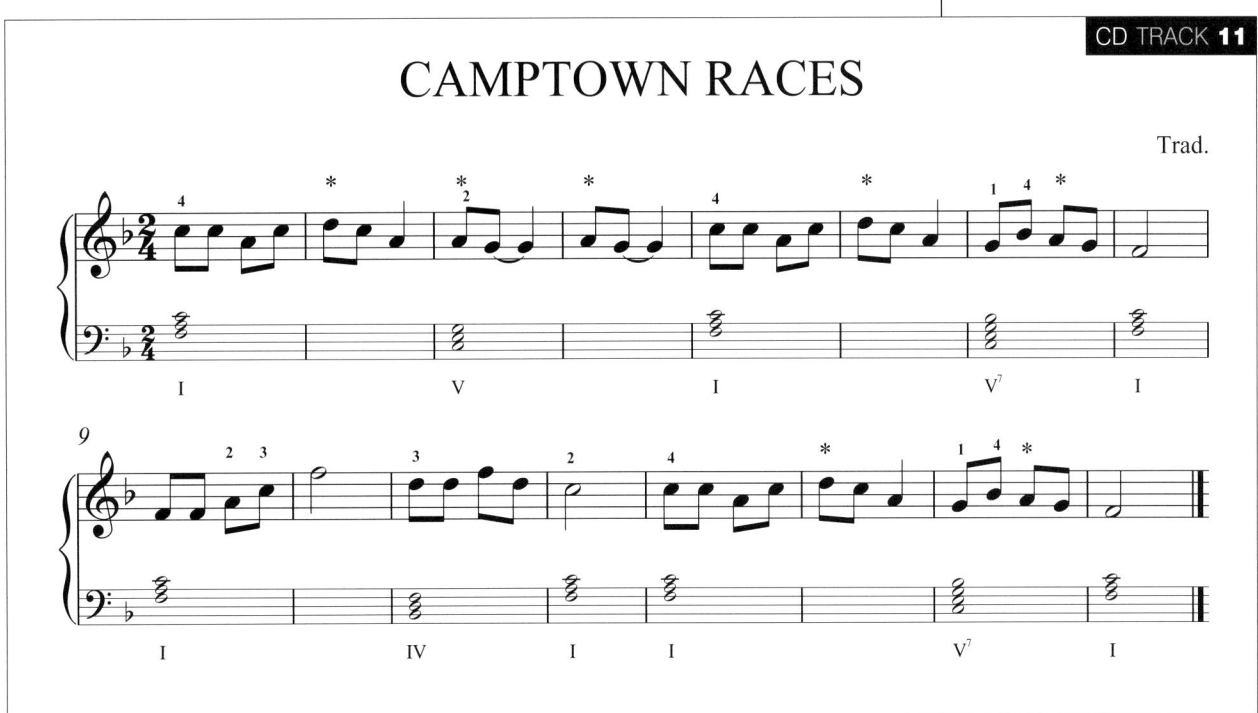

immediately by stepwise movement to a note that is a harmony note (relative to the same chord). ('Escape notes' are the one exception to this – see below.) You can see that this happens in every case here.

Classical music also classifies the types of non-harmony notes that can occur in a melody in more precise ways. The most common type are **passing notes**: with these the non-harmony note is approached and quitted by step. In the above example all the non-harmony notes are passing notes, and because they all occur on (rather than between) beats they are called **accented passing notes.**

Now for a couple of minor-key examples. The first is 'Hatikva' (over the page), a classic Jewish melody based on the harmonic minor scale. (Only the first part of this tune is given here.) In this case you can see that the non-harmony notes in bars 1 and 5 occur between beats, so they're what we call **unaccented passing notes**. The same goes for the non-harmony note in bar 2 and the first one in bar 6, except that in these cases the notes before and after are the same, so that we hear the non-harmony note as moving by step away from and back to a harmony note: this makes it an **auxiliary note**. (More specifically, a **lower auxiliary**, as it moves to the note a step below the harmony note, whereas an **upper auxiliary** moves to the note a step above and back.)

Now take a look at the non-harmony notes in bars 4 and 8. In each case the first is clearly another lower auxiliary note, but what about the second? It doesn't move by step to the next note, so it can't be a passing note. It's what's known as an **escape note** – a note that precedes a step or a leap with one (or more) steps in the opposite direction.

Finally, consider the second non-harmony note in bar 6. This note also doesn't

UNIT 7 | SECTION 3

move by step to the next note so it, too, can't be a passing note, but neither is it an escape note. Hence it falls outside of what's acceptable under the strictest application of classical rules. (Note that the melody in question is a traditional Jewish folk tune rather than the work of a classical composer.)

Now look at our second minor-key example. It's the classic English melody 'Scarborough Fair'. This melody has a strongly modal character. (The combination of flattened seventh but unflattened sixth relative to the major scale identifies it as the Dorian mode in the first half, but this shifts to the Aeolian mode in the second half, with the flattened sixth of the scale appearing as a bass note towards the end.) Apart from the upper auxiliary in bar 3 and the unaccented passing notes in bars 11 and 15, it contains several examples of non-harmony notes not resolved by step (see bars 5, 6, and 14) but which are not 'escape notes'. In bar 10 note how the non-harmony note precedes an instance of the same note as a harmony note on a stronger beat, so in this case we hear the preceding instance of the same note as a decorative **anticipation** of this. However, in the other three cases this does not happen, and this means that they are not in line with strict classical principles. (This is hardly surprising here, given that the melody almost certainly comes from the period before tonal harmony was fully established as the basis for classical music. It's also worth noting that these problematic notes all correspond to either the seventh or sixth of the chord beneath them: under the looser approach of jazz, rock, and some latter styles of classical music this allows them

to be viewed as harmony notes, providing we think of the chords themselves as including the seventh or sixth. We'll discuss this more in the next unit.)

Bar 7 shows another way of using non-harmony notes typical of classical music. In this case the note in question (the B) is approached by a leap but quitted (and resolved) by step. This is known as an **appoggiatura**. The resolution (to C-sharp) moves stepwise in one direction before leaping in the other direction (to A), so we also have here another instance of an **escape note**. (Sometimes we encounter the reverse movement as well: the melody first leaps past the note to which it's really heading, then finally gets to the latter via stepwise movement in the opposite direction to the leap. This is a **cambiata**.)

There remains one more commonly used formula in classical music for the treatment of non-harmony notes – the **suspension**. However, because of the especially important role that suspensions play in contrapuntal music, we'll put off exploring this to the next section.

The key point is that grasping the harmonic implications of a melody enables us to hear some notes as decorative and others as more structural, based on how they stand relative to the chords implied by the melody itself.

5) Melodic continuation

When improvising melody lines there are many possible techniques we can use to continue a melodic line beyond an initial idea. Taking a closer look at a couple of the preceding examples will give us some ideas about how we can do this. Here's 'Camptown Races' again, this time showing how phrase structure and other features contribute to its unfolding:

UNIT 7 | SECTION 3

First we have a two-bar idea, characterised by a combination of repeated notes, a leap of a third, and then stepwise movement. This forms the first half of a four-bar phrase.

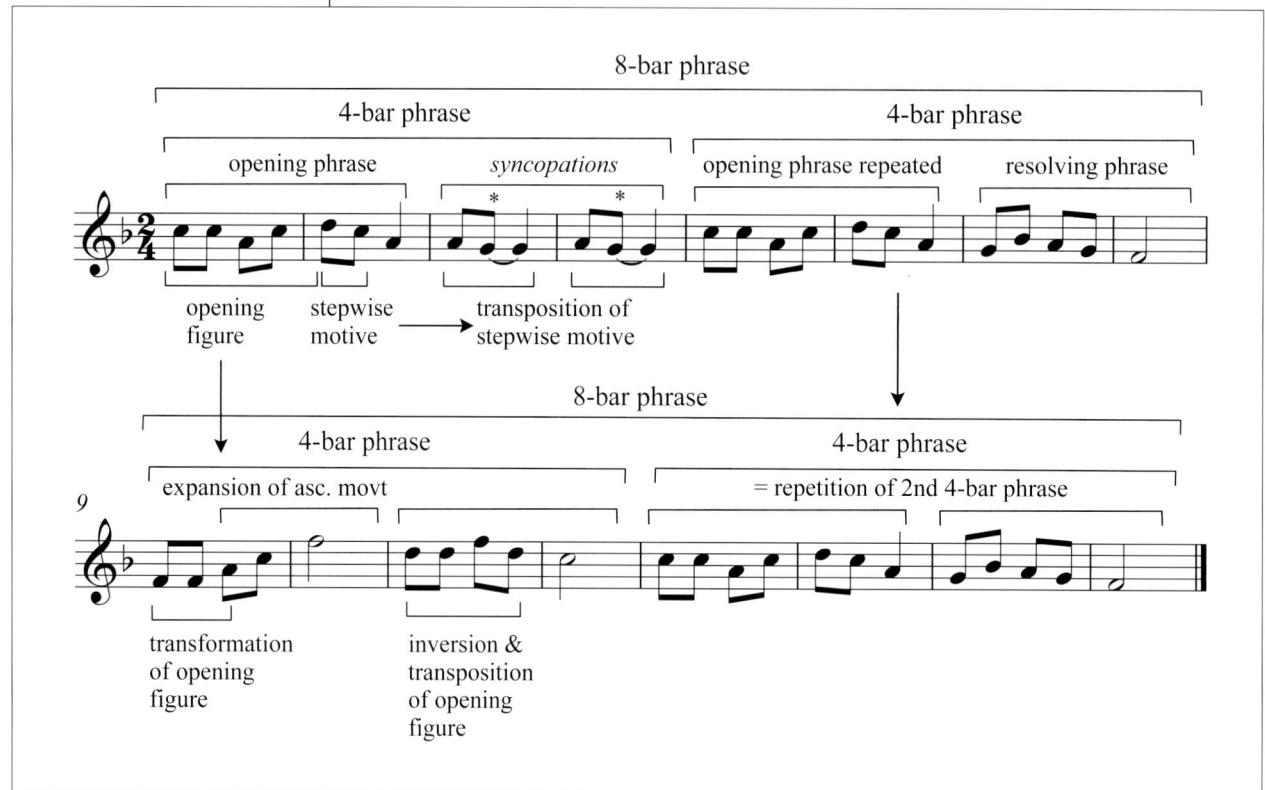

In the second half of this four-bar structure the stepwise figure at the start of bar 2 is then developed as a separate **motive**. The motive is **transposed**, with the second note held on over the beat time to produce a **syncopation** that generates a sense of rhythmic tension that must then be resolved in the next four-bar phrase. The latter repeats the opening idea but follows it with a phrase that answers the melodic character of the preceding material more clearly than the first time round, while also resolving the overall contour and harmonic implications of the eight-bar structure by descending stepwise to the tonic over an implied perfect cadence.

The second eight-bar structure then seeks to maintain the musical interest of the line by introducing a further level of contrast with the opening. The first eight bars featured isolated leaps of a third combined with stepwise movement. Now the opening idea is **transformed** in various ways (eg, the lowering of the repeated notes so that they are a third below rather than a third above the next note). The rising leap of a third in the original shape is **extended** into an ascending one-octave arpeggio figure, thanks to which the compass of the line is expanded in an upwards direction. In bar 11 the same opening figure is then restated but **transposed** to a higher pitch. It is also subjected to a change known as melodic **inversion** in which ascending movements are replaced by descending ones of equivalent size, and vice versa.

Finally we have a repeat of the second four-bar phrase, whose melodic resolution and implied harmonic resolution now serve to round off the whole 16-bar structure. The overall feeling is that a balance has been achieved between unity and continuity on the one hand and variety and contrast on the other.

Now here's 'Scarborough Fair' again, but with the phrase structure and other features of the melodic unfolding marked.

In this case we also have a regular phrase structure with four-bar phrases linked to create eight-bar units that in turn create a 16-bar structure. Each four-bar phrase begins with two bars featuring a dance-like rhythm, followed by one bar of more continuous

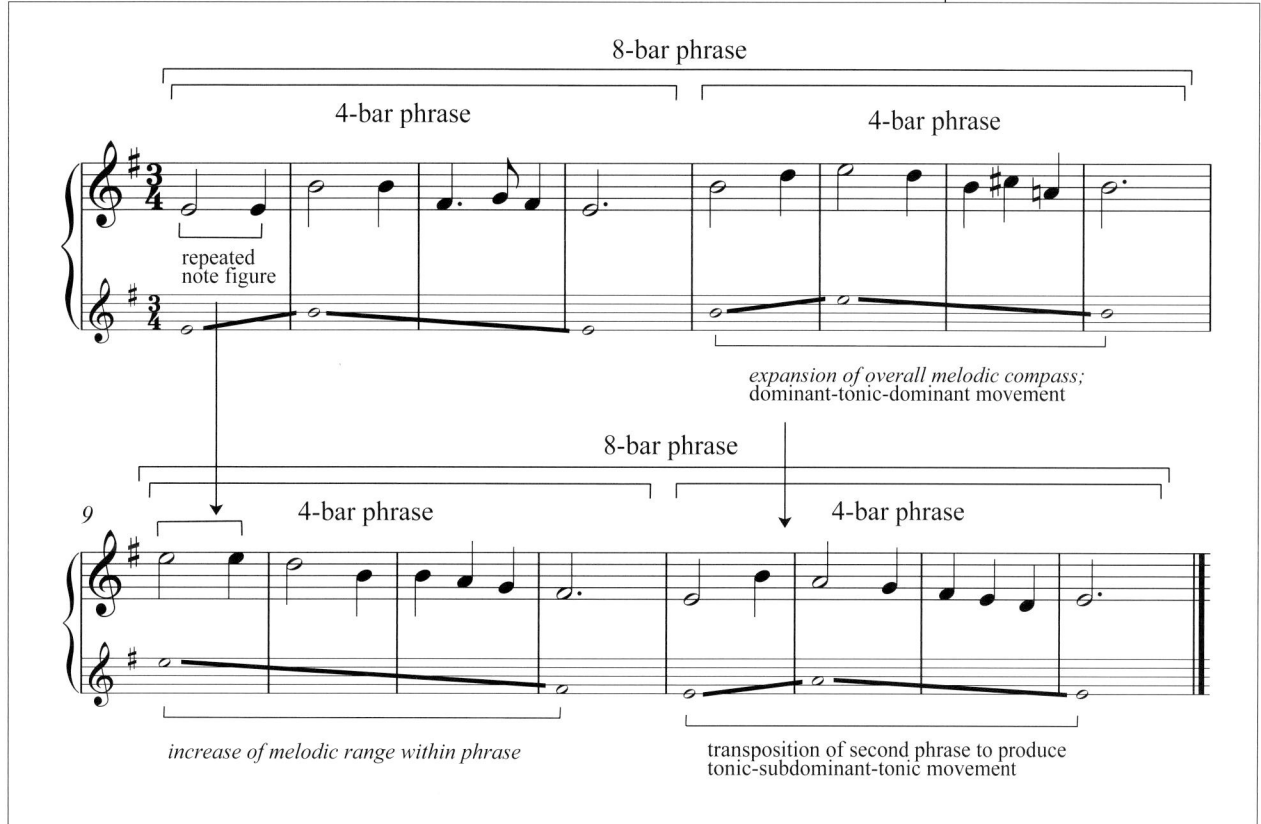

rhythmic movement leading to a held note in the fourth bar. Nevertheless, with each new phrase there's **variation** in the melodic shape and compass.

Note how the first and third phrases begin with a repeated-note figure, whereas the second and fourth replace this with an ascending leap. What's striking is how the melodic outline and compass evolve from one phrase to the next: this is what gives the melody its overall feeling of inevitability and balance, so it's highlighted here on the lower staff.

An important role is also played by **transposition**: the third phrase begins by transposing the opening up an octave, before moving down towards the same A that appears at the end of bar 2. Meanwhile the fourth phrase transposes the essential notes of the second phrase down a perfect fifth: this means that the underlying movement from dominant to tonic to dominant in bars 5-8 becomes a movement from tonic to subdominant to tonic in bars 13-16. This in turn creates a powerful sense of melodic resolution at the end of the whole 16-bar structure.

Now it's time to get to work applying some of these techniques in practice, as part of what's involved when improvising. In the exercise on the opposite page each four-bar phrase calls for an answering phrase of equivalent length. The harmonic implications are pretty straightforward, but to make it easier they're shown using Roman numerals, and the key is indicated.

Exercise 7.4
First play through each four-bar phrase several times, so you develop a feeling for where it wants to go. It can also help to play the chords for the whole eight-bar sequence through a few times in your left hand, as simple triads. This will give you a feeling for the harmonic structure of the overall phrase, which will help you to decide how the melody should be continued.

Exercise 7.5
Now try improvising your own four-bar opening phrases, and afterwards see if you can continue them using a similar approach to that of the previous exercise. Once again, it can help to explore the harmonic structure first, and to play through the first phrase several times before attempting a continuation.

Countermelody

Now that we've learned about how solo melodies work it's time to look at what's involved in combining a melody with other things. The first stage of this involves exploring simple forms of **polyphony** – that's the name for a musical texture in which two or more independent melody lines are combined.

In classical music there are special techniques for combining melodies together to produce a satisfying texture: the overall name for these is **counterpoint**. The aim of good counterpoint is to make sure that at any point in time the different melodic parts are clearly audible independently of one another, while at the same time producing satisfying combinations of sounds. This means paying careful attention to the way the lines are related, not just in terms of consonance and dissonance, but also in terms of melodic shape and rhythm.

The best way to learn about counterpoint is to begin with a simple melodic part given in advance, and to learn to create another melody sounding alongside it. The given melody is known as the **cantus** (short for cantus firmus, which means 'fixed song' in Latin), while the new part that we have to create is known as the **countermelody** (or the **counterpoint**). It's worth remembering that the art of improvising a countermelody is thought to have been central to the training of musicians in much of the period of early classical music (ie, the late Middle Ages).

> In its earlier stages of development classical music mostly consisted of polyphonic textures, created using a very strict style of counterpoint. Because later styles of classical music evolved out of these earlier polyphonic styles, they are also based around an understanding of contrapuntal relations between parts, even when this is not obvious from the music itself. That's why the best route to learning to improvise in any classical style is to begin by learning to improvise simple countermelodies. Above all, this will sensitise your musical ear to the subtle ways in which classical music handles consonance and dissonance in respect of the relations between melodic parts. This in turn provides the proper basis for understanding how techniques of melodic decoration work in classical music – techniques central to classical improvisation. Keep in mind, though, that you don't need to become fluent in this to benefit from it as an improviser: even just learning the basic rules and hearing the difference they make will help when you come to explore how melody works over chords and a bassline.

When studying counterpoint for the purpose of improvisation we follow the same procedure as when learning to compose it. Each of the four basic forms of contrapuntal combination – known as different **species** of counterpoint – is first explored separately. Only then can we experiment with mixing them up to make what's called **florid counterpoint**. Of course improvising requires us to make decisions much more quickly than composing, so it's necessary to accept some practical limitations:

- We'll apply the rules of counterpoint a bit more loosely than when composing (though the really essential principles remain the same).
- We'll limit the exercise to two-part textures. (Since it's the contrapuntal relationship between just two parts that serves as the basis for the subsequent development in classical music of the special relationship between the melody and the bassline, this isn't a serious constraint.)
- In classical counterpoint the countermelody can be added above or below the cantus. Here we just focus on adding it above. That's because improvising a countermelody above a cantus offers the best preparation for improvising a melody above a bassline or chords, which is the basis of later classical styles.

This allows us to focus on learning how to improvise a countermelody in the right hand while playing the given line or cantus in the left hand. When studying individual species of counterpoint the cantus is always given as a rhythmically straightforward line that consists of just equal whole notes. It invariably starts on the Tonic or Dominant and always ends on the Tonic, usually preceded by the Supertonic. For the sake of consistency with later harmonic developments in classical music, it's best to focus initially on using just the major and harmonic minor scales. (Afterwards you can try out all of the same techniques again, using the melodic minor scale or modes such as Aeolian or Dorian instead.)

In all forms of counterpoint we try to achieve a balance between different kinds of relation between the movements of the individual parts. There are three possible relations:

- In **similar motion** the parts move together in the same direction.
- In **oblique motion** one part moves while the other does not.
- In **contrary motion** the parts move in opposite directions at the same time.

In practice this means avoiding excessive reliance on just one of these forms of movement. However, we must be especially careful to avoid extended passages of either similar or oblique motion. Contrary motion is the least problematic and can be used more extensively, though some variety is still preferable.

1) First Species

In First Species the countermelody and the cantus move together simultaneously in the simplest possible rhythmic relationship, with one whole note sounding in the former for each whole note in the latter. The golden rule is that in each case the two notes sounding together must form a consonance – an octave, perfect fifth, major or minor third, or major or minor sixth. (Note that for the purposes of counterpoint the interval of a perfect fourth counts as a dissonance.) Apart from this, there are a few other rules you need to keep in mind. (Some of these will apply to other species of counterpoint as well.)

- Follow the basic principles of melodic shape mentioned at the start of this unit.
- Avoid consecutive octaves and fifths.
- Octaves and fifths should not be approached in similar motion (ie, both parts moving in the same direction) unless the upper part moves by step.

> Note that in counterpoint there's also another interval that counts as a consonance: it's what we call a **unison**. A unison occurs when two voices or instruments sing the same pitch simultaneously. Of course this is an impossibility when realising counterpoint on a keyboard instrument like the piano, but it's important nevertheless. The chief reference point for early classical music was polyphonic vocal textures with several voices singing together (so that they can sing in unison if they wish). Because of this fact, even when creating or hearing such textures on the piano we operate as if such a possibility existed. However, unisons can only be used in the very first and last bars, so the rest of the time you can forget about them.

- When both parts move by step, make sure that a note in one part and the next note in the other part don't form an interval of an augmented fourth.
- When the parts move in similar motion don't use more than three consecutive thirds or sixths.
- Don't double the leading note (ie, the seventh of the scale).
- In the closing cadence, if the cantus descends by step from the supertonic to the tonic then the countermelody should ascend by step from the leading note to the tonic.

Finally there are three other issues to consider:

- Overlapping and crossing of parts. In strict counterpoint the parts may cross, but may not overlap. (Overlapping of parts occurs when the lower part moves above where the upper part was just beforehand, but remains below where it is now, or where the upper part moves below where the lower part was just beforehand, but remains above where it is now.) However, crossing of parts is also best avoided when improvising counterpoint on modern keyboard instruments as it makes fingering difficult and may require crossing of the hands.
- Harmonic implications. Historically, the classical system of chord-based harmony emerged gradually out of the polyphonic textures that resulted when early classical composers and improvisers made use of species counterpoint. For this reason, although such techniques predate chordal harmony, they are usually employed with at least some reference to the harmonic (ie, chordal) implications that result. This means, above all, being aware of the fact that when an interval implies a particular chord, this may be in either root position or first inversion, depending on which progression is more desirable. (See Unit Four for guidelines about what makes for a good chord progression.) We've already seen that chord III and chord VII in root position are best avoided. So when we encounter the third or seventh of the scale in the lower part we'll treat that note as the third rather than the root of the chord – as implying I^b or V^b (instead of III or VII). It's also worth realising that the second and fourth of the scale can each occur as either the root of a chord (II and IV respectively) or the third (VII^b and II^b respectively). When using the melodic minor scale we have to be aware that the ascending form of the scale has a raised sixth. As with the raised seventh of the harmonic minor, this can't be treated as a root, so we always understand it as the third of a first inversion chord (IV^b).
- Metrical implications. Due to its lack of fully defined harmonic implications, early classical polyphony is often metrically vague. This is especially the case with First Species, in as much as there are no rhythmic subdivisions whatsoever within the basic time value of a whole note. Keeping the metre vague is an advantage when first learning to improvise polyphonic textures, as it simplifies things, but where there are harmonic implications these will often suggest a metrical grouping of two, three or four whole notes. (The implied metre is shown in the examples and

exercises below by using conventional barlines before metrically stressed beats and dashed barlines the rest of the time.)

Below and on pages 210-211 are examples of successful First Species counterpoint, using first the major scale, then the harmonic minor, and finally the melodic minor, followed by some exercises to help you practice this. (Remember that the lower part here is always the cantus and the upper part the countermelody.)

Note the figure '6' placed under certain notes in the lower part: this indicates that the implied harmony at those points will be a chord in first inversion rather than root position. It's an example of what is known as **figured bass** notation.

> **Figured bass** notation was widely used in written out keyboard music of the 17th and 18th centuries. It meant that keyboard players wishing to improvise their own textures and melodies above a given bassline could read off the harmonic implications without any problems. Numbers placed below the bassline indicate the implied chords by stating what intervals are formed between the bass note and other notes sounding as part of the chord. These follow the same logic as the traditional numbering used with Roman numerals to indicate chord inversions. It's worth turning back to Unit Four to make sure you're familiar with this. Hence, for example, '6' is short for 'six-three', which indicates first inversion, while an absence of any numbers indicates root position.

D major

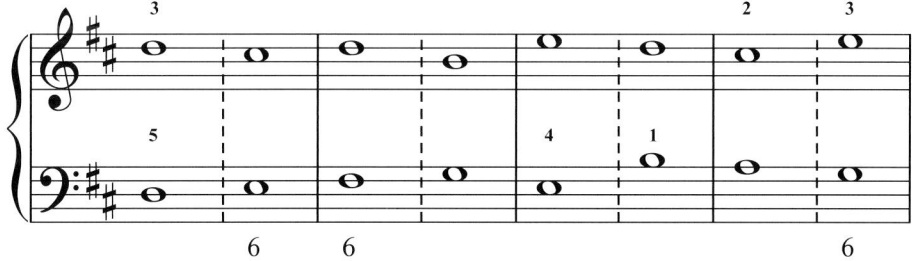

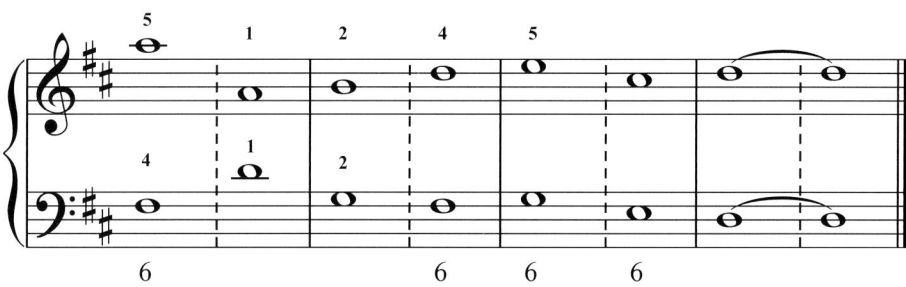

UNIT 7 | SECTION 3

CD TRACK 15 — F major

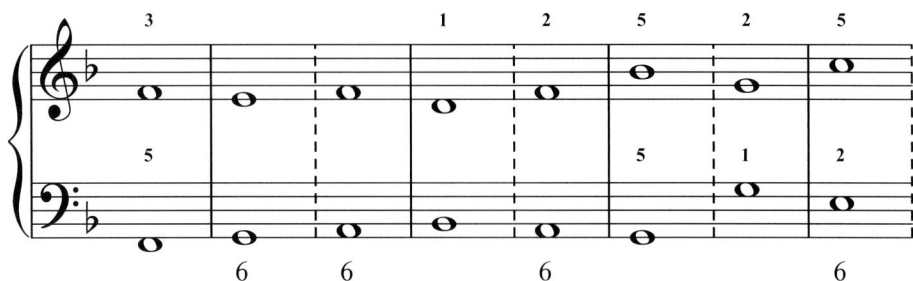

CD TRACK 16 — A minor

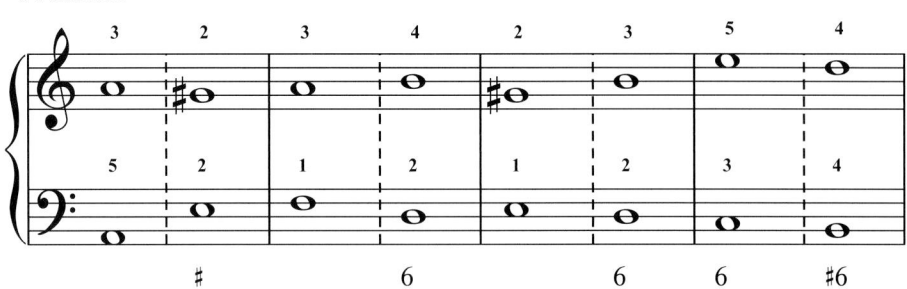

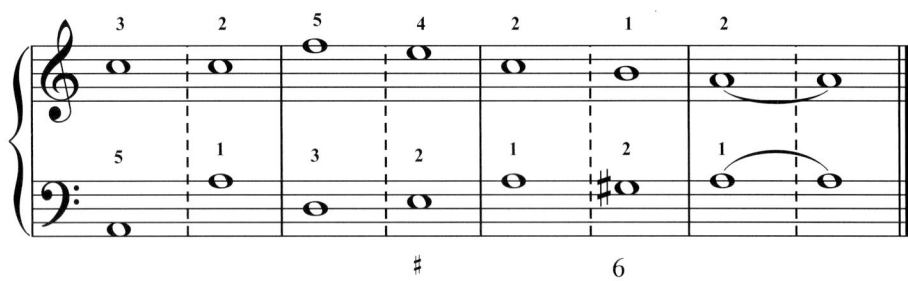

In the minor-key examples on these pages you'll also see some accidentals placed beneath the music: in figured bass these indicate that the chords contain notes that must be altered from the key signature to correspond to the degrees of the minor scale

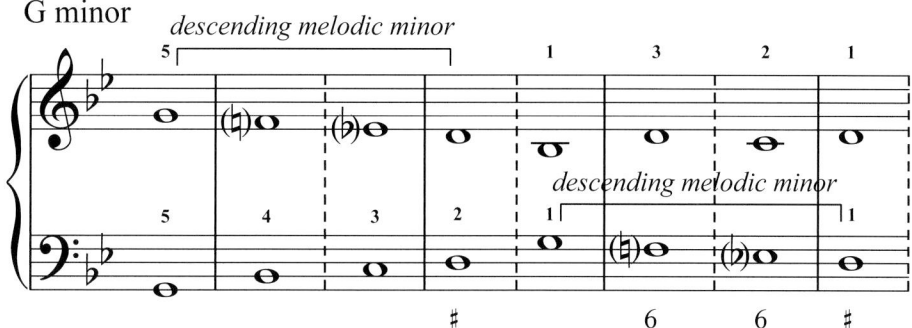

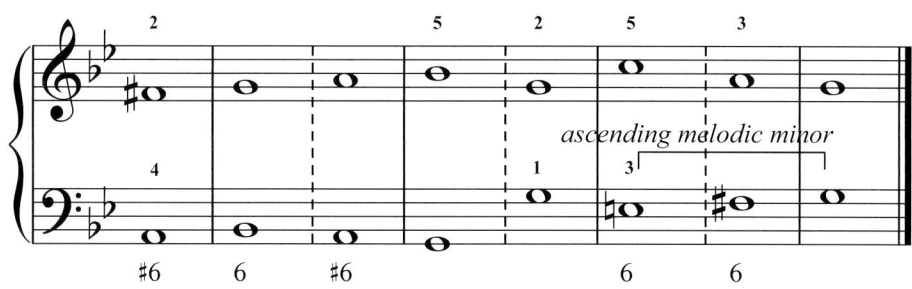

being used. This affects the seventh of the harmonic minor scale, or the sixth and seventh of the ascending melodic minor scale. However, when modes are used other scale degrees may be altered too.

Note carefully the use of the melodic minor scale in the last example – it's only used for specific melodic situations, not for the entire texture:

- The minor seventh from the descending form is reserved for stepwise descending passages involving the seventh of the scale.
- The major sixth from the ascending form is reserved for stepwise ascending passages involving the sixth of the scale.
- In almost all other circumstances the harmonic minor scale is used.

Now practise transposing these model examples at the piano into as many keys as possible. This will help you to get familiar with typical contrapuntal combinations in First Species in a variety of keys.

Exercise 7.6

Play through each of these left-hand lines (next page) very slowly as many times as you need to, trying gradually to introduce elements of countermelody above them in First Species. Don't worry if you can't improvise a complete countermelody straight away. Even if you only manage to sustain the counterpoint for a few bars at a time, that's already a great achievement. Listen

UNIT 7 | SECTION 3

a) C major

b) G major

c) D minor

d) E minor

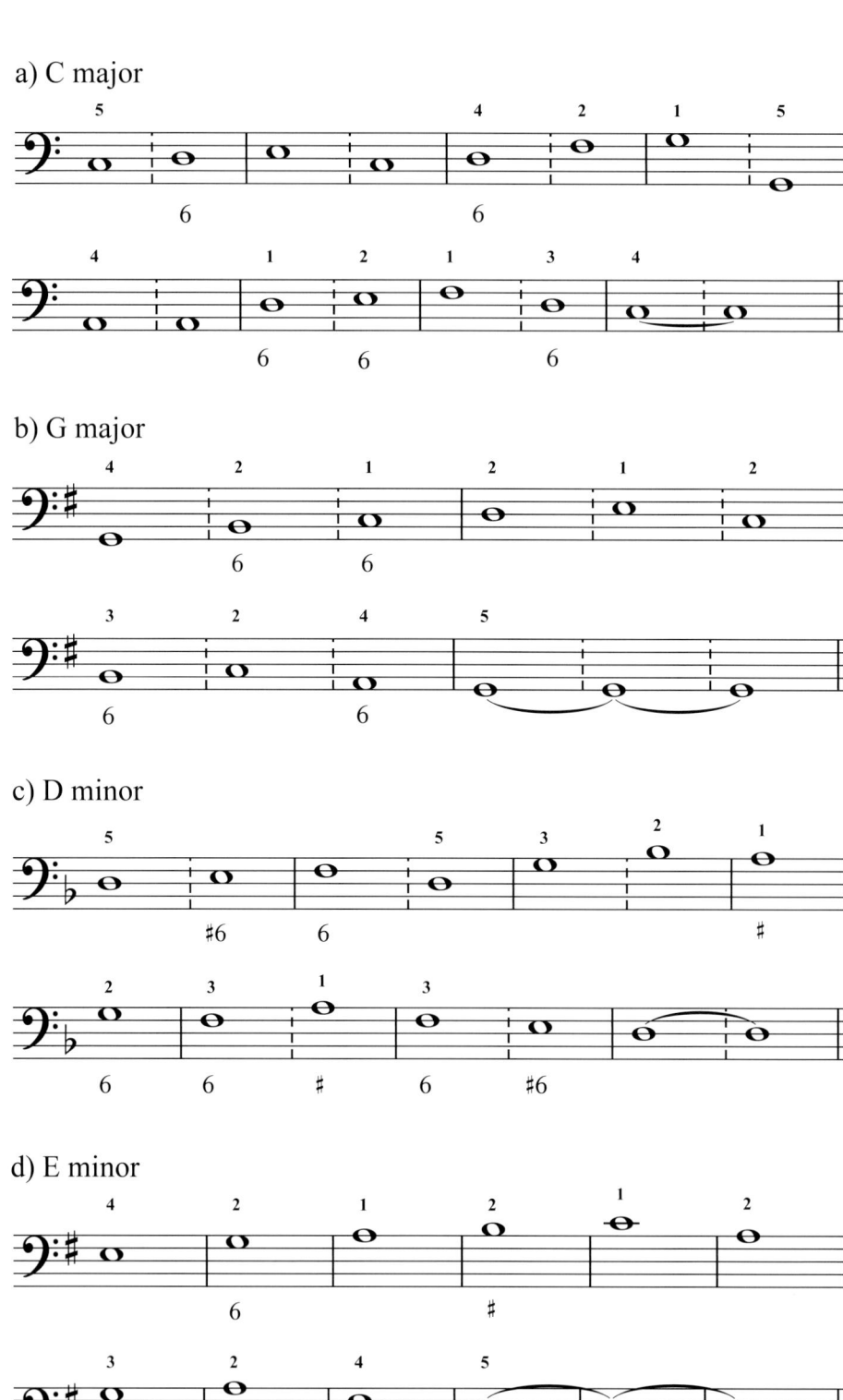

for effects that should be avoided, and try to hear the difference when the countermelody satisfies all the rules given above. When you think you've arrived at a satisfactory counterpoint, try transposing it into as many other keys as possible. (If necessary first write the notes out in the original key, so you can see them above the cantus.)

2) Second Species

In Second Species the rhythmic relationship between the two parts takes the form of two notes of equal length in the countermelody for each note in the cantus. Hence the notes of the countermelody are normally written as half-notes (minims).

In the countermelody it is the first half-note of each bar that actually sounds at the same time as the note in the cantus, and this note must form a consonance with the latter. However, the second half-note in the bar may either form another consonance with the cantus or a dissonance, and different rules apply depending on which of these is the case:

- If the second half-note forms a consonance then it can be approached and left by step or by a leap. However, if it's followed by a leap make sure this is in the opposite direction to the preceding movement (which will most likely be a step).
- If the second half-note forms a dissonance then it must be approached and left by step, just like an unaccented passing note.

In Second Species the problem of avoiding consecutive fifths and octaves is a bit more complicated. As the next example shows, they can occur in three ways:

- As the intervals formed between the cantus and the first half-note of countermelody in successive bars.
- As the succession of intervals formed by the cantus and second half-note of countermelody in one bar and by the cantus and first half-note of countermelody in the next bar.
- As the intervals formed between the cantus and the second half-note of countermelody in successive bars.

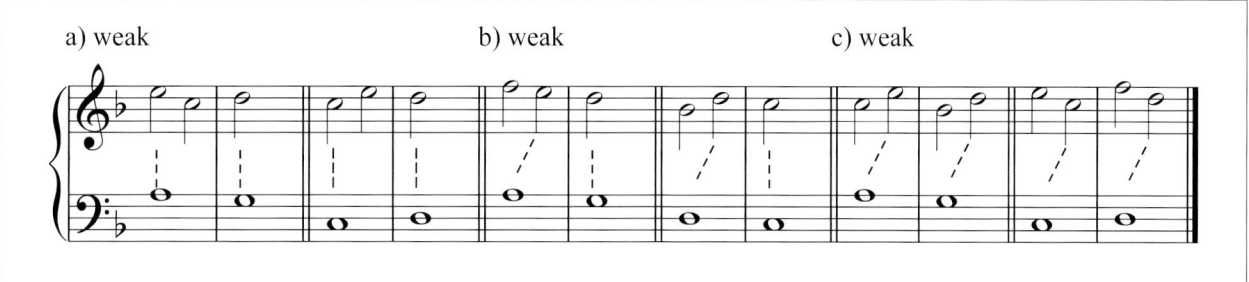

Generally you should avoid all of these, but with (c) there are exceptions, as the next example demonstrates. If the two half-notes in question are not in both cases the highest or lowest notes in the bar, then (c) is acceptable. See (i) below.

It's also okay if one or other of the bars has the countermelody moving to a note on the second half-note that's heard as part of the same harmony as the preceding note. This is worth knowing about, because there's also a rule that says that when we move from a sixth above the bass to a fifth this can be heard as continuing the same harmony rather than changing it, so this then also counts as a case where (c) is then allowed. See (ii) below.

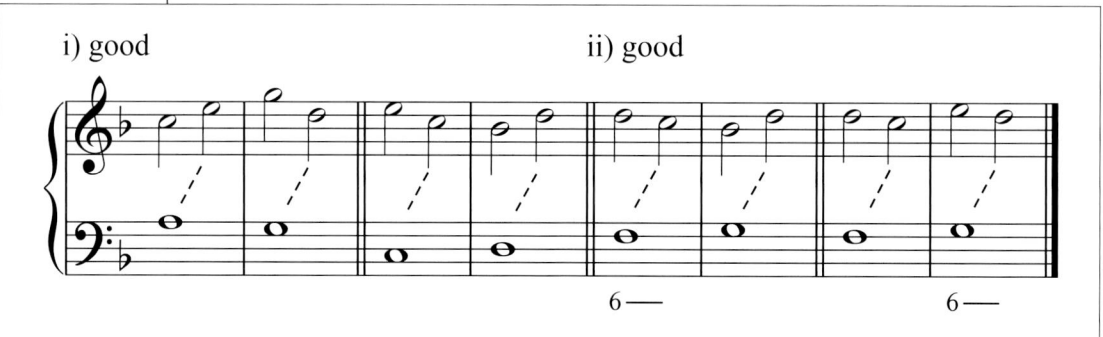

Here are a couple of examples of Second Species counterpoint written out for you to play through, followed by some exercises to practise this.

SECTION 3 | UNIT 7

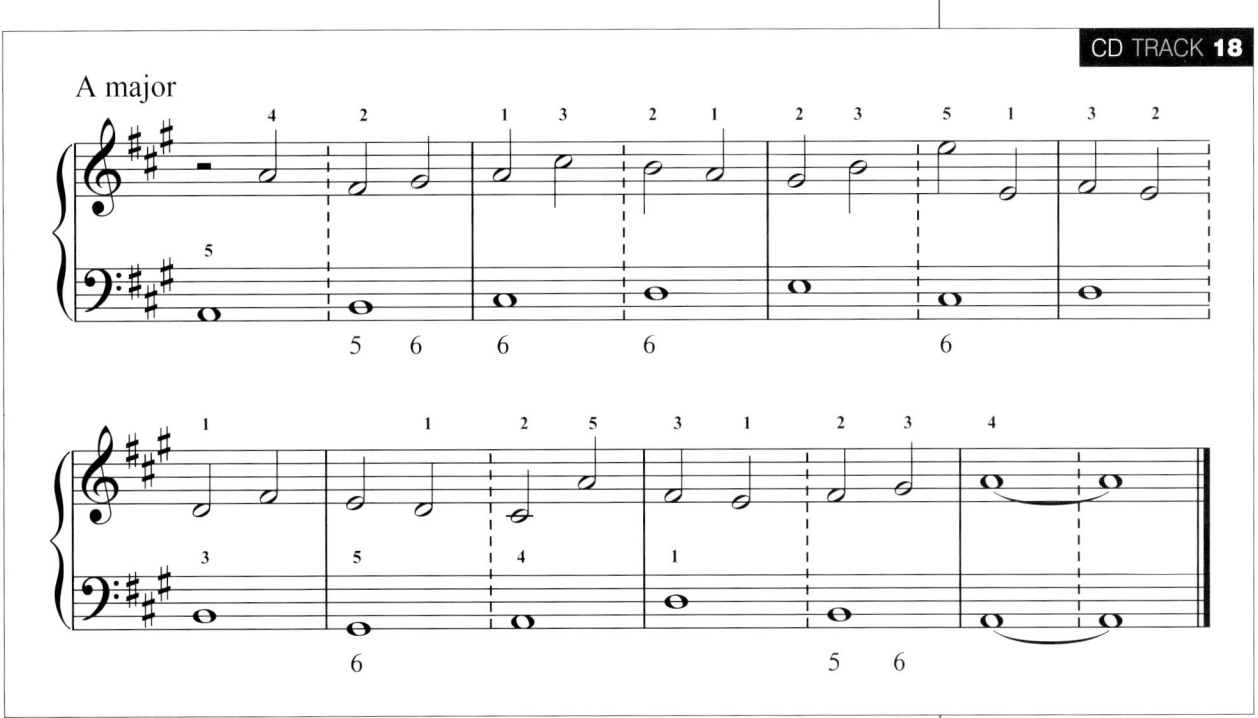

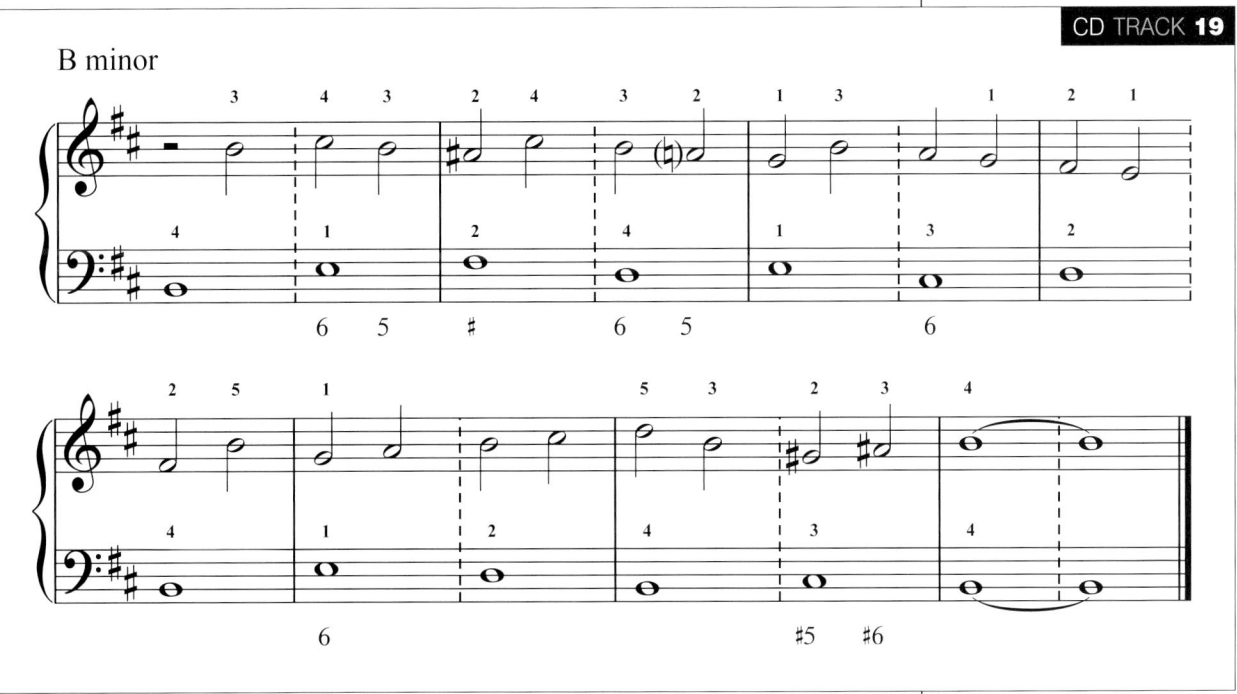

Exercise 7.7
In each of these two exercises the first half-note of each bar of countermelody in Second Species is provided, and you need to fill in the second, except at the very start, where both half-notes are given in the first full bar of countermelody. Asterisks mark the places where a half-note must be added. Once again, play through the material several times slowly before attempting to add the additional notes.

3) Third Species

In Third Species the countermelody has four equal notes to each note of the cantus. Hence if the cantus is thought of as written out in whole notes, we should think of the countermelody as consisting of quarter-notes (crotchets). (It's worth restating that this is only relevant when dealing with written examples. When you come to improvise independently of these you won't need to think in terms of specific time values.) While the possible grouping of notes in the cantus into larger metrical patterns can be left relatively unexplored here, at least for practice purposes, we can't avoid noting that the rhythmic subdivision of each individual note of the cantus into four is itself enough to imply a metrical hierarchy, equivalent to simple duple time.

Third Species counterpoint, even when limited to two parts, introduces a number of further complications. In written composition these can be dealt with by formulating rules that specify which sorts of contrapuntal combination are effective, acceptable, or strictly to be avoided. However, even here the idea that only a finite number of successful combinations exists plays an important role, so one can also learn to apply these in a more or less formulaic fashion. Because this more formulaic approach is especially helpful when improvising 'on the fly', we'll make even more use of it here than is normally the case. Even so, it's important to be aware of why certain combinations do or don't work, so the basic rules of Third Species are still worth getting to know:

- The first note of every bar in the countermelody must be consonant with the cantus.
- Make sure the very first note of countermelody forms a consonance with the cantus, even if it doesn't start on the first beat of the bar.
- Always finish with a movement from leading note to tonic in the countermelody.
- Avoid consecutive fifths and octaves, where the interval in question occurs between any note of the countermelody and the cantus in the first of two bars, and between the first note of the countermelody and the cantus in the second one.

Apart from these general rules, there are some additional guidelines for how to deal with the fact that notes in the countermelody other than the first of each bar can, in principle, be either consonant or dissonant against the cantus.

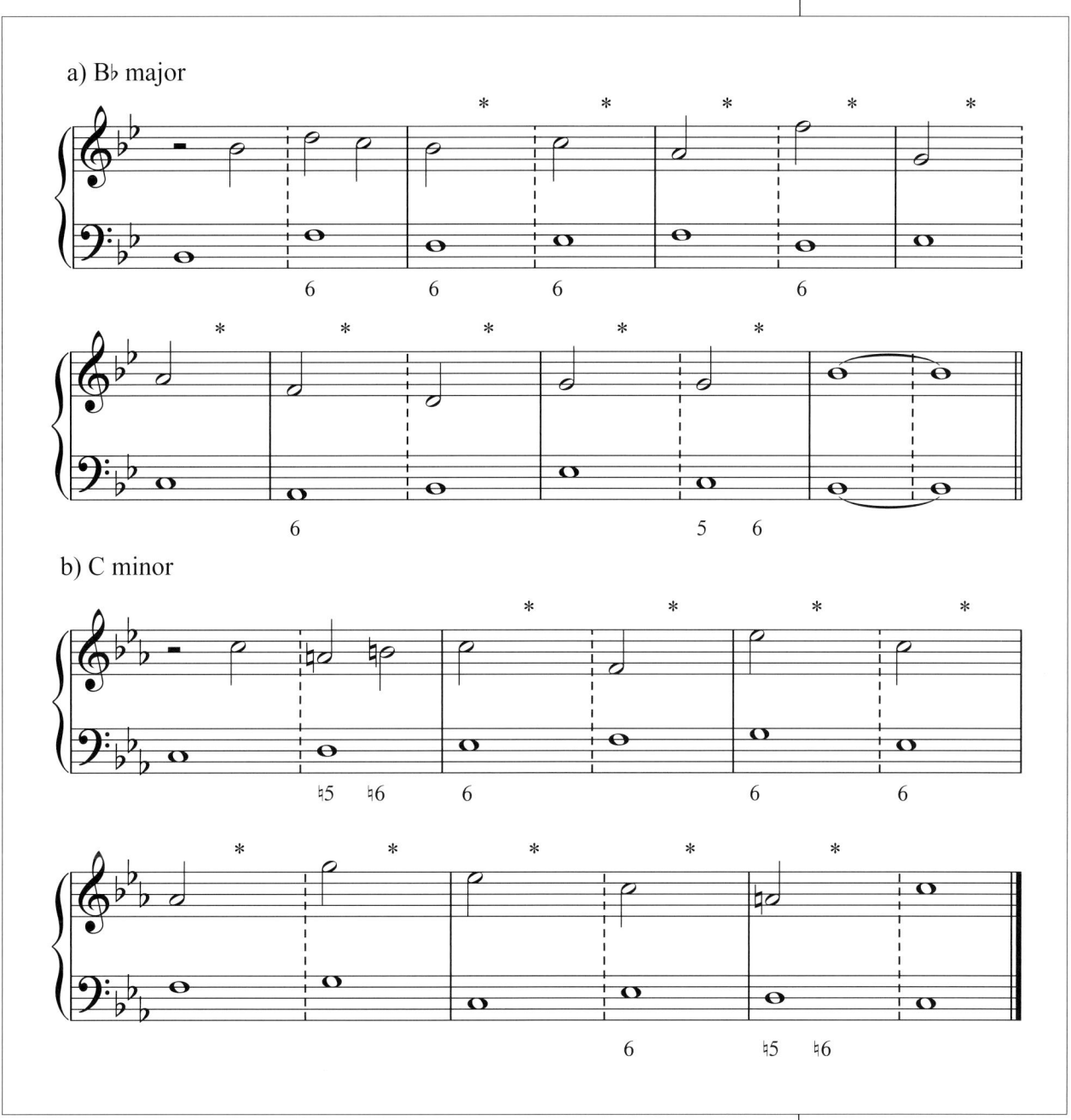

- Avoid conflict between the succession of consonances and dissonances and the metrical hierarchy: if the second and fourth notes are consonant, the third should be so too.
- Approach and leave all dissonant notes through stepwise movement (ie, treat them as passing notes).
- Two passing notes in direct succession should be followed by movement in the same direction that arrives at a harmony note.
- Avoid bars in which the countermelody consists entirely of leaps.
- Avoid a bar of stepwise movement in one direction followed by a leap in the same direction to the first note of the next bar.

The problem is that these guidelines don't cover all the cases, as the question of what does or doesn't work can also depend on the specific harmonic implications. So it's here that we need to make use of the formulaic approach, by actually spelling out some additional figures that can be used even though they don't necessarily fulfil the guidelines mentioned above.

The most important case of this is the contrapuntal formula known as **Nota Cambiata**: if the first and fourth quarter-notes are consonant, with the latter a third lower than the former, we may follow a stepwise descending movement to a dissonance with a further downward leap of two steps – providing that this in turn is followed by stepwise movement back up to the consonant fourth note. (Compare this to the description of a cambiata as a way of treating non-harmony notes in a melody, given in the first section of this unit.) In the example below, (a) and (b) represent standard instances of this, while (c) is an acceptable variation in which the fourth quarter-note is dissonant rather than the second and third ones.

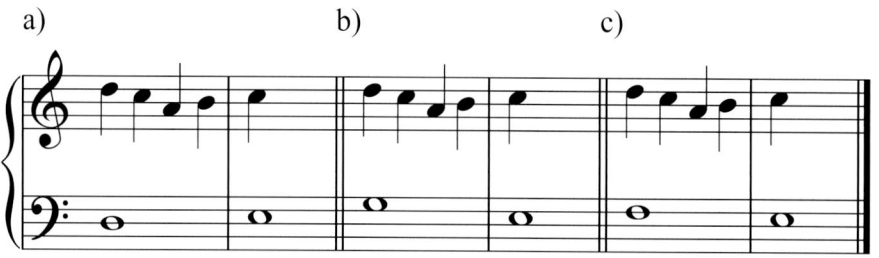

Something similar is possible when the first and fourth notes in the bar are the same: the countermelody can move up a step to a dissonance before leaping down a third and then moving stepwise back up. However, the effect isn't so interesting musically, so it's best not to use it too often (except perhaps in the bar before the final cadence, where it's harmonically effective).

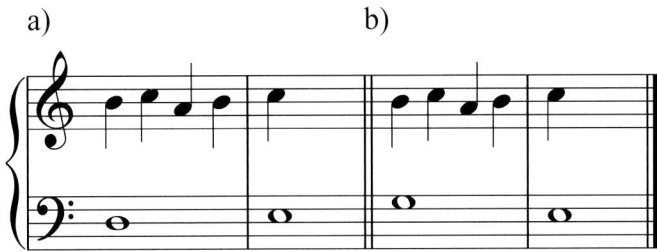

It's also important to keep in mind the harmonic implications when handling consecutive fifths and octaves. If, as in (a) below, the consecutive intervals don't correspond to different chords, we can still accept them, even though they may not fulfil the rules mentioned above. Likewise, we can accept consecutive fifths if the first of them

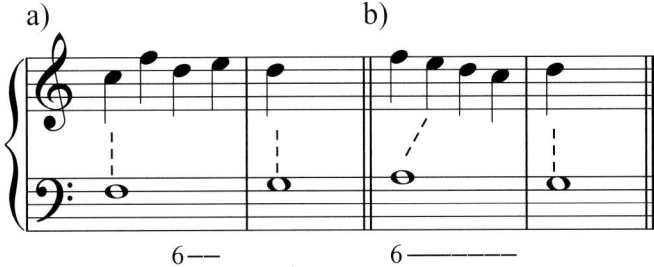

occurs in the way shown in (b), so long as the harmonic implication created by the sixth on the first beat is strong enough to make us hear the next note as a non-harmony note, even when it's a consonance.

Finally, the limited options for a satisfactory closing cadence in Third Species mean that its worth just memorising the different possibilities and treating them as fixed formulas:

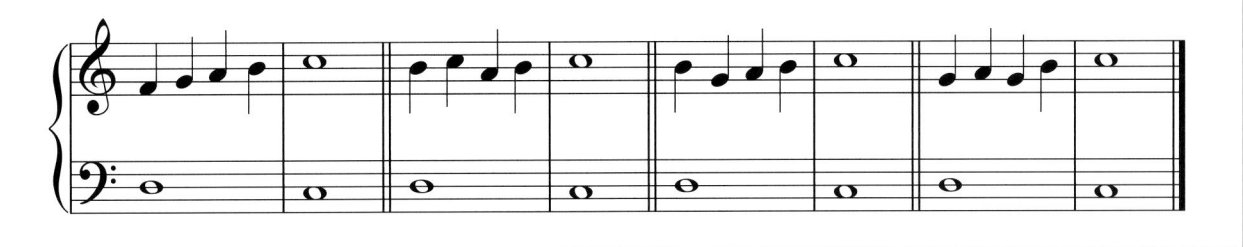

UNIT 7 | SECTION 3

Here are a couple of examples of Third Species counterpoint for you to play through, followed by some exercises for practising this.

CD TRACK 20

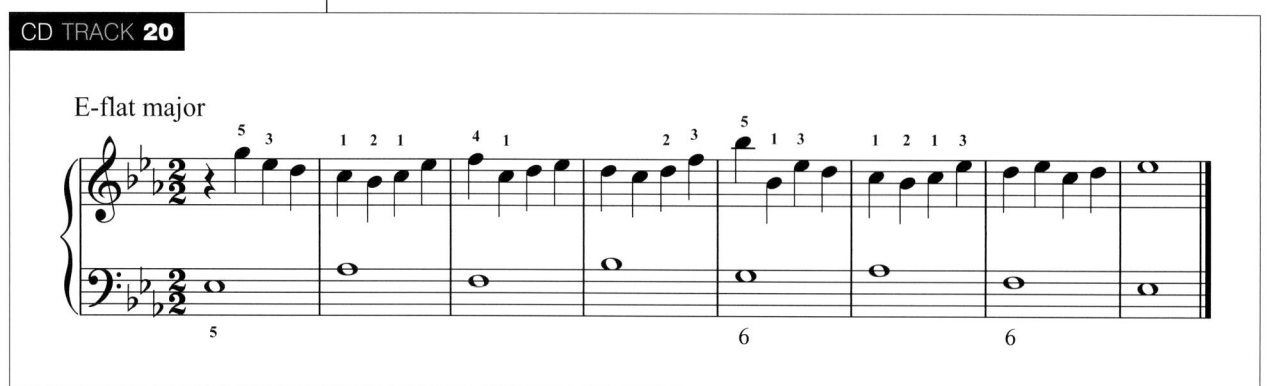

CD TRACK 21

Exercise 7.8
In these two exercises the first quarter-note of each bar of countermelody in Third Species is provided, and you just need to fill in the rest, except at the very start. Asterisks mark the places where a half-note must be added. Once more, play through the material several times slowly before attempting to add the additional notes.

UNIT 7 | SECTION 3

4) Fourth Species

In Fourth Species, as in First, the countermelody consists of one note for each note of the cantus. However, the rhythmic relationship between the two parts is different owing to the fact that the notes of the countermelody are syncopated: each begins halfway through the bar and is held over past the first beat of the next bar, as in the following example:

While the first and last notes in the countermelody must always be consonant with the cantus, others can be dissonant, unlike in First Species. However, they must be prepared and resolved in a specific way, so that they form in each case a **suspension**. The note that will form a dissonance against the cantus must first appear as a consonance when it occurs halfway through the bar, with the dissonance arising as a result of the move in the cantus to a new note at the start of the next bar. It must then be resolved through the countermelody moving downwards by step, halfway through the new bar.

There are three basic forms of suspension: 4-3, 7-6, and 9-8. Note that the 9-8 suspension can occur over an implied root position chord or an implied first inversion chord. (Remember that as with figured bass these numbers refer to the intervals formed between the countermelody and the lower part or bass, which are independent of whether the implied chord is understood to be in root position or first inversion.) Here they are. (There are also a couple in the previous example. See if you can identify them.)

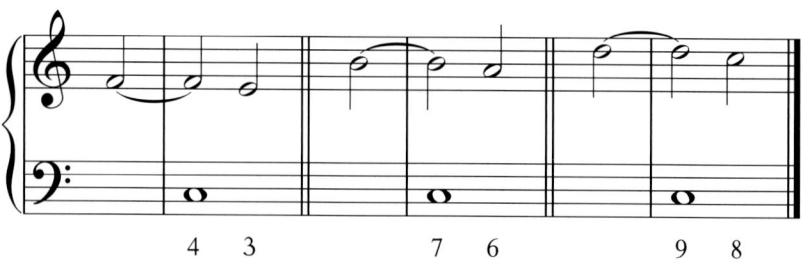

> From the point of view of classical improvisation it doesn't make much sense to get too involved in studying how Fourth Species counterpoint works as a self-contained form of polyphonic texture. What matters is that you grasp the origins of the suspension in this kind of contrapuntal relationship, and become sensitive to the rules governing its successful use. The real point is that it's easier to grasp the essence of the latter in the simplified context of Fourth Species counterpoint than in that of fully developed classical melodies, with their more varied rhythmic and harmonic structures.

You won't need to master the art of improvising counterpoint in Fourth Species to get the benefit of it as an improviser: what's useful, at least for most purposes, are just the principles for handling suspensions that it gives rise to. These aren't too hard to grasp, but are worth remembering:

- Avoid suspended dissonances that form an interval of a tritone with the cantus.
- Always finish with a movement from leading note to tonic in the countermelody.
- When preparing a 9-8 suspension avoid having an octave between the preparation and the cantus in the previous bar.
- In textures with more than two parts don't let the note to which a suspension resolves be present elsewhere in the texture at the same time, unless it's in the bass (as in 9-8).
- As with previous species, where the movement of the countermelody implies a change of harmony mid-bar you needn't worry about consecutive fifths or octaves between successive bars.

5) Fifth Species or florid counterpoint

The study of strict counterpoint normally culminates in Fifth Species, which is a more elaborate or 'florid' mixture of the other four species, similar to that actually used in the 16th century. (That's the period from which the models used to teach strict counterpoint are normally taken.) Apart from some general rules for combining the species, it involves getting to know some variants of the existing species and formulas that are mostly used for stylistic reasons. As our aim here is just to get familiar with the contrapuntal origins of the classical understanding of how melody relates to harmony and basslines, rather than to learn to imitate earlier styles for their own sake, we needn't be too concerned about this. However, it's certainly worth getting to know the more ornamental ways in which suspensions can be resolved in florid counterpoint, as these can give you a good insight into the origins of the classical approach to melodic decoration, which is particularly important when improvising:

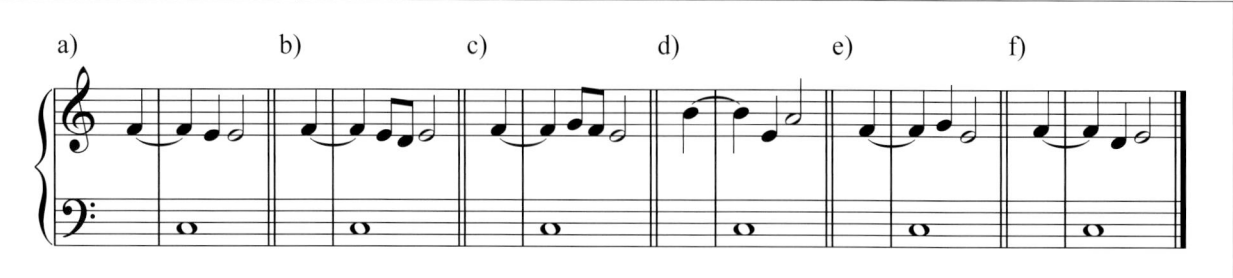

In (a) the resolution is anticipated on the second quarter-note of the bar, while in (b) and (c) two eighth-notes are interpolated before the resolution. (It's important that they are each approached and left by step.) In (d) the countermelody leaps onto and away from a note in the implied chord other than that to which the suspension itself resolves, while in (e) and (f) it moves up one step and down two, or down two steps and up one, between the suspension and its resolution.

Melody and bass

In the next stage of exploring how classical melody and harmony furnish a basis for piano improvising we'll think of the cantus more explicitly as a bassline. That means treating it as having more specific harmonic implications, while being aware that any melody we improvise over it still has a contrapuntal character. (In other words, it remains a countermelody of sorts.) First off, let's just focus on how to make a melody work over it. Then in the next section we'll look at improvising chord structures over a bass too.

> It's this two-sided approach, in which we think of a melody simultaneously as unfolding the harmonic implications of a bassline and as working in counterpoint to the bass, that is the essential and distinctive feature of the classical approach. It became standard practice in Europe in the 17th and 18th centuries, and has remained central to mainstream Western classical music (and, on a rather basic level, some aspects of popular music) ever since.

Take a look at the bassline below. It's from one of the most famous works of classical music from the 17th century (ie, the period known as the Baroque era): Pachelbel's *Canon*.

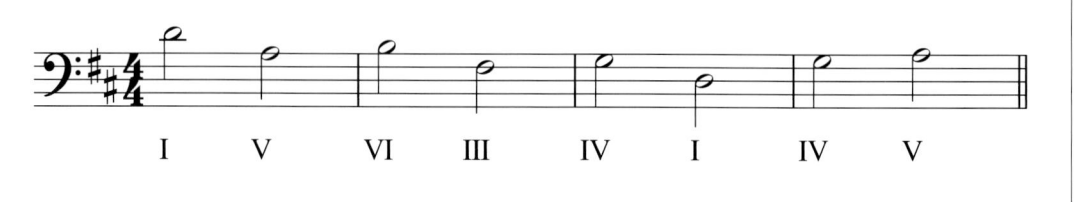

The chords have been marked as Roman numerals beneath the music. (It's in the key of D major.) Just to make it easier to grasp, here they are as simple triads:

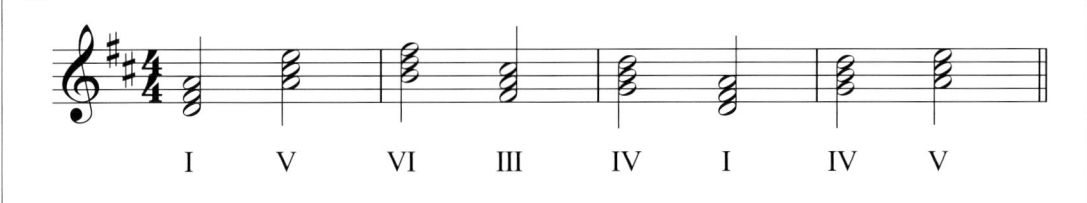

As a model for what we ourselves might do with simple basslines such as this, let's take a look at what the composer himself does. (It will help if you play through each of the following examples yourself on the piano.) Here are the first four bars. Note that while the time-values are half-notes rather than whole notes, the one-against-one rhythmic relationship between the parts still makes it count as First Species counterpoint.

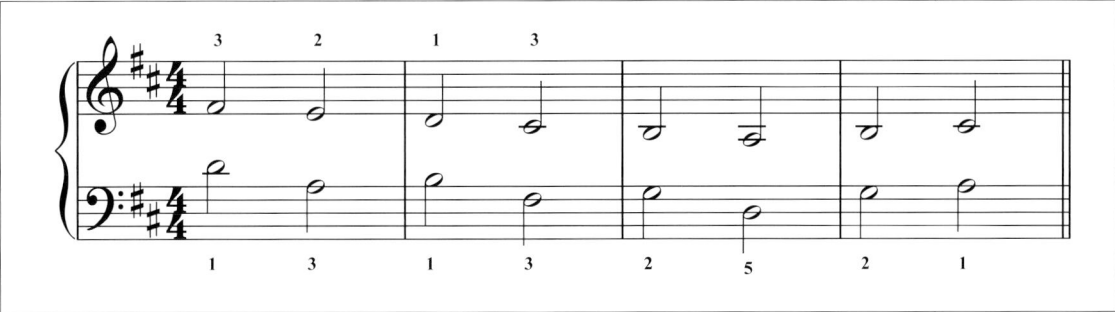

The next four bars add a third part which fills out the harmony. (Note that it also repeats the opening melody of the first four bars, this time an octave higher.) As you can see, no dissonances or non-harmony notes at all have been introduced so far.

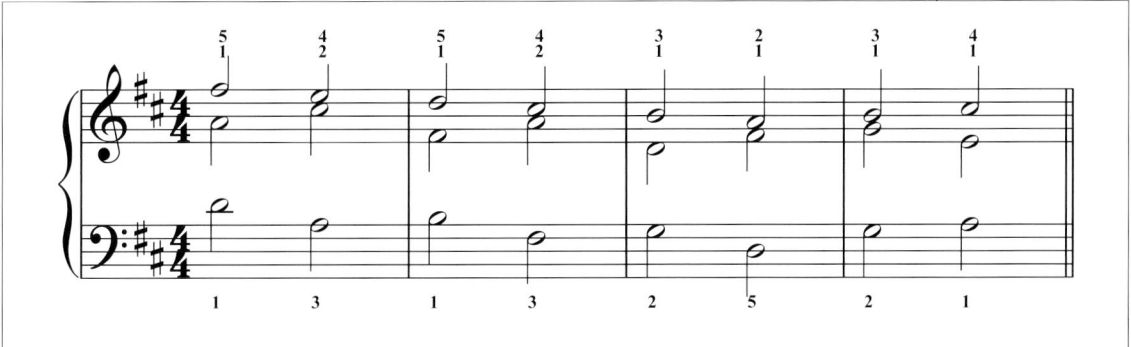

UNIT 7 | SECTION 3

> The technique of letting each part copy the music that has just appeared in another part (usually transposed to a different pitch, but not always an octave), is known as imitation. It's the most important technique for contrapuntal development in classical music. A piece in which each part enters in turn imitating the material of the previous one is known as a canon.

In the next four bars a second countermelody is introduced, this time moving in Second Species (ie, two notes against one), over both the bass and the original countermelody. (You'll find you need to practice the left-hand fingering by itself here before you can play the next few examples through. See the section on scale-fingering in the Appendix as well – especially the Scale of D major in thirds.) In this case there are still no dissonant notes that are not harmony notes:

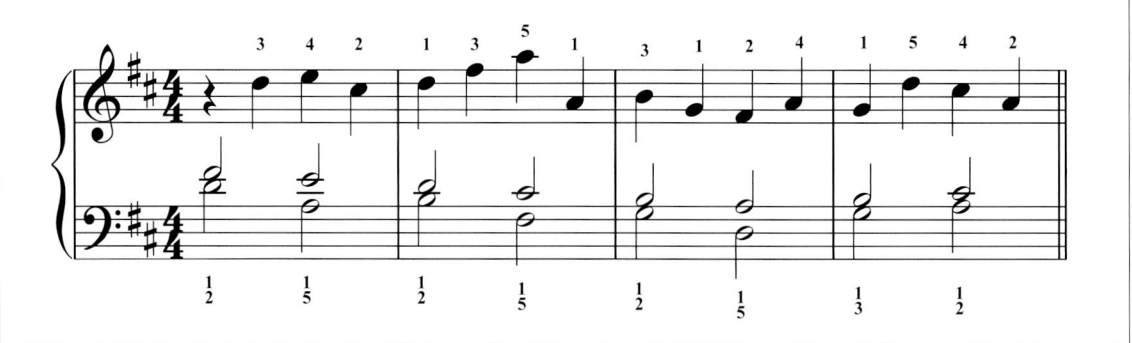

Now this gets followed by a more florid line that mixes eighth-note (quaver) passages (Third Species, with passing notes) with quarter-notes:

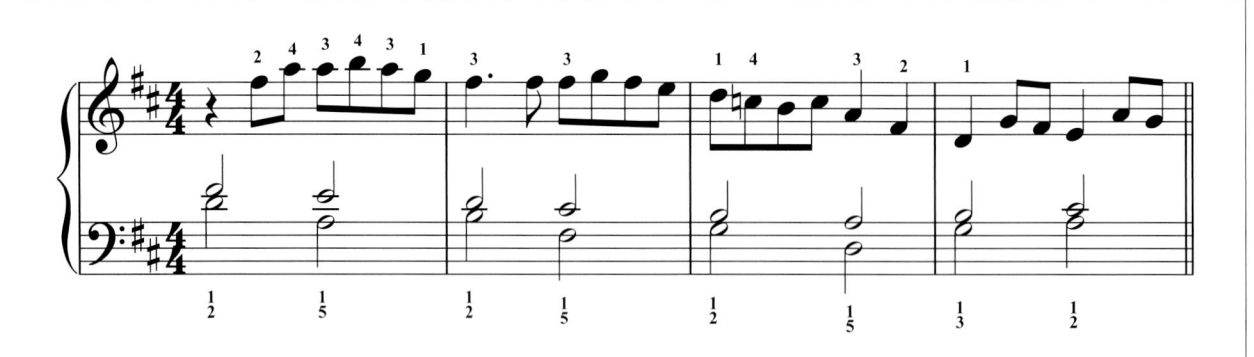

Finally, here comes what looks like the second countermelody again, only this time it's quickly varied as it reaches its high point, with a dotted rhythm and an altered shape, so that in some places different notes are used to realise the same harmony:

SECTION 3 UNIT 7

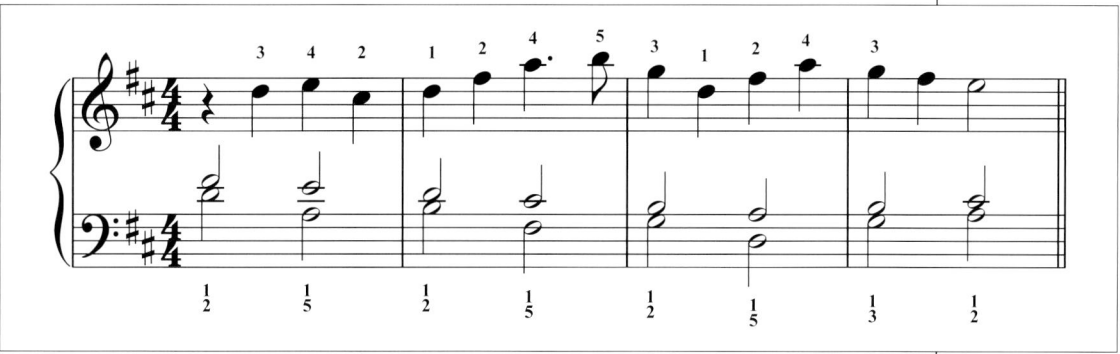

Now here are all of those phrases together, so you can hear how they unfold one after another as a single stretch of music, as in Pachelbel's original composition (but arranged for piano):

CANON

Pachelbel

CD TRACK 23

UNIT 7 | SECTION 3

The entry point to improvising over basslines is to take something familiar like this, remove the elaborations so that only the absolutely essential notes of the melody are retained, and then play around by introducing your own embellishments and variations, keeping the original structure as a reference point and comparing versions to see what works and what doesn't. (We'll discuss specific techniques you can use for varying a melody at the end of this unit.) Here are some exercises for that, using the material we've just been looking at.

Exercise 7.9.
Try improvising your own alternative First Species countermelodies here (in half-notes) over the bassline, in each case using the notes given as a guide. Note how the possible continuations vary depending on how you finger the opening material, as this determines the initial position of your hand. In some cases alternative fingerings are given so that you can explore multiple hand positions. Experiment freely with your own fingerings as well. Although the original treats all of the bass notes as roots of chords, you can try substituting first inversion chords where appropriate too – especially when you see the third or fourth of the scale in the bass. As in the previous exercises, asterisks mark the places where notes must be added.

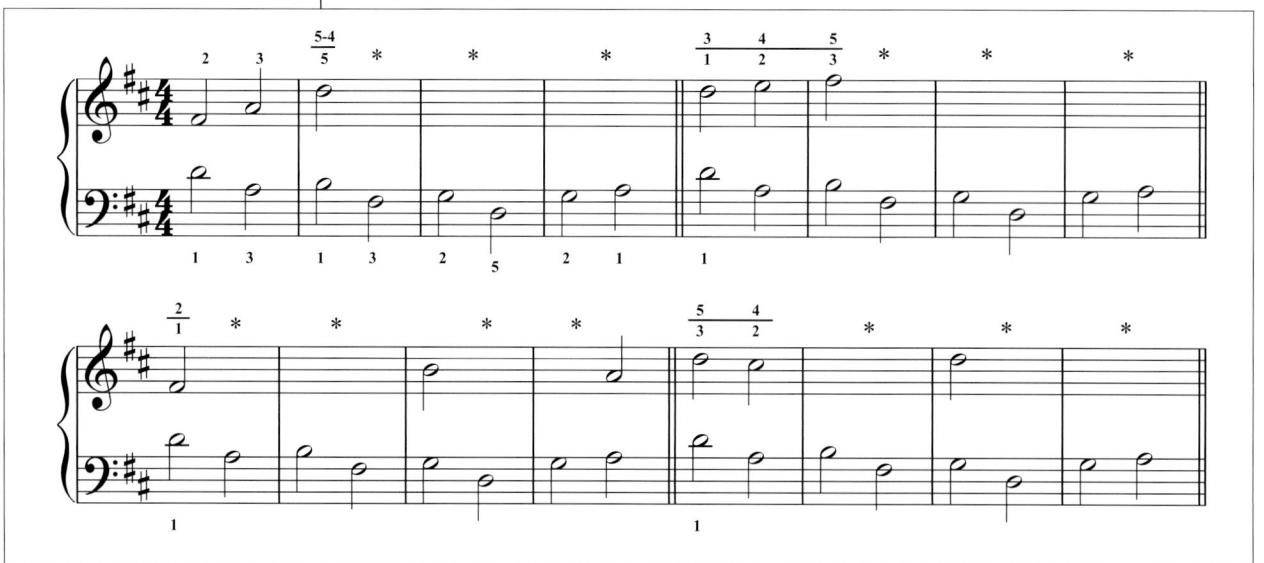

SECTION 3 | UNIT 7

Exercise 7.10.
Now try improvising your own alternative Second Species countermelodies (in quarter-notes) over the bassline here, once again using the notes given as a guide. Here, too, try a variety of fingerings, and experiment with introducing first inversion chords as a harmonic basis for the countermelody in some places.

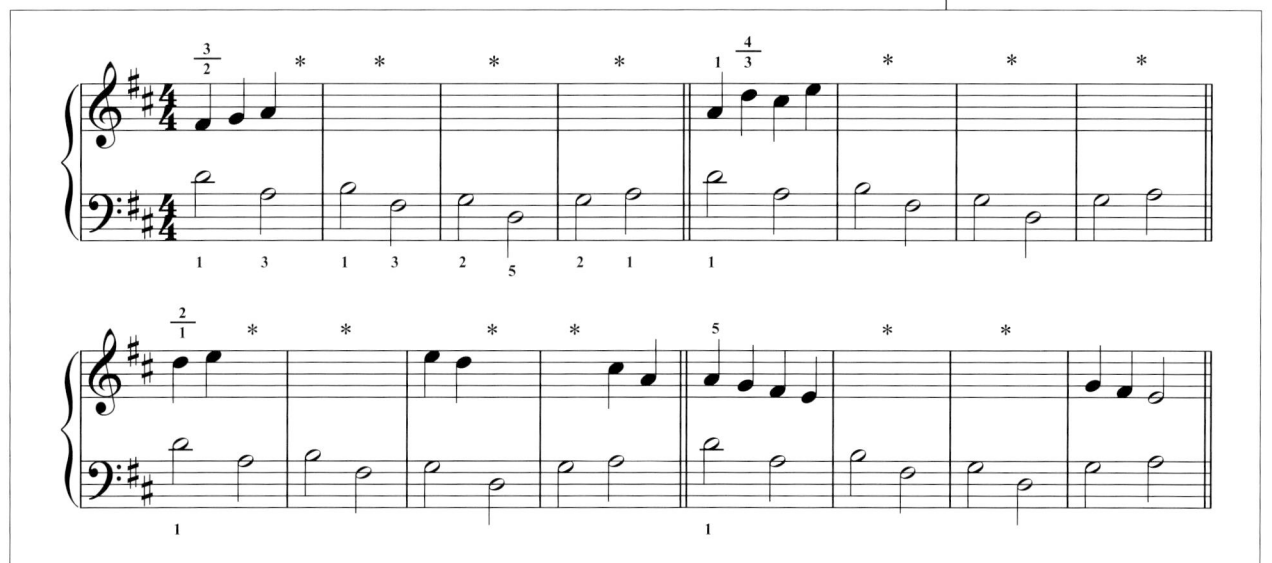

Exercise 7.11.

This time try improvising your own Third Species countermelodies (in eighth-notes) using the notes given as a guide.

SECTION 3 | UNIT 7

Exercise 7.12.
Now here comes the most important stage of all! You should have memorised the bassline in your left hand by now, so close the book and try improvising your own florid (ie, rhythmically free) countermelodies against the left hand (playing the latter from memory so you can focus totally on what your right hand is doing).

Hopefully you can see that each of the first three contrapuntal species corresponds to an additional degree of elaboration, requiring more embellishment in order to maintain the rhythmic texture. It's especially important to understand this in improvised counterpoint: that's because trying out each species in ascending order prepares you for the next by familiarising you with the possible consonances between the parts before you embellish them further.

Now let's look at another approach to developing countermelodies over a bassline. Here's 'Scarborough Fair' again, but this time we'll focus on the harmonic implications of the bassline, and just use the most important notes of the melody as jumping off points for melodic improvisation. (This technique of cutting down a melody line to its bare essentials before embellishing these in our own way is known as **melodic reduction** – we'll explore it in more depth in Unit Nine.) Play through the structure a few times to get familiar with it, remembering that the key is E minor:

UNIT 7 | SECTION 3

Right now we're just interested in seeing how the unfolding of an improvised melody line over a bass can be guided by the chords the latter implies. The next example leaves just the bass in the left hand. The chord notes are thought of as lying around the existing melody notes in the right hand, and this enables us to think of them as possible points the melody can pass through on its way to the next harmony.

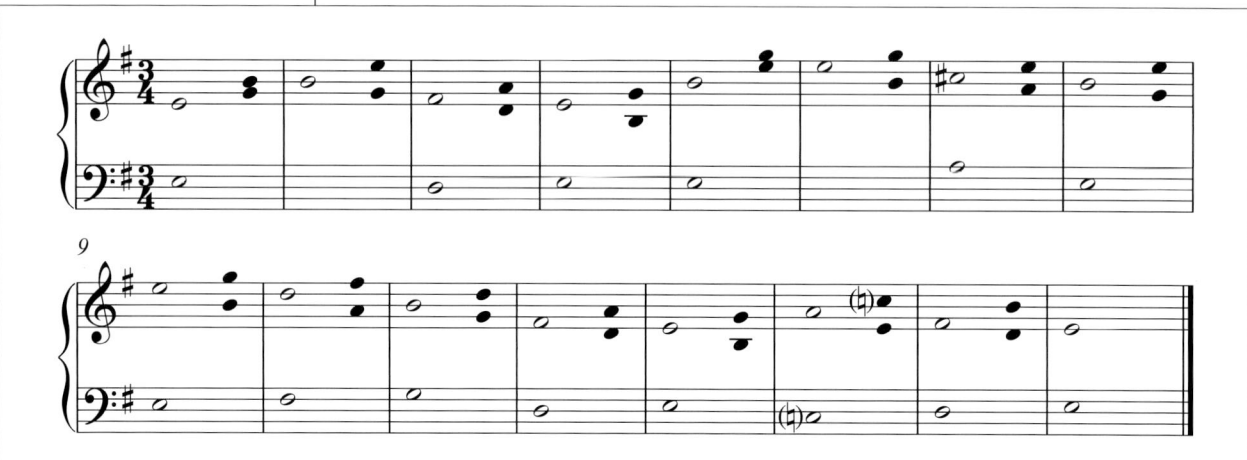

Here's an example where one additional note is added in the right hand for each note in the bass. Note that while the right-hand rhythm consists of half-notes alternating with quarter-notes, the contrapuntal effect remains essentially the same as with two equal notes in the countermelody against one in the cantus: ie, Second Species. (Note that the last of each group of four bars isn't elaborated at this stage: it's better to retain a clear sense of where each four-bar phrase ends and the next begins.)

CD TRACK 24

Next we can introduce passing notes around the new harmony notes that have just been incorporated into the melodic outline:

It's worth noting the variety of ways in which this can be done, so here's another version of the same thing:

Here's a version where the outline is elaborated using further notes from the chords:

In practice, however, the requirement for melodies to balance stepwise movement with leaps means that it's best to aim for a mix of elaboration through passing notes and elaboration through introducing additional harmony notes. The next example shows one way of doing this:

Exercise 7.13.
Now it's your turn to try your hand at improvising some countermelodies based on the bassline and implied chords of Scarborough Fair. Here are a couple of alternative outlines for you to work with. First play through the given material several times, until you've got it 'under your skin'. Then gradually introduce additional notes into the melody as you are playing it, becoming a little more ambitious each time. Try to retain as much rhythmic fluency as you can: it will certainly help to maintain a strong sense of pulse with a clearly accented first beat of the bar. (The bass has been 'figured' to remind you which implied chords are first inversion triads instead of root position ones. The key is still E minor.)

Chords and bass

Now that we've explored putting a countermelody over a bass, let's see what's involved in improvising chords over one. In classical music this practice became very common during the 17th century, owing to the practice of writing keyboard parts (known as 'continuo' parts) in scores in which only the bassline was specified, accompanied by figured-bass symbols of the kind we've already encountered. This allowed keyboard players to choose for themselves how to realise the harmonic implications of the bassline as an actual chordal texture.

We've already explored chord layout, voice leading, and chord progressions in Unit Four, and now here's our chance to see how some of those skills can be usefully applied when improvising. We're going to take the basslines from the melodies already used in this section and see how they can be turned into chordal textures. Let's start with 'Camptown Races', as it offers an exceptionally straightforward harmonic structure in a major key. Here's the bassline again, with the chord symbols below:

All the chords are in root position here, so there are no inversions to worry about. The main issues, then, are avoiding consecutive fifths or octaves and ensuring smooth melodic movement in the upper parts. When improvising we don't always have time to think through all the relationships between the parts, so it can help to follow some more general guidelines that at least reduce the risk of consecutives:

- If the bass moves by step, the upper parts should either stay fixed or move in the opposite direction to the bass (by step or by a leap)
- If the bass moves by a leap, the upper parts should either stay fixed or move by step (in either direction)

If necessary we can further simplify things if we think of the texture as consisting principally of a relationship between the bass and the remaining notes of each chord, taking the latter as a single unit. This works especially well when the texture is laid out with three notes in the right hand and one in the left. In that case, it can be sufficient for most purposes just to follow these more straightforward guidelines:

- Aim wherever possible for contrary or oblique motion between the bassline (ie, the left hand) and the upper parts (ie, the right hand).
- Avoid laying out the upper three parts so that they form consecutive root position triads (as this generates parallel fifths within the right hand).

Of course, these guidelines don't cover all the possibilities: for example, parallel thirds and sixths are fine between parts. Another issue when improvising chords over a bassline is the fact that the top part tends to stand out melodically, so where possible it should have a form that works with the structure of the chord sequence. The following harmonisation of the bassline from 'Camptown Races' shows one way to do this:

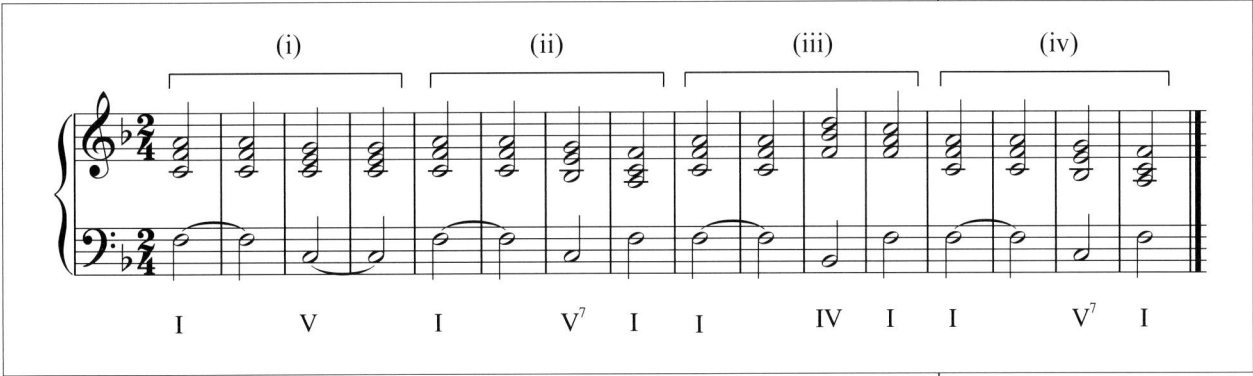

You can see that the material is divided into four four-bar units. The first features a stepwise descent in the top part. The next begins with the same movement but continues it down a further step. The third returns to the opening layout once again. (Because the same chord occurs at the end of the previous four bars and at the start of this unit, a change of layout is needed here to mark the structural division.) The leap down to the root of chord IV – a new chord in the sequence here – is matched by an upwards leap to a higher note in the top part. The fourth four-bar unit once again takes us back to the opening layout and repeats the movement of the second one, taking us back nicely to the tonic in the top part.

Notice, however, that wherever the chord is held for two bars we end up having to repeat the right-hand chord to maintain a consistent rhythmic texture, and the effect is not so interesting. Here's an alternative version where we shift the chord layout in the right hand with each new bar to avoid this:

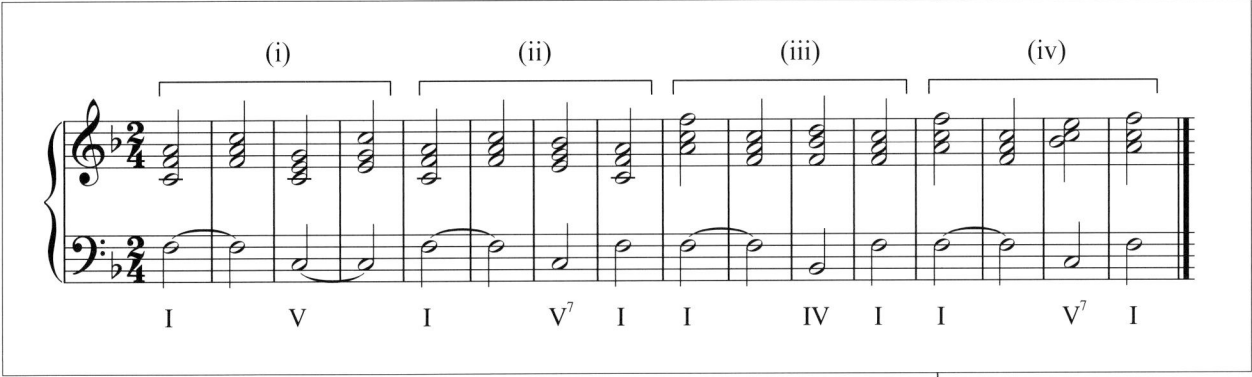

In this case the second four-bar unit recommences the pattern established at the outset in the right hand before changing to a stepwise descent. The third four-bar unit then introduces a textural contrast by turning the opening right-hand shift of position around (from ascending to descending), and this is rounded off in the last four bars by a stepwise ascent in the top part from leading tone to tonic.

Exercise 7.14.
Try coming up with your own harmonisations of the 'Camptown Races' bassline now. First focus on producing a texture with three notes in the right hand and one in the left. Then, when you feel confident enough, try improvising a similar texture with two notes in each hand – it's much harder but will make you more aware of relations between the upper parts.

Let's follow that by taking the bassline and chords from Pachelbel's *Canon* we were exploring earlier in the unit and seeing what we can do with them. Here they are again:

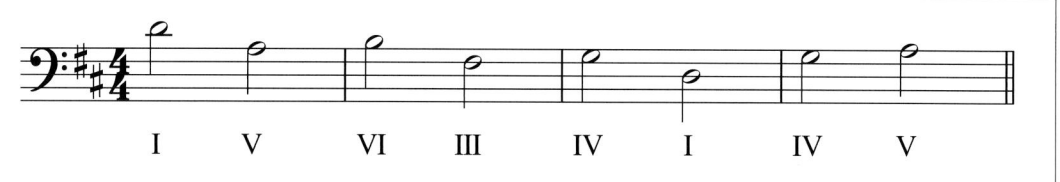

Note how each of the first three bars consists of a two-chord progression linking two root-position chords with a descending leap of a perfect fourth in the bass. That means that in each bar the interval between the roots is the same, even if the chords themselves are not. Now recall what we learned in Unit Four: the same voice-leading formula works between almost any two chords, providing the interval between the roots is the same and the inversions are unchanged. This means that whatever formula we use for the first pair of chords can simply be reused over the next two pairs as well, as in the next set of examples:

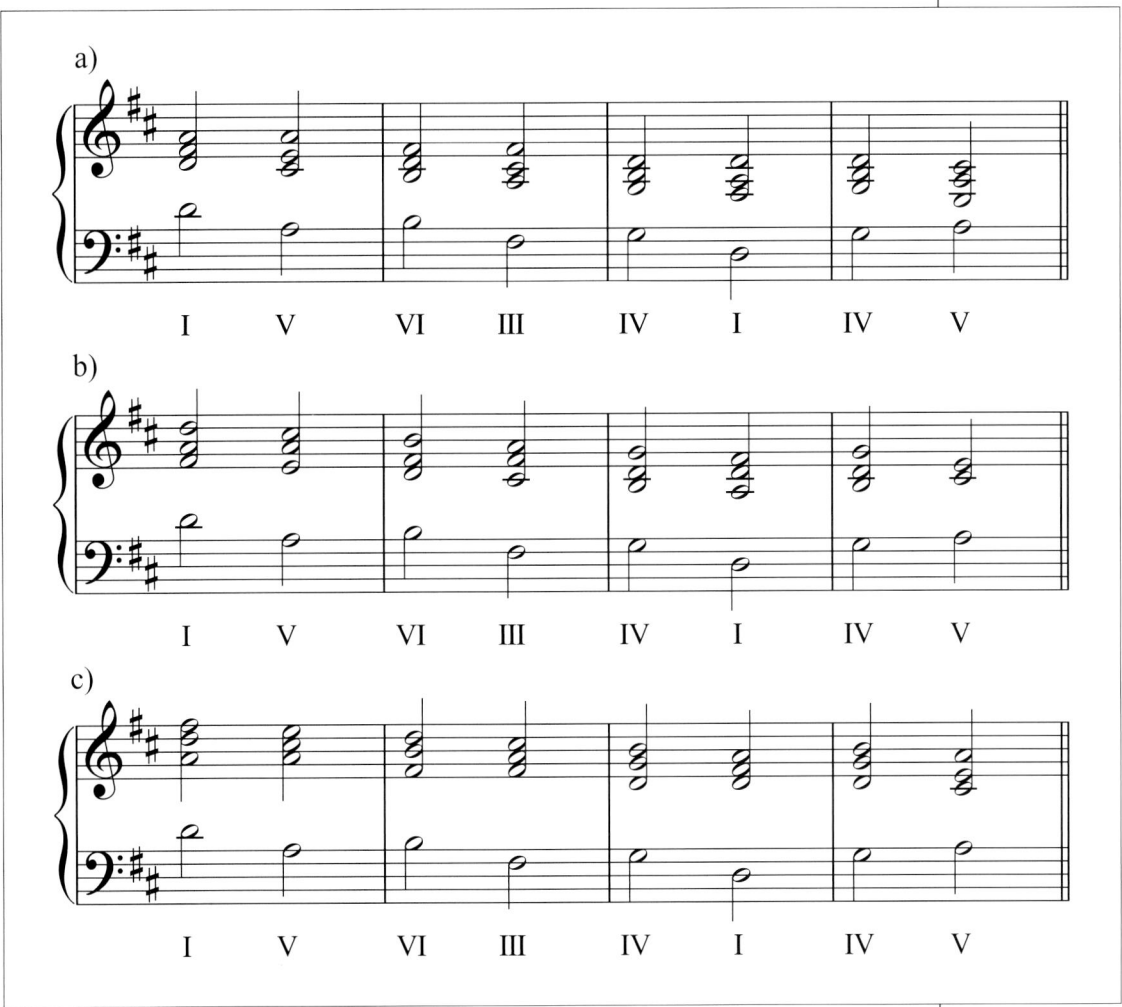

Take a look at the top part in each of the above examples. In (a) the voice leading produces a top part with repeated notes, which consequently lacks melodic interest. In this respect (b) and (c) are definitely better. Placing the third of the chord at the top in the first chord of each bar, as in (c), is best, since it sets off the top part more effectively than simply doubling the root, which is already given in the bass. (Note that this version gives us a top part similar to that used by Pachelbel as a countermelody in First Species, except that unlike the composer we've harmonised the fourth bar in each case so that consecutives are avoided.)

Okay, that has shown just how easy it can be to make use of voice-leading formulas over a bassline, but we might also try something more interesting here. For example, we could alter the voice leading to give a more interesting top line (instead of just reproducing the same relation to the bass in each of these bars). Here are a couple of examples:

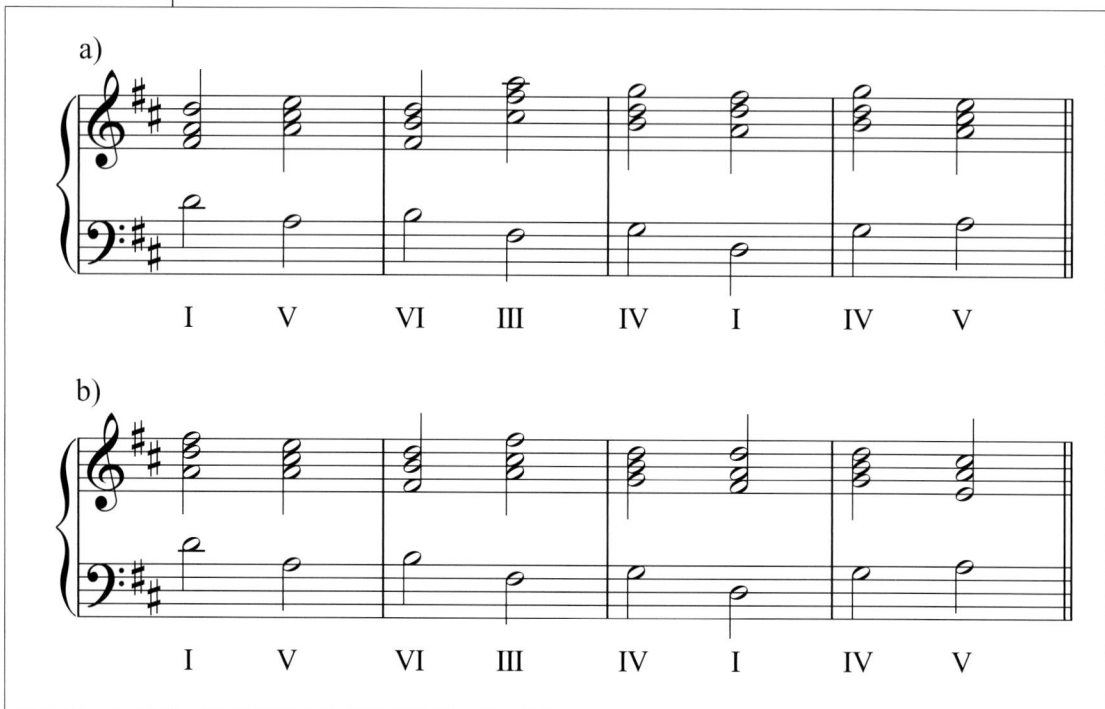

Note how the right-hand chords tend to move in contrary motion to the bassline, especially when the latter moves by step, and that when the two hands do move in parallel, the right hand avoids moving by a similar interval to the bass. Either way, when putting three notes in the right hand we avoid producing successive triads in the same inversion there. That way there can't be any consecutives between the three upper parts.

Exercise 7.14.
Try out your own harmonisations of the Pachelbel Canon bassline. Can you find any other alternatives to those given here that also work?

SECTION 3 | UNIT 7

Now let's take a slightly harder example, this time in a minor key. Here's the bassline and chord symbols for 'Hatikva':

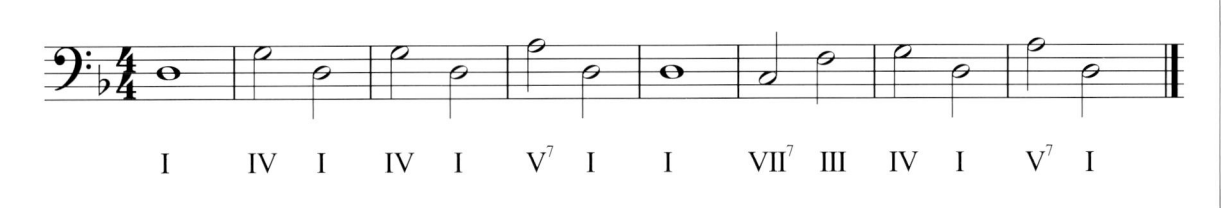

First let's look at the structure of the chord progression here. Apart from bars 2 and 6, the chords in the first four bars and in the second four bars are identical. Bar 6 represents an interesting departure from what has gone before as the progression from VII⁷ to III seems to suggest a kind of brief modulation from D minor to the relative major (F major) or, at least, a change of scale (from D harmonic minor to the descending melodic minor on D). (We'll discuss what such transient modulations really amount to later in this unit.)

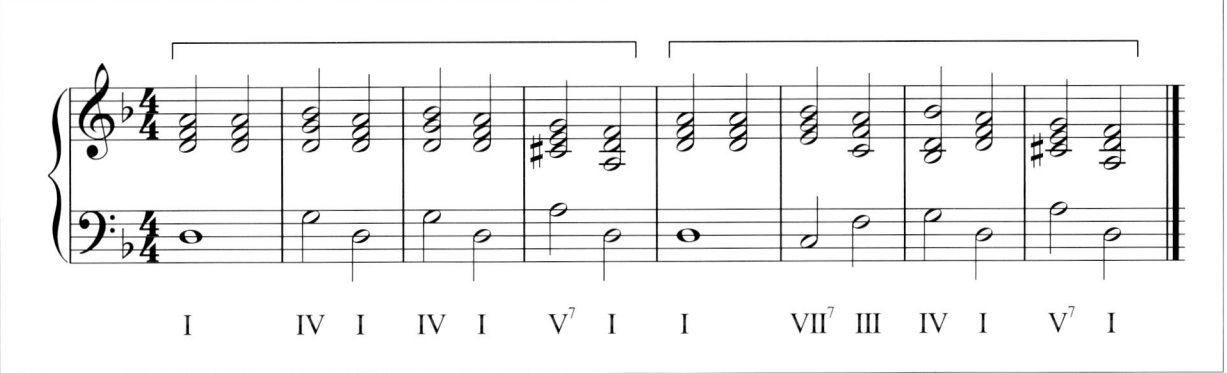

In this case the choices are fairly clear:

1 The bassline moves by leaps rather than steps, except between bars 6 and 7, so we can let the upper parts move in similar or contrary motion to the bass, so long as they keep wherever possible to stepwise movement.
2 Starting with the fifth on top in the initial chord I makes sense, as then we can move nicely by step to the highly expressive sixth of the minor scale (= the minor third of chord IV). By contrast, starting with the third on top would only take us by step to the root of IV (= less interesting), while having the root on top would lead to repetition as this note is also in chord IV.
3 After that, the descent in the top part through G (the seventh of V) to F (the third of I) follows naturally in bar 4, as by this stage we need some melodic development in the top part, and the stepwise descent rounds of the first four-bar phrase.

4 Because the second four-bar phrase runs parallel to the first, except for the harmony in bar 6, it's natural to aim for a similar realisation. Keeping the top part the same, even in bar 6, actually throws the spotlight on the changed harmony there. (Fortunately, the notes required belong to these chords as well!) Note, though, that the first chord in bar 7 has to have an alternative layout this time round to avoid consecutives.

Finally, here are the bassline and chords for 'Scarborough Fair', which, as we've seen, have a modal minor-key feel:

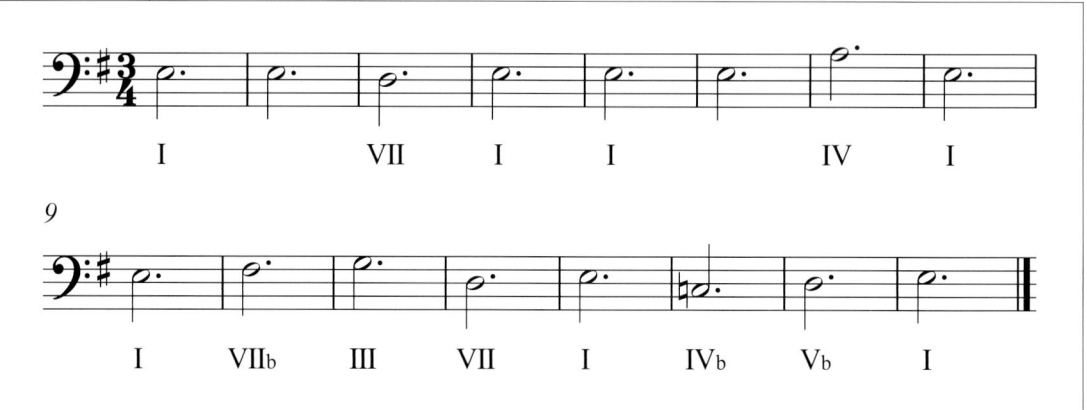

This time we'll need to be more careful when realising the harmony: apart from the presence of first inversion chords in the second half, together with the shift of mode from Dorian to Aeolian that comes with the lowered sixth (ie, C-natural instead of C-sharp) in bar 14, we've a got a lot of stepwise movement in the bass. This makes it more likely that consecutives will arise between the bass and the upper parts, so we have to make sure all of the latter move in contrary (or, at least, oblique) motion relative to the bass, where possible. When harmonising with three notes in the right and one in the bass we can achieve most of this by aiming for as much contrary motion as possible between the hands and varying the positions of successive chords outlined in the right hand. Here are a couple of realisations. Notice how (b) achieves a more effective top line than (a) thanks to its avoidance of repeated notes and use of more stepwise movement.

Exercise 7.15.
Try out your own harmonisations of the 'Scarborough Fair' bassline.

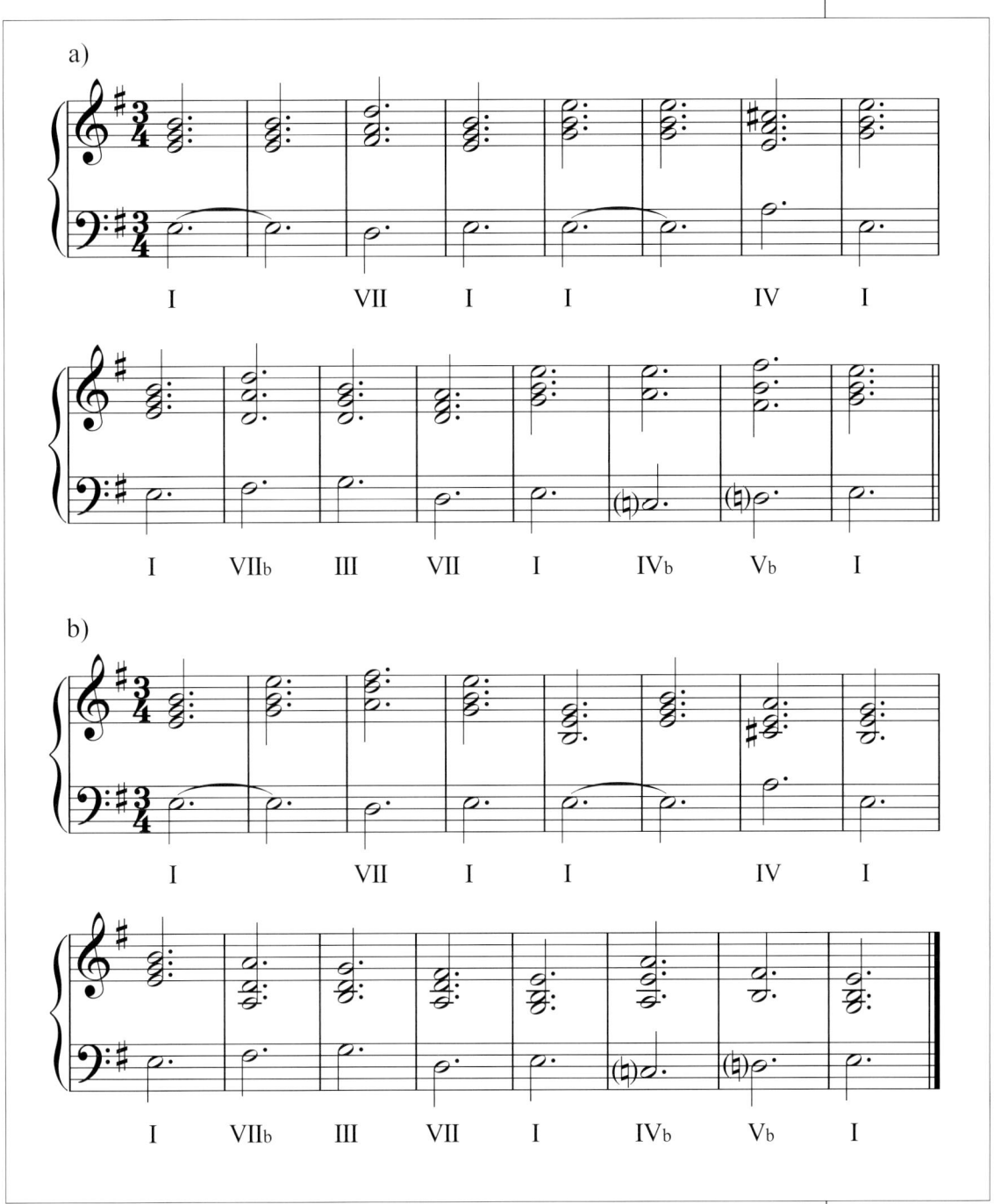

UNIT 7 | SECTION 3

> The art of realising chords over a figured bass, or above a bassline with functional chord symbols added (using Roman numerals), is known in classical music as keyboard harmony. That's really short for 'harmonisation at the keyboard'. You can find many good text books devoted to teaching the skills involved, and if you want to take classical improvising further as a major element of your own pianistic approach then it's certainly worth getting hold of one of these and working through it.

The next stage in exploring the classical approach is to take an existing set of chords (with an implied or stated bassline) and see how a melody can be improvised above them. However, before we can do this we need to learn a bit more about classical harmony.

Extended harmony

We've already learned how chords are built from triads on different notes of the scale for the key we're improvising in. However, once classical harmony developed it quickly began to evolve: in particular, composers and improvisers from the 17th century right through to the 19th century looked to expand the harmonic resources available within a key, and they found a number of ways of doing this. In the 20th century some of these approaches were then taken further in jazz, while others were developed in new ways in modern classical music. (We'll explore these in due course.) Let's take a look at the basic methods that classical music has used to expand its range of harmonic possibilities. (You'll need to be reasonably familiar with these if you want to understand the remaining sections of this book.) The methods we'll explore here are the following:

- Chord extensions (and their inversions).
- Chromatic alteration and borrowed chords.
- Secondary harmony (and passing modulations).

1) Chord extensions

We learned about dominant seventh and diminished seventh chords in Unit Four. Now it's time to see how the technique of adding extra notes to a triad to give it a more complex harmonic character can be more widely applied in classical music. The first step is to realise that we can build seventh chords on each and every step of the major or minor scale (opposite page, top).

Note the particular type of seventh chord that results for each scale degree. (The names of these seventh chord types are shown above the chords in the example, abbreviated slightly. We'll discuss the relationship between the different types of seventh chord, and the special symbols used to indicate these, in the next unit, as it's more immediately relevant to jazz than to classical music.) Although we can make use of all

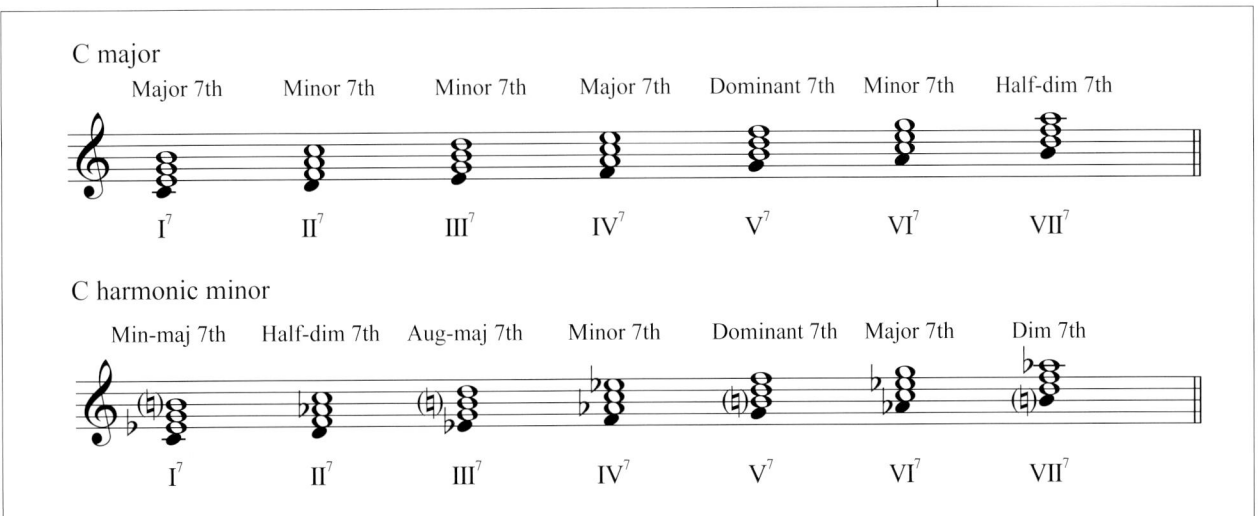

of the seventh chords that appear over the major scale, not all of those that appear over the harmonic minor scale are useful in a standard classical context: chords with a major seventh over a minor triad (I) or a major seventh over an augmented triad (III) are mostly avoided here, even though they are widely used in jazz.

Notice how the dominant seventh chord appears on V over both the major and harmonic minor scales. Apart from this the most widely used seventh chords in classical music are minor and major seventh chords and diminished seventh chords. (Note how the last of these appears only appears in the minor, on VII).

Half-diminished seventh chords (with a diminished fifth and minor seventh) are also used for expressive effect, particularly in late Romantic music – especially as this chord appears in the minor on II, which is a scale degree that lends itself especially well to seventh chords in either a major or minor key. The reason for this is that chord II^7 in first inversion corresponds to IV in root position with an added sixth. Often it's more natural for us to hear it as this, because of the importance of the subdominant as a counter-pole to both the tonic and dominant within the overall structure of diatonic harmony:

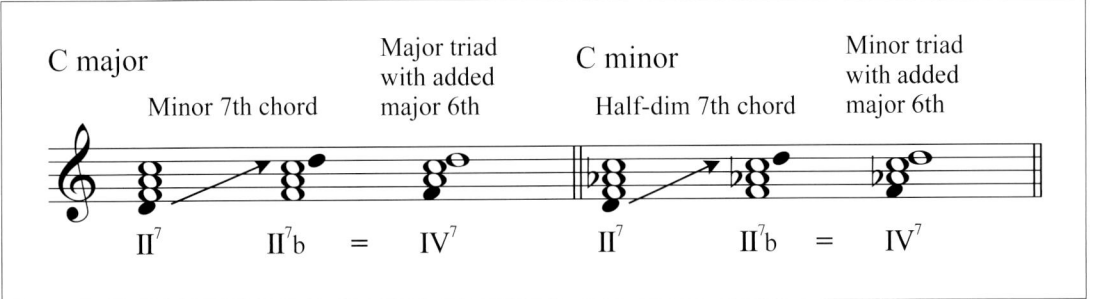

As a result, seventh chords tend to appear much more frequently on II than on any other scale degrees – apart, that is, from the dominant seventh on V and the diminished seventh chord on VII. (Hearing II^7 as chord IV with a sixth added means hearing it as an **added-note chord**. We'll discuss such chords more in the next unit, as they play a bigger role in jazz than in classical music, even though they originate in the latter.)

When dealing with seventh chords it's worth knowing how their different inversions get shown, both in figured bass and in the older and newer systems for indicating chord structure using Roman numerals:

Inversion of seventh chord	Old Roman numeral system and figured bass	New Roman numeral system
Root position	7	7
First inversion (ie, third in bass)	6 5	7b
Second inversion (ie, fifth in bass)	4 3	7c
Third inversion (ie, seventh in bass)	4 2	7d

Note that the process by which we generate a seventh chord from a triad (by adding a note a third above the existing ones) can be taken further to produce chords with a ninth, 11th or 13th above the root. (These chords normally include the seventh as well, as otherwise they tend to be heard as triads with added notes.)

From the late 18th century onwards the dominant seventh chord was frequently extended to include the ninth, and especially the flattened ninth, even in a major key. This was a way of intensifying the tension of the dominant before a resolution. Adding the unflattened ninth to the dominant chord in a major key produces a richer, more colourful flavour with only a fairly gentle dissonance, whereas adding the flattened ninth creates a sharp dissonance, and thus more tension, as the ninth sounds against the root. Both can be effective. (The example below shows typical resolutions to I.)

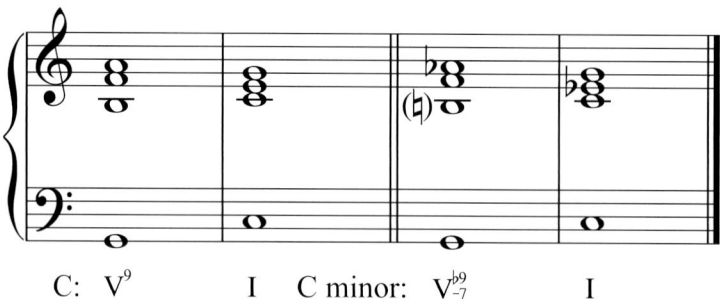

C: V^9 I   C minor: V$^{♭9}_{-7}$ I

It's rare for ninth chords to be used in inversions or as extensions of chords other than the dominant seventh, except, perhaps, in advanced tonal harmony of the kind practised by early 20th century composers such as Debussy, Ravel, and Schoenberg.

Note that seventh chords built on VII in a major or minor key tend to be interpreted in classical harmony as **incomplete dominant** ninth chords, which means dominant ninth chords with the root implied but not sounded. Hence we can think of them as having V rather than VII as their root. This means they can function in cadences and other progressions where V is called for.

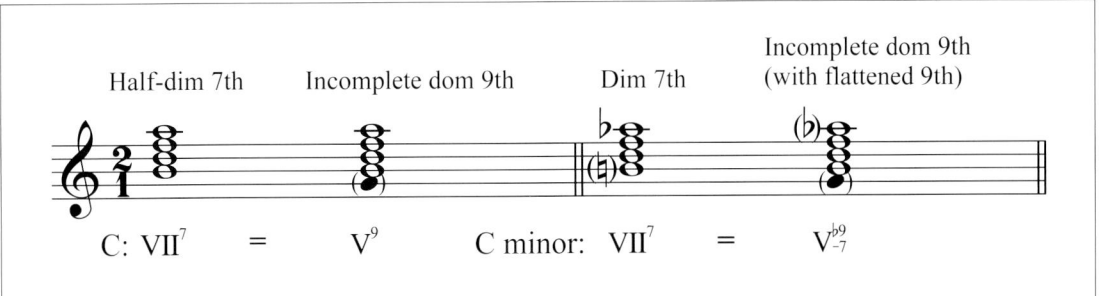

2) Chromatic alteration and borrowed chords

The next method we need to look at involves changing existing notes in the chord rather than adding new ones. We can chromatically alter one or more notes in the chord – usually only one – without entirely sacrificing its identity. (Remember, chromatic alteration means raising or lowering a note by just one semitone.) The most common form of this occurs when we take the version of the same chord that would exist if we were using a different type of scale based on the same keynote: for example, we may use the version of the chord that occurs in the minor scale, even though the music is actually in the major key, or vice versa. The chords which result are called **borrowed chords**.

The most common examples in a major key involve introducing the flattened sixth from the harmonic or descending melodic minor. This can result in (a) a minor triad on IV, (b) a major triad on ♭VI (instead of a minor triad on VI), (c) a diminished seventh chord on VII, heard as an incomplete dominant seventh with flattened ninth, or (d) a dominant seventh with flattened ninth with the root present. Using a minor triad on IV is especially effective in a major key when it is followed immediately by I. Using ♭VI in a major key is an effective preparation for V, thanks to the fact that the bass can then move down by a half-step from one root to the next. These are shown below. In all of the following examples first play the examples through several times as written, until you've memorised them. Then try playing the same progressions with the upper parts rearranged so that different notes sound on top, but avoiding consecutives. Then try transposing them into other keys.

Note how the Roman numeral chord symbols in the above example indicate the

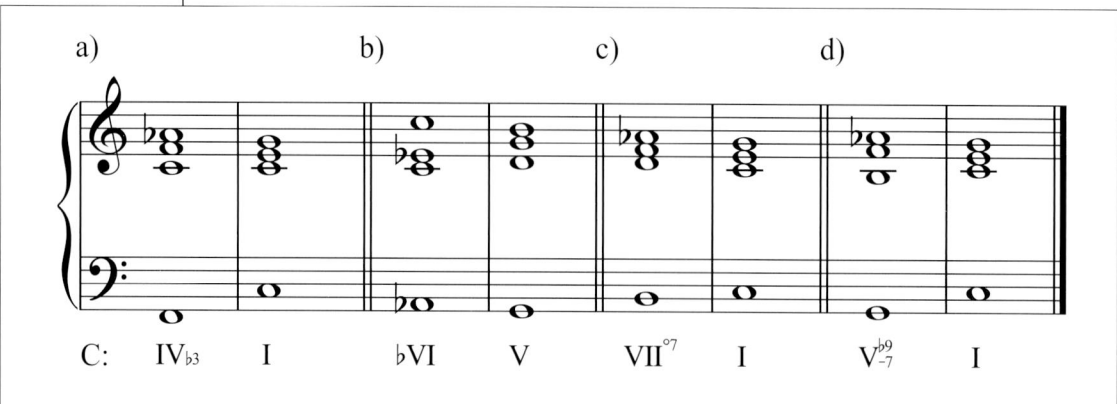

borrowed chords by specifying the chromatic alterations required from the normal major-key chords on the same scale degrees. (In the case of the diminished seventh chord, we indicate the presence of a diminished interval above the root/bass using a small circle: as °7.)

In a minor key the most common instance of a borrowed chord is the **Tierce de Picardie** effect, in which a major triad on I is substituted for the normal minor triad as the resolution of a perfect (a) or plagal (b) cadence:

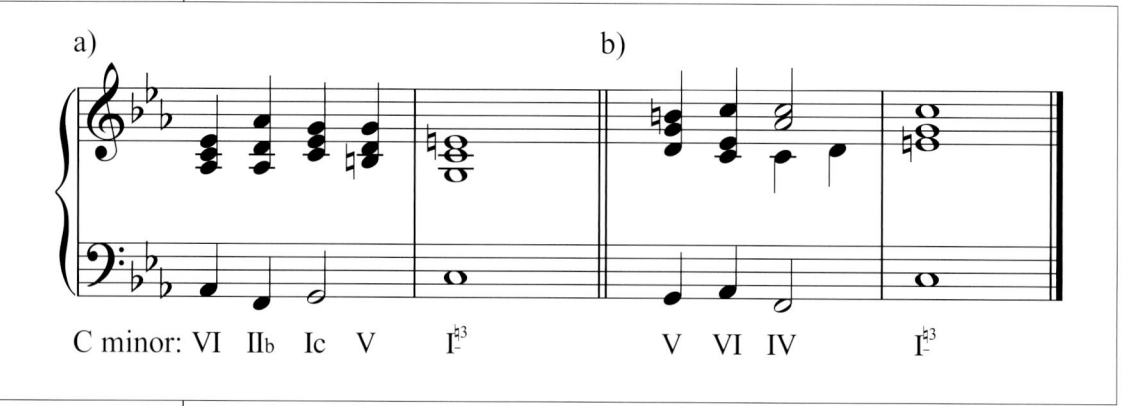

Some other forms of chromatic alteration are also frequently used in a minor key. The **Neapolitan sixth** is a chord based on the flattened second degree (♭II). A such it runs parallel to the effect of changing VI to ♭VI in a major key (see above). However, the voice leading requires it to be in first inversion, to avoid a tritone leap in the bass to the root of the next chord, which is almost always V:

Finally, we have a kind of chromatically altered chord featuring the combination of the flattened sixth of the scale (as in the harmonic minor) and raised fourth, which together produce an interval of an augmented sixth. (That's a major sixth that's been enlarged by one semitone.) Hence it's known as an **augmented sixth chord**. It can be used in either a major or minor key, and comes in three versions, as shown below. These

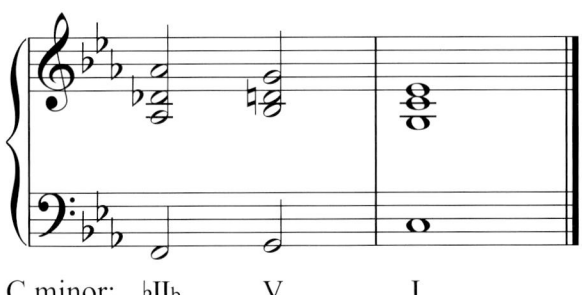

are (a) the **Italian sixth**, (b) the **German sixth**, and (c) the **French sixth**. These all typically resolve to V, with the raised fourth moving up a semitone to the dominant and the tonic moving down a semitone to the leading tone. In each case the process of deriving the chord from a normal chord in the minor scale is first shown. It's worth realising that (a) and (b) are derived by alteration and inversion from, respectively, chord IV and IV^7 of the minor scale, which we've learned is also commonly used as a borrowed chord in the major. By contrast, (c) is figured here as an alteration and inversion of chord II^7 in the minor. However, you should remember what we noted earlier, which is that II^7 tends to be heard as IV with an added sixth instead, in order to give it the significance of representing the subdominant counter-pole within the key. Hence we can also think of (c) as a version of IV, so that it, too, lends itself naturally to being transferred into a major key.

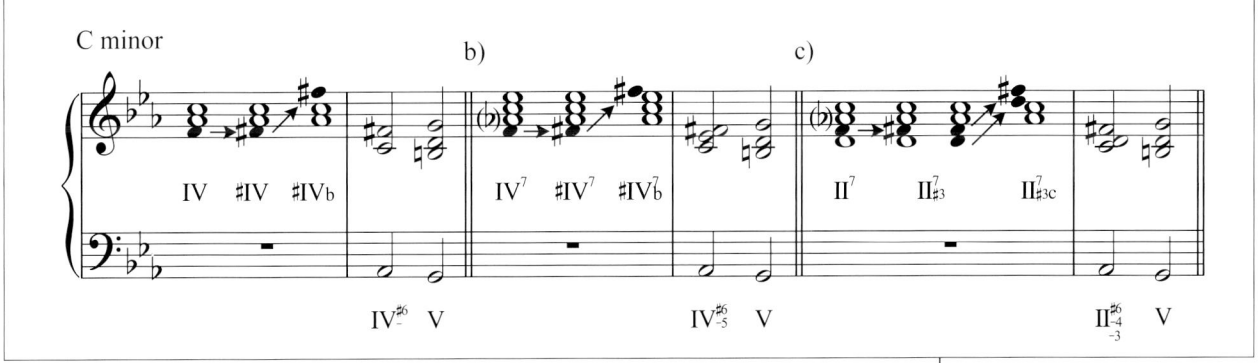

3) Secondary harmony

The third basic method that classical music uses to expand its range of harmonic possibilities involves creating harmonies in which a chord other than the tonic (I) is treated as if it were itself, temporarily, a tonic. There's a standard way of doing this: we take the chord that would be the dominant (V) relative to the key implied by this, and make whatever chromatic alterations are necessary for it to sound exactly as it would if the music really were in that key. However the music continues afterwards in the original key. Hence it seems as if the music was briefly passing through an alternative key, ie, modulating. If our sense that this is so is strong enough, we may call this a **passing modulation**. When a chord is employed as a dominant relative to a chord other than the tonic it's known as a secondary dominant, and this may take the form of any of the standard variations of dominant harmony already discussed – with or without a seventh, a ninth, or a flattened ninth, with the latter complete or incomplete (eg, appearing as a diminished seventh chord).

The next example shows the basic forms of these chords in C major and minor, in ascending order – realised here as dominant seventh chords. (Note that VII, typically a diminished triad, is not normally used as a temporary tonic in a major key, and is only treated this way in a minor key when it corresponds to the flattened seventh of the scale (as in the descending melodic minor scale). Likewise, in a minor key we don't treat II this way as it, too, is a diminished triad.) Try transposing all of these into as many other keys as you can.

Secondary dominants may also resolve onto forms of the chord treated as a tonic that are themselves altered (relative to what they should be in the original key). Chords II, III, and VI, which are minor in a major key, may be treated as major triads when preceded by their respective secondary dominants, producing a very bright effect.

In a minor key, we notice a very dark effect when major chords III and VI (and VII, if based on the descending melodic minor scale) are replaced by minor chords, as they may be when preceded by secondary dominants. (We can also switch V from a major to a minor chord in either a major or a minor key, but this is much less common as it threatens to undermine our sense of the real key of the music, producing a conclusive modulation rather than merely a passing one.)

Melody and chords (I)

Now we're ready to take some existing chords and see how a melody can be improvised above them. There are two different ways of doing this: one which seeks to preserve a strict contrapuntal relation between the melody and the actual bassline (as in standard classical practice) and another which adopts a looser approach, simply taking the chords in root position and seeing how an improvised melody can work over them (as in some kinds of jazz). We'll explore the first option now, and the second one in the final section of this unit.

UNIT 7 | SECTION 3

Here's the first 19 bars of J.S. Bach's keyboard classic, the 'Prelude In C major' from Book One of his *Forty-Eight Preludes and Fugues*. Amongst other things it's one of the most perfect examples of the use of extended harmony in classical music:

Now here are just the block chords that this texture is based on, with the chord functions shown underneath using Roman numerals:

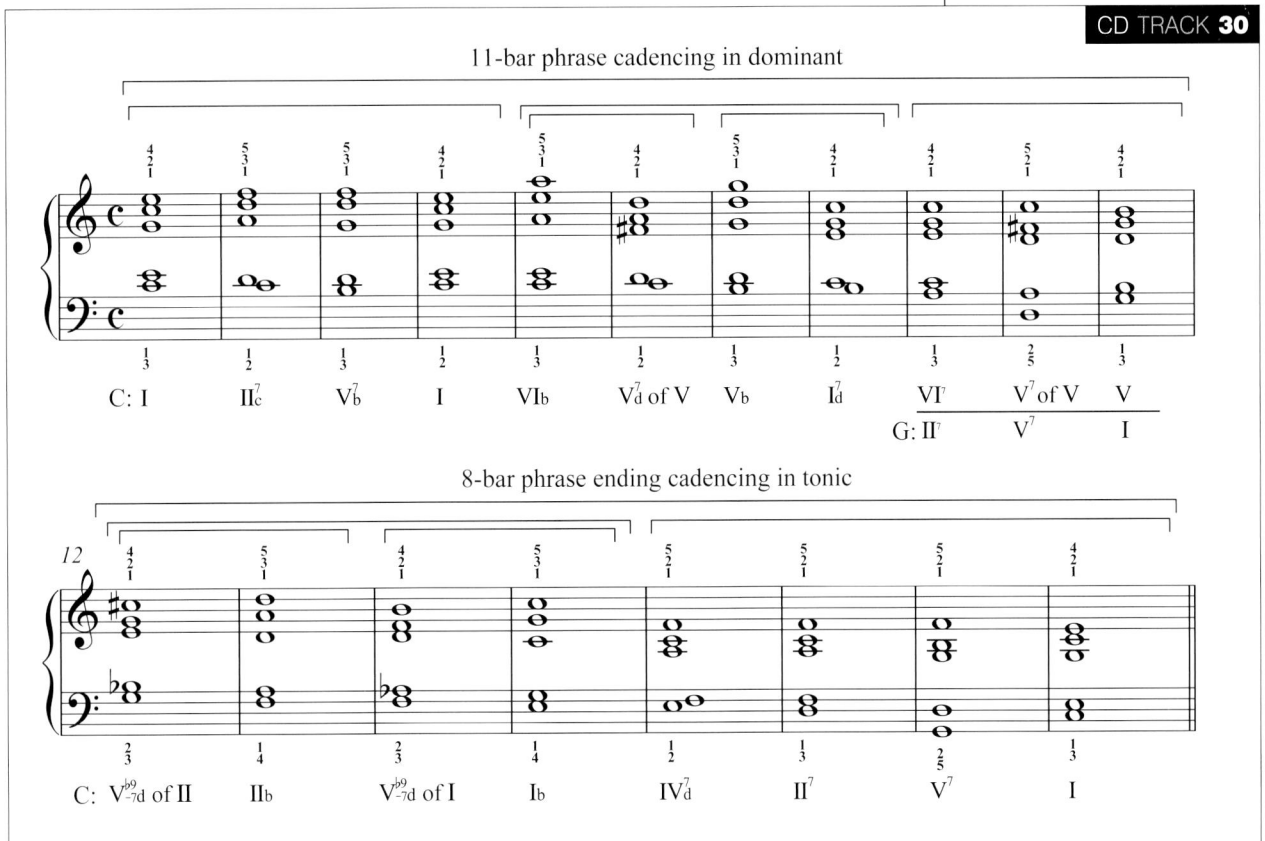

The first thing to do when improvising over a chord sequence is to get a firm grasp of its structure – so let's analyse this one. As you can see in the above example, here we have two large phrases: the first lasts for 11 bars and takes us from the home key (C major) to a perfect cadence in the dominant key (G major). The second takes us straight back in the direction of the home key rather than continuing in the key of the dominant, eventually ending with a perfect cadence in C major. (This reveals the move to G major to have been only a passing modulation.)

Within each of these overarching phrases we can also see some important structural features. The first 11 bars begin with a four-bar phrase that starts and finishes on chord I. (Note how Bach links the second chord to the first by retaining the same note in the bass – the root of I becomes the seventh of II in third inversion.) This is followed by another four-bar phrase, consisting of a two-bar progression repeated sequentially a step lower. (Here, too, we have a progression occurring over a repeated bass note, with the third of a first-inversion triad each time becoming the seventh of a seventh chord in third inversion.) The final three-bar phrase of the first eleven bars gives us a standard II-

V-I perfect cadence in the dominant, with chord VI in C functioning as the pivot chord that can also be heard as II in G.

The second large phrase, consisting of eight bars, also breaks down into smaller units. Of these, the first four-bar phrase (bars 12-15), like bars 5-8, uses a two-bar progression repeated sequentially a step lower. This time a diminished seventh chord (= incomplete dominant seventh with a flattened ninth in third inversion) resolves via stepwise movement in the bass to the tonic: note how the first time round this V-I progression involves V of II moving to II (ie, secondary harmony), but the effect of then repeating it a step lower is that the same structure comes out as V moving to I. Hence the effect of the sequence is to return us firmly to C major. You should be able to see how the technique of reusing the root of a chord in the bass as the seventh of the next chord (as in bars 1-2, 5-6 and 7-8) returns again, linking the last chord of bars 12-15 to the first chord of the final cadential progression. The latter then exactly reproduces the whole of the last five bars of the first phrase (bars 7-11) a perfect fifth lower so that it creates an equivalent cadential progression in the home key.

Notice how we've identified the structure of the music just from the harmony itself. This means that any melody improvised over these chords must reflect this structure. The simplest way to accomplish this is to use the top voice of the chords as a **melodic skeleton**. This skeleton will then function as a series of signposts that guide us as we improvise. You'll find this occurs quite naturally when we are improvising around chords with the standard division of three parts in the right hand and one in the left, as the most natural thing to do then is for the right hand to embellish the top part anyway.

So here are bars 1-11 again, with the top part highlighted as a skeleton for improvising. (When working with just this opening fragment you'll find it easier to feel how the structure works if you hold the last chord on for one more bar so that the last unit becomes a four-bar phrase, just like the preceding ones. (See below.) Bach's deliberate use of a three-bar phrase, though irregular, makes sense as part of the longer-term structure of the music as a whole.)

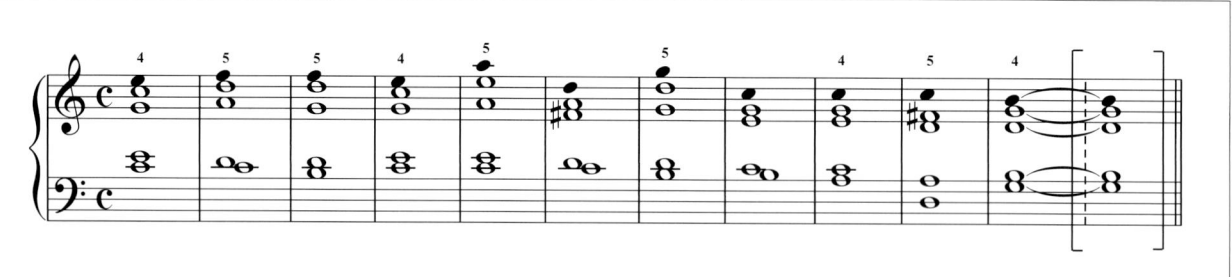

Now let's start off with the simplest possible ways of improvising around this, which involve stepwise elaboration of each move between notes of the skeleton. To get a sense of the different possibilities, we'll focus initially on just the first few bars, keeping the rhythm undefined. (As you work through the following examples, see how many different rhythms you can find to make the top part sound effective.) Here are a few obvious options for the first move in the skeleton.

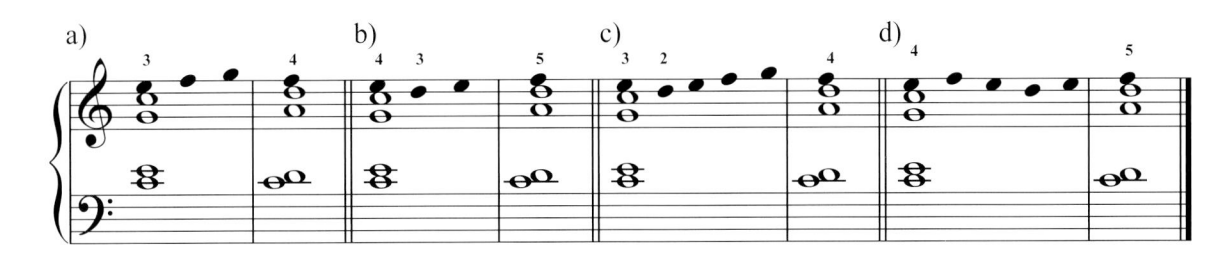

As you can see, we sometimes alter the fingering on the top note of a chord in the right hand to facilitate the fingering of subsequent notes: this requires you to anticipate the direction of the melody and its implications for fingering as you sound the chord:
- If you think the melody will go mainly up next, 'shift down' with the fingers (change the right-hand fingering on the top note of the chord in the direction of the thumb).
- If you think the melody will go mainly down next, 'shift up' with the fingers (change the right-hand fingering on the top chord-note in the direction of the little finger).

If this means releasing other notes in the chord, that's usually fine – use the sustaining pedal to ensure that those notes sound for as long as possible, but avoid blurring the melody with over-pedalling. (You should be especially careful about this when the melody moves by step rather than leaping between harmony notes.)

Each embellishment will suggest an answering embellishment of the next two notes of the melodic skeleton, hopefully resulting in a nicely rounded four-bar melodic phrase:

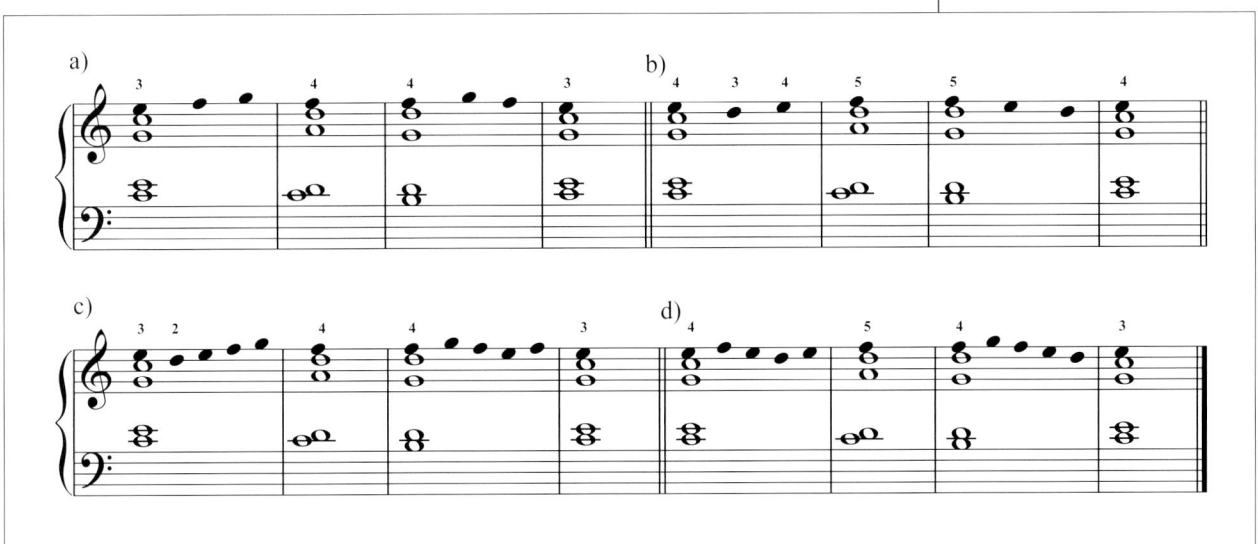

Leaps between harmony notes that belong to the same chord are also acceptable, and these make possible additional stepwise embellishments:

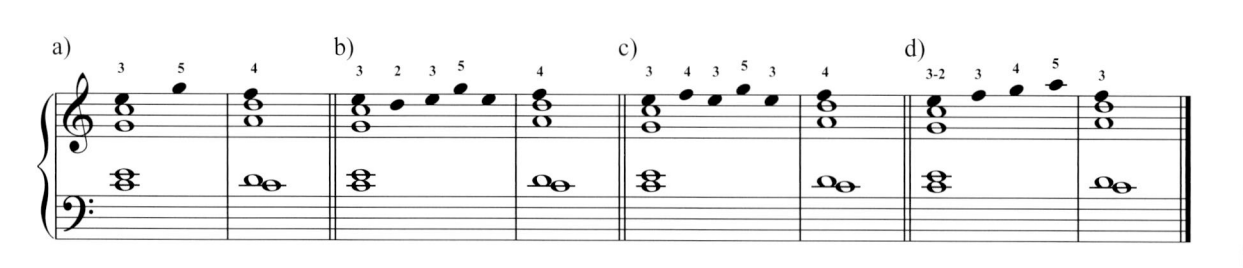

These, too, suggest answering embellishments that should aim to achieve satisfactory four-bar phrases:

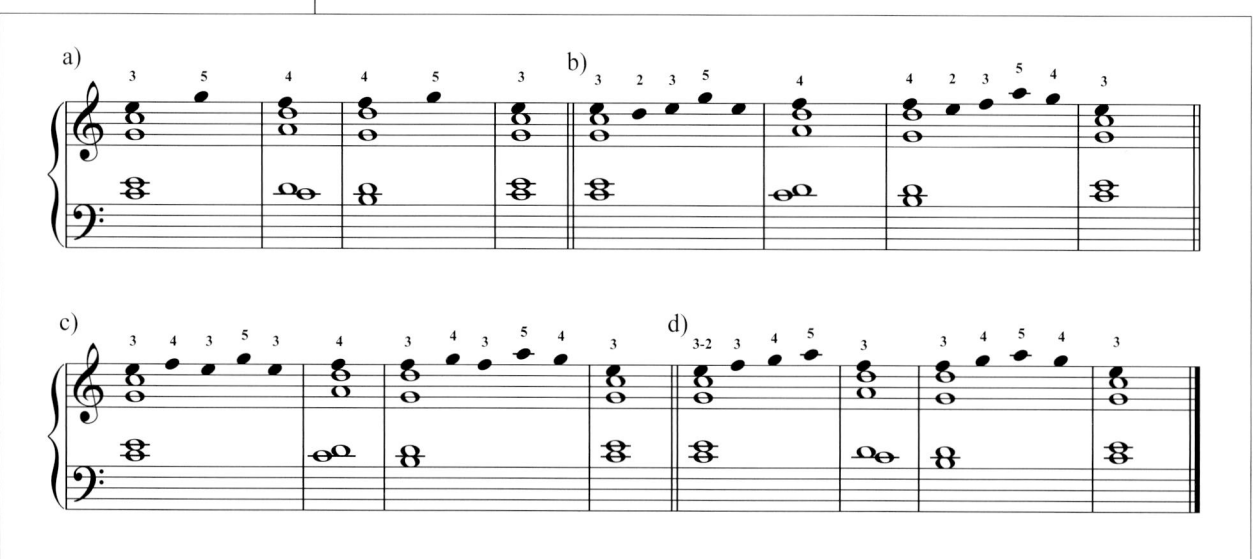

Now we'll take the whole of the first 11 bars (with final bar extended over for one extra bar, to make 12) and see what a longer embellishment could look like. Note how the melody reflects the chromatic alterations introduced by the harmony in bars 6 and 10.

And here's an example of what we could then do with the next eight bars.

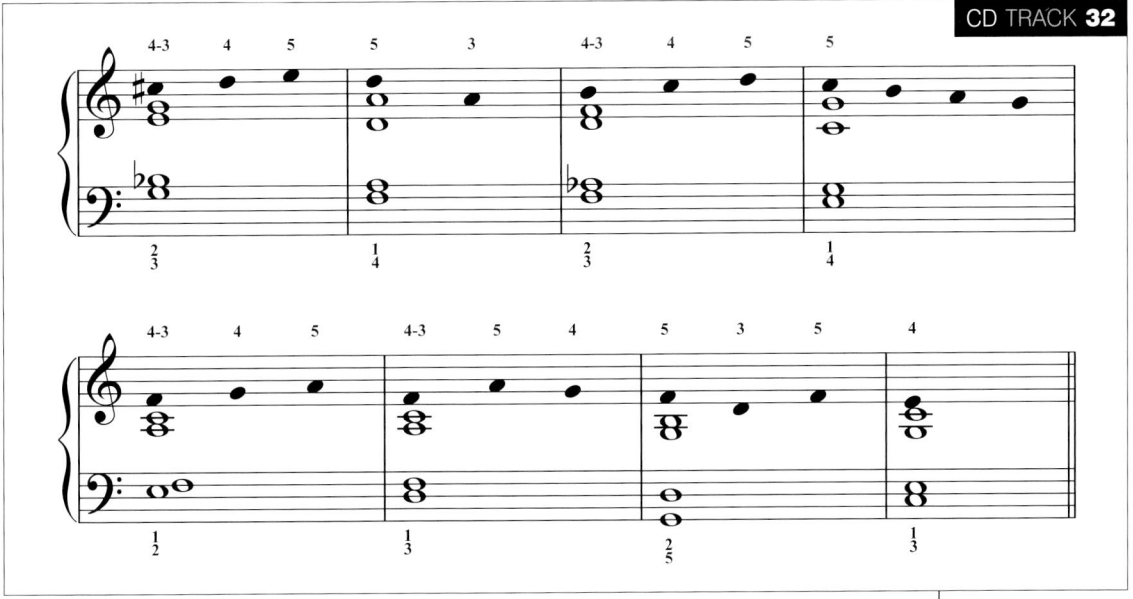

UNIT 7 | SECTION 3

Exercise 7.16.
Now it's your turn. First try improvising your own melody lines over the chords of the Bach given earlier. Afterwards, if you want more practice at this, get hold of a copy of the whole piece and work out the underlying chords (as we did here) for the remaining bars. Then use the top part as a melodic skeleton for improvising over these.

The next step is to free up the right hand by transferring some or all of the harmony into the left hand. Remember that in classical music especially you must still be aware of the relationship between the melody and the other parts, so having a melodic skeleton is still a good idea. The simplest method is to retain just the top part in the right hand as a skeleton and move the rest into the left hand wherever possible, as shown in the next example:

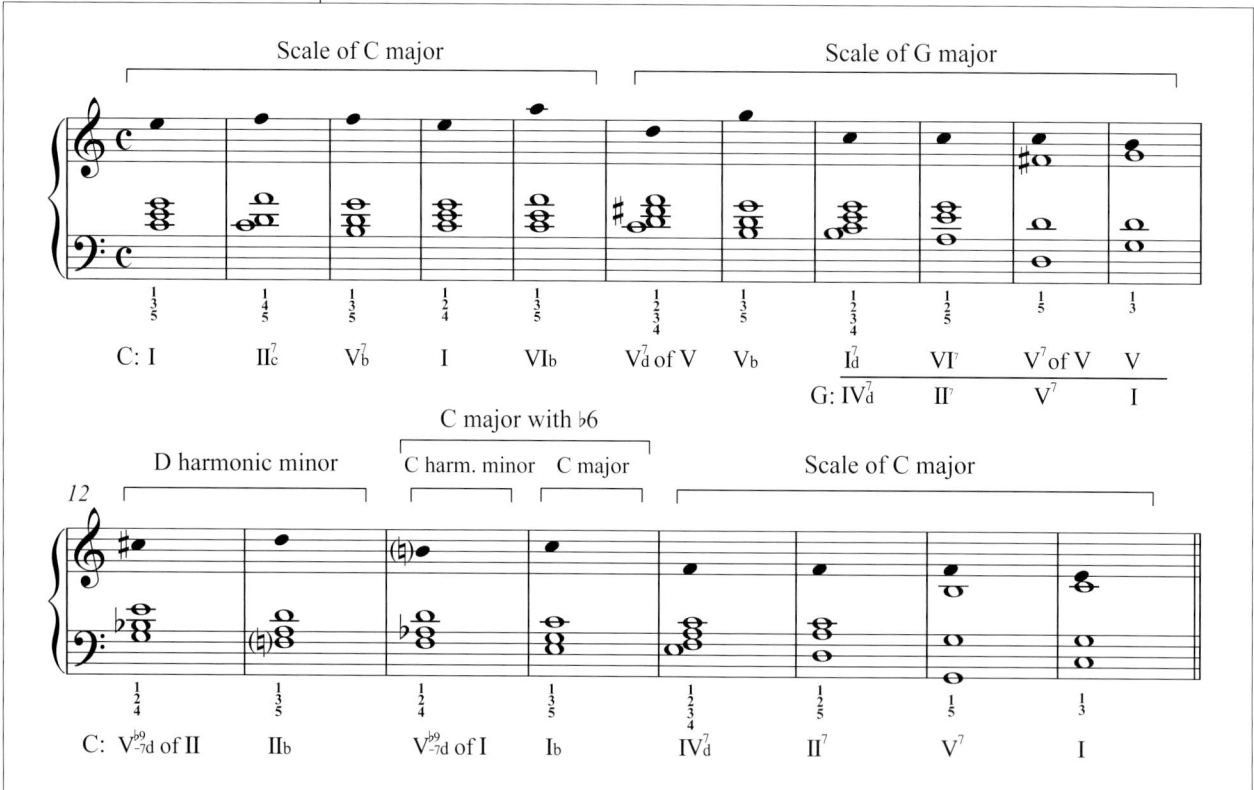

Once you've freed up your right hand to improvise around the skeleton, you need to know what notes to use. The presence of secondary and chromatic harmony, implying passing modulations, as well as more lasting modulations, means that the scale of the home key won't work over every chord. That's why the choice of scale for improvising is shown above the chords in the last example.

Note how the diminished seventh chord resolving to a chord of C major in bars 14-

15 implies a mixture of major and minor elements: the B-natural and A-flat in bar 14 imply C harmonic minor, but the E-natural in the next bar clearly suggests C major. We can understand this in two ways, both of which make musical sense:

- As implying a succession of two scales: first C minor (bar 14), then C major (bar 15).
- As implying one scale: C major with a chromatically altered sixth (A-flat) for bars 14 and 15.

Exercise 7.17. CD Track 33

Try improvising around the skeleton in the previous example, paying careful attention to the indications of what scale to use. (For a demo of how this might sound, listen to Track 33 on the CD.)

CD TRACK 33

Note that you can also extract other parts from the texture to serve as a skeleton, or borrow material freely from different parts at different times, as in the next example. (The left hand chords then need to be re-voiced to avoid unsatisfactory doublings, etc.). The implied scales for melodic improvising are unaffected by this.

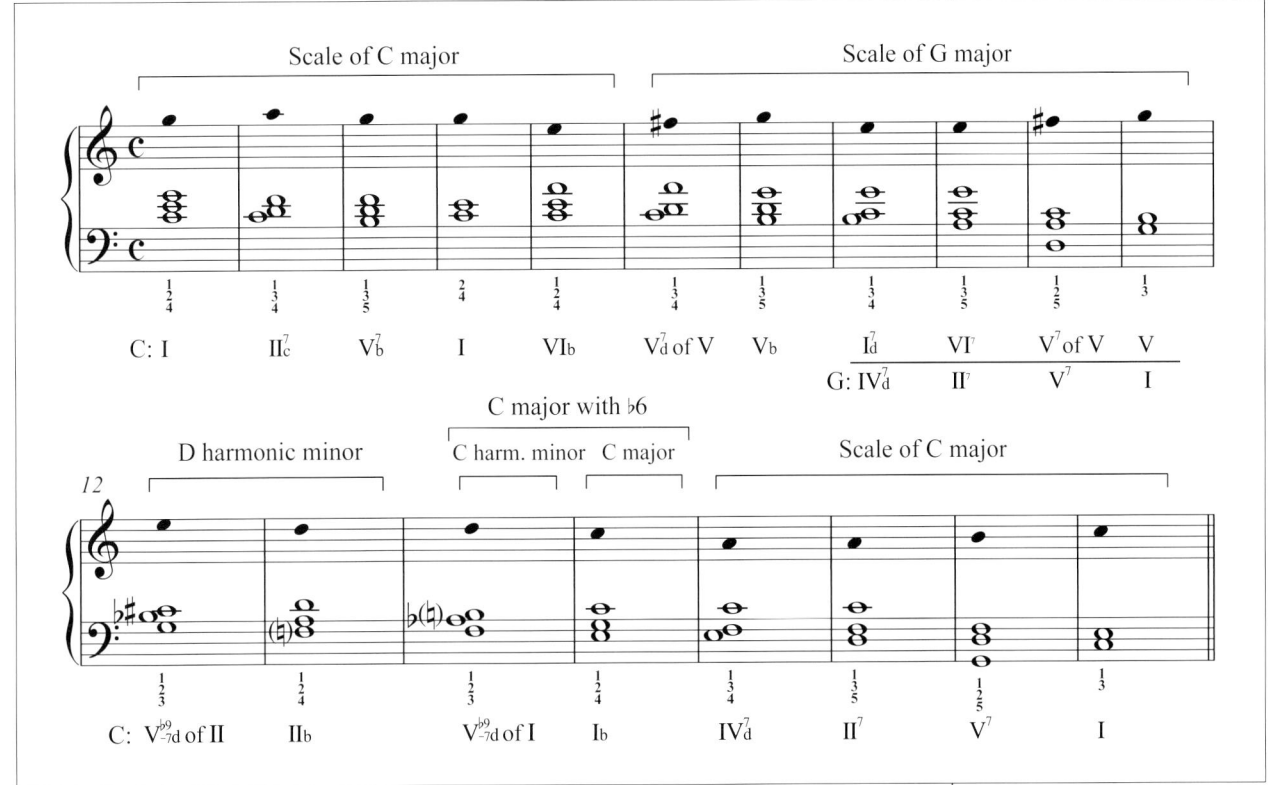

UNIT 7 SECTION 3

CD TRACK 34

Exercise 7.18. CD Track 34
Try improvising around the alternative skeleton given in the previous example. (For a demo of how this might sound, listen to Track 34 on the CD.) Then try to extract your own skeleton from the harmony and improvise around that.

The next step in freeing up the right hand is to transfer all the harmony into the left hand. However, this already takes us in the direction of the looser approach to the relationship between melody and harmony mentioned earlier, so we won't look at this until the final section of this unit.

> Many keyboard preludes from the Baroque period can be used as a source of good chord sequences for improvising. There's a reason for that: the Baroque prelude was a genre that was often itself improvised, and this was done by taking harmonic formulas that were easy to memorise and turning them into different keyboard textures. Hence the chord structures make especially good harmonic sense by themselves and are well suited to embellishment.

Melodic variation

The term **variation** has a specific meaning in classical music. It's used as the collective name for the techniques that composers and improvisers make use of when they want to derive an extended stretch of music from a given musical theme by presenting it in a series of altered versions. In fact, one of the most basic ways of extending any musical idea is to restate it, changing some aspects but leaving others the same, so that it sounds different but is still recognisable. We can vary melodies, textures and harmonic structures, but the most important of these for improvising is, without any doubt, the variation of a melody. (We'll explore the others in later parts of this book). Taking just melody as our starting point, there are a number of kinds of variation we can apply:

- Melodic embellishment = introducing additional material into the melodic line itself.
- Rhythmic variation = change of rhythm and/or metre.
- Reharmonisation = altering the chords or tonality implied by the melody.
- Change of colour and texture = change of register or articulation; doubling of melody.

> Many of these techniques are also used in jazz: so much so that some people claim jazz improvisation is based on the same techniques as classical variation. However, while it does use these same techniques, jazz is not normally pursuing what classical musicians mean by 'variation'. We'll go into this more in the next unit.

The first two of these normally go together, but not always in the same way. Melodic embellishment means adding extras notes, so the rhythm also gets more elaborated, but the underlying rhythmic structure and metre are not normally affected. On the other hand, rhythmic variation usually involves some sort of structural change to the rhythm and/or metre, which usually then also entails adding or removing some notes from the melody itself, affecting the latter's shape but not changing it fundamentally.

Here's one of the melodies from earlier in this unit being varied through melodic embellishment. It's 'Camptown Races'.

In this case the variation consists mainly of introducing lower auxiliary notes (eg, bars 1-2) or escape notes (bars 3-4). Now here's 'Scarborough Fair' with melodic embellishments and a few rhythmic variations:

Note how in three of the four-bar phrases eighth-notes are used to create a 'lead-in' effect on the upbeat preceding the first strong beat of the phrase. This produces a variation of the rhythmic structure, as each phrase now starts in the middle of the previous bar – creating an **anacrusis** effect. Note also how the **appoggiatura** (B) at the start of bar 7 has been changed to an eighth-note to make it more emphatic, while a similar figure has been added in bar 10 (though here it's actually a **suspension** as the dissonance is prepared in the preceding bar). One of the most natural ways to embellish a melody is for leaps to be filled in with stepwise movement, as in bar 5 of the above example.

Rhythmic variation may involve altering the subdivision of beats, or special effects such as syncopation or anacrusis. Replacing even divisions of a beat with dotted rhythms, or replacing divisions into two or four with triplets that divide the beat into equal thirds can also effective. A more fundamental change consists of altering the metre itself, either by changing the number of beats in a bar or switching between simple and compound time. Here's the opening of 'Camptown Races', in compound instead of simple time:

And here's 'Scarborough Fair', moved from simple triple time into simple duple. Notice how the note-repetitions and syncopations introduced to accommodate the three-notes-per-bar feel of the original tune leave room for melodic embellishments too:

Now here's a very simple reharmonisation of 'Camptown Races' that puts it from major into minor. This time the rhythm is simplified, with repeated notes omitted to support the more reflective feel of a minor tonality, but the basic shape of the tune remains recognisable:

In the next example some parts of 'Scarborough Fair' have been reharmonised by substituting alternative chords. In bar 8 chord I is replaced by V, creating an imperfect instead of a plagal cadence, and in the bar 9 chord I has been replaced again, this time by VI (a common substitute for I, as we saw in Unit Four.) A more adventurous variation is introduced in the final four bars, using a Neapolitan sixth (♭II) in bar 14 and a borrowed major triad on I (Tierce de Picardie) in the final bar. The voice-leading is realised below so you can hear the precise effect of the reharmonisations:

> It's also worth knowing that **classical reharmonisation** of a melody isn't quite the same as **jazz reharmonisation** of a chord sequence, though the two are related. In classical music a melody may be restated with only the harmony altered, or with a change of tonality or mode (eg, from major to minor or vice versa) that leaves the melodic shapes and intervals broadly the same. In jazz, however, reharmonisation of a chord structure involves taking a familiar sequence of harmonies and deliberately substituting other chords, just so that entirely new melodic possibilities are created.

Varying the texture or colour of a melody normally involves changes to the overall texture or colour of the music, for example by changing dynamics and articulation, or doubling the line in octaves, thirds, or sixths. We'll explore these possibilities in the section on colour and texture in Unit Nine.

Exercise 7.19.
Now get hold of the sheet music for some well known melodies you really like. First practise each one till you can play it fluently from memory. Then look and see if you can analyse the harmony. (Can you figure the chords as Roman Numerals under the music?) Try varying the melody as you play it, experimenting with the techniques mentioned above. To begin with, keep the harmony unchanged. Later on, try varying the harmony too.

Melody and chords (II)
Now for the second approach to improvising a melody above chords. This involves a significant loosening up of the relationship between melody and harmony, since we focus more on how melody notes sound in relation to a given chord (with its stated or implied root), and less on how they relate contrapuntally to the actual melodic unfolding of the bass. The big advantage is that this allows us to put all of the harmony into the left hand if we want to, leaving the right hand free to explore melodic possibilities of improvisation.

This approach is most typical of jazz – the focus of the next unit – but it's also worth exploring how it works with the sort of melodic and harmonic material we're already familiar with, as then you can see how it relates to the classical techniques discussed here.

SECTION 3 | UNIT 7

> Relating a melody just to chords rather than to a specific bassline is the first step in the direction of the much looser approach to improvising found in jazz. It's especially useful if you want to get involved in open-ended group-based improvising – what jazz and rock musicians call **jamming** – since it allows the bassline to be varied independently of the melody above it. Even so, the most exciting improvising only happens when you've mastered both approaches and can move between them or mix them up quite freely.

Basically we ignore any actual bassline and just treat all chords as in root-position: as having an implied or stated root in the bass. Consonance and dissonance in the melody are now treated as depending on the interval between the melody note and the root of the chord, though they also vary with the type of chord, as the chart shows:

	Interval above root of a major triad:	Interval above root of a minor triad:	Interval above root of a diminished triad:
Strong dissonances: avoid or resolve immediately	Perfect 4th	Minor 6th, major 7th	Minor 2nd (9th)
Weak dissonances: need not be avoided, but should resolve	Major 2nd, major 6th, major 7th	Major 2nd, perfect 4th, major 6th, minor 7th	Perfect 4th, minor 6th, minor 7th
Consonances: already resolved	Major 3rd, perfect 5th, octave	Minor 3rd, perfect 5th, octave	Minor 3rd, diminished 5th

Note that the intervals that form strong dissonances over these triads will also do so over seventh chords containing the same triads. Hence a perfect fourth will be a strong dissonance over a dominant seventh, a minor sixth will be very dissonant over a seventh chord built on a minor triad, and a minor second (or minor ninth) will sound highly dissonant over a diminished seventh chord. (In each case this is because the melody note forms an interval of a minor ninth with one of the notes in the chord.)

To see how this works in practice, here are the same chords from the Bach prelude we were exploring earlier, only this time shifted entirely into the left hand. A good way to grasp their implications for our melodic improvising is to think of the scale we use as starting on the note that's the root of the chord. The example on page 266 shows this. (Note how the chords are now figured as in root position regardless of which note actually sounds at the bottom, since in each case the root is implied as the bass note.)

Of course we can also think in terms of a skeleton, consisting perhaps of notes that stand in consonant relations to the roots of the chords, if we want to. Either way, we've lots more freedom now to decide for ourselves how we want to proceed, as the notes don't fulfil an essential role in the harmonic texture. We can even just allow our fingers to explore the keys for themselves, guided just by our ears, which will tell us when we should head for a note that's consonant with the harmony.

Exercise 7.20. CD Track 36
Now have a go at improvising freely in your right hand over the material in the previous example, using the appropriate scale for each chord and bearing in mind which notes count as strong or weak dissonances against the harmony. (For a demo of how this might sound, listen to Track 36 on the CD.)

> **'Creative' vs 'stylistic' improvisation.** This unit has concentrated on exploring the basic and essential skills you need to explore improvising in your own way while keeping within the overall framework of mainstream classical music. However, classical improvisation is sometimes practised in another way, which aims chiefly to reproduce the exact character of particular historical styles. Classical musicians call this 'stylistic improvisation'. It's mostly used as a basis for training performers and musicologists, to gain a better understanding of particular styles, though of course you can also do it for fun. Such an approach requires more detailed knowledge of particular historical periods, genres and styles – and so lies outside the scope of this volume.

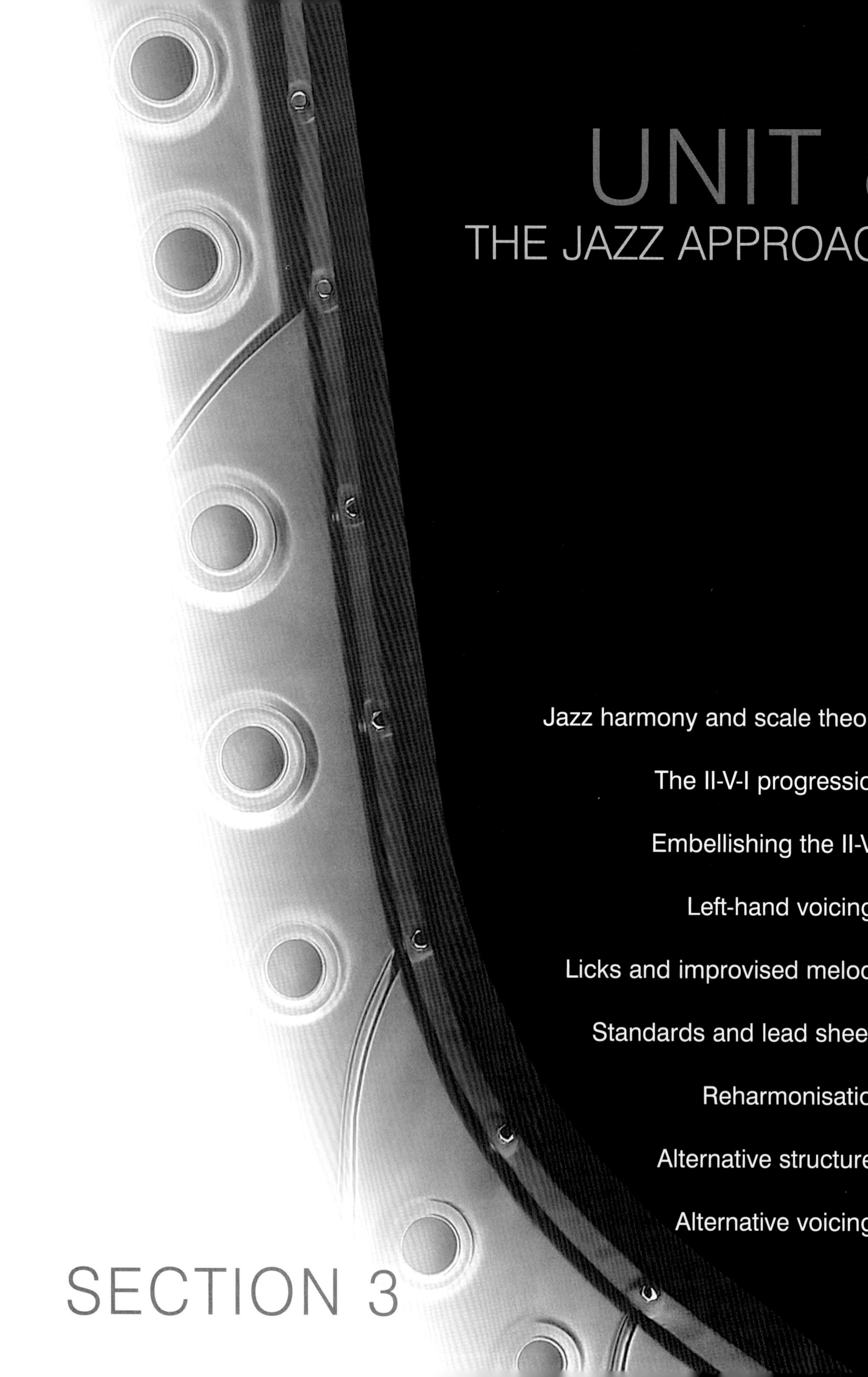

UNIT 8
THE JAZZ APPROACH

Jazz harmony and scale theory

The II-V-I progression

Embellishing the II-V-I

Left-hand voicings

Licks and improvised melody

Standards and lead sheets

Reharmonisation

Alternative structures

Alternative voicings

SECTION 3

SECTION 3 | UNIT 8

Jazz harmony and scale theory

If you've chosen to work through the previous unit before starting this one, you'll know that classical improvisation involves a three-way relationship between melody, chords, and bass. This means that in the classical approach we have to pay careful attention to how the melody relates to the surrounding texture not just harmonically but also contrapuntally. The fundamental contrast with the jazz approach is that in the latter we try to minimise, or even eliminate, the contrapuntal aspect of this relationship. The idea is to gain more freedom and flexibility as regards melodic improvising over the chords themselves. We've already had a taste of how this works, using classical harmony, at the end of the last unit. However, in jazz this becomes standard, so it requires a different way of thinking about how chords themselves work and how they relate to scales.

> Just as the previous unit aimed to present the fundamentals of the classical approach without trying to copy specific styles (as in so-called 'stylistic improvisation'), this unit presents the fundamentals of the jazz approach in a way that's largely independent of any particular type of jazz. Nearly all books that teach jazz focus on giving transcriptions of voicings and solos by individual jazz artists, encouraging you to copy these and learn by example, without explaining how they really work. Of course it's good to explore that approach if you want to cultivate a particular style, and you certainly should listen to as much jazz as possible and try copying things you like the sound of, but it's better to do it by ear than working from transcriptions in a book. What a book can offer, however, is help with mastering the essential melodic and harmonic structures of jazz, and with understanding the principles behind them.

In order to suppress the contrapuntal implications that arise when a melody unfolds over simple chords and a bass line, jazz broadens the concept of what counts as chord to include more than just the triad. We've already seen how dominant and diminished seventh chords (and thus, by implication, also dominant ninth chords) were introduced into classical music to raise the level of harmonic tension, especially of dominant harmony. We've also seen other cases of the use of seventh chords in classical music. (Think of the chords in the Bach prelude that we were improvising over in the previous unit: they included seventh chords built on other major and minor triads as well as on the dominant.)

In the second half of the 19th century such chords came to be more and more widely used in classical music itself. By the time jazz began to evolve, in the early decades of the 20th century, composers like Debussy and Ravel had gone a stage further and were making use of such chords without bothering to resolve the dissonances created by adding the seventh or sixth to triads. Jazz took this over and made it the norm, so that from the outset we think of the chord itself as including the seventh – as being a seventh chord rather than a triad.

Indeed, jazz musicians then went even further: they began to think of each chord as including all of the possible **chord extensions** it could have when we add notes to the chord by stacking them in thirds above one another – ie, the seventh, ninth, 11th (= fourth) and 13th (= sixth) – while keeping in mind the scale of the key of the music. So exceptional effects in classical harmony came to count as part of the basic harmonic framework of jazz.

This allowed jazz to be much more flexible in its treatment of dissonance. Once it is accepted as normal for chords to include notes other than the basic triad, some dissonance becomes a standard, permanent feature of the harmonic texture. Against this background the need to resolve dissonances that occur contrapuntally between the melody and other voices in the texture is greatly reduced.

At the same time, the inclusion of dissonances into chords means that many of the classical principles of voice-leading lose their significance, since for the most part we can no longer perceive the difference they are supposed to make in terms of ensuring continuity and evenness of harmonic texture. This means we're free both to improvise melodies without worrying about the contrapuntal treatment of dissonance, and to develop chordal textures and harmonisations without worrying about the refinements of chord layout and voice-leading. As far as the latter are concerned, only the crudest principles still apply. These can be fulfilled just by keeping to certain basic and recurring formulas that define how particular chords are laid out when they appear in the most common progressions. Once a jazz musician is completely familiar with these formulas in all the different keys he or she can call upon them automatically while improvising and there's no need to worry about whether any rules are being broken or not.

1) Jazz chord theory

> The relationship between scales and chords in jazz has two aspects: on the one hand, as in classical music, chords are constructed out of scales, so scales are the basis for chords. On the other hand, once we actually get going with jazz improvising we find that the chords also furnish the basis for turning scales into melody. So where do we start, with chords or scales? Here we'll start with how chords come from scales, as this follows the same logic as classical harmony. Then we'll explore how jazz transforms chords into melody.

Whether talking about scales or chords, in jazz we always use the diatonic major scale as a basic reference point. Then we indicate other scales and harmonic relationships by thinking of them as alterations from this. Here are the total set of chord extensions we get if we superimpose intervals of a third using just notes from the major scale based on the note that is also the root of the chord – in this case C major. Note that this gives us a chord containing all seven notes of the scale:

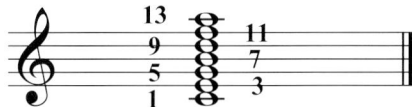

Now let's see what happens if we build a seventh chord on each step of the scale. Here, as with classical harmony, we normally create chords using notes from the overall scale for the key, in this case C major. (However, in view of the frequent use of the diminished seventh chord in major-key music, in both classical and jazz, we'll also include this here as an alternative seventh chord on VII, in spite of the fact that it involves a chromatic alteration from the major scale.)

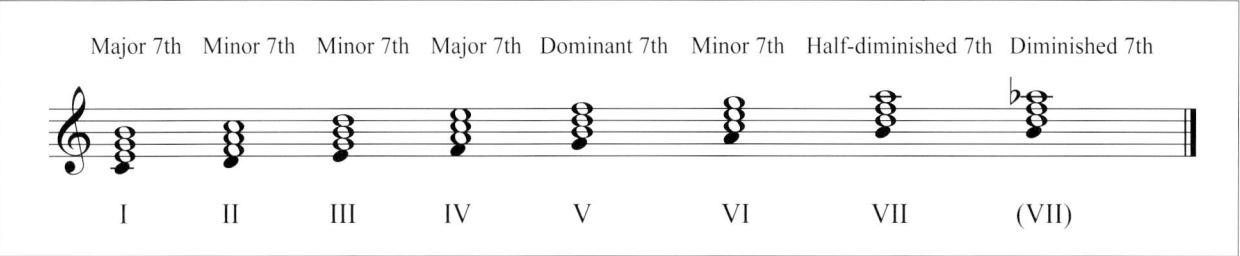

The result is that depending on which degree of the major scale the chord is built on, the type of seventh chord is different. To grasp the different kinds of seventh chord it's best to see how they look over a common root. Then it becomes obvious that each of them corresponds to a stage in a series of **chromatic alterations** of the form that a seventh chord takes when it occurs on the tonic in a major key (ie, as chord I). Starting from this, each of the others flattens one more note by a semitone, until the third, fifth and seventh are all flattened relative to the major scale and tonic chord. Finally, a diminished seventh chord type flattens the seventh of the chord yet again.

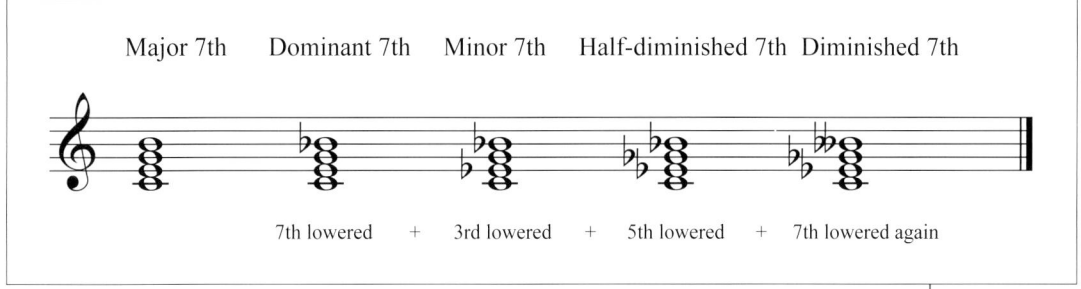

The following table highlights how the notes within each type of seventh chord stand relative to the major scale based on the same note as the root of the chord:

Chord				
Major seventh chord	1	3	5	7
Dominant seventh chord	1	3	5	♭7
Minor seventh chord	1	♭3	5	♭7
Half-diminished chord	1	♭3	♭5	♭7
Diminished chord	1	♭3	♭5	♭♭7

Now here's a table to show the chord symbols used in jazz to indicate the different types of triad and/or seventh chord.

Chord type	Notation
Major triad	C or C$^\Delta$
Major 7th	Cmaj7, CM7, C$^{\Delta 7}$ or C$^\Delta$
Dominant 7th	C^7
Minor triad	Cmin, Cm or C$^-$
Minor 7th	Cmin7, Cm7, C^{-7} or C$^-$
Diminished triad	Cdim or C$^\circ$
Half-diminished 7th	Cm7♭5 or C$^{\varnothing 7}$
Diminished 7th	Cdim7 or C^{o7}
Augmented triad	Caug, C$^{\sharp 5}$, C$^+$ or C^{+5}

These are related to the symbols used in classical Roman numeral notation, but there are also important differences. The most important of these is that in jazz they come after the letter name of the actual root of the chord, rather than a numeral indicating the scale degree of the key this root represents. In other words, chord symbols in jazz and other modern non-classical styles like rock or pop are always key-specific. Another is that inversions are indicated using what are known as **slash chords**: the name of the chord is followed by the letter name of the actual bass note, separated by a slash. A chord of C major in first inversion is written as C/E, in second inversion as C/G, etc.

Apart from extending triads into seventh chords, jazz also uses the technique of simply adding more notes to a triad without regard to their position in the series of superimposed thirds that's used when we wish to extend the structure of the triad itself. The result is what are called **added-note chords**. The most common note to be added is the sixth, but the fourth may also be used. (Also, occasionally, the second, though this is more common in heavy rock styles – the sort that regularly omit the third from chords to make them more strident.) Complications arise, however, owing to the fact that these notes are identical to the 13th and 11th, which also appear as chord extensions. Whether we think of them as added notes or extensions therefore depends on the type of harmony, as the table shows:

Major triad or seventh chord	9th	(Added 2nd)	Added 4th	Added 6th
Dominant seventh chord	9th	11th	13th	
Minor triad or seventh chord	9th		11th	Added 6th

These are the foundations of the jazz approach to understanding chords. How chords then get laid out and used is mostly a matter of their role in actual progressions. We'll take a look at that after we've first explored the rudiments of how scales work in jazz.

2) Jazz scale theory

Whereas classical music treats the major and minor scales as equally basic, jazz operates differently. Firstly, it regards the major scale as the basic form of the diatonic scale, and tends to regard minor-key harmony as a secondary option. (In fact, as we'll see in practice later, chords based on the minor scale frequently function as alternative harmonisations for chord progressions that are actually in a major key.)

Secondly, like other non-classical styles (eg, rock and pop), it operates with a hierarchy of scales in which certain structures are treated as more basic than others, and as embedded in one other. This reflects the fact that the musical materials of jazz and jazz-influenced styles originally came out of a fusion of diverse traditions: for example, the diatonic harmonies of European and North American classical music; the folk melodies and religious hymns of white settlers, which feature the pentatonic (five-note) scale; and the blues idiom brought to cities in America after the emancipation of the slaves, with its distinctive use of flattened scale degrees over major-key harmony for an 'out-of-tune' effect, corresponding to the **blues scale**.

In jazz, rock, and pop this idea of a hierarchy of scales involves thinking of the pentatonic (five-note) scale – common to a great many folk traditions around the world – as embedded within the diatonic scale.

For each kind of diatonic scale (ie, major or minor) there is a version of the pentatonic scale that begins on the same note and can be thought of as present within it:

Major pentatonic (within major scale)

Minor pentatonic (within minor scale)

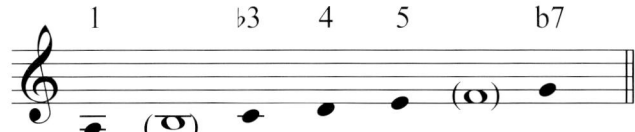

UNIT 8 | SECTION 3

Note that the pentatonic minor scale contains the flattened seventh and so is only present within those forms of the minor scale that also have the seventh flattened relative to the major scale (ie, the rock minor, and the descending melodic minor scale of classical music, as well as the version of the minor scale based on the Dorian mode).

Then if we also think of the tonic triad as a still more basic structure within the pentatonic scale, and of all of these as embedded in turn in the chromatic scale, we get a hierarchical model of how different kinds of scale relate to each other in major-key music:

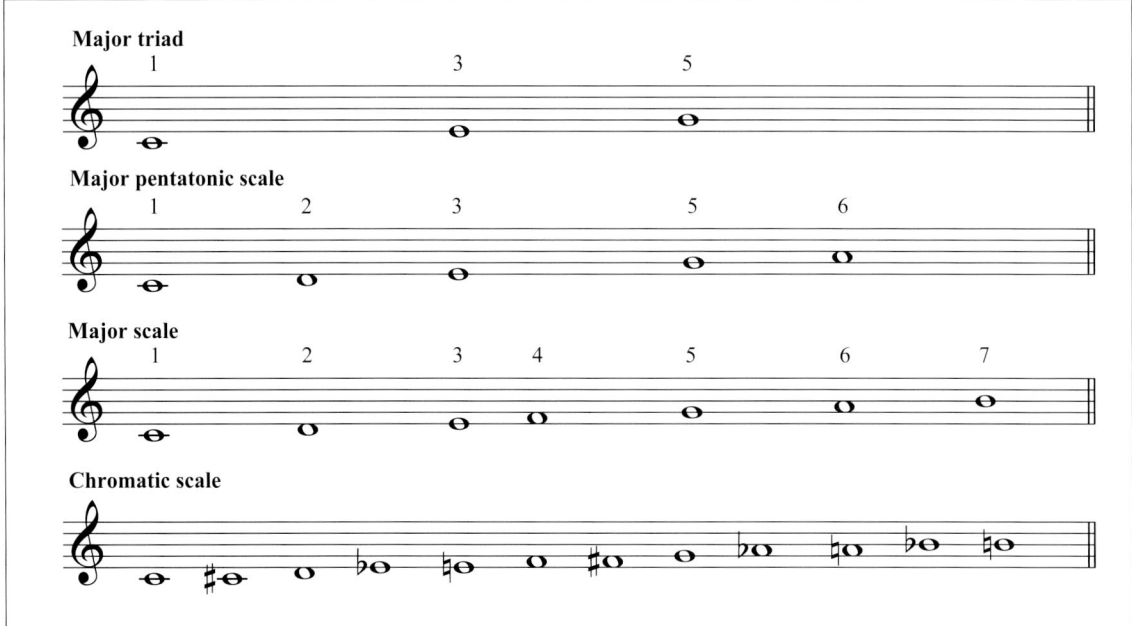

We can think of the minor triad and minor pentatonic scale, together with the various kinds of minor scale, as forming a similar hierarchy (opposite page). This also allows us to understand how the blues scale relates to the different elements of minor-key music.

However, it's important to remember that the blues scale, which often appears in jazz and rock as well as in blues music itself, is actually used over major-key harmony. (We'll explore the blues idiom in more depth in Unit Ten.)

Notice how the different minor scales listed in the example include the rock minor, the classical harmonic minor, the minor scale based on the Dorian mode, and the jazz minor. These all figure in jazz, but in different ways.

- The classical harmonic minor scale can be used when a traditional minor-key harmonic feel is called for.
- The jazz minor can be used as a source of scale material for advanced reharmonisations of chords in a major key. (See the section on reharmonisation near the end of this unit.)

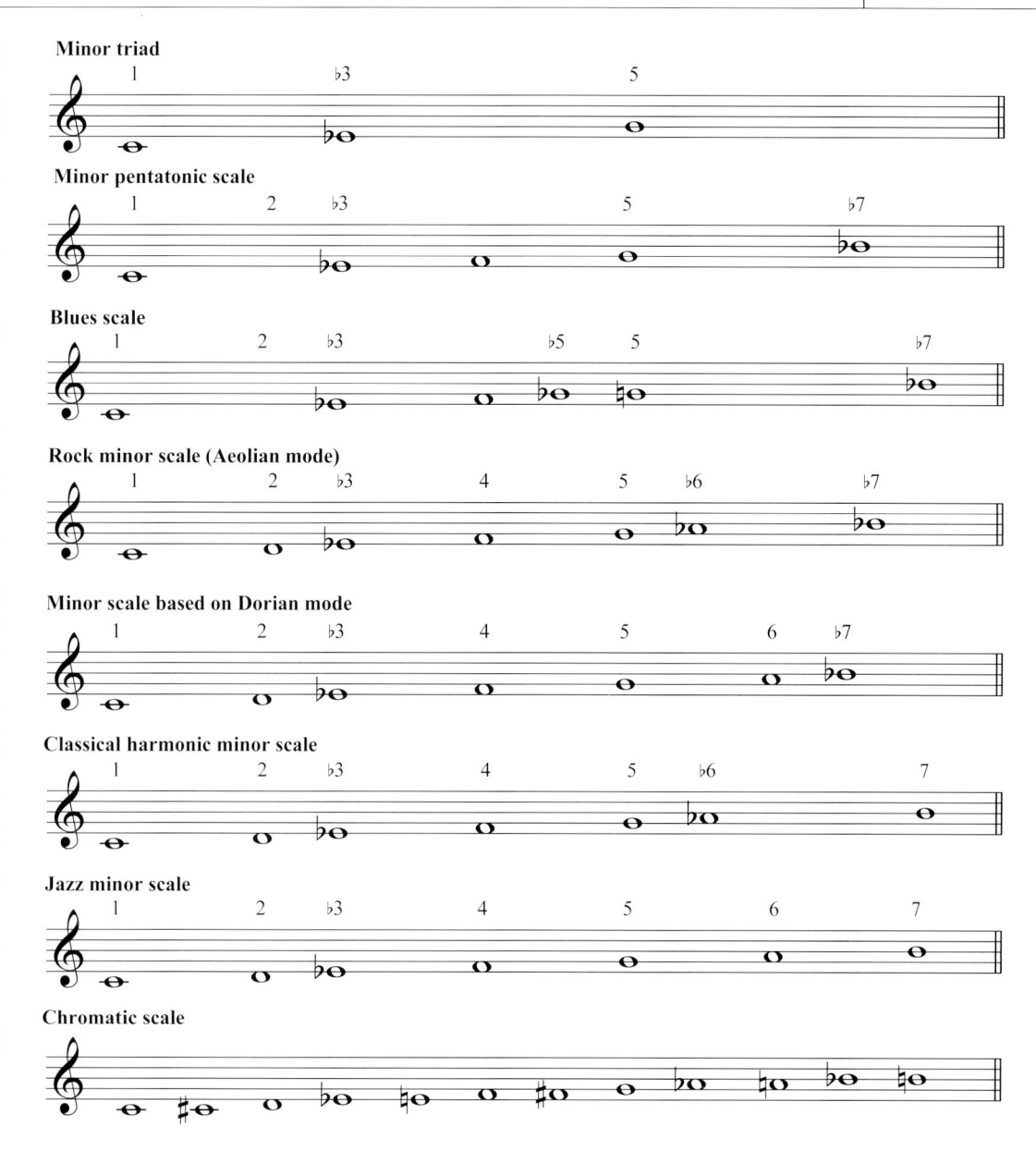

- The rock minor and the version of the minor scale based on the Dorian mode play an important role in **modal jazz** (see Unit Ten).

Jazz can also use a range of scales in which individual chromatic notes are inserted alongside the notes normally present in any of the diatonic major or minor scales: these are known as **bebop scales** owing to their important role in the jazz style known as bebop (which we'll explore in Unit Ten). Remember, though, that for the most part jazz harmony operates in a major key.

The next important aspect of jazz theory involves the relationship between chords and scales, and what are known in jazz as **modes**.

3) Putting scales and chords together

We've seen how jazz harmony uses chord extensions and added-notes, so scale-notes can be included in a chord even when they're not part of the triad for that chord. The result is that the contrapuntal dissonances between a melody and other parts in the harmony become largely inaudible. Then, when we start improvising a melody over these chords, we needn't worry about the rules of counterpoint: instead we can focus on how our melody sounds against the particular chord we're playing. (This is partly why jazz often gives listeners the impression of being music that's more strongly focused on the present moment. However, to some degree this is an illusion, as the underlying harmony remains part of a structure that reaches across time to create a sense of progression.)

This focus on how a melody sounds in relation to the particular chord that accompanies it finds practical expression in a special way of treating the relationship between the overall scale of the music and the particular chord sounding at any moment. Basically, we think of the scale as source material for a series of other scales consisting of the same notes, but each starting on a different degree of the original one. We then make use of the scale whose first note happens to correspond to the root of the chord at that moment to improvise over that chord.

Because the overall scale in jazz is usually a diatonic major scale, in effect we are using a major scale, but starting on steps other than the tonic (though starting on the tonic still also counts as an option here). The result is a series of different scales which correspond to the old **church modes** used in the earliest religious music in Europe. For this reason in jazz we also call them **modes**.

Here are the seven different modes we get when we keep to the notes of the scale of C major, but start (and end) on each degree of the scale in turn. (The alterations relative to a major scale starting on the same note are shown above each scale.) The different modes are still known by their old-fashioned Greek names.

By thinking of a scale as a mode by starting on the note that's the root of the chord, rather than on the one that's the tonic of the key, we are made to think about how the scale works over just that harmony, from the point of view of which notes sound functionally more or less resolved, and which notes are more or less dissonant.

Although we can think of each mode as just a reordering of the notes of the scale of the key we're in, it's also useful to try thinking of it as a scale in its own right. For example, each mode has its own distinctive sequence of whole-steps (tones) and half-steps (semitones). Here it can help to see how the modes look when they start on the same note, rather than being in the same key. In this case each one will be derived from a major scale in a different key (p278).

Modes in C major

Ionian - I

Dorian - II

Phrygian - III

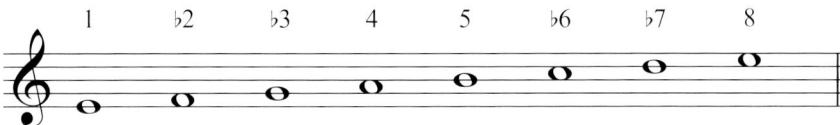

Lydian - IV

Mixolydian - V

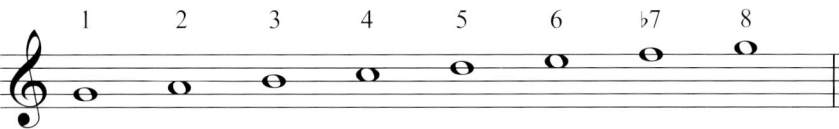

Aeolian - VI

Locrian - VII

UNIT 8 | SECTION 3

Modes on C (with implied keys)

Ionian (= C major)

Dorian (= B♭ major)

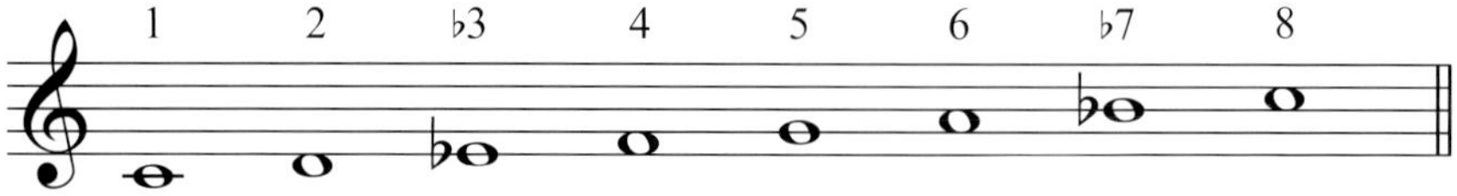

Phrygian (= A♭ major)

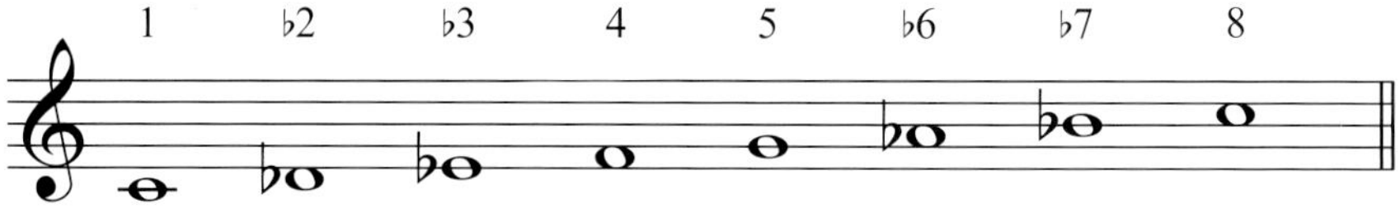

Lydian (= G major)

Mixolydian (= F major)

Aeolian (E♭ major)

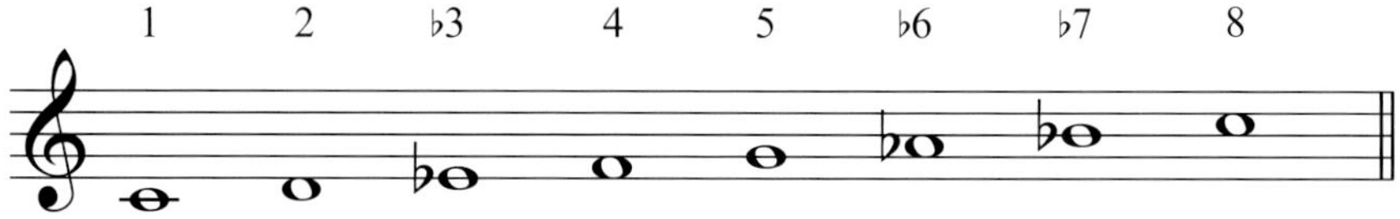

Locrian (D♭ major)

Looking at the number of notes raised or flattened relative to the major scale on the same note, we see that some modes are more closely related to the major scale than others, since they involve fewer alterations. This in turn functions as an indication of how close or far away on the Circle of Fifths their implied keys will be from that of the major scale on the same note.

So let's see how the different modes stand relative to a major scale on the same starting note, from the point of view of where their implied keys are located on the Circle of Fifths:

Mode	Alterations to major scale					Implied key when starting on C
Lydian					♯4	G
Ionian (= MAJOR SCALE)						C
Mixolydian				♭7		F
Dorian	♭3			♭7		B♭
Aeolian	♭3		♭6	♭7		E♭
Phrygian	♭2	♭3		♭6	♭7	A♭
Locrian	♭♭	♭3	♭5	♭6	♭7	D♭

Note how we get exactly the opposite order of modes if we take them in the form they have when based on the notes of a single major scale (rather than a single starting note), and list them in terms of how the resulting starting notes, corresponding to roots of chords in the key of that major scale, relate to the Circle of Fifths:

Mode	Alterations to major scale					Corresponding chord
Locrian	♭2	♭3	b5	♭6	♭7	VII
Phrygian	♭2	♭3		♭6	♭7	III
Aeolian	♭3			♭6	♭7	VI
Dorian	♭3			♭7		II
Mixolydian				♭7		V
Ionian (= MAJOR SCALE)						I
Lydian					♯4	IV

This second order is the one in which the modes appear when they correspond to chords in a progression with roots descending through the Circle of Fifths towards the tonic (and then, in the case of chord IV, beyond it). This is important because, as we saw in Unit Four, progressions with roots descending by fifths are the strongest and most common ones of all. That's true for both classical and jazz, but in jazz they also serve as the basis for a special kind of formulaic progression from which most other progressions are derived, and this is also used as a basis for defining the most commonly used forms of chord layout and voice-leading. It's known as the **II-V-I progression**, and we're going to explore it in the next section.

Because each chord in jazz can, in theory, include all the possible chord extensions made available by the notes of the scale on which it is built, the notes of each mode also correspond to the notes of a chord with a particular structure resulting from what sort of seventh, ninth, 11th, and 13th it has, as well as the more basic triad beneath these. Even so, certain notes in a mode can still stand out as exceptionally dissonant against the chord – usually because they form an interval of a minor ninth in relation to one of the more basic notes in the chord (ie, the root, third, or fifth). In jazz these correspond to the only dissonances we still have to worry about: they're known as **avoid notes**. Either we avoid them altogether (over the chords in question), or we treat them as needing to be resolved by stepwise movement to more consonant notes – just like in classical music.

The next example shows the entire series of extensions for each chord, together with the corresponding modes. This time they're presented in a special sequence that begins and ends on the tonic, with the roots of the chords descending by intervals of a fifth within the scale of the key – once again in C major. (This is still the order shown in the second diagram above, except that here we start with I, move down to IV at the bottom, then jump up to VII at the top of the list before passing downwards through the

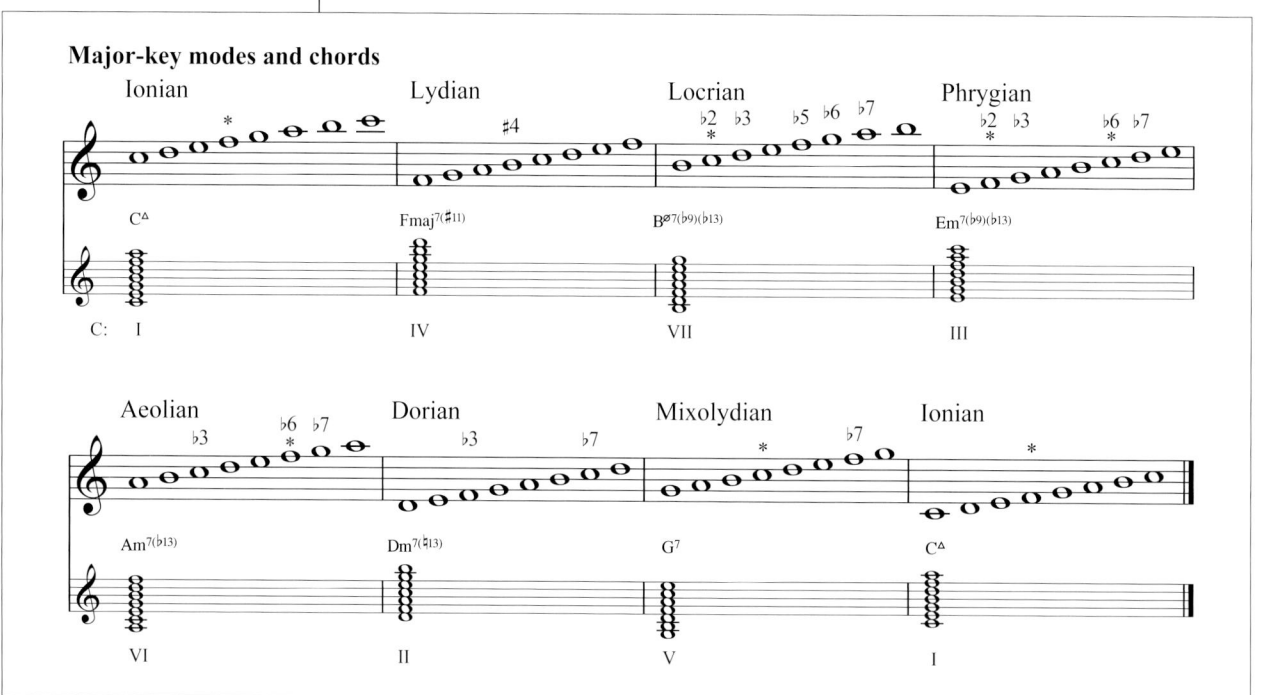

other chords to get back to I.)

Avoid notes are indicated here with an asterisk. If we find that we need to make prominent use of a scale degree that corresponds to an avoid note, then a common practice in jazz is to raise it by a semitone. (This softens the dissonance to acceptable proportions.) The next table shows this. When such chromatic alterations are used consistently over a period of time we start to hear them as belonging to the scale, and they may also then be introduced as chromatic alterations of the harmony itself. Sometimes the result is that one of the other modes is, in effect, then being used. (In the case of both III and VI, as you can see from the table below, this is the Dorian mode, which normally would appear on II. One consequence of this is that many jazz pianists opt to just treat all minor triads as if they were II chords. Then they use the Dorian mode to improvise over all of them.)

Mode	Chord	Raised note(s):	Resulting scale
Lydian		IV	none
Ionian (= MAJOR SCALE)	I	4th/11th	Lydian
Mixolydian	V	4th/11th	Lydian dominant
Dorian	II	none	
Aeolian	VI	6th/13th	Dorian
Phrygian	III	6th/13th; 2nd/9th	Dorian
Locrian	VII	2nd/9th	Locrian-♯2

In the cases of the Mixolydian (V) and Locrian (VII) modes, new scales are the result. These, along with other scales containing notes foreign to the key, are derived from the jazz minor scale by a similar process to that through which the modes are derived from the major scale. Such scales, and the chromatically altered chords that go with them, tend to be associated with alternative harmonisations – known in jazz as **reharmonisations** – of existing chord progressions. We'll explore these later in this unit.

The II-V-I progression

At the centre of the jazz approach to harmony lies the II-V-I progression. It's a neat chord sequence in which the three most important types of seventh chord – minor seventh, dominant seventh and major seventh follow directly on from one another in a logical movement that involves the level of harmonic tension first increasing (as we move from II to V) and then being resolved (thanks to the move from V to I, equivalent to a perfect cadence). At the same time the bass line delivers the strongest possible root-progression, as it falls by intervals of a perfect fifth (or rises by intervals a perfect fourth – the same thing).

The other thing that's special about this is that the shift from a seventh chord to another with a root a fifth lower allows us to make use of a fixed voice-leading formula that's invaluable for piano improvisers. Of course many other progressions are also used in jazz, but what's important is that they are often realised using the voice-leading structures typical of the II-V-I.

The simplest version of this progression involves three-part harmony, with the fifth of each chord omitted. At each stage of the voice-leading the seventh of a chord falls by one scale-step to the third of the next chord, while at the same time the third of the first chord is retained as the seventh of the next. The result is perfectly smooth voice-leading that can be used for any root progression involving descent by fifths, and that's easy to remember visually in any key. Either of the two upper parts may be placed on top of the texture. Here it is in the key of C major. Note the use of jazz chord symbols above the music. (Roman numeral chord symbols have been placed beneath the music as well for clarity, even though they are not commonly used in jazz.)

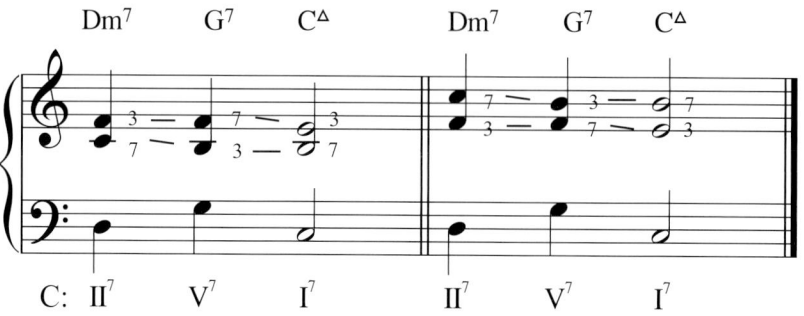

One feature of the above is the way each of the upper parts alternates between being the third of one chord and the seventh of the next (as shown above). When we move to four-part harmony, the texture gets richer, and the additional voice follows a similar logic, this time alternating between being the fifth of one chord and the ninth of the next. (Each chord is required to have the third and seventh to be identifiable, so in four parts we can either add the fifth or the ninth too, but there's no room for both.)

In practice it makes sense to use the fifth on chords II and I and reserve the more dissonant ninth for the V chord in between, as this latter is supposed to be the point of maximum tension in the progression. Again, any of the three voices can be placed on top.

Note how the chord symbols above don't indicate whether the ninth is present or not. This is because in jazz it's assumed that chord extensions such as the ninth, 11th, or 13th may be present, so they're only shown in the chord symbols when this is necessary to indicate specific chromatic alterations from the major scale.

> Keep in mind that chord symbols in jazz indicate the type of chord and the root of the chord, but not which notes are actually sounded: that's always down to the player's individual choice of layout for the chord – what jazz musicians call its voicing. The type of **voicings** used are often one of the distinguishing hallmarks of a particular pianist's style.

To be a good jazz player you really need to familiarise yourself with the basic voice-leading structures associated with the II-V-I. On the one hand, you need to get to know how it looks on the keyboard and how it feels in your hands as you play it. On the other hand, you need to get confident with playing it in all the different keys.

> Remember, in jazz it's not enough just to know in theory how a progression should go. When improvising you've really got to have the chords in your fingers or, more precisely, in what psychologists and music teachers call your muscular memory. That way you can call on them immediately and spontaneously, whenever you want. To get to that level of fluency you must acquire a firm sense of how the voicings and progressions look and feel, physically, as you're playing them. So it's no good just knowing what notes they have. On the piano this is affected by the key you're in, owing to the different configurations of black and white notes, so practising progressions extensively across all of the different keys is absolutely essential.

The first thing to do is to try taking it through all the keys using the same voicing arrangement. It can help to vary the sequence of the keys. Each of the following exercises takes you through the twelve major keys following a different route.

UNIT 8 | SECTION 3

Exercise 8.1

Here's the II-V-I in a key sequence moving down the Circle of Fifths. Each key is a perfect fifth lower than the previous one. (Note that if we continue further like this we wind up back in C major again.) Try each version several times until you can play it from memory. Then try playing it with the book closed. Finally, try closing your eyes each time you play it, just feeling where to put your fingers in each key.

Exercise 8.2

Now here's a similar exercise moving through keys a semitone lower. This is also a common key movement in jazz. Note how here, too, continuing the sequence further will bring us back to C major again.

UNIT 8 — SECTION 3

Exercise 8.3

Now here are some other key sequences you can try. This time round, see if you can produce the progressions in the required keys from memory.
First let's try taking the II-V-I through keys a whole tone lower, which gives us two series of six keys each: (1) C B♭ A♭ G♭ E D; (2) B A G F E♭ D♭.
  Now we'll move through keys a minor third lower, which gives us three series of four keys each. (1) C A F♯ E♭; (2) B A♭ F D; (3) B♭ G E D♭.
Finally, let's try taking the II-V-I through a sequence of keys a major third lower, which produces four series of three keys each: (1) C A♭ E; (2) B G E♭; (3) B♭ F♯ D; (4) A F D♭.

Exercise 8.4 (opposite page)

Here's another important variation. This time the II-V-I follows the same key sequence as in the first of the preceding exercises – ie, moving down the Circle of Fifths. However, the layout of the voicings alternates from one key to the next, making for greater melodic continuity in the top part across the different transpositions. It's a bit more difficult, but certainly worth trying, as successive II-V-I progressions in jazz are more often than not voiced differently for just this reason.

Now we need to take this whole process a stage further, so as to make ourselves even more familiar with how the underlying structure of the voice-leading looks and feels. (Remember, our aim is to reach the point where we can play these structures without having to think about them at all.) Basically there are two things we can do to achieve this:

- Practise the voice-leading formula across a wider range of progressions than just II-V-I, while staying in a single key.
- Play the II-V-I progression while improvising simple melodic embellishments of the top part at the same time, moving from key to key.

  We'll explore the first option right away, and pursue the second option in the next section.

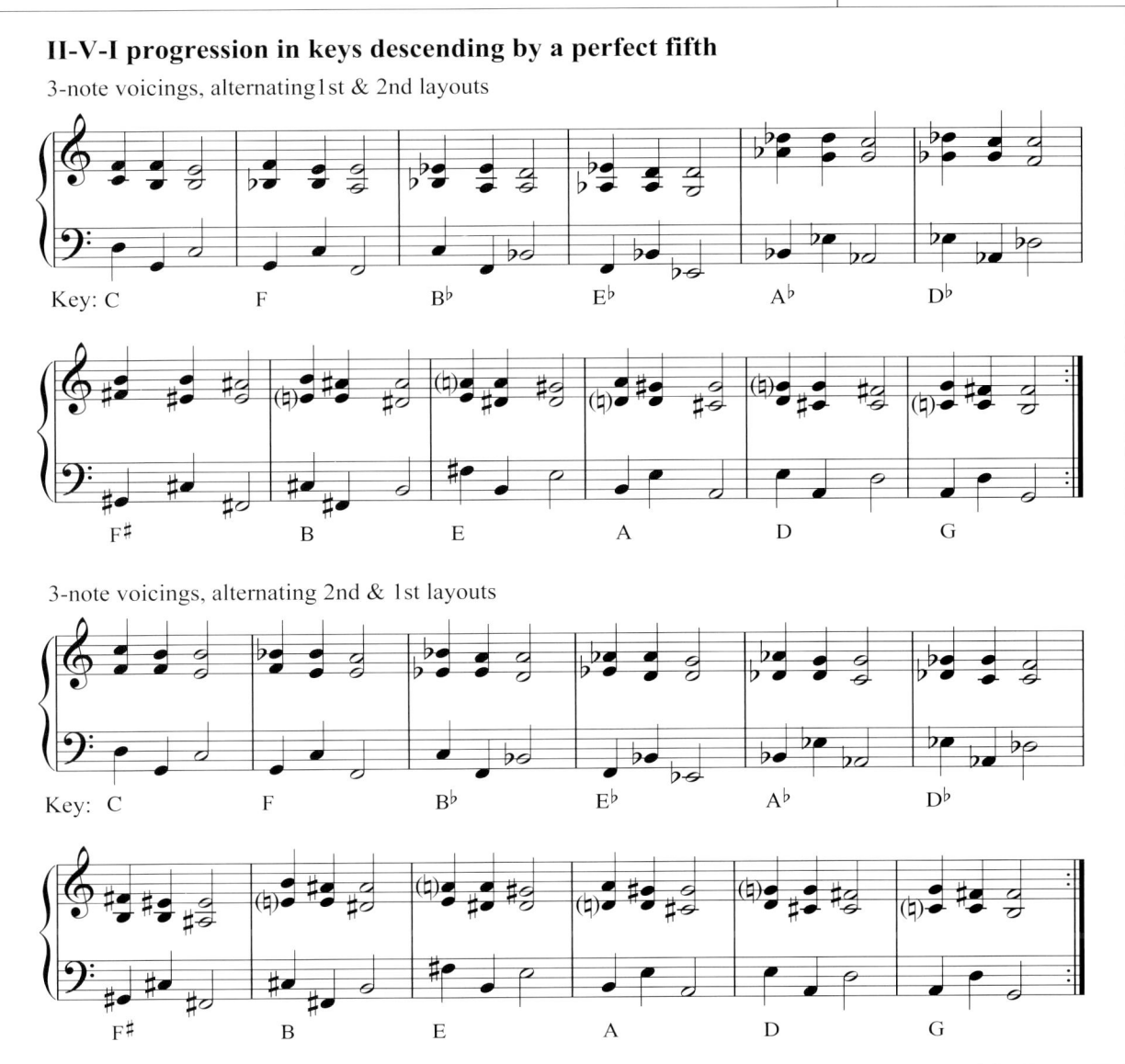

The next exercise uses the eight-chord sequence introduced earlier in this unit (starting and ending on I), in which all the root-progressions move down in fifths (or up in fourths), just as in the II-V-I itself. This time, though, the actual voice-leading formula typical of the II-V-I is applied to all of the root progressions in the longer sequence too. Note also how the fingering remains the same wherever the formula is applied.

UNIT 8 | SECTION 3

SECTION 3 | UNIT 8

Exercise 8.5
Here's the eight-chord sequence in the various possible voice-leading arrangements, in C major. When you've mastered this, try taking each arrangement through all the other keys, first moving through keys a fifth lower, then keys a semitone lower, then keys a whole tone, minor third, or major third lower – just as with the II-V-I. As your hands become more and more familiar with the voice leading you should need to think less and less about transposition and can just let the hands reproduce the shifts automatically, in the scale of each new key. (Before you try each new key, make sure you are confident about the scale it requires.)

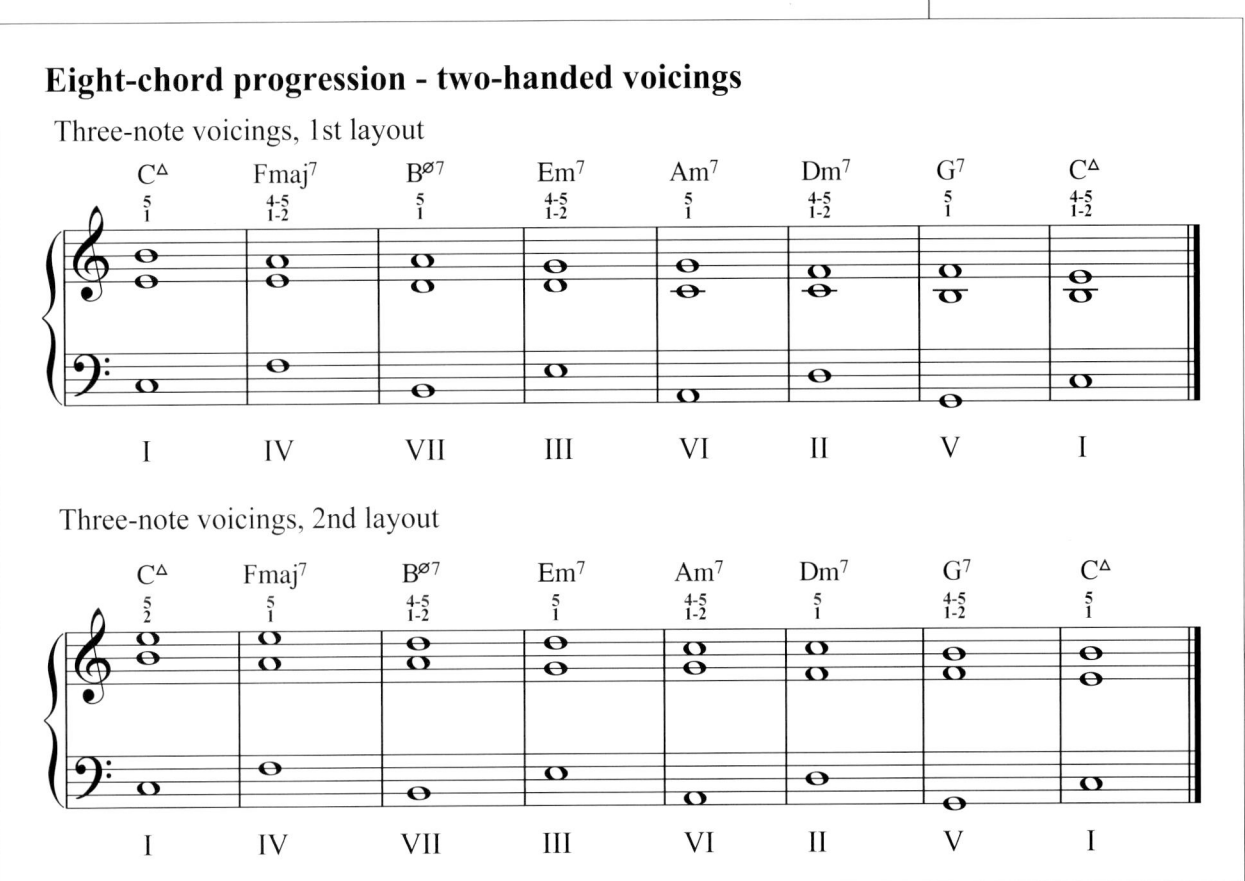

continued over page

UNIT 8 | SECTION 3

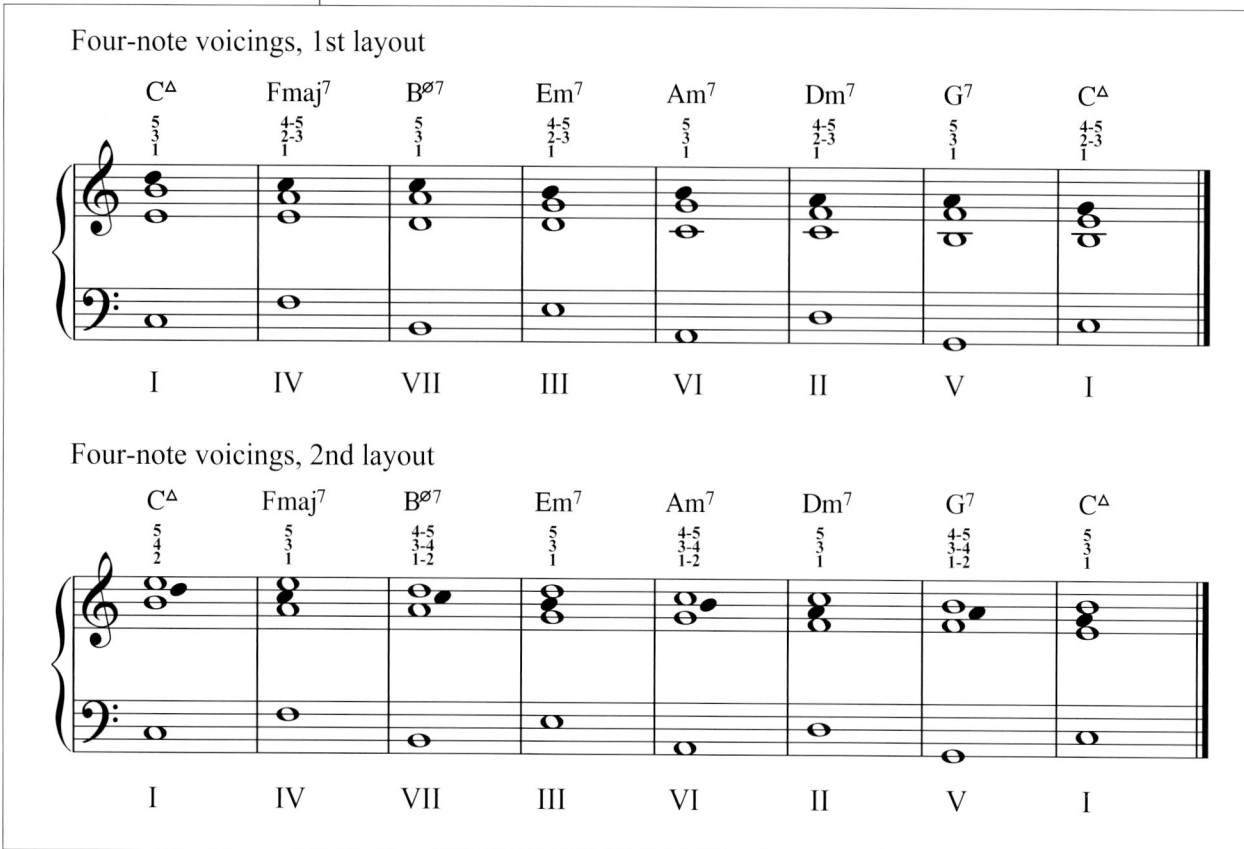

Embellishing the II-V-I

Embellishing progressions, even by adding just simple stepwise melodic movements to the top part, is an effective way to consolidate your knowledge of the progressions themselves. It's also the natural starting point for the kind of melodic improvising that is typical of jazz.

To begin with, let's just take some simple embellishment figures and try reproducing each one in different keys: you can use the harmonic sequences given in the preceding exercises as a basis for this. Basically, there are three possible approaches:

- Stepwise embellishment keeping to the notes of the (diatonic) scale of the key.
- Stepwise chromatic embellishment – involving chromatic stepwise movement away from and back to the notes of the (diatonic) scale of the key.
- Chord-based embellishment – involving melodic leaps between notes of the chord itself (ie, the triad and the seventh, and to a lesser extent other chord extensions as well).

To give you an idea of what this can look, feel, and sound like, here are a few simple examples based on three-note voicings. Although in practice the three methods are

SECTION 3 | UNIT 8

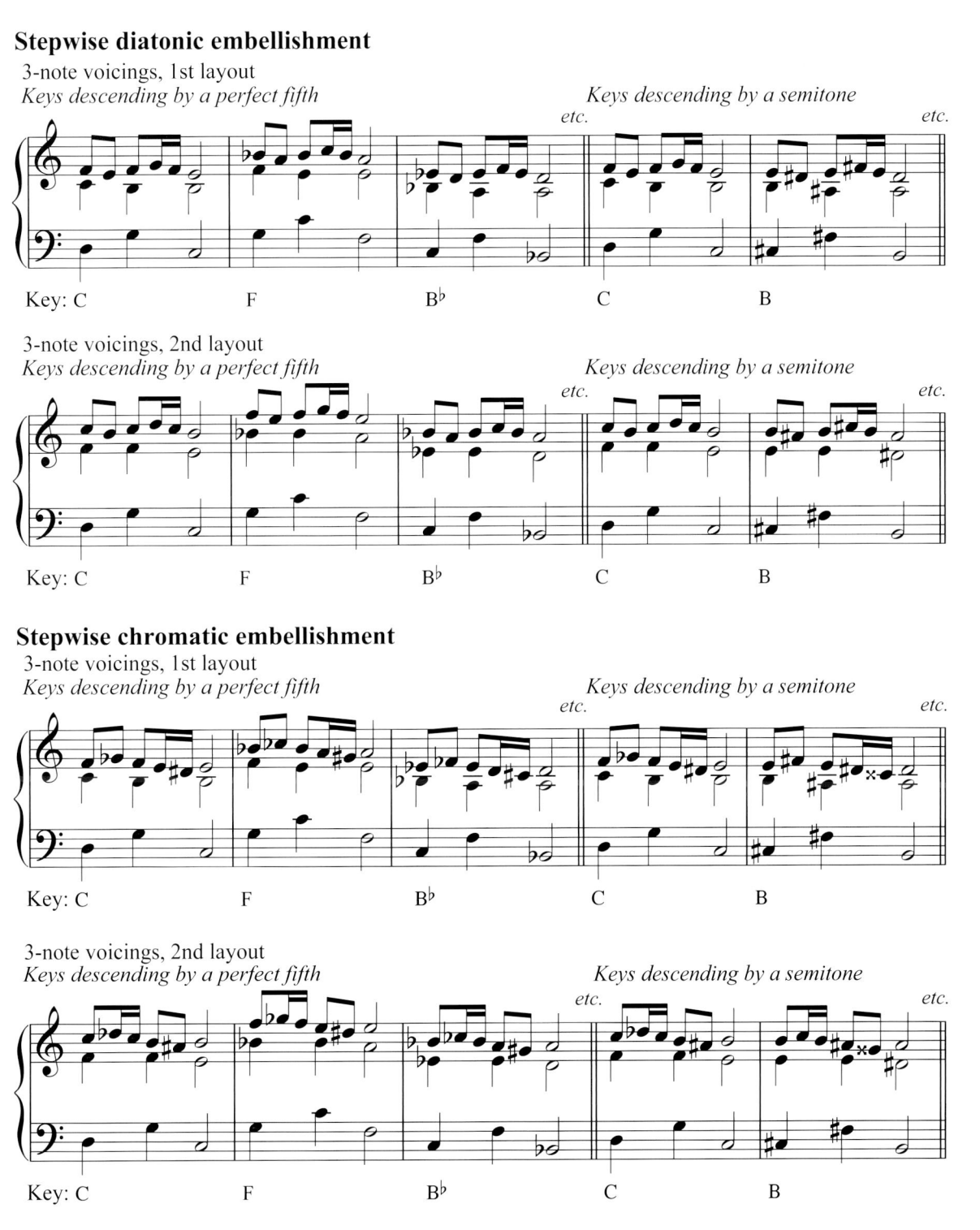

continued over page

UNIT 8 | SECTION 3

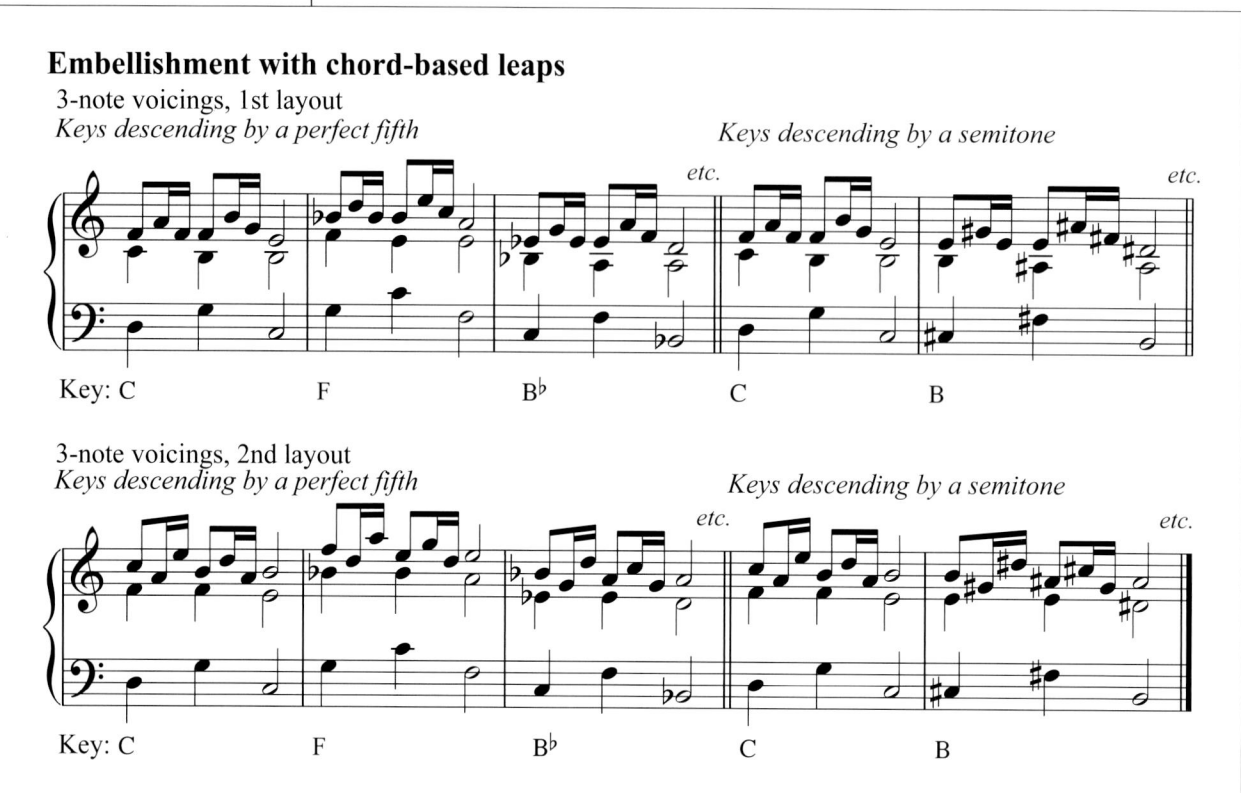

normally mixed up, we'll show separate examples of each. Try adding the extra part to make four-note voicings yourself. Treat the rhythm loosely, remembering that in jazz these rhythms would be played with swing.

Exercise 8.6
Practise improvising your own short embellishment figures over the top part in Exercises 8.1 and 8.2. See if you can transpose each figure and take it right through the whole 12-key sequence.

Once you've got the hang of this, the next stage is to try improvising more extended melodic phrases. We can do this over more extended progressions like the eight-chord sequence at the end of the previous section, or we can aim for phrases that run over two or more successive II-V-I progressions in different keys. Both are worth exploring. Here are some examples of the former (opposite page). Note how this time the three kinds of melodic embellishment mentioned above are mixed up. The same embellishments are shown here, first over three-note voicings, then four-note ones, to help you see how the extra part fits into the texture.

Note how adding the ninth to the half-diminished chord at the start of bar 2 creates a strong dissonance, as it corresponds to an avoid note – one that clashes strongly with the root. In the first four-part texture it sounds okay, but in the second the fact that this

part has been moved to lower down in the texture, so as to leave the embellished part on top, makes the effect more pronounced. Here, then it would make sense to substitute a raised ninth (in this case C-sharp).

Notice that if we do the same in the first four-part texture in the above example, then the C-sharp in the top part will no longer be heard as a chromatic embellishment, as it will now be part of the scale implied by the chord beneath it. The result is a sweeter, brighter, and smoother flavour. The effect is too sweet for some, but if you like it enough to want to use it a lot, you might as well go ahead and just treat these notes as permanently raised within the scales used over the chords. The next example demonstrates how embellishments can look when we do this using the same eight-chord sequence as before. The raised notes are now also reflected in the jazz chord symbols placed above the music.

CD TRACK 38

Embellishment with chromatically raised avoid notes

Now for the other option – where extended phrases run over two or more II-V-I progressions and so, in effect, contain modulations. This is where progressions that maintain continuity of voice-leading in the top part as we pass between keys prove really useful. The best examples are the chromatically descending key-sequence shown in Exercise 8.2 and the key-sequence in Exercise 8.4 that mixes up different layouts to ensure continuity in the top part while modulating down the Circle of Fifths. Here are some examples (p297-8). Once more, the different types of embellishment are mixed together for a more richly varied effect. This time each II-V-I extends over two bars, giving more space for embellishment of the individual chords, and three- and four-note voicings are also intermixed to vary the effect. (Note how melodic phrases stretching over two successive II-V-I progressions can be repeated sequentially a step lower over the next pair of II-V-I progressions as well, with variations. This can be an effective way of building a longer line, but be careful – it can quickly sound predictable if overused.)

SECTION 3 UNIT 8

Mixed embellishment over successive II-V-I progressions

continued over page

Exercise 8.7
Now have a go at improvising your own longer phrases (running over two or more instances of the II-V-I progression), based on embellishments of the top part of the sequences in Exercises 8.2 and 8.4. If you like the effect it produces, try systematically raising the avoid notes as well.

Left-hand voicings

So far we've looked at how the II-V-I and related progressions work with the chords split between the hands as **two-handed voicings**. When improvising jazz, though, we often want the right hand entirely free of any role in realising the chords, so it can roam about the keyboard without having to come back to a specific point every time a new chord gets played. So it's useful to have a way of producing the entire chord in the left hand alone. Jazz has a special set of formulas for this, known as **left-hand voicings**. These work on the basis that many of the notes in the chord – including the root – can be implied without having actually to be sounded. (In the case of the root, though, this is often not an issue, as in ensemble jazz it will typically be sounded by a separate instrument anyway – usually the double bass.)

As with two-handed voicings, we must first learn the left-hand formulas for II-V-I progressions by taking them through all the possible keys, applying them across longer sequences, and mixing up the different variants to get a feel for how they link together. Here are the two basic options for II-V-I. In each case the final I chord can also be realised in two possible ways – as a more dissonant voicing or a more resolved one. (The second option is written in treble clef here for ease of reading; it's still played by the left hand, of course.)

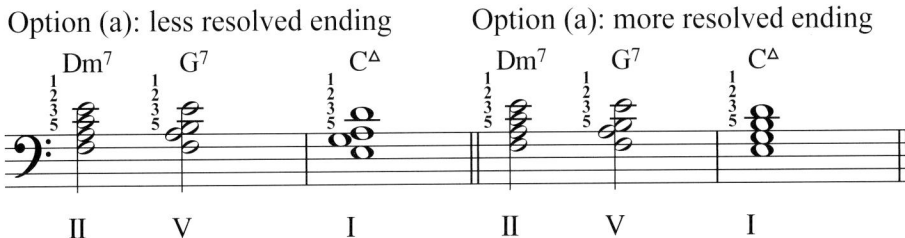

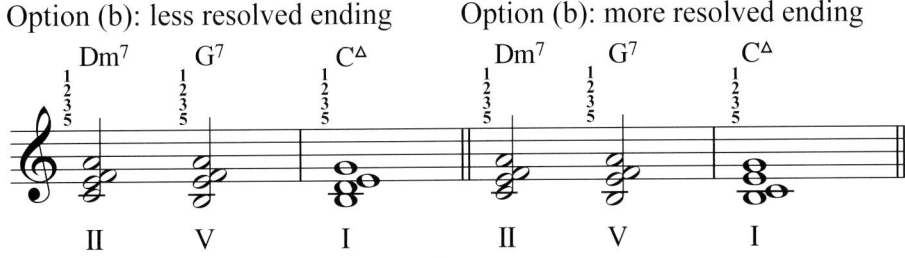

These two options are distinguished by whether the fifth finger plays third–seventh–third or seventh–third–seventh at the bottom of the three chords. Note also how each progression contains a part in which the fifth of one chord becomes the ninth of the next before descending stepwise to give us the fifth again, just as in four-note two-handed voicings. Meanwhile a new alternation is now added alongside this, in which the ninth of one chord becomes the 13th of the next before moving down by step to become the ninth of the next one again.

Which of these options we use depends on how they sound in the particular key in which we are playing. Sometimes one of them will take us too high or too low, resulting in a lack of sonority or a muddy texture, while the other one will lie nearer to the optimum register for the voicing in question. However, it's also a matter of personal taste, mood, and context. Type (a) voicings generally tend to sound a little bit fuller and a little less 'scrunchy' than type (b) ones. The more dissonant, less resolved ending has become the more widely used option in both cases, so we'll mainly use this in subsequent examples and exercises. Note how the type (a) voicings involve first moving just the second finger down one scale-step, and then doing the same with all the fingers (including the second once again). Meanwhile the type (b) voicings involve first moving just the fifth finger down by a scale-step, and then doing the same for the remaining fingers (so in this case not the fifth again).

Exercise 8.8 (opposite page)
Here are left-hand voicings of each type for the II-V-I, in a key sequence moving down the Circle of Fifths. Try each option several times until you can play it from memory right through all 12 keys and back to C major again. Then try with the book closed, and then with your eyes closed, just feeling where to put your fingers in each key. Make a note of which keys produce good sonorities for these voicings, and which make them sound too thin or too muddy as a result of being too high or low.

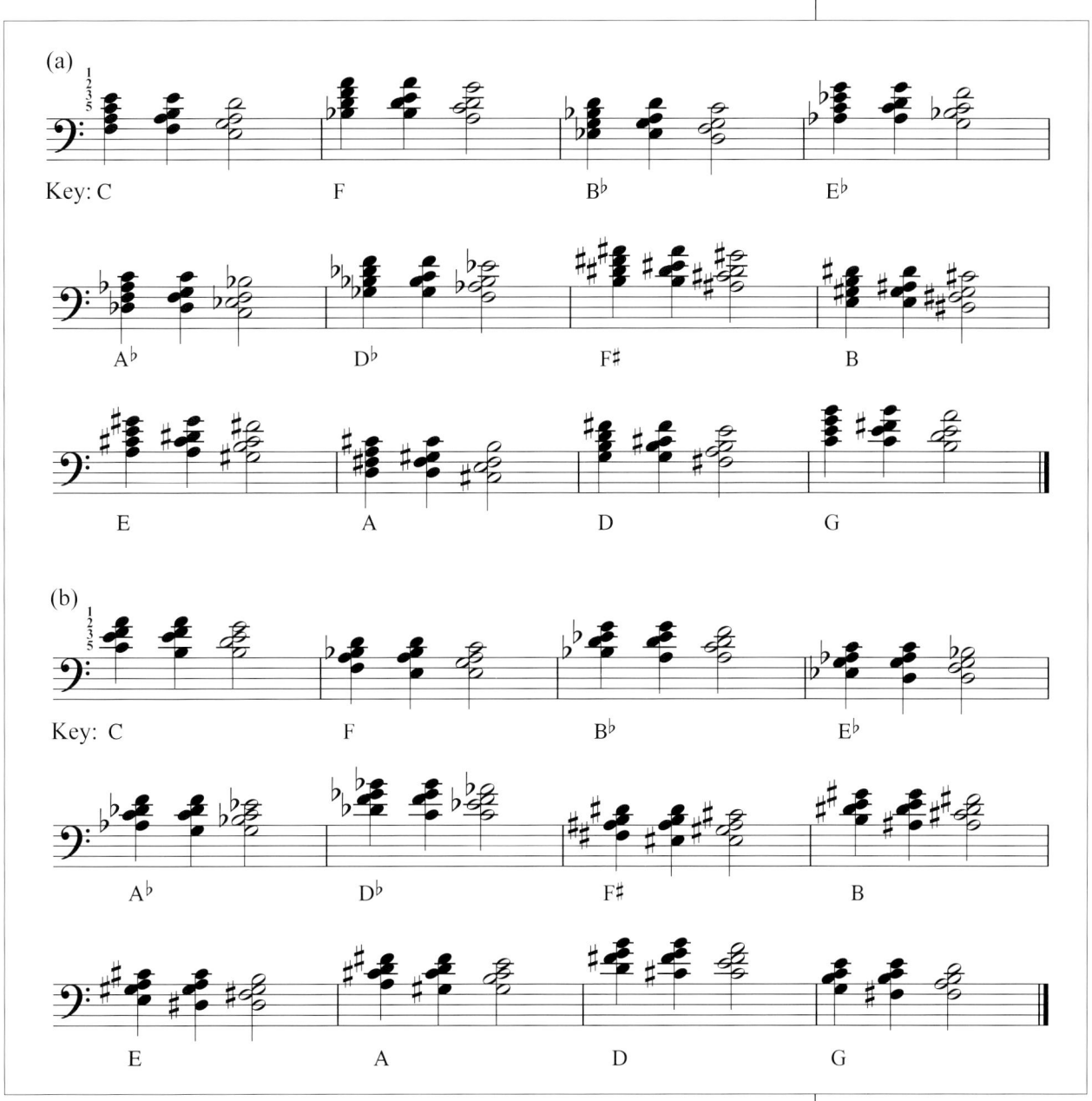

Exercise 8.9
Now here's a similar exercise moving through keys a semitone lower. As with the two-handed voicings, it's also worth trying other key sequences. (See Exercise 8.3 in the preceding section for these.) Try shifting the individual voicings up and down an octave to see how this changes their sonority.

Exercise 8.10

Now we'll alternate between the two options as we move down the Circle of Fifths, for greater continuity of register, texture, and voice-leading, first starting with type (a), then starting with type (b).

Finally, to get a really good feel for how voice-leading works in these progressions we can apply the left-hand formula for the II-V-I over a more extended sequence of similar root-progressions: the eight-chord sequence that we used for a similar purpose in the previous section. Here, in the next exercise, are left-hand voicings for that sequence, for each of the two possible voicing options. The II-V-I at the end is arranged here so as to maintain the same voice-leading formula as the rest of the sequence – a straightforward alternation between two kinds of shift: either we move the upper two notes down a step, or we move down the lower two, keeping the other two unchanged. To make this clearer the chords have been labelled here as 'x' and 'y'. You can see that when 'x' moves to 'y' it's always the bottom two notes of the chord that move down a step, and when 'y' moves to 'x' it's always the top two. (Note also how chord V has lost its 13th here. In a simple II-V-I this is used to enhance the tension of the dominant prior to its resolution, but the example below shows how behind this lies a more basic voice-leading formula for linking chords with roots a fifth apart – one which gets modified when we add the 13th to the dominant.)

Exercise 8.11
Here's the eight-chord progression in C major used earlier, this time arranged as left-hand voicings, in each variant. Optional chromatic alterations are shown using accidentals in brackets: these are raised avoid notes of the sort discussed earlier. Playing the sequence through without the alterations will help you memorise the voice-leading more easily, but you may feel that some of the

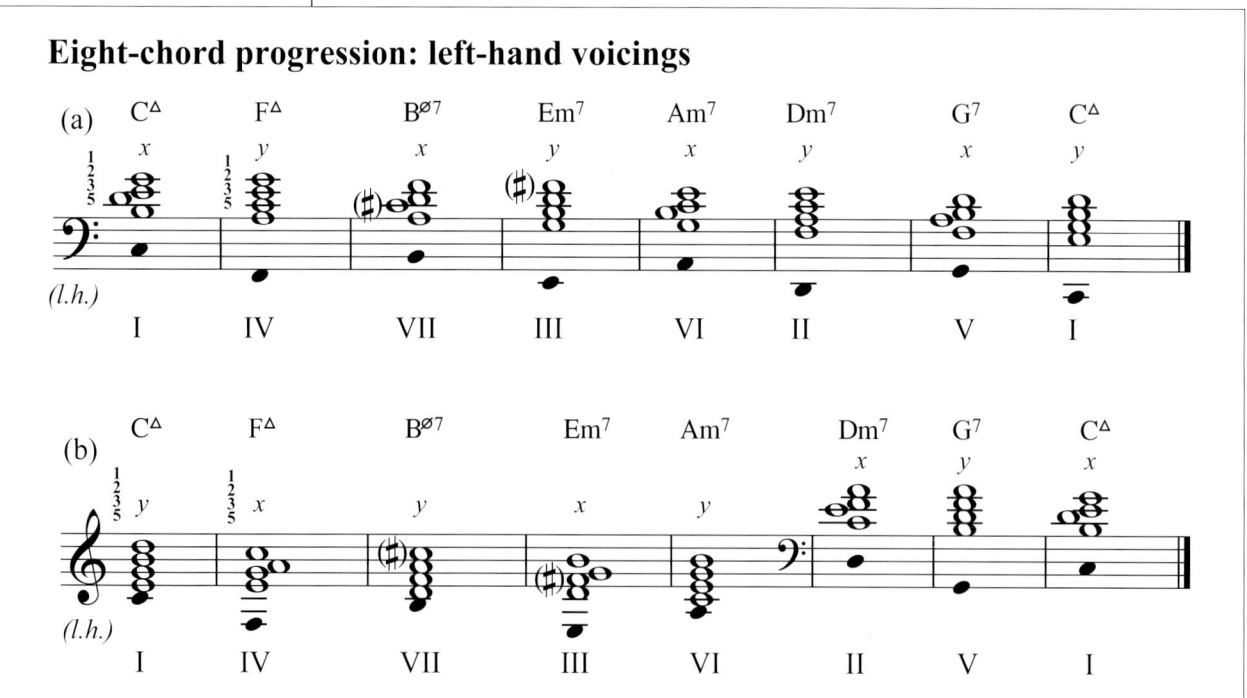

chords sound better with the alterations, especially when the roots sound at the same time. The roots of the chords are shown below, so why not try adding them with your right hand (crossing over your left), to hear how the voicings would sound against a bass line? When you've done this, try transposing the sequence to other keys.

Another approach to freeing up the right hand is to strip the left-hand voicings right down to just two. (We usually do this omitting the fifth of the chord.) This is a feature associated with the jazz pianist Bud Powell. Hence the fact that these are often known as **Bud Powell voicings**. This has a big advantage: because the left hand plays fewer notes it can move lower down without producing a muddy texture, which in turn opens up the sonorous middle register of the piano for the right hand to use melodically. Some three-note voicings can also be used this way, though they may involve large stretches. (Such voicings involving intervals of a tenth were typical of the early style of jazz known as 'stride'.) Here's the same eight-chord sequence as in the previous exercise, with the chords arranged in these ways.

Exercise 8.12
Play through these left-hand arrangements for the eight-chord progression, then try transposing them through other keys. Unless you've a very large hand you'll need to 'spread' the chords with tenths in the second variant. Use sustaining pedal to help with this, assisted by a lateral hand movement similar to that used in one-octave arpeggios.

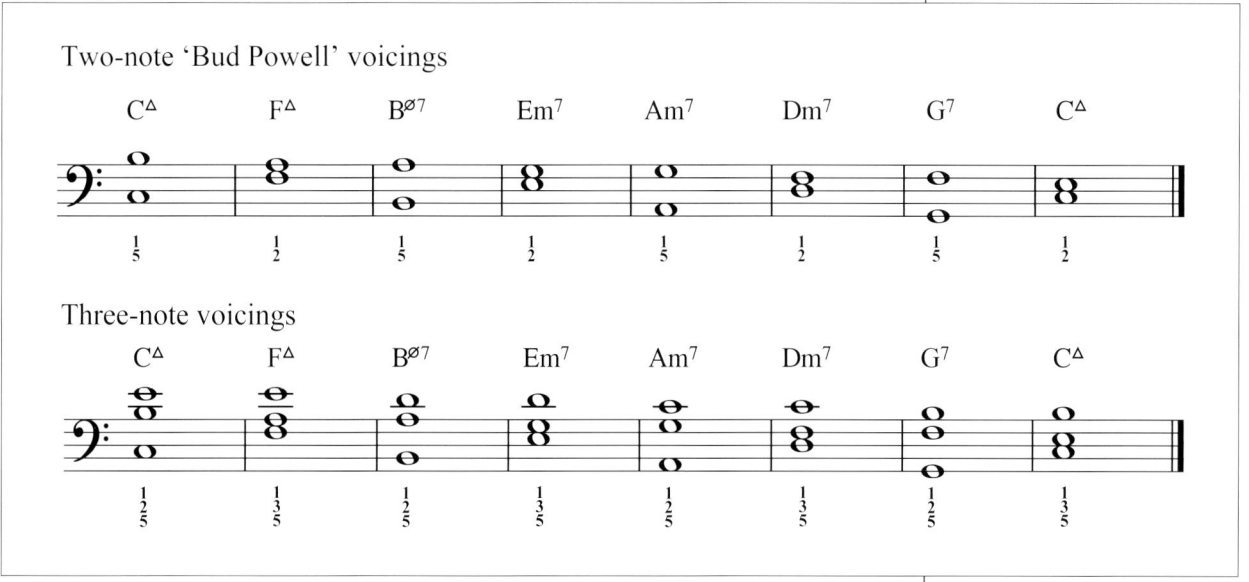

UNIT 8 | SECTION 3

Although left-hand voicings enable us to pursue right-hand melodic improvising more freely with respect to sounding the chords, we still need to preserve some harmonic reference points, and this is where the idea of using **modes** proves useful in jazz. As we saw when improvising over the Bach prelude in the previous unit, thinking of the scale as having the root of the chord as its starting note, instead of the tonic of the key, helps to maintain an awareness of how the melodic line stands relative to the chord over which it unfolds. The next exercise gives you the modes arranged over the eight-chord sequence with left-hand voicings. The first voice-leading formula is shown in C major, the second in F major.

Exercise 8.13 (opposite page)
Try holding down each chord in the left hand as you play the corresponding mode in the right. Listen to how the different scale-notes sound against each chord. Then see if you can improvise in the right hand over each chord, thinking all the time in terms of the mode for that chord, rather than in terms of the original scale of the key.

The next exercise shows you how the right-hand modes look over the start of a modulating series of II-V-I progressions. In this case we're limited to just three modes (Dorian, Mixolydian, Ionian), but must reproduce them in changing keys (modulating down the Circle of Fifths here). Note how the left-hand voicings alternate between the two variants of the voice-leading formula to maintain continuity of register and texture between successive keys. The first sequence starts with a type (a) formula, the second with type (b).

Exercise 8.14 (p308-9)
Once again, hold down the chords and play the corresponding modes in the right hand to hear how the scale-notes sound against each chord. See if you can continue each sequence through more keys by transposing the modes along with the chords. (If you need help, you'll find the same sequences of left-hand chords going through all keys in Exercise 8.10.) Then try improvising over each II-V-I, thinking of the modes. Look out for key changes: when they happen make sure you change the notes in the scale accordingly.

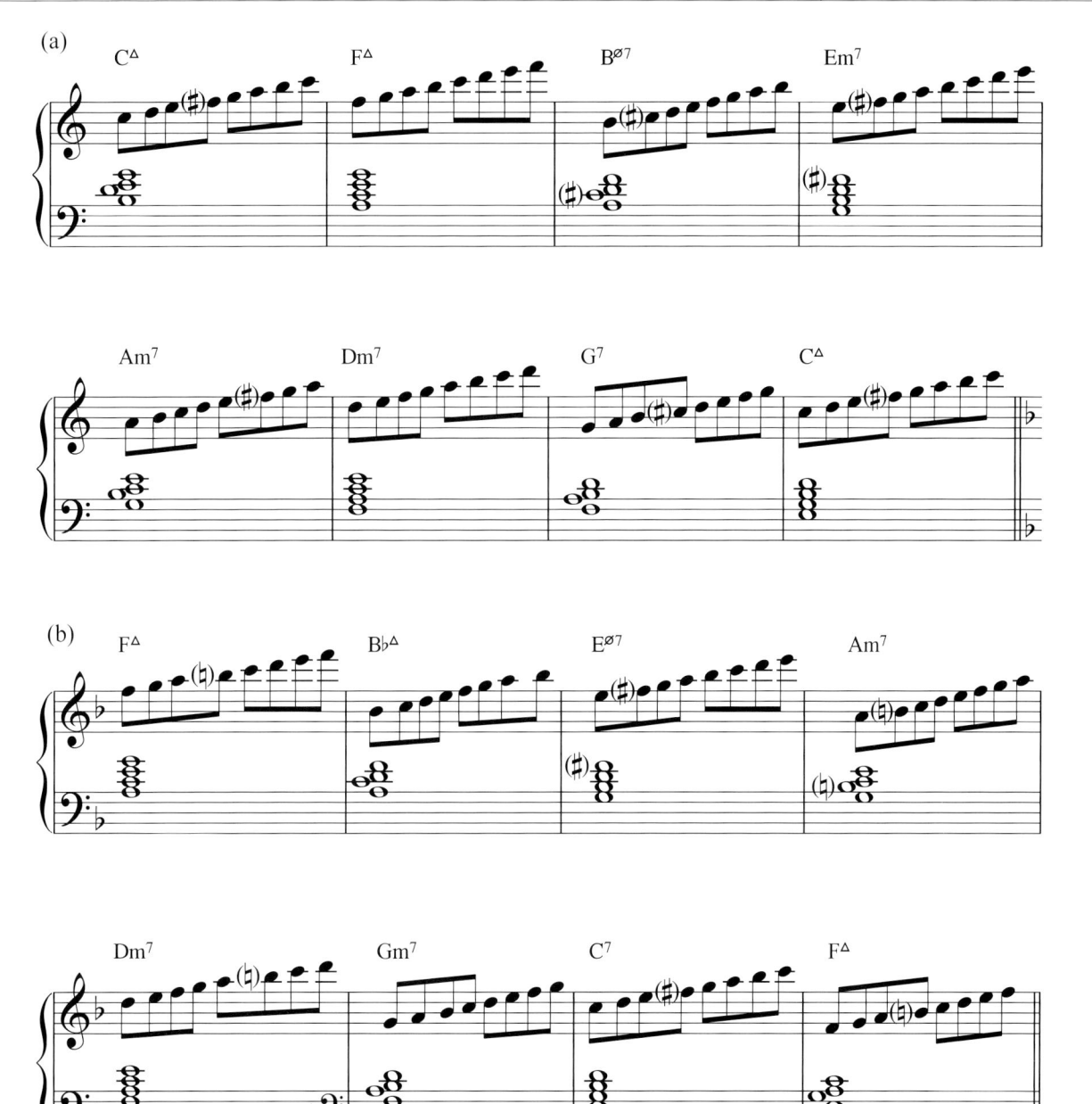

Modes over left-hand voicings for II-V-I progressions: type (b) then type (a)

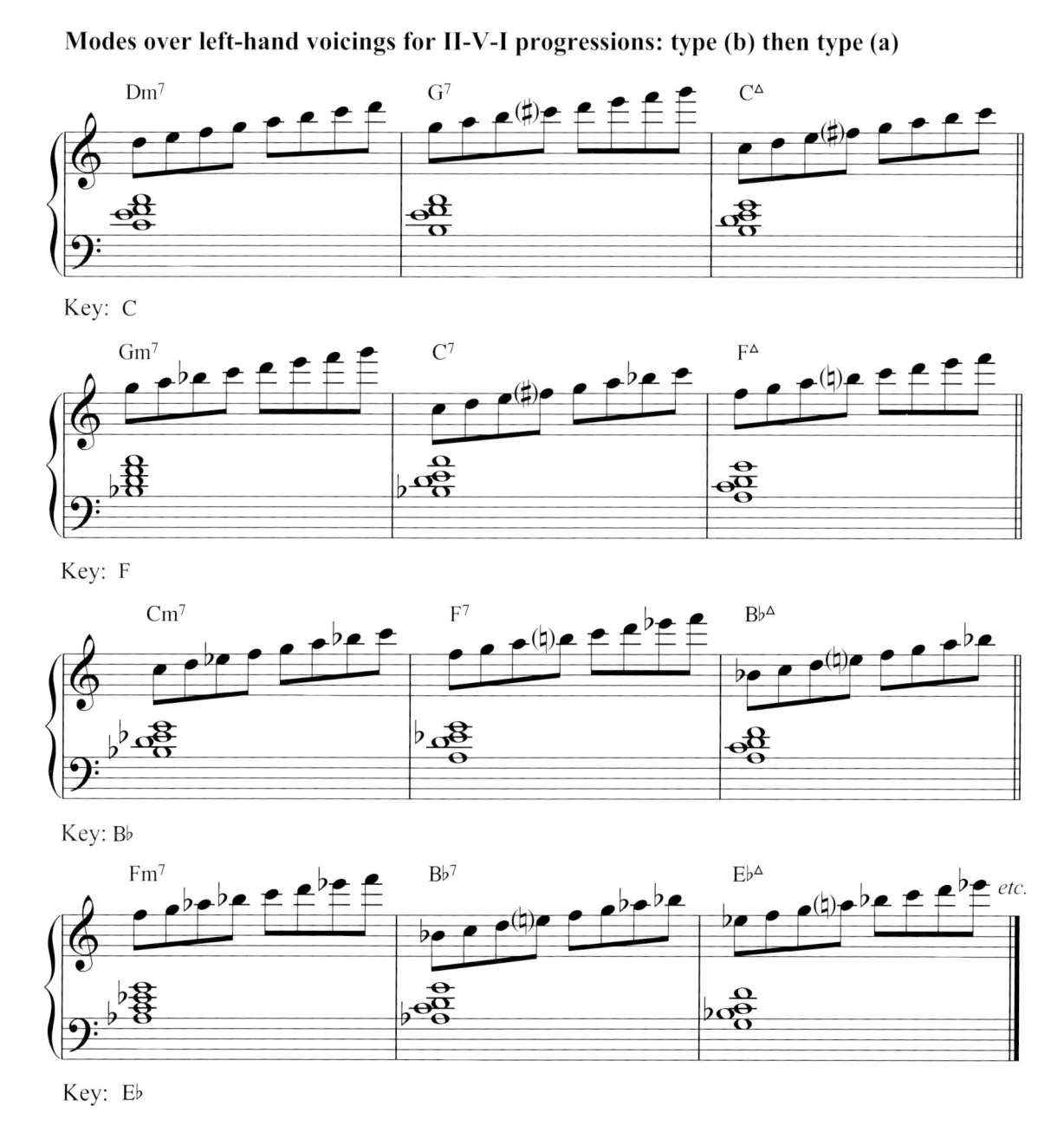

Licks and improvised melody

Apart from embellishing a given melody line (or just the top part of a given chordal texture), jazz improvisers like to make use of melodic figures built directly out of scales and/or chords themselves. These are known as **licks**.

> **Licks** can be improvised on the spot, but in jazz they also play an important role by providing pre-prepared material for improvising. Each player has a personal repertoire of licks that they take around in their head from one performance to the next and can use whenever they need to. Often the element of improvisation in performance lies in the way they're stitched together on the spot to produce something that sounds like a completely spontaneous line, but which is really a patchwork of already existing ideas. However, this doesn't necessarily mean licks aren't improvised too. On the contrary, they'll probably first have been discovered in previous sessions through improvising, either during or outside of a performance.

Understanding how licks work in jazz is complicated by two factors:

- They're more than just melodic patterns used to create a texture (as in 'passage work' in classical music), but not yet a fully worked-out melody.

- They live in the 'grey zone' between scales and chords: just like scale-based melodies, they can outline the sort of complex shapes that mix steps with leaps, but like chord-based figurations or patterns they often outline harmonically defined structures too.

To really make sense of this you need to know that licks were originally used in jazz as raw material for use while improvising around a given melody line – usually one taken from a well-known song (called a **standard**). Later on, many jazz musicians preferred to forget about the original melody of the song and just take the chord sequence associated with it (known in jazz parlance as **the changes**), an approach known as **contrafaction**. They then used this as a basis for freer forms of improvising. However, the basic approach to improvising in jazz still reflects what's involved when we try to improvise around a given tune.

The key concept here is that of **melodic paraphrase**: jazz musicians improvise alternative melodic shapes over the chords connected with a tune to those of the tune itself. However, they are closely enough related to the latter (harmonically, melodically and/or rhythmically) to make us hear them with the original tune at least partly in mind.

It's important to understand how this differs from related procedures in classical music, where the idea of **melodic variation** involves some rather similar features. (We looked at the topic of classical melodic variation in the previous unit. If you're not sure about it, go back and have another look at the material there.)

In classical variation technique there's an original musical idea or 'theme' whose underlying structure is preserved through all the variations we make on it, so we always hear these variations with reference to the theme itself – as embellishments or alterations of it.

In jazz paraphrase technique, however, the melodic material the improviser creates counts as being just as important as the original tune – if not even more important.

So whereas classical variations are best thought of as exploring the potential of the original tune as a way of revealing different perspectives on the original material itself, jazz paraphrasing is really more about treating the original as no more than raw material – or even just as a 'means to an end' – the real goal being the improvising itself.

> Jazz **paraphrase** and classical **variation** both play a big role in improvisation. The difference between them is subtle but important. One way to sum it up is like this: whereas a classical musician is more likely to want to improvise (variations) on a theme or melody, a jazz musician is more likely to want to improvise around it.

In the classical approach, then, there's a clear hierarchy – one that places the original material on a higher level of importance than the variations of the improviser. In jazz, no such hierarchy exists. In practice, though, jazz also often makes use of elements of classical variation. (It's not always possible to make an absolutely clear-cut distinction between the two.) Even so, the central role of paraphrase in jazz means jazz improvisers are naturally drawn to material whose structure cuts across the line separating a melody from a melodically unfolding texture or pattern.

One example of this is the way basic techniques for developing licks often blur the distinction between scales and chords, especially by using **pentatonic scales** and what are known as **'four-note scales'** (though the latter could equally be called 'four-note chordal patterns'). Let's take a look at these.

By now you should be familiar with the idea of a pentatonic scale, which in a major key leaves out the fourth and seventh of the diatonic major scale. However, there are more options than this. Firstly, we can build pentatonic scales on other degrees of the scale of the key, not just the tonic. Secondly, we can explore the various modes of each pentatonic scale.

The major pentatonic scales on the fourth or fifth degrees of a major scale don't involve any notes foreign to that scale, so they're also useful. Note that in jazz theory we refer to these different pentatonic scales within a key in the same way as we refer to different chords within a key, using Roman numerals that stand for the degrees of the original diatonic scale that defines the actual key: eg, 'I-pentatonic', 'IV-pentatonic' and 'V-pentatonic'.

Major pentatonic scales (in a major key)

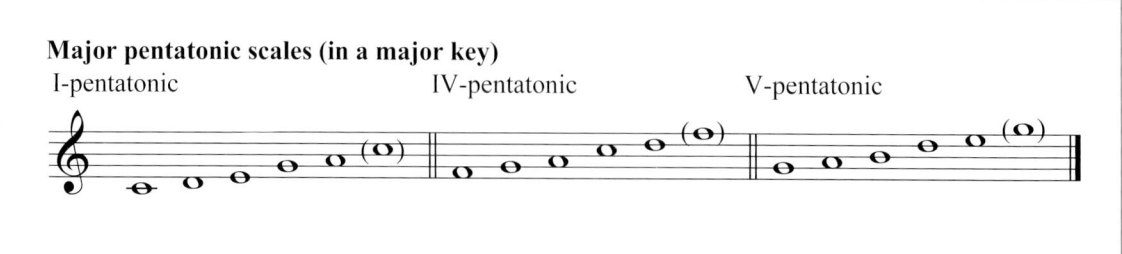

We can also use other kinds of pentatonic scale: ones that, when based on a particular degree of the major scale, don't result in notes foreign to the key being introduced. For each of the three major pentatonic scales there's a minor pentatonic scale that starts two steps lower that also stays within the key, since it uses exactly the same notes:

Minor pentatonic scales (in a major key)

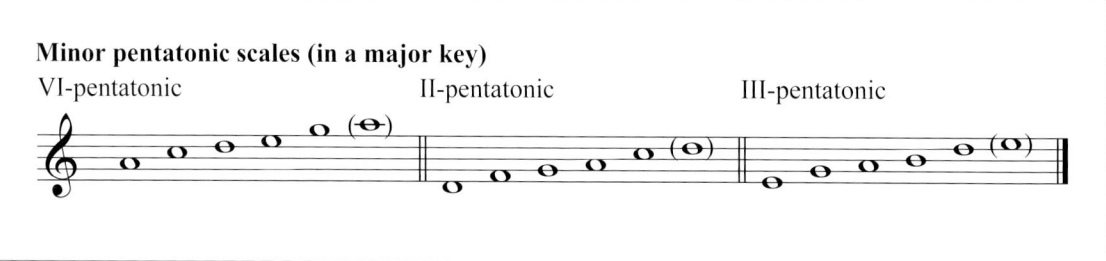

If these minor pentatonic scales contain exactly the same notes as the major pentatonic scales two steps higher, then we can also think of them as just modes of the latter. Here, then are all of the modes for each of the three major pentatonic scales:

Modes of pentatonic scales (in a major key)

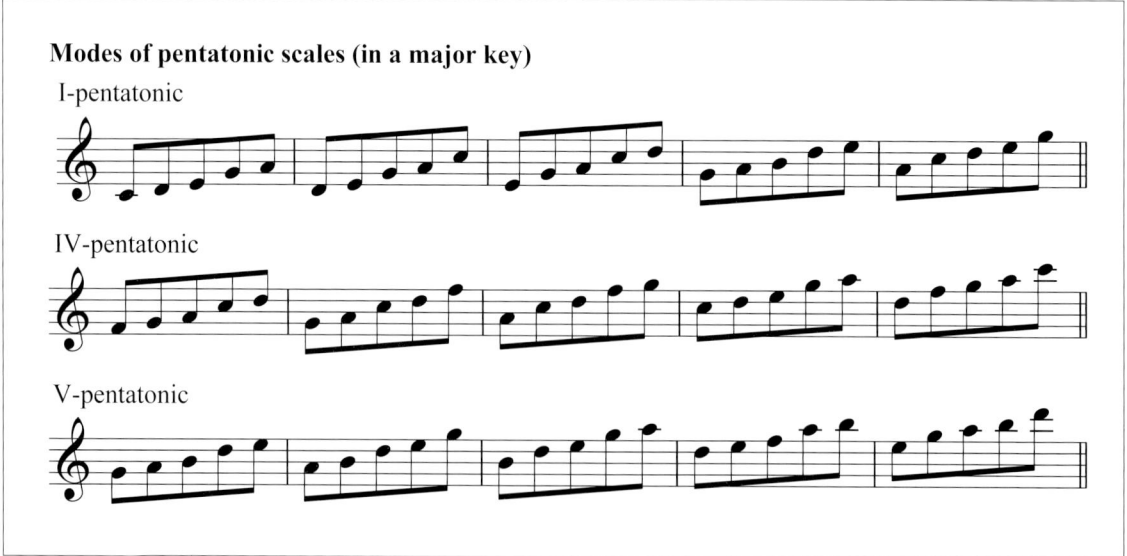

Not all of these pentatonic scales work equally well over all of the basic chords in jazz. As far as the major pentatonic scales (and their modes) are concerned:

- Over chord II, pentatonic scales on I, IV, and V all sound good, but V sounds best as it contains more interesting chord extensions – the sixth and ninth.
- Over chord V, only the pentatonic scale on V works well, as the others contain an avoid note (a fourth above the root of the chord); moreover, V also has the ninth and 13th which are interesting chord extensions.
- Over chord I, pentatonic scales on I and V both sound good, whereas the one on IV contains an avoid note (the fourth of the scale). But V sounds best as it contains the more colourful seventh and ninth of the chord.

In short, then, the pentatonic scale on V sounds best over all three of the chords of the II-V-I. (There's a straightforward reason for this: it corresponds to the major scale with the avoid notes occurring over V and I removed and, of course, there are no avoid notes over II.)

Another kind of pentatonic scale used in jazz is the rather oriental-sounding **in-sen scale**, normally built on the third of the major scale. It can be used over any unaltered major-key chords, but sounds best over II or V, as it contains the avoid note that occurs over chord I. There's also a useful variant which chromatically raises the avoid note occurring over chord V. Likewise, a major pentatonic scale on II is useful as it contains the sharpened fourth of the scale, corresponding to the chromatically raised version of the avoid note over I.

Alternative pentatonic scales
In-sen scale starting on III   Adapted in-sen on III (raised avoid note over V)   Major pentatonic on II (raised avoid note over I)

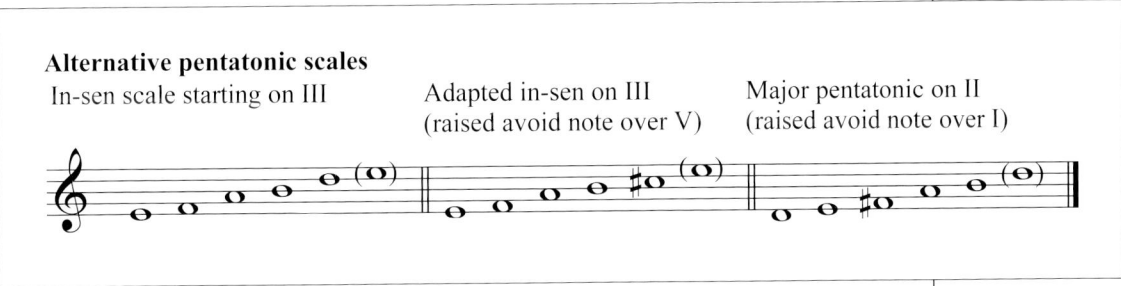

UNIT 8 | SECTION 3

Now let's consider so-called 'four-note scales'. These most commonly consist of a minor triad with an added major sixth. The most common examples are the structures we get when we build them on the second, third, and sixth degrees of the major scale. Note how the four-note structure built on the third degree has the raised version of the avoid note occurring over chord V, while that built on the sixth has the raised version of the avoid note over I.

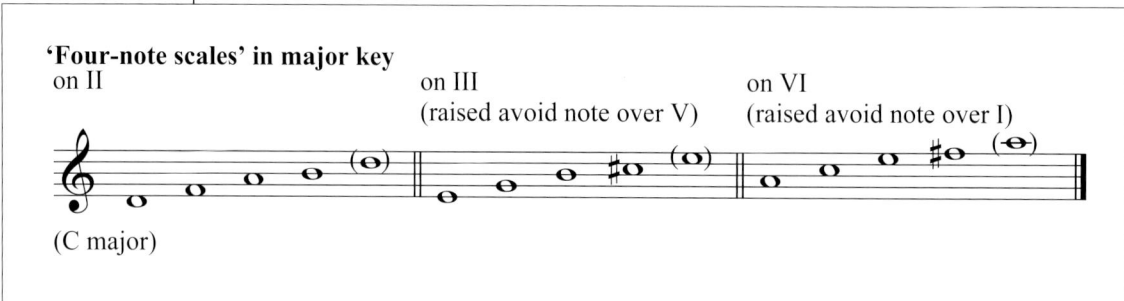

Jazz musicians often treat these more like arpeggiated chords than scales, creating patterns by moving through different inversions – just like broken chords or arpeggios in classical piano music. For example:

Using pentatonic and 'four-note' scales alongside elements of the diatonic and chromatic scales breaks down the sharp distinction between scales and chords, or between melody and harmony, in the way that's necessary if you want to engage in the kind of playful melodic 'doodling' or paraphrase that's the essence of jazz improvising.

SECTION 3 | UNIT 8

> **Pick 'n' mix.** Riffs and licks are often most effective when they mix different sorts of material together: eg, diatonic, pentatonic, four-note, and chromatic scales, and arpeggiated triads or seventh chords. But don't forget that riffs and licks are also very much about generating particular qualities of shape and movement: you can even think of them as ways of getting about the keyboard through playing notes. So you should also pay attention to the ways in which they contribute to rhythm and texture. Try taking the each riff or lick that you come up with through different registers – in different keys or just different octaves – to see what changes of colour and/or texture result. Above all, listen to as much jazz as possible.

If you want to develop an individual voice as a jazz improviser, you should try your hand at making up your own licks as soon as possible. Although it's essential to listen to how experienced jazz musicians build their solo improvisations out of their licks, it's not enough just to be able to reproduce their techniques. What matters is that you get engaged in exploring and playing with ideas, shapes, and sequences yourself, seeing what happens when you add (or remove) bits of this or that type of scale, move them around the keyboard, try them over different chords, chord progressions, or chord-voicings, etc. The hardest thing is getting started, but the next few exercises should help with this.

Exercise 8.15 (p316)
This is the first of several exercises in 'guided improvisation'. The score tells you what notes are available to be used over each progression, but not what you should do with them. We'll start with nothing more than the simplest possible melodic structure that works over a II-V-I progression – the 'V-pentatonic'. Try to see what you can do with just the material given. Note that when we move to a key a fifth lower only one note of the pentatonic scale changes: any of the other four can serve as a link-note between successive II-V-I progressions. (The one that can't is highlighted as an unfilled notehead.) At the same time, each major pentatonic contains a 'four-note scale' – shown in brackets – corresponding to major triad on V with an added sixth. You may also carry each scale over into other octaves.

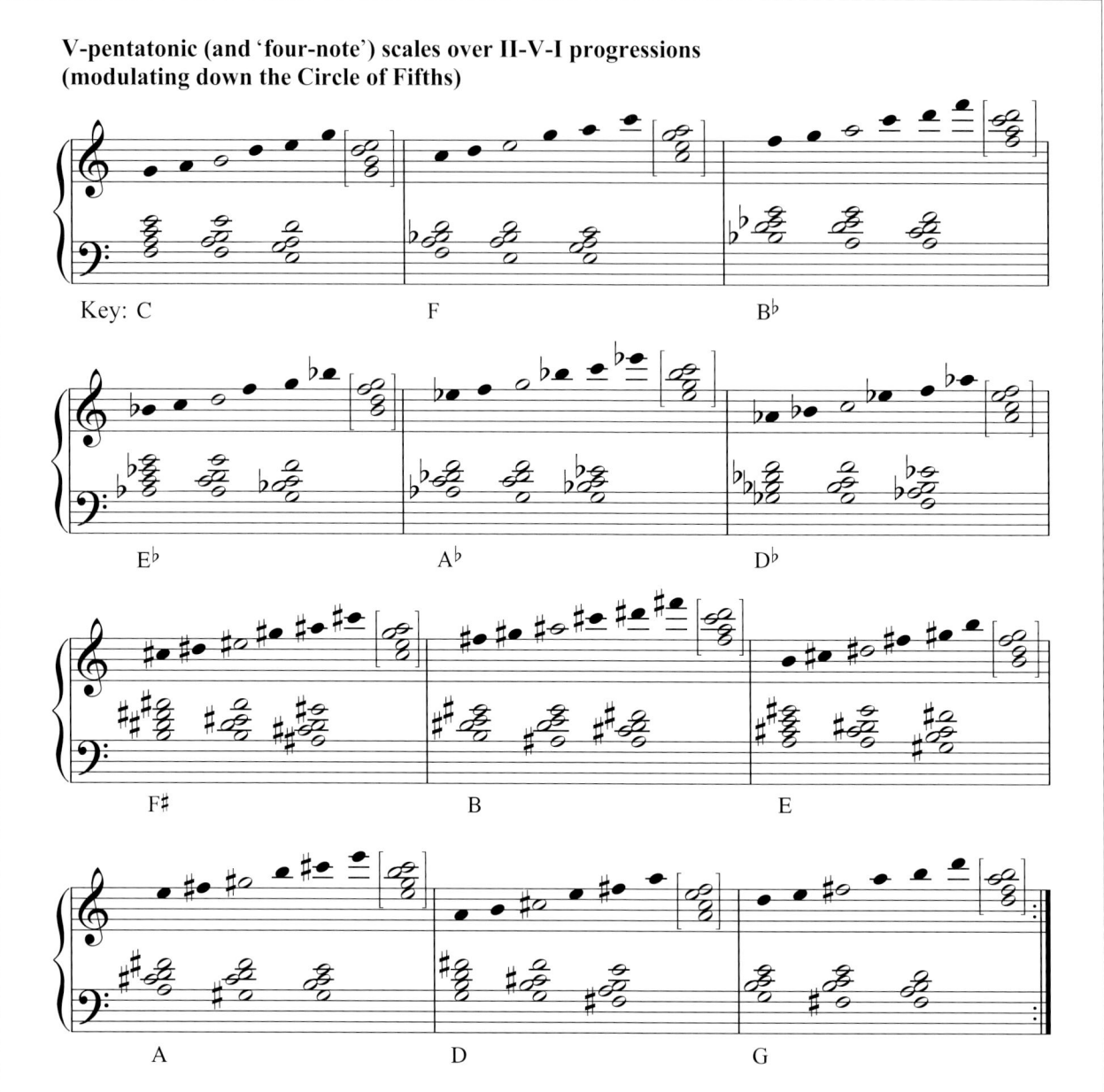

Exercise 8.16

Now here's the same material, but with the scales appearing with different scale-degrees at the bottom in successive keys (equivalent to different modes of the same pentatonic scale). This encourages you to focus on what's possible within a single area of the piano, even as the scales, chords, and keys change around it, rather than just transposing scales and licks mechanically from one key to the next.

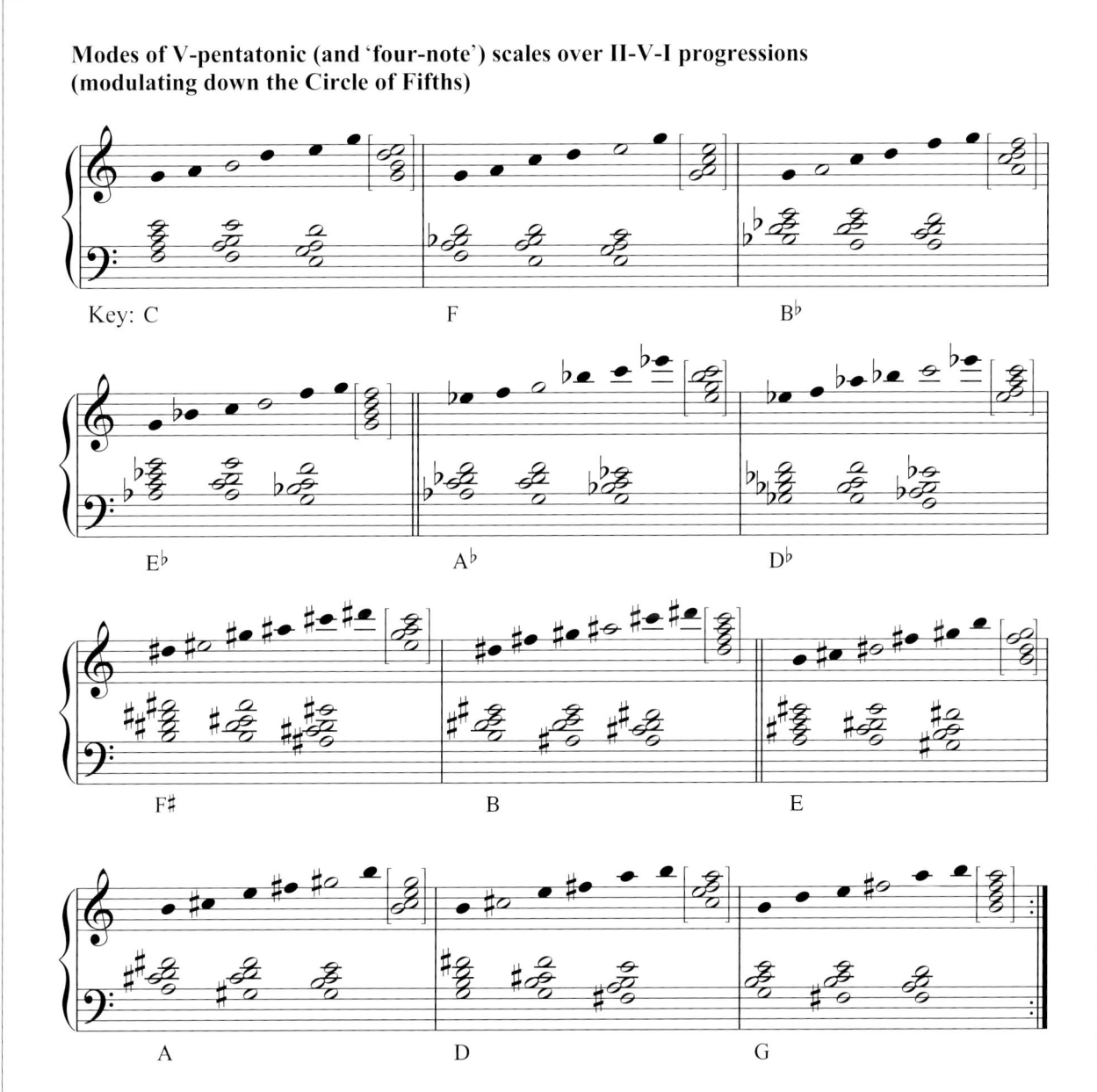

You might be tempted to think that the logical next stage in enriching the materials at our disposal would be to introduce the remaining notes of the diatonic major scale for each key. However, in jazz this isn't so – partly because these additional notes are precisely the avoid notes over V and I we're likely to want to steer clear of, and partly for another reason: in jazz, unlike in classical, it's both acceptable and effective for chromatic embellishments to be applied directly to pentatonic material, bypassing the diatonic scale altogether. Before we try that, though, it's worth knowing the forms that chromatic embellishments can take in jazz:

- Chromatic passing notes: one or two notes from the chromatic scale are used to create stepwise chromatic movement between adjacent notes of the diatonic or pentatonic scales (ie, notes separated by either a whole tone or a minor third).
- Chromatic auxiliary notes: stepwise movement from a note of the diatonic or pentatonic scale to a chromatically adjacent one and back again.
- Chromatic appoggiaturas: instead of moving straight to a note from the diatonic or pentatonic scale, we first play a chromatically adjacent note, quickly moving from the latter to the former – as if correcting a mistake. (This effect is also related to the use of glissando effects in blues piano playing – see Unit Ten for more about this.)

The next two pages (p319-320) contain a couple of examples to show how some licks based on the scale material from the previous exercise look and sound before and after they've been chromatically embellished in the ways just mentioned. Note how the melodic contour and rhythm of the line sometimes get adjusted, to throw the chromatic elements better into relief or make more rhythmic space for them.

SECTION 3 | UNIT 8

UNIT 8 | SECTION 3

Exercise 8.17

Now see if you can add chromatic embellishments to some of your licks as you improvise using the material of the last two exercises.

Exercise 8.18 (p321-2)

This is a similar exercise, but more advanced: the scale material changes slightly from one chord to the next within each II-V-I, using each of the three alternative forms of pentatonic scale mentioned above in turn.

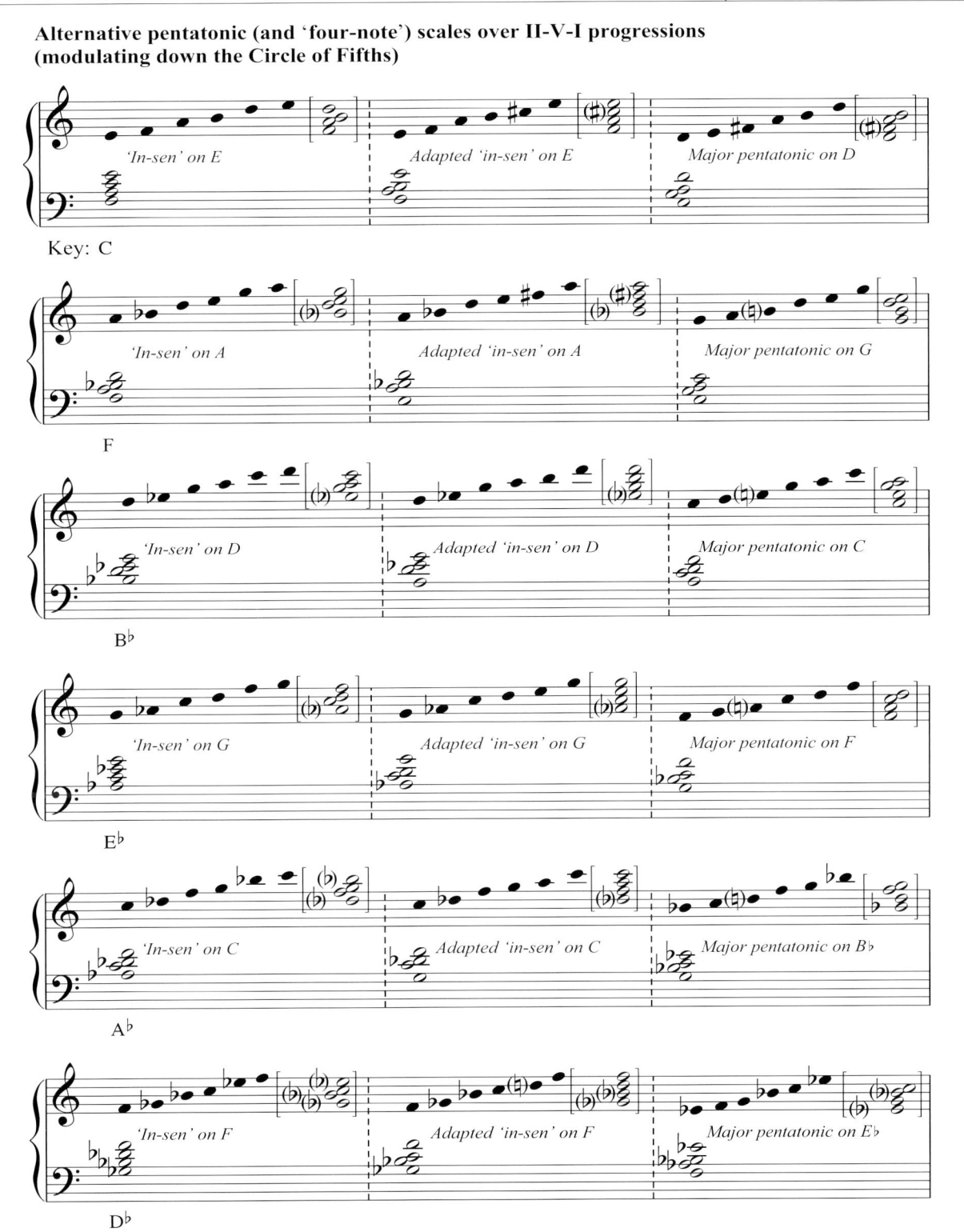

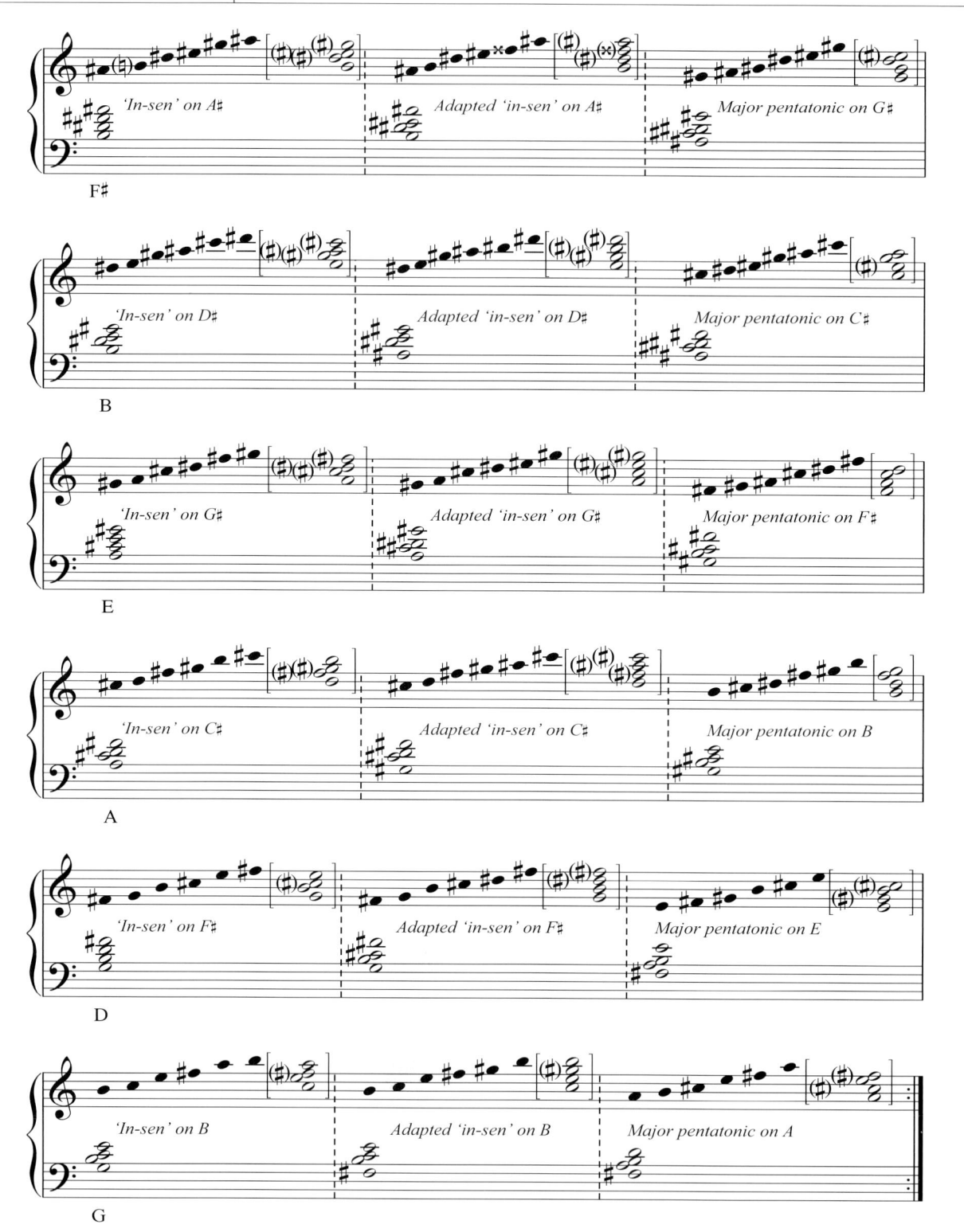

Exercise 8.19

Now here's the first part of the last exercise again, but, as before, the scale material appears in different modes in each key to help you focus on exploring a single area of the piano in the right hand as you pass through successive II-V-I progressions. (You can still experiment with carrying over the scales into other octaves, though.) Only the first four keys are given: try to continue the pattern yourself through all the remaining keys. (You may use the scales given in the previous exercise as a guide.)

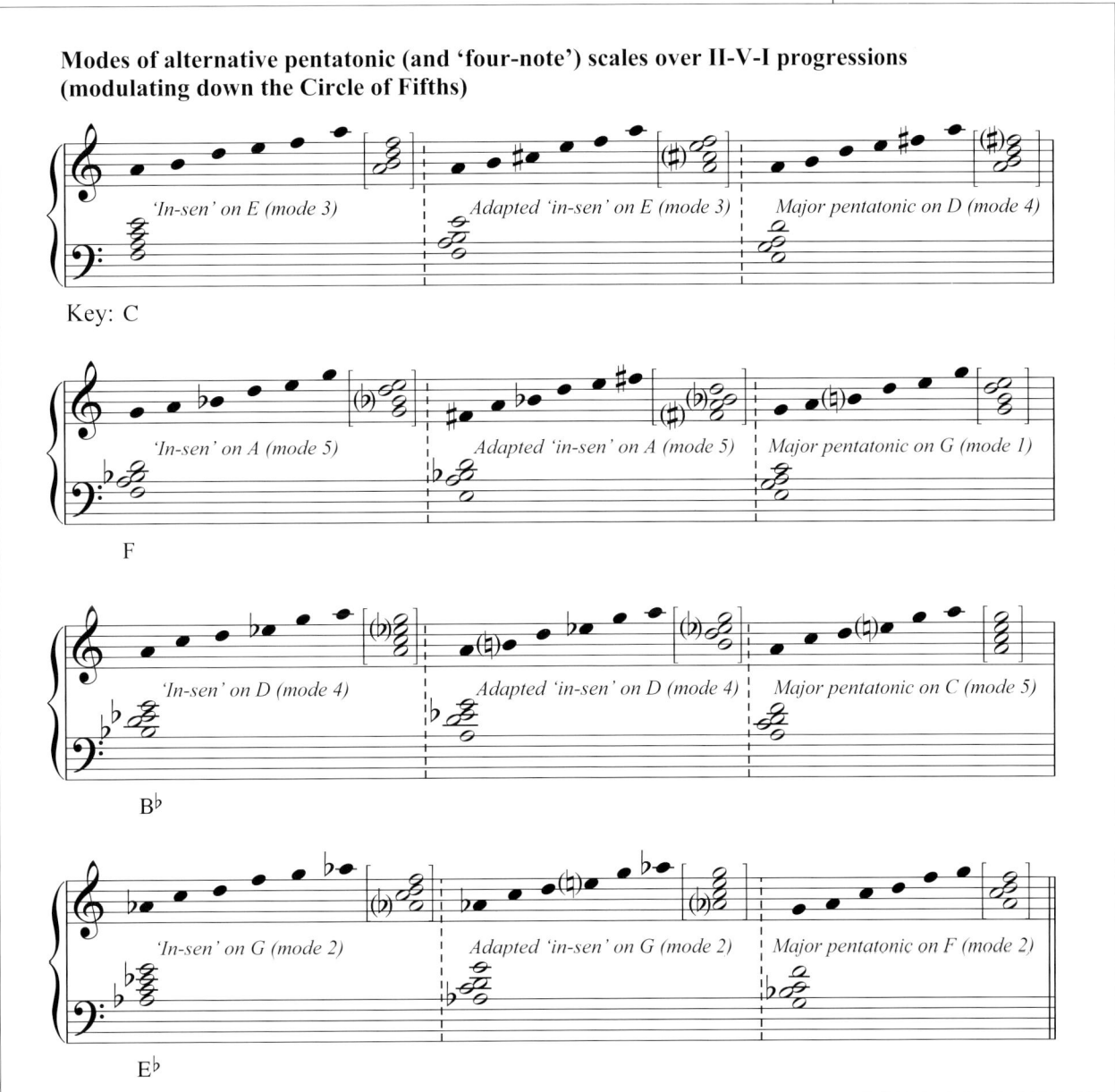

Modes of alternative pentatonic (and 'four-note') scales over II-V-I progressions (modulating down the Circle of Fifths)

continued over page

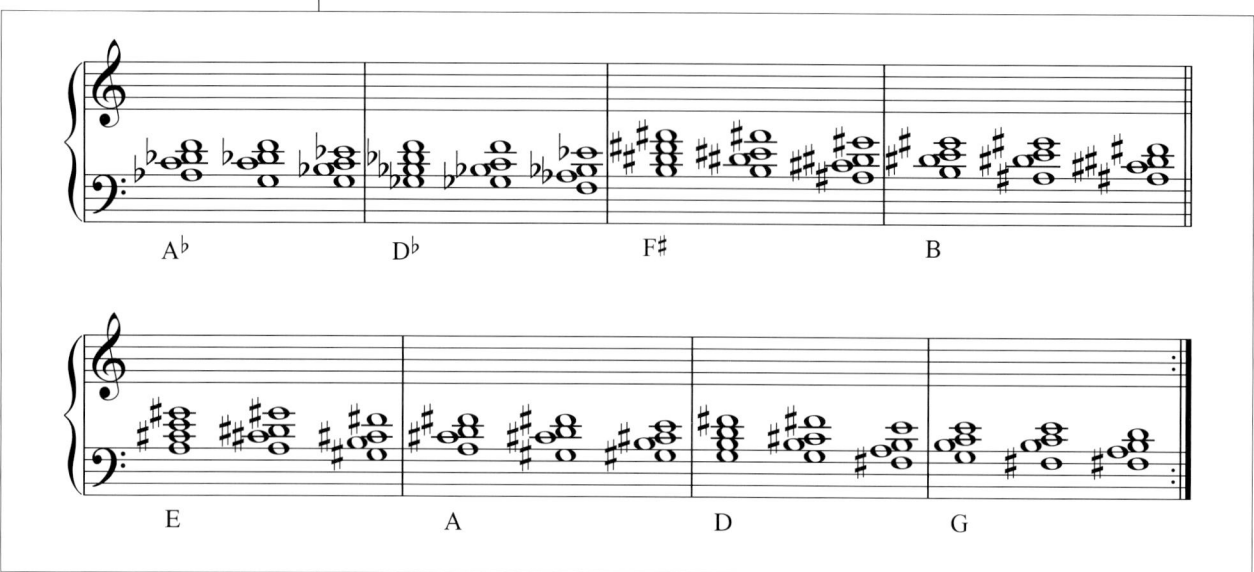

On the opposite page are some similar licks to those shown earlier, adapted to reflect the more advanced scale material in the last exercise. Listen to how they sound compared to the related licks shown before.

Exercise 8.20
Now try adding chromatic embellishments to your licks as you improvise using the material in the previous couple of exercises.

> Like voicings, your choice of what licks to use will sometimes be affected by the key you are in, though for different reasons. With voicings this is because the register that a voicing takes on in a particular key can have consequences for its colouristic qualities. With licks it is because melodic figures that are straightforward to play in some keys can turn out to be technically awkward in others, thanks to the changed configurations of black and white keys involved, which in turn affects what fingerings are practically possible. That's why many players reserve different licks for different sets of keys.

Having explored some of the options for using pentatonic scales over II-V-I progressions – without and then with chromatic embellishment – we're now ready to move on to improvising with diatonic scales. This means using either the modes of the major scale itself, or the changed versions of these modes that result when raised avoid notes get to count as notes within the scales themselves.

The next two exercises give you raw material for improvising with these. However, it's important to remember that within each diatonic scale (or its modes, or its versions with raised avoid notes) pentatonic scales are still present – embedded as a more basic element that you'll probably want to highlight a lot of the time. Indeed, just avoiding the avoid notes by placing them off the beats will itself introduce a pentatonic flavour. (Note also how you aren't necessarily limited to alluding to the pentatonic scale on V here, as those on I and IV are also available – at least in the unaltered forms of the diatonic scale and its modes.)

Exercise 8.21

Once again this is an exercise in 'guided improvisation'. The diatonic major scale (corresponding to the major scale of the key) is given over each chord in the II-V-I, but in the form of the appropriate mode for the chord in question. (Avoid notes are highlighted with unfilled noteheads.) Try working out your own licks first without, then with, chromatic embellishment. The scales are given for just the first four keys. Work out the rest yourself!

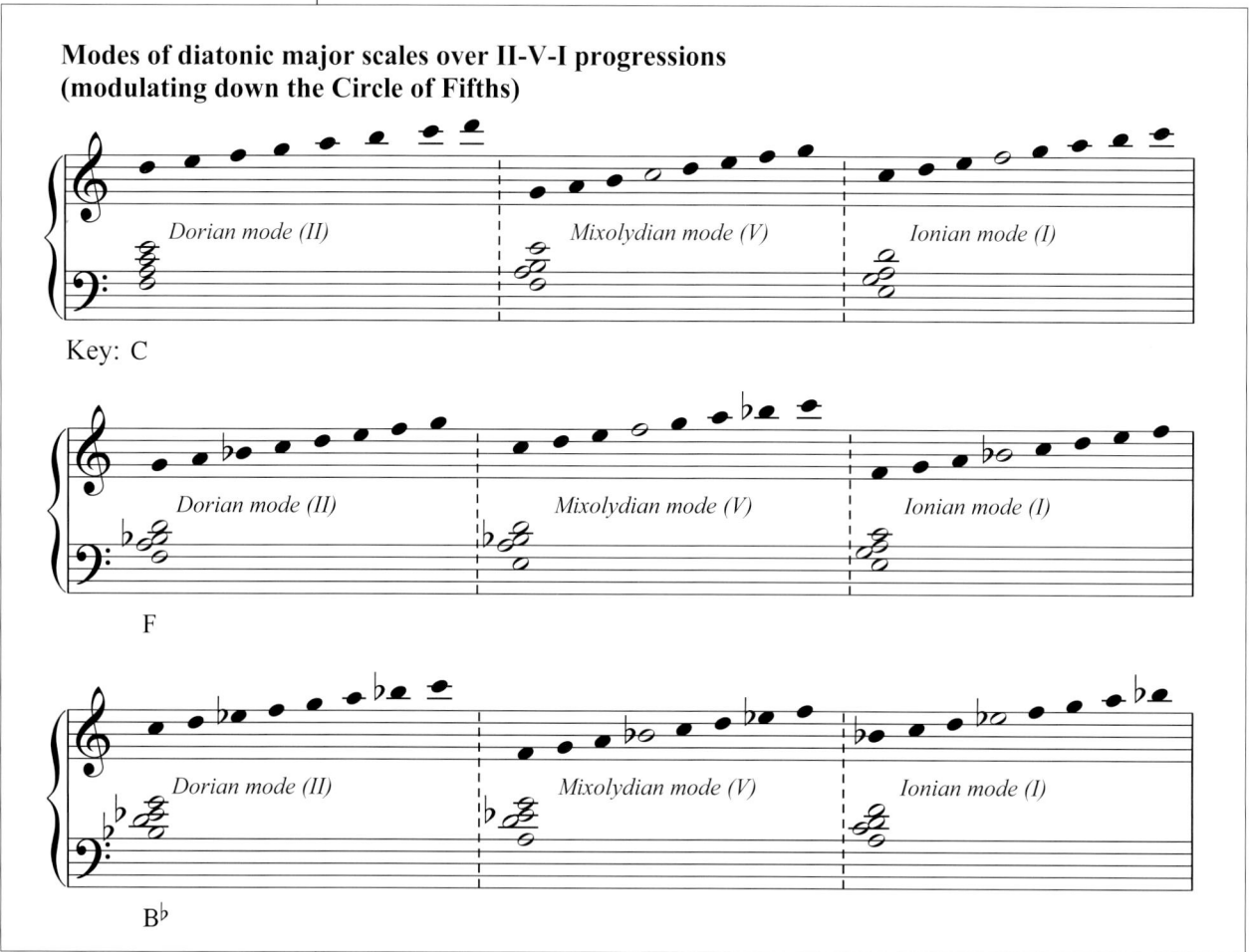

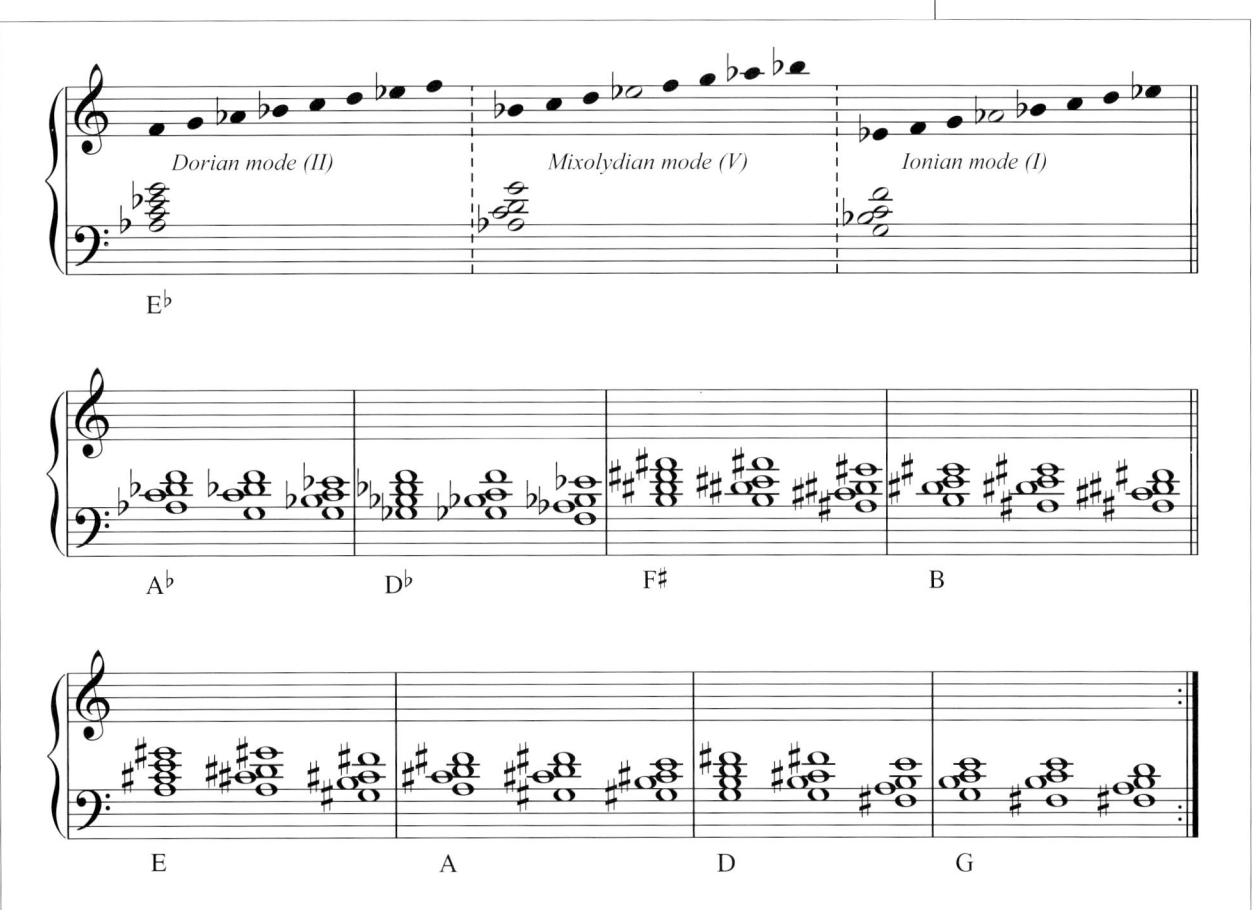

Exercise 8.22

And here's a similar exercise with chromatically raised avoid notes counting as part of the scales to be used, so that they then correspond to alternative modes. (The resulting scale over V is called the Lydian dominant and is used a great deal in jazz. We'll examine its origins more carefully later in the unit.) Try making use of the 'four-note scales' shown in brackets as well. (Note how these are also shown here with the starting note of the mode at the bottom, though you can use them starting on the other notes too. Can you see how over V and I they contain the raised avoid notes?) Then experiment with adding chromaticism, keeping in mind that because the raised avoid notes now count as part of the scale they, too, can be chromatically embellished. Here, too, the scales are only shown for the first four keys, so you'll have to work out the rest yourself.

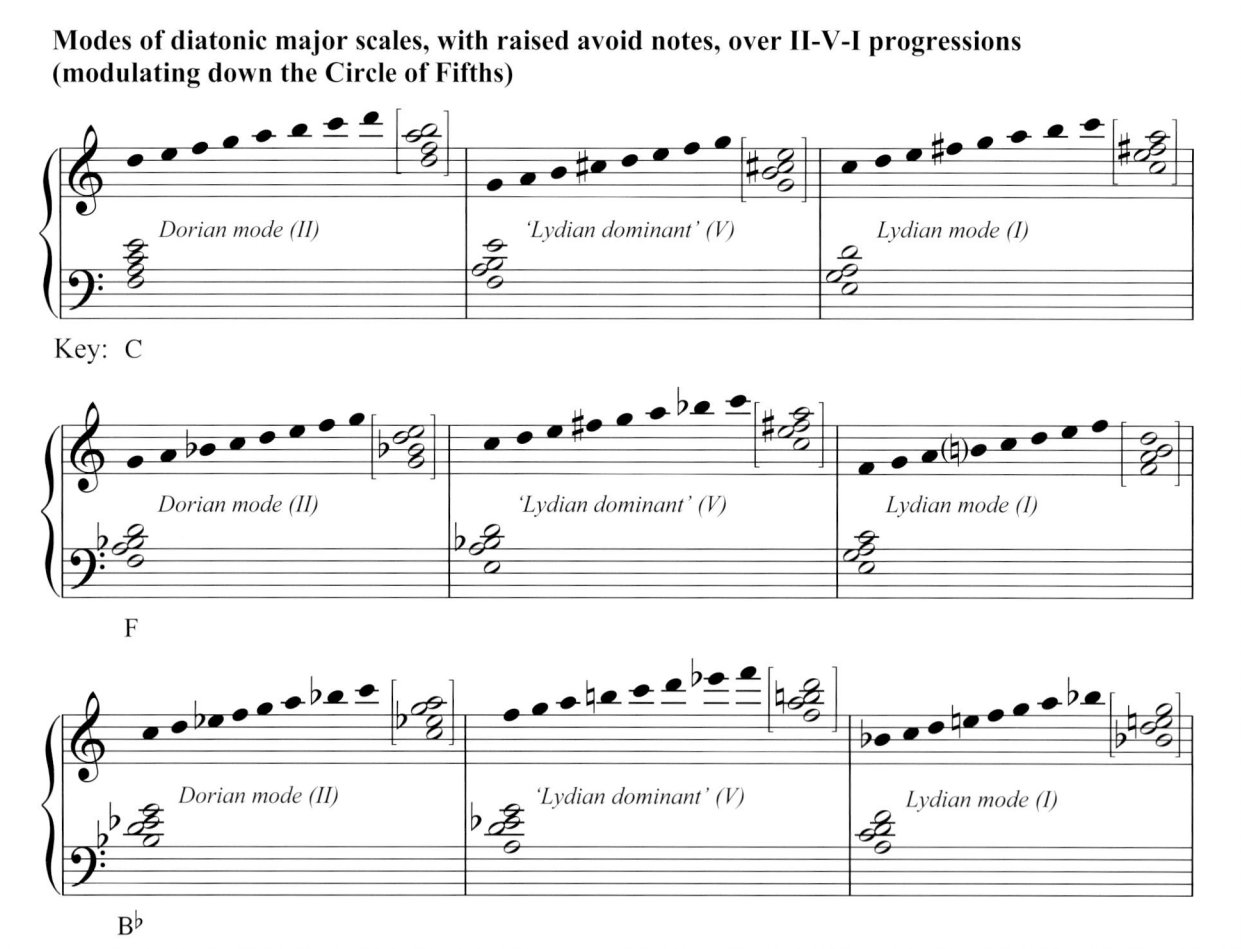

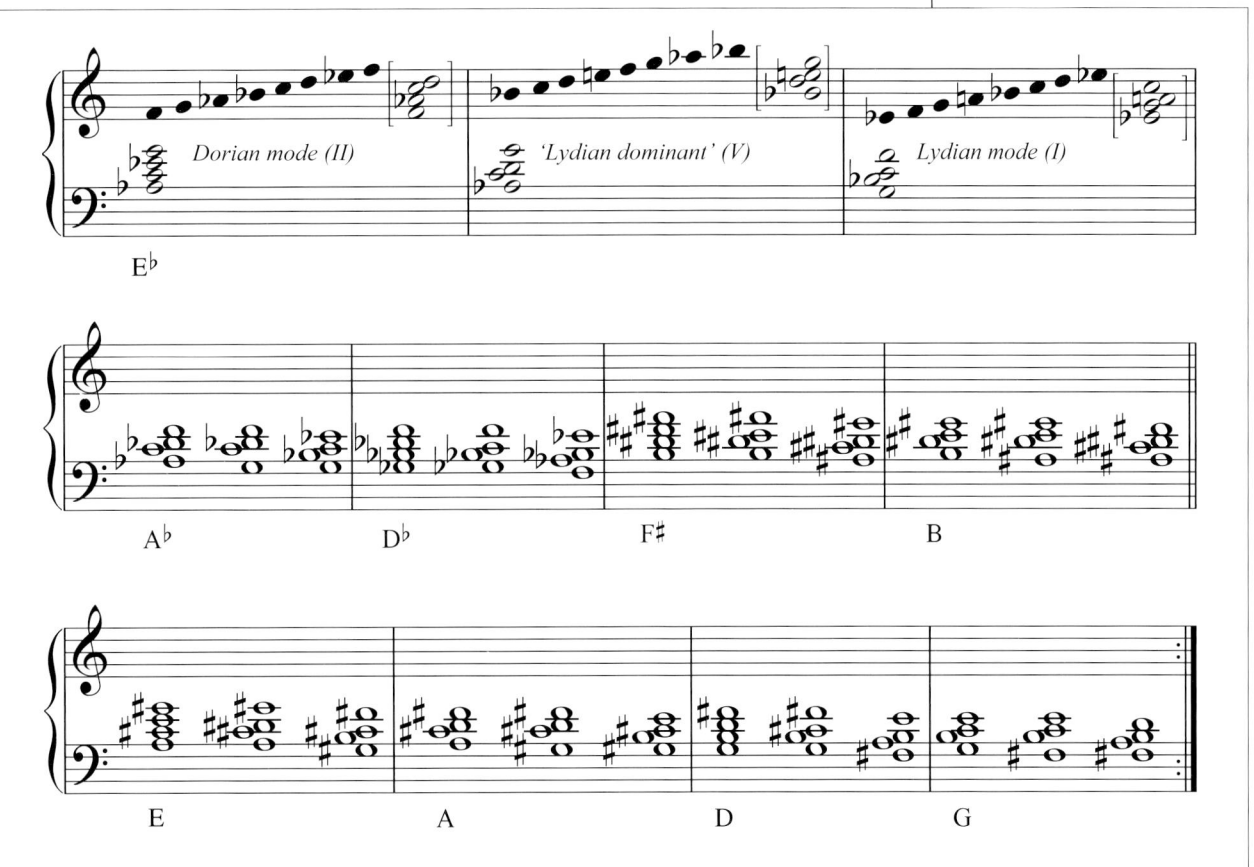

If we take the three modes of the diatonic major scale, but with the raised versions of the avoid notes on V and I included, as in the last exercise, we get three distinct scales (each containing a slightly different set of pitches) – one for each chord in the II-V-I – just like with the alternative pentatonic scales featured earlier. This means that each scale has a definite association with one of the chords in the II-V-I, simply by virtue of what notes it has – or, more precisely, what raised notes it does or doesn't have. So if we want to keep things really simple when improvising with the major scale, all we need focus on is which raised avoid notes to introduce or leave out:

- On II: no raised notes at all.
- On V: chromatically raise the first degree of the major scale of the key.
- On I: chromatically raise the fourth degree of the major scale of the key.

We haven't said anything so far about what makes a good lick. You'll find lots of books that give advice about this, but the suggestions they give usually boil down to the idea of copying a small number of standard formulas. Formulas have always played a big role in improvised music – see the introduction to this book for more about that – but frankly, where licks are concerned you shouldn't need to use them, provided you've understood the essential points of how scale and chords are used, along with the idea of chromatic embellishment. The whole point of learning the harmonic formulas and scales in jazz is so you can let go and just doodle freely with them without losing musical sense.

You, should, though, aim to give your melody lines and figures a sense of harmonic directedness (or 'directionality'). We'll explore what this means at the start of the next unit – especially the idea of **goal notes** – but here's a basic technique that'll help get you going.

Aim to arrive at the next chord change on a chord note, preferably the third of the chord. As you approach the change, decide whether you want to emphasise or delay the chord note (third). You emphasise the chord note (third) by playing it on the beat, followed by a change of melodic direction or movement from ascending to descending or vice versa, or from stepwise to leaps or vice versa. You delay the chord note (third) by first playing a note one scale-step or semitone away, and then quickly moving to the chord note – as if you'd accidentally missed the chord note first time round and wanted to correct the mistake. Alternatively, you can play a note on one side of the chord note, then a note on the other (also one scale step or semitone away), then move straight to the chord note (third) itself.

Actually each of these options – emphasising and delaying – is just a different way of giving prominence to the chord note. The real point of these techniques, though, is the effect they have on your handling of the material that comes before and after. You should find that the notes you improvise just beforehand follow a trajectory that feels like it's leading them naturally towards the new chord note, while the notes you improvise just afterwards feel like they are already moving away and towards something else.

There's one more technique we should mention when talking about licks and melodic improvising: it's the deliberate use of melody notes that are foreign to the scale that actually fits with the harmony beneath it. Such notes are known in jazz as **off-notes**. For every seven-note scale, there are five off-notes. These notes will certainly sound strange or out-of-place over the chord, which is why we mostly steer clear of them. However, sometimes it can be interesting to deliberately pick out one or more of these notes and let the melody pass through them, to create a specific effect. It can sound as though the melody has 'got lost' for a moment before finding its way again, or it can give the music a 'wacky' or unpredictable feel.

Sometimes off-notes are useful just to prevent the melody line from sounding predictable. On the other hand, use them too often and you'll see that they quickly lose their 'shock value' and threaten to undermine the harmonic structure and direction of the music. The table below shows the off-notes for the seven modes of a major scale, plus the most commonly used alternative scales derived from the jazz minor scale:

Scale off-notes

Major (Ionian)	♭2	♭3	–	♭5	♭6	♭7
Dorian	♭2	3	–	♭5	♭6	7
Phrygian	2	3	–	♭5	6	7
Lydian	♭2	♭3	4	–	♭6	♭7
Mixolydian	♭2	♭3	–	♭5	♭6	7
Aeolian	♭2	3	–	♭5	6	7
Locrian	2	3	–	5	6	7
Locrian #2	♭2	3	–	5	6	7
Lydian dominant	♭2	♭3	4	–	♭6	7
Altered scale	2	–	4	5	6	7
Diminished scale (half-step/whole-step)	2	–	4	5	–	♭7

Exercise 8.23
Finally, go back and work through again all of the possibilities shown here for right-hand improvisation over left-hand voicings, but this time following the alternative key-sequences mentioned earlier: try descending through keys a semitone lower, a whole tone lower, a minor third lower, and a major third lower. (Pay special attention to the last of these, as this kind of modulation plays an important role in some later styles of jazz.)

> **Keep a diary**. Not like Samuel Pepys did, but a lick diary! This gives you a permanent record of your ideas that you can come back to again and again. It means you can monitor your progress by comparing yourself now to what you were doing several months (or years) ago. That way you won't suffer from being 'trapped in the present'. The best way to go about this is to jot ideas down on manuscript paper, as loosely or precisely as you wish. But if you don't like that, use recording equipment. Mike up your instrument, then set up an MP3, CD, or computer-based recording system that you're happy to leave switched on in record mode while you play. It's worth cataloguing your recordings so you can come back to them later and know when they were made. Or why not try both methods at the same time?

Standards and lead sheets
Traditionally, jazz musicians mostly improvised around the melodies in well-known hit songs, which they refer to as **standards**. These can be learned and played from a **lead sheet** – a reduced version of the song, typically used by non-classical performers as a starting point for working out their own arrangements. However, jazz musicians have

increasingly come to focus on just the chord changes in the songs – often in versions adapted by previous jazz artists. These will often be written down using no more than an empty staff with a time signature and chord symbols – known as a **chord chart**.

You'll find lead sheets for jazz standards in the kind of published collections known as **fake books** or **real books**. However, don't take the chord symbols in these too literally. They tend to include only the most basic structures, and assume that the individual player will decide how to make the harmony more stylish and interesting.

It's also worth knowing that they follow some slightly different conventions from those in force in written classical music. The key signature is often only given for the first line of music, yet it affects all of the subsequent music (at least until the next key signature). Diagonal strokes or slashes may be used to indicate beats of a bar (in which case it may also be referred to as a **slash chart**), and the melody itself is normally placed in a register corresponding to notes close to the middle of a staff with the treble clef, for ease of reading. (Of course, you're free to transpose it to other octaves if you wish.) If you work with a singer or other instrumentalist then it'll be down to you to transpose the melody and/or chords into other keys – so you can play in the key best for them.

The most famous and widely used example of jazz chord changes adapted for improvising from a well-known standard are '**Rhythm Changes**'. (The name reflects the fact that they're derived from George Gershwin's hit song, 'I've Got Rhythm'.) These have also served as a basis for many famous jazz **heads** (ie, melodies composed by jazz musicians on the basis of existing chords, which are then themselves used as starting points for improvisation). Like the **12-bar blues**, which we'll consider in Unit Ten, they're often employed as a starting point for group improvising when jazz musicians first get together, so you should certainly be familiar with them. On the opposite page is the original, most basic version of the changes, shown as a slash chart.

Note the overall form, typical of songs and chord structures in jazz: an eight-bar **verse** or 'A-section' at the start, immediately repeated, followed by a contrasting eight-bar **bridge** or 'B-section', followed in turn by the eight-bar verse one more time, producing a 32-bar AABA structure. (This is known as **jazz song form**.)

To see why this sequence of chords is so handy just take note of the implications of the recurring VI-II-V-I progression in the verse: raising the avoid note in VI allows us to treat chord VI as having equivalent implications for melodic improvisation as chord II (ie, Dorian mode). That means we can harmonise all four chords with voicings from the II-V-I formula (just transposing voicings for II up a perfect fifth to get equivalent voicings for VI).

What's more, because the avoid note over VI is the same pitch as the avoid note over I, the pentatonic scale starting on V (which works over all of the II-V-I because it leaves out the avoid notes over both V and I) will also work over VI. That means that (if we want to) we can use just the pentatonic scale on V to improvise over the whole of bars 1-4, as well as bars 7-8 (both in the version leading back to the repeat and in the

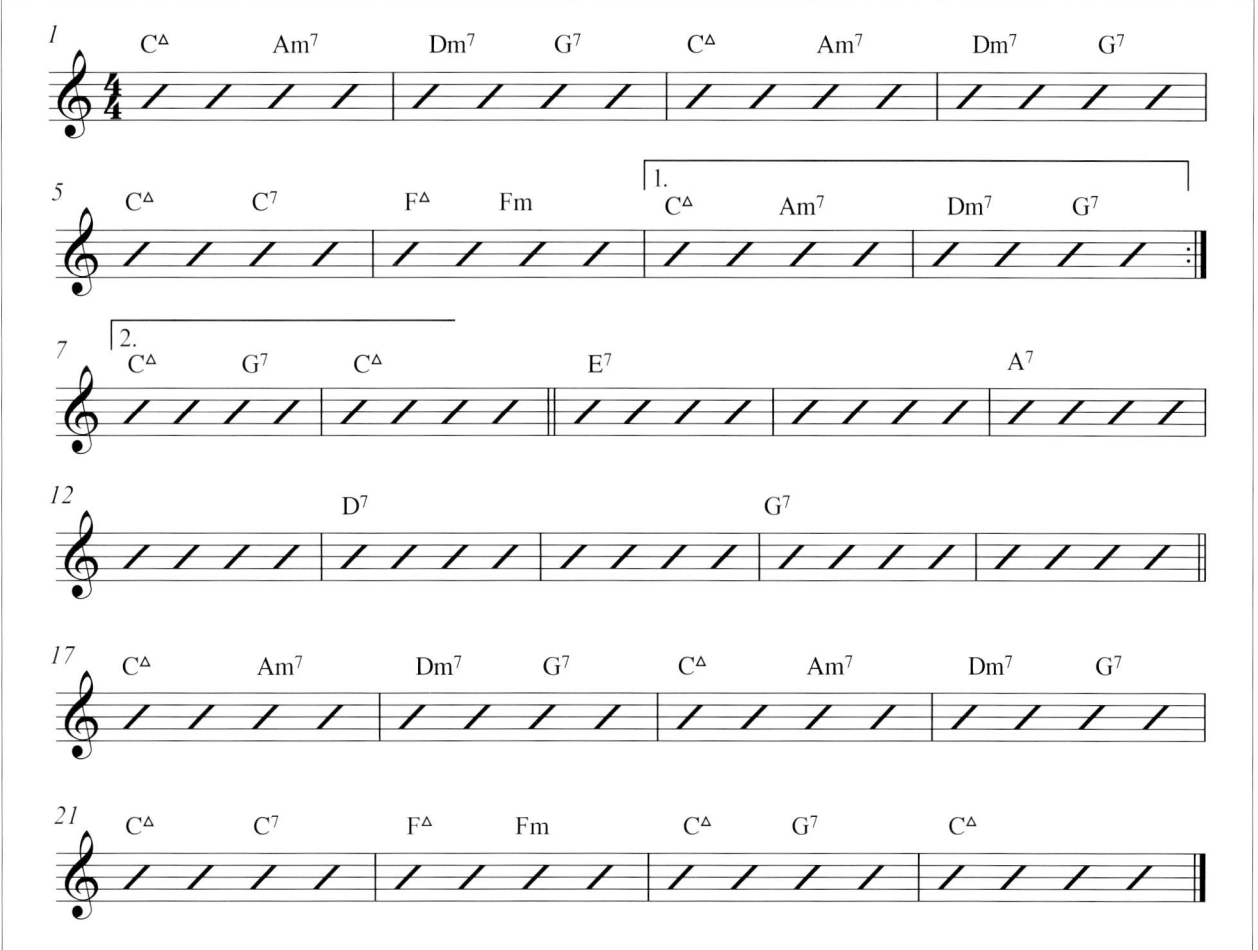

final cadence). (Of course, we can also use the appropriate modes of the diatonic major scale as well, if we like – with or without raised avoid notes.)

The one place where we need to think more carefully about what scales to use to embellish or improvise over the chords is bars 5-6:

- The C7 and F△ chords introduce a passing modulation to F major, so it's best to treat them as a V-I in the key of F. In that case we can just use a pentatonic scale on V of F – ie, the major pentatonic starting on C. But we can also use Mixolydian or Lydian dominant over the C7 chord, and F major (or F Lydian to give us the raised avoid note) over the F△ chord. And these can be used together, since V pentatonic is present within those other scales.

- Use F jazz minor over the F minor chord in bar 6 – this keeps the B-flat from the key of F major (which is no longer an avoid note), but also has the flattened third (A-flat) of the F minor chord itself. (We'll discuss the treatment of minor chords and the jazz minor scale in more detail in the next section.)

After just stringing together II-V-I progressions in successive keys, as we did earlier in the unit, the next logical step is to play through the first eight bars of the 'Rhythm Changes' over and over again, exploring the different possibilities. It means working with a slightly longer structure (that starts with I and moves through VI), while bars 5 and 6 will force you to think about how jazz voice-leading sometimes needs to be adapted to work with other chord progressions and in modulations. The next example shows a straightforward arrangement of the chords for the verse, using two-handed voicings:

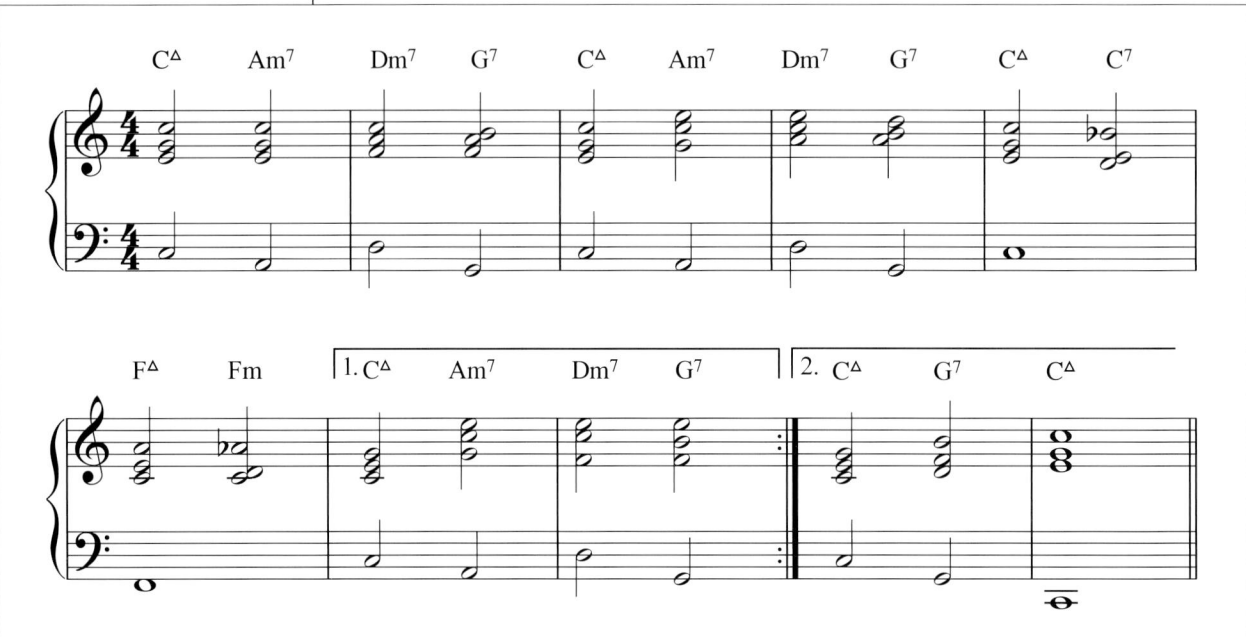

Exercise 8.24

Play through the verse for 'Rhythm Changes' as many times as you want, seeing how many different harmonisations you can come up with using two-handed voicings. When you're feeling confident about this, try embellishing the top part in the right hand with some stepwise movements, chromaticism, and chord-based leaps, just as we did with the II-V-I progression earlier on in the unit. Finally, try the same in other keys. If necessary, transpose the chord symbols in the chart into other keys, writing them out to create new chord charts that you can then use as a guide.

We can also try left-hand voicings for the 'Rhythm Changes', to free up our right hand for improvising – just as we did with the II-V-I and eight-chord progressions before. Once again, we'll need to adapt the voice-leading formulas to make sense of the opening I and VI chords, not to mention the chords in bars 5 and 6. The next example demonstrates this, with the repeat of the verse written out in full to show an alternative realisation of the harmony the second time round:

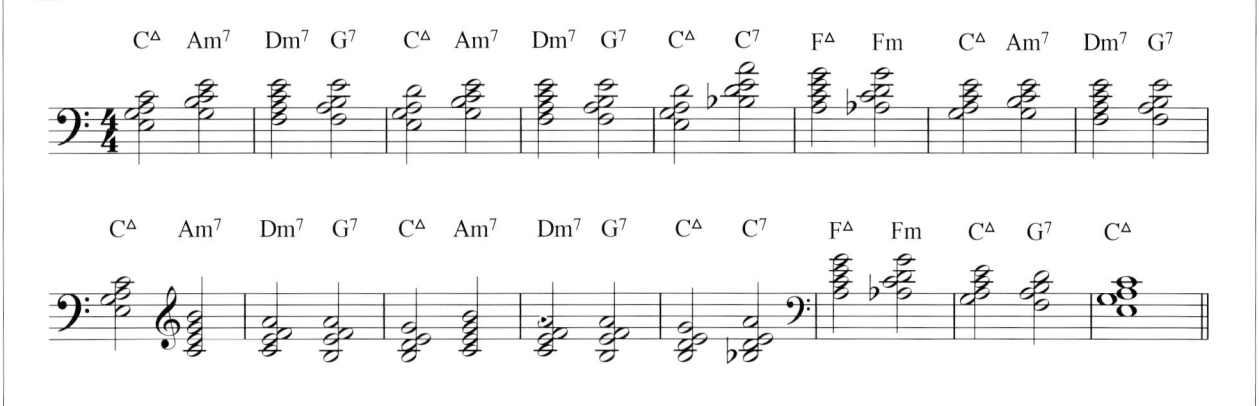

Our choice of scales for improvising over these voicings will be the same as with the embellishments of two-handed voicings discussed above.

Exercise 8.25
Now take the left-hand harmonisation of the verse of 'Rhythm Changes' given in the previous example and improvise over it with your right hand. Once again, see if you can transpose the whole sequence into other keys, creating alternative realisations of the chords and improvising over these too.

Now let's turn our attention to the eight-bar 'B-section' or bridge. The first thing to note is that it's quite a different kind of structure, consisting as it does of just a series of dominant seventh chords. Taken individually each implies a modulatory movement down the Circle of Fifths. Together they eventually bring us back to the dominant of the home key, ready for a repeat of the verse. Apart from the shifting key centre, what's striking is that the sequence of chords has no harmonic interest in itself. (In effect, there's no progression within a key, only a progression of keys here.) Yet this is typical for jazz bridge sections. Because all of the chords are instances of unresolved dominant harmony, with only one chord per key, they offer the improviser a great deal of scope. That's because dominant harmony, with its highly unresolved nature, lends itself particularly well to the kind of ambiguous harmonic structures jazz musicians like to substitute for existing chords in standards. This brings us to the subject of jazz **reharmonisation** – which we'll examine in the next section.

> **Verse and bridge**: in jazz song form, whereas the verse offers a melody and chords that are good for improvising around, the bridge is usually reserved for a freer approach: it's here that individual musicians take turns to perform solo breaks featuring their own distinctive material. Hence the need for more open-ended harmonic structures to support this.

UNIT 8 | SECTION 3

Just before we get involved in learning how to reharmonise structures like these, it's worth seeing how simple it is to voice a sequence of modulating dominant seventh chords using the voicings we already know. As you can see from the example below, alternating the third and seventh of successive chords in the top part provides a good basis for two-handed voicings, with the fifth and ninth alternating below in one of the inner parts, just like in II-V-I. Note how putting the more dissonant ninth on the second and fourth chords in the sequence gives us a greater level of tension on the final chord of the bridge than would be the case if we voiced the sequence the other way around, making for a stronger sense of arrival when the music then returns back to the home key (on I) to restart the verse.

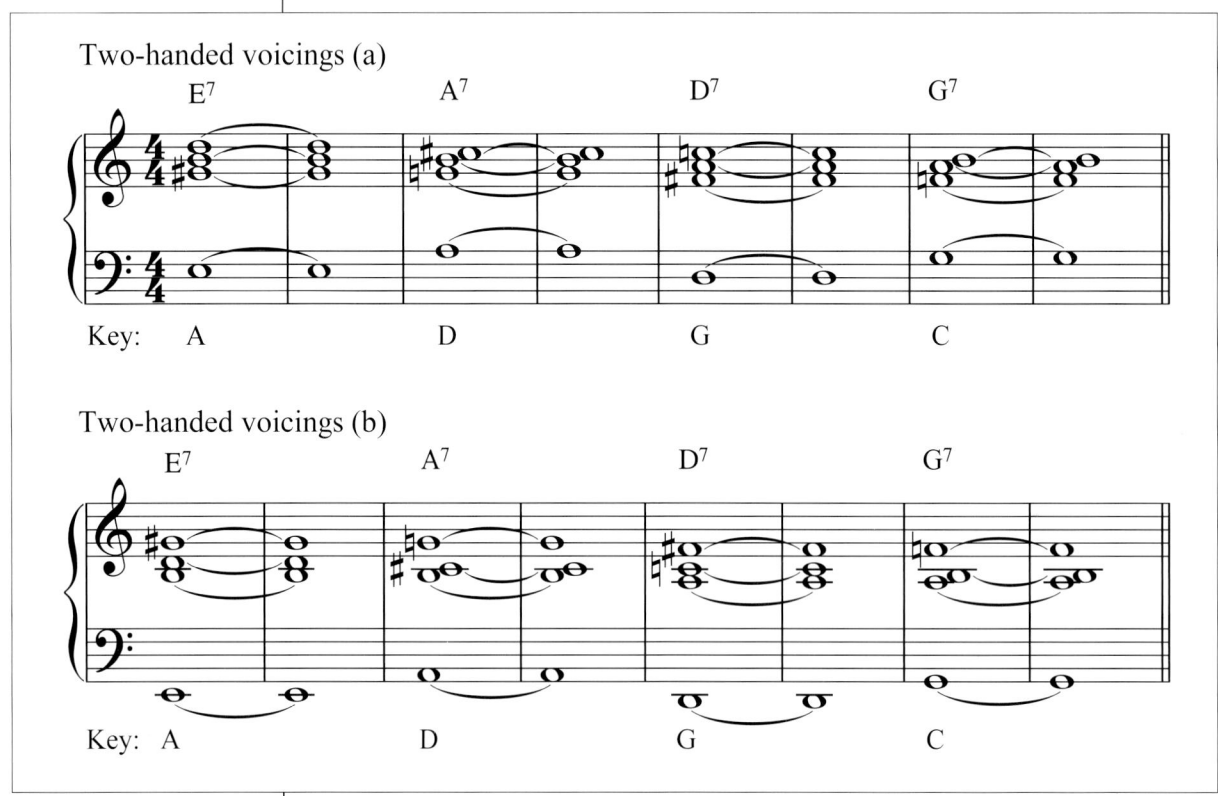

Alternating the two types of left-hand voicing for V chords also works well, as the next example shows:

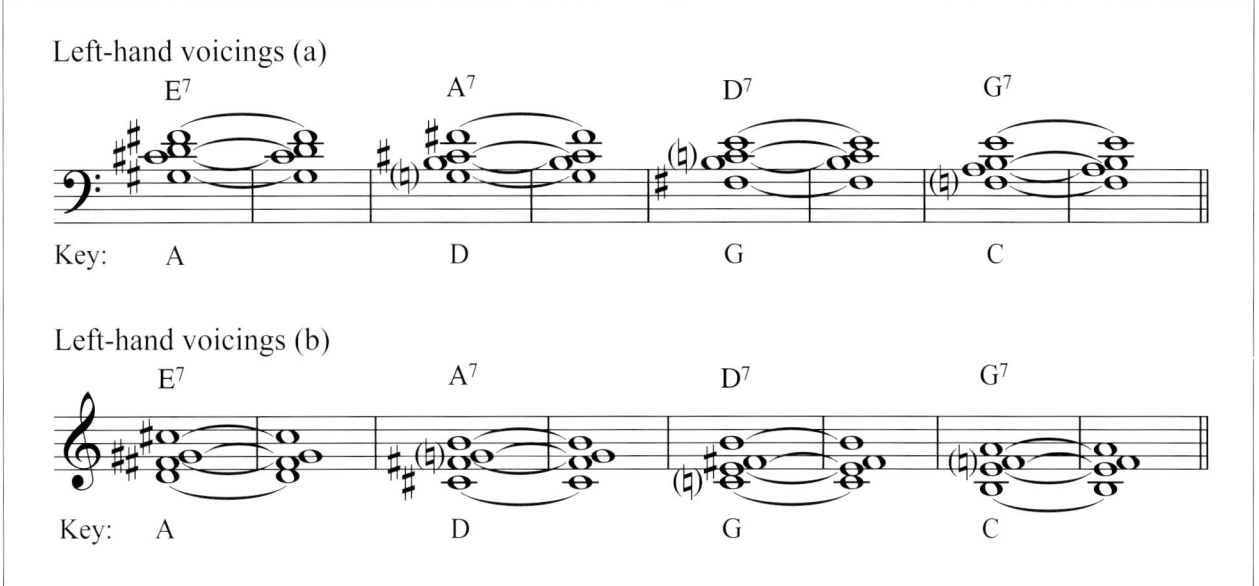

Exercise 8.26
Take the harmonisations of the bridge of 'Rhythm Changes' (shown in the two previous examples) and try embellishing and improvising over them. Once again, try other keys too.

Reharmonisation
Here's another, slightly later version of the 'Rhythm Changes' – one that became popular as a basis for jazz improvising from the 1930s onwards:

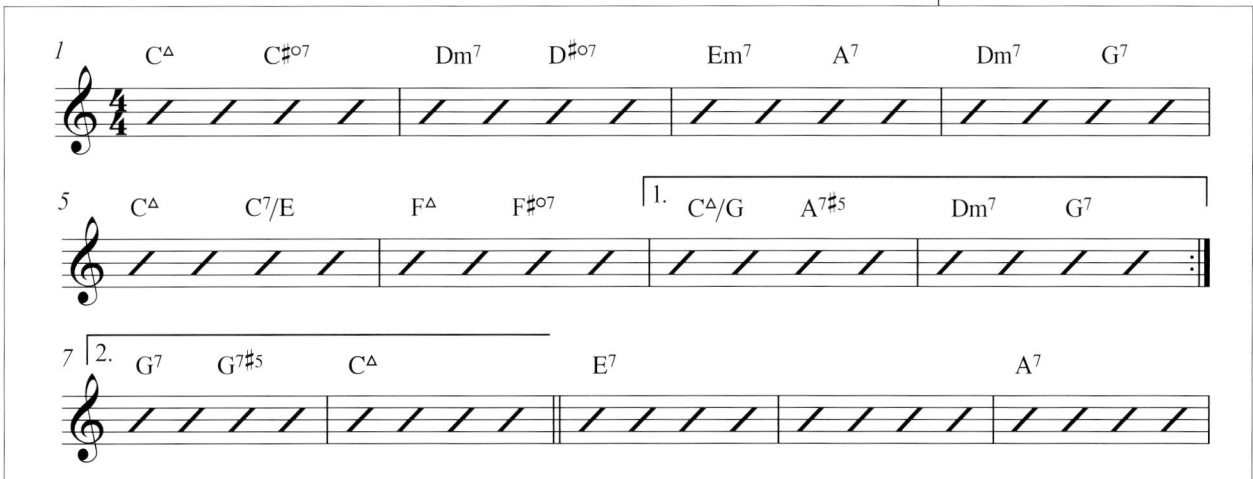

continued over page

UNIT 8 | SECTION 3

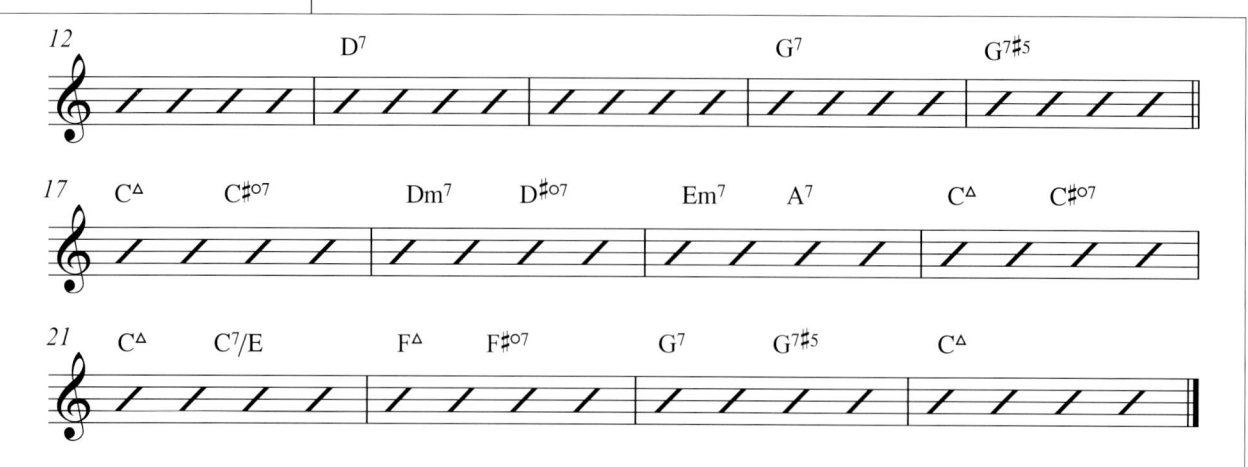

Compare the changes here to those in the original version, as shown in the preceding section. (The key is still C major.) Let's consider the different ways in which the harmony has been altered:

- In the opening I-VI-II-V (bars 1-2), both VI (Am7) and V (G7) have been replaced by diminished seventh chords on roots a semitone (half-step) above that of the preceding chord, and a semitone below that of the next chord: this creates a stepwise chromatic movement in the implied bass. A similar effect appears in the second half of bar 6.
- In the next I-VI-II-V (bars 3-4), I (C△) has been replaced by III (Em7) and VI (Am7) has been changed into V of II (A7), suggesting a passing modulation to the supertonic. We can also hear the Em7 chord as II of II, so together these make a II-V progression in the key of D, followed in the next bar by a similar II-V progression a step lower in the key of C. This type of effect, in which a short progression is reproduced a step lower or higher (one or more times), is common in both classical music and jazz, and is sometimes called a **harmonic sequence** (by analogy with the idea of a melodic sequence). The particular version of this here is especially popular amongst jazz players.
- In the second half of bar 5 and at the start of bar 7 (first time round), chords have been changed from root position to first or second inversion (indicated as slash chords), again creating a stepwise chromatic movement in the implied bass.
- In the next I-VI-II-V (bars 7-8, first-time bars), apart from the change of inversion on C△, the Am7 chord has once again been changed into A7, but this time with the addition of an augmented fifth as well: we'll discuss what this means in a moment.
- In bar 7 (of the second-time bars), and in the second-to-last bar, the G7 chord has been moved back to the start of the bar, and then halfway through the bar has an augmented fifth added to it.

Although these alterations to the original chords are now regarded as more or less permanent features of the 'Rhythm Changes' sequence, the truth is they're a result of jazz performers adapting existing changes (ie, those shown earlier): welcome to the world of **jazz reharmonisation**.

As you can see, this may involve inserting **additional** chords between existing ones, or replacing the latter with **alternative** harmonies. In the latter case, we may opt to play a different type of chord (built on the same scale degree as the original one and somehow functionally equivalent to it) or simply a new chord that, for one reason or another, works equally well in the same context – in which case we're making what's known as a **chord substitution**. (This last term should ring a bell, as we mentioned it back in Unit Four. The idea that the secondary triads II, III, and VI can each 'stand in' for the primary triad two scale-steps higher in classical harmony is an example of the same logic: roughly speaking, the idea is that one chord can take on the function normally associated with another, more basic one, if it's closely enough related.)

In this section we're going to consider the most common options for reharmonising the individual chord-functions of the II-V-I progression (and other chords that, in jazz, can be seen as functioning in ways that are analogous to these). We'll also explore some other more general techniques used by jazz musicians. However, if we want to make sense of the implications of the resulting harmonisations for our improvising we must first expand our knowledge of jazz scale theory a bit.

1) Alternative scale-chord combinations

Let's begin by mentioning two kinds of scale that are different from any we've discussed so far: the **diminished scale** and the **whole-tone scale**.

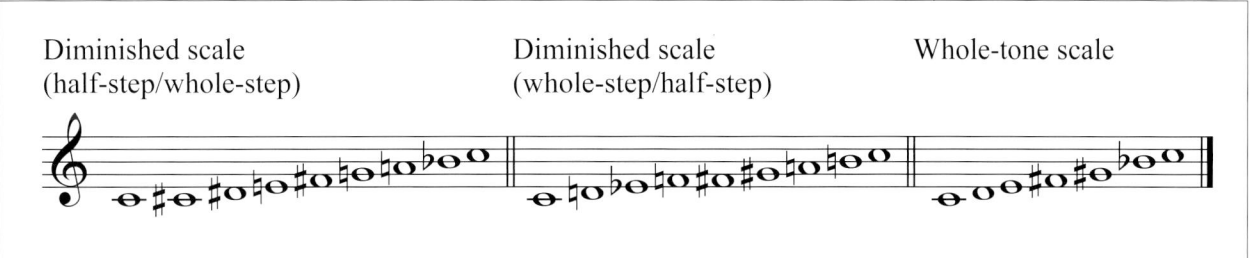

Note how the diminished scale alternates half-step and whole-step intervals, starting in one version with a half-step and in the other with a whole step. Meanwhile, the whole-tone scale consists of nothing but whole-tone steps. Even so, they share a distinctive feature: they can only be transposed a small number of times before arriving back at a scale containing exactly the same pitches (even if it starts in a different place). You can see that transposing a diminished scale up or down a semitone or a tone will generate a distinct scale, but transposing it by a minor third we get a scale with exactly the same notes as the original. (Transposing it by a minor third plus a semitone will produce a scale with the same notes as transposing it by just a semitone, transposing by a minor third plus a tone will be the same as just transposing by a tone, and so on.)

Modes of jazz minor scale *in* C

Jazz minor (mode 1)

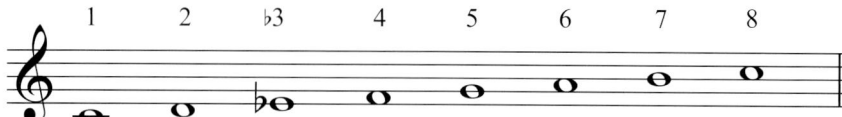

'Dorian ♭2' (mode 2)

'Lydian augmented' (mode 3)

'Lydian dominant' (mode 4)

'Mixolydian ♭6' (mode 5)

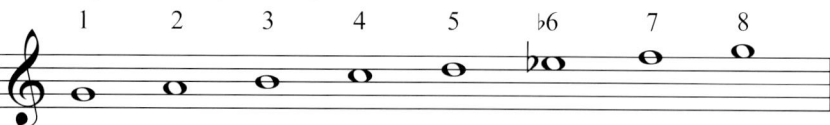

'Half-diminished' or 'Locrian ♮2' (mode 6)

'Altered' (mode 7)

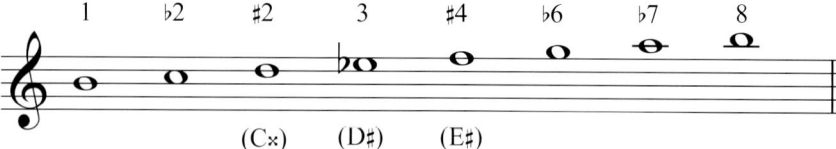

Similarly, transposing the whole-tone scale by a semitone gives us a new scale, but transposing by a tone gives us the same notes as we started with, etc. This means that chords built on these scales are potentially ambiguous as to the key they are in: exactly the same chord can, in principle, belong to any of four diminished scales, and thus four keys, or to any of six whole-tone scales and thus six keys. This is particularly useful in the case of diminished-scale harmony, as we'll see later.

The other thing we need to learn about right now is connected with the special role played in jazz by the **jazz minor scale**. Like the major scale, we think of this as providing a series of distinctive scale-types, each corresponding to one of its modes. We may refer to these as the **jazz minor modes** (opposite page).

To highlight the differences between these more clearly here they are again, this time all starting on a single note (C):

Modes of jazz minor scale *on* C

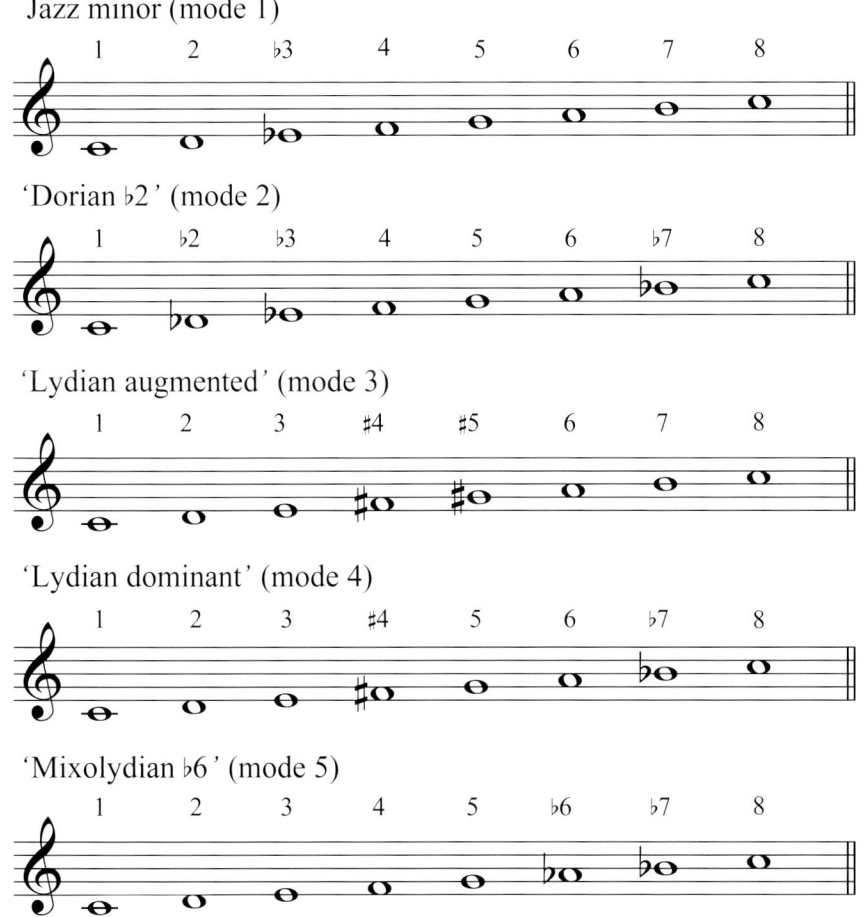

Jazz minor (mode 1)

'Dorian ♭2' (mode 2)

'Lydian augmented' (mode 3)

'Lydian dominant' (mode 4)

'Mixolydian ♭6' (mode 5)

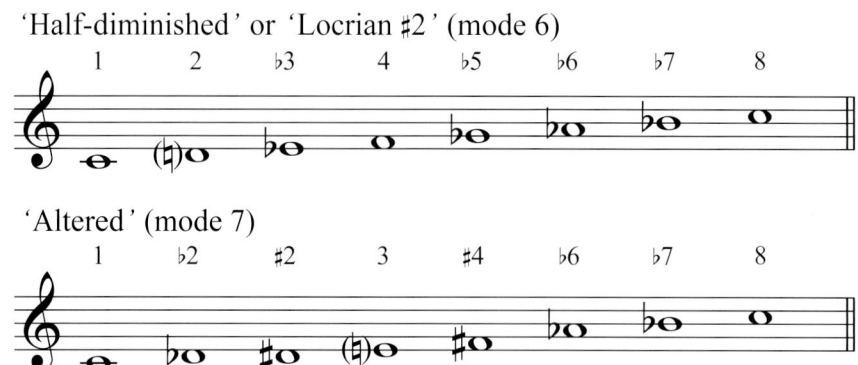

The key point is that each of the scale-types represented by a mode of the jazz minor scale corresponds to a more advanced type of chord – one that can be used to reharmonise the essential chords of jazz (ie, II, V, and I, as well as their substitutes). Learning the scale and the harmonisation it relates to at one and the same time makes sense, as it allows us to see straight away what possibilities for melodic improvising are created by each of these alternative chord structures.

The next example shows the standard alternative harmonisations that make use of either modes of the jazz minor or the whole-tone or diminished scales mentioned earlier. (Avoid notes are shown with asterisks. Of the seven modes of the jazz minor, only the fifth mode isn't represented here. That's because it doesn't generate any further alternative harmonisation that we could hear as playing the role of II, V, or I in a major key. Instead, we just hear the harmonies it produces as part of the tonality of the jazz minor scale itself. This means the options it corresponds to are identical to those offered by the first mode, ie, the jazz minor scale itself.) Each scale for improvising is placed above an unvoiced version of the corresponding alternative harmonisation of II, V, or I: see opposite page.

Each of these chord structures is based around an existing chord from major-key harmony that's been chromatically altered in some way. Let's consider each of them in turn and see what difference they make to the II-V-I arrangements we're already familiar with.

a) II with ♭5: this is II as a half-diminished chord. Like the use of a minor chord IV in a major key that's common in classical music, this is an example of a 'borrowed chord', since it's been taken over from chord II of the minor key with the same keynote. (Note that it contains the flattened sixth of the scale, like minor chord IV, but also like V$^{7♭9}$, making the latter a popular follow-on chord. (See the subsequent examples below for options when realising and improvising over V chords with ♭9). Apart from offering an alternative, more wistful harmonic colour in a major key, it may also show up as II in jazz for a more simple reason, which is that some jazz actually operates (classical-style) in a minor key. (When it does, this may involve chords based on the harmonic minor scale, as in classical music, or harmony based on modes with a strong minor-

key character – just like the Aeolian mode, which functions as the standard minor scale in a lot of rock and folk-based music. Note that II will be half-diminished in the Aeolian mode or rock minor, but not in the Dorian mode.)

b) II/V with ♭9: this is a chromatically altered version of a special kind of harmonic structure specific to jazz, called a 'sus chord' – see below for more on this.

c) V with ♯11/♭5: Lydian dominant. This is the most basic alternative chord-scale combination for use on V. All it involves is chromatically raising the note of the Mixolydian mode that's an avoid note over V – the fourth of the mode, or 11th of the chord. Because ♯11 is enharmonically equivalent to ♭5, it's also a popular choice for improvising over V^7 chords that contain ♭5. Because of this it plays an important role in a technique we'll be discussing a little later on: that of tritone substitution. Because the chromatic alteration here corresponds to the raised avoid note (♯4) it does not appear in the standard voicings, which remain unchanged. (Even if we choose to think of the chords as containing ♭5 rather than ♯11, this will not show up in the voicings here. This is because, as we saw earlier, the standard voice-leading formulas always alternate between the fifth and ninth, with the ninth invariably appearing in the V chord itself in order to heighten the sense of resolution when chord I follows on after. This means that the fifth is almost always absent from the voicing for V.

d) (First option) V with ♯11/♭5 and ♭9: using ♭9 was already a popular option for increasing tension in dominant harmony in classical music of the early 19th century (eg, Beethoven and Schubert). Using the half-tone/whole-tone diminished scale over it adds ♯11/♭5 as well. (Once again, we'll see later that this is important because of tritone substitution.) Remember, diminished scales have another advantage, which is that the same scale can be used in four different keys (each a minor third apart). Hence any V chord harmonised using notes from this scale immediately becomes potentially ambiguous between four different keys and can be used as a basis for modulation between them.

d) (Second option) V with ♯11/♭5 and ♭9, as a diminished seventh chord on VII. Just as a diminished seventh chord on VII is treated in classical harmony as an incomplete $V^{7♭9}$ (with the root missing), we can think of a diminished seventh chord on VII containing notes from the whole-tone/half-tone diminished scale beginning on VII as producing an identical set of notes to the chord-scale combination in the preceding example. It thus has similar implications as a way of harmonising V that combines the tension of the highly dissonant ♭9 with the enharmonic ambiguity of ♯11/♭5 and the key-ambiguity of the diminished scale (in this case the whole-tone/half-tone diminished scale). As with classical harmony, the most common motivation for using this alternative to a harmonisation of V that keeps the root in the bass is the fact that a diminished seventh chord on VII allows stepwise chromatic bassline movement to (and from) chord I. As we'll see in due course, this is especially important in jazz, due to the role played by stepwise chromatic voice-leading of the sort called chromatic approach.

e) **V with ♯11/♭5, ♭9, and ♯5/♭13**. Alongside the Lydian dominant over V⁷♯¹¹ (see above), this is one of the most important alternatives for V in jazz: the scale used is known in jazz as the **altered scale**, and the corresponding chord structure is known as an **alt chord**. Note how it contains the dissonant ♭9, the enharmonically ambiguous ♯11/♭5, and the enharmonically ambiguous ♯5/♭13 that implies some sort of augmented triad. The resulting sonority is highly tense and unstable, but with a strong urge to resolve to I, making it especially popular with improvisers working in bebop and post-bebop styles. A special feature of this scale is the fact that it has identical notes to those of the Lydian dominant in the key a tritone away, making these two scales interchangeable. Once again, this is of immense value because of the role that it can play in facilitating tritone substitution (see below). Standard two-hand voicings for V afford very limited scope for including some or all of the alterations essential to defining altered-scale harmony in effective voicings; jazz pianists tend to opt for the more flexible voicings made possible thanks to 'alternative structures' of the sort discussed in the next section. Here, though, are some left-hand voicings adapted to give alt chords on V:

f) V with ♯11/♭5 and ♯5/♭13: this option, like the previous one, gives us both the enharmonically ambiguous ♯11/♭5 and the enharmonically ambiguous ♯5/♭13, but this time without the more dissonant ♭9. The corresponding scale is the whole-tone scale, which as we've seen is also ambiguous as to key. This option offers a less strident and more 'spaced out' alternative to altered-scale harmony for realising V chords with ♯5 such as those encountered earlier in the reharmonised version of the 'Rhythm Changes'.

g) I with ♭3: here the result of the chromatic alteration is simply the replacement of the major triad that forms the basis for a standard major seventh chord on I with a minor triad, producing a minor triad with a major seventh, sometimes known as a 'minor-major seventh chord'. This chord is typically used in jazz to suggest a resolution onto I in a minor key.

h) IV with ♯5: this corresponds to an augmented triad, featuring a raised fifth alongside the raised fourth of the Lydian mode. The resulting 'Lydian-augmented' scale offers an atmospheric alternative to the Lydian mode, not just over IV, but also (as in the example below) over I, where it also implies inclusion of the chromatically raised avoid note (the fourth) into the scale itself:

Exercise 8.27
Now practise introducing some of the alternative harmonisations just mentioned into the various sequences taking the II-V-I through all 12 keys shown earlier. When you feel the time's right, try embellishing and improvising over them, using the corresponding alternative scale-material. (Leave out those alternative harmonisations for which no examples have been given so far. We're going to explore how these work a little later on – once we're familiar with the 'alternative structures' jazz pianists use as a ready source of voicings for them.)

This way of using alternative scales to generate not just different harmonisations but also the scale-material needed to improvise over them, while still keeping the underlying functional feel of II, V, and I, is central to the modern-day jazz approach. However, it certainly doesn't account for everything jazz musicians do by way of reharmonisation. They also make use of chord substitution (ie, the substitution of functionally different chords for the original ones) and chord insertion. We'll look at these in a moment.

Exercise 8.28
We've already seen how the original 'Rhythm Changes' chords were reharmonised to produce an alternative version – one that itself then became a standard chord sequence for jazz improvisation. Now see if you can make use of some of the options just mentioned to develop alternative reharmonisations of either the original version or the 'standard reharmonisation'. Then try embellishing and improvising over these with the corresponding scale-material. First try switching from two-handed voicings to left-hand voicings as you move from the verse to the bridge, so the right hand opens up into freer melodic improvising in the latter. Then try left-hand voicings throughout, with your right-hand improvising more freely for the duration of the whole sequence.

2) Chord substitution and chord insertion

Chord substitution and chord insertion are distinct but interrelated techniques. More often than not, the same harmonic principles operate in both cases. The four most commonly used techniques are the following:

- Introduction of secondary dominants (V of V).
- Tritone substitution.
- Substitute major seventh chords.
- Chromatic approach.

You should remember secondary dominants from Unit Four, where we looked at the idea of a passing modulation involving the dominant (V) of a chord other than the tonic (I).

- In jazz, the general idea is that any minor chord or V chord sounds good when preceded by its V (ie, its secondary dominant). However, whether the secondary dominant is used as a substitute for the chord coming before that of which it is the dominant, or is just inserted in front it as an additional change, depends on the role played by the chord it would replace. If the latter is essential for the overall chord structure, then instead of substituting the secondary dominant we insert it (see below). A good rule of thumb for when to use secondary dominants as substitutions is the following: any minor chord followed by a chord on a root a perfect fifth lower can be replaced by V of the chord that follows it.

Typically, what this means in practice is that:

- II can be replaced by V of V when followed by V.
- VI can be replaced by V of II when followed by II.
- III can be replaced by V of VI when followed by VI.

Now go back and compare the two versions of the chords for 'Rhythm Changes' shown earlier in the unit: see if you can identify at least one instance of this technique being used there. Note that these chord substitutions reflect the privileged role that modulations descending through the Circle of Fifths play in jazz as a way of structuring key-relations.

> When substituting a secondary dominant for an existing chord, always keep in mind that it replaces (or is inserted after) the chord preceding the chord of which it's the dominant.

Next we'll look at **tritone substitution**, which plays a big role in bebop and post-bebop jazz. Remember how the distinctive feature of the II-V-I is the way the roots progress through descending perfect fifths (or ascending perfect fourths), so each chord is followed by a chord with a root a perfect fifth lower (or perfect fourth higher). This makes for an unusually strong harmonic progression, but jazz also regards progressions with roots descending in semitones (ie, stepwise chromatic movement) as especially strong. When we replace a chord that's followed by a chord with a root a perfect fifth lower with the chord whose root is a tritone (ie, augmented fourth or diminished fifth) away, the root progression changes from a descending perfect fifth to a descending semitone. This means that substituting a chord a tritone away allows us to move freely between root progressions based on descending fifths and root progressions based on chromatic stepwise descent. Since both kinds of progression are very strong, a powerful sense of harmonic continuity is maintained in spite of the resulting alterations to the existing chord structure.

The most common chord in the II-V-I to be subjected to tritone substitution is definitely V, but as the examples below show, we can also apply it to II and V, or just to II itself.

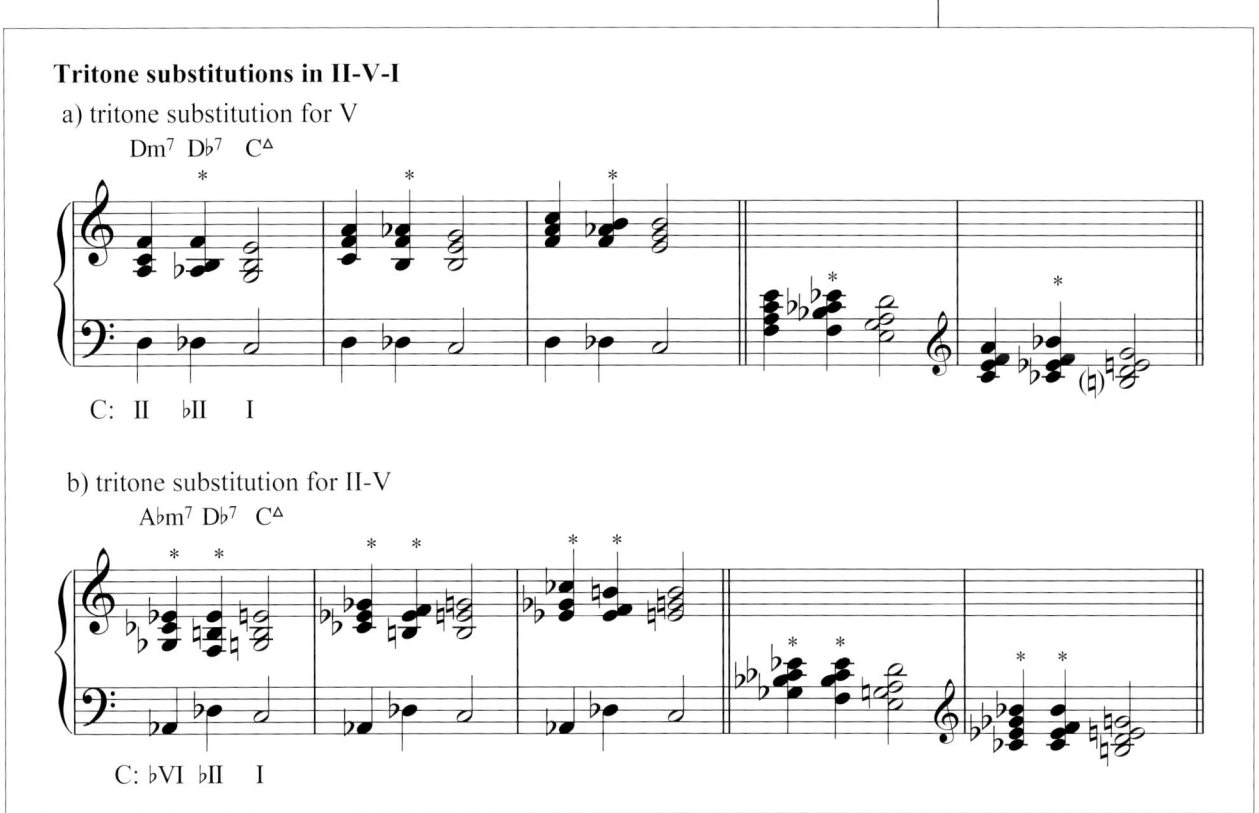

continued over page

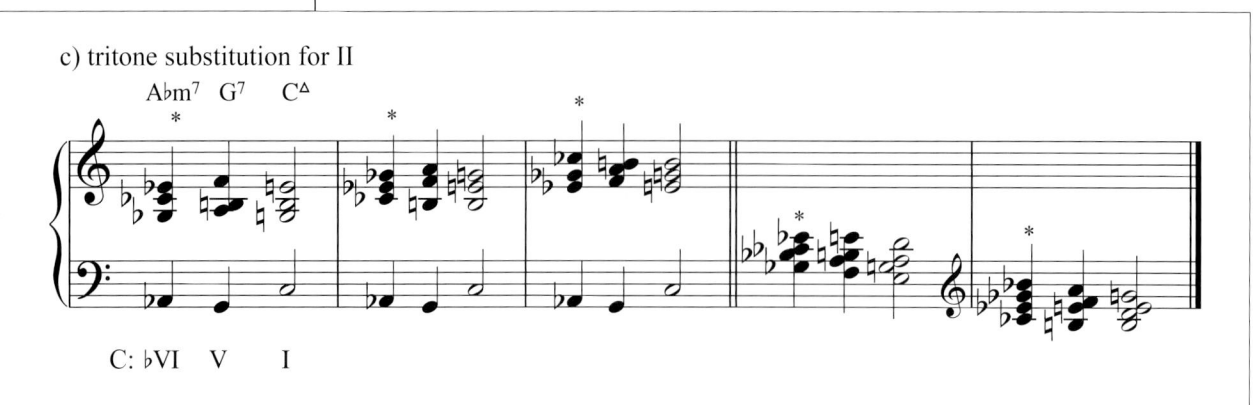

c) tritone substitution for II

C: ♭VI V I

Note how the two-handed voicings for ♭II (the tritone substitution for V) sound better in (b) than in (a): this is because they contain the ninth of the chord, just as chord V did in these voicings, so the substitute chord retains the relatively high level of harmonic tension displayed by V in the original progression. It's worth knowing that we can also voice ♭II this way when only V has been subjected to tritone substitution, as in (a) above, if we alter the voice-leading:

Revoiced tritone substitution for V

C: II ♭II I

The scales used over these tritone substitutions will be the same ones used over these chords in equivalent progressions in their own key:

- ♭II will still be treated as V in the key a tritone away – eg, using the Mixolydian mode or alternatives such as the Lydian dominant or altered scales, based on the root of the chord.
- ♭VI will still be treated as II in the key a tritone away – using the Dorian mode based on the root of the chord.

Now look again at (a) in the set of examples of tritone substitution shown above. Note how with the two-handed voicings the only change (outside of the bass) to the existing voicing of V is that A (the ninth of V) gets dropped by a half-step (semitone) to A-flat (the fifth of ♭II). Since V^7 often appears with a flattened ninth anyway, in many cases no change at all is required to the upper parts – the right hand – and merely changing the root is enough. This kind of interchangeability between some or all of the notes in dominant chords a tritone away is taken further in modern jazz harmony: it's known as **tritone interchangeability.**

The basis for tritone interchangeability is the fact that the key elements of a V chord apart from the root, ie, the third and seventh, lie a tritone apart, so transposing the chord by a tritone simply results in them exchanging roles (partly thanks to enharmonic equivalence):

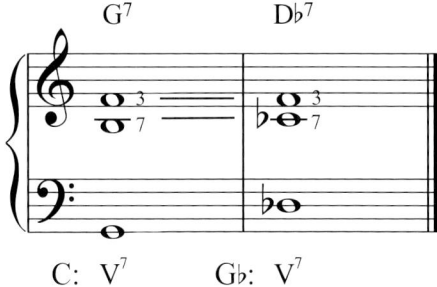

If we now go back and look at the left-hand voicings above, we can also notice some other useful features of how chord V functions. When substituting ♭II the best way to preserve the unresolved character of the dominant relative to the chords before and after is to make sure that ♭II is voiced to include similar chord-extensions to those in the left-hand voicing for V: ie, the ninth and 13th. The ninth of ♭II corresponds to the flattened 13th of V, while conversely the 13th of ♭II corresponds to the raised ninth of V. This means an alternative harmonisation of V that already contains these alterations will automatically work as chord V in the key a tritone away:

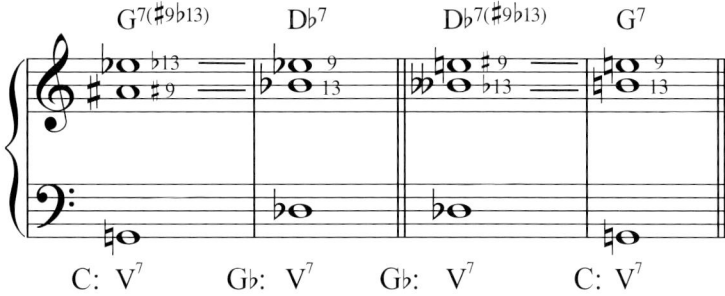

We've already seen how the altered scale contains both a sharpened ninth and a flattened 13th – as well as the sharpened 11th, which allows the tonic of the key a tritone away to also be present in the scale. This is the basis for the special role played by both alt chords and the altered scale in relation to tritone interchangeability of V chords: alt chords over V can work as $V^{7(\sharp 11)}$ chords over ♭II, and conversely alt chords over ♭II will work as $V^{7(\sharp 11)}$ chords over V. Similarly, the notes of the altered scale over V are identical to those of the Lydian dominant over V a tritone away (= ♭II in the key), and vice versa:

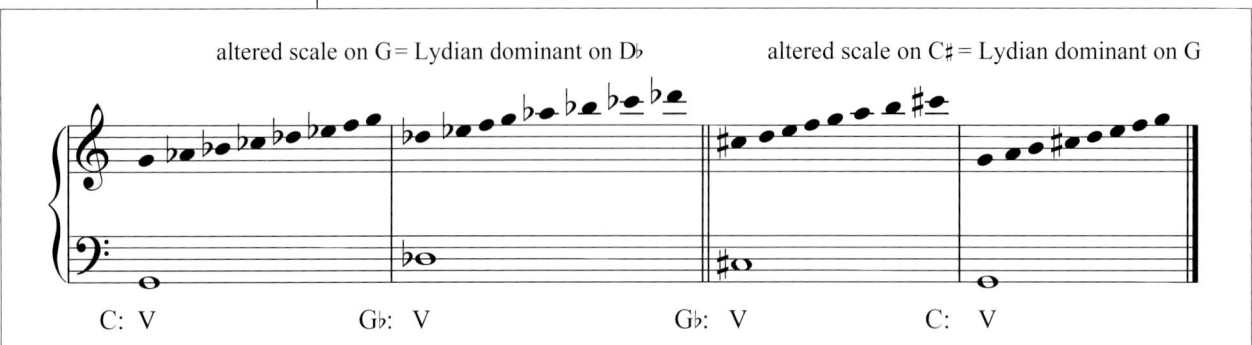

We'll look at the two-handed voicings for these tritone substitutions involving alt chords later, as they involve the alternative structures discussed in the next section. However, you can see how neatly it works by looking at how the following left-hand voicings correspond across keys a tritone apart. (Try playing the scales from the previous example over these chords).

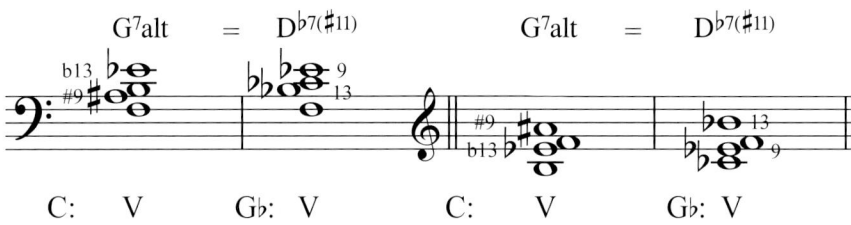

The third kind of substitution is **major seventh chord substitution**, which involves substituting a major seventh chord for an existing minor triad (below). The idea here is that the top note in the chord – which may also be a melody note – can be recoloured to make it more expressive by changing the chord beneath it. In jazz there's a general understanding that the seventh and third of a chord are more harmonically colourful and expressive than the fifth or the root. Replacing a triad with a major seventh chord based on the root two diatonic scale steps lower means that if the top note was the fifth of the

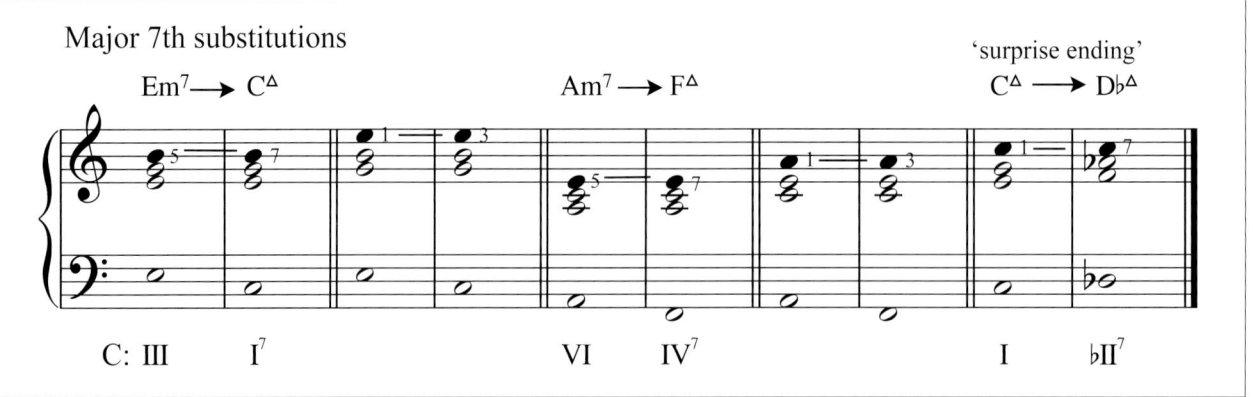

chord it will now be the seventh, and if it was the root it'll now be the third. If the root is in the top part, a more striking substitution can also be used to achieve a recolouring effect: we substitute the major seventh chord on bII for chord I. This substitution is usually reserved for the final chord I of a jazz improvisation, where it gives rise to a 'surprise ending' effect. However, it's easily overused – then it sounds more clichéd than surprising.

Finally let's consider the technique known as **chromatic approach**. This involves replacing the chord before a given major or minor (or sometimes dominant) chord with a diminished seventh chord – one whose root is a semitone (half-step) below that of the next chord. The result is stepwise ascending bassline movement between the two chords, which corresponds to a leading tone moving to a tonic in the key of which the second chord would be chord I. Hence it is also a form of secondary harmony (ie, chord VII of whatever the second chord is). If we recall that a diminished seventh chord on VII also counts as an incomplete dominant (with flattened ninth), then we can also think of these chords as another way to introduce secondary dominants as chord substitutions. (Have a look once again at the two versions of 'Rhythm Changes' shown earlier as slash charts. Compare them and see if you can identify the places where this technique has been used to generate some of the alterations to the original changes.)

Both chromatic approach and the use of secondary dominants can be used much more freely once we think of them as techniques for inserting additional chords rather than just principles for replacing existing ones. There's an amazingly simple rule here. Before any major, minor or dominant chord, feel free to insert either the dominant of that chord (ie, its V) or a diminished seventh chord whose root is a semitone (half-step) lower than the given chord (ie, its VII).

It's worth mentioning three additional techniques used in jazz reharmonisation. The first of these amounts to something between substitution and insertion: whenever we have a V chord not already preceded by a II chord, we can replace it with II-V. In terms of the pure sequence of chords, II is here being inserted between V and the chord that would otherwise have preceded it, but in terms of harmonic rhythm V is here being replaced by II (as the chord occurring on the principal point in the metrical structure – even though it still occurs afterwards).

The second of these techniques looks a bit like a reversal of this. Jazz often uses a kind of fusion of II and V into a single chord, known as a **sus chord**. Technically, this is a V chord with an added fourth, but this needs some explanation. You should remember that over dominant harmony one of the chord extensions that can occur is the 11th (which is the alternative way of referring to the fourth). However, as we've seen, this is an avoid note, so in order for it to count as part of the V chord it must be raised chromatically. If we place the unraised fourth or 11th over the chord it must therefore be understood in some other way: instead of thinking of it as a chord extension, we treat it as an unprepared and unresolved suspension. The idea is that if the V chord with an added fourth were in fact preceded by II we would be able to hear the fourth as the seventh of II, held over onto V as a suspended dissonance. At the same time, jazz voicings for V typically contain the seventh and ninth as well, and these notes correspond to the third and fifth of II. (This gives us three notes belonging to II sounding over the root of V.) The result is an arrangement of notes on the keyboard with a striking and easy-to-remember shape: a major triad in the right hand that corresponds to IV, over a dominant bass, so the root of the right hand triad is a whole tone lower than the actual root of the V chord:

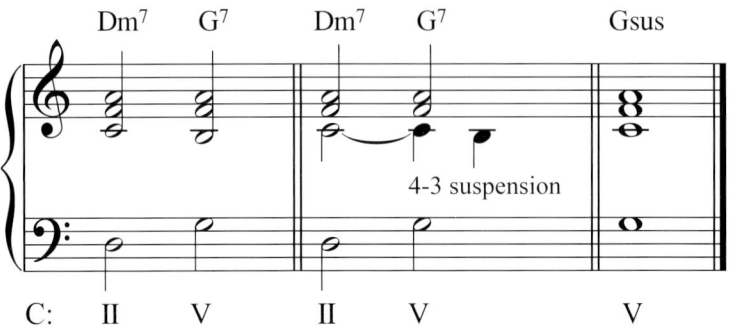

Jazz improvisers love chord structures that are easy to recall because of how they look on the keyboard and how they feel under the fingers. That's why, as we'll see in the next section, this method of breaking down a more complex harmonic structure into a bass note with a functionally unrelated triad over it plays a big role in more advanced jazz approaches to pianistic harmony.

Exercise 8.29
Here you've got a sus chord in place of II and V, resolving to I. Practise taking each version of the progression through all the different keys, just like with II-V-I. (Follow the same key sequences explored earlier, modulating/transposing a fifth down each time, then a semitone down, then a major second, etc.) Note how the third variant of the voice-leading sounds less effective, at least as a resolution: the placing of the fourth (the avoid note) over V in the top part makes this chord even more unstable, while the presence of the seventh at the top of chord I means that in terms of the scale of the key the top part ends on its least resolved note, the leading note.

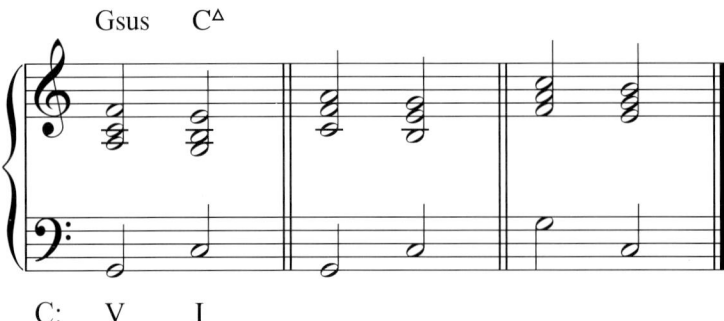

The third additional reharmonisation technique is one introduced fairly late on in the development of jazz by that great jazzman, John Coltrane. In his tune 'Giant Steps', Coltrane made use of direct modulation between keys a major third apart. This was an exciting new development for jazz improvisers, though already familiar in classical music from the 19th century onwards. It became known as **Coltrane changes**. Other jazz musicians subsequently experimented with direct modulations between keys a minor third apart as well. The following example shows how II-V-I or V-I progressions can be juxtaposed in keys a major third apart in this way. Try realising the progressions yourself using the voicings covered earlier in the unit:

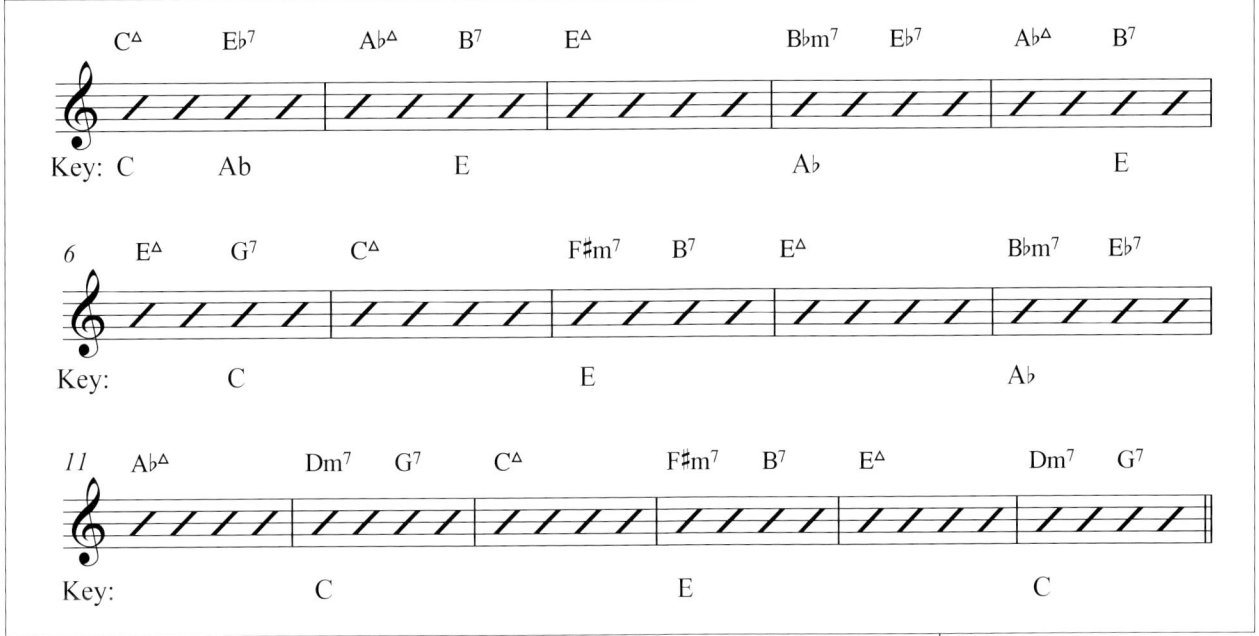

Coltrane then interpolated some of these changes into the middle of II-V-I progressions to reharmonise them, as in the following example:

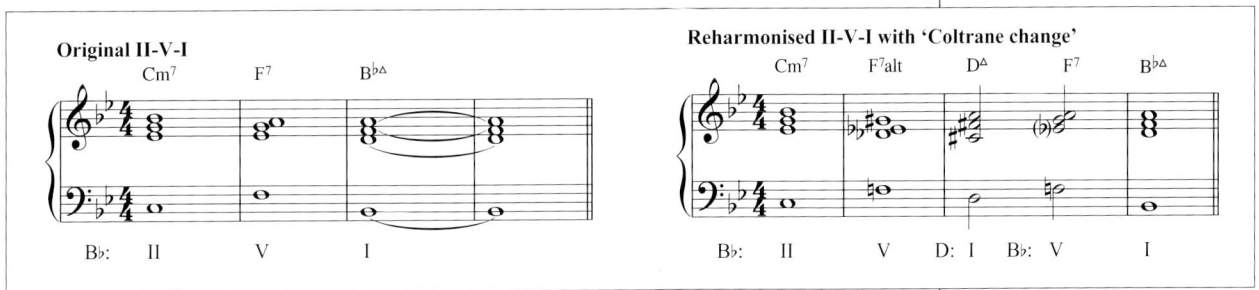

Exercise 8.30
Now take the original version of the 'Rhythm Changes' chord sequence and try applying for yourself the chord substitution and insertion techniques discussed in the preceding section.

Alternative structures

These are chord-like structures chosen for their intrinsic harmonic character and practical ease of execution, which in jazz is treated as being at least partly independent of how they function as chords in a particular key. The basic idea is that the same configuration of notes may correspond to several different chords at the same time, depending on the root. Because the latter need not be present and can be taken as just implied, the resulting chords tend to be ambiguous in themselves as regards their functional significance.

> It's tempting to think of these 'alternative structures' as more like voicings than chords: ie, as particular kinds of harmonic effect that are more specific than the differences produced by the functional system of chords themselves. Yet as we'll see later, they're also more than just alternative voicings, since they themselves can be voiced in various ways. Hence they really inhabit a sort of grey zone between chords and voicings, without really corresponding to either.

To really grasp how this works you need to remember that in jazz any one chord-function (eg, I, II, III, etc.) can be thought of as having chord notes and extensions corresponding to any or all of the seven notes of the scale from which it's built. That means any selection from the notes of that scale, played together as a voicing, could, in theory, form part of a chord built on any step of the scale. Normally we identify voicings by thinking of them as specific realisations of particular chord-functions (eg, I, II, III, etc.). However, if the same set of notes played together can correspond to several different chord functions, depending on which note counts as the root, then these harmonic structures really are ambiguous in themselves. This has some important practical consequences for more advanced approaches to jazz improvisation:

1. Because chords in jazz are mostly assumed to be in root position, what then defines the actual functional identity of the chord is just the presence of a particular note at the bottom of the texture, in the bass, which is assumed to be the root.
2. Chords and bass often stand in a rather loose relationship to one another in jazz anyway, as a result of the bass lines either being played by a separate player or being left unstated and only implied in solo piano playing.
3. So where a voicing has a definite sounding character, and can be easily recalled and realised, independently of which bass note it sounds over (and thus which

note is heard as its root, and which chord function it is heard as realising), it makes practical sense to first learn the voicing without reference to its harmonic function in any specific key, treating it as a fixed set of notes that are harmonically ambiguous.

That's how we arrive at the 'alternative structures' discussed in this section.

a) 'So What' chords

The first of these structures is known as a **'So What' chord**, named after the Miles Davis tune in which they were used by Bill Evans. It refers to an arrangement of five notes, normally played with three in the right and two in the left, characterised by a specific spacing of intervals. We can think of it as three intervals of a fourth with one interval of a third placed on top, but we can also think of it as a major triad in second inversion played over an interval of a fourth. In its most common form it functions as a II chord, but its harmonically ambiguous character, combined with the jazz idea that the root of a chord can be taken as implied even when not actually present, allows it to function as several different chords at the same time.

(Notice also that each of these root-specific chords can function in several keys. For example, the Dm7 chord could be II in C, VI in F, III in B-flat, or even I in a version of D minor using either the Dorian mode or the natural ('rock') minor scale. Likewise, the same arrangement of notes thought of as a B♭△ chord (minus the root) can be I in B-flat or IV in F, and as E♭△♯4 can be I in E-flat or IV in B-flat.)

We can also move the whole 'So What' chord structure up and down within a given scale, so that the underlying shape is reproduced on different degrees of the scale. This produces other arrangements of notes, some of which are also ambiguous, while others have clearly defined functions (p358).

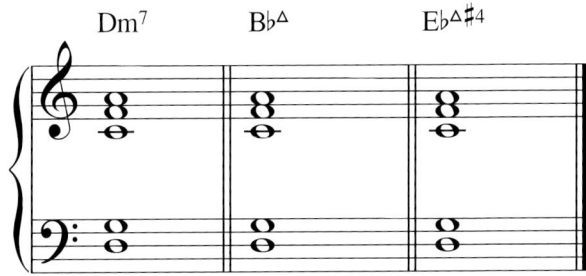

One of the effects of this is that some chords contain different kinds of fourth or third, which means intervals like the tritone and minor ninth can then show up as present in the resulting chord. This produces more dissonant versions of the structure, such as those on F and B in the example (shown with asterisks). These must be handled with care, and are unlikely to be used outside of the specific kinds of modal improvising that occur in some more modern jazz styles.

UNIT 8 | SECTION 3

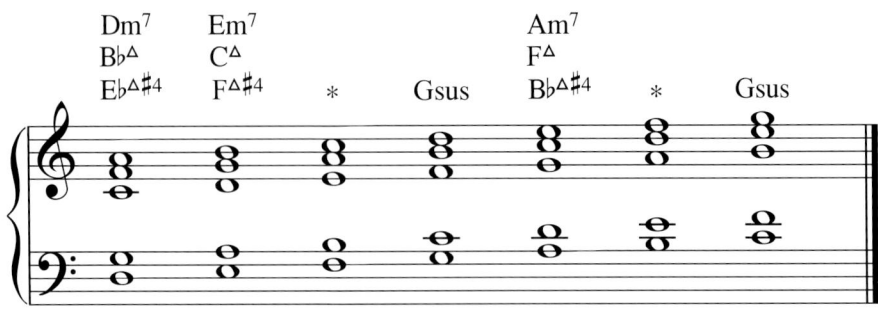

The most common use of the 'So What' chord structure is as a stand-in for a II chord with the fifth of the chord in the top voice as a melody note. However, the fact that a version of this structure can be used with each note of the scale on top means we can use it to harmonise a series of melody notes by simply shifting the chord shape up and down so it moves in parallel with the melody itself. When whole chords move in parallel with the melody in this way, we get what's known as **parallelism**.

The above example shows two ways in which this can occur. The first keeps to the notes of the diatonic scale, resulting in changes to the intervals in some of the chords. The second shows a more radical form of parallelism, in which each of the chords retains the exact set of intervals present when the structure appears as a minor seventh chord on II, even when this requires it to contain notes outside the diatonic scale. Both forms of parallelism are widely used in jazz, not just with 'So What' chords but also with the other kinds of alternative structure discussed here. Play them through and hear how different they sound.

b) Fourth chords

The second kind of alternative structure that plays an important role in jazz is **fourth chords**. Classical triads consist of intervals of a third, so the only time we get an interval of a fourth in a chord is between the fifth and the root. The standard chord extensions used in jazz tend to maintain this feature, since they are typically stacked on top of one another in thirds, as the seventh, ninth, 11th, and 13th of the chord. But notice how the jazz sus chord voicing shown earlier included two intervals of a fourth below a third, while the 'So What' chord structures just discussed involve three fourths below a third. We can take this a step further by simply building chords entirely out of fourths, and then seeing what possible harmonic implications they can have. (In classical theory the same technique is referred to as **quartal harmony**.) The next example shows fourth chords built on each step of the major scale, together with their typical functional implications. Notice how we tend to treat the bottom note of the structure as being either the third of a major or minor chord (with an added sixth or ninth), or as the seventh of a V^7 chord, or as the root or ninth of a sus chord on V, all in the key of the scale used. (The topmost notes in the chords are placed in brackets: omitting them gives extra options for using these chords when harmonising a melody, as different notes then appear in the top part. Note also the different sonorities we get, depending on whether we use four-note, five-note or six-note versions of the chords.)

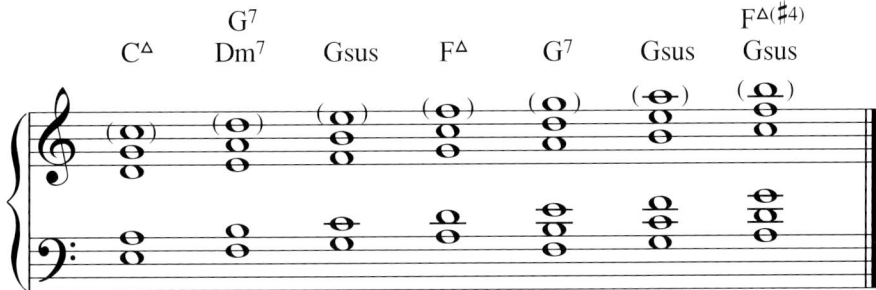

As the following example shows, fourth chords also lend themselves to parallelism.

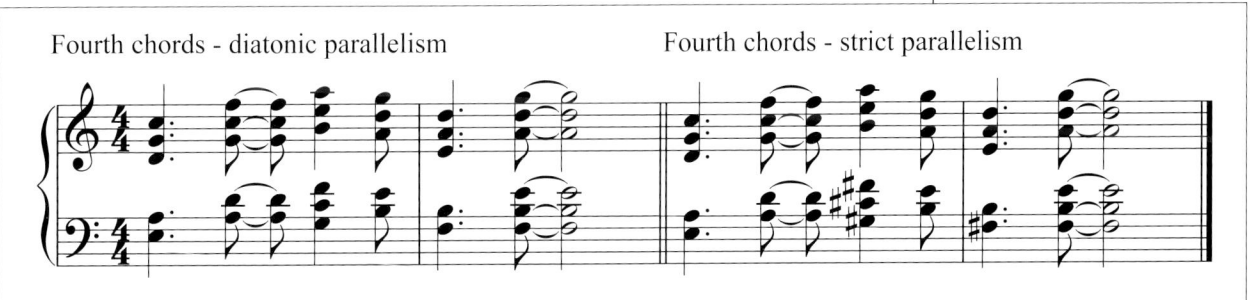

c) Upper structures

We've seen that in jazz dominant harmony often gets reharmonised with multiple chromatic alterations designed to increase the level of unresolved tension in the chord. Left-hand voicings, as we found when looking at alt chords, contain insufficient notes to allow us to realise the full complexity of these alternative harmonisations, so we tend to prefer two-handed voicings for these. Using two handed-voicings – as we've already seen with 'So What' chords – also allows us to break down a complex chord into an easily remembered (and more easily transposable) combination of a two-note structure in the left hand and an unrelated triad in the right.

It makes even more sense to use this same approach when realising alt chords and other alternative V-chord harmonisations. The resulting harmonies are known in jazz theory as **upper structures**. Each one consists of a tritone in the left hand – the third and seventh of chord V – with a major or minor triad played over it in the right hand.

The interval that we get by counting upwards from the root of the V chord to the implied root of the right-hand triad is used to define each particular upper structure. Along with the major or minor character of the right-hand triad, it also gives its name to the structure. (As far as the latter is concerned, we assume that if this is not stated, then the chord is major). Hence, for example, a harmony consisting of a major triad whose root is a major second above the root of the V chord is known as 'upper structure II', while a harmony consisting of a minor triad whose root is an augmented fourth above the root of the V chord is known as as 'upper structure ♯IV minor'.

If, as is sometimes the case, the resulting structure turns out to be interchangeable with a less interesting version of V in the key a tritone away, then it becomes obligatory to include the root of the actual V chord in the structure to ensure that we do not just hear it as the simpler V chord in the other key.

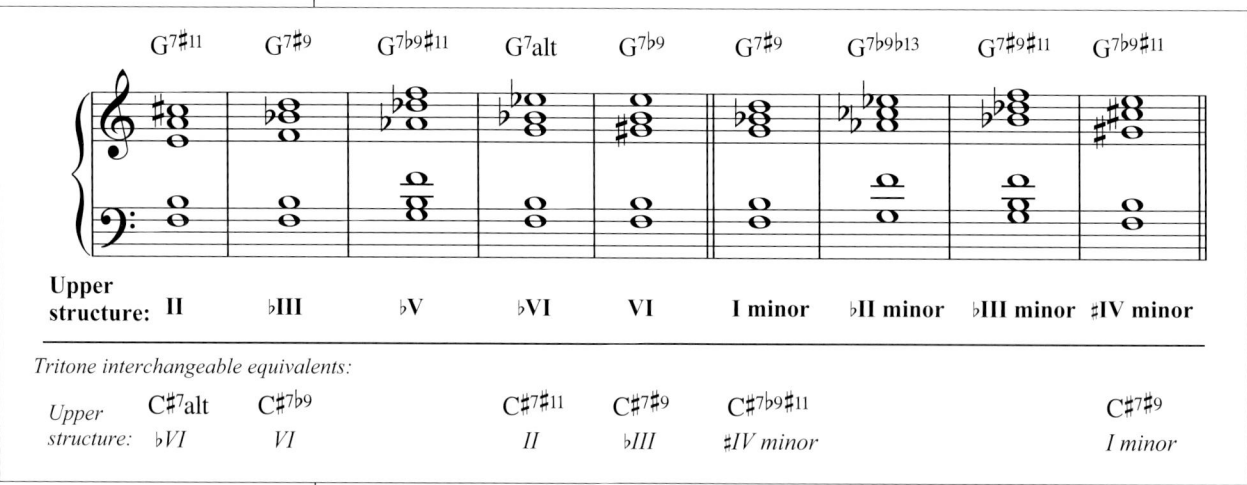

The table opposite shows which upper structures work for the various possible harmonisations of V resulting from the most common chromatic alterations used, together with the corresponding scales for improvising. (The most important options are highlighted in bold.)

Note that where an upper structure doesn't include the avoid note on V (ie, the fourth above the root) we're free to assume that this note will be raised chromatically in order for the harmonic implications of the chord to be consistent with the scale.

Remember also that some V chord alterations are more likely to turn up in jazz chord structures as diminished seventh chords on VII than as V chords themselves – especially when chord substitution using the principle of chromatic approach is already in use. Where an upper structure corresponds to one of these diminished seventh chords, this is shown in the last column of the table.

Chord V alterations	Upper structures	Scales for improvising	Dim 7th equivalent
♭9 (+ ♯4 as raised avoid note)	'VI'	diminished scale on V (half-tone/whole-tone) = diminished scale on VII (whole-tone/half-tone)	= VII°
♯9 (+ ♯4 as raised avoid note)	'♭III' 'I minor'		
♯11	II	Lydian dominant	
♭9 ♯11	'♭V' '♯IV minor'	diminished scale on V (half-tone/whole-tone) = diminished scale on VII (whole-tone/half-tone)	= VII°
♭9 ♭13 (+ ♯4 as raised avoid note)	'♭II minor'	Altered scale	
♭9 ♯9 ♯11 ♭13	'♭VI'	Altered scale	
♭9 ♯11	'♭V' '♯IV minor'	diminished scale on V (half-tone/whole-tone) = diminished scale on VII (whole-tone/half-tone)	= VII°
♯9 ♯11	'♭III minor'		

Upper structures are not the same as voicings, since we can change the layout of the chord without changing which upper structure it corresponds to. We'll explore voicings more in the next section.

Exercise 8.31
Try playing each of the structures shown in the previous example, preceded by a II-chord voicing and followed by a I-chord voicing. Have a go at improvising over the resulting V chords using the scales shown in the table. Then transpose the resulting progressions and scales into other keys and do the same there.

Alternative voicings
Reharmonisation involves changing/adapting the structure of individual chords, but this is not the only way in which we can create new possibilities for colour, texture, and mood in jazz. The way a chord is voiced (ie, the choice of chord layout) also plays a very important role. There are two key points to remember about chord voicings:

- The character of a chord voicing will be different in different keys, since its positioning relative to different registers of the piano will vary depending on which key it's in.
- The voicing you choose will have implications for both the range and audibility of any melody line you want to play over it.

As far as the first of these is concerned, only experience and experimentation will teach you which voicings sound good in particular keys. As far as the second is concerned, you should be aware of the following issues:

UNIT 8 SECTION 3

- Avoid voicings that extend too high – ie, too far into 'right-hand territory'. These will sound thin and colourless, won't produce a texture sonorous enough to support a properly projected melody line, and may limit the audibility of the melody line, which is forced up into the higher, less penetrating register of the instrument, just to stay clear of the chord-notes.
- Avoid voicings that group two or more notes close together low down in the register where the left-hand normally plays chord-notes: these will sound muddy and colourless or can drown out the melody line above them by being over-sonorous.

> Don't worry, as you develop your skills as a jazz improviser, you'll quickly discover which voicings you want to use in each key. The choice of voicings relative to keys is often one of the features that distinguishes a jazz pianist's personal style from that of other players. This often translates into an overall sense of lightness, heaviness, smoothness, or scrunchiness of texture that can be a hallmark of a particular player's style. The most important thing is to let your ear be your guide.

Apart from the issue of register, when deciding how to voice an individual chord it is also worth paying attention to the following points: which chord-notes are included, omitted, or doubled (just as in the classical approach to chord-layout discussed in Unit Four); which notes lie at the bottom or top of the chord. Notes lower down have a more prominent role in determining the overall harmonic character of the chord sonority. Notes higher up are more prominent as individual notes.

Notice that what gives a chord its expressive character or colour isn't just the pitches (notes in a scale) it contains. Above all it's the intervals between those pitches: the most prominent interval in a chord is usually the one formed by the lowest and highest notes, or between the implied root and the top note. (Hence, the more expressive or colourful this interval is, the more interesting the chord will be.)

Jazz musicians like to focus on the voicing of chords as if they were isolated units of sound whose characteristics are independent of what comes before or after them. That partly makes sense, given the emphasis in jazz on treating each harmony as a kind of source material for melodic improvisation, where its internal harmonic qualities are more important than its role as part of a longer term harmonic progression. However, this is also potentially misleading. The fact is, what works harmonically depends on what comes before and after, not just at the level of chord functions but also at that of chord voicings. Much as some jazz theorists would like to, we can't (and shouldn't) separate voicings from voice-leading. So in practice another important consideration when choosing a voicing is how well it links to the voicings of the chords that immediately precede and succeed it.

Just as in classical chord layout, we can distinguish between **close-position voicing** and **open-position voicing**. The former tends to stack chord notes (apart from the bass note) together as closely as possible, typically at intervals of a third but sometimes using intervals of a second or a fourth. The latter has the chord notes more widely spaced, often including larger intervals between adjacent notes in the chord.

> **The minor ninth rule**: if a jazz voicing contains an interval of a minor ninth, you should generally avoid it, unless it's between the root and ♭9 of a V chord.

Look back at the examples used throughout this unit so far to illustrate jazz harmony and you'll see that they're nearly all in close-position voicing, no matter whether they're split between the two hands or just intended for the left hand alone. With left-hand voicings, as we've already seen, the only option for thinning out the texture is to adopt the Bud Powell approach – leaving out everything but the third or seventh over the root. With two-handed voicings, there are more possibilities, but only if we break away from the three-plus-one format and vary the distribution of notes between the hands in a more fluid and flexible way – one that may be specific to each chord. The downside of this is that it's harder to sustain satisfactory voice-leading, as the voice-leading formulas jazz musicians rely on no longer translate into the same fingering patterns every time. You'll need to be more aware of the actual harmonic significance of what is happening in individual parts of the texture – in the way classical improvisers tend to be.

When voicing chords, keep in mind the following general principles:

- The most effective note to have at the top will usually be either the third or seventh, or any higher extension present (ie, the ninth, 11th or 13th) if not too dissonant.
- Higher notes can be grouped closer together or farther apart, but keep lower notes spaced well apart.
- Dissonant intervals within a chord will sound more dissonant the closer together their constituent notes are, less dissonant the farther apart they are.

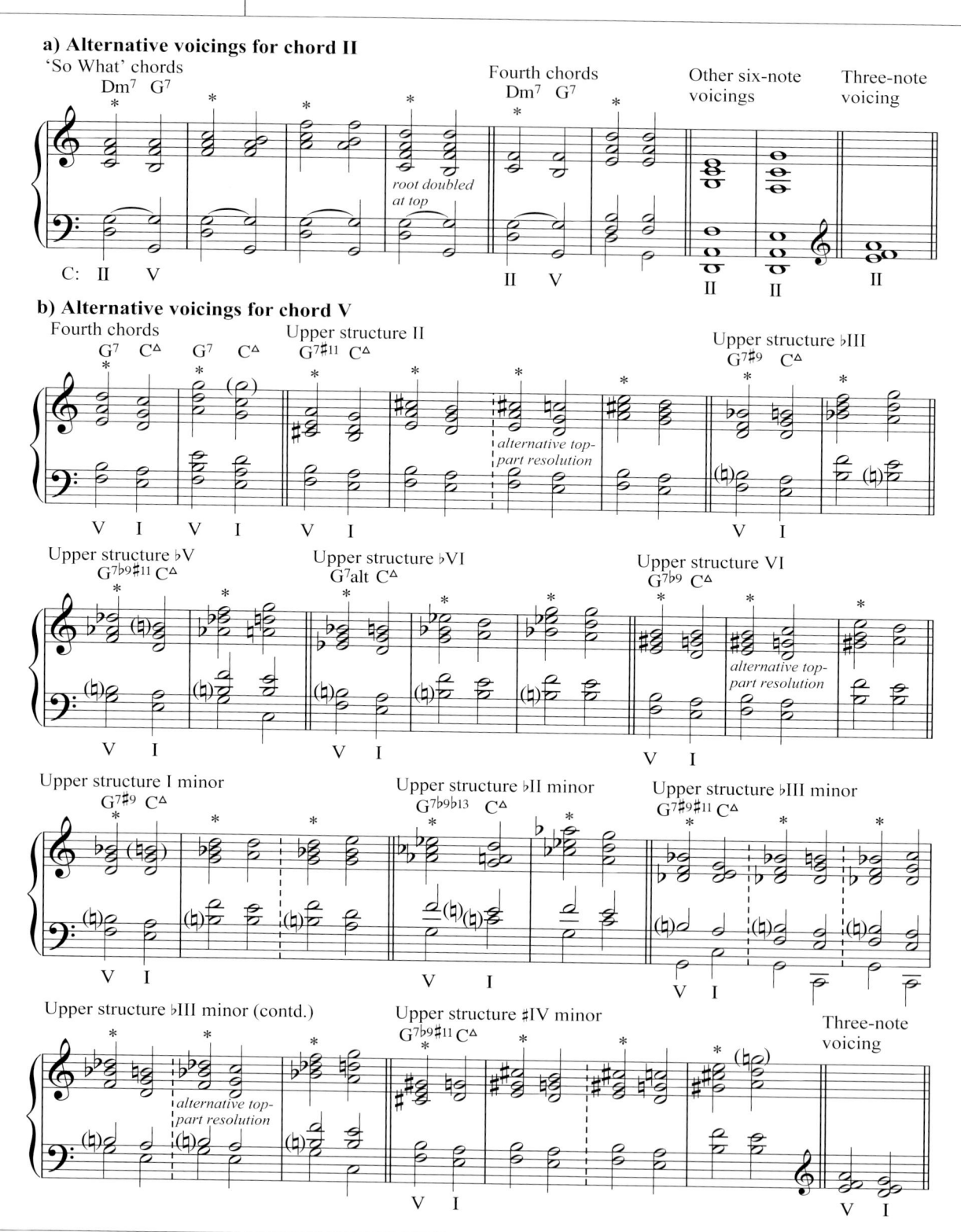

Exercise 8.32

The material on these two pages provides a range of typical alternative voicings to those we've already come across in the context of the standard voice-leading formulas shown earlier. Most voicing options here (marked with asterisks) are linked to the alternative structures explored in the previous section – as are the suggested follow-on voicings. Play them through carefully and consider how they sound. Then try introducing them into short II-V-I progressions – in a range of keys. Make a mental note of how they strike you in terms of voice-leading and register, as well as which keys you think they sound best in. Then try using them to develop your own realisations of the 'Rhythm Changes' sequence – first using just the original version of the chords, then using the reharmonised version given earlier. Finally, try combining the reharmonisation techniques mentioned earlier with the alternative voicings mentioned in this section. At each stage focus initially on just realising the chords – only afterwards see if you can improvise over them.

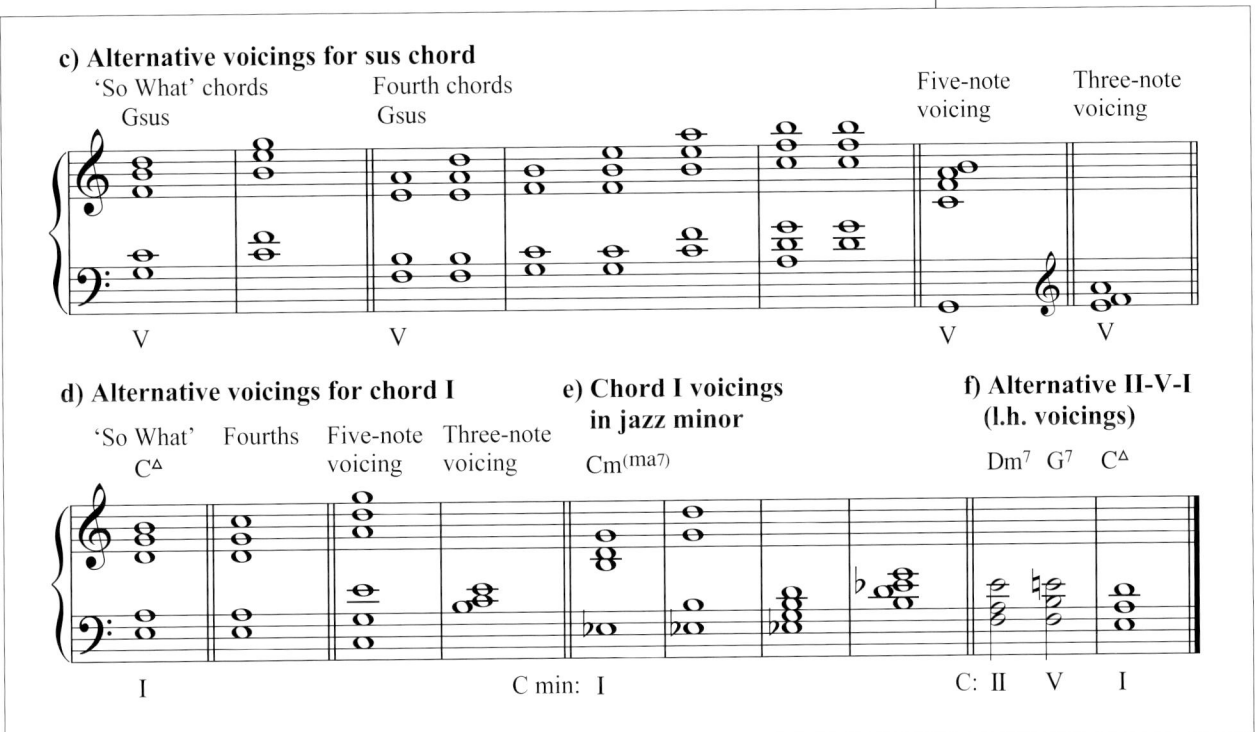

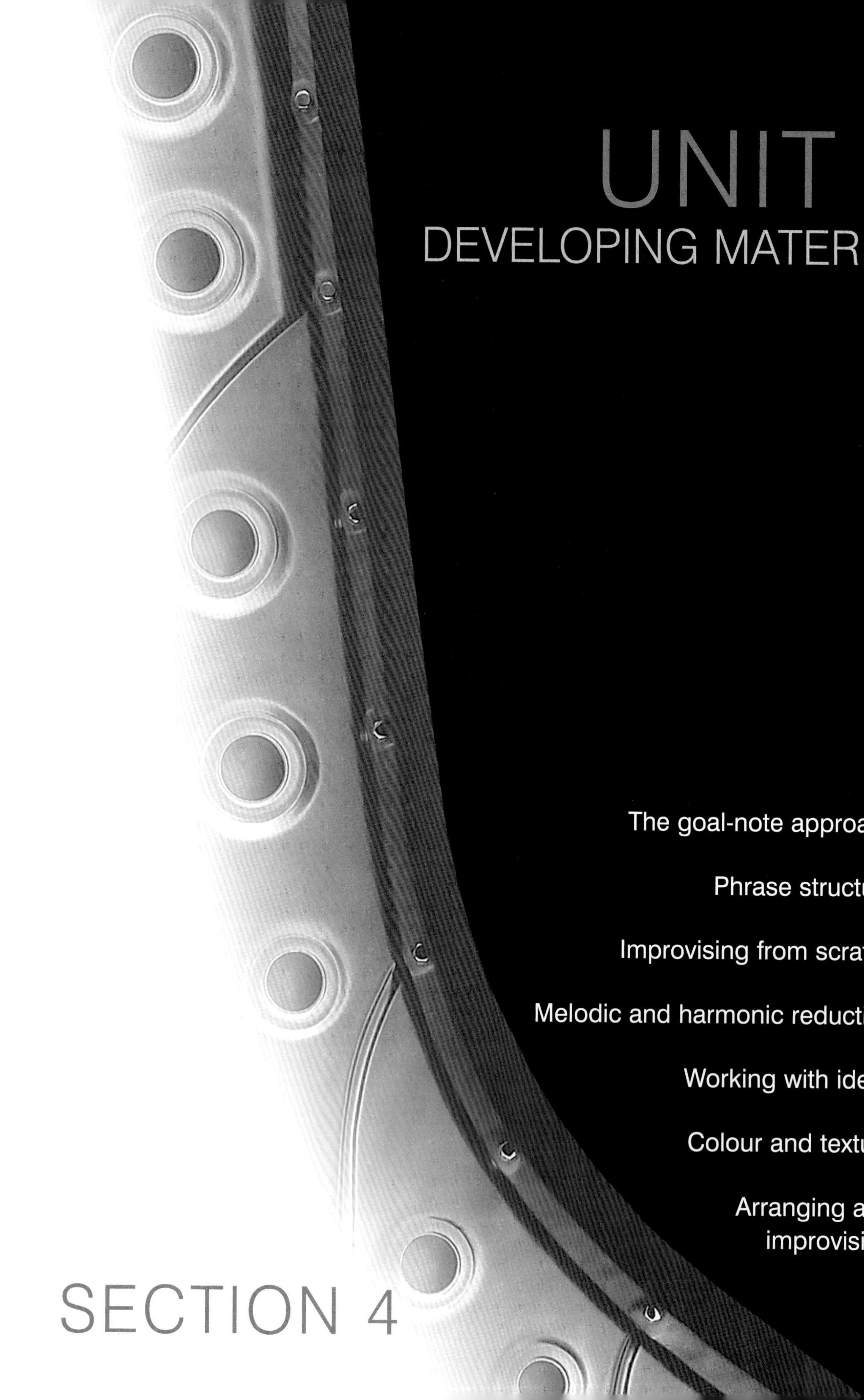

UNIT 9
DEVELOPING MATERIAL

The goal-note approach

Phrase structure

Improvising from scratch

Melodic and harmonic reduction

Working with ideas

Colour and texture

Arranging and improvising

SECTION 4

SECTION 4 UNIT 9

The goal-note approach

> The last two units of this book deal with a range of issues connected to improvising, many of which cut across the boundaries separating classical, jazz, and other musical styles. However, they do assume that by now you're familiar with the basic principles of both the classical and jazz approaches to harmony, melody, and counterpoint, as covered in the previous two units.

In Unit Seven we looked at the distinctive way in which classical improvisation approaches the relationship of melody to harmony, focusing on the important role played by the contrapuntal treatment of dissonance. In Unit Eight we then explored the contrasting approach to melody and harmony typical of jazz. We saw there how extended and altered chords can be used to create a context in which dissonance can be handled more freely. In this unit the focus will be on building your overall confidence and flexibility as an improviser, by helping you to acquire a range of skills connected with developing and maintaining a flow of ideas while improvising. First we need to look at how the classical and jazz approaches to improvising compare.

Classical music's stricter approach to dissonance allows us to experience the expressive effects of contrapuntal dissonance and resolution a lot more vividly and precisely than in jazz. However, from an improviser's point of view this comes at a price: melodic improvisation has to stick closely to the harmonic implications of the underlying chords, and when it departs from these it is constrained by some fairly exacting rules about how a melody can be embellished, especially in terms of its contrapuntal implications.

At the same time, though, by ensuring that an improvised melody line remains closely tied to the underlying structure of the harmony, these constraints do serve to strengthen the overall sense of direction the melody has. As we saw in Unit Seven, the way this works is that we feel the melody heading towards particular harmony notes, and at the same time these notes function as landmarks in the unfolding of a larger structure. The result is that we feel the melody is really going somewhere.

Jazz contrasts with this. On the one hand, it confines itself to a much simpler set of underlying chord functions – chiefly II, V, and I, understood to be in root position regardless of the actual bass – that mostly follow a standard set of formulaic progressions (like II-V-I). Often the structure of longer chord sequences is also familiar, especially if they've been taken from popular songs, and/or have been regularly recycled as source material by other jazz players. On the other hand, jazz treats each of these chord-functions as generating its own distinctive scale (or mode) for improvising, and it allows for quite a few variations in the way each chord function is realised. Each of these in turn also gives rise to differences in the scale used for improvising, which is nevertheless still heard with reference to the underlying chord function, as part of a harmonically directed progression.

The obvious advantage of the jazz approach is that it opens up a great deal more scope, not only for using the resulting scales to improvise, but also for varying how familiar chord structures are realised, using reharmonisation.

Yet, as with the classical approach, there's a significant downside: because each scale corresponds to its own chord, we mainly hear what goes on when we improvise melodically over that chord as harmonically significant relative to that chord, rather than hearing it as playing a role in the unfolding of a larger harmonic and melodic structure. The result is that our sense of a musical structure unfolding and being shaped by the choices we make while improvising gets split in two: we identify the overall, longer-term structure of the music with what the harmony (including the key structure) implies, while only identifying melodic shapes and movements with the more local and immediate sense of direction these have relative to the harmony sounding beneath them (and the scale generated by this).

From the point of view of melodic improvisation, then, jazz gives greater flexibility to develop and explore melody as it works over individual chords, but affords less scope for exploring how melody can itself contribute to the unfolding of a larger structure. Melodically, we can feel 'trapped in the chord'. Given how insulated the larger unfolding of the music is from what we happen to do when improvising melodically over individual chords, this extra freedom can start to seem rather superficial.

In spite of these important differences between jazz and classical music, there's also a significant point of contact between them, which may help us to move in the direction of getting the best of both worlds, whichever tradition or style we, personally, most like to work in. It corresponds to a method known in jazz as the **goal-note approach**. So maybe we can, after all, combine something of the more structurally integrated character of classical improvisation with something of the freedom and flexibility of jazz.

We've already seen something of how this works in Unit Seven, where we looked at how extracting a melodic skeleton from an existing melody or harmonic texture can furnish a framework that enables us to improvise variations on the original music from which these were taken. (This technique of stripping down a melody to its basic skeleton, or stripping down a harmonic texture to its simplest underlying chord structures, is known as **reduction**. We'll explore a wider range of things we can do with it in the next section.)

As we've already seen, having a melodic and/or harmonic skeleton of this kind in place makes it much easier to give a sense of direction to our melodic improvising: wherever we are in the structure in terms of our melodic improvising, there's always some definite place we have to aim to get to, at or around a point in time in the approaching future, whose distance from the present can be felt by us in metrical terms.

In the earlier stages of learning jazz improvisation, teachers often make use of a related idea: they suggest that wherever you are in the unfolding structure, you should try to think forward to the next chord and choose a note from that to aim for. In other words, you should **project** (in your mind) a note that belongs to the chord after the one you're actually improvising over, and use this note as a goal to head towards as you play over the current chord.

This is what jazz musicians and teachers have in mind when they talk about the goal-note approach and, whether they are aware of it or not, it plays a large role in the way jazz players go about improvising. To really understand the implications of this, it's worth comparing how it works in practice with the equivalent in classical playing. You should get a sense of this from working through this and the following two sections of this unit.

Here's the A section (or verse) of 'Rhythm Changes', in the standard reharmonised version once again. This time the chord-notes are shown, so we can see how they might be used to help a jazz player project goal notes as he or she improvises over the unfolding harmony.

The basic principle in jazz is that because the third and seventh are the notes that define the functional character of each chord type (since they indicate which kind of seventh chord it is), we should always make it our aim to arrive at one of these notes on or around the beat where the change to the new chord occurs. (Exceptions are when either of these notes is specifically present in the bass – indicated by a slash chord – or when another note becomes more expressively significant through chromatic alteration.) Hence these notes are highlighted (using filled noteheads) in the example below:

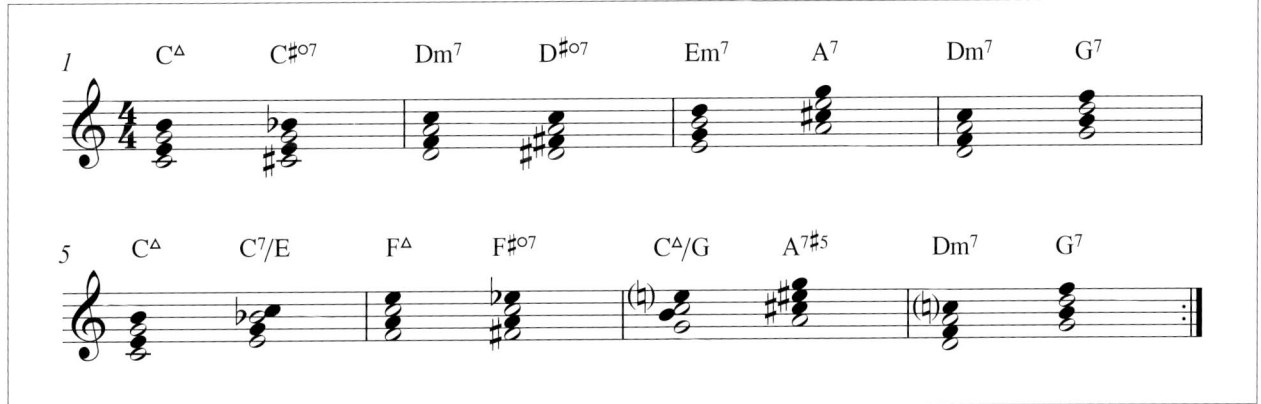

The simplest way to apply this is by using two-handed voicings, as each chord automatically has its third and seventh present in the right hand as part of the voicing, with one or other of these notes usually brought into prominence on top of the chord. The next example, which also serves as material for an exercise practising this, shows two takes of the verse, each with a different realisation of the voicings. Note how each version generates a distinct top part, whose notes may then serve as goal notes when improvising over the changes. The position within the chords of the notes considered preferable as goal notes is indicated on a smaller staff, beneath the music:

UNIT 9 | SECTION 4

CD TRACK 43

SECTION 4 UNIT 9

Exercise 9.1 CD Track 44
Take the above versions of the verse of 'Rhythm Changes' and explore how you can improvise on the basis of the top part by filling it in with stepwise movements and leaps. Try to feel how the notes you play establish a trajectory beginning from the top note in the preceding chord but headed towards that of the next one – even before you've reached the latter. Try as many keys as possible. (Listening to the demo track first may help get you started. You'll hear just the two-handed voicings first, followed by a sample improvisation. Listen to how the goal-note framework remains audible within the improvised line, giving it direction as the music unfolds from one chord change to the next.)

Now let's take this a stage further. On p372 are the same chords realised as left-hand voicings, with another series of goal notes above them, as reference points for the right hand as it improvises. (Note how the latter now cover a wider melodic compass, reflecting the increased freedom of the right hand to move across the keyboard when not required to help realise the chords themselves.) Once again, two versions are given, which may correspond to successive takes of the verse, and which may serve as material for an exercise.

Exercise 9.2 CD Track 46
Now explore improvising over the left-hand voicings in the above example, using the notes in the right hand as goal notes that you feel yourself heading towards. Try this in a range of keys. (Once again, a demo track is provided, consisting this time of just the left-hand voicings with the goal-notes sounding above them, followed by a sample improvisation. Can you hear how the goal-note framework informs the melodic improvising?)

These examples and exercises provide you with a fixed framework of goal-notes to work with, but in practice jazz improvisers also make decisions about which goal-note to head for next as they go along. Hence you need to get used to the idea of thinking about this as you play.

Exercise 9.3
Now turn right back to the very first example in this unit. See if you can generate your own series of goal notes as you improvise your own two-handed voicings based on the chords in the first eight bars of 'Rhythm Changes'. Then take just the left-hand voicings from the last example given above (as used in the previous exercise): this time ignore the right-hand goal-notes and again see if you can make decisions about what goal-notes to head for as you go along.

Exercise 9.4
Now it's time to revisit some of your own reharmonisations of the 'Rhythm

UNIT 9 | SECTION 4

Changes' chords from the previous unit. Have a look and see if you can work out some alternative goal-note structures based on these. Try writing them down and using them as a framework for more improvising. Then see if you can improvise over the same reharmonisations, but only deciding which goal-notes to head for as you go along.

Now that we've had a look at how the goal-note approach works in jazz, it's time to consider how the corresponding elements within classical improvising differ from this. Amongst other things, this means getting clear about the essential role that phrase structure plays in classical music, and experiencing the practical consequences of this – not just for improvisation on a given structure (such as we've already tried in Unit Seven), but also for improvising from scratch.

Phrase structure

Back in Unit Seven we tried improvising simple countermelodies, first over a cantus, then over chords. We also saw how the chords of Bach's 'Prelude In C Major' could be used to produce a melodic skeleton rather similar to those used in the last section to illustrate the jazz approach. If, however, we want to grasp the way in which classical improvising uses methods comparable to the goal-note approach in jazz, we'll need to understand another important aspect of music we've not said much about yet: **phrase structure**. In case you've forgotten, this is the name for the division of the music into shorter and longer sections, subsections and phrases or, looked at from the opposite perspective, the way shorter phrases are grouped together into longer phrases, which in turn are grouped together to form subsections, sections, etc.

Phrase structure isn't something we have to think about much when improvising jazz. Why?

- Because both jazz standards and the other chord sequences used as a basis for jazz improvisation tend to be chosen for their regular and easy-to-recognise sectional structure, which is created by the changes themselves.
- Because in jazz the changes themselves imply a structure at the level of harmony and metre that's more basic than whatever happens above it melodically, so even if the improvised melody goes against the phrase structure implied by the harmony and metre themselves, the latter need not be adjusted; instead the music simply operates on two levels simultaneously.

In jazz the basic structure will mostly remain the same, whatever you do melodically. This means that when you project goal notes while improvising you mostly need only think one chord ahead of where you are. At its simplest, then, all you need do is pick out any suitable note to aim for from the next chord (eg, the third or seventh), head towards it, and see what happens!

In classical music things are rather different. Unlike jazz, classical music treats melody, harmony, and rhythm (or metre) as parts of a single integral whole. What's more, this integral whole is articulated in terms of phrase structure, not merely the harmony or melody taken in isolation. So when the music unfolds, whatever happens in any of these can require adjustment of the others to ensure that a coherent phrase structure is maintained. At the same time, as we've already noted, melodic shapes tend to be more tightly integrated into the longer-term structure unfolded by the music. (This is especially true of music from the second half of the 18th century, and the first quarter of the 19th century – what's known as the Classical period of classical music – but it's also generally the case with other kinds of classical music too.)

Provided that classical improvising keeps to variations and/or embellishments of existing material, the implications of this aren't too complicated. When improvising on a given chord structure:

- Make sure the goal notes you project (or obtain through reduction of existing music) are consistent with the phrase structure implied by the existing material.
- Make sure your improvised embellishments and variations of the unfolding melodic skeleton outlined by these goal notes fit with the phrase structure implied by the existing material.

You should already have some sense of how the second of these two points works from Unit Seven, where we tried our hand at embellishing a melodic skeleton based on the top notes of the chords of Bach's 'Prelude In C Major'. If you don't yet feel confident about that, try working through that material again, this time noting carefully how the melodic skeleton was first broken down into phrases to reflect the phrase structure implied by the chords themselves, before being embellished in ways that were then made to be consistent with this.

The first of these two points takes us further, since it corresponds to the next stage in developing classical improvisation skills – where we try projecting our own goal notes based on an existing chord structure, while keeping in mind the phrase-structure implications of the latter.

Let's take a couple of model examples and follow them closely through the various stages of development to see how this works in practice. For each example, there's

1. A given chord structure, shown in a table that indicates its phrase structure.
2. A model showing how goal-notes can be projected (using the notes from the chords) to form a melodic outline that's designed to complement the phrase structure.
3. A keyboard realisation, giving a simple harmonisation that could serve as a framework for subsequent melodic embellishment and improvisation.
4. Preliminary exercises to help you developing a melody line from the outline.
5. A demo track giving a straightforward sample improvisation based on the material shown (in case you need it to get started with your own improvising).

SECTION 4 UNIT 9

Our first model begins with a 32-bar structure in a major key. Note how it follows the most typical and regular phrase-structure pattern available, with each section or phrase subdivided into two equal parts, which are in turn divided in the same way, etc. The result is a question-and-answer structure, rather like a dialogue, juxtaposing four-bar harmonic phrases, as highlighted in the table below. This is one of the features we should aim to reflect in the choice of goal-notes and, more specifically, in the melodic outline created by the latter.

1-4	I	IV	V	I				
5-8					VI	II	V	I
9-12	I	IV	V	I				
13-16					I	VI	V7 of V	V
17-20	I	IV	V	I				
21-24					IV	II	V7 of VI	VI
25-28	I	IV	V	I				
29-32					V7 of II	II	V7	I

Note how the same four-bar chord structure forms the first half of each eight-bar phrase, but is followed by a different four-bar answering structure each time. That's not typical of classical structures, but for teaching and learning purposes it offers a useful transition stage as we move away from simple variation and embellishment of existing, fixed structures (such as we explored in Unit Seven), and towards the kind of improvising where the player makes more significant decisions about how the music will unfold, and where it will go next.

On p376 you can see how we can project goal-notes based on these chords to form a melodic contour or skeleton that will guide us while improvising, followed by a keyboard realisation of the harmony to fit with the resulting top line in the texture. (It's in C major, but you should be able to transpose it to other keys by now. Remember, some adjustments to chord layout may be needed to compensate for register shifts resulting from transposition.)

Exercise 9.5 CD Track 48

The next stage is to practise improvising around the melodic outline in the above example. First listen to the demo track: it gives a sample of how this might sound, in the Classical style of the late 18th and early 19th centuries. (That's the period of great improvisers such as Mozart and Beethoven. Notice especially the dramatic cadenza-like material at the end.) Since the preceding track allows you to hear the unembellished structure by itself, exactly as it appears in the second half of the last example, you might also listen to that first. Then try playing through the preliminary material below (p377), which gives two sets of basic embellishments (similar to those practised in Unit Seven): first stepwise elaboration with passing notes, then alternative chord-notes that can serve as a basis for embellishing

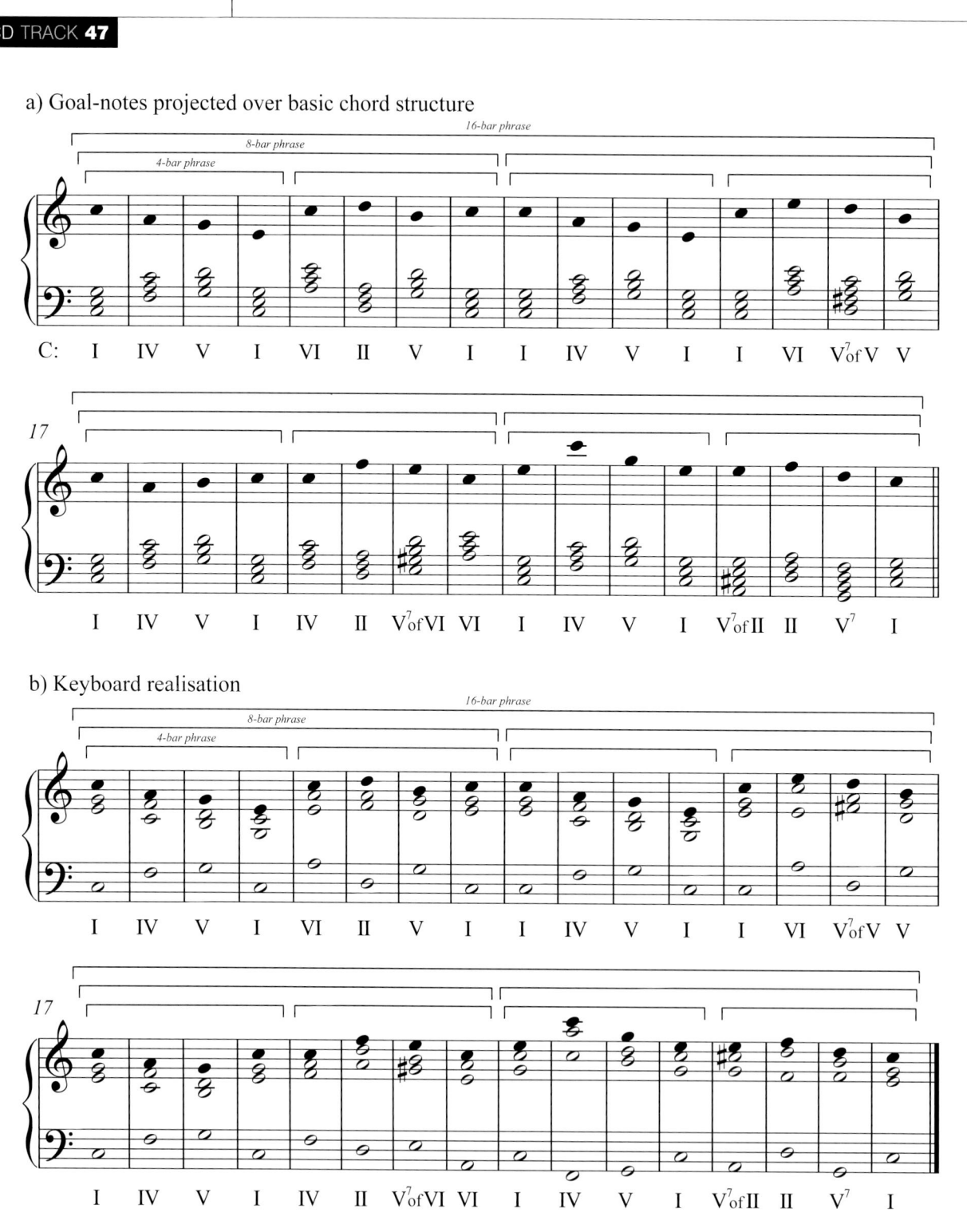

with melodic leaps. No timing is specified: try out a variety of metres (simple and compound duple, triple and quadruple time). As soon as you feel your improvising suggests a metre, try to identify it and make use of the other rhythmic possibilities it offers. (See Unit Six for examples of these.) Finally, transpose everything into other keys, improvising in them too. You may also try making up your own goal notes to use 'on the fly' – as you are improvising over these same chords.

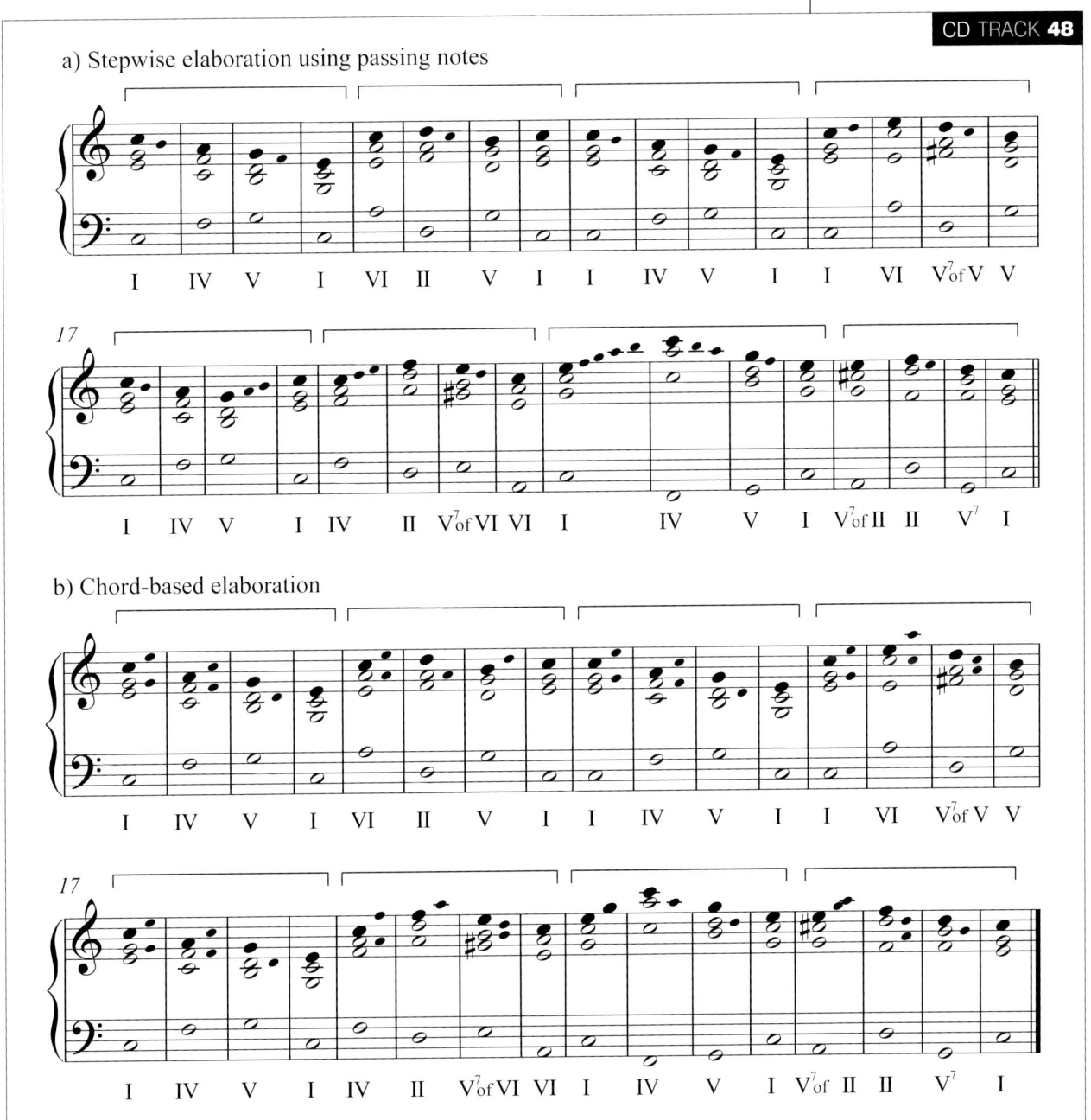

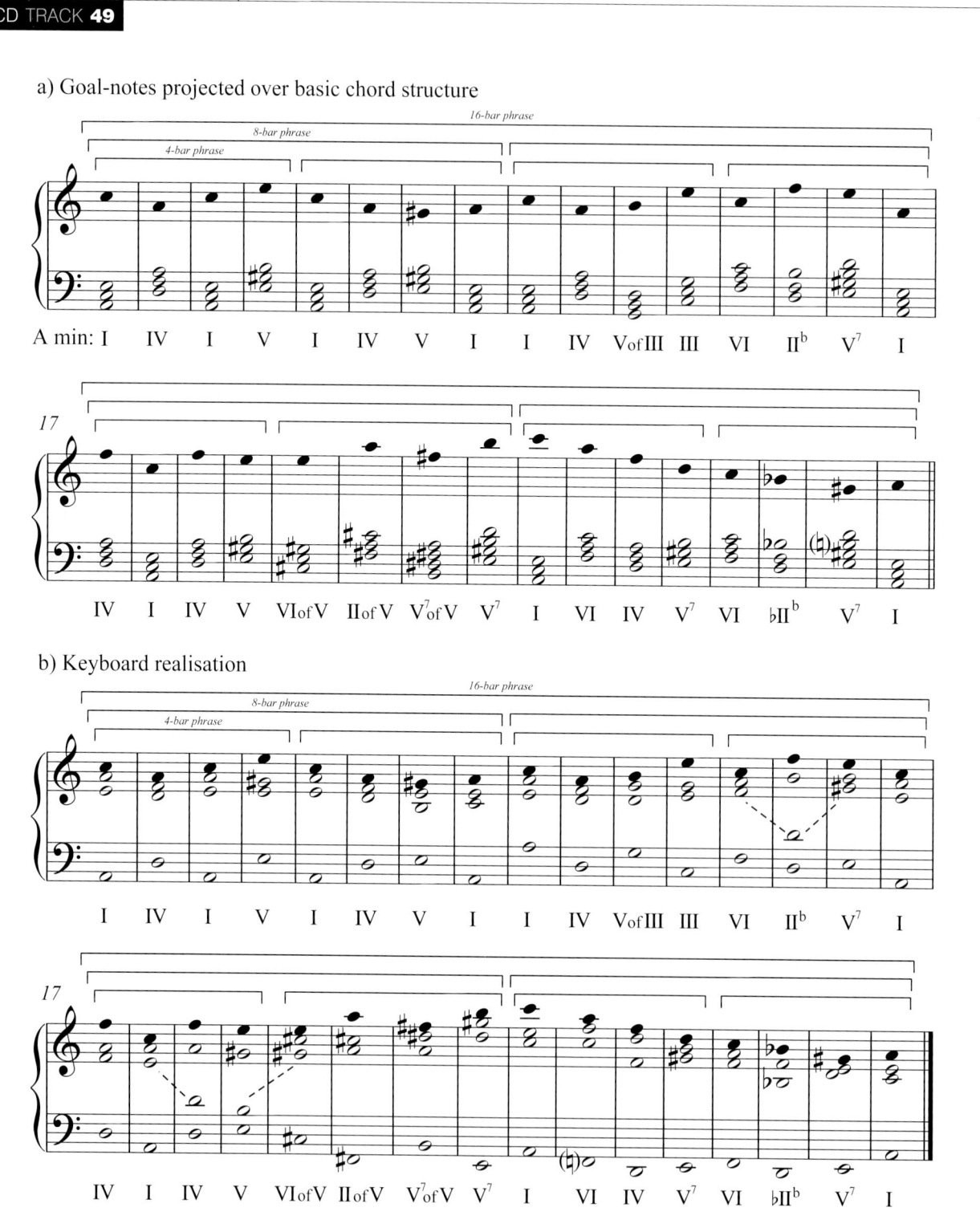

The next model is not quite so straightforward: it's in a minor key, and moves more quickly away from repetition of the opening chord structure. Once again we're dealing with a 32-bar structure with regular subdivisions. This time notice how the last four bars of the first 16-bar phrase reappear with a variation (Neapolitan ♭II♭ replacing ordinary II♭) at the end of the second 16-bar phrase.

1-4	I	IV	I	V				
5-8					I	IV	V	I
9-12	I	IV	V7 of III	III				
13-16					VI	IIb	V7	I
17-20	IV	I	IV	V				
21-24					VI of V	II of V	V7 of V	V
25-28	I	VI	IV	V7				
29-32					VI	♭IIb	V7	I

Opposite is the example of projected goal-notes based on the chords, together with a realisation of the harmony to fit with this. (This time it's in A minor: once again, try transposing it to other keys.) Note how some of the intervals and shapes outlined by the goal notes at the start get developed thematically: they reappear later on over different chords (especially the motive of the falling third). This helps to build a degree of unity into the framework of your improvisation, which in turn then gives you more flexibility to do exactly what you want as you elaborate more complex melodic shapes around the skeleton.

Exercise 9.6, p380 CD Track 50

As with the first model example, the next stage is to practise improvising around the melodic outline, followed by making up your own goal notes, as you improvise over these chords. It's best to take this in stages. First listen to the demo track for some inspiration. (Once again, the preceding track gives you the unembellished structure by itself, exactly as it appears in the second half of the last example, so you can listen to this beforehand if you want to. Like the previous demo, this one is in the style of classical improvising from the late 18th and early 19th centuries. Notice especially the dramatic use of rapid scale-runs, register changes, and expressive melodic decoration, as well as the very loose musical form – known as 'free fantasia'.) The preliminary material below will then get you started by giving you basic stepwise embellishments and alternative chord-notes for embellishing with leaps. As with the previous exercise, try out different metres and make use of the range of rhythmic possibilities each one offers and, finally, try out the material in other keys too.

UNIT 9 | SECTION 4

CD TRACK 50

a) Stepwise elaboration using passing notes

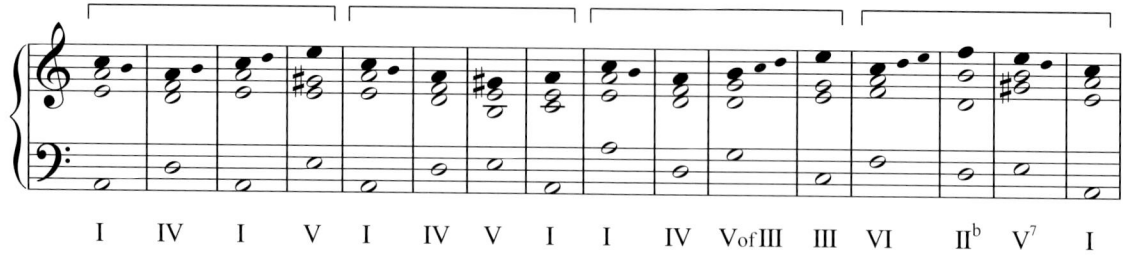

b) Chord-based elaboration

In classical improvisation the main challenge comes from the fact that we generally don't want to limit ourselves to just varying or embellishing existing material. Why? Because much more than jazz, the language of classical music has evolved in ways that reflect compositional as well as improvisational possibilities, making its available structures less suited to the kinds of wide-ranging, open-ended variation typical of jazz. (This is especially true of harmony: even though classical harmony also uses a range of formulas, there's no equivalent to the practically all-pervasive role in jazz of the II-V-I.)

> Some theorists, notably Heinrich Schenker, have argued that a small set of cadence-like contrapuntal formulas underlie all the more complex structures typical of mainstream classical tonal music, but this is disputed. Even if it's partly true, these formulas certainly don't generate the kind of possibilities for reharmonisation and open-ended improvisation using chord-based scales that we see in jazz. Schenker's model may be useful for analysing the ways in which the carefully balanced melodic contours of composed classical music can be heard as being ultimately derived from harmonic-contrapuntal formulas just like those that serve as the basis for classical improvisation. However, it can't tell us much about the role the latter play in classical improvising itself.

For this reason, techniques of variation and embellishment in classical music rarely penetrate beneath the surface level (or levels) of structure in the music, whereas in jazz they do (even if the structures in question are, as a consequence, less well-defined). The most obvious way to get around this – if we find it problematic – is to improvise classical music from scratch – with no overall structure for the music defined in advance. This is certainly more challenging, particularly as it's complicated by the more integrated character of classical music mentioned earlier. (We'll see how in the next section.)

Improvising from scratch according to classical principles offers another important angle on improvising, because it's only here that we're really brought face to face with just how different the classical and jazz approaches are. So even if you ultimately find improvising from scratch isn't for you, and end up doing something else when you improvise at the piano, you'll benefit from having tried it.

Improvising from scratch

When improvising from scratch, we must still project goal-notes for the melody to head towards, but these must now contribute to creating an unfolding structure with consistent harmonic, melodic, and metrical implications. The problem is that it's not so easy to make the sort of coordinated judgements about how these different aspects work together that the classical approach involves when the projections of goal notes reflect decisions we're making as we play (ie, decisions made 'on the fly').

So we need to try to understand what it means in practice to make decisions that fundamentally affect the structure of the music we are playing, as we are playing it – something that takes us to the heart of what is involved in improvising.

> **Improvising from scratch: classical vs jazz.** Although jazz is more closely linked to improvisation than classical music in people's minds, its heavy dependence on the idea of varying existing harmonic material makes improvising from scratch problematic, as making use of familiar pre-given structures just seems to be one of the things that defines it. By treating harmonic and metrical structure as more basic than, and therefore largely independent of, melodic structure, jazz makes improvising from scratch fairly pointless anyway, since even with these structures in place we have enormous flexibility. Some modern jazz players certainly try improvising without them, as in so-called 'free jazz', but this raises a lot of questions. Is it still jazz? Are they really improvising the structure itself? Or have they replaced the given structure of a standard with one they've composed themselves, even if they've never written the latter down?

A good entry-point to this fairly challenging area is the idea of **decision-hierarchies**. The basic idea is that at each point in our ongoing improvising, we can decide which aspect of the musical structure gets projected first. This then serves as our initial reference point for projecting an overall sense of phrase structure, relative to which other aspects of the music are then determined. The only way to understand this properly is to see how it works in practice. (At the end of this section we'll consider the pros and cons of analysing what goes on when we improvise in terms of decision-making.)

The next example shows a melodic idea already partly unfolded over an opening chord sequence – one based on the first of the model examples we've just been exploring.

The structure of both the melody and the harmony form an opening two-bar phrase, such as is typically answered by another two-bar phrase. Together these will make a four-bar unit that, in turn, will probably form the first half of a larger eight-bar phrase. This will also then form part of a larger structure – typically a 16-bar one. (Not all classical music follows this symmetrical model of phrase structure, but if you're just starting to explore how phrase structure works in classical music it's best to keep to it until you feel confident about the role phrase structure is going to play in your improvising. Then you can start experimenting with irregular and non-symmetrical phrase structures.)

First let's be clear about exactly how the decisions we make relate to the different levels of the phrase-structure hierarchy.

- How we complete the first four-bar phrase depends on the form of the second two-bar phrase; and the completion of the first four-bar phrase will then determine what possibilities make sense for the second four-bar phrase.
- Likewise, how we complete the first eight-bar phrase depends on the form of the second four-bar phrase; and the completion of the first eight-bar phrase will then determine what possibilities make sense for the second eight-bar phrase.
- And so on for larger elements of the phrase structure.

Now's the moment to see how adopting a particular hierarchy of decision-making can limit the otherwise potentially unlimited alternatives that arise in the early stages of creating a musical structure from scratch. We'll start with the decisions we make when completing the first four-bar phrase, by adding a second two-bar phrase to follow on from the existing one.

Initially, we must decide whether to project the second phrase in the first instance as a purely harmonic structure or a purely melodic structure.

Of course, harmony and melody are closely interrelated, so as soon as we project one of these elements we will want to consider its implications for the other. Even, so, the fact remains that in practice (when improvising from scratch) we just have to project one or other of them first. Hence the first step in the decision-hierarchy will concern the initial projection of the answering phrase in terms of either melody or harmony.

Let's say we first decide to project the phrase structure as just harmony. This already suggests two obvious options, given as (a) and (b) below. (These are not exhaustive, but they are the simplest options, so for simplicity's sake we'll limit ourselves to them.)

It's worth noting that each of these already has implications for the possible harmonic unfolding of the next four-bar phrase (and, in turn, for the larger eight-bar structure of which both four-bar phrases are parts), as the example on page 384 shows.

Most of these options are entailed by the need to counterbalance the V-I or I-V progressions in bars 3-4 with a complementary cadence in bars 7-8. If the first four-bar phrase ends with V-I, then it's natural to reverse this into an imperfect cadence on V at the end of the next phrase. Equally, if the first one ends with I-V we'll probably want to reverse this and use V-I to complete the next phrase. (There are other options here, of course, but they are less straightforward.) Note that the option of V of V going to V in bars 7-8 also amounts to a reversal of I-V, since it corresponds to V-I in the dominant key.

We are now faced with a decision as to which of these purely harmonic options for completing the first four bars we want to pursue. (We'll assume that in themselves they are equally good.) However, that doesn't make this the next decision we actually take.

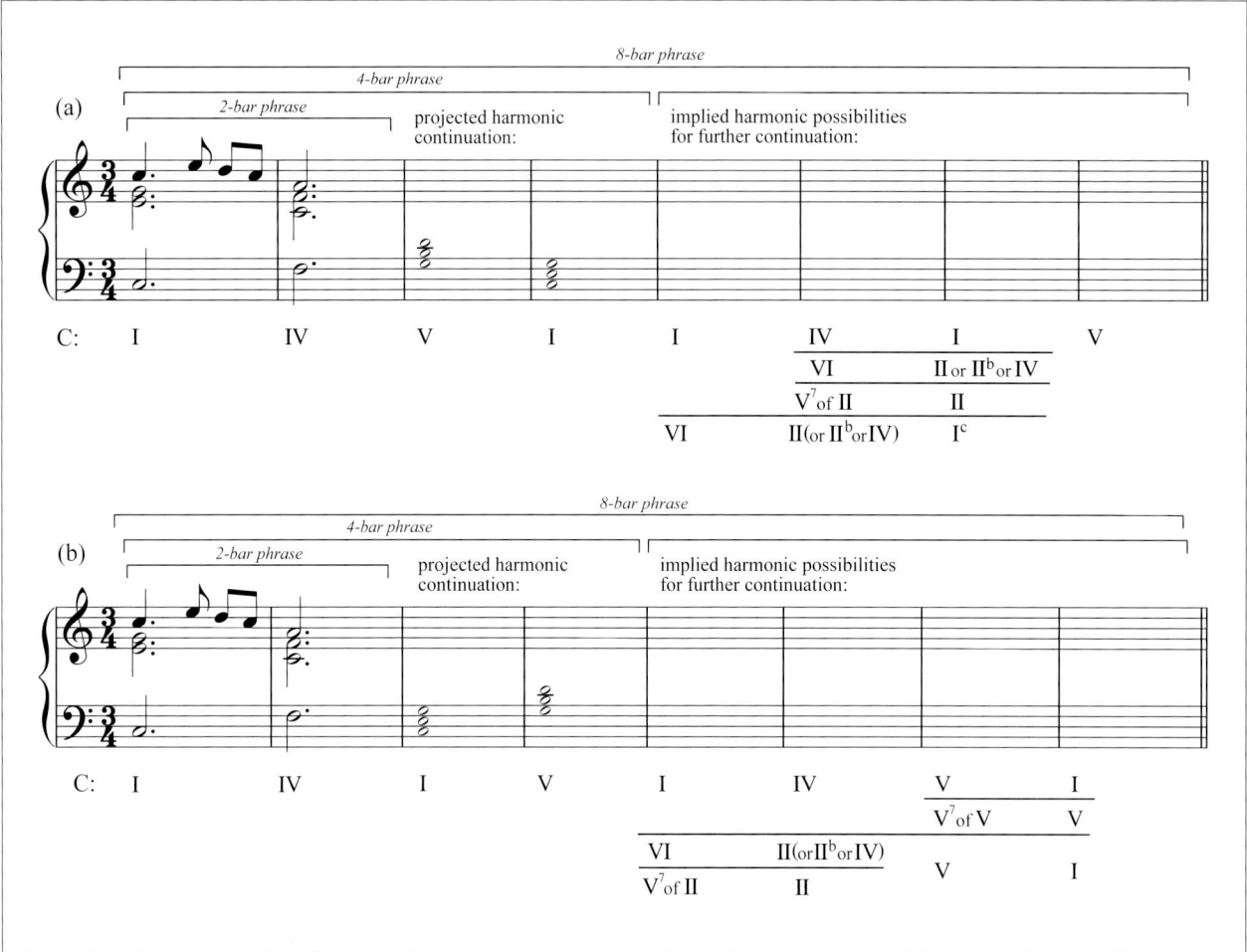

First we should consider two other factors:

1. We'll want to take into account the subsequent possibilities for harmonic development they open up. (Remember: in classical music short-term structures are much more tightly integrated into longer-term structures than in jazz.)
2. We may not know which of these implied eight-bar harmonic structures we want until we know what melodic implications we're dealing with. (Remember: in classical music different aspects such as harmony and melody are absolutely interdependent.)

Hence, given our initial choice, the second step will be to decide whether these further harmonic implications are sufficient to determine which completion we go for, or not. So there are two possible scenarios here, depending on whether the answer to that question is 'yes' or 'no'. We'll consider each of these in a moment, but let's summarise them both first:

The 'yes' scenario: if the harmonic implications already tell us which harmonic completion to go for, we can choose and project an eight-bar chord structure straight away. Only afterwards will we think about what goal notes to project, to improvise a melody over this.

The 'no' scenario: if we can't tell just from the harmonic implications which harmonic completion would be best, then it will be the options for melodic unfolding that guide us in choosing this – at least for the first four-bar phrase. So to decide this we'll also need to know in advance what melodic completions each of these harmonic structures allows us.

Now let's take a closer look at what's involved in each of these cases.

(i) The 'yes' scenario: harmony alone decides structure

When choosing between harmonic continuations that are all 'possible' (in the sense that they make musical sense in themselves), it's often helpful to ask yourself whether a particular option would work better at a later stage in the unfolding of the improvisation, rather than at the opening:

- In both (a) and (b) of the above example, introducing V^{7}of II into the opening eight-bar phrase feels premature, since it already implies an expansion or complication of the underlying tonality to include a passing modulation to the supertonic.
- Indeed the entire V^{7}of II - II - V sequence, with its implied root progression of descending fifths, suggests a preparation for a return to I such as we'd expect to encounter after a period of harmonic development that's taken us away from the home key, rather than at the very outset.
- Equally, the option for (a) that finishes with a cadential six-four (I^c-V) produces a cadence that feels far too emphatic for the end of an opening eight-bar phrase, and would work better during a final reprise (ie, restatement) of the opening material, when cadences are used to help create an overall sense of resolution and closure.

On the other hand, you'll also often find that a particular option may be eliminated on the basis of its intrinsic qualities, even though it's 'musically correct':

- In both (a) and (b) the continuations using just primary chords (I, IV and V) sound bland and uninteresting, even though they lead to harmonically coherent resolutions within the eight-bar phrase, as they introduce no new harmonic elements.
- The same goes (to a lesser extent) for the version of (b) in which bars 5-6 restate the opening two chords (even though these are then followed by a more interesting development in the form of V of V going to V, it's too late).

In both of these cases we're left feeling that this music isn't going anywhere interesting. If that's how it seems after just six or eight bars, don't be surprised if people choose not to stick around to hear the rest of your improvisation.

Exercise 9.6
To explore this option in practice, just take each of the possible eight-bar chord structures in the preceding example, decide which works best for you, and use it as a basis for projecting your own goal notes as a guide for continuing the given melodic opening. Then improvise eight-bar melodic phrases based on this, realising the harmony yourself.

(ii) The 'no' scenario: harmony and melody together decide structure

As we said, in this case we'll want first to explore what specific melodic completions of the opening four-bar phrase are possible, given each of the options for completing it harmonically.

The next two examples (opposite page) demonstrate this, using the same opening material. Four melodic possibilities in terms of goal notes are first shown, given the two options for harmonic completion of the first four-bar phrase. Each of these may then have implications for the next four-bar phrase, and thus for the overall eight-bar structure whose exact course of harmonic development we haven't yet committed ourselves to.

Here, too, we're likely to find ourselves wanting to choose between alternative melodic continuations that are all 'musically correct' in principle. Once again, it can help to ask which of these options work better at the particular stage in the larger unfolding of the music we're at:

- Some sound better as opening material, arousing our expectations as listeners without taking us too far from the initial material too quickly (which could be disorientating).
- Others involve the sorts of more radical development more appropriate once the musical unfolding is more fully under way.
- Others create a more powerful sense of melodic closure, which could be more effective towards the end of an extended section of music, or as the entire improvisation nears its end.

You'll normally find that some options for melodic continuation can be ruled out straight away on purely melodic grounds. Which ones these are will depend on what overall effect you are aiming for. For example:

- The final goal note projected for the opening four-bar phrase in (a_1) makes the music feel as though it's going to be just going round in circles, as it's the same as the structurally important first note.

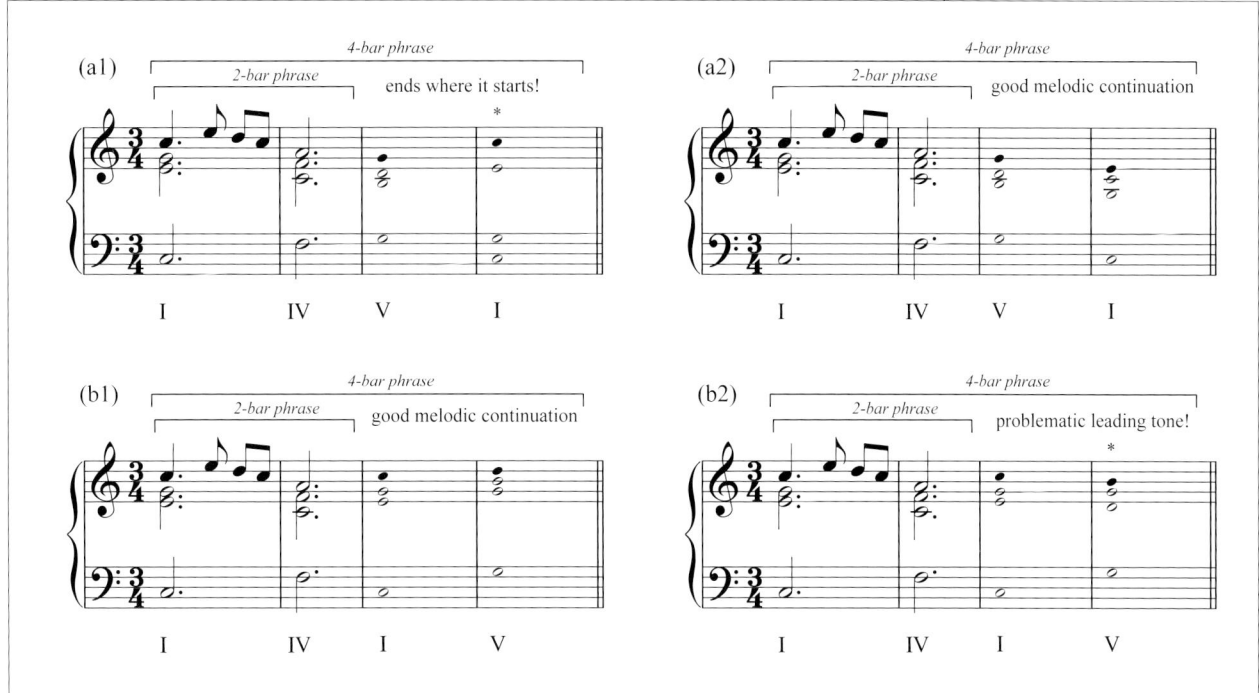

- The melodic contour of (a2) wouldn't work well as a basis for a dramatic opening as there's nothing to counterbalance the falling trajectory of the goal notes, producing a lack of melodic tension; however, it could work as part of a longer, lyrical phrase, if answered straight away by a rising four-bar phrase.
- The final goal note projected for the opening four-bar phrase in (b2) will make the melodic continuation of the opening too unresolved for this early stage in the music's unfolding, as it's the leading note.

This means that for most purposes (a1) and (b2) will be ruled out as melodic completions of the first four-bar phrase, leaving just (a2) and (b1). If we keep in mind which harmonic continuations have already been ruled out as unsuitable on purely harmonic grounds, we're left with a single possible harmonic continuation for each of these. The next example (p388) shows how these can then be used as a basis for deciding what viable melodic continuations are available for the second four-bar phrase, in the form of further projections of goal notes that could serve as a guide when improvising a continuation of the melody line.

Now that we can see what sort of eight-bar phrase is likely to emerge from each of these openings, given its implications for the continuation of the music's harmonic structure, we're a lot better placed to decide which of these options will fit best with our intuitions about the longer-term unfolding of our improvisation.

UNIT 9 | SECTION 4

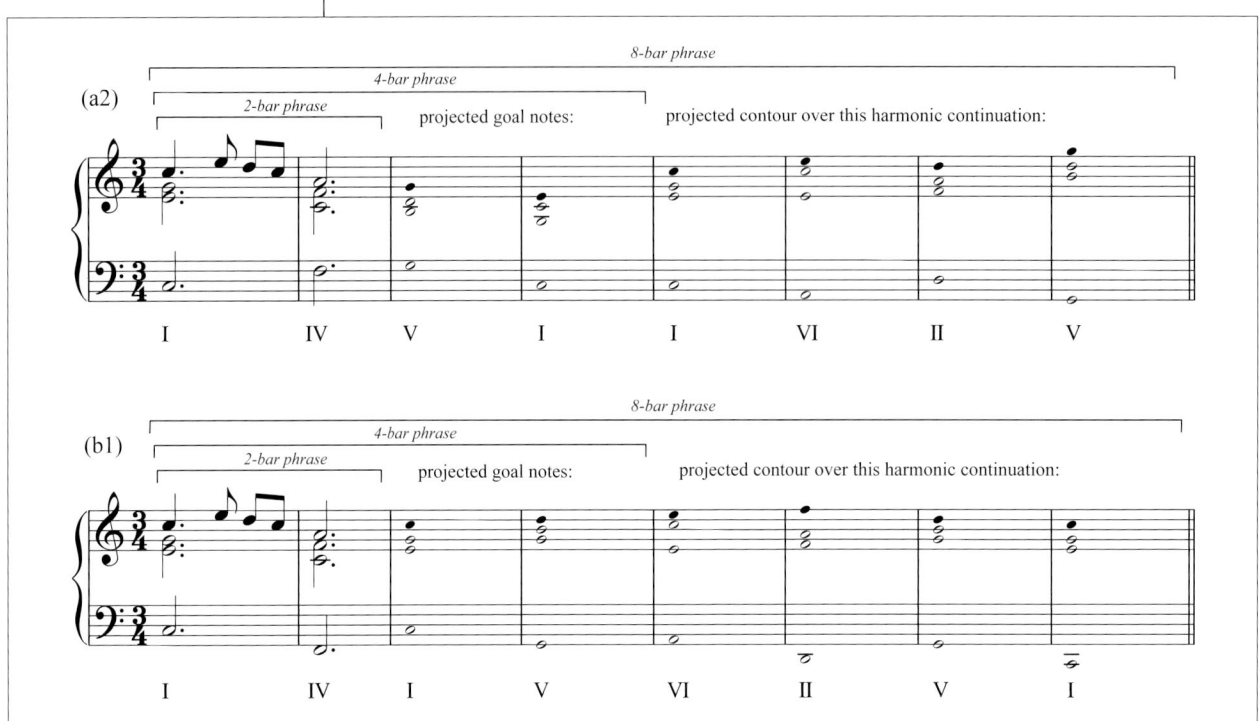

> When improvising classical music from scratch it's tempting just to decide on a particular harmonic continuation, regardless of its implications for any possible melodic continuation, or vice versa, thinking that you'll somehow get everything else to fit with this in due course. Do this, though, and you've lost sight of the subtlety of the classical approach. Instead, it's better to aim constantly to compare the options for melodic continuation in a way that reflects an awareness of their implications for harmonic continuation – and vice versa, of course.

Exercise 9.7
Play through both of the options in the previous example. Then try and project some alternative melodic continuations (in terms of goal notes) based on each harmonic continuation, and some alternative harmonisations that would work with each melodic continuation. Which of these would be suitable as continuations of an opening phrase in an improvisation? Where else might they be placed in relation to the larger unfolding of the music? In each case, feel free also to elaborate an improvised melody line on the basis of the material, and to try out your ideas in a range of keys.

Now lets reverse-track right back to our very first decision, which was to project the phrase structure for the first four bars in the first instance as just harmony. What happens if we take the other option and first project a series of goal notes for melodic improvising without reference to any given chord structure – simply focusing on the shape they make and the harmonic implications suggested by the melody line itself?

Well, it's pretty simple: this time everything in the decision-hierarchy works the other way round (in respect of the relationship between melody and harmony). Now the question is: does the implied subsequent melodic unfolding of each optional (melodic) completion of the first phrase tell us which harmonic completion of that phrase we should opt for, or not?

- If the answer's 'yes', we can straight away select and project an entire eight-bar structure of goal notes, knowing that this has determined which of the available acceptable harmonic completions of the first four-bar phrase we're going to pursue. This in turn narrows down the options for harmonic continuation in respect of the next phrase.

Exercise 9.8
Take the original two-bar opening material and try out a variety of melodic completions of the first four-bar phrase, based on each of the two possible harmonic completions shown earlier (I-IV-V-I and I-IV-I-V). Now project further possible goal notes based just on this and see whether they imply good harmonic continuations for the second four-bar phrase. Finally, see how many different eight-bar melodic phrases you can improvise based on these combinations of goal-notes and chords, and transpose these into other keys.

- If the answer to the last question is 'no', then it will be the possibilities for harmonic unfolding that will guide us in choosing between the different acceptable options for completing the first four-bar phrase melodically. That means first exploring what specific harmonic completions of the opening four-bar phrase are possible, given these melodic options.

In this case, what goal notes we project for the subsequent unfolding of our improvised melody will reflect not just our choice of melodic completion for the opening phrase, but also the choice of harmonic completion that helped determine this. Note that the overall outcome is that the first four-bar phrase gets defined as a complete structure, both melodically and harmonically, before any choices are made about the subsequent melodic direction of the music. As a result, when we come to make those choices, we will also have to make sure they do justice to the harmonic implications of the completed opening phrase.

At this point, then, it's more than likely that we'll want to project an approximate chord structure for the eight-bar phrase. This could mean just knowing which cadence we want to end on, and/or what key we'd like to be in, when we've completed the phrase. But as we decide this we'll probably want to have some idea about what's going to happen harmonically over the rest of the improvisation – especially in terms of key structure (ie, modulations) and the type of chord structures used. This can and should make a difference to the decisions we make even at this early stage.

Exercise 9.9
Take the original two-bar opening material again, but this time forget about the harmonic continuations we've explored so far. Instead, focus on exploring how each of your own melodic continuations (involving the projection of goal notes to define a melodic outline) suggests its own harmonic completion of the phrase. Then try to project a continuation of the melodic structure based on each of these harmonic structures and its chordal implications.

This section should have given you a taste of what's involved in improvising music from scratch according to classical principles of harmonic and melodic structure, but it's not a comprehensive exploration of what's involved. Why not? Because the kind of complex decision-making sequences we've come across here represent something artificial. It's not that these choices are not present in classical improvising: they are, though not, mostly, as choices we make. Instead, they've been settled in advance, as classical improvising, even when carried out from scratch, invariably occurs within more specific boundaries that implicitly dictate many of the choices we would otherwise have to make ourselves. These boundaries spring from some or all of the following:

- A historically specific musical style – eg, Renaissance, Baroque, Classical, or Romantic, as well as more precise subcategories of these.
- A specific musical idiom – eg, certain kinds of lyrical, dramatic, narrative or dance-based music.
- A particular genre – eg, prelude, fantasia, intemezzo, rhapsody, etc.

We'll discuss issues of style (and, to a certain extent, idiom and genre) in the final unit of this book. But by now you're probably wondering why we've taken the trouble to analyse these structures of decision-making, if in practice they're mostly settled in advance of our actual improvising. It's worth explaining why, as this sheds important light on the rest of this unit.

- You need to understand properly the features that make classical music fundamentally different from jazz, to see why classical improvising from scratch makes no practical sense outside of specific styles, idioms and genres.
- In the past, classical musicians learned about these features by studying improvisation and composition alongside one another as elements of a single larger practice. (Composing tends to make one much more aware of these implicit choices, as you have a great deal more scope for exploring alternative options in your imagination before deciding how the music will actually unfold.)

- Studying the decision-making process involved in improvising from scratch is the nearest we can get to that, short of making a study of the art of classical composing itself (which would be ideal, but which lies outside the scope of this book).
- Only when you've grasped these differences between classical music and jazz can you see that without the more specific contexts furnished by particular styles, idioms, and genres, we would actually have to make a whole lot of decisions about the structural unfolding of the music ourselves, while improvising – which, at least for ordinary folks, is impossible.
- This is why classical improvisers, if they still want to go beyond mere surface variation and embellishment of a given structure, need a technique that will allow them to do so while still taking such a structure as a starting point. That's why **reduction** – the subject of the next section – plays a central role in most forms of improvisation outside of jazz.

> Although the more highly integrated structures of classical music are harder to cope with when improvising from scratch than when composing, making us more dependent in turn on the boundaries imposed by a given style, genre, or idiom, this isn't the whole story as to why classical improvising can run into problems when it proceeds from scratch. To benefit from working in a specific style, idiom or genre we must immerse ourselves in it over an extended period of time. This wasn't much of a problem for classical greats like Bach, Handel, Mozart, Beethoven, Chopin, and Liszt: in their time, only specific idioms or genres relevant to a particular style were available, so they devoted their whole lives to exploring these, becoming familiar with all the options by reworking the same material over and over again. These days we live in a much more multi-faceted culture: there's a huge range of musical styles, idioms, and genres to choose between – past and present, both within and beyond the Western tradition. Extended immersion in a particular style is now only an option for experts specialising in the recreation of specific historical improvisation practices – as what classical musicians call 'stylistic improvisation'.

Melodic and harmonic reduction

The basic idea of melodic and harmonic reduction is simple. First we take an existing piece of music that we'd like to use as a basis for improvising; then we reduce its melodic contour and/or chord structure to the barest essentials; this in turn allows us to explore our own elaborations of the basic structures that remain, in place of those responsible for giving the existing music its more familiar or exact form.

To appreciate how melodic and harmonic reduction can work, let's take an extremely well known melody – the one commonly associated with the hymn text 'Amazing Grace'.

UNIT 9 | SECTION 4

Indeed, you can already learn something useful about why melodic and harmonic reduction are natural tools for any improviser working in the Western musical tradition (of both folk and classical music) just by comparing different versions of this classic. Each of the three arrangements below sets the same text to the same melody, but does so in a way that reflects a distinct phase in the development of Western music.

Let's start with a pretty standard kind of arrangement of the sort you'll hear played in North American churches nowadays. (You can listen to the arrangements on the CD, but from the point of view of the improvisation exercises that follow it's better to play them through yourself on the piano.)

CD TRACK 51

AMAZING GRACE

Traditional

Notice the dominant seventh on chord I (making this V of IV) in bars 2 and 9, which clearly shows the influence of blues-based harmony in this arrangement, and the unresolved ninth on the last beat of bar 2, which resembles the use of chord extensions in jazz. (We'll explore blues harmony more in Unit Ten.) The apparent changes of inversion of chord I also follow a logic similar to that of jazz: they aren't significant since they always follow on from root position versions of the same chord, which remains implied as the actual bass, and have almost no contrapuntal significance.

Compare that to the next version, an arrangement made for use in English church services during the 19th century:

You can see that this uses harmonic effects more typical of mainstream classical music, such as the substitution of chord VI for I (in bars 3 and 12) and the use of chords in a range of inversions to enhance the the melodic continuity of the bass line (I^b in bars 7, 9 and 11, I^c in bars 2 and 13, V^{7d} in bar 6). Notice also the more contrapuntal character of the melodic elaboration in the inner parts and bass.

Finally, here's a transcription of a three-part vocal ensemble version that reflects the highly distinctive, vernacular yet polyphonic style of country church singing ('psalmody') that was popular throughout the 18th century in England and parts of North America:

AMAZING GRACE

Traditional

In this example the melodic and harmonic elements are simpler: there's an emphasis on the pentatonic scale and a reduction of the harmony to little more than variations of chord I, with occasional moves to chord V. This, together with the use of parallel and open fifths (chords with the third omitted) brings the style closer to folk music, while nevertheless maintaining a distinctive contrapuntal texture in which each part retains its own melodic interest and echoes the others.

If we place the three versions of the melody line above one another, as in the next example, we can see that they share almost exactly the same underlying skeleton (except for a small divergence in bars 9 and 10).

Note how practically all of the notes on the strong first beat of the metre belong to the tonic triad (or, failing this, the major pentatonic scale based on the tonic. This is a common feature of certain families of European folk melodies, especially those originally designed to be played on solo instruments (such as the bagpipes) that 'harmonise' the melody by playing it against a single continuous pitch – a drone – or in folk ensembles that create similar effects. (More often than not, the drone functions as a kind of tonic.) It's also worth noting that the closer the arrangement is to preserving this effect – as with the 18th-century version shown above – the more 'folksy' it sounds, in terms of style.

Now let's put this melodic skeleton over a representation (using functional Roman numeral chord notation) of the three different versions of the harmony in these arrangements, to better see how this aspect has been varied:

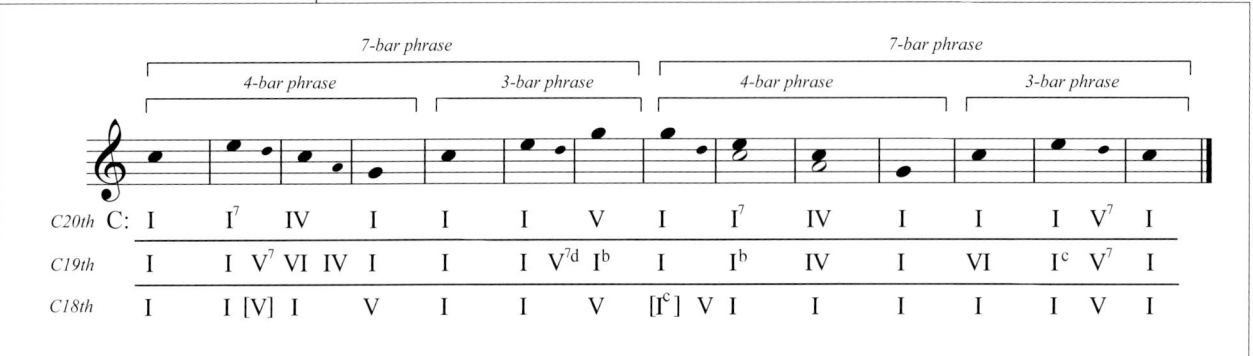

Comparing these three versions of the chord structure allows us to see that while each of them has important elements in common with one or both of the others, each is, nevertheless, in important respects different. It's tempting to assume that the differences between alternative harmonisations of the same melody will always be merely decorative, but as these cases show, this is not necessarily the case. That's because melodies often contain at least some basic harmonic ambiguities. This is especially likely to be so if they originate from particular periods or styles (in Western musical culture) in which harmonic structure had to be treated more loosely to accommodate strong influences coming from folk melody traditions.

In practical terms this means we have three possible reductions of the tune for 'Amazing Grace' instead of one: each of them could, in theory, be a starting point for improvising. Let's first take the melodic skeleton and just add a very simple realisation of each set of chord changes to see how it sounds (opposite page).

Now we'll explore the potential of each one in turn, starting with the reduction of the 20th century American-style arrangement.

You'll have noticed by now that the phrase structure of 'Amazing Grace' doesn't conform to the symmetrical models explored in previous sections of this unit: instead we have two seven-bar phrases, each divided into a four-bar phrase followed by a three-bar one. This is an issue with this first reduction, as the opening four changes themselves establish a regular pattern with a strongly rhythmic feel. (In fact this chord sequence has its origins in the opening chords of the blues and is widely used in blues-influenced styles, including jazz, gospel, and rock.) It's repeated in the first four bars of the second seven-bar phrase too, but both times it's disrupted by the three-bar phrase coming after.

Because the chords here strongly suggest an improvisation in a blues-influenced style, it makes sense to alter the phrase structure straight away to a more regular 16-bar one that will support the regular rhythmic pattern of chord changes over the entire course of the material (opposite page, bottom).

a)

C: I I7 IV I I I V I I7 IV I I I V7 I

b)

C: I I V7 VI IV I I I V7d Ib I Ib IV I VI Ic V7 I

c)

C: I I [V] I V I I V [Ic] V I I I I I V I

16-bar phrase
8-bar phrase
8-bar phrase
4-bar phrase
4-bar phrase
4-bar phrase
4-bar phrase
C: I I7 IV I I I V I I7 IV I I I V7 I

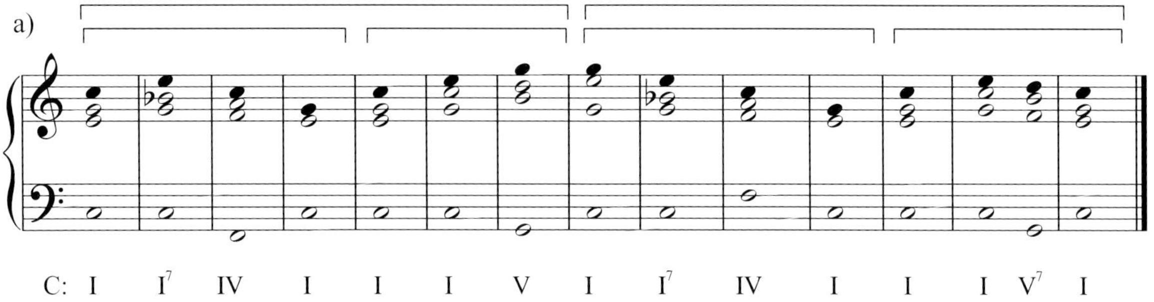

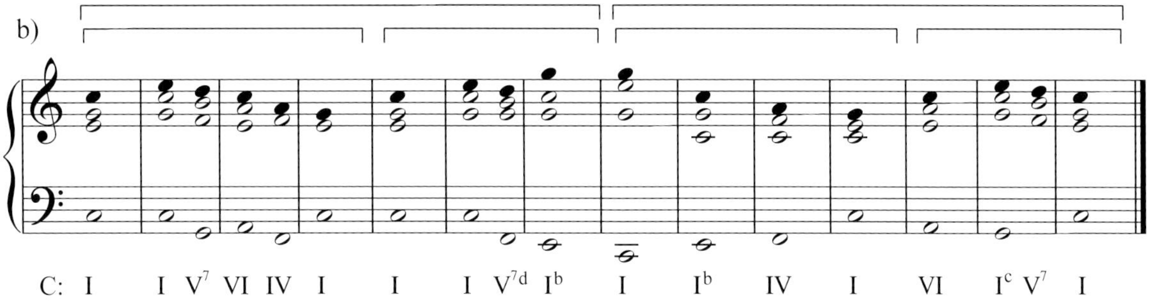

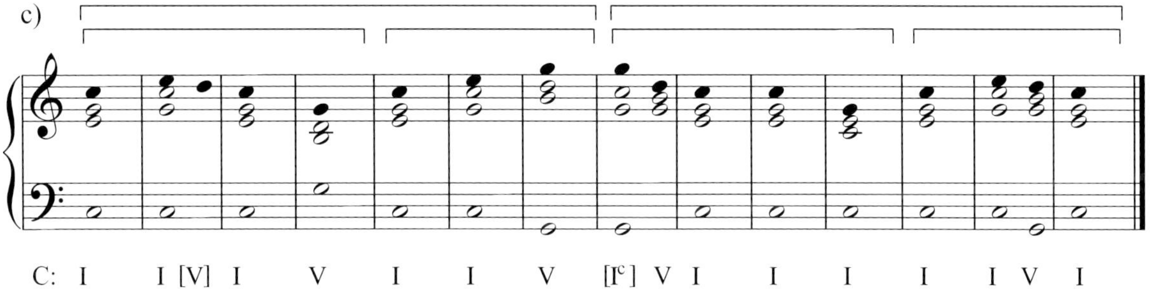

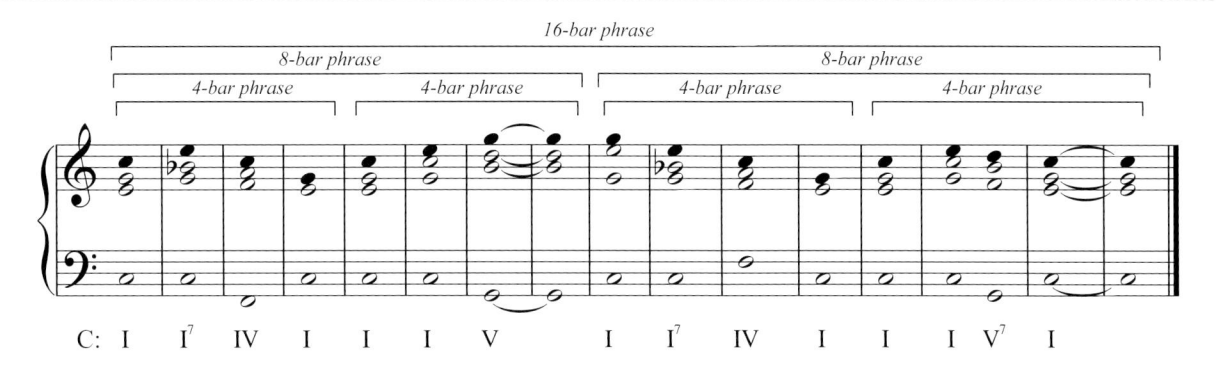

UNIT 9 | SECTION 4

This reduction is obviously suited to being used for jazz improvising, so let's start by introducing some straightforward jazz voicings into the realisation of the harmony.

Exercise 9.10 CD Track 54
Opposite are two sets of jazz voicings for the 16-bar version of the reduction shown above: first two-handed voicings (with the melodic skeleton absorbed into the top part of the chords), then left-hand voicings. Play through each and improvise over them, using the melodic skeleton as a source of goal notes to give you a sense of overall melodic shape and direction. (It's entirely up to you to decide how strictly or loosely you follow the skeleton. Often it works best when we stick to it more closely at first, and then adopt a progressively freer approach as we gain in confidence and begin to see more clearly where our own ideas want to take us.) If you feel short on inspiration or ideas, try listening to the demo track first.

Remember what we said before: the point of making a reduction from an existing piece of music to a more basic structure is that it then gives you more options to elaborate that structure in your own way, without losing the underlying sense of coherence and direction that comes from the structure itself. In jazz, of course, a lot of this potential is connected with the increased options for reharmonisation. The next exercise gives you a version using some of the standard reharmonisation options mentioned in the previous unit. Here they are:

- Bar 6-8: V replaced by II-V, with II preceded in turn by a secondary dominant (V of II in place of I);
- Bar 10: tritone substitution of G♭^{7} (= ♭II of IV) for C^7 (= V^7 of IV);
- Bar 13: classical substitution of a secondary triad for the related primary triad (VI for I), followed by a diminished seventh chord justified by stepwise chromatic approach in the bass to the root of the substitute chord in the next bar;
- Bar 14: V replaced by II-V once again;
- Bars 15-16: I replaced by a major seventh chord on ♭II = the 'surprise ending' reharmonisation for when the tonic appears as the closing note of the melody line.

Exercise 9.11, p400 CD Track 55
Now play through the simple reharmonisation below in each realisation, and then try improvising around it. If you're short of ideas, the demo track will give you a feel for some of the possibilities here.

Now let's see what a further development of these reharmonisations, using alternative scale material involving chromatic alterations, modes of the jazz minor scale, etc, might look like. First here are the additional reharmonisations:

- Bar 2: V⁷ reharmonised as V⁷alt;
- Bar 5: I (C^Δ) replaced by V of V of II (E⁷#5) = V of the chord (V of II) in the next bar ;
- Bar 6: V⁷ of II reharmonised as V⁷♭9;
- Bar 8: V⁷ reharmonised as V⁷#11;
- Bar 10: V⁷ of ♭II (= existing tritone substitution for I⁷) reharmonised as V⁷#11 of ♭II;
- Bar 12: a major seventh substitution, this time reharmonising the fifth as a major seventh (on ♭VI);
- Bar 14 (1): minor seventh chord on II (Dm7) reharmonised as a half-diminished seventh chord (D⌀7);

- Bar 14 (2): V^7 reharmonised as V^{7}alt;
- Bar 15-16: note the removal of the existing major seventh subsitution (♭II), which in this case would reduce the effectiveness of Valt in the preceding bar (as tritone interchangeability between V^{7}alt and ♭II$^{7♯11}$ means the two chords now share too many notes to form a resolution).

SECTION 4 | UNIT 9

Exercise 9.12 CD Track 56

Here's the more advanced reharmonisation. As a guide, some suggested scales for improvising over the more advanced chords are indicated. Once again, the demo track gives a flavour of what can be done here.

UNIT 9 | SECTION 4

Let's now turn to the second reduction of 'Amazing Grace', based on the 19th-century version shown earlier. In this case there's less reason to consider adapting the phrase structure to produce a more regular 16-bar phrase, as the more contrapuntally elaborated texture makes the harmonic rhythm more fluid. In the earlier stages of learning to improvise over reductions you'll find that it's worth 'straightening out' irregular phrase structures, as a more regular structure tends to provide a more flexible harmonic basis for improvising.

At the same time, though, this may itself create problematic features that then call for further adjustments. This is illustrated by what happens when we do this to the 19th-century version of 'Amazing Grace':

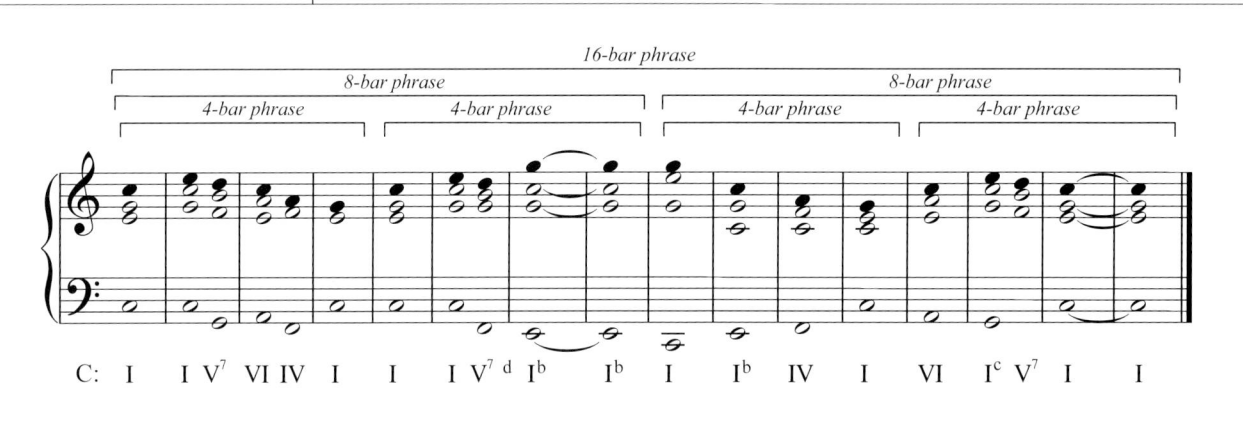

Here the existing phrase structure makes it natural to add an extra bar at the end of each seven-bar phrase, giving us a neat structure of two eight-bar phrases, and the easiest way to do this, as we saw with the previous reduction, is to prolong the final chord of each seven-bar phrase by one extra bar. However, the result here is two bars of I^b at the end of the first eight-bar phrase, followed by a bar of I and another bar of I^b at the start of the next one. This means a lack of significant harmonic development as we pass from the end of the first phrase to the start of the second, which diminishes the musical effectiveness of the structure as a whole.

Note that in the original 14-bar version the unexpectedly shorter three-bar phrase at the end of the first half means that a similar problem is largely avoided: the abbreviated phrase structure compensates for the lack of development in the harmony by moving us on to the new melodic phrase more quickly than we expect. (That's a perfect example of how phrase structure is used flexibly in classical music to accommodate subtle features of melodic or harmonic development.) The weakness of the 16-bar version could, perhaps, be rectified by making changes to the chord structure in bars 7-10. However, for our purposes right now it makes better sense to keep to the original harmonic structure as it appears in the 14-bar version.

> The fact that a reduction gives us a structure in which harmony and melody are already coordinated with respect to phrase structure means we can improvise according to classical principles without struggling to make the complex decisions explored in the last section. Classical composers have more time to work through those choices, but as we've seen, unless you're a specialist in a particular historical style, idiom or genre, then from the point of view of improvising this is unrealistic. Using a reduction leaves us free to focus on elaborating the different melodic, harmonic, and contrapuntal possibilities that a given structure allows for. At the same time it affords much more flexibility and scope for exploring your own ideas than simply embellishing or varying an existing piece of music.

When improvising using a skeleton the most straightforward approach to melody is to introduce melodic figures just ahead of the goal notes that then approach these more or less directly or indirectly, using a combination of simple stepwise movement and/or leaps (based on chord-notes). Notice how the same elaborations can be realised in different metres, for different overall effects:

See below how transferring this into a slightly more complex metre such as simple quadruple or compound duple time makes it natural for us to add further melodic elaborations. At the same time, though, the lengthening of individual bars relative to the

harmonic rhythm makes us more aware of the lack of harmony development at certain points in the structure. We should then compensate for this by introducing more melodic elaboration – eg, the bassline elaborations shown in the example. (Failing this, some sort of modification of the harmony will be required, just like with the 16-bar version.)

As we gain confidence in improvising over structures like these, it can be fun to take the reduction process further. In the examples so far what's been removed is only the surface layer of embellishment in the music – what in technical terms is referred to as the **foreground**. Further reduction involves uncovering even more basic structures. As the next example shows, we can remove melodic and harmonic elements within the skeleton itself that are less than absolutely essential, where these themselves can be seen as resulting from decorative embellishments of more basic melodic movements or reharmonisations of simpler chord progressions. Such elements are known as the **middleground** texture or structure. Removing these exposes the most fundamental elements of the structure, which often turn out to be surprisingly simple – what's known as the structural **background**.

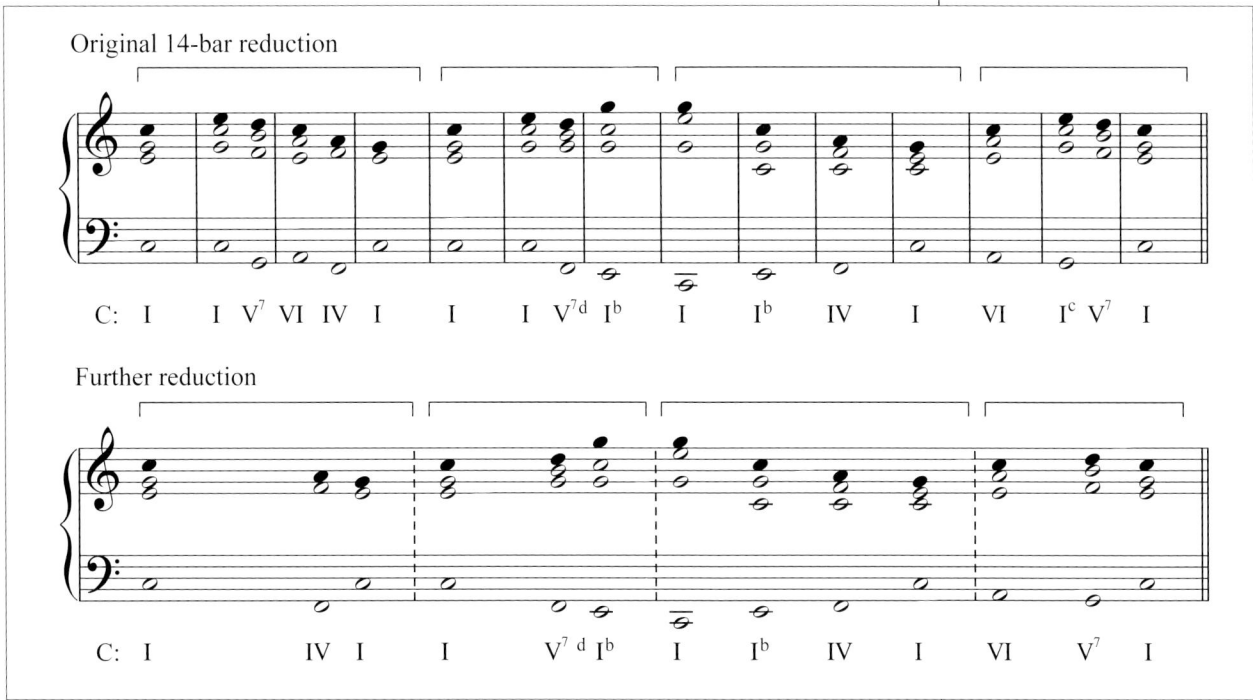

There may be several stages to this process of reducing music to its most basic level. (For example, the next example shows a second stage of reduction that happens to include the removal of any references to a structure of bar-divisions.) It's interesting from the point of view of analysing how music is put together to follow this through as far as it can go, but for improvising it often makes more sense to stop somewhere along the line, because the more we strip pieces down the less differentiated they become.

Once we've made a further reduction of some sort we're in a position to consider alternative forms of elaboration of the middleground (as well as the foreground). This may involve inserting new goal notes into the melodic skeleton, or new chords (or substitutions), or relocating the basic material relative to phrase-structure divisions and/or metrical divisions and subdivisions. Let's start with the last option first.

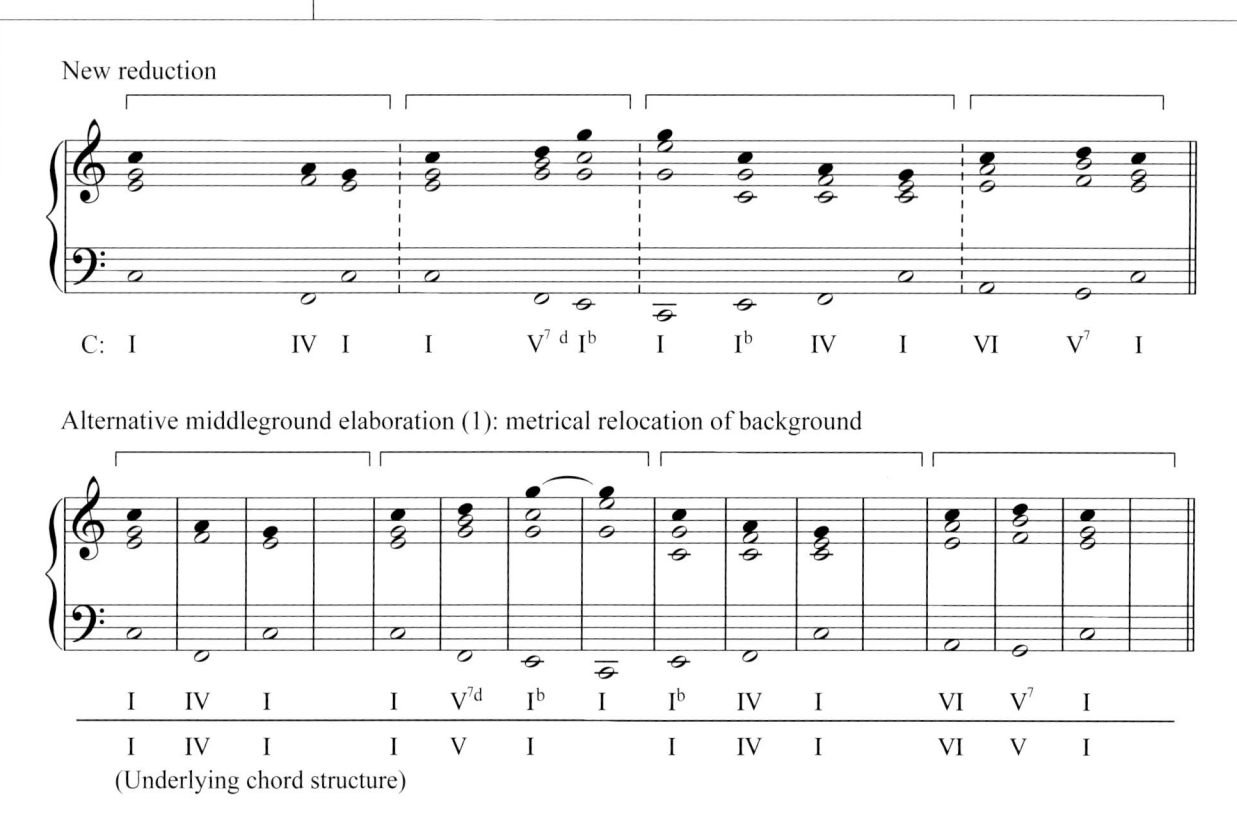

Here the background structure has been relocated into a more regular 16-bar framework. Note how this already begins to solve the problem mentioned earlier when we were discussing the consequences of adjusting the original 14-bar structure to make it more regular. In fact, stripping it down to a more basic level before trying to turn it into a 16-bar structure gives us more scope to adapt the harmony to the latter.

The next example illustrates a simple way of doing this, in which some extra chords are introduced, in this case without changing the melodic skeleton. (In this case each additional chord is put somewhere in the middle of one of the basic three-chord background progressions, whose final chord in each case must then be pushed back to the next bar, where it would have still been sounding anyway. In others things may not be so simple: we may find we have to adjust the basic structure of the goal notes as well.)

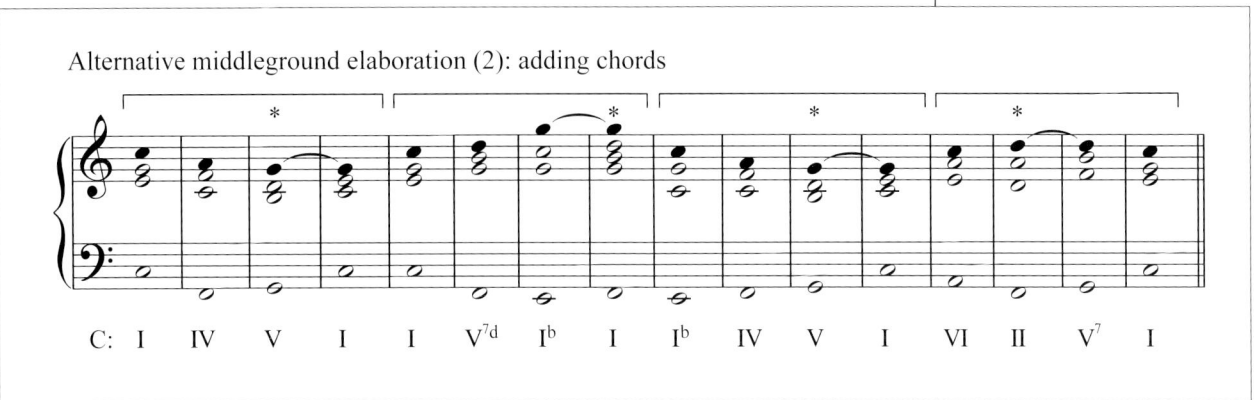

What we now have is an alternative 16-bar framework – one which at some level remains the same as the one extracted from the 19th-century version of 'Amazing Grace', but which in some important respects offers more scope as a starting point for improvisation. Notice the simplicity of the melodic skeleton, in which the goal-notes are now grouped together into three-note contours.

If we feel confident enough, we can opt to make this our new point of departure for improvising – just letting the rest of the music take shape as we play. If not, systematically adding further elaborations of the middleground to produce a progressively more specific structure will gradually bring us back towards the type of playing scenarios we've explored earlier – where our improvising is confined to varying and embellishing the 'surface' or 'foreground' of the music.

Note how even small additions can make a structure more inspiring as a starting point for exploring our ideas while we are actually playing. The next example adds just one note to the first, second, and fourth phrases of the skeleton, but this is enough to give the melodic contour a more individual and expressive character.

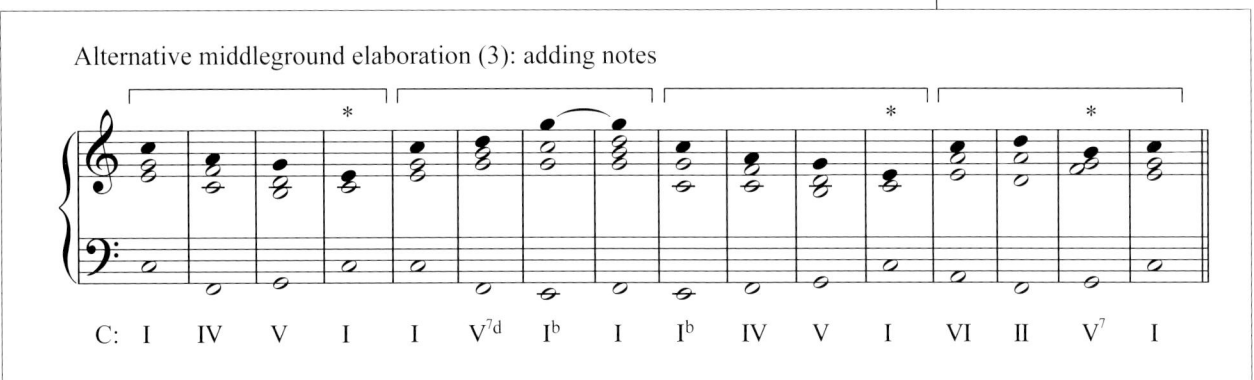

Now let's take a look at the third version of the reduction of 'Amazing Grace': the one based on the 18th-century choral arrangement shown earlier (as a piano transcription). The influence of folk music can be clearly heard here in the very simple and rather static character of the harmony. This gives it its charming, 'folksy' feel, and moreover removes the need to keep to the 14-bar structure just to compensate for a lack of harmonic movement towards the middle of the structure, as we did when first exploring the reduction of the 19th century version (though there's nothing to prevent us opting for this if we wish to.)

> The 18th-century arrangement of 'Amazing Grace' used here as a starting point for improvisation shows that vernacular styles of music making in Western culture – ie, those practised by ordinary people as part of their everyday culture, rather than just by professional artists – need not be limited to simple solo melodies or melodies with chords, as modern folk and popular music might tend to suggest. Such arrangements (eg, the 'West Gallery' tradition) reflect a rich musical culture in which high art was blended with everyday folk music-making, and professional composing with amateur improvising. West Gallery music is the term now used to refer to the sacred music of 18th-century provincial English parish churches and nonconformist chapels, performed by and often written specifically for amateurs.

Here's the existing reduction, which in this case we've chosen to adapt so as to make a more regular 16-bar phrase, followed by a further reduction:

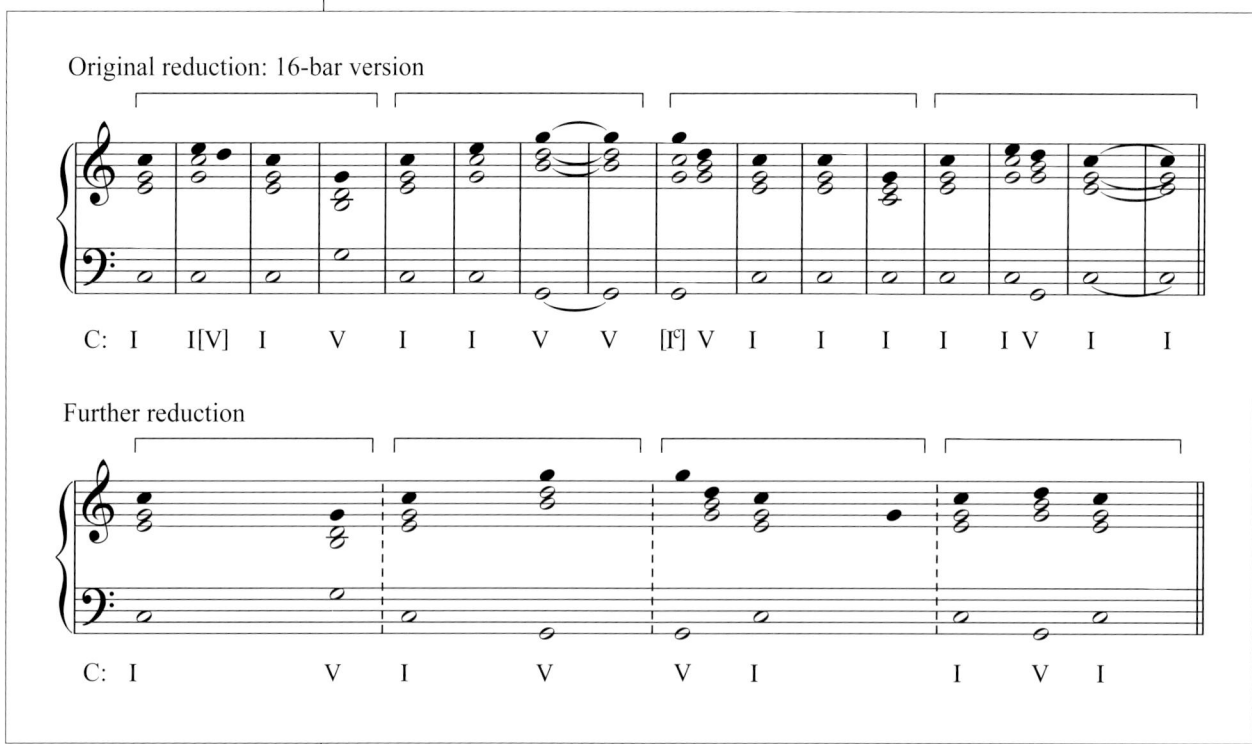

At the level of this further reduction we get a simple juxtaposition of chords I and V. This makes the role of melodic contour more important in determining the overall sense of shape and movement. If we focus on this we then see that a further reduction is possible, as the contour in the third part of the structure contains an anticipatory decoration of the larger melodic descent from the high point (the high G), through D, to the final C.

Making this extra reduction exposes an even more basic contour and, with this, the underlying movement of the harmony, which we can now see consists of two movements from I to V followed by a single movement from V to I. (Note how in this case the melodic reduction guides the harmonic one. Which of these takes priority can be a matter of the style and structure of the music, but also of what we're looking to end up with as a starting point for improvisation.)

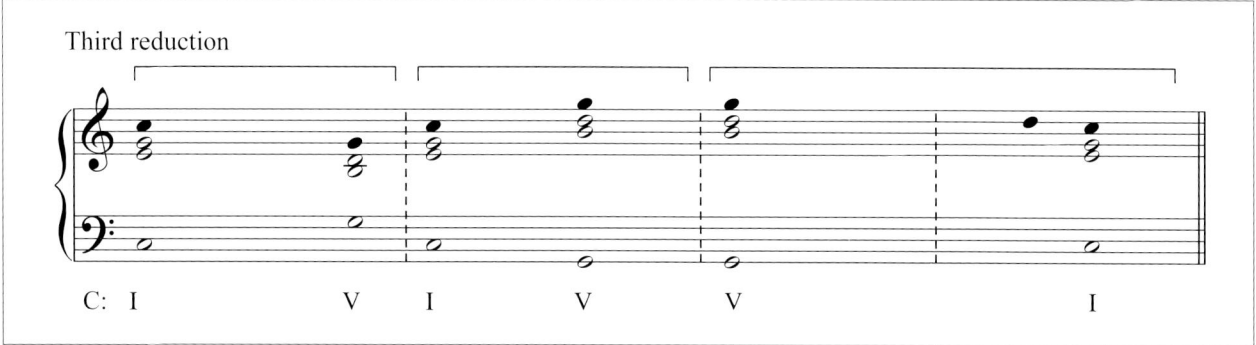

A structure like this can serve as a starting point for alternative middleground elaborations. As with the reduction of the 19th-century arrangement, we can begin by repositioning the elements relative to a basic structure of metrical divisions, generating a more defined phrase structure. In this case this is done by making the two chords of each harmonic movement span an entire four-bar or eight-bar phrase:

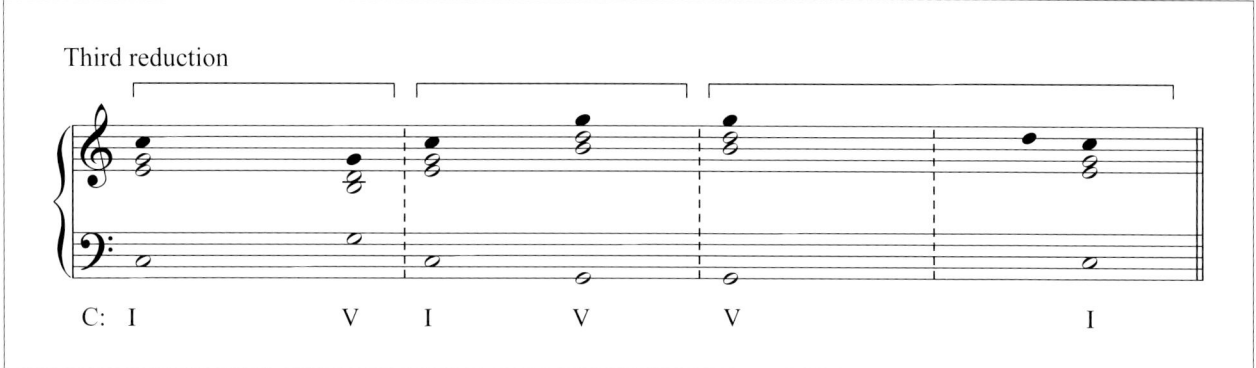

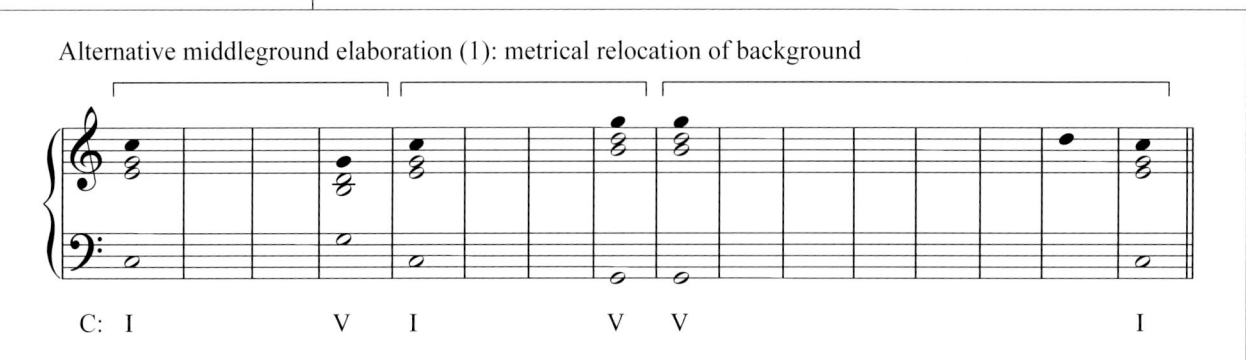

Alternative middleground elaboration (1): metrical relocation of background

As before, we can then add chords and/or additional goal notes, as the example opposite (p411) illustrates. In this particular middleground elaboration, the fact that the first half of the background ends on V while the second half starts on the same chord is seen as offering a good pretext for a modulation to the dominant and back to the tonic. The first version of this elaboration introduces just chords, while the second allows additional goal notes to emerge naturally from the implied voice-leading in the second half. Note how these form a stepwise descent between the melody notes of the background structure. The third variant illustrates a further option for middleground elaboration, with some of the notes in this stepwise descent delayed to create a series of expressive suspensions. The effect of this is to establish some goal notes as harmonically unresolved, heightening the level of expressive tension in this part of the structure.

Alternatively, we might well decide that what's interesting about the reduced structure here is precisely its harmonic simplicity and vagueness, which are partly responsible for the charmingly 'folksy' feel of the original 18th-century polyphonic arrangement. In that case it'll make more sense to retain these and treat the background structure as largely melodic in its implications.

This second line of approach offers a good starting point for a more folk-oriented style. Such improvising makes greater use of modal and/or pentatonic scale material, whose harmonic implications may be more ambiguous. (See Unit Ten for more discussion of the role of modes and pentatonic scales in different styles such as folk, rock, and some kinds of classical music.) When we opt for that, it can make sense to elaborate the middleground largely in terms of melodic contour, as the example on p412 illustrates.

Alternative middleground elaboration (2): adding chords

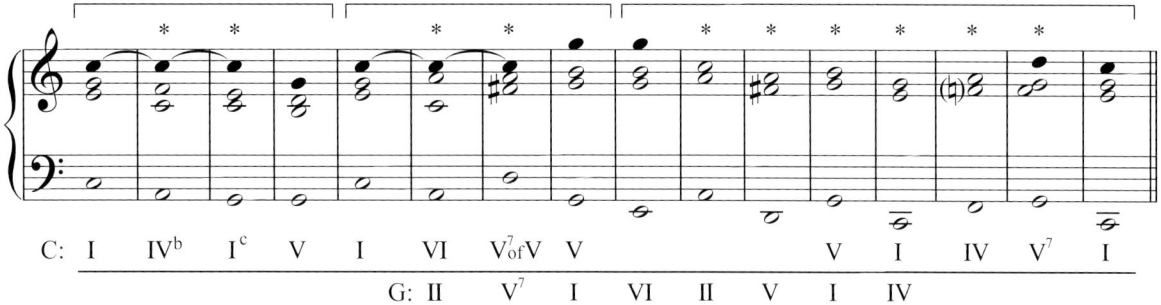

Alternative middleground elaboration (3): adding goal notes

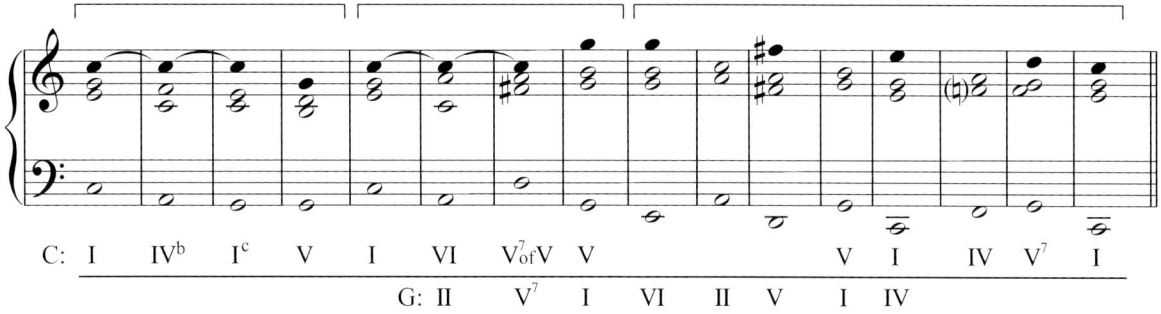

Alternative middleground elaboration (4): rhythmic displacement of goal notes to form suspensions

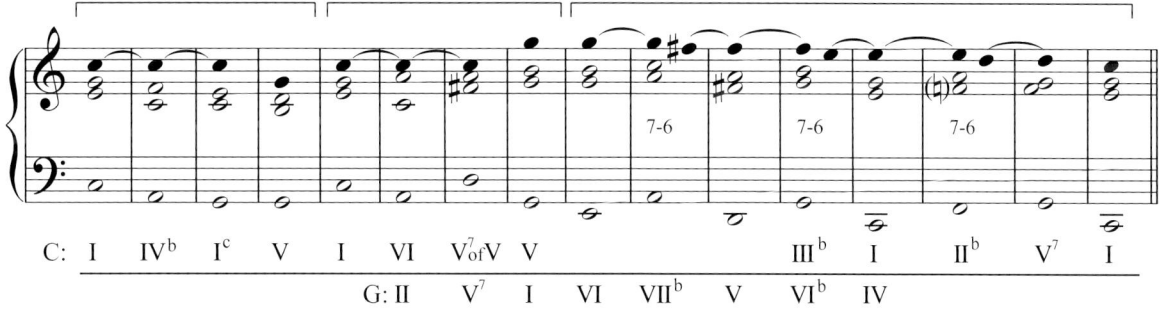

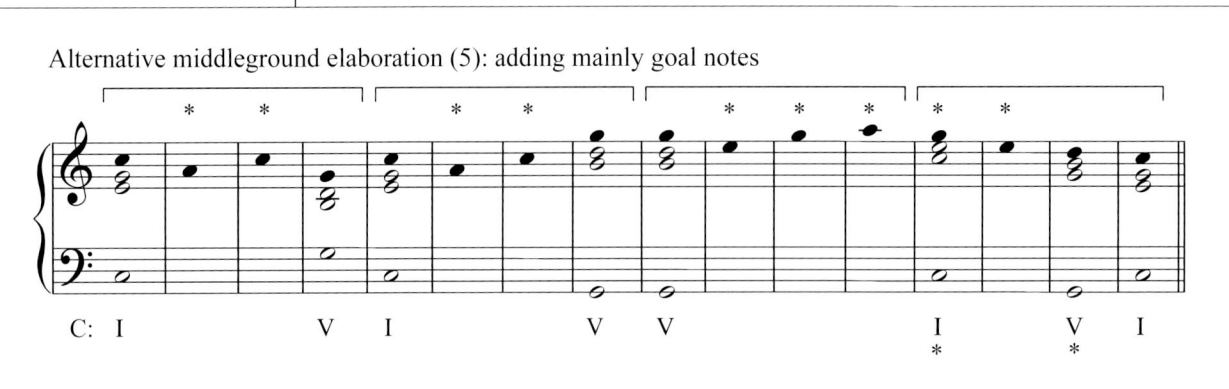

Alternative middleground elaboration (5): adding mainly goal notes

Only two chords have been added – to give a slightly clearer sense of harmonic direction towards the end. Note how the contour is elaborated using notes from the pentatonic major scale (on C, the keynote), without regard to whether these count as belonging to the chords (ie, triads) beneath them: the sixth and ninth above the root are treated as no more in need of stepwise resolution than the third or fifth. This looser understanding of what works harmonically over a chord is already familiar to us from jazz. That's no great surprise, considering jazz is itself partly derived from folk-based sources.

It's also worth comparing the four phrases of the melodic middleground to see how they unfold according to a kind of logic:

- Each phrase begins with a falling minor third.
- The second phrase is the same as the first, except that the final leap is inverted.
- The third phrase repeats the phrases at a higher pitch, but replacing the final leap with a rising stepwise movement.
- The fourth phrase repeats the beginning of the third phrase, replacing the remaining steps or leaps with falling stepwise movement.

Having a skeleton in place that itself unfolds in a logical or natural way is sure to increase the sense of coherence and direction that our improvising should have if it is to be effective. The question of how ideas can then be developed further (at the level of foreground elaboration) while preserving this will be the focus of the next section.

Let's finish with some exercises to practice the material just covered. The example right shows a straightforward arrangement of a well-known traditional Irish melody:

Exercise 9.13 CD Track 60

The material for this exercise shows an initial reduction of 'Londonderry Air' for you to improvise around. Note how in this case the metre of the original melody is preserved in the reduction. Listening to the demo track may help to get you started – it's in a folk style that preserves some features of the Irish or Celtic folk tradition from which the melody comes. (The use of spread chords resembles a Celtic harp, while the rhythmically loose melody is the sort of thing often heard played on Celtic pipes. The extensive use of the pentatonic scale is also typical of this kind of folk style.)

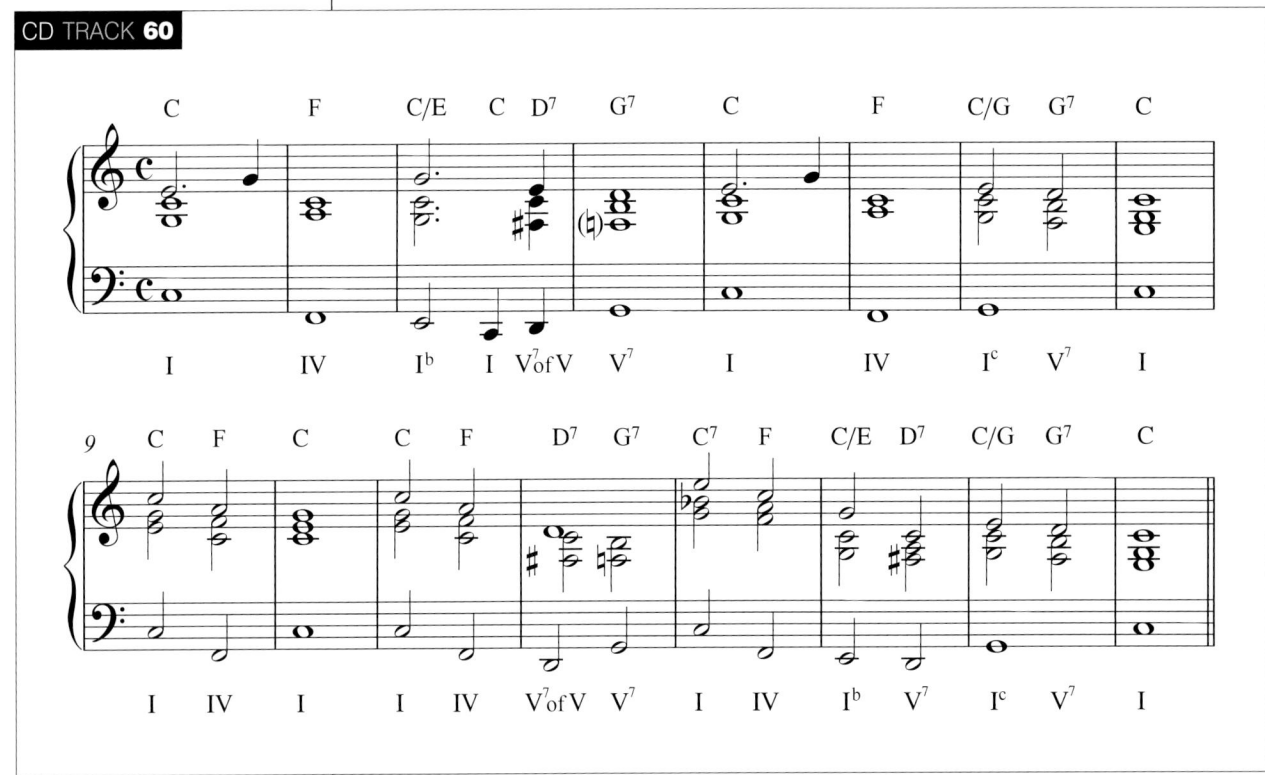

Exercise 9.14 CD Track 61

The material for this exercise shows a further reduction of 'Londonderry Air', this time at a level at which metrical structure is no longer specified. First try to work out your own alternative middleground elaborations of the reduction, and then try improvising around these, experimenting with different metres. Finally, try some improvisations based on just the background reduction itself. The demo track may give you some ideas. (Note that if we improvise directly around the background reduction itself, then the simplicity of the structure will need to be counterbalanced by elaborating some other aspects of the music. The demo shows one way to go about this: it makes use of a rhythmically elaborate rock style called 'halftime groove', where each beat gets subdivided into quarters rather than halves to generate a more highly syncopated feel.)

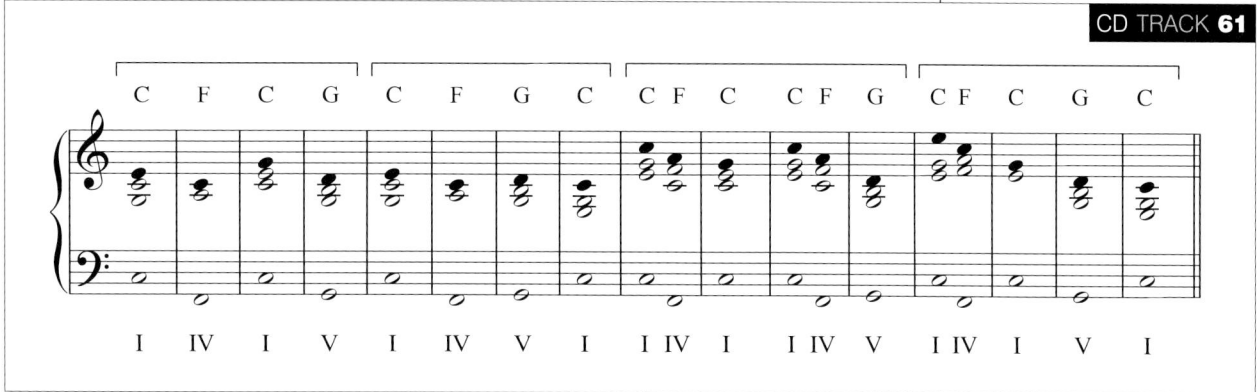

Exercise 9.15

Now here's an extreme reduction of 'Londonderry Air', similar to that created earlier for 'Amazing Grace'. Once again, try out different middleground elaborations as a basis for improvising. (You may also see if you can cope with the challenge of improvising freely over the background itself. Note that its simplicity may require you to elaborate your own middleground structures.)

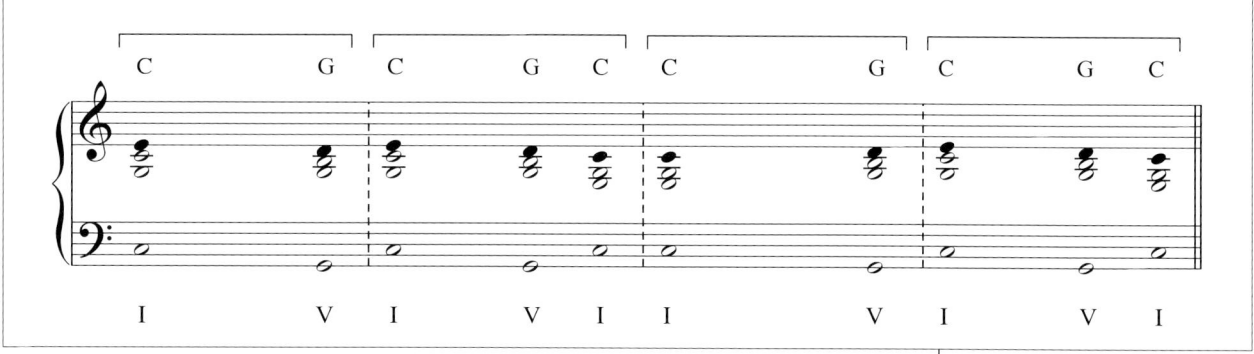

UNIT 9   SECTION 4

Exercise 9.16
Now take some other fairly simple pieces of music you like and try making similar reductions and elaborations yourself, before improvising around these.

> In this section we've only covered a few of the possible ways in which structures can be first reduced and then adapted (through alternative middleground elaborations) to provide fertile starting points for improvising. Once we've arrived at such a starting point there are, of course, many other techniques we can also apply, as we turn these structures into fully-fledged music. Some of these will be explored in the rest of this unit: not just as they relate to the melodic unfolding of ideas, but also in terms of the colouristic and textural effects that can be created out of them.

Working with ideas

Each time you sit down to improvise you'll probably be hoping to come out with some great musical ideas: perhaps a really catchy theme, or a memorable chord sequence – or maybe a rhythmic pattern that's just fun to play. That's natural, but it can also lead to problems. Why? Because these days the very idea of improvising tends to go hand in hand with another idea – the notion that when you make music, write poetry, or do anything else creative, you're doing the sort of thing that can be a spontaneous expression of your personal feelings, your state of mind, or even your personality.

At first glance it's hard to see that there could be a problem with this. Say, for example, you produce a melody that's really original and absolutely dead cool: we can hear that it relates to this or that existing style, but we can also recognise that you've created something special, with qualities that go beyond what's typical. Great. However, it's tempting to think of this as expressing something about how you feel or who you are, in the same kind of direct way that we think of a smile or a frown as directly revealing what a person feels about something. Then it's natural to believe you've succeeded in making public some characteristics of yourself that would, quite probably, otherwise not have been fully recognised by people around you. If you happen to be convinced that your own improvising is, or could be, something that others regard as special, or if they do actually regard it as special, then this shows that they could, will, or do regard you as special too. And who doesn't want that?

Yet this way of thinking can be as cruel as it can be kind. The same 'logic' that says you're special because the music you improvise is special says you're 'nothing special' if the music you improvise 'ain't special'. That puts you under a lot of pressure to prove things about yourself every time you sit down in front of those keys. And as far as good improvising is concerned this kind of pressure of self-expectation is enemy number one: it can make you self-conscious, tense, and worried, just when you want to be as playful, relaxed, and open to new options as it's possible to be.

It also implies that since most of the time we never really know what others think about our improvising – for example, because they may not get to hear it, or may not tell us what they think when they do hear it – we never really get to know what they think, or would think, about us, given what our improvising is supposed to reveal about us. We're left thinking such lonely thoughts as "I think my improvising's brilliant, so I must be brilliant." That's not much fun because, let's face it, what most of us want is to be recognised by others as the great genius we secretly already believe ourselves to be. Once the realisation clicks in that it's hard, if not impossible, to get to the point where others do recognise this, we can easily get disillusioned and start wondering whether it's time to give up.

The only way to avoid these problems is to recognise that they come from fallacious ways of thinking about what goes on when we make music, or do anything else, that we find expressive in ways that seem to reveal something about us as people. It's not that making music or other things reveals nothing – it's just that it's not as simple and straightforward as the comparison with our direct expressions of feelings through physical appearances suggests. It's this simplistic model that makes the kind of destructive ways of thinking mentioned above, which musicians and creative people often fall into, seem compelling.

From a practical standpoint there's an even bigger reason to reject this way of thinking, which is that it tends to confuse us as to the nature of what really goes on when we improvise music. The idea that we express ourselves through making music in the same way as we do through, say, smiling when we're happy or crying when we're sad, encourages us to think of improvisation in terms of spontaneity. We get the idea that improvisation is something spontaneous, whereas composition is something carefully planned. This notion of improvisation became popular in the early 19th century, as part of the wider cultural movement known as Romanticism. (However, if you've read the introduction to this book you'll also know that it led to a craze for improvising that actually resulted in the disappearance of improvising from classical concert music, as audiences got sick of the empty virtuosity and melodramatic emotionalism it brought with it – surely not a good result from the improviser's point of view.)

Equating improvisation with just the spontaneous aspect of making music – whatever that really means – makes it impossible to appreciate what's really involved when we do it, because we can't then make sense of what it means to develop musical ideas in the way that we actually do. This is because musical ideas are developed by improvisers in two different but interconnected ways at the same time:

- There's the working out of ideas (and the possibilities they open up) that occurs before, during, and across one or more improvisations.
- There's the working through of ideas (and the possibilities they open up) that occurs as one particular individual improvisation unfolds.

Working out your ideas means exploring and defining your ideas as a result of repeated attempts to make use of them. It's cumulative, since the more we do it, the more aware we become of the musical potential our raw material has, in terms of how it can be varied and transformed, how it contrasts with the alternatives, etc. Working through your ideas, on the other hand, refers to the way in which the actual music you're making as you improvise unfolds and realises these possibilities over time.

Clearly, if you think that the defining feature of improvisation is that musical ideas emerge and get developed in an entirely spontaneous way as we play, then you've left no room to acknowledge the role played by the broader process of working out ideas over time that typically stretches across many instances of improvised performing. You'll probably think that all that matters is how your ideas are worked through as you are improvising. Many people start out thinking that this is what improvisation amounts to, but it just isn't like that!

Both working ideas out and working ideas through are present in all music making, but how big a role each of them plays in shaping the way we think about ideas and their development varies from one musical culture or practice to the next. It tends to reflect the relative importance given to improvising and composing within the musical culture, but it also has implications for how ideas are treated in particular styles, both in terms of how they are worked out and how they are worked through.

> **Working out** and **working through.** We can also make this distinction for composed music, although here both elements are largely determined in advance of the actual realisation of the music (ie, its being performed). Then we can see that what really distinguishes improvised music from composed music has nothing to do with whether it's written down or not: it's just that in the former, how our musical ideas are worked through is at least partly determined as the music unfolds – as we are playing it – while in the latter this is hardly the case, if at all.

The best way to grasp these implications is to relate what goes on in different kinds of improvised music to the different roles we can think of a musical idea as playing, as we develop it, within or beyond the context of an actual perfomance.

The two basic ways of understanding the role of ideas in music are as **blocks** and as **threads**:

- Blocks are self-sufficient units that can be combined into larger structures (within which they are, normally, to some extent still identifiable as themselves).
- Threads are shorter stretches of musical material that can be woven together into a single longer stretch of material (within which they normally need not still be identifiable as themselves).

If we compare how musical phrases are put together in different classical traditions and in jazz, we can see that some of them tend more towards the model of musical ideas as building blocks, while others tend more towards the model of them as threads. As the diagram illustrates, the greater the role (or higher the status) of improvisation in the culture, the closer its model of an idea will be to threads, while the greater the role of composition, the closer it will be to that of blocks.

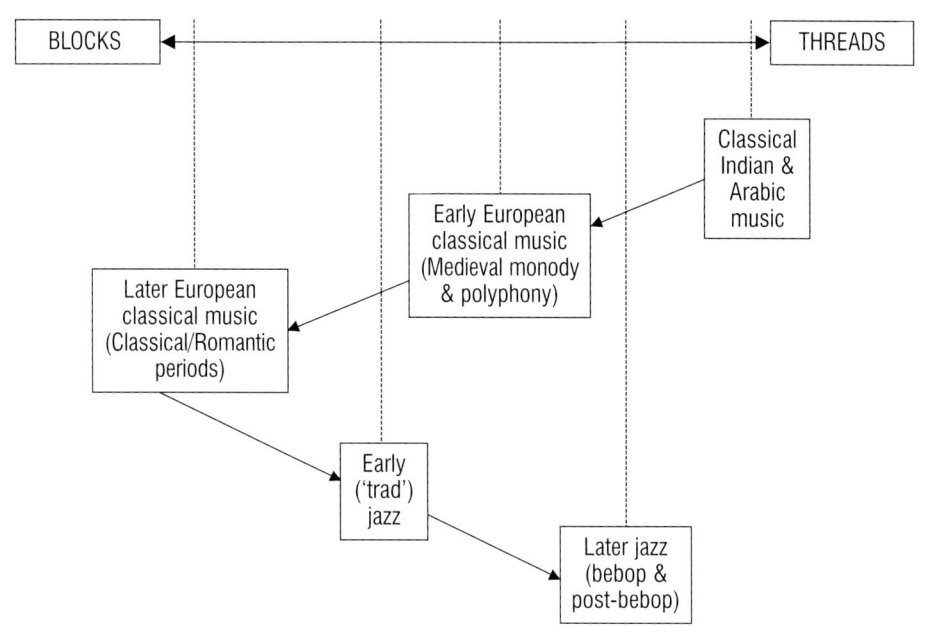

As you can see, there's also a clear path of evolution. It starts from Middle Eastern and Indian classical musics that date back to before the beginnings of Western classical music, and which influenced the latter in its early stages via Ancient Greek and then Byzantine culture: in these styles the greater role played by improvisation is manifested in a strong emphasis on treating musical material as threads. (Try listening to some music of this kind and you'll instantly perceive what we're talking about here – any attempt to carve up the melody line into self-contained motives or themes that fit together as parts of larger phrases seems arbitrary.)

The next stage is represented by early European classical music (and also by a great many European folk music idioms): here individual phrases tend to be separated from one another (like blocks), but aren't yet used systematically to build larger phrase structures.

Then come the Classical and Romantic periods of European classical music. (The Baroque period can be seen as a transition between the two stages of development, merging elements of both kinds of treatment of musical ideas in a very specific way that gives such music its distinctive quality of melodic unfolding.) Here we see a strict emphasis on phrase structure, with the building-block model of ideas most clearly in evidence. (It's no coincidence that these were the times when changes occurred that would eventually lead to the decline of improvisation as an element of Western art music, and the emergence of the composer as the exclusive role model for artistic creativity in music.)

After this comes traditional jazz (from the 1920s through to the 1940s), in which we see the beginnings of a move back in the opposite direction as melodic structures get loosened up as a result of being used as the basis for improvised jazz soloing.

Finally we arrive at bebop and modern jazz, in which we find ourselves encountering a much more fluid approach to melodic structure which, though otherwise different in many respects, shares the same thread-like way of developing melodic ideas as we find in the earliest non-European classical styles. (The diagram isn't meant to be exhaustive: it just shows one important and clearly identifiable line of development in the history of music – there are surely others too.)

The degree to which our notion of a musical idea approximates to the building-block or the thread model has consequences for how we approach developing ideas. What's more, these are pretty much the same consequences, whether we're doing so in the context of working them out or in that of working them through. However, before exploring some of these in practice it's worth mentioning a striking difference between how these two aspects stand in relation to each other in classical music on the one hand and in jazz on the other:

- In classical improvising, working ideas out and working them through generally remain distinct.
- In jazz improvising, working ideas out and working them through are to some extent mixed or merged together.

What does this mean? Well, to make sense of it, let's compare improvising to painting or drawing a picture. What's the difference between what a professional artist does, when working to fulfil a commission, and what someone does who's just doodling to pass the time of day? Normally the pro first does sketch after sketch – some of which may even go as far as looking like fully worked-out paintings – just to see how this or that idea works in practice. Only when they've done this to their satisfaction will they settle on making one possible version into the final finished picture. The doodler, on the other hand, doesn't care about making a finished picture at all: you can watch them just covering the same piece of paper with one drawing after another for the sake of the sheer fun of doing just that.

A classical improviser is much more like the pro artist than the doodler: there's a usually a clear boundary between trying out ideas to see how they work, which usually happens when practising or rehearsing, and letting those ideas develop in a particular way as an actual performance unfolds.

The opposite extreme from this isn't jazz improvising – at least not when the latter happens in a concert. It's **jamming** – something that most non-classical musicians do, whether they specifically play jazz or not. Just like doodling, we do it for its own sake, so there's no distinction between rehearsal and performance. That means there's no strict distinction between working out your ideas in rehearsal and working through your ideas as a particular improvisation unfolds.

Jamming usually takes place over an already familiar chord structure that gets repeated over and over again. (For example, the **12-bar blues**, which we'll look at in the next unit.) Jazz players also jam a lot, so when they improvise as part of a performance it tends to have a lot in common with jamming. The repetitive structure of the jazz song form – which cycles through the AABA structure over and over again – is handy here, as it allows them to keep coming back to the same material, trying out new variations and departures each time. So jazz improvising – and to a lesser extent other styles such as rock and pop, too – has something in common with jamming and something in common with classical improvising. This in turn means the distinction between working ideas out (in advance of an improvised performance, or over a series of these), and working ideas through, is sometimes relevant and sometimes not.

Now let's come back to the issue of what goes on when we try to work out or work through ideas in styles whose approach to developing ideas reflects the greater or lesser influence that improvisation has had in shaping the overall musical culture to which they belong. The diagram earlier highlighted four stages of development in what might loosely be called 'Western music', each corresponding to a different degree of emphasis on the model of musical ideas as 'blocks' or as 'threads'. (We've excluded classical Indian and Arabic music as these require systems of tuning and instruments that can't be 'translated' into what's possible on the modern piano.) Here are the stages of evolution once again:

STAGE OF EVOLUTION	APPROACH TO DEVELOPING IDEAS
Early European classical music (Medieval monody & polyphony)	Separate phrases (= blocks), but no hierarchical phrase structure (= threads)
Later European classical music (Classical/Romantic periods)	Separate themes and motifs (= blocks), with hierarchical phrase structure (= blocks)
Early ('trad') jazz	Continuous use of licks (= threads), loosely based around existing melodies with some phrase structure (= blocks)
Later jazz (bebop & post-bebop)	Continuous use of licks, motifs and scale-figures (= threads), without regard to anything more than the structure implied by the chords themselves

Now let's take a simple idea and see how it works when developed in terms of each of these approaches. In each case, we can identify the same three stages in the process of arriving at an actual improvisation based on the development of one or more initial ideas:

1 Working out the ideas themselves (as more or less like threads or blocks, depending on the style).

UNIT 9 | SECTION 4

2 Working out possible ways in which these ideas could be worked through: ie, different possible ways in which they could unfold as part of a longer improvised line.
3 Working through the ideas as the actual improvisation unfolds.

Here's the initial material – a four-note figure based on the C major pentatonic scale:

The approach typical of the earlier stages in the development of Western classical music requires us to develop a string of separate phrases out of a figure like this, without embedding them in a larger phrase structure. As we work our ideas out, then, the first thing is to focus on identifying a range of possible phrases – or variations on the given phrase – that will eventually work as a simple succession of ideas:

The next thing we need to do is to work out ways in which this material could be worked through. Here, too, we need to focus on creating a sequence of linked phrases rather than on combining a given phrase with others (or with variations of itself) to produce larger units.

The example below shows just two of the many possibilities. Note how the first option involves phrases of varying length, making it harder to group the phrases into larger units in the sort of way that would generate a phrase structure built of treating ideas as blocks. (You'll find this feature in many traditional folk melodies, as well as in many of the melody lines of medieval classical music.) Hence the effect is of a pure succession of ideas. By contrast, the second option uses phrases of identical length, with an implied skeleton of goal notes formed by the sequence of long notes that come at the ends of the phrases. This already hints at the possibility of a very simple form of phrase structure emerging. Nevertheless, this possibility is not realised due to the lack of rhythmic-metrical differentiation between and within phrases. Hence the effect one again is largely that of a pure linear sequence of ideas.

Finally comes the stage where we sit down and aim to create a more or less definitive improvised performance. That needn't mean a public performance though: unless you're really confident about what you're doing it's best to think of it as just the point where you try to 'commit' yourself to following a single line of development through as far as it'll go. Remember, if it's not a public performance you can still approach the whole thing in a pretty relaxed way: if the music doesn't turn out as you were hoping it would, just 'uncommit' yourself and start over again!

Exercise 9.17
Play around with the ideas shown above: see if you can discover more possibilities and listen to find out which ideas and sequences of ideas appeal to you most. Then make your own improvisations as particular ways of working through some of these. Don't worry about arriving at a single definitive version, though. Instead, treat it as more like 'doodling'. Only when you feel really confident about your ideas should you consider trying to improvise a final version for others to hear. For this style of working with ideas it's probably best to keep to a single-line (monodic) texture, but this can be executed in either hand. (Transpose the material down an octave if you wish to bring it into the part of the keyboard more accessible to the left hand.)

In contrast to the last two examples, the approach typical of the next stage in the development of Western classical music does require us to work out phrases in such a way that they can be embedded in a larger structure. The next example illustrates a few of the different techniques that could be used to develop our initial idea in this kind of way.

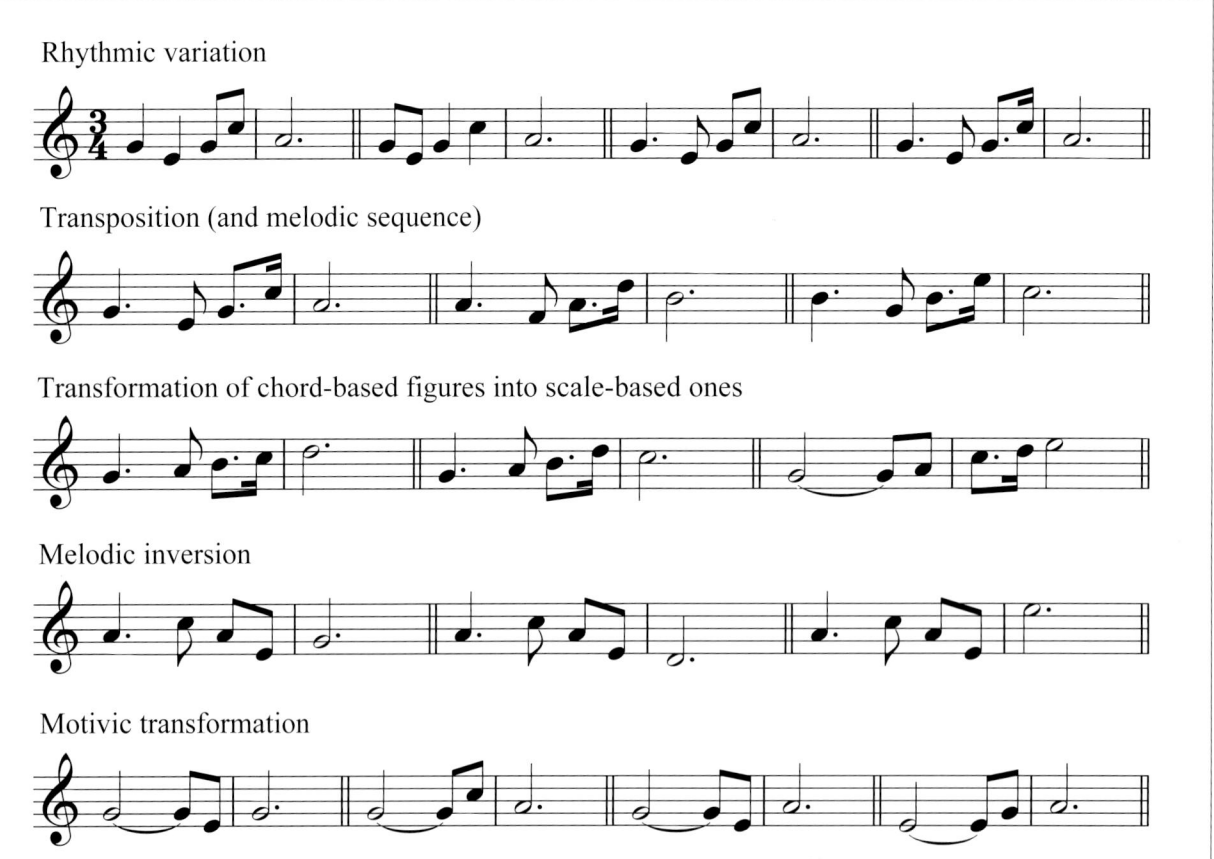

Note the increased differentiation of melodic ideas from the point of view of metre and rhythm: this plays an essential role in defining how they can fit together as blocks to make larger units.

When it comes to exploring ways of working through these ideas, two techniques can often prove indispensable. These are: (a) putting complementary phrases next to each other for a question-and-answer effect, and (b) letting larger phrases grow out of smaller motifs.

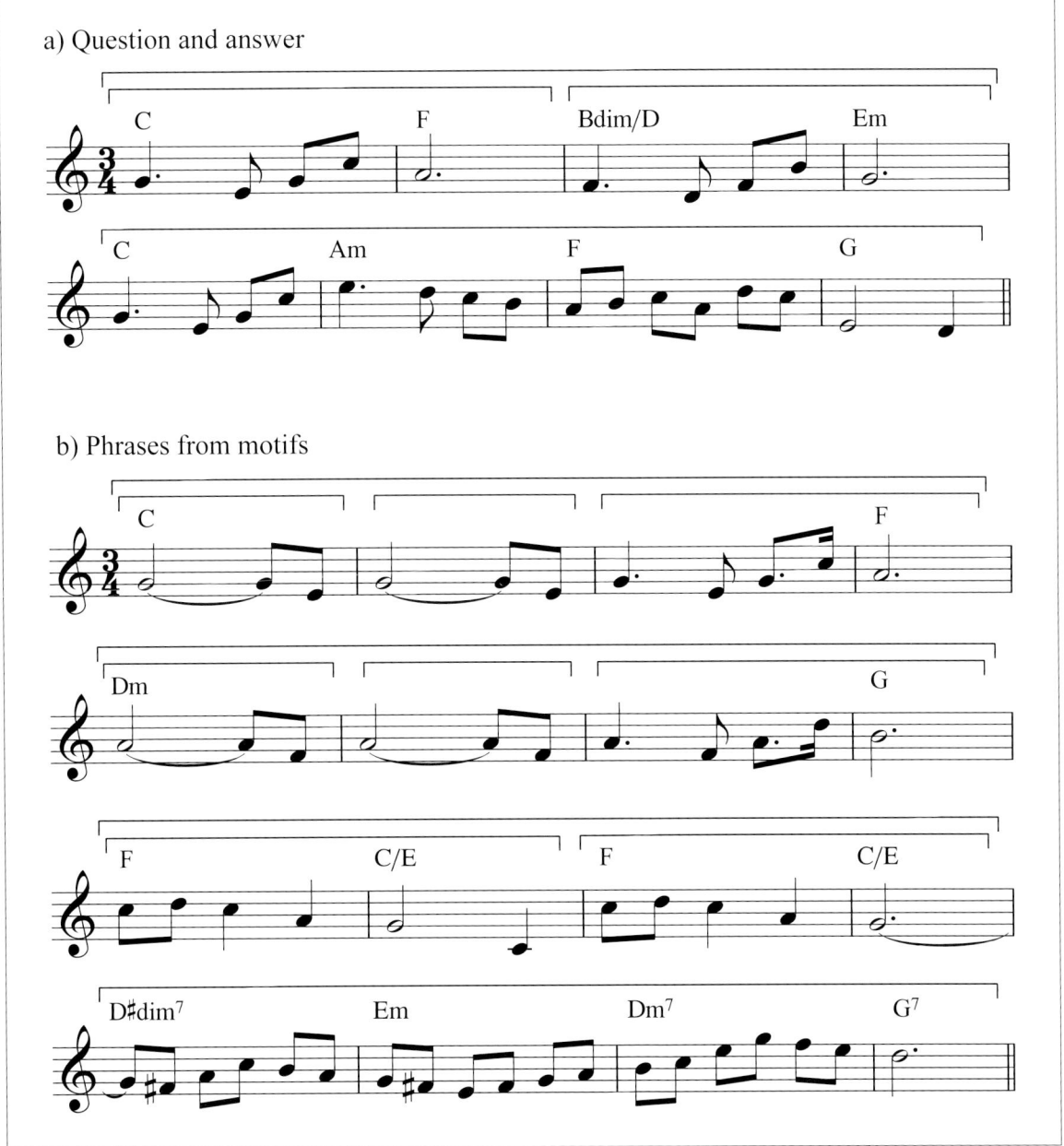

Exercise 9.18

Now try working out your ideas in a classical style that uses the building-block approach to developing material. First just work on the ideas, then try out options for how they can be worked through as part of a longer improvised structure. Explore both the question-and-answer and phrases-from-motives techniques.

The third approach to consider is that which we encounter in mainstream traditional

jazz (and perhaps also to some extent in classical music of the later Romantic period – from Chopin and Liszt onwards). Here musical ideas in the form of licks are threaded together to form a continuous line, which is nevertheless loosely based around an existing melody and/or chord structure – one which itself implies a fairly simple phrase structure. How we thread licks together will of course depend on the particular harmony and melodic skeleton provided by the existing melody. However, in jazz the first stage is just to work out the possible variations and ways of combining licks independently of this.

Remember what we said in Unit Eight: licks exist in the grey area between fully defined musical themes on the one hand, and raw materials like scales and arpeggiated chords on the other. It can also be helpful to first explore the shapes without them being defined straight away in terms of rhythm or metre. The example on the opposite page shows how our initial idea can be varied to produce a range of possible figures.

Then we simply play around with the different ways these figures can be strung together, as the following example demonstrates. Notice they still haven't been placed in any relationship to metre or rhythm:

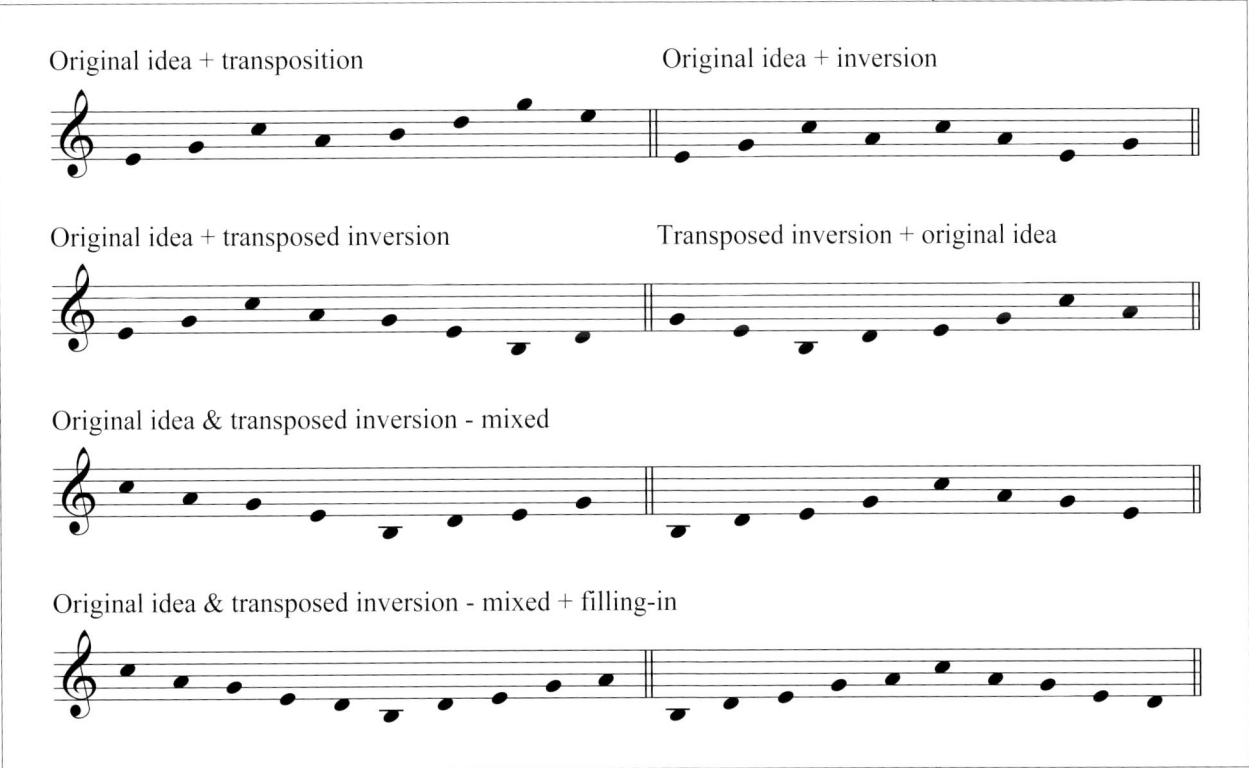

Fitting these shapes into the swung rhythms typical of jazz will then produce further variations, as we can see if we take a simple two-bar version of the figure as a starting point:

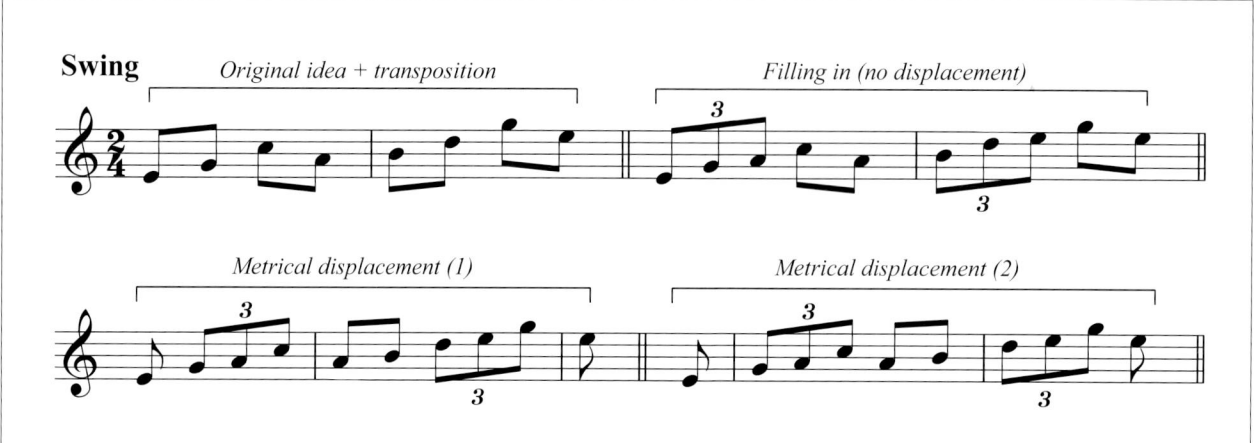

Once we've arrived at a sense of how a lick can be developed in terms of both its shape and its relationship to metre, we can start to thread ideas together into a longer line. In traditional jazz this is usually done with reference to an existing melody as well as chords, using the goal-note approach discussed earlier. All we do is use licks to take us from one goal note to the next, creating whatever shapes we want in between by combining them freely. The next example illustrates this, using the first eight bars of one of the reductions of 'Londonderry Air' created earlier:

Now here's the first four bars of the same reduction in a later jazz style – the sort of thing a bebop player might improvise. This time the phrase structure suggested by the original melody is pretty much buried beneath a continuous stream of figures created by threading licks together, interspersed with scale and chord fragments.

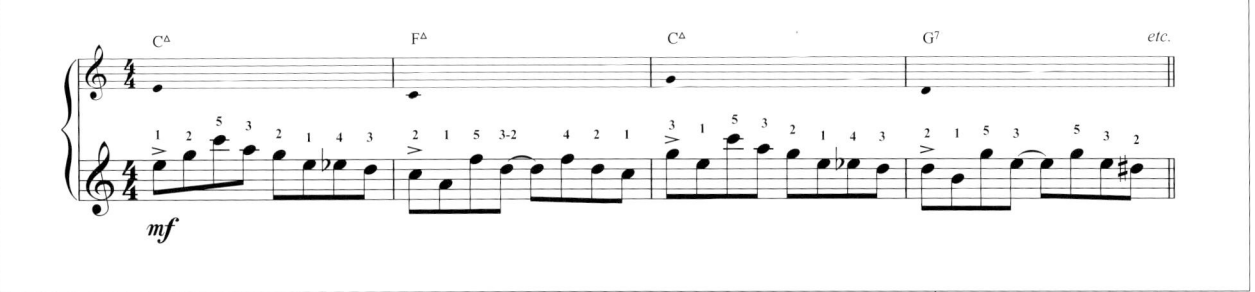

Exercise 9.19
Now try working out your ideas in a jazz style, using the thread-based approach to developing material. First just work out some licks that you like, then try joining them together into longer stretches of material. Finally, try out options for working them through as part of a longer improvised structure. Only consider trying to improvise a final version for others to hear when you feel confident about your ideas. Alternatively, you might prefer to try jamming in a jazz style with some other musicians. (For this, see the the 12-bar blues sequence later in the book.)

> Remember, not all styles make an equally sharp division between the final stage of development, where ideas are worked through as part of an actual improvised performance, and the preceding stages, where ideas (and options for working them through) are worked out. Classical music tends to make a sharp distinction, whereas jamming (like doodling) makes no distinction, and jazz lies somewhere in between. So why not experiment with mixing up these approaches and styles to see what works best for you? Nowadays many jazz musicians have moved away from 'live' jamming and are closer to the classical model, treating a final performance as the only definitive improvisation, and exclusively preparing for that. But why not try the opposite? Try musical doodling (or jamming) using a classical approach. See what happens when you let the line between rehearsal and performance get blurred in these styles too. This can also help you to loosen up as a player in any style.

UNIT 9 | SECTION 4

Colour and texture

Jazz and classical approaches to piano improvising handle colour and texture in different ways, but the best way to understand these is to see them as part of a single larger process of evolution.

The basic format for jazz textures is a melodic line unfolding against a chord-based accompaniment that also usually performs a rhythmic function. The exact nature of the latter depends on whether the pianist plays solo or as part of a group. If the former, then the accompaniment, which is normally mainly in the left hand, must provide the entire basis for the rhythmic texture that is supposed to support the melody and drive the music forwards. There are two ways in which this can be done:

- Rhythmically active bassline plus chords.
- Rhythmically active chords only (with bass line implied).

Bassline plus chords is the traditional approach to left-hand texture in jazz. It derives from earlier classical styles of left hand accompaniment common in 19th-century piano music. These typically alternate a bass note on the first beat of the bar (or on any other point in the metre where a chord change occurs) with chords in the lower-middle register of the piano.

Traditional jazz piano does the same, but tries to give the bass line a more prominent rhythmic character of its own – like that which we typically get from the

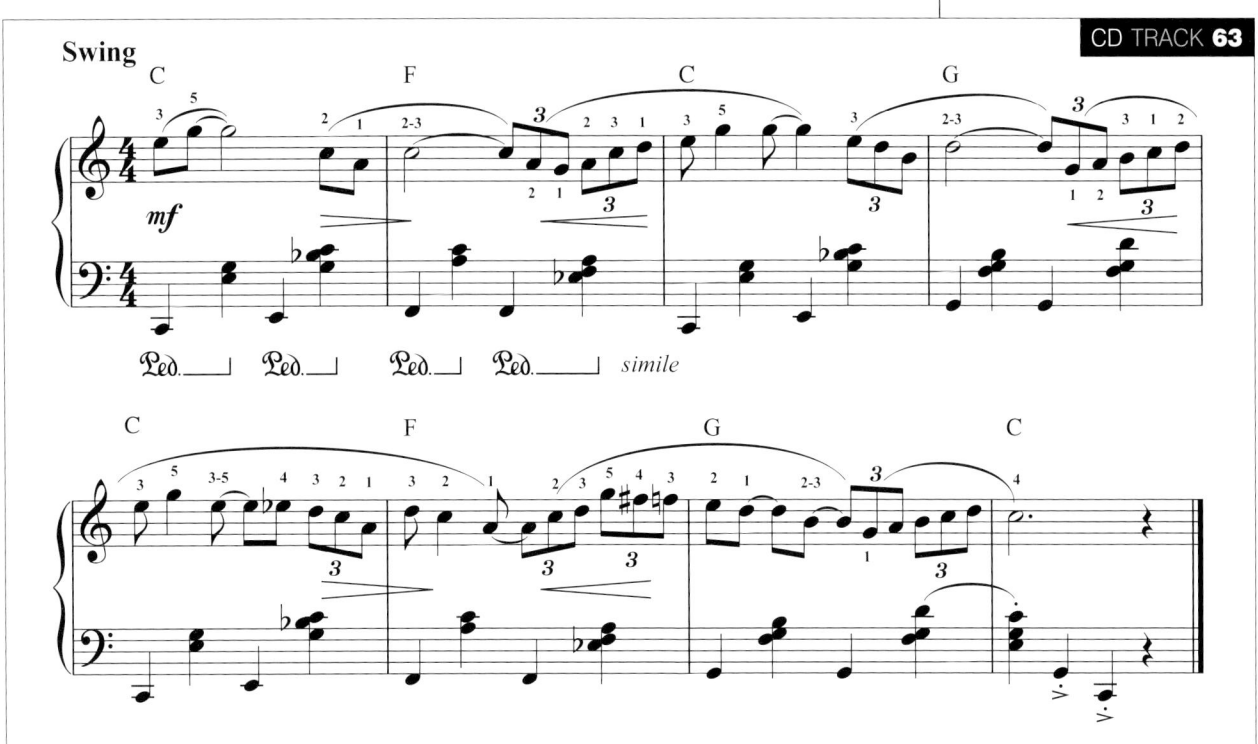

double bass in a jazz ensemble. This style is known as 'stride'. (You'll also come across this left-hand style in ragtime – the immediate precursor of jazz.)

Here are the classical and trad jazz versions of the working through shown in the previous section, this time over typical left-hand textures of this sort. Note how the jazz version adds some dominant sevenths to reinforce the texture, left and above.

The rhythmically active bass line in left-hand 'stride' piano is related to another feature of early jazz, the well-known 'walking bass' effect. Here the left hand goes in further in imitating the effect of a double bass in a jazz ensemble, and any chords must be incorporated into the right hand. Note how the left-hand texture makes use of chord outlines and stepwise movements, with the latter based on both diatonic and chromatic scales (p432, top).

Later jazz styles tend to move away from the bassline plus chords formula, focusing instead on the second option, chords only. This is especially so with bebop. The chords themselves may often be syncopated, to ensure the texture they create adds rhythmic drive to the music (p432, bottom).

Note how when played at speed the distinction between melody and accompaniment gets blurred here. This is a result of the combination of less defined melodic material and denser harmonies. We start to hear both together as just a single indivisible texture. (Around the same time as bebop emerged in the 1950s, classical composers were also experimenting with dissolving the boundary between melody and harmony, using 'pointillistic' textures.)

The jazz model of pianistic texture has always kept to the format of right-hand melody and left-hand chordal accompaniment, but it's worth keeping in mind that it didn't invent this from scratch – it inherited it from classical music. Hence it links in to a more extended process of evolution as regards texture in Western keyboard music.

The Renaissance saw musical textures emerge from a long period dominated first by **monody** (ie, single-line texture) and then **polyphony** (ie, independent lines combined), thanks to the introduction of a new texture, **homophony** (ie, a single melody line supported by block chords). The result was a new kind of **polyphonic-homophonic format** that allowed melodies to be accompanied by chords while still treating this combination as also forming a polyphonic texture. Hence voice-leading was treated with almost as much care as in pure polyphonic music, and the possibilities for contrapuntal relations between melody and bass (and other parts in the chordal texture) were explored. (This also meant that in subsequent classical styles melodies were not always placed in the top part – in contrast to jazz.)

> The polyphonic-homophonic format became the template for piano music right through to the early 20th century, when jazz borrowed and adapted it. Knowing about the stages it passed through before this will give you a better understanding of the possibilities it offers – even for jazz. Even if jazz doesn't often make use of these other possibilities, they remain latent in the format itself, so we shouldn't think of them as just a feature of classical idioms.

The next example shows a straightforward melodic theme presented in polyphonic-homophonic format, in the style of earlier classical music of the Renaissance and Baroque periods. The first version shows the melody accompanied by just plain chords, while the second (p434) adds some elaboration of the bass line:

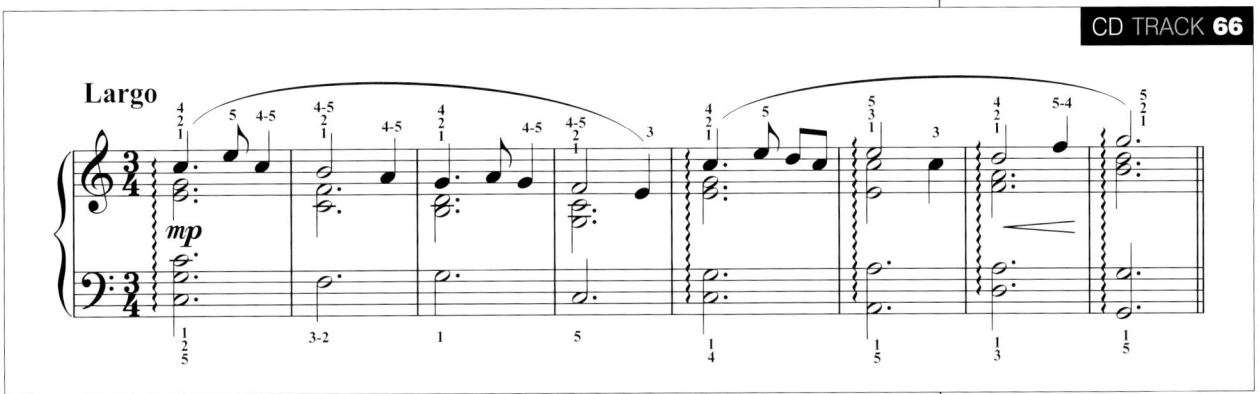

CD TRACK **66**

CD TRACK 67

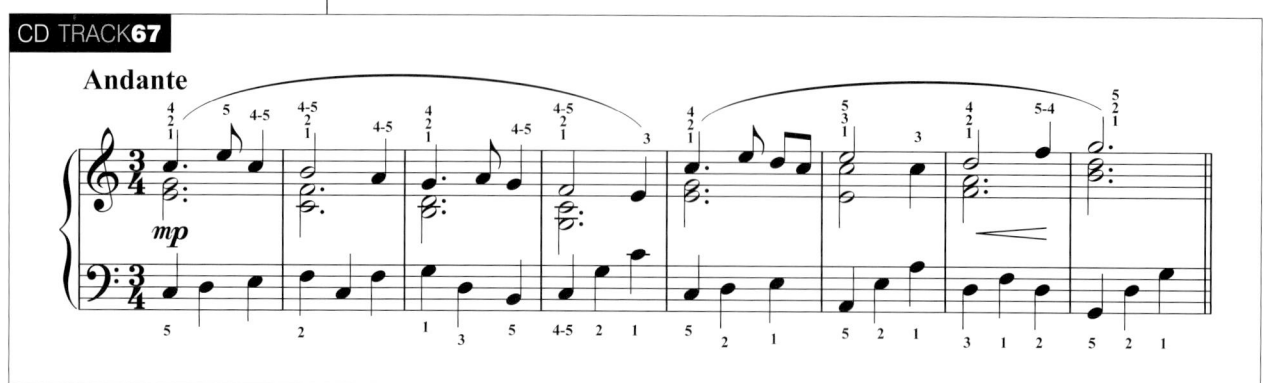

The next stage of evolution of classical polyphonic-harmonic texture occurred in what's known as the Classical period of classical music, and consisted of the introduction of simple broken-chord textures to form a flowing accompaniment, usually in a regular rhythmic pattern known as an 'Alberti bass'. (This was used together with the existing options.)

CD TRACK 68

Romantic period music then went on to develop this into a much wider range of textures. (This reflected the emergence of the modern piano, with its more enhanced resonance and sustaining pedal, in the late 18th and early 19th centuries.) The examples below (p436-7) illustrate this.

First we have a texture that exploits the sustaining pedal: this enables the left hand to move between bass notes and chords in the middle register. Then we have a couple of examples of more flowing textures that also make use of the pedal to achieve continuity and, in some cases, an accumulation of sound. (Note how the right hand may double the melody in thirds or sixths to further enrich the texture, or in octaves to make sure it penetrates through the texture when needed.) Finally we have a split-hands texture, enabling the accompaniment to surround the melody with a 'halo' of sound. These more elaborate textures – which often also cover an expanded compass – are a feature of later Romantic music. They are difficult to realise from scratch when improvising, but you should certainly be aware of them as possibilities.

The expanded compass of Romantic piano textures brings with it an expanded colouristic palette: you can see this especially from the last two examples (p437). Allowing the bass to travel down into the lowest register of the piano can be an effective way of adding a feeling of darkness or sonorous depth to the texture, while moving texture or melody up into the highest registers adds a sense of lightness and/or brightness. These colouristic qualities are in turn coloured by the harmony itself.

In jazz the issue of colour also surfaces in a way that's closely connected to register. We've already noted the interdependence of right hand and left hand as regards sonority: the denser voicings typical of jazz tend to sound too muddy when played too low, but move them up past the middle of the piano and we deny this register to the melody, forcing the latter up into a thinner register where it's less likely to penetrate through the texture. (Also, the flowing character of jazz melody normally makes it impractical to try to reinforce the melody with octave doublings.) The only solution is to pay careful attention to your voicings and make sure to adapt them (rather than mechanically transposing them) as you move across different keys.

When improvising using either the classical or the jazz approach, you'll quickly discover just how important the role of the **bassline movement** is. Basically, the more elaborate the texture, the more likely we are to have to rely on the bass to maintain continuity and progression. There's a simple reason for this: when improvising complex accompanying textures it's impossible to fully manage voice-leading in the inner parts in line with either classical principles or jazz formulas. Effective bassline movement – especially stepwise diatonic or chromatic movement – can come to the rescue here, as it serves to bind successive harmonies together into coherent progressions even when these other elements are not fully realised.

UNIT 9 | SECTION 4

CD TRACK 69

CD TRACK 70

SECTION 4 | UNIT 9

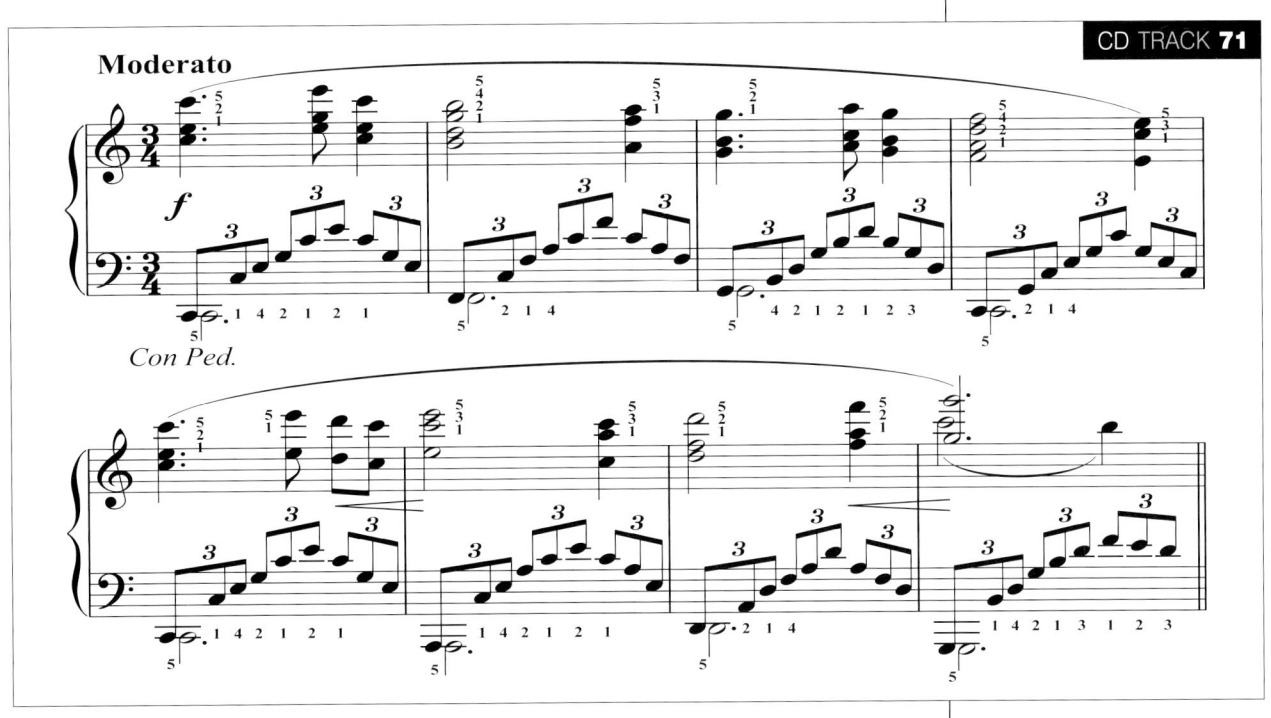

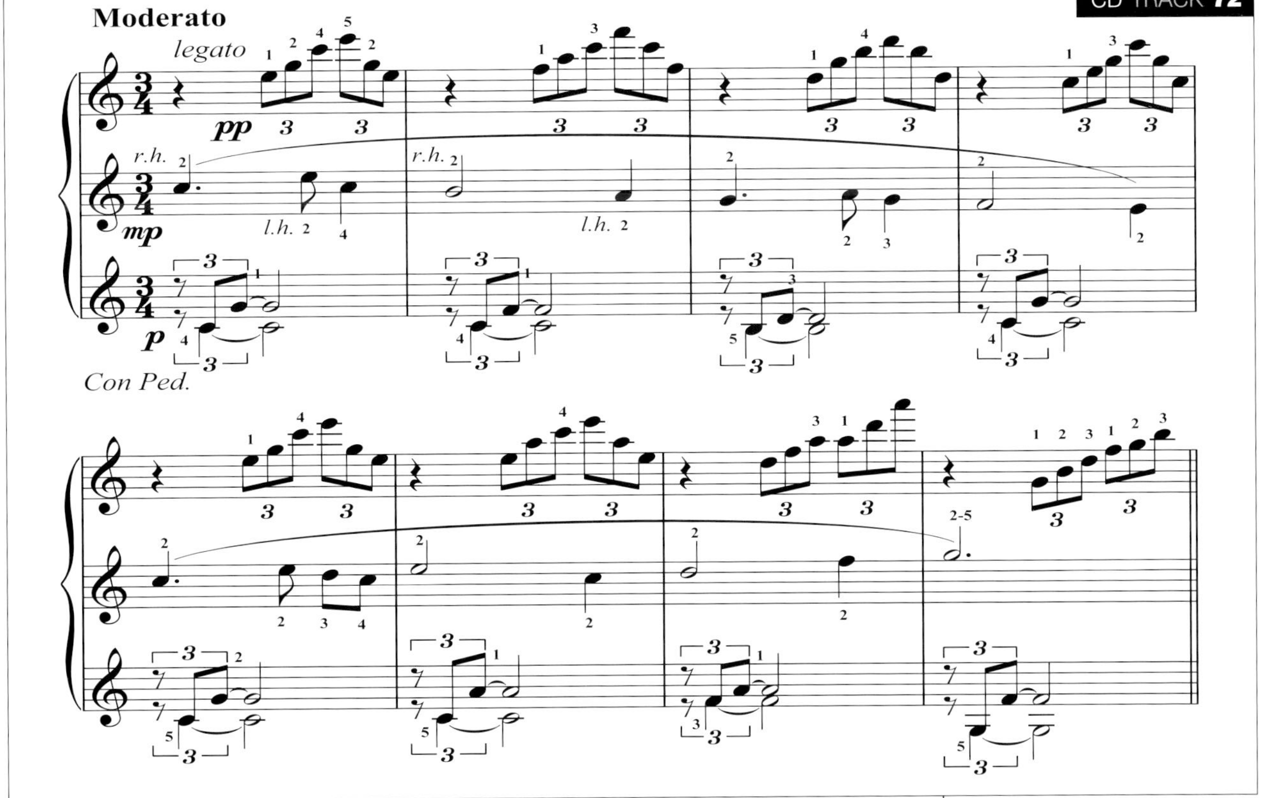

UNIT 9 | SECTION 4

From the improviser's point of view, then, it's really worth becoming familiar with a number of formulaic progressions based on bassline continuity. These can then be called upon as and when needed. (You should therefore practise transposing all of the sample progressions below into all keys.) Here they are.

Stepwise diatonic descent – major key: note how the same kind of progression involving a root-position chord and then a first inversion over a root a fifth higher gets reused throughout the first sequence. The second sequence shows how a succession of first-inversion chords can be used over a descending bass without fear of consecutives.

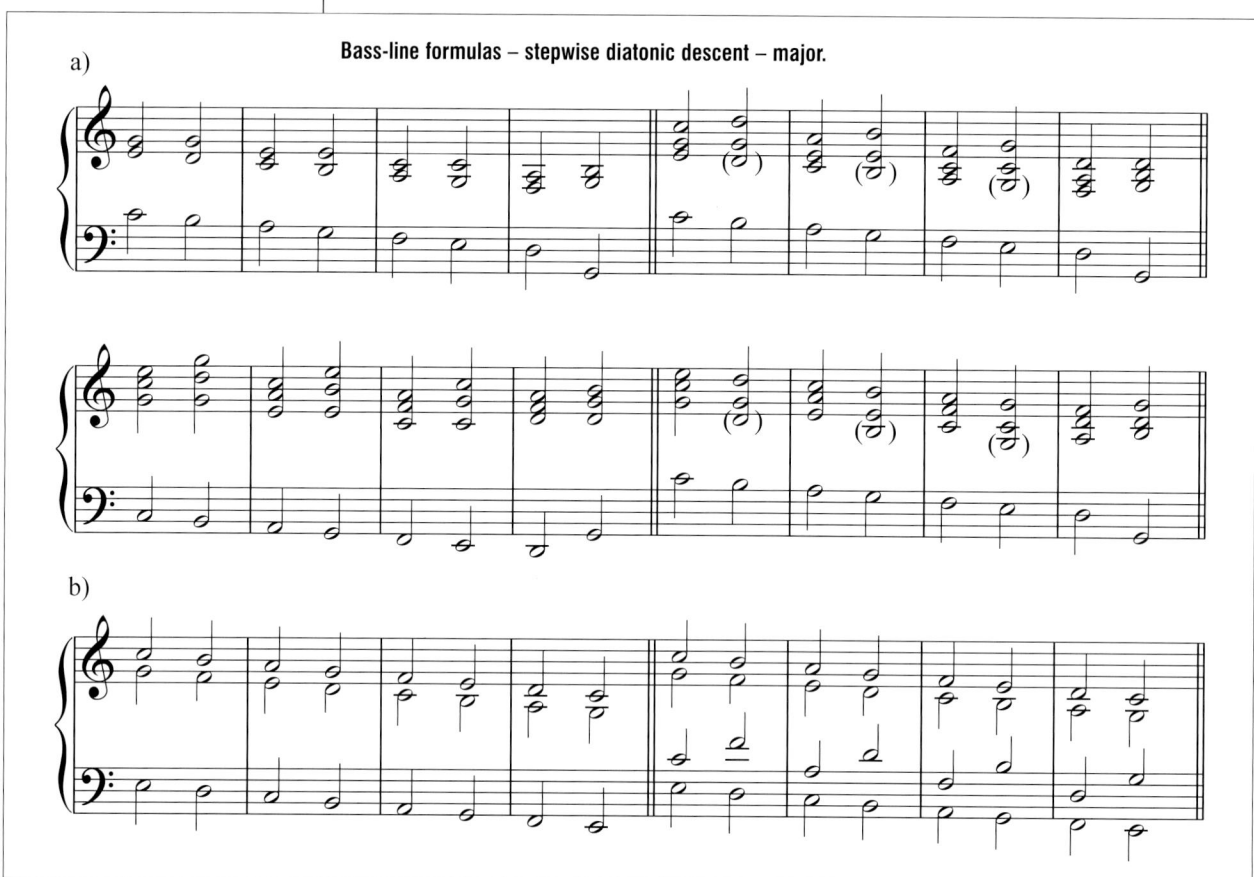

Stepwise diatonic descent – minor key (opposite, top): note here how the descending melodic minor scale generates the stepwise movement in the bass, while the harmonic minor provides a more effective source for the dominant harmony that comes later in the sequence.

Stepwise chromatic descent – minor key (opposite, bottom): chromatically descending bass lines are more likely to be used in a minor key than a major key. Differences in the timing (relative to the bass) of descending movements in the upper parts can give rise to interesting variations in the resulting chords.

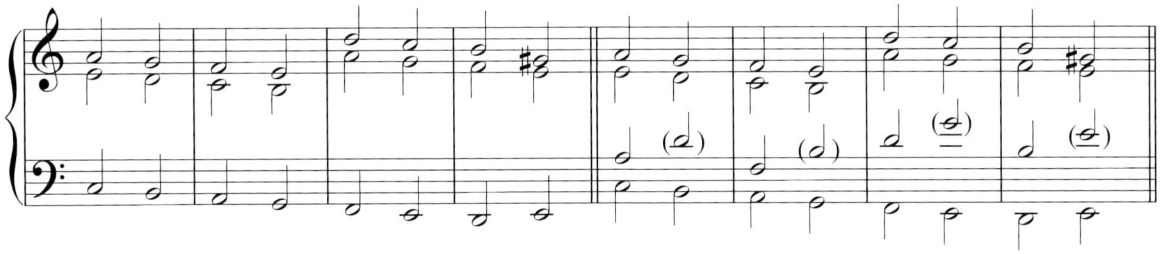

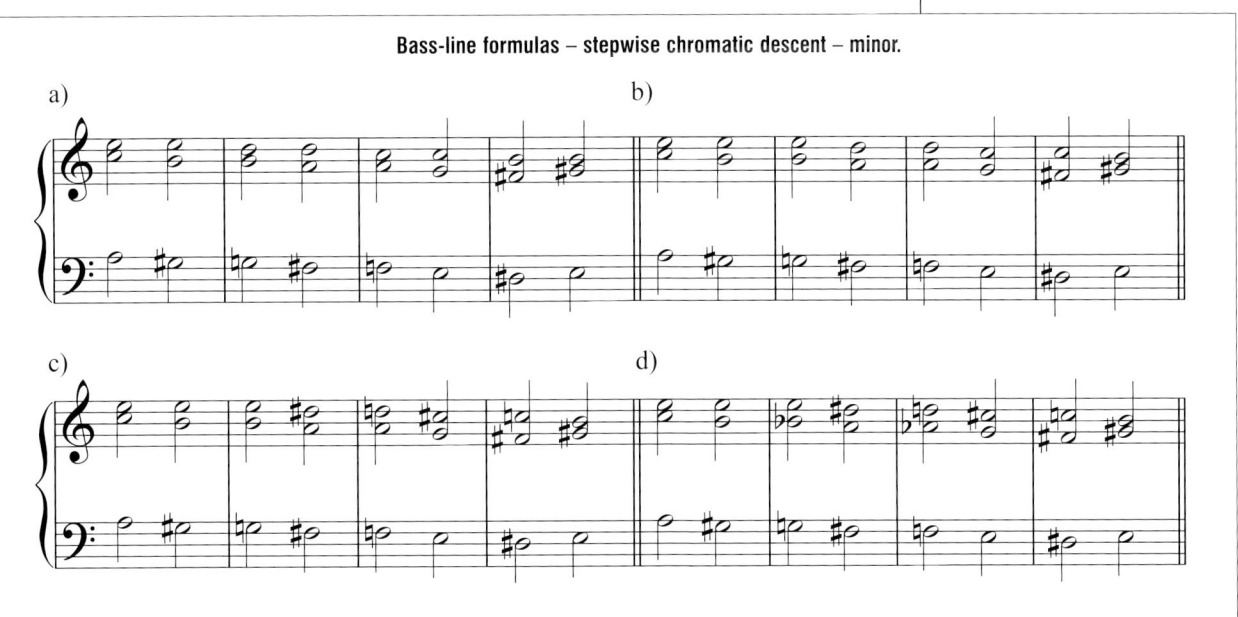

Stepwise chromatic descent – major key: in a major key chromatically descending bass lines produce the kind of forceful progressions typically encountered in rock music. Notice the alternative approach to V at the end, using a Neapolitan sixth:

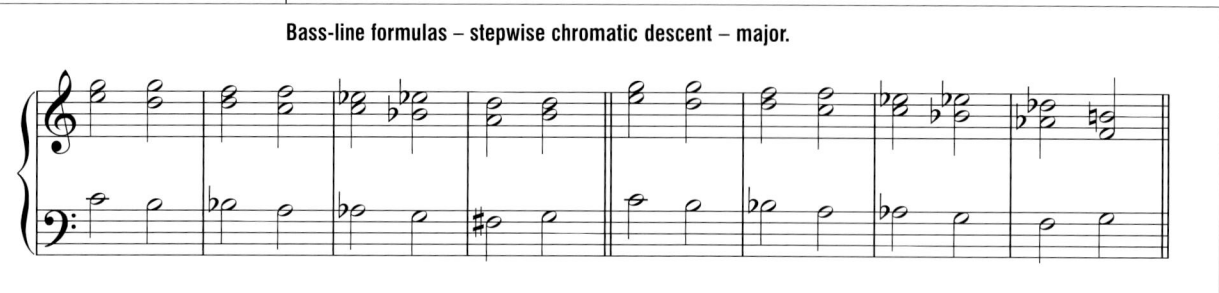

Bass-line formulas – stepwise chromatic descent – major.

Stepwise diatonic ascent – major key: these alternative arrangements of the same sequence show how a succession of first-inversion chords can be used over a stepwise ascending bass without fear of consecutives:

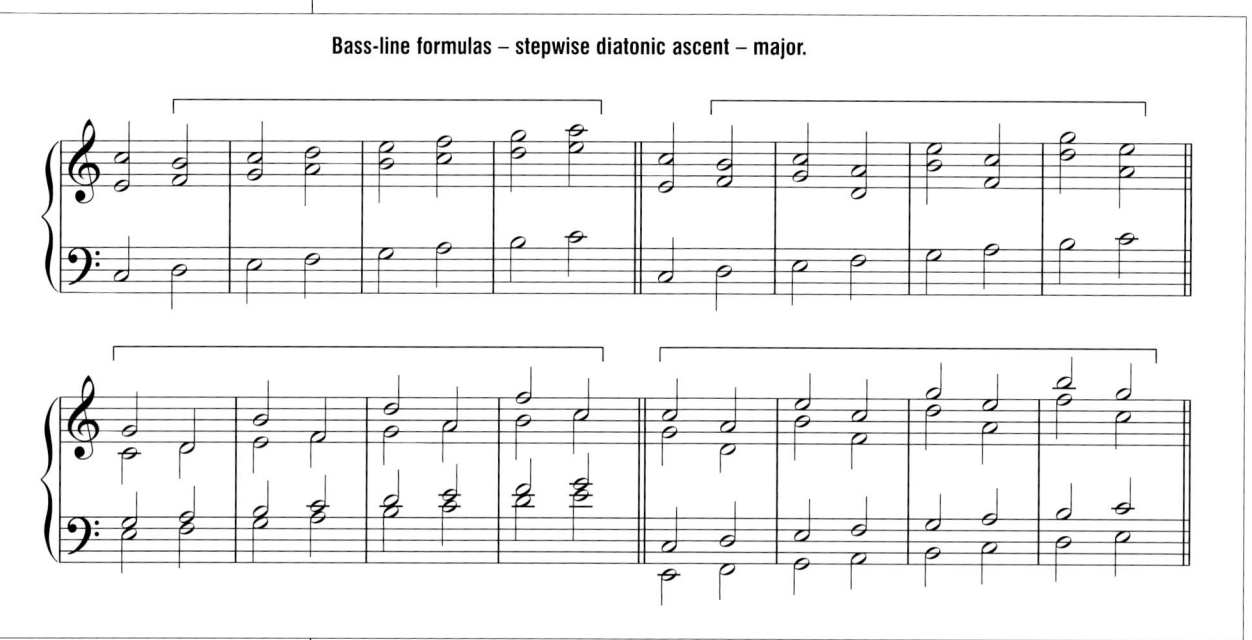

Bass-line formulas – stepwise diatonic ascent – major.

Stepwise diatonic ascent – minor key: this is more complex, owing to the variety of forms of the minor scale available. Option (a) uses only notes from the ascending melodic minor, but the effect is somewhat static. Option (b) uses notes from the descending melodic minor, even though the voices ascend – hence we hear it as a modal (Aeolian) effect; once again it's rather static. To achieve a stronger sense of progression over ascending minor-key bass lines, we tend to treat the chords as forming more localised progressions, drawing notes from whichever form of the minor scale fits with the local implications of the bass line. The most effective way to generate a sense of harmonic direction is to use a diminished triad in first inversion whose bass moves up a step to form a first-inversion triad on the root a step higher, as in (c). The resulting VII^b-I^b progression is powerful because we hear the chord VII as an incomplete V^7 of the following chord. Hence the effect is similar to that of a secondary dominant resolving. (A similar effect plays a big role in jazz arranging: see the discussion of the 'four-way close' technique below.)

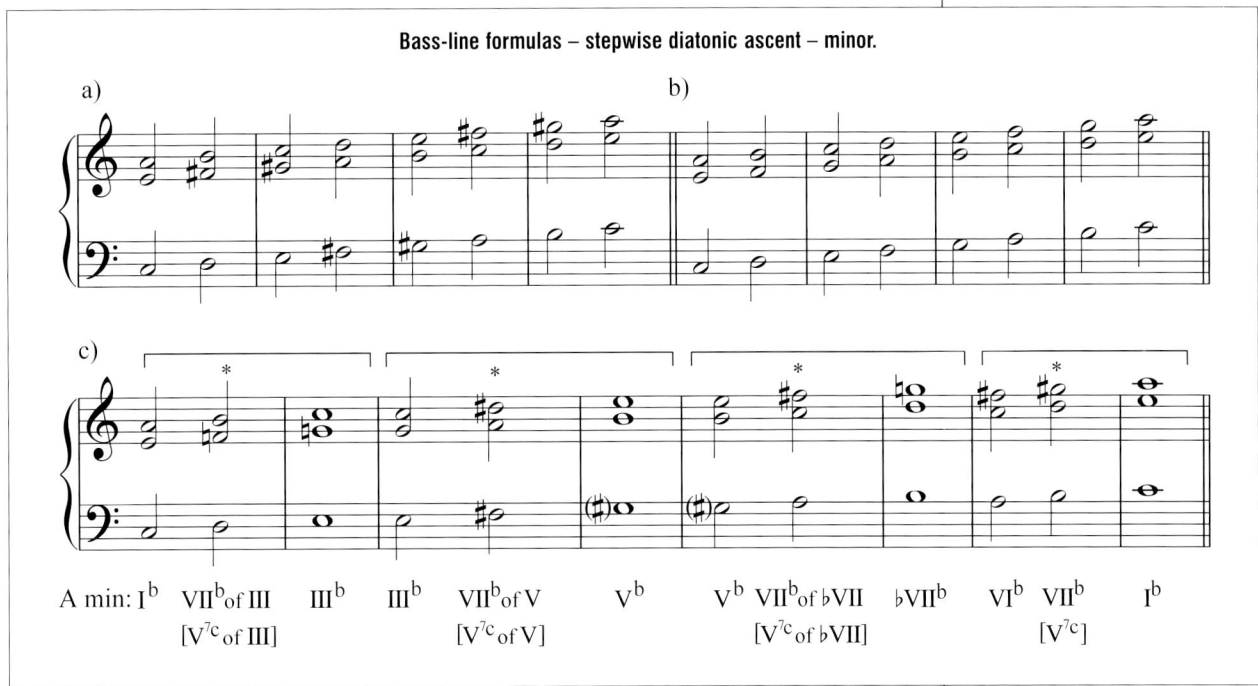

Stepwise chromatic ascent – major and minor keys (p442): ascending chromatic bass lines tend to follow a similar principle of harmonising chords to form local progressions that imply secondary dominants resolving. This is the case regardless of whether the key is major or minor. Note how these chords may show up as diminished or half-diminished seventh chords on VII of the chord that follows. (Diminished sevenths are more likely to be used in minor keys than in major ones.)

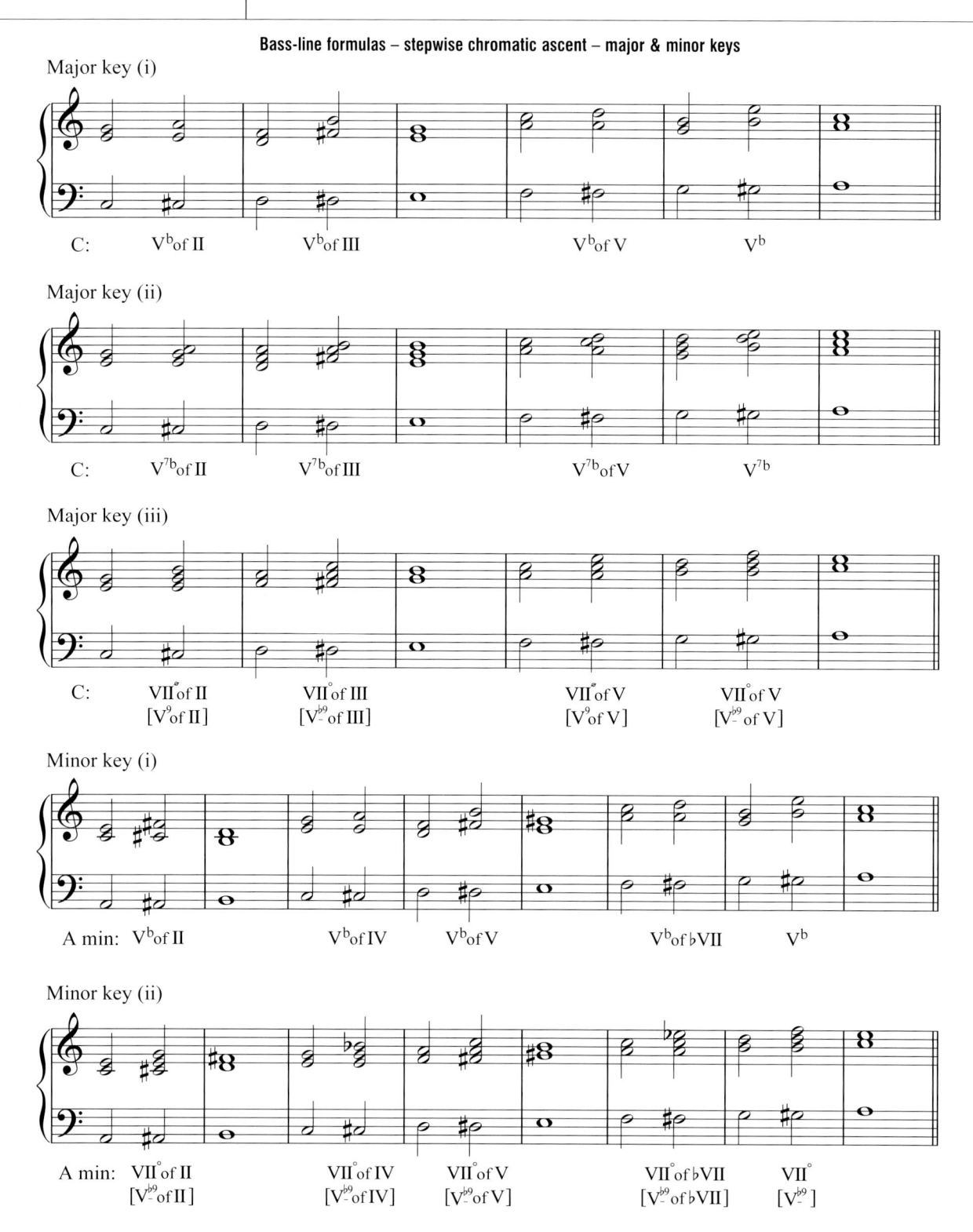

SECTION 4 | UNIT 9

Exercise 9.20
Now take some of these formulaic progressions over stepwise bass-line movement and see if you can turn them into flowing textures similar to those shown earlier.

The use of diminished seventh chords above stepwise bassline movement in the above examples resembles a common arranging technique in jazz called **four-way close**. This is often employed when scoring parts for four saxophones in jazz ensembles, but is also useful when harmonising a melody on piano when we want the hands to move in parallel motion – an effect known as **locked hands**.

In four-way close we move upwards or downwards between inversions of an added sixth, minor seventh, or dominant seventh chord by interspersing diminished seventh chords built on the scale notes that lie between the bass notes of the other chords. (Where necessary we insert a chromatic passing note to ensure a regular alternation between the diminished seventh chords and the other kind of chord – normally the raised fifth of the scale.)

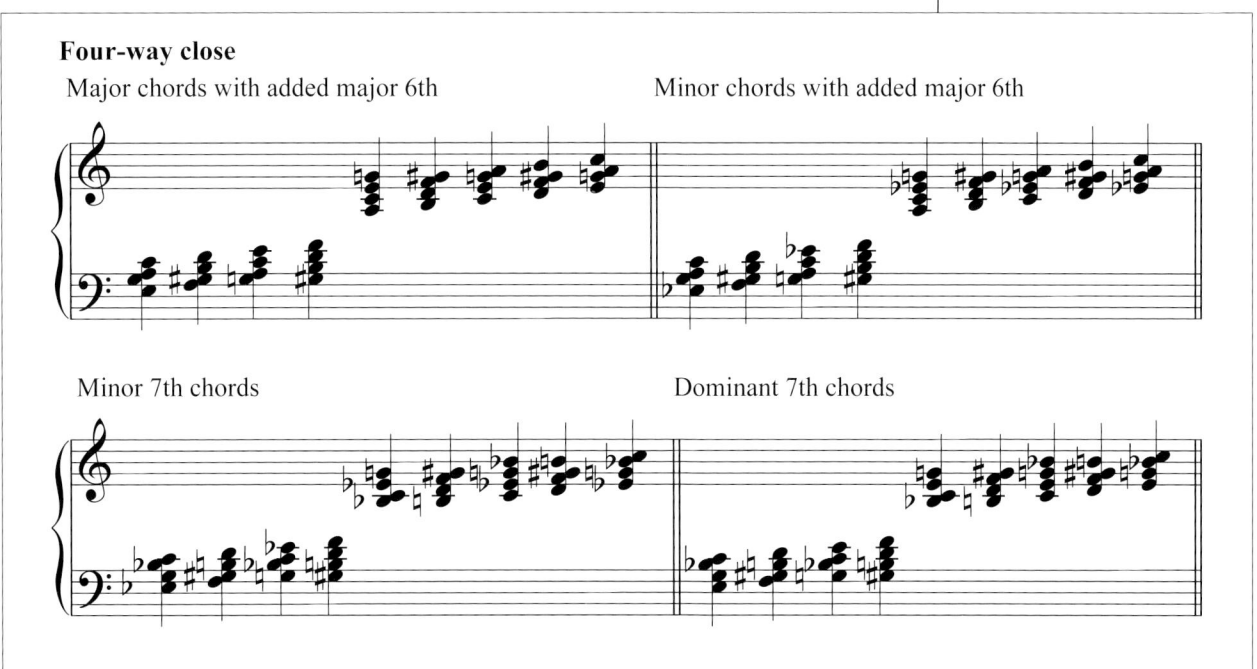

We can realise this on the piano by doubling the top part an octave lower in the bass. As the chords move in parallel with the top part, this normally means that the bass line doubles the melody – an effect associated with the pianist George Shearing (see p444).

UNIT 9 | SECTION 4

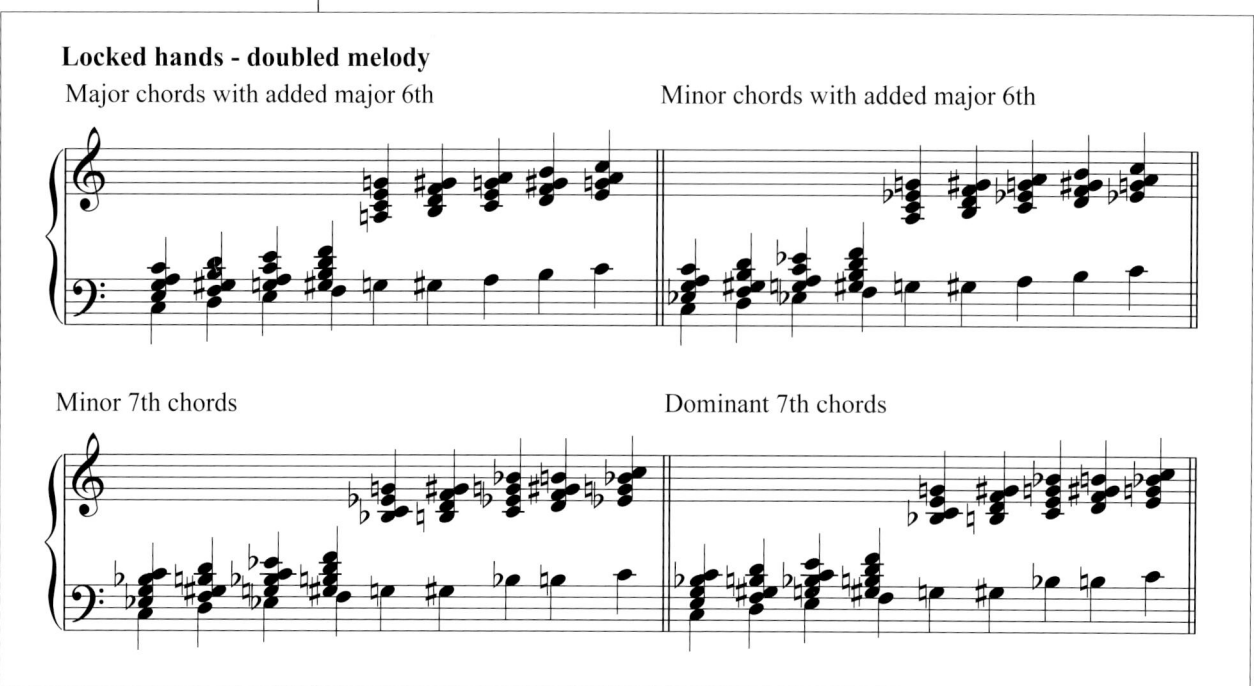

Often, though, it's more effective to take the second note from the top of each chord and drop it by an octave to make the bass – an effect known as **drop two**:

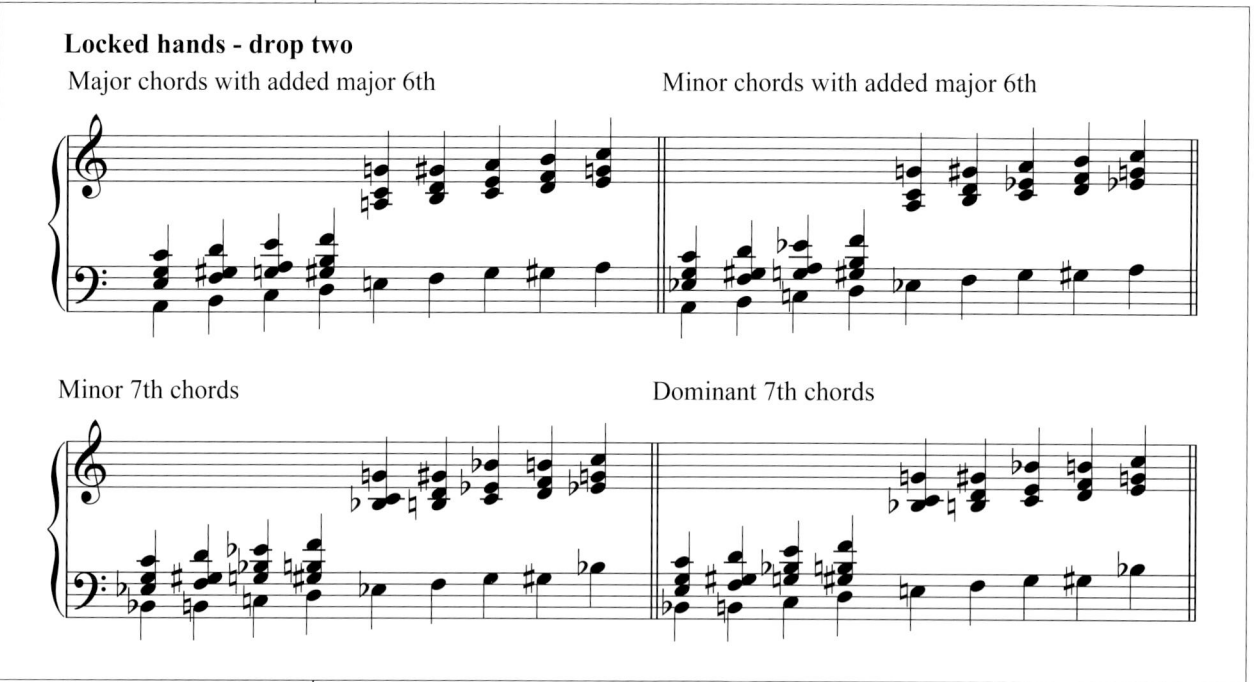

SECTION 4 UNIT 9

Bassline movement may also play an important role in another way – through being withheld when we are expecting it, as a way of building a sense of expectation and tension. Basically, we let the chords change above it but keep the bass note itself fixed, as what's known as a **pedal point**. The most common form this takes is for the dominant of the key to be held on for some time in the bass as chords change over it, until finally it resolves to the tonic. A fine example of a dominant pedal point is offered by the second part of Bach's 'Prelude In C major' (from Book I of his *Forty-Eight Preludes And Fugues*) – the piece we used as a starting point for improvising in Unit Seven:

UNIT 9 | SECTION 4

Note how the move to the tonic in the bass, when it eventually comes (in bar 32), leads to another pedal point, this time on the tonic, creating a staggered sense of harmonic resolution as the music reaches its conclusion. Tonic pedal points can also be effective as a way of delaying harmonic movement in the opening stages of a piece, in a way that generates a heightened sense of expectation, as the opening of another 'Prelude In C major' by Bach – this time from Book II of his *Forty-Eight Preludes And Fugues* – demonstrates:

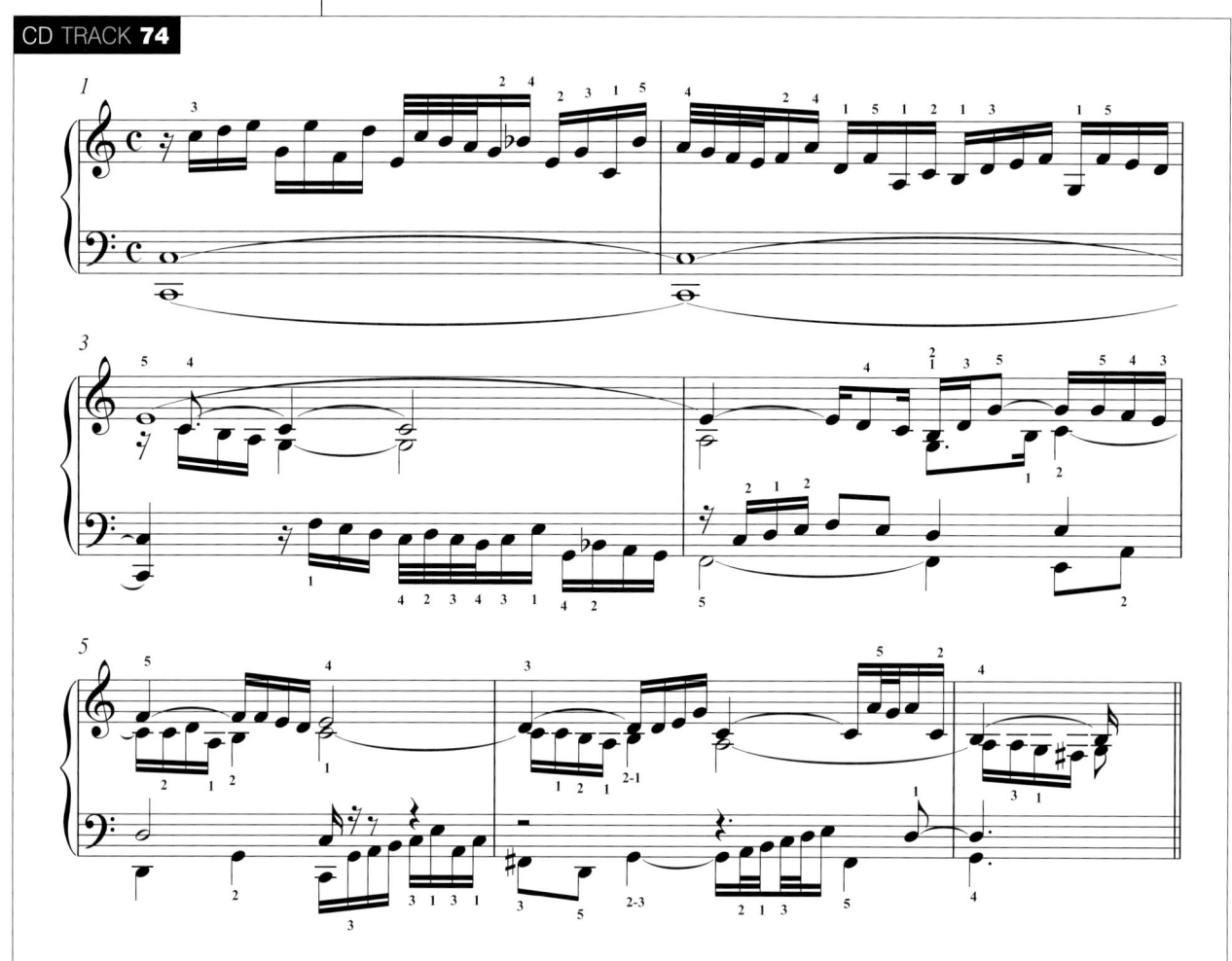

CD TRACK 74

Arranging and improvising

So far in this book we've explored approaches that focus on melodic improvisation – mostly over a given structure of harmony and metre of the sort furnished either by a jazz standard or a classical reduction. Now let's turn the tables: we'll take the melody as given, along with the basic harmony, and see what we can do to create interesting pianistic textures around this.

Since the process of realising a given melody and chords as a specific texture is normally associated with what professional arrangers do, this is where arranging and improvising overlap. In fact there's a more familiar term for this: busking. (Now 'busking' also means playing music on street-corners, etc, for money.) To explore this we'll take as our material some melodies from one of the most exceptional sources of folk melody in the Western world – one that has always involved elements of improvisation: the Neapolitan song tradition from Southern Italy (Naples).

Here's one of their most memorable melodies, 'Te Voglio Bene Assaje', shown with chord symbols above, rather like a jazz standard when presented in the form of a lead sheet:

Let's start by trying out a couple of simple arrangements for the first four bars:

The first one realises the harmony as inner parts in the right hand with just the bass notes in the left hand, while the second uses a standard alternating pattern of bass notes and chords in the left hand.

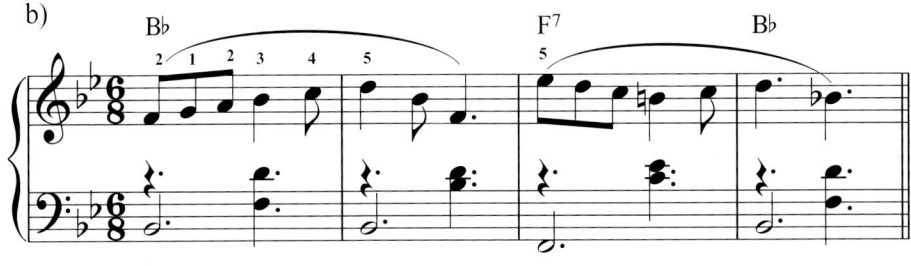

The first version sounds acceptable, but the potential of the left hand to contribute to the texture is unexplored. Also, fitting the rest of the harmony in the right hand along with the melody means that all of the upper parts are obliged to remain close together throughout, preventing the melody from being projected into the foreground of the texture as effectively it could otherwise be.

The second version avoids these problems by using a standard left-hand pattern of alternating bass notes and chords. However, this, too, has its limitations. Although the melody is now more clearly audible above the rest of the texture, the fact that the first beat of each bar has just a melody note and a bass note sounding together means that we are denied a full realisation of the harmony at the moment when each new chord arrives. As a result, the effect of the chord changes is weakened.

Now here's a version of the whole song which addresses all of these issues by combining elements of the two approaches just discussed. Note how much more effective the results are:

Although this sounds a lot better, there's still some work to be done before we can say we've created a really satisfactory arrangement. For example, notice how the right-hand melody initiates a sense of flowing eighth-note (quaver) movement right at the start – yet this isn't developed further by anything in the accompaniment. Adding some eighth-note figures based on the chord notes in the left hand in those places where the melody itself lacks eighth-note movement will address this, making the whole texture more fluid and less pedestrian:

Now take a look at the last eight bars or so. Notice that bars 17-18 are a repeat of bars 13-14, only leading this time to a pause on an extended dominant harmony (halfway through bar 19) which prepares us in turn for the final resolution. Both the repetition and the build-up to the climactic caesura pause call for an intensification of some kind. The next example shows how we can achieve this with doubling of the melody and an expansion of texture in terms of both compass and the number of notes used to fill out the chords:

UNIT 9 | SECTION 4

Now here's a final version (opposite page). Note the further addition of some semiquaver movement in bars 11-12, once again adding variety as the melody repeats itself (and also complimenting the increased harmonic tension created by the diminished seventh chords here). Note also the cadenza-like decorative treatment of the final extended dominant chord with the pause: in both the Italian folksong tradition and the Italian operatic tradition this was the moment when the solo singer would show off their ability to improvise.

Now here are a couple more great Neapolitan melodies, in lead-sheet format, so you can practise working out your own arrangements of them.

Exercise 9.21 CD Track 77
The first one is 'La Luisella'. This calls for a flowing accompaniment along similar lines to the song we've just been looking at. Note the shift to B minor (the relative minor) in bar 9, and the unusual harmonies on the caesura pauses in bars 12 and 16 – unusual because they're not dominant chords. Doubling the melody in thirds may also be effective in places where it's not too flowing (eg, bars 1-2 and 5-6).

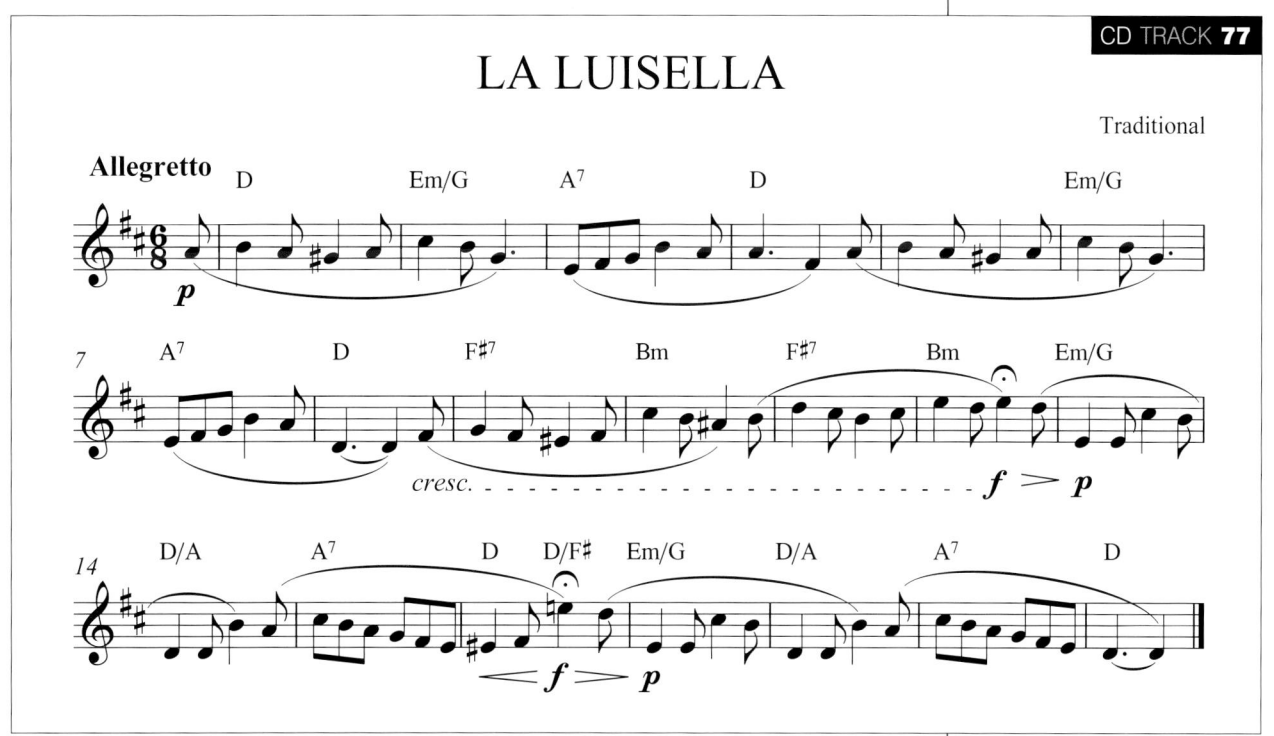

UNIT 9 | SECTION 4

Exercise 9.22 CD Track 78

Now for an absolute all-time classic: 'Napole Mio'. Once again, the song has a lilting flow characteristic of the way compound duple time is used in Neapolitan melodies. In this case, though, the chord structure is more demanding, partly thanks to the augmented triad (bar 1) and some faster chord changes (eg, bar 5). Notice also the C chord with a raised 13th in bar 16: this is a simplified way of notating an augmented sixth chord that is strictly the first inversion of a seventh chord on the chromatically raised fourth of the scale (here A-sharp, in E minor). You can save yourself a headache by realising that enharmonic equivalence makes the resulting chord the same as a V7 on C. Note also the use of a diminished seventh chord in bar 22: this resembles the use of such chords in the jazz technique of four-way close discussed earlier. (We could likewise harmonise the G-sharp earlier in the same bar with a diminished seventh chord, this time with a B in the bass.) As with the first of these songs, extended dominant harmony is indicated for some of the notes marked with caesura pauses (bars 8 and 24): consider this an open invitation to improvise your own decorative ornamentations or, in the case of the penultimate bar, even a full cadenza.

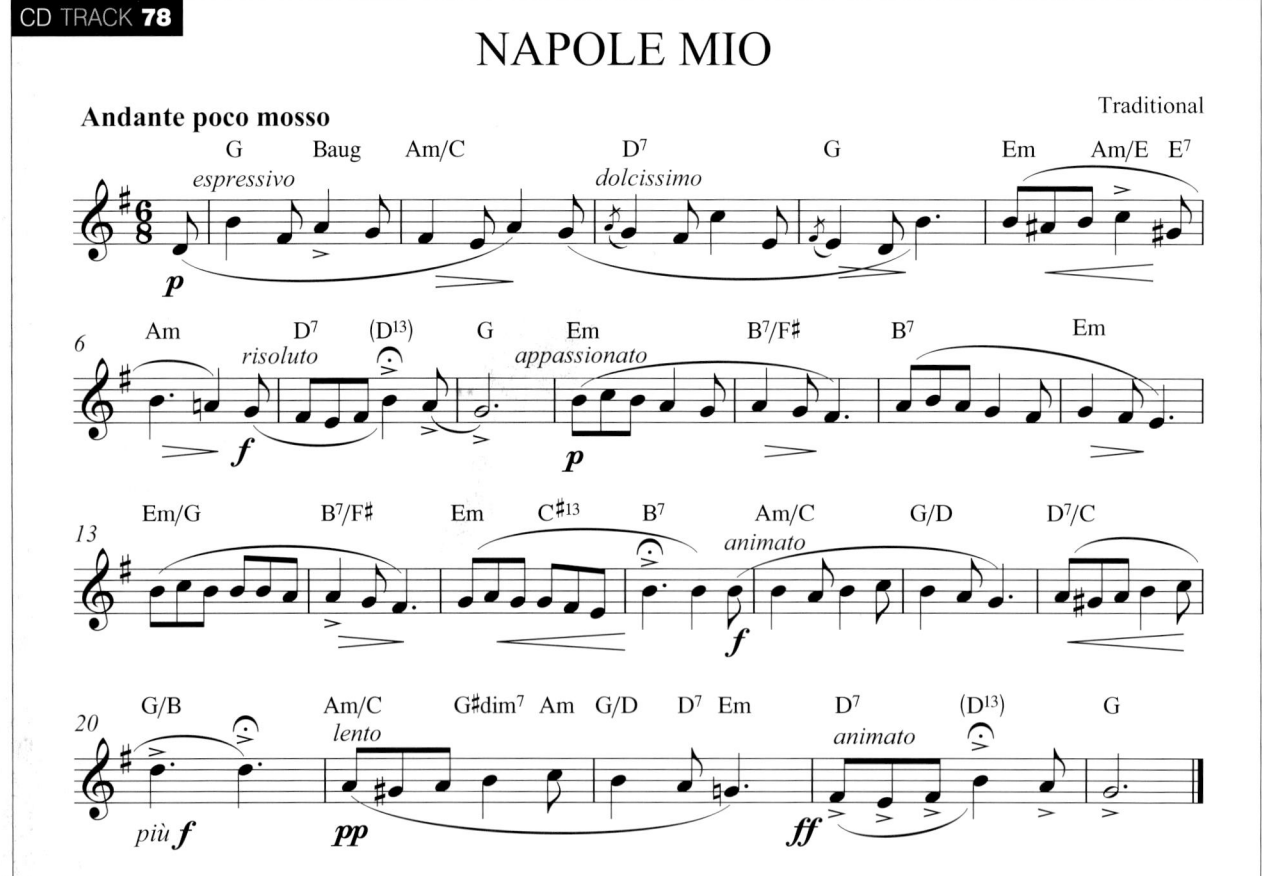

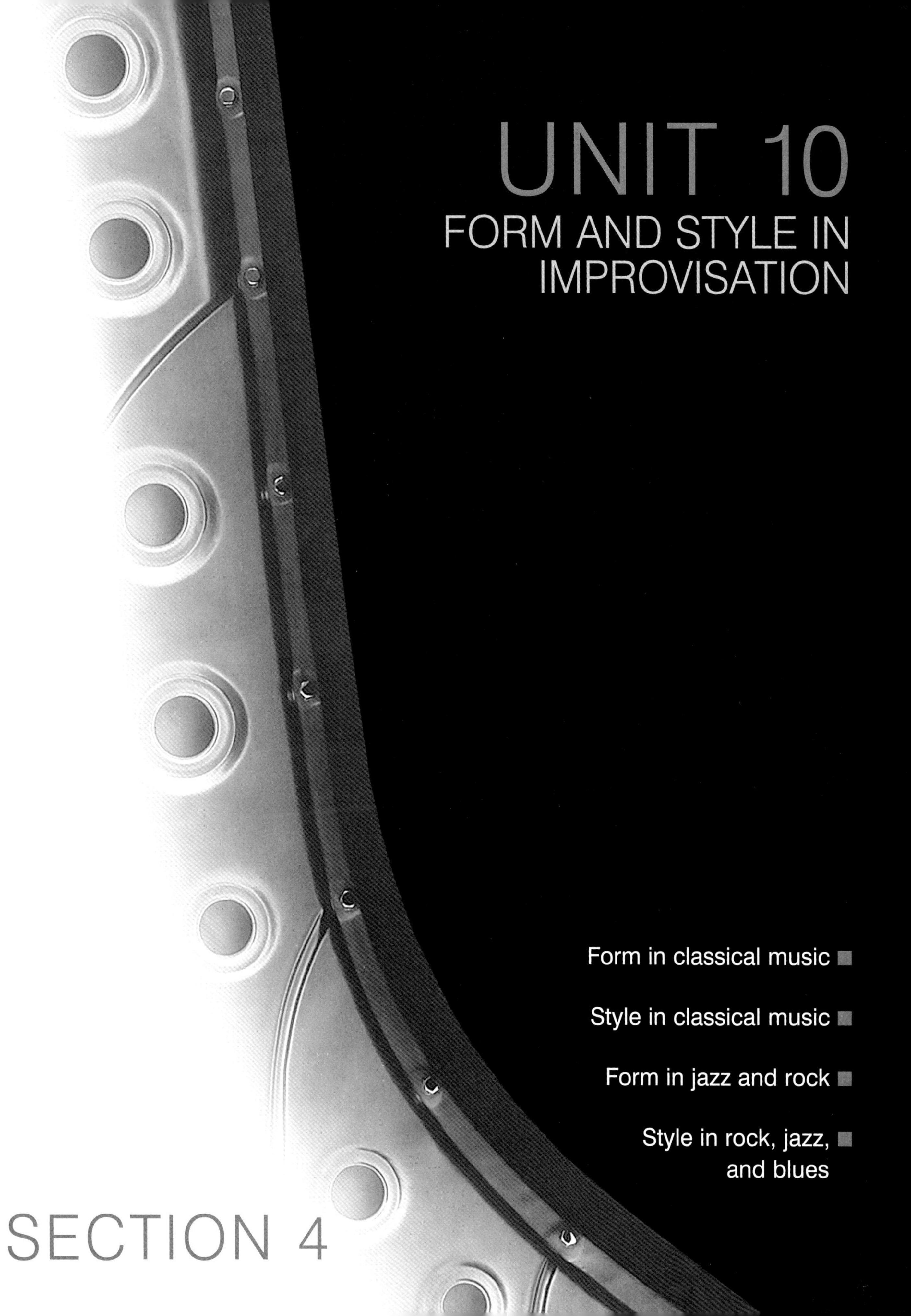

UNIT 10
FORM AND STYLE IN IMPROVISATION

- Form in classical music
- Style in classical music
- Form in jazz and rock
- Style in rock, jazz, and blues

SECTION 4

Form in classical music

All musical cultures have some sort of concept of **musical form**, by which they mean ways in which the unfolding of music over time can be organised. However, making sense of how form works when we improvise using the classical approach isn't straightforward. That's because it's linked to the changing relationship that improvising and composing have had with one another throughout the history of the Western art-music tradition.

This relationship went through an important shift around the time of the Renaissance. The development of elaborate but highly consonant polyphonic textures led away from the medieval practice of treating improvisation and composition as essentially interdependent elements of a single practice (as in medieval discanting). Renaissance church music, in particular, required a level of control over dissonance that could only be achieved through carefully planned composing. This led to a belief that composed music, rather than improvised music, best exemplified the rules and conventions governing what works in musical textures. So composed music then began to set the standards for the musical culture as a whole. Meanwhile, improvised music came to be seen as an exceptional case: a product of special circumstances, in which musicians were allowed to deviate from these standards to achieve some particular artistic effects.

This change in the status of improvisation immediately preceded two other important developments. Firstly, the Baroque period (approximately 1600-1750) saw the emergence of more sophisticated instruments that allowed a new culture of instrumental virtuosity to develop, especially where stringed and keyboard instruments were concerned. In short, instrumental music took off and developed in a big way. The result was that players began to identify improvised music making with the sort of freer approaches to musical form that allowed them to concentrate on exploring the virtuoso potential of their instruments.

Secondly, the same period saw a shift in emphasis as regards the relationship between words and music. Whereas the most elevated forms of Renaissance vocal music (ie, church music) treated words as secondary and music as primary, a new approach emerged in which the words were now seen as more important. This led to a more dramatic approach to the setting of words to music, with greater freedom in the use of harmony and treatment of dissonance and more emphasis on the dramatic expressive potential of solo melody lines. This new style quickly became popular, thanks to the growing success of opera, in which it had a natural place. What's more, it offered a new model for melodies generally – including those in instrumental music. The result was that instrumental performers came to see melody as a self-sufficient medium, capable of expressive drama in its own right. They soon came to see improvisation as offering the basis for a stronger relationship between the dramatic, expressive aspect of music and the immediacy of actual performances.

This set of connections, linking together improvisation, freer forms, and the expressive immediacy of performance, continued right through into the Romantic art music of the 19th century. It's even still there in our musical culture today (especially, perhaps, in certain areas of popular culture). So in classical music we still tend to expect improvisations to reflect familiar classical forms in a much freer and looser way than other music, with more emphasis placed on the expressive drama of performance and/or on displays of virtuosity – and paying less attention to the unfolding of large-scale structures.

> Improvising using the classical approach often involves making indirect reference to classical musical forms. The forms are primarily defined by their role in composed music, so we only expect those forms to be partly realised in improvisation, or to be realised in a different – often much freer or less predictable – kind of way.

As far as learning to improvise on the piano using the classical approach is concerned, there are two possible methods. One is to study specific classical forms and formal conventions as they exist in relation to particular styles of classical music. Then, when we improvise in that style, we do so against the background of the particular rules for handling form that were in place when that style was in common use: applying them, or deliberately stretching, loosening, or even ignoring them, as we see fit, much as an improviser familiar with that style would have done in the past. That makes sense if you just want to precisely recreate specific improvising practices from the past. If, however, you're looking for a way to develop your own ideas and style, which is what this book is all about, then that's not so relevant.

A better approach is to look for more basic and common features of how form works in Western classical music. Then you can explore how these can be used in the indirect and looser way mentioned above, just as the more specific forms associated with past styles were. These general principles and models can inform your improvising, no matter what style you end up with, but if you want them to they can also serve as a valuable foil, giving you that sense of inhabiting a special realm of freedom which is what improvising in the classical tradition has come to be mostly about.

The rest of this section explores these more basic concepts connected with form in Western music. First we'll look at the concept of form itself, and its relationship to improvisation. Then we'll examine the more specific categories you need to know about to grasp how form works in classical music.

1) Improvisation and the concept of musical form

This term refers to how music is organised, but in practice there are several distinct things we may mean by it. The central idea, though, is that the parts or stages of a composition or improvisation should come together to form a coherent whole – a combination of parts that isn't arbitrary. Here we'll consider the three conceptions of form in music most relevant to classical improvising.

a) Organic form

These days form is most often understood in a way that takes the natural world as a model. For example, we all know that a living body or plant is a whole that is 'more than the sum of its parts', because it has a structure that can only be properly appreciated when we see how all of its elements come together to enable it to function as a living organism. There are several reasons for why this particular conception has dominated our understanding of form in music over the last couple of centuries or so. One of them, though, is that it fits rather neatly with an approach that treats composition rather than improvisation as primary, since it encourages us to think of music as the end-product of a process of putting together – literally 'com-posing' – ideas or elements to make a larger unity, independently of what goes on in an actual musical performance.

When we think of classical improvisation as involving a loosening up, or even a partial rejection, of standard forms, it's really just this particular conception of form that we have in mind. It's important to realise that there are others too, whose role in improvisation is not affected by this, and whose importance may even be increased rather than diminished as a consequence of how classical forms are made use of in classical improvising.

b) Dramatic form

This is the conception of form Aristotle (the philosopher) had in mind when he tried to describe what makes for a good drama (in his work entitled *Poetics*). (Back in Ancient Greece, drama chiefly meant tragedy, but his ideas would be just as valid today for the kind of drama we see presented at the movies or on TV.) He thought the most basic requirement was **unity of action**, and he meant more by this than just a structure consisting of a particular arrangement of parts. What he had in mind was the idea that a drama unfolds a specific series of events that, because of their very nature, together form an indivisible whole, with a distinct beginning, middle and end. It's the job of the dramatist to make sure these events are presented in a way that makes absolutely clear how they stand in relation to this whole – thus helping an audience to grasp their real significance.

This is relevant to music on many levels. In general terms it reminds us that good musical form is more than just having a neat arrangement of ideas or sections – it's the art of presenting these over time in a way that shows that, taken in sequence, they amount to more than just a succession of smaller units. So just stringing ideas together – even if they make for some quite good contrasts with one another – isn't 'form' in Aristotle's sense.

More specifically, it reminds us that there's a deeper sense in which music, like drama, should 'hang together' and make sense, however undefined or loose its structure may be – the (perhaps rather mysterious) level at which it presents a kind of human drama in sound. That's why good improvisers always pay careful attention to the 'psychological' drama of their improvisation, frequently modelling this around a kind of emotional narrative with a clearly defined trajectory of tension, leading first to a climax, then to a sense of resolution. We expect this emotional narrative to be psychologically plausible – to make sense in terms of how we would expect human feelings to evolve in response to events in the real world – but we also expect it to be more than just predictable.

c) Discursive form

This is another notion of form in music – one that's definitely worth being aware of when you improvise: it's the idea that music is organised not in the way an organism is, or as a kind of drama, but in the way a conversation is. It's what sophisticated music critics and musicologists mostly have in mind when they speak of a **musical discourse**. According to this conception, we can understand what happens in music as reflecting choices a person makes as they select from a set of options which we've all learned are the only acceptable options in that particular kind of musical context. The idea is that this resembles what happens when we talk to one another, since there are limited options for things to say that will make sense, given the situation in which we are conversing and the rules of the language we're using.

It's questionable whether music can ever really amount to anything like what goes on in a real conversation – though it can certainly sound like one at times, in ways that may be important in themselves. It's true that we often have the impression that how musicians react to one another's playing – 'trading licks' in jazz or responding to each other's expressive interpretations in classical performances – is a kind of conversation. However, this is not really a conversation happening in the music itself. For one thing, it depends on our sense of who is responsible for producing this or that phrase or idea, which already takes us out of a purely musical realm. For another, it's not clear whether anything is actually being conveyed or accomplished when this goes on in music making, whereas it's clear that this is so when people speak to one another.

The idea of a discourse actually happening within music probably only makes sense as a metaphor. Even so, like many metaphors, it can reveal something important. In this case it highlights the sense in which we hear music not just as unfolding a structure that can possess a certain quality of logical coherence or necessity, but also as taking a particular course whose significance is linked to our awareness that it could have just as easily unfolded in some other way. Hearing music like this means appreciating its form or structure as a play on different possible forms that the music could have (or could have had) – some more in line with our expectations than others, some realised and others not.

This playful approach to form naturally goes hand in hand with the kind of loosened-up approach to structure that's a feature of most classical improvising today. In fact, thinking about form in these terms reminds us that not everything in music needs to sound (or be) absolutely logical and necessary, so we really shouldn't focus on that aspect too much. This thought can help to make us more relaxed and confident as we sit down at the piano to improvise.

Whichever conception of form we attach the most importance to, it's worth keeping in mind that all form in music revolves around the same basic things: the stuff of musical form consists of the similarities and contrasts between elements or aspects of music that develop as the music unfolds. In practice this can mean thematic contrasts between different kinds of musical idea, contrasts of key and tonality (eg, major vs minor, diatonic vs chromatic, modal), and contrasts of colour and texture (often achieved through changes of rhythm, register, tone colour, articulation, volume, etc).

2) Classical formal categories
Now let's take a look at the specific types of form used in classical music, and how they can be adapted to serve the needs of improvisers.

a) Binary form
This is the simplest form in classical music, and is found especially in many dances and other shorter pieces from the Renaissance and Baroque periods. Basically, as the name suggests, it consists of two sections: in the first part the music starts out from an initial key and/or idea and moves to a contrasting key and/or idea; in the second part it makes a 'return journey' back from these to end up in the home key, often restating the initial idea near the end. We can also make use of this idea in the context of the looser approach to form of classical improvising. The best way to do this is to forget about the strict division into sections and focus on the underlying idea of a 'journey' away from and back to the 'place' we start from. The music will still fall into two phases:

1st phase	1st key (and 1st idea) – transition (and/or development) – 2nd key
2nd phase	2nd key (and 2nd idea) – transition (and/or development) – 1st key (and 1st idea)

From an improviser's point of view this is one of the most useful frameworks for exploring material, precisely because it's so simple and therefore so flexible. Note that the form can be understood either purely in terms of key relationships (so that the music need not involve thematic contrast and is therefore 'monothematic'), or in terms of thematic relationships as well. (In theory it could also be articulated purely in terms of thematic contrasts, but this is unlikely, as normally a contrast between musical ideas is accompanied by some sort of key contrast as well – at least in classical music from the Renaissance onwards.) Binary form is also an excellent basis for organising shorter sections within a longer improvisation.

b) Ternary form
This came to play a more important role in music from the 18th century onwards – especially once the operatic aria, which is usually in this form, had come to prominence. It has also provided the basis for many of the more complex forms used in classical music since that time. It involves the idea of a self-contained section (known as the 'A section') followed by a contrasting section (the 'B section'), which is then followed in turn by a repeat of the first section (known as the 'Da Capo' – that's the Italian instruction

telling musicians to repeat from the start). An important difference from Binary Form is that in Ternary Form each section is complete in itself, rather than making a transition to a point from which the next section can then begin. Each section may therefore also be understood as having its own internal structure – often consisting of two phases in binary form. That means Ternary Form is typically a two-level structure, since it involves not just the arrangement of the sections relative to one another but also the arrangement of material within each section.

This can be problematic when improvising: to realise such a form, we would need to accurately recall and repeat substantial stretches of music during the course of a performance. Hence it's more useful as a model for how an improvisation might be planned, at the level of the underlying structures that can be worked out ahead of an actual improvised performance, either when using the techniques of melodic and harmonic reduction explored in Unit Nine, or just in terms of establishing a rough sequence for how one's musical ideas will follow on from one another, or even just an overall key structure for an extended improvisation. The table below gives an example of what these kinds of plan might look like. (In this case the material within each section is assumed to be organised according to Binary Form.)

	A	**B**	**A** (repeated)
1st phase	1st key (and 1st idea) • transition/development • 2nd key	3rd key (and 3rd idea) • transition/development • 4th key	
2nd phase	2nd key (and 2nd idea) • transition/development) • 1st key (and 1st idea)	4th key (and 4th idea) • transition/development) • 3rd key (and 3rd idea)	

c) Variation form

The growing importance of instrumental music during the Baroque period meant that by the end of this phase in the development of classical music another kind of musical form had emerged as important: the 'theme and variations' or 'variation form' as it's also known. This form lends itself very well to a certain kind of improvised or semi-improvised approach to music making. That's because it consists of a series of short sections or movements based on a common underlying harmonic and melodic structure, which tend to refer back to a single initial musical idea (the 'theme'), but which vary other aspects of the music, like texture, rhythm (and metre), tonality, and the melodic foreground (through decoration). Actually something like this had already emerged in the Renaissance period, when instrumentalists frequently improvised variations over a recurring bassline – known as the 'ground' – rather like in jazz.

We've already seen how classical improvising is at its most straightforward when one plays around with a given structure rather than trying to make music up from scratch, and that's exactly what this form is all about, so it naturally became one of the main options for improvisers throughout the ensuing Classical period of Western art music. (Composed sets of variations from this period – the later 18th and early 19th centuries – are therefore probably one of the best guides to how people like Mozart and Beethoven sounded when they improvised.)

At the same time, though, we've also seen that this equating of improvisation with the decorative embellishment and variation of surface features of the music represents a big limitation from the point of view of improvising itself: that's why serious classical players tend to resort to the techniques of melodic and harmonic reduction to open up a wider range of possibilities with respect to some given material. The lesson we can learn from this is that the most fruitful way to approach the formal concept of 'variations on a theme' when improvising is first to clearly establish a reduced structure that will be the real basis for one's variations, and to then prepare (in advance of actually improvising) a range of options for how this structure can be realised at the middleground level – in terms of harmonic development, melodic outlines, metre, and texture.

d) Sonata form

The next major development in classical form was the emergence in the 18th century of what came later to be known as 'sonata form'. We can think of this form as a more complex version of ternary form, since it involves the underlying model of a three-part ABA structure with the first section repeated. However, it is more complex than this. For a start, the first section – known as the 'Exposition' – normally revolves around a thematic contrast between (at least) two distinct musical ideas (or groups of ideas), presented in contrasting keys. The next section, the 'Development', then takes these same ideas further, subjecting them to a variety of processes of transformation, usually including a series of key changes. The third main section, the 'Recapitulation' or 'Reprise', then restates the material from the first section, but with an altered key structure designed to ensure that this time round the second idea (or group of ideas) appears in the home key of the movement as a whole (ie, the tonic). The structure may be further enriched by the addition of an introductory section and/or a further concluding section (known as a Coda).

Sonata form poses an even bigger challenge to the improviser than ternary form, due to the complex thematic and tonal relations that need to be maintained over an extended period of time for it to work. Hence the reaction of improvising musicians at the time (and after) was to treat this as a form essentially designed for composed music, whose significance for improvisation was indirect. Hence sonata form became one of the strongest examples of a classical form that was deliberately alluded to without being actually followed in improvisations of the 18th and 19th centuries. The idea of producing an improvised or composed work of equivalent proportions to a sonata-form movement but not actually strictly following this form even had its own name: it was called a **fantasia**. Some composers (such as Beethoven and Schubert) attempted to blend elements of the sonata and elements of the fantasia in some of their compositions. (We can see this as a comparatively late example of the two-way influence that improvising and composing still had on one another in classical music at that time.)

The idea of producing an improvisation or composition that's significant just because it's not cast in the form everyone expects – namely, sonata form – has lost part of its significance today, because we no longer expect all extended instrumental music to be in this form anyway. However, it's still worth knowing about it, as it embodies in a very clear way a more basic idea that's still useful – the idea of building a structure around distinction between musical **statement** and **development**. One of the most effective techniques for sustaining an extended improvisation, even in a form that's pretty loose, is to juxtapose passages in which ideas are simply stated (with relatively stable harmony) with ones where they are transformed (and harmony is relatively unstable). This remains probably the most effective way of maintaining psychological interest over a longer stretch of music, though it's worth keeping in mind that it also generates a need for some sort of definitive resolution towards the end of the improvisation.

e) Song form

The same period that saw the development of the sonata-form movement also saw the emergence of classical song form, not only as a basis for song settings but also for many lyrical slow movements in instrumental music. Classical song form has links to the more basic form that most songs – and many poems – tend to have, which is an alternation between a verse (whose words, and sometimes music as well, are varied each time) and a chorus (which stays the same each time it comes round). The technical name for this is **strophic form**.

Of course, this form now plays a huge role in popular music – we'll see that in the next section. However, in classical music it's main relevance to improvisation is that it opened the way for Romantic composers of the early 19th century to start using a new type of approach, assembling short, separate movements into a sequence, linked together by an overarching narrative. This was typified by the song-cycle, but soon came to be copied by instrumental composers (eg, Schumann). This blurring of the boundaries separating individual movements from one another encouraged later Romantic composers to explore shorter forms that have a deliberately fragmentary or incomplete character. At the same time a new approach to operatic music (pioneered by Wagner) meant stage dramas could be accompanied by continuous music that unfolded in a much more fluid way, instead of being divided up into smaller units like arias, duets, etc.

These two developments led composed music of the late 19th century towards a much looser approach to form and structure, rather similar to what we find in improvised music of the preceding periods. This means that even though improvisation pretty much disappeared from public concert life during this period, many of its distinctive features reappeared in the guise of composed music. So the composed music of this time can be a great source of ideas for classical improvising, and many of the techniques used to maintain a fluid sense of continuity there are invaluable to improvisers today – especially as regards extended harmony, chromatic voice-leading, and modulation.

(We've already seen that quite a few of these techniques have been taken over and adapted to form elements of the jazz approach, but it's worth knowing they can be used independently of jazz.)

Style in classical music

The approach taken throughout this book has been to focus on techniques and fundamentals that can be useful in any style of improvisation. The idea is that you can make whatever use you want of the things you learn about in this book, to develop your own style. However, as we've seen with non-classical improvising, a lot of techniques that get used are style-specific, so knowing the technique means knowing the style too. The same goes for classical improvising.

The main difference is that style in classical music is more heavily bound up with history, as it has evolved over a much longer period of time than modern non-classical styles themselves. It's not just a question of style but also of history. As an improviser trying to develop your own style, it's good to be able to draw freely on all the stylistic resources offered by classical music – which means all the historical periods – even if your aim isn't just to imitate or recreate them. But that still means understanding something about the historical context in which they occurred. That's why this section presents an overview of the development of different styles within classical music, from a historical point of view.

1) Medieval and Renaissance music

Western classical and non-classical music as we know it today evolved gradually from Medieval **plainchant** – religious chanting in which the only permitted harmonic effects were intervals of a perfect fifth and octave between lines moving in parallel. With the development of Medieval music, the role of the interval of a third shifted: it ceased to be seen as an unacceptable dissonance and instead came to be regarded as a consonance. This meant that 15th and 16th-century Renaissance composers were able to begin to explore the harmonic potential of combining melodic lines into a single texture to create polyphony. This was followed by a growing emphasis on harmonic progressions in which the roots of successive chords moved in intervals of a perfect fifth (or its inversion, a perfect fourth). The stress on tonic and dominant that forms the basis for modern tonal harmony resulted from this. At the same time the modal approach of earlier Renaissance music began to fade away. During this period a more reliable and consistent system for notating music was also developed.

This means that music of the Renaissance period reflects two important developments: firstly, the exploration and refinement of polyphony (and counterpoint), and secondly the emergence of a new approach to tonal harmony, treating it as an increasingly important structural feature in its own right. One important thing that eventually came from this was a new understanding of the relationship between melody and harmony – something that marks the beginning of the next stage in the evolution of Western music, the Baroque period.

Of course the piano had not yet been invented during this period. Instead, the only keyboard instruments available were the precursors of the piano: keyed instruments such as the clavichord, virginals, spinet, and smaller harpsichords. The music written for these reflects an emphasis on the polyphonic working out of ideas through imitation (where one part in the texture copies the previous one after a time-delay) over short passages, but also displays an emerging awareness of how tonal harmony can function as an organising principle. Keyboard music flourished during the later stages of the Renaissance, and especially so in Tudor and Elizabethan England – where it existed alongside the rich literary culture that eventually culminated in Shakespeare. To see what English keyboard compositions of this time look like, have a look at two important collections: the *Mulliner Book* and the *Fitzwilliam Virginal Book*. The first of these dates from the middle of the 16th century and features plainsong lines that are developed using either imitative counterpoint or ornamental lines. The second dates from later in the century and features additional techniques such as the 'English variation', where short patterns are also used as the basis for imitative or decorative development.

Apart from the intrinsic artistic value of the music itself, the chief relevance of Renaissance music to contemporary improvising pianists lies in the fact that it reflects a culture in which composed and improvised music making had not yet become as clearly separated as they subsequently would be. This is reflected in the loose, improvisatory, partly episodic quality of the musical structures used. New ideas are often introduced and developed fairly briefly, before moving on to others that in turn also contribute to a consistent overall character and mood. This shows that the loose approach to melody, harmony, and structure typical of jazz need not be the only paradigm for how structures unfold that is consistent with what you can realistically do when improvising.

> CD Track 66 illustrates the simple, chord-based textures that are a feature of early keyboard music. It's worth keeping in mind, though, that these were often extravagantly embellished on the spur of the moment during performances.

2) Baroque music

The Baroque period lasted from the early 17th century until the first half of the 18th century. It coincided with the emergence of the modern system of tonal harmony, together with a greater emphasis on virtuoso instrumental writing and those kinds of dramatic musical expression through solo melody associated with opera. Lines often unfold continuously without clear phrase divisions, and were extensively embellished through decorative ornamentation by performers. Baroque keyboard music was mostly written for the harpsichord, whose dynamics and articulation were fixed. This meant there were no expressive markings in the score. If you play works from this time on the piano you must therefore decide yourself what is appropriate in the way of expressive

UNIT 10 SECTION 4

articulation and dynamics. The instrumental music of this period often reflected popular dance forms, so a firm sense of metre and pulse should be maintained even when the music is highly decorative.

The term **Baroque** refers on the one hand to a distinctive style in the arts generally, and on the other hand to a historical period of classical art music. In the former case it emphasises dynamic and fluid forms, and dramatic expression. In contrast to the Renaissance period (which is more 'classicist' in its emphasis on harmony and proportion), the Baroque stresses sensual imagery and the drama of human experience.

During its later stages it evolved into a lighter, more playful style: **Rococo**. The nearest equivalent in music is the mid-18th century **Galant** style, which marks the transition between the Baroque and Classical periods in Western art music. Here we see an increasing emphasis on phrase structure and dramatic use of form in instrumental music, combined with the emergence of a new, much more intensely expressive approach to improvising and performing, as typified by the keyboard performances of C.P.E. Bach. That provided the basis for the eventual emergence of the Romantic style of expressive and virtuosic improvisation which reached its peak in the early 19th century. You can read C.P.E. Bach's thoughts about keyboard performance and improvisation in his treatise *Essay On The True Art Of Playing Keyboard Instruments*.

Baroque music has a great deal to offer improvisers today. On the one hand there is the fully developed tonal system, incorporating and reconciling diatonic and chromatic aspects of harmony into a single unified system of scales, chords, and key relations, whose most perfect embodiment is, arguably, the works of J.S. Bach. On the other hand there is the richly contrapuntal character of the music, with its strong awareness of how melodic lines work against one another rhythmically as well as harmonically, combined with the powerful new feeling for melody as dramatic expression, linked to opera and to the idea of a homophonic texture where the solo line is in the foreground and the harmony plays a supporting role. Baroque music also gives us the first clear manifestation of the kind of harmony that gives a special role to the bassline. Many of the harmonic techniques used in both later classical music and in jazz owe their origins to the Baroque understanding of the role of the bassline in linking chords together to make coherent and well-directed progressions. The importance of the Circle of Fifths, and (to a lesser extent) of chromatic connections, are features that link jazz harmony and voice-leading back to Baroque music.

> CD Track 67 illustrates the role of the bassline in Baroque keyboard style: note how it is elaborated melodically to create an effective counterpoint to the right-hand melody while also providing the basis for the unfolding chord structure.

3) The Classical style

'Classical style' doesn't mean the style of classical music as a whole, but the style of the music of the 'Classical period'. This is roughly the second half of the 18th century and first quarter of the 19th century. What it really corresponds to, above all, is the music of great composers like Haydn, Mozart, and Beethoven, and perhaps Schubert. The term 'Classical' can be misleading: it comes from the idea of 'classicism' and 'classical' ideals – ideals of harmony, proportion and rationality – values thought to be most clearly embodied in the culture and art of ancient Greek and Roman civilisations. By contrast, these composers were seen in their own time as moving away from, rather than towards, such ideals, as by the standards of their day they were challenging existing traditions and exploring new and more difficult musical forms.

More than Baroque music (and perhaps Romantic music, too) music of the Classical period unfolds as a kind of argument or discourse, balancing successive musical phrases. Hence phrase structure plays a much bigger role. The harmonic structure of the music revolves around the tonic-dominant relationship, particularly at the level of key relations, though the relationship of a minor key to its relative major is also important. Thematic contrasts are much more clearly defined and developed than in preceding or succeeding periods, and piano textures (such as the famous Alberti bass) are elaborated in order to support a melodic line while retaining rhythmic flow. Scales and arpeggios are used a great deal as what is called **passage work** – this is transitional material whose role is to sustain and unfold the larger musical structure of key relations, making it an important element of the music, in spite of the fact that it is devoid of thematic significance in itself.

Above all, Classical period music offers improvisers today interesting models of how complex forms (eg, sonata form, slow movement form, rondo, minuet and trio) can be elaborated for dramatic effect, even if such forms cannot be sustained in the context of improvised performance. As we observed earlier in this unit, such forms can be present in the background as a reference point, even when a looser approach is adopted. This was the approach to improvisation of classical composer-improvisers such as Mozart and Beethoven, who would often extemporise 'free fantasias' in which ideas, thematic contrasts, key relations, and virtuoso passage work similar to those in their compositions would be explored more freely and adventurously, playing on the unfulfilled expectations of listeners familiar with the composed forms of the time.

> CD Track 68 illustrates a standard Classical-period texture in which a right-hand melody is supported by a flowing left-hand texture based on chordal patterns. However, for more extended examples of the classical approach during this period, try CD Tracks 48 and 50. The latter illustrates the kind of improvising associated with the use of 'free fantasia' form as a starting point for lyrical and dramatic expressive effects.

4) Romantic period music

Romanticism was a cultural, artistic and political movement that swept through Europe towards the end of the 18th century – beginning around the time of the French Revolution in France and the Industrial Revolution in Britain. It came in the wake of a period characterised by rationalism and an emphasis on science, known as the Enlightenment, and was partly a reaction to this. (However, only partly, since its emphasis on 'subjective' feelings was itself an offshoot of 18th-century intellectual and artistic developments that owed their existence to the rationalism of the Enlightenment.)

We can already see some elements of Romanticism in Beethoven's earlier works, such as his famous 'Moonlight' Sonata. There's a definite shift of emphasis away from the interplay of musical ideas, and towards emotion and atmosphere for their own sake. Melodies tend to be simpler but more dramatically expressive, while pianistic textures are more complex and less clearly defined, and often make a lot more use of the sustaining pedal. Composers such as Mendelssohn and Schumann took this further, opening the way for the more virtuosic pianistic styles of great pianist-composers like Chopin and Liszt, in which the capacity of the modern piano to sustain highly elaborate textures and a much wider palette of colouristic effects was explored to much greater degree.

In the late 19th century the features typical of Romanticism were taken to an extreme. Wagner, in particular, replaced the stricter musical forms previously used in opera with a continuous stream of unfolding textures and motives that functioned as a musical commentary on events happening on stage. He also pioneered a new approach to harmony, involving much freer use of dissonance and chromatic alteration, that exploited the different ways in which chords could be connected through chromatic voice-leading. This was the first step towards the stylistic upheavals of 20th-century classical music.

Romantic period music stands in a complex relationship to our culture today. On the one hand, classical music has mostly moved on from 19th-century musical styles – though how quickly or slowly, and how far it has done so, has varied enormously with different composers and different local cultures. At the same time, many of the ideas and ideals associated with Romanticism as a wider cultural movement have remained beneath the surface of modern culture, and remain a powerful influence within contemporary popular culture. Hence it's not surprising to find that qualities associated above all with music of the Romantic period show up in modern popular styles such as rock and pop: the colouristic emphasis on harmony, on expressive melody and melodic nuances, not to mention the use of narratives to frame lyrical expressions of feeling, as in rock and pop ballads.

Beyond this, classical music from the Romantic period is relevant to piano improvisers today on account of its far-reaching exploration of the piano as a source of colour and texture – a feature taken further by some 20th-century music, especially that of so-called 'impressionist' composers like Ravel and Debussy.

> The semi-improvised arrangements of Italian folksongs on CD Tracks 75-78 illustrate many elements of improvised Romantic piano style – especially its emphasis on expressive melody supported by rich and colourful textures involving extensive use of the sustaining pedal. For other examples of Romantic piano texture, listen to CD Tracks 69-72.

5) 20th-century classical music

The 20th century saw revolutionary developments in the language of classical music. Composers like Schoenberg, Stravinsky, and Bartok developed new ways of working with rhythm, metre, and harmony, as well as exploring the textural possibilities of instruments (and of the modern orchestra) for their own sake. Schoenberg began writing music that was athematic (ie, with no distinguishable musical themes) and atonal (ie, with no stable key centres). Stravinsky explored polyrhythms (simultaneous but independent rhythmic and metrical structures) and polytonality (music in several keys at once).

The 1930s saw the emergence of another tendency, neoclassicism, in which past styles were parodied or played with in other ironic ways. The 1950s and 1960s saw the development of a new experimental avant-garde, which was reacting against the growing influence of commercialised popular music, while the 1960s also brought the first examples of interaction between avant-garde and popular music.

By the 1970s many (but certainly not all) composers were rejecting the more extreme innovations of post-war modern music in favour of neo-Romantic styles, or alternative approaches such as minimalism that overtly reflect the influence of popular and ethnic music. The 1980s and 1990s saw a shift towards what is sometimes described as 'postmodernism' – which means a move away from modernist experimentation and towards a more eclectic, multicultural, multilayered approach to style, often involving a complex and ambiguous relationship both to Western art music of the past and to the music of other cultures. What is more, many of these more recent developments in classical music now seem to coexist, rather than superseding one another in any sort of linear fashion, adding to the many-sided and complicated character of contemporary classical musical culture.

Both the richness and the still controversial character of many of the developments in classical music over the course of the 20th century (and since) make it impossible to sum up its implications for improvisers today. What one does or does not take from this complex series of developments may largely depend on one's own relationship to the culture we all find ourselves in today, how open-minded one is, and maybe also what one is looking for at a more personal level.

Improvisation itself figured for a while in experimental classical music (of the 1960s), thanks to the interest of some composers in mysticism, chance-based music making, alternative forms of notation, and novel kinds of open-ended form that allowed elements of a work to be played in different sequences on different occasions. However, most of these developments have faded from the contemporary music scene, and their musical significance tends to be far removed from the mainstream – hence the fact that they have not been explored earlier in this book. If improvisation appears within the sphere of contemporary classical music making today, it's much more likely to be in the context of one or other of the cultural crossovers that have occurred, linking classical music to jazz, rock, or other non-classical styles. In these areas the possibilities for improvising will no doubt reflect elements of how improvisation figures in the individual styles themselves, but their interaction may also give rise to new and unforeseeable possibilities.

Form in jazz & rock

Form in both jazz and rock has its origins in the kind of simple strophic structure already mentioned. This was a feature of European and North American folksongs long before it began to be developed by classical music as the basis for the sort of art-songs (often known by their German name, *Lieder*) discussed in the previous section.

The basic structure of this form revolves around a story (or some other sequence of thoughts, images, etc, expressed in words), which alternates with a commentary. The story unfolds from one **verse** to the next, usually with new words set to the same music. Meanwhile the commentary takes the form of a contrasting **chorus** section. Here the same words typically recur with the same music each time – though their significance may alter as the context provided by the narrative or argument of the lyrics unfolds.

> The term chorus, and the idea of interspersing regular commentaries into an unfolding story or drama which this refers to, both come from Ancient Greek drama – especially tragedy. The 'chorus' was the name for the stage-character or performers whose job was to comment on events to the audience just after they occurred – often showing the audience what sort of response was appropriate through singing and dancing. The basic effect remains the same in modern popular songs: a shift from simply keeping track of events or thoughts as they are presented on stage or in song to a focus on interpretation – on 'what it all adds up to'. This means adopting a perspective that, paradoxically, is usually more reflective and detached but at the same time a lot more intensely emotional. The fact that this idea from Ancient Greek culture has survived to become the main device in modern popular songs surely tells us something interesting about our culture today.

By the time of the emergence of jazz, this form had come to play a major role not just in classical music, but also in popular forms of entertainment such as variety theatre, as well as in the kind of songs and hymns typically sung at home and at church by ordinary folk, or as part of different kinds of amateur music making.

Jazz took this form as it existed in the popular songs of the early 20th century and adapted it. Such songs typically included an additional section known as a **bridge**: this was introduced after two or three alternations of the verse and chorus, and consisted of new material, followed by either a return to another verse or a move straight to a final chorus. Jazz kept the verse and the bridge, but left out the chorus, creating the AABA structure of two verses, middle-eight (bridge) and a final third verse that we all know today – the standard 32-bar jazz song form.

From an improviser's point of view the advantage of this form is its simplicity and familiarity, which leave the jazz player free to do what he or she wants, without worrying about whether the listener will keep track of where they've got to in the structure. The repetitions of the verse give scope for **variation**, while the bridge leaves room for **contrast**. Furthermore, jazz players are free to cycle through the whole of this form as many times as they wish, each time giving space for solo improvising to a different member of an ensemble, or using each new 'take' as an opportunity to try some new angle on the original material.

Some more modern jazz attempts to introduce elements of the kind of approach to form that evolved in 19th century classical music: in particular, the use of small recurring motifs to create a sense of unity over the course of extended improvisations. This is not really an essential feature of the jazz approach, but makes sense if a player wishes to move jazz away from its traditional basis in popular songs and towards the kind of more extended, developmental approach to form found in a lot of classical music of the last two centuries. This can be understood as part of a wider process of 'classicising' jazz – introducing elements of art-music culture into jazz as a way of bringing it closer to the mainstream of Western culture. This is something that some jazz musicians feel is necessary if they are to be able to explore their more serious artistic ambitions within jazz, but others may equally feel that it means losing sight of the essence of what jazz was originally really about.

Strophic song forms play an even greater role in modern rock and pop styles than they do in jazz. This is because these kinds of music have largely evolved around the rock and pop song as their main genre. This means that purely instrumental music in these areas, when it happens at all, tends to be modelled on songs in the same style. It often functions as a kind of 'song without words', copying the effects of a real song-structure, right down to the specific effects associated with the alternation of verse and chorus, or the use of an intro, bridge, or coda. Improvisation in pop, and to some extent also in rock, typically plays a supporting role, with instrumental riffs and licks being added alongside or between phrases of the vocal line to add texture or form a continuous musical commentary.

One area where form becomes a significant concern for improvisation in these styles is where a performer is required to deliver an extended solo **break**, which may well be improvised. This is more likely to happen in rock music than pop, but is less likely to involve piano, due to the guitar-centred nature of most rock music. Nevertheless, a rock pianist performing an extended solo improvisation needs to be sensitive to what we described earlier in this unit as dramatic form. The use of riffs, licks, and grooves, as well as register, volume, harmony, and melodic ideas, must all be calculated to effectively maintain and build on an audience's interest.

This is usually done by 'upping the tension' in stages, progressively introducing more elaborate textures, stronger backbeat and/or syncopation effects, and striking key changes. A common technique is to copy what often happens in pop and rock songs themselves: as the material comes back for the last time around (ie, the last verse), we make an abrupt modulation to a brighter key – usually a whole tone or semitone higher. Improvisers may make several such moves in succession to maintain or build tension. One of the main differences between how form works in classical music and in styles like rock and pop is that in the former we typically expect the music eventually to get back to the initial (or principal) key centre, whereas in the latter we don't.

Another area where form plays a role is **jamming**. This is what rock, pop, and jazz musicians do when they get together informally to try out ideas and have fun by improvising together. It's usually done by taking a well-known set of chords or a well-known song and using this structure as a common point of reference. Just like with jazz song form, we can cycle through the structure as many times as we want, taking turns to improvise solos or accompanying licks, or just contributing some nice voicings or an interesting bassline riff to the supporting texture.

> One of the great things about jamming is that you can have different musicians improvising together who start out from different styles that they are familiar with, only to arrive at a common approach. This is often how new and original approaches emerge in modern popular music. It's rather like what happens in poetry: writers encounter the different ways people use language by speaking to them in everyday conversations, and this forces them to open up and adapt to new possibilities in ordinary language, which then makes for a richer poetic language. That's why contact with a vernacular is so important for all art forms. Jamming is one of the few areas in music making today where this is still a possibility, as classical music has shifted its focus towards the more professionalised sphere of concerts and away from those sorts of amateur music making and improvised approaches that don't easily relate to that.

By far the most commonly used structure for this is **12-bar blues**. It's employed by musicians of all kinds who play in modern, non-classical styles – not just by those who play in the blues idiom, as the name might suggest. So if you want to get involved in any of these styles you should get really familiar with it. We'll be looking at this in the next section.

Style in rock, jazz, and blues

The 12-bar blues is the main model that has influenced how chord structures are used in rock and jazz – even when the style is one that doesn't particularly show the influence of the blues idiom.

Looking at how we can use this to improvise in different non-classical styles can help us to unlock the essential differences not only between non-classical and classical harmony, but also between different non-classical styles themselves. Here's the basic structure:

| I | I | I | I | IV | IV | I | I | V | IV | I | I :||

But this got changed just a little, in the 1930s, to:

| I | IV | I | I | IV | IV | I | I | V | IV | I | V :||

The first thing we can learn from these two sequences is that the basic logic according to which harmony works in rock, pop, blues, and jazz is slightly different from that of mainstream classical music.

In the 18th century classical music evolved towards a paradigm which clearly took the dominant as the main counter-pole to the tonic, with other options understood against the background of this central relationship. Although the resulting hierarchy of key and chord relationships then got loosened up a lot, due to the developments that occurred in the 19th century, it remains as the basic guiding principle of mainstream classical harmony.

In these modern, non-classical styles, however, the subdominant tends to function as an equally important counter-pole – especially in blues-based harmony. Indeed one of the most distinctive features of the blues sequences above is the sudden switch from V to IV in bars 9-10. This would be unthinkable in classical harmony, as it represents a 'trumping' of the dominant by the subdominant.

Note, however, that in the second version – more likely to be used by jazz, rock, and pop musicians, and anyone else who plays in styles other than just the 'pure' blues itself – the sequence still ends on V. It thus still treats the dominant as the eventual point of arrival, prior to the return to the tonic that will inevitably occur when we go back to the beginning to repeat the entire structure. However, there's a strong feeling that the 'upbeat' pull of the dominant towards brighter keys has been weakened by the prominence of the subdominant, which seems to be dragging the tonality back down in the opposite direction. The original effect was to create a powerful feeling of being weighed down by an inescapable burden – the chief expressive effect of the original blues idiom. It's interesting to note that this same effect continues to underlie a great deal of modern rock, pop, and jazz, even when these styles appear 'upbeat' and positive. (It's also interesting to note that most musicians now have opted to play the slightly more optimistic second version, in which the sequence does finally make it through to the dominant in bar 12.)

There's a whole lot of things we can do with this structure, depending on the style we're operating in. In the blues idiom itself, all of these chords would be dominant sevenths. (Don't worry about that for now – we'll explore blues itself later in this unit.) However, when improvising or jamming using this sequence it's best to think of it as just a series of straight triads that can be altered, extended, or substituted to suit whatever style we're playing in.

1) Pop

A straightforward pop-style treatment of the sequence in C major might look like this:

| C	| C	| F	| C	|
| F	| F	| C	| Am	|
| G	| F	| C	| G7	:||

Notice that the harmony avoids any obvious blues element in the individual chords themselves: the only dominant seventh chord is in bar 12, where the G chord actually

CD TRACK 79

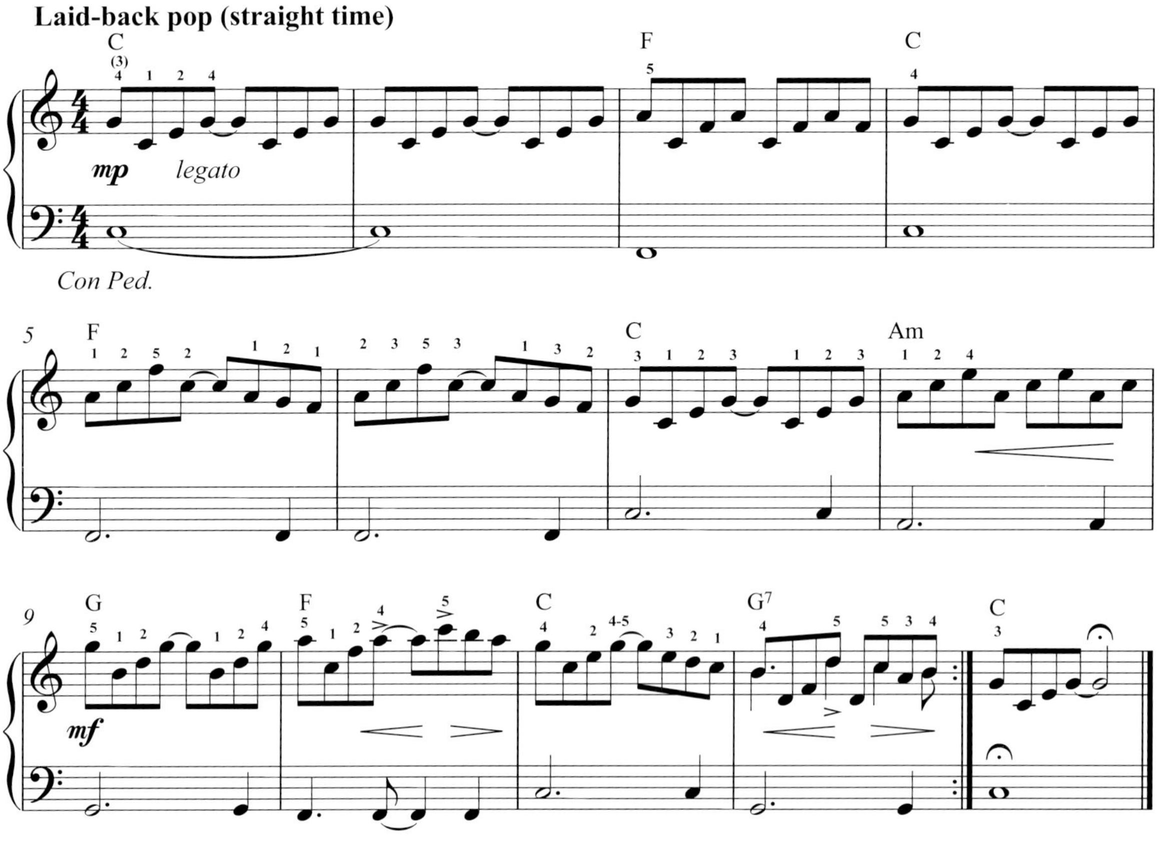

functions as a traditional dominant, in contrast to all the rest, including V in bar 9, which gives way to IV and thus can't properly be heard in these terms. Note also how the only other complication to the harmony is a simple classical substitution of VI for I, which is reserved for late on in the sequence (bar 8), so that its effect will be felt more strongly as a contrast to the extreme simplicity of the harmony in the preceding bars, which is limited to just two chords. (In this case the first IV chord is inserted in bar 3 instead of bar 2, as sometimes happens.)

This way of introducing secondary triads or other 'light' additions only after a sense of extreme harmonic simplicity and directness has first been established – if at all – is the hallmark of many 'pop' styles: especially (but not only) those influenced by American folk and 'country' idioms. We would expect any piano realisation to aim for a similar feel in terms of texture and rhythm, perhaps by placing very simple guitar-style chord figurations in the middle register, with only gentle syncopation (opposite page).

Any further elaboration of this texture (below) would remain limited to the introduction of small melodic figurations, some simple added-note harmonies and sus chords, and possibly the odd raised fourth (or ninth) over major triads or dominant

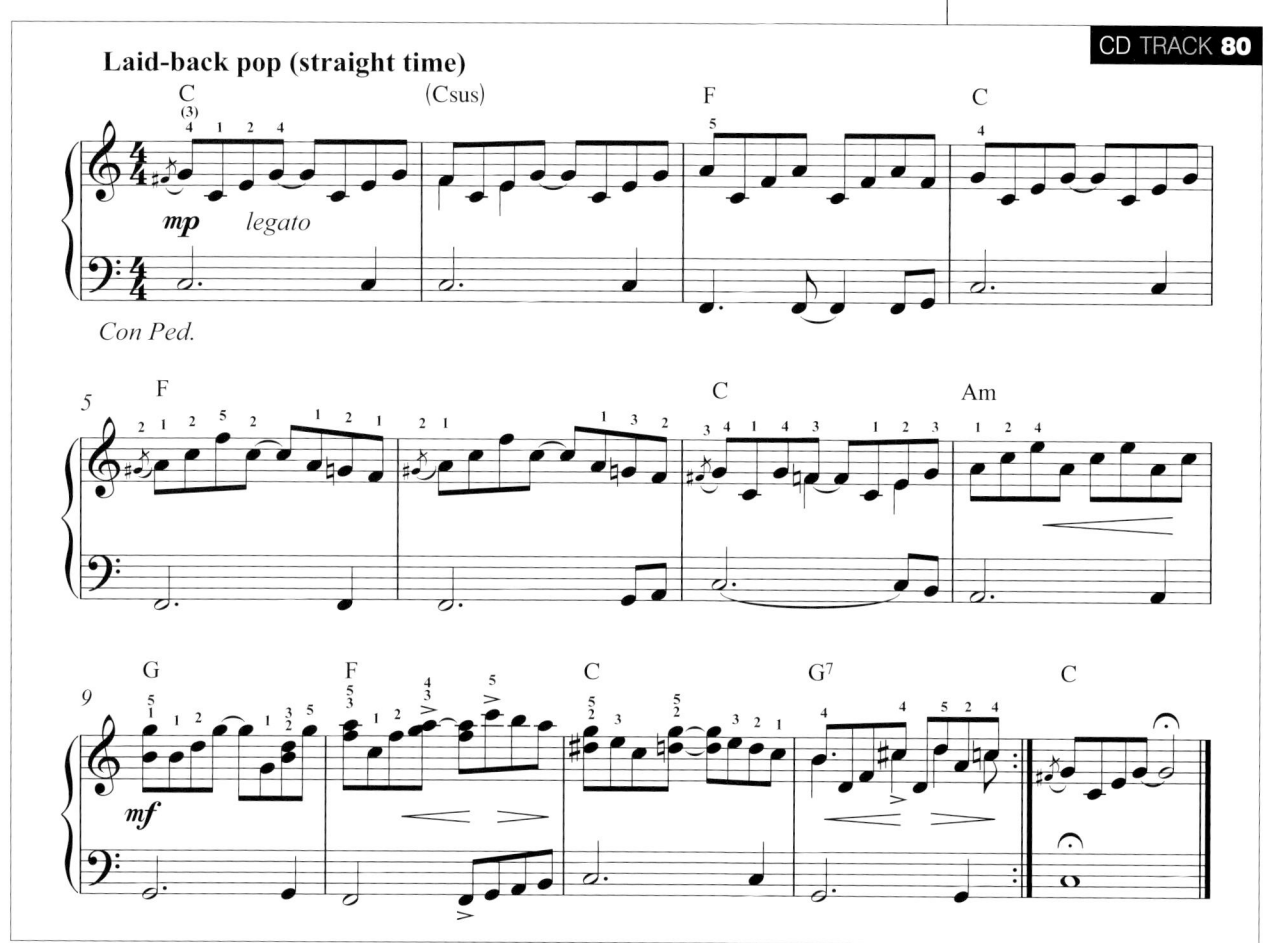

chords (particularly in 'country' style pop). The left hand, which plays a role equivalent to a bass instrument in an ensemble here, might also add some stepwise figures or additional repetitions of notes, just to propel the rhythm forward.

Exercise 10.1
Now try your own pop-style realisations of the 12-bar blues, using the chord progressions shown above. Remember, keep the harmony simple, and make the listener wait before you introduce any significant harmonic departures.
Experiment with adding the odd decorative melodic figuration here and there, or a few simple added-note harmonies and sus chords. Listen to some of your favourite pop songs and then try improvising simple textures like the ones shown above, based on the grooves in those songs. Try working in a range of speeds, time signatures, and keys too.

2) Rock
Now let's see what a typical straight rock version of the chords might look like:

C	Csus4	Fsus2	C
B♭sus2	F	A♭sus2	E♭
G	F	Am7	Dm7 G7

As with pop, the stress is on harmonic simplicity, but note this time the use of sus2 and sus4 chords in the earlier stages and minor seventh chords later on. The former add some roughness and stridency, while the latter add mellowness, but also allow the harmony to blossom out into something more richly colourful as it builds to the final V chord. Note especially the use of ♭VII in bar 5. This is a typical rock feature: it can be analysed as another device for reinforcing the subdominant as an alternative counter-pole to the dominant, as IV of IV. (Hence the move to IV straight after, and the fact that these two chords correspond to two bars of chord IV in the original sequence.)

Most rock exists on a stylistic continuum between 'hard' and 'soft'. The harder the 'sound', the more we go for sus chords and simple triads, and an emphasis on ♭VII. (This can also mean using the Mixolydian mode as a basis for major-key harmony and melody, or the rock minor or Dorian for minor key music. All these include ♭VII.)

The softer the 'sound', the more we tend to go for minor seventh chords. At the extreme 'soft' end, we might even indulge in the odd major seventh. But these should definitely be handled with care: their sweetness tends to undermine the rough-edged, slightly 'nasty' feel that's important to many rock styles.

The same logic applies with texture, which in rock is determined essentially by the rhythmic feel of the music. That means **grooves** with either a harder or softer **backbeat**. (The backbeat is the stressed second and fourth beats of a bar, as distinct from the natural metrical stress on the first and third beats in quadruple time.

In a rock group the rhythm section will provide this, but in solo piano the texture must generate the backbeat feel itself.) There are loads of rock piano textures and grooves that correspond to different sub-styles of rock – too many to explore in this book. Note, though, that the general approach behind piano rock grooves is to import elements of the logic of drumming into the traditional relationship between the hands. There are two main ways to do this.

1) LAYERED GROOVES: One hand plays a more active rhythm, while the other supports it, accentuating a simpler outline – sometimes just the backbeat – that falls on some of the same beats or subdivisions.

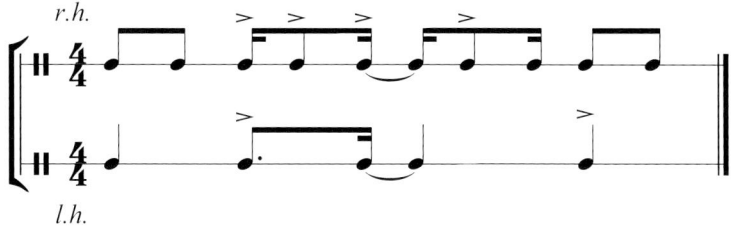

2) LINEAR GROOVES: Here we divide a single continuous rhythm, or stream of equal subdivisions, between the two hands. Positioning the hands in distinct registers of the piano then results in a separation effect: we hear two separate rhythms working against each other, often with a considerable degree of syncopation.

Of course we can also mix these:

How we realise harmony and grooves as piano textures in a rock style also depends to some extent on how 'hard' or 'soft' the rock effect is that we're aiming at. Rock piano mostly means solo piano, because rock bands are usually electric guitar-based, and both these and the drum kit tend to drown out instruments like the piano. Of course there are lots of standardised groove-based piano styles around now, but is it really so interesting to copy what's already out there?

A more interesting approach is to explore creating your own grooves first – focusing on the basic techniques mentioned above – and then see for yourself how these can be made to work over your own versions of harmonic sequences like 12-bar blues. Layered grooves like the one shown above naturally divide up between the hands, with chords in the right and bass-line patterns in the left:

On the other hand, linear grooves call for a more creative and flexible approach to dividing up the texture between the hands, as the following example demonstrates. Note how the chord used here has been developed into an alternation with the second-inversion triad on the same bass note – a common effect in rock that also gives the harmony a strong subdominant feel. The second bar shows the same material, written

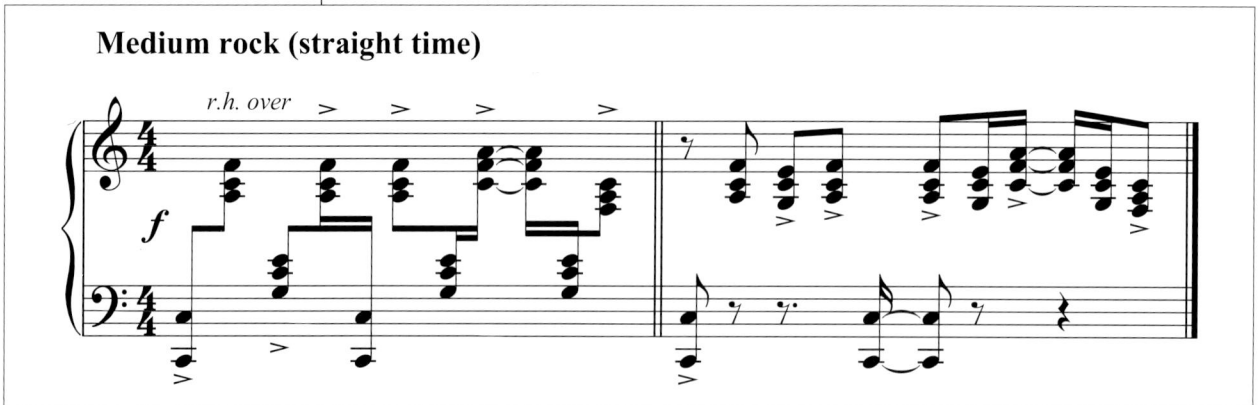

in a more traditional way to highlight the division of the texture into chords and bass (which is what hear), rather than the division between the hands (which is what we do).

Of course, **riffs** also play a major role in rock music, though these normally tend to be worked out ahead of a performance or jam session as a basis for improvisation, rather than being improvised themselves. The paradigm for melodic improvisation in rock is, of course, the kind of soloing that a lead guitar in a band does, which mainly consists of fast scale and chord-based runs, usually with an even stronger emphasis on the pentatonic scale than in jazz. Note the following important difference:

- Jazz mainly uses pentatonic scales that leave out avoid notes, which often means a pentatonic scale based on a different starting note from the root of the chord (eg, pentatonic major on V over chord I).
- Rock uses the pentatonic scale on a starting note that's the root of the chord, or on a starting note a perfect fourth above the root.

There's a simple reason for this, which is also worth knowing about. Rock, especially at the 'harder' end of the spectrum, doesn't worry so much about avoid notes. But unless a very 'soft rock' effect is wanted, it's best to avoid pentatonic scales that include a major seventh above the root, as these are too 'nice'. Also, certain pentatonics work especially well over the sus chords rock players are so fond of. Remember:

- A major pentatonic starting on the same note as the root of a sus2 major chord will sound great.
- A major pentatonic starting on the note a perfect fourth above a sus4 major chord will sound great.

Having said this, rock-guitar-style soloing on a piano tends to sound like a poor imitation of the real thing. In solo piano rock improvising it's therefore generally better to focus on building interesting textures and riffs as an accompaniment to a melody.

> For a taste of rock-style piano improvising at the softer end of the hard-soft rock spectrum, but with a lively syncopated groove, try CD Track 61.

Exercise 10.2.
Now try your own rock-style realisations, using the progressions for the 12-bar blues presented earlier. Remember, keep the harmony simple, and focus on achieving and maintaining the right level of rhythmic intensity. Then add decorative melodic figurations and sus chords, before exploring some left-hand riffs and integrating them into your playing. Find some great rock numbers and try improvising in a similar way over the grooves in those songs. Think about how the

piano can imitate elements of the rock ensemble texture like guitar riffs, bass effects, and even drum kit patterns. Try a range of speeds, time signatures, and keys.

3) Jazz

Okay, so what would a jazz player do with the 12-bar blues chord sequence? The first thing to note is that jazz is more closely connected with the blues idiom from which this sequence originally comes. That means it's more likely to reflect elements of blues harmony in its way of handling the chords, though it need not do so.

Here's a jazz version with some fairly typical elements of jazz reharmonisation that you should recognise from Unit Eight, with only a light blues feel. This is mainly achieved through the use of dominant seventh chords in bars 9 and 10.

C△	F△♯4	C△	Gm7 C7♭9
F△	F♯°7	C/G	C△
G7	F7 E7	Am7 A♭m7	D♭7 G7♭9

Remember we said that in classical harmony the V chord in bar 9 would be problematic when treated as dominant harmony, just because it's followed directly by IV. So adding the dominant seventh here will be heard as a definite blues effect, as will the 'sliding' of the chord-shape down to IV and then III in the following bar. (This technique is derived from the blues guitar style, where it's natural to slide the hand down the fretboard with the fingers locked in the same chord shape.)

Now compare this to a more strongly blues-influenced version, where many more chords get the dominant seventh treatment:

C7	F7	C7	Gm7 C7
F7	F♯°7	C/G	E⌀7 A7
Dm7	G7	C7 E♭7	A♭7 G7

Now let's compare a version in a later jazz style – the sort of thing a bebop (or 'bop', for short) player might improvise over. Notice how chords functioning as dominants relative to whatever follows them get turned into alt or 7♯11 chords, while Lydian harmony (as in bar 2 of the first jazz version shown above) gets turned into a dominant seventh with an augmented feel (ie, a sharpened 11th, and a flattened 13th that's actually heard as a raised fifth).

C△	F7♯11♭13	C△	Gm7 Calt
F7	F♯°7	C/G	A♭7♯11
G7	F7 E7	Am7 A♭m7	D♭7♯11 Galt

We've already looked at some of things bebop players might do when improvising in Unit Eight, but what, exactly, would a bebop player play over these chords?

Apart from using the voicings and reharmonisation techniques explored earlier, they would use special **bebop scales** to generate fast scale-based runs. These add one extra note to the normal seven-note diatonic scales and modes of more traditional jazz. The fact that the scale then has an even number of notes per octave ensures a more regular and predictable correlation between scale-degrees and beats of the bar when improvising. Here are the main examples. Bebop scales for chords in the same II-V progression keep the same added note, which also then corresponds to the raised avoid note (the fourth) on chord I in a major key.

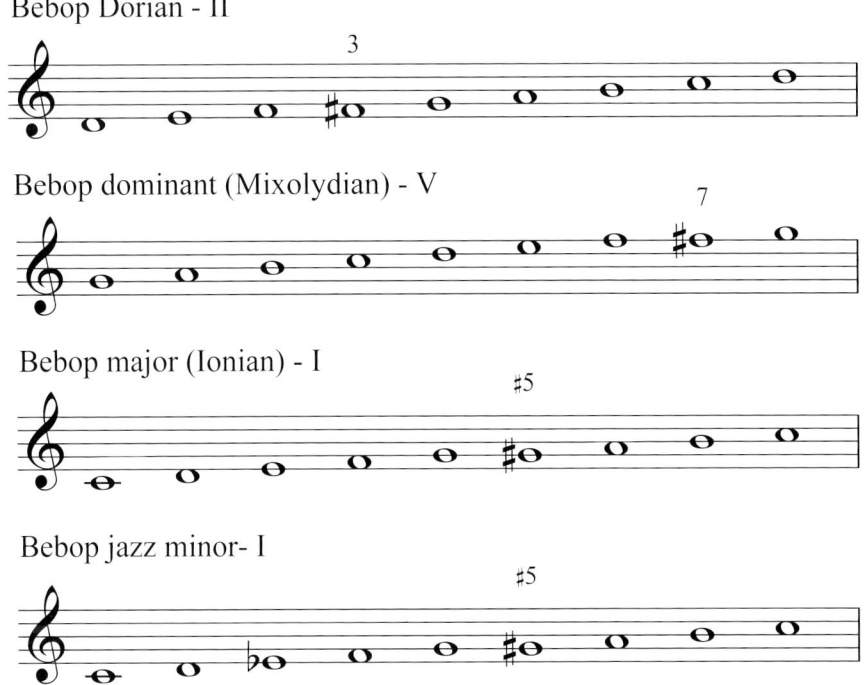

Exercise 10.3.
Now try your some bebop-style jazz improvisations over the 12-bar blues. First listen to great pianists like Bud Powell and Thelonious Monk, or, for a more mellow and minimalistic aproach, the wonderful Bill Evans. The melodic style should be rapid-fire, racy, with lots of scale-figurations and quirky voicings. Try a range of keys.

Fusion styles such as **jazz-rock** mix elements of the rock and pop techniques discussed in this section with the jazz approach to harmony and improvisation already covered earlier in this book. However, if that's what interests you, it's best to work out your own fusion by starting out with these styles themselves, rather than copying other people's. Other fusions, such as Latin jazz or Latin rock, require you to first be familiar with the basic elements of Latin-style music.

4) Latin jazz

> 'Latin' is short for 'Latin-American' – the name for popular and folk-based music from Cuba, the Caribbean, Mexico, Panama, Argentina, Brazil, and other parts of the northern mainland of the South American continent. Most of these places were once Spanish or Portuguese colonies, where coffee, sugar, and cotton plantations were run using slave labour from Africa. The result was a melting pot of different ethnic cultures: Hispanic and even Arabic influences alongside African and native Indian ones, followed later in some cases by the additional influence of jazz, which itself took from some of these styles in its earlier stages. The distinctive dance-based styles and rhythms that emerged from this are the main feature of Latin music: not just world-famous ones like salsa and samba, but also tango, mariachi, calypso, reggae, and merengue.

As far as improvisation is concerned, the most significant of the Latin styles is without doubt **Latin jazz**. A lot of jazz is influenced by Latin music's unique and exciting rhythmic feel, but it's worth also being aware that Latin musicians, when improvising, often make use of harmonic and melodic techniques drawn from jazz. This means that in practice it's hard to say where Latin-influenced jazz stops, and jazz-influenced Latin (involving improvisation) begins. Typically, though, Latin jazz involves one or both of the following two possibilities:

- Improvising with jazz scales and harmonies over a Latin groove.
- Improvising with jazz scales and harmonies around Latin standards.

In this book we'll focus on the first option. What goes on here is pretty much like in mainstream jazz, but with the important difference that it all happens in straight time, using the characteristic syncopated rhythms of Latin music, rather than the swung rhythms of ordinary jazz. If you come to this with a knowledge of the latter already in place then it's basically a question of learning new sets of rhythmic patterns – **grooves**. Each of these has its own rhythmic 'feel' that reflects one or other of the well-known Latin dance forms. Some Latin grooves seem to be associated with music that's fast and demonically furious, but in practice most of them can be played at a variety of speeds.

Let's start with **salsa**, which has an Afro-Cuban base. The main pattern here is the 'clave' (pronounced 'clah-veh'), which alternates basic three-note and two-note rhythmic formulas in either 'forward clave' (3+2) or 'reverse clave' (2+3):

Forward clave (3+2)

Reverse clave (2+3)

A variation on this that became associated with the style known as **bossa nova** uses just 'forward clave', but delays the final attack, making the pattern less defined and rather more flexible:

Samba, on the other hand, has a more primitive, hypnotic character. Note how over the course of a two-bar cycle it starts on the beat, goes through repeated syncopations, and then recovers the beat again, driven on relentlessly by a repeated dotted-rhythm pattern beneath, known as the samba 'feet'.

Jazz chords, played either as left-hand voicings or two-handed voicings, will work well when played to these rhythms, or to variations on them. When arranging or improvising around a jazz standard in a Latin style, you may find the melody line doesn't fit so naturally, and needs to be adapted rhythmically.

Exercise 10.4.
Okay, so now it's time to 'go Latin'. First take the three jazz-style versions of the sequence shown earlier in the unit and work out your own realisations of the harmony using left-hand and/or two-handed voicings. (You should be able to do that if you've reached this stage in the book.) Then try improvising textures and right-hand melodies using the straight-time Latin grooves shown here, rather than swung jazz rhythms.

5) Blues

Blues, as we've already seen, has had a major influence on jazz and other kinds of modern non-classical music. It mostly uses the fixed 12-bar harmonic sequence we're already familiar with, repeated with variations: the **12-bar blues**. In blues, however, all of the chords played in the unreharmonised version of the sequence tend to get treated as dominant sevenths.

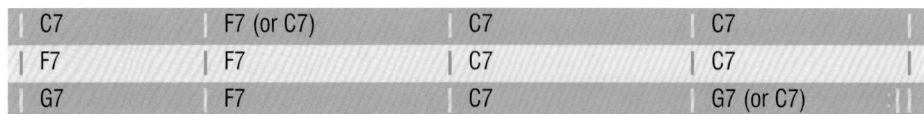

C7	F7 (or C7)	C7	C7
F7	F7	C7	C7
G7	F7	C7	G7 (or C7)

Note that these chords are still closer to what we'd expect in a major key than in a minor one. However, the special **blues scale** that blues players make use of to improvise over these is closer to a minor scale. It's like a minor pentatonic with an additional note, the flattened fifth, present along with the normal fifth.

Blues scale on C

Playing either the minor third, flattened fifth, or flattened seventh will produce a grating tension when played over a major chord. This tension between major and minor harmonic implications is the classic 'out-of-tune' effect, with these notes referred to as 'blue notes'.

Blues pianists generally improvise by combining melodic elaborations of right-hand material with a range of repetitive rhythmic patterns in the left hand whose driving rhythm is what essentially holds the music together, even when the right hand plays around the beat. The latter effect, known as **leaning on the beat**, is also a distinctive feature of blues: right-hand notes and phrases are delivered just after the beat, with a slight delay. This effect added to the downbeat mood of the original blues.

Even so, the driving rhythms of blues piano can often point towards a more upbeat feel, anticipating the rhythmic character of rock. This is especially true for **boogie-woogie** left-hand patterns, whose physically demanding character makes them incompatible with playing in other styles – especially classical music. That's why they're not explored in this book. Nevertheless, here are some blues-style left-hand patterns or grooves you can safely make use of (opposite page). Each pattern can be simply transposed to fit the chord required. (In blues we treat issues of voice-leading extremely loosely, so implied or sounding consecutive fifths or octaves tend to be accepted.)

Note that these patterns can be played straight or with swing. Straight-eight effects are much more likely to be associated with an up-tempo (ie, faster, more upbeat) blues idiom, while swing is typical for medium-speed and slower blues. Remember also that

the more downbeat (ie, slow, heavy, serious) the style, the more we lean on the beat in the right hand. At the other end of the spectrum, faster, driving straight-eight styles may do the opposite, **pushing the beat** – this means playing right-hand material just ahead of the beat to further intensify the strong upbeat feel of the music.

Apart from these patterns, an important left-hand option for medium-tempo blues playing is the **walking bass**. Here we link roots of chords on the first beats of bars by playing rhythmically even quarter-notes (crotchets) throughout. These move mostly in stepwise movement, or so that they outline chords. Notice how stepwise movement involves the Mixolydian mode (sometimes with chromatic additions) rather than the major scale, while outlined chords are normally dominant sevenths. Here are some examples:

Walking bass figures

Blues playing employs a wide repertoire of formulaic patterns as a basis for what the right hand does. These include grace-note figures (often played by sliding the same fingers from black keys onto neighbouring white keys), parallel thirds and sixths, and repeated-note figures:

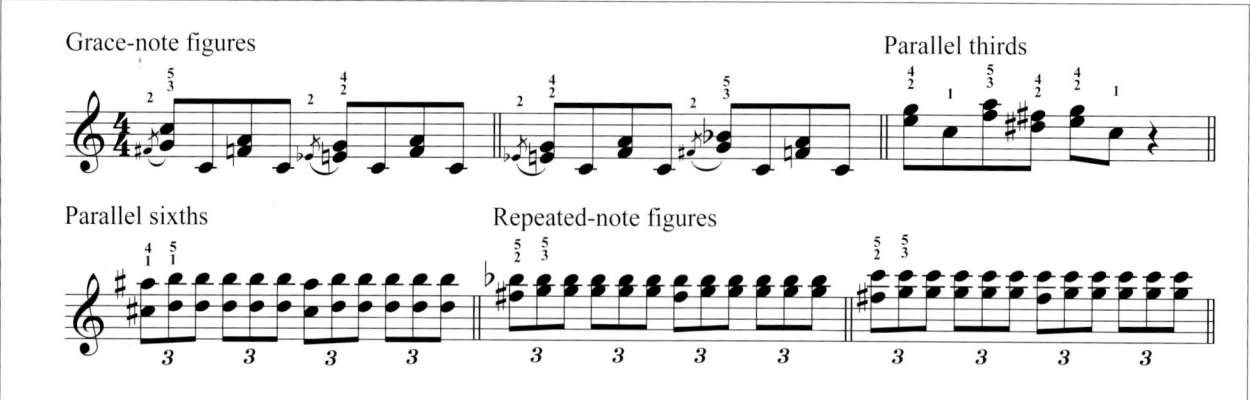

Soloing uses the blues scale, but often takes the form of recurring licks such as the following. Those shown here, in which fingers cross over the thumb in a distinctive way, are known as 'crossover' or 'resolving' licks:

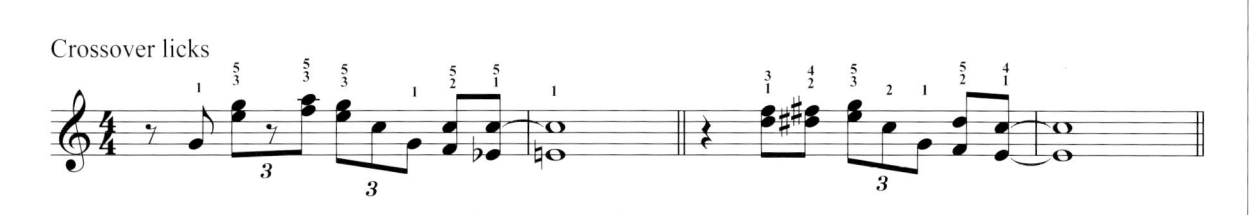

Tremolos, which on the piano can consist of rapid alternations between two notes, pairs of notes, or chords, are also a feature of blues playing.

Conclusion

Well done! You've made it through to the end of the book. Hopefully it's been an enjoyable and instructive journey through lots of different musical forms, exciting styles, and interesting techniques. The main aim throughout has been to give a firm grasp of the essential concepts involved in piano improvisation in different traditions, so you can choose how far and in what ways you draw on each one.

Above all, you should be clear now about the differences between the underlying methods of classical and jazz piano improvisation, and the pros and cons of each of them. Maybe you've already sensed that each approach has great things to offer, in which case it's a pity to feel tied to just one or other of them.

Yes, classical improvising involves more discipline, but sticking with it will bring a subtler feeling for how melody relates to harmony in your playing. Listeners will definitely appreciate that, even if they can't say exactly why your playing stands out as more distinctive and individual (and refined) than other people's. Understanding the logic of the classical approach will also enable you to see how your own improvising links up with the rich repertoire of composed classical music that is one of the high points of our culture. That cannot be a bad thing.

On the other hand there's no denying the immense flexibility that jazz improvising allows for: its looser approach to the relationship between melody and harmony makes it easy to have fun, just playing around with ideas, scales, and harmonies, in the sort of open-ended and relaxed way that makes improvising into a voyage of personal self-discovery. It's easy to forget that this kind of playful experimentation is where all musical creativity begins – a reason why improvising remains an essential competence for musicians today.

It certainly is the case that you need to acquire a good deal of skill and knowledge before you can improvise well – that's the reason for having a book like this. However, jazz reminds us of a more basic truth, which is that improvising (on the piano or any other instrument) ultimately ought to be the most natural thing in the world. If that's right, then it's also the sort of thing anyone serious about enjoying music-making should definitely learn to do.

CD TRACK LISTING

TRACK

1	'The Drunken Sailor' (1) p180		40	Jazz improvisation over II-V-Is (1) p319
2	'The Drunken Sailor' (2) p180		41	Jazz improvisation over II-V-Is (2) p320
3	'The Drunken Sailor' (3) p180		42	Jazz improvisation over II-V-Is (3) p325
4	'The Drunken Sailor' (4) p180		43	'Rhythm Changes' 2-handed voicings & goal-note skeleton p370
5	'The Irish Washerwoman' p181		44	'Rhythm Changes' improvisation (1) p371
6	'Kalinka' p182		45	'Rhythm Changes' left-hand voicings & goal-note skeleton p371-372
7	'La Cucaracha' (1) p184		46	'Rhythm Changes' improvisation (2) p371
8	'La Cucaracha' (2) p184		47	Classical chords & goal-note skeleton – C major p375-376
9	Harmonic rhythm: 2/4, 3/4 & 4/4 time p185		48	Classical improvisation (1) – Andante p375-377
10	'When The Saints Go Marching In' p187		49	Classical chords & goal-note skeleton – A minor p378
11	'Camptown Races' – melody p199		50	Classical improvisation (2) – Largo p379-380
12	'Hatikva' – melody p200		51	'Amazing Grace' C20th US church style p392
13	'Scarborough Fair' – melody p201		52	'Amazing Grace' C19th European church style p393
14	First species – D major p209		53	'Amazing Grace' C18th vernacular church style p394
15	First species – F major p210		54	'Amazing Grace' C20th jazz improvisation (1) p398-399
16	First species – A minor p210		55	'Amazing Grace' C20th jazz improvisation (2) p398-400
17	First species – G minor p211		56	'Amazing Grace' C20th jazz improvisation (3) p401
18	Second species – A major p215		57	'Amazing Grace' C19th classical elaboration (1) p403
19	Second species – B minor p215		58	'Amazing Grace' C19th – classical elaboration (2) p404
20	Third species – E flat major p220		59	'Londonderry Air' p413
21	Third species – G minor p220		60	'Londonderry Air' folk-style improvisation p414
22	Fourth species – E major p222		61	'Londonderry Air' halftime rock-style improvisation p415
23	Pachelbel 'Canon' – opening p227		62	Andante – classical working through p430-431
24	'Scarborough Fair' – melodic variation (1) p232		63	Swing/stride – trad jazz working through p430-431
25	'Scarborough Fair' – melodic variation (2) p233		64	Swing/walking bass – trad jazz working through p432
26	'Scarborough Fair' – melodic variation (3) p233		65	Fast swing – bebop-style working through p432
27	'Scarborough Fair' – melodic variation (4) p234		66	Classical texture – Renaissance style: Largo p433-434
28	'Scarborough Fair' – melodic variation (5) p234		67	Classical texture – Baroque style: Andante p433-434
29	Bach 'Prelude in C' bars 1-19 p252		68	Classical texture – Classical-period style: Allegretto p434
30	Bach 'Prelude in C' bars 1-19 – block chords p253		69	Classical texture – early Romantic style (1): Moderato p436
31	Bach 'Prelude in C' bars 1-11 – simple decorations p257		70	Classical texture – early Romantic style (2): Moderato p436
32	Bach 'Prelude in C' bars 12-19 – simple decorations p257		71	Classical texture – later Romantic style (1): Moderato p437
33	Bach 'Prelude in C' improvisation 1 p259		72	Classical texture – later Romantic style (2): Moderato p437
34	Bach 'Prelude in C' improvisation 2 p260		73	Bach 'Prelude in C' bars 24-35 p445
35	'Scarborough Fair' – harmonisation p263		74	Bach 'Prelude in C' (Book 2 of '48') bars 1-7 p446
36	Bach 'Prelude in C' improvisation 3 p267		75	'Te Voglio Bene Assaje' – simple arrangement p449
37	8-chord jazz embellishments: 3-note voicings (a/b), 4-note voicings (a/b) p295		76	'Te Voglio Bene Assaje' – advanced arrangement p452
38	8-chord jazz embellishments: raised avoid notes p296		77	'La Luisella' – arrangement p453
39	II-V-I jazz embellishments: keys descending by semitones, by 5ths – (a) p297 keys descending by semitones, by 5ths – (b) p298		78	'Napole Mio' – arrangement p454
			79	12-bar blues – laid-back pop (1) p474
			80	12-bar blues – laid-back pop (2) p475